W9-DIT-931

LEONARD COHEN
ON LEONARD COHEN

LEONARD COHEN ON LEONARD COHEN
INTERVIEWS AND ENCOUNTERS

EDITED BY JEFF BURGER

An A Cappella Book

Copyright © 2014 by Jeff Burger

Foreword copyright © 2014 by Suzanne Vega

First edition

Published by Chicago Review Press, Incorporated

814 North Franklin Street

Chicago, Illinois 60610

ISBN 978-1-61374-758-2

A list of credits and copyright notices for the individual pieces in this collection can be found on pages 585–90.

Interior and cover design: Jon Hahn

Cover photograph: © Ann Johansson/Corbis

Library of Congress Cataloging-in-Publication Data

Cohen, Leonard, 1934-

  Leonard Cohen on Leonard Cohen : interviews and encounters / edited by Jeff Burger. — First edition.

    pages cm

  Includes index.

  ISBN 978-1-61374-758-2 (cloth)

  1. Cohen, Leonard, 1934—Interviews. 2. Singers—Canada—Interviews. 3. Composers—Canada—Interviews. 4. Poets, Canadian—20th century—Interviews. I. Burger, Jeff, editor. II. Title.

  ML410.C734A5 2014

  782.42164092—dc23

  [B]

2013034568

Printed in the United States of America

5 4 3 2 1

For Madeleine

CONTENTS

PART III · THE NINETIES

Cohen issues *The Future* and a book of poems and songs,
then climbs Mount Baldy to try out the life of a monk.

FOREWORD

I've had the chance to talk to Leonard Cohen on a few occasions, some private and some public.

You should know, and you'll see in this book, that he tends to speak in complete sentences, with careful and appropriate vocabulary. Mr. Cohen is a bit formal, in fact.

This is true even after a bottle or two of wine. We did an interview together once. A room was reserved somewhere on the record company lot, where we sat for more than an hour and bantered. He asked me questions about an album of mine that was just being released. The result was funny, dense; he was being provocative and asking (fair) questions about my personal life, and the world of the songs, that I wasn't inclined to answer. Especially since we were being recorded for radio.

After the interview was over and we went out to dinner, though, I decided I would probably reveal what he wanted to know. But to my surprise, I found that although he continued to be flirtatious, he no longer pushed to know, and I didn't pull. So all was left unrevealed. Although he had been candid during the interview, it was still definitely a kind of performance as he was more polite, congenial, and friendly in private.

But still somewhat formal.

I asked him once about his preference for wearing suits. "My father was a tailor," he said. "I am not trying to be Paul Bunyan."

One Saturday I ran into him at a hotel in Los Angeles. He invited me to breakfast by the pool at ten the next morning. I showed up on time. I wondered whether he would wear one of his well-known suits. He showed up wearing jeans, a T-shirt, cowboy boots, possibly a fedora, and a tailored jacket.

"Would you like to hear a song I'm working on?"

"Of course!" I said.

Without looking at any papers, he then proceeded to recite for the next eight minutes a perfectly metered, perfectly rhymed song. (Unfortunately, I can't remember which one.) I sat, mesmerized.

Then, as I watched, first one girl in a bikini came out behind him and then another. They arranged themselves around the pool for a day of sunning.

By the end of the song, there were probably nine girls in bikinis around the pool.

"You'll never guess what happened!" I said to him, and joyfully described the scene right beyond his back.

Without turning around to see, he just shrugged and smiled.

"It works every time," he said.

When I was a teenager, I was the only one of my friends who listened to him, which I did fervently, every day after school. I felt that he was my friend, and this feeling was not changed by meeting him. I loved his darkness and complexity, his fearlessness of song choices. It has been strange to witness his rise in the world. Now I must share him with thousands of people at Radio City and Madison Square Garden.

And with you! Enjoy this book and the eloquence of the man.

—SUZANNE VEGA
New York City, 2013

PREFACE

How many of the 701 people inducted into the Rock and Roll Hall of Fame by 2013 hit their peaks in their mid- and late seventies? Maybe just one: Leonard Cohen, who, at age seventy-three, began his first tour in fifteen years in 2008, the same year he was inducted into the Hall of Fame. Since then, he has performed all over the world to some of his largest audiences ever; released three popular DVDs, *Live in London, Songs from the Road,* and *Live at the Isle of Wight 1970*; and issued the most successful album of his nearly half-century recording career, the emotive *Old Ideas.* That 2012 recording—only his twelfth studio collection—climbed higher on the charts than any of its predecessors, reaching number one in nearly a dozen countries and the two or three position in others, including the United States.

Besides peaking late, Cohen started late, at least as a recording artist. Born in Montreal on September 21, 1934, he didn't release his first album until he was thirty-three. We won't dwell in these pages on what he did before that age, as his early years are well covered in several biographies, most notably Sylvie Simmons's *I'm Your Man.* Suffice it to say that his youth provided strong hints of the direction his life would take. He was a poetry fan by high school and showed particular interest in the work of Federico García Lorca. He also learned guitar and formed a country-folk group, the Buckskin Boys. Then, in the early 1950s, while an undergraduate at McGill University, he published his first poems and won a literary competition.

After graduating from McGill, Cohen flirted with the idea of becoming an attorney (can you imagine?) and attended one term at the university's law school. Then he spent a year at Columbia University in New York. But he became increasingly focused on fiction and poetry. He published his first book of poems, *Let Us Compare Mythologies*, in 1956. The following year, he returned from New York to Montreal and began taking odd jobs so he could concentrate on his writing. Four years later, in 1961, he published a second book of poetry, *The Spice-Box of Earth*, which ultimately found its way into many college students' backpacks and did much to enhance his prospects. *The Favorite Game*, his first novel, followed in 1963 and *Beautiful Losers*, another novel, arrived in 1966.

But Cohen didn't release his debut album, *Songs of Leonard Cohen*, until December 27, 1967. And it took him a long time to develop into the performer he is today. You could certainly hear songwriting brilliance—and the influence of a literary background—in "Suzanne," "So Long, Marianne," and many of his other early creations; but Cohen onstage in the early years was by all accounts a tentative and limited performer. Today, critics call his strikingly deep voice "a force of nature" and he appears with a magnificent group of backing musicians and singers who beautifully complement his singing. Watching the video of his performance at the Isle of Wight festival in 1970, though, you'd have to conclude that he was getting by at the time largely on the considerable strength of his lyrics and personality.

In the decades since then, he has sold more than 21 million albums and built a large and devoted fan base. He has been the subject of many documentary films and tribute albums and has seen his songs featured in more than fifty films and covered more than thirteen hundred times by such admirers as Judy Collins, Bob Dylan, Johnny Cash, Joe Cocker, Rufus Wainwright, Nick Cave, Jennifer Warnes, Sting, R.E.M., Concrete Blonde, and Jeff Buckley.

But Cohen's story is far from all happy. Though the cloud appears to have lifted in recent years, he suffered from clinical depression for decades. And while relationships clearly matter a lot to him, he has had a long series of failed ones and has never married. Moreover, he found his retirement savings reduced to about $150,000 in 2004, after Kelley

Lynch—his manager of seventeen years and one-time lover—misappropriated a reported $5 million. (In May 2006, Cohen won a $7.3 million civil suit against Lynch. Sylvie Simmons reported in 2012 that "through the various legal proceedings, Leonard had recovered some of his lost money, though nothing like all of it." Lynch, meanwhile, was convicted in 2012 of harassing Cohen and sentenced to an eighteen-month jail term.)

There have been musical stumbling blocks as well. In 1977, he collaborated with legendary producer Phil Spector on *Death of a Ladies' Man*, an album that many critics—and the singer himself—consider a serious blunder. And then there was 1984's *Various Positions*, which was anything but a mistake—it was, in fact, frequently brilliant—but which Columbia Records deemed not good enough for US release. (The label distributed it only in Canada and Europe, though an independent company subsequently issued it in the United States; it finally entered the Columbia catalog in 1990.)

Cohen talks thoughtfully and in detail about all these ups and downs in the interviews that follow, many of which have not previously appeared in print or in English. And the man who emerges from these conversations is as complicated and surprising as his career has been. He once said he "dislikes talking" but at times he is positively loquacious. Indeed, there were years when he seemed to give no-time-limit interviews—often in his own home—to almost anyone who asked. Then there were the years when he retreated to a Zen monastery; was ordained as a monk with the Dharma name "Jikan," meaning "the Silent One"; and for long stretches gave no interviews at all. (During one thirteen-year period, which ended in 2006, he made absolutely no public appearances.) In the many new reminiscences provided for this book, quite a few journalists recall him as the most charming and gentlemanly individual they've ever met; a couple of others remember questionable behavior and ostensibly drunken rants. As for the content of the conversations themselves, who else would discuss the "Talmudic sense of human possibility" in one interview and oral sex with Janis Joplin in another?

Cohen's emotional state varies as much in these conversations as his subject matter, but his moods can be hard to read, particularly in his early and middle years. Half a century ago, he was already developing a reputation for being depressed—and for protesting that he didn't deserve that reputation. "If we assume the role of melancholy too enthusiastically, we lose a great deal of life," he told the Canadian Broadcasting Corporation's Jed Adams in a brief radio conversation that aired on June 16, 1961. "Yes, there are things to protest against and things to hate but there are a vast range of things to enjoy, beginning with our bodies and ending with ideas. . . . If we refuse those or if we disdain them, then we are just as guilty as those who live complacently."

When Adams expressed surprise that Cohen didn't seem angry about anything, he replied, "There are lots of things that anger me [but] let us not destroy ourselves with hostility, let us not become paranoiac. If there are things to fight against, let's do it in health and in sanity. I don't want to become a mad poet, I want to become a healthy man that can face the things that are around me."

Cohen seemed earnest throughout this interview, but when he talked with the CBC's Bill McNeill for a December 19, 1963, radio broadcast, he sounded somewhat like the early Bob Dylan, who was known for putting on reporters with silly answers to serious if sometimes inane questions. Cohen said he'd been living on the Greek island of Hydra for four or five years "but I keep coming back to Canada to get sick. But it's a very special divine kind of sickness that's absolutely necessary for my life." Asked whether he was preoccupied with sex, he said, "A man's a fool if he isn't. But I didn't write this thing [*The Favorite Game*] to titillate, although if it does titillate, it's an extra bonus."

When journalist Beryl Fox talked with Cohen for CBC-TV on May 8, 1966, you couldn't miss the twinkle in his eye. He told Fox he'd pondered getting a tattoo and when she asked "Where?" he deadpanned, "There's this place on Saint Lawrence Boulevard." He also mentioned that "sometimes I go down the street and when I'm not in a particularly liturgical mood blessing everything, I divorce everybody . . . in all the houses and I see people bursting out of the front doors and running in different directions and I feel that I've really cleaned up the streets . . . just divorcing people. A lot of people want a divorce."

As comments like these suggest, Cohen in his early and mid-period interviews could be alternately sarcastic, cynical, or playful. He could also be less than fully candid, perhaps even with himself; he sometimes seems more focused on projecting a persona than on speaking from the heart. But hang in there; he is never less than interesting, even—or sometimes particularly—when he's repeating or contradicting himself. And there comes a time, starting around the late 1990s, when he begins to refer to his longtime public image as a "cover story." At that point, he increasingly discards the cover and talks much more openly about his depressions, his relationships, and his career.

I've never met him, but after reading the interviews and interview-based features collected here, I feel as if I've spent many revealing hours in his company over many years. I suspect you will, too.

I've standardized style in the pages that follow with regard to numbers, punctuation, and the like; Americanized British spellings; and fixed some grammatical and factual errors, especially outside of quotes. But I've preserved the original magazine and newspaper articles as much as possible and have not done the kind of editing I'd do to a previously unpublished manuscript. I've fiddled just a bit more with the transcripts of audio and video recordings, to remove redundancies and transform the spoken word into something that's workable in print. To the extent possible, interviews appear in the order they occurred; when the interview date is unknown, the publication or airdate dictates placement.

My thanks to everyone at Chicago Review Press, particularly senior editor Yuval Taylor and project editor Amelia Estrich. This is my second book with the folks at CRP, and I still think they're terrific. Thanks, also, to all of those who contributed articles and audio and video recordings and transcripts to this book. Special thanks to the many who provided new reflections and reminiscences and to Alberto Manzano for his help with photography and translations. Thank you to Kathryn Duys for transcribing and translating French passages and to the fans who maintain such helpful websites as leonardcohenfiles.com, leonardcohenforum.com, and 1heckofaguy.com.

My gratitude goes to my coworkers at AIN Publications, especially colleague extraordinaire Jennifer Leach English. Thanks to my brother and sister, Todd Burger and Amy Downs, and to my lifelong friend Ken

Terry. And thanks always to my wife, Madeleine Beresford, and children, Andre and Myriam, all of whom resisted the urge to complain—well, *mostly* resisted the urge—when I disappeared into my home office for hours and days at a time.

Finally, thanks to Leonard Cohen for contributing to the soundtrack of our lives for nearly half a century. I'm glad he's now receiving the degree of praise he has long deserved. As I write this, he is seventy-nine years old, and I know he can't go on forever. But as he sings, "You'll be hearing from me baby, long after I'm gone / I'll be speaking to you sweetly, from a window in the Tower of Song."

—JEFF BURGER
Ridgewood, New Jersey, 2013

PART I

THE SIXTIES AND SEVENTIES

Cohen draws attention with his poetry and fiction, then picks up a guitar and delivers classics like "Suzanne," "Sisters of Mercy," "Bird on the Wire," and "Famous Blue Raincoat."

TV INTERVIEW

ADRIENNE CLARKSON | May 23, 1966, *Take 30*, CBC (Canada)

Though Leonard Cohen gave a few brief interviews in the early sixties (several of which are quoted in this book's preface), he spent most of the period living in semi-seclusion on the Greek island of Hydra. He was nearly as reclusive in the late sixties and early seventies, when he granted only the occasional interview.

One such interview was with the Canadian Broadcasting Corporation's Adrienne Clarkson, who decades later would describe herself as a Leonard Cohen groupie who has been to dozens of his concerts all over the world. Clarkson talked with Cohen shortly after the publication of his second novel, *Beautiful Losers*. At the time, Cohen's debut album release was still a year and a half away, but the thirty-one-year-old artist was already receiving lots of attention for his novels and poetry, particularly in his native Canada. As the introduction to Clarkson's interview makes clear, however, that attention wasn't exactly all favorable. —Ed.

Adrienne Clarkson: Listen to what some of the critics said about his latest book.

Announcer: [*reads from reviews.*] "This is, among other things, the most revolting book ever written in Canada." [Robert Fulford, *Toronto Daily Star.*] "I have just read Leonard Cohen's new novel, *Beautiful Losers*, and have had to wash my mind." [Gladys Taylor, *Toronto Telegram.*] "Verbal masturbation." [The *Globe and Mail.*] "We've had overdrill and overkill and now we have oversex." [The *Globe and Mail.*] "At its best *Losers* is a sluggish stream of concupiscence exposition of . . . nausea." [*Time.*]

[*Cohen reads a poem.*]

AC: How does it affect you when you read a poem that you've forgotten? Is it like reading a poem by someone else?

Leonard Cohen: Well, this time I was just faking it because for the purposes of continuity I had to read this poem but I hadn't read it for some time, and I left out a verse and I'd forgotten the meaning of the whole poem.

AC: Does it in any way disturb you? Isn't every poem a part of you as a poet?

LC: It doesn't disturb me 'cause I don't think anything was at stake. But I think that the message comes through with the body, with the eyes, and the voice. You could really be reading the instructions from a shoe-polish can.

AC: What's the point of writing poetry if you could just as well read instructions on how to polish your shoes?

LC: It depends. If you want people to have shiny shoes, you want to write those kinds of very good instructions. And if you want to polish other parts of yourself, you do it with poetry.

AC: How can you relate the creating of a work of art with an act of polishing shoes?

LC: It depends on where you're looking. It depends exactly where you've got your binoculars trained. If you stand far enough away, it's probably the same thing. You know the story of that juggler who performed his acrobatics and plate balancing in front of a statue of the virgin? Well, I think it really comes down to that. You really do what sings.

AC: Is that the key to your diversity?

LC: I'm all in one place.

AC: You may seem so to yourself. But you must admit that for other people looking at you, the poet, the novelist, the man who lives in a white house on the [Greek] island of Hydra, scion of a Jewish family from Montreal, pop singer, and writer of pop songs . . . all these things may add up to Leonard Cohen but they do look rather complex at first.

LC: Well, I think the borders have faded between a lot of endeavors and people are no longer capable of those kinds of poses, like the poet on the mountain with the cape or the singer catering to the masses. All those kinds of expression are completely meaningless. It's just a matter of what your hand falls on and if you can make what your hand falls on sing then you can just do it. If someone offered me a building to design now, I'd take it up. If someone offered me a small country to govern, I'd take it. Anything going I'd like to try.

AC: Would you feel bad that maybe the building you designed would fall down or the country that you were trying to govern would turn into chaos?

LC: I don't think the building would fall down and I have perhaps an arrogant dream that the country would [endure] . . . I knew a fellow [*Michael X. —Ed.*] who was trying to take over a country. He's a friend of mine in England. He's the head of a large Negro movement there and he will probably take over a country soon. I asked him what the purpose of his government will be and he said, "It will be to protect the people from government because they're fine as they are. Just let 'em alone and my government will just keep everything away."

Things are really a lot more substantial than we think. And I think that my building would probably last. It would either last or fall down depending on the needs of the people inside it. Some people may want a building to collapse over them at a specific time. A friend of mine designed a mural for a coffee shop in Montreal with a special glue on it. This glue dried every winter and the mural fell to pieces and he would have to be engaged to repair the mural. He said, "Cars are designed with built-in obsolescence—why not murals?"

AC: What about poetry?

LC: I think that history and time pretty much build obsolescence into poetry unless it's really the great stuff and you never know whether you're hitting that.

AC: Don't you ever?

LC: Sometimes you know about it. But I'm not interested in posterity, which somebody said is a kind of paltry form of eternity. I'd like to see headlines . . . instead of the Spencer case [*An apparent reference to Vancouver mail clerk George Victor Spencer, who was caught collecting information for the Soviet Union. —Ed.*], something like "[Canadian painter Harold] Town Finishes Painting Today." I'd like the stuff I do to have that kind of horizontal immediacy rather than something that is going to be around for a long time. I'm not interested in an insurance plan for my work.

AC: What about the kind of diversity that you want to do? Do you want to write musical comedies like Town wants to do?

LC: Oh, yes, sure. I'd like to write a musical comedy.

AC: What would it be about?

LC: I'd really have to fall on an idea. But I'd like to do that. Maybe Town would sing the lead.

AC: Does he sing?

LC: All the time. He's a very good singer.

AC: Do you mean with notes and everything?

LC: He's not tied down to anything.

AC: Does that help—to sing?

LC: I think it helps everything.

AC: Does that mean you have to opt out of society? It's a terrible phrase but it's the only way I know how to put it to you.

LC: Well, it's a good trick if you can manage it, but I don't know anybody who's managed to do that. Everybody's on the crust of this star. I don't know anybody who's opting out, except a couple of astronauts and they always come back. And they bring their own smoked-meat sandwiches with them. Nobody really wants to leave.

AC: When you go off to your house in Hydra, do you want to leave? Do you leave things behind?

LC: Well, I have no plans to go back there. I've been in Greece off and on for six years now. I've just been discovering Toronto for the past couple of days. It's really nice.

AC: Is it exciting?

LC: I think it's a happy revolution.

AC: A revolution?

LC: Well, that's how we describe all phenomena today. But there's a quiet one in Quebec and I think there's a happy one here. I was walking on Yorkville Street and it was jammed with beautiful, beautiful people last night. I thought maybe it could spread to the [other] streets and maybe even . . . where's the money district? Bay Street?

AC: King and Bay.

LC: King and Bay. I thought maybe they could take that over soon, too.

AC: Do people need the kind of happiness that you can sing about?

LC: I don't establish any of those criteria for happiness. I just like to sing. I don't have a program to establish with my singing. I just like to get up and sing my piece and sit down, listen to other people.

AC: Do you actually not make value judgments about what you like to do better or less? Right now you're writing songs. You're not writing poetry, you're not writing a novel, so you're liking [songs] better.

LC: I've got a new book of poems ready to go out . . . but I don't want to be glutting the market with my work so I'm holding that back a while. No, everything keeps on going or it stops. You know when you're happy. There's been so much talk about the mechanics of happiness—psychiatry and pills and positive thinking and ideology—but I really think that the mechanism is there. All you have to do is get quiet for a moment or two and you know where you are.

AC: And so this knowing where you are . . . you don't need the help of anything like drugs or liquor?

LC: It's not a matter of the help. You can cooperate with the vision that alcohol gives you. You can cooperate with the vision that LSD gives you. All those things are just made out of plants and they're there for us and I think we ought to use them. But also there's another kind of high to get from refusing to use them. There are all kinds of possibilities. Asceticism is a nice high, too. Voluptuousness is a high. Alcohol is a high. [Harold] Town gets beautiful under alcohol. I just get kind of stupid and generally throw up. But some people get beautiful with alcohol.

AC: Do you see things in terms of highs and lows or is this just an appeal to sensation?

LC: It's not just a matter of sensation. What I mean by high is not a manic phase of swinging, knocking down buildings, and laughing hysterically. I mean that you're situated somehow. There's a nice balance. You're in the center of your own orbit or as Dylan said, you fade into your own parade.

AC: In one of your poems ["Why I Happen to Be Free," in *Flowers for Hitler*], you say, "Now more than ever I want enemies." This is in your poem about how people conspire to make you free. Do you feel this way about the criticisms of your book?

LC: Oh yes. I'd feel pretty lousy if I were praised by a lot of the people that have come down pretty heavy on me. I think, first of all, in a way there's a war on.

AC: What kind of war?

LC: Well, it's an old, old war and I think that I'd join the other side if I tried to describe it too articulately, but I think you know what I mean—that there's a war on, and if I have to choose sides, which I don't generally like to do, I'd just as well be defined as I have been by the establishment press.

AC: Thank you, Leonard Cohen.

COHEN CLIP

On Self-Discipline

"It takes a fantastic inner compulsion [to write]. Nobody writes who doesn't really drive himself. I feel secretly that I am much more highly disciplined than anybody I meet. I know what it is to sit down at a desk for long periods of time and lay it on. *Beautiful Losers* I wrote every day until it was finished. I wrote a minimum of four hours a day and a maximum of twenty. The last two weeks I worked twenty hours a day. That was when I flipped out."

—from "Is the World (or Anybody) Ready for Leonard Cohen?"
by Jon Ruddy, *Maclean's* (Canada), October 1966

AFTER THE WIPEOUT,
A RENEWAL

SANDRA DJWA | February 3, 1967, the *Ubyssey* (Vancouver, Canada)

By the time Sandra Djwa interviewed the then thirty-two-year-old Cohen, he was on the verge of receiving serious acclaim for his music. The release of his first album, *Songs of Leonard Cohen*, remained more than ten months away, but Judy Collins's recordings of his "Dress Rehearsal Rag" and "Suzanne" appeared shortly before this conversation. (Both were on her November 1966 sixth album, *In My Life*, which spent thirty-four weeks on the US pop charts.)

The interview, which Djwa conducted while earning her PhD at the University of British Columbia, ran on page eight of the school's student newspaper and was not touted on the front page. When I emailed current editor Jonny Wakefield to ask about including the piece here, he replied, "Wow, we had an interview with Leonard Cohen?"

Djwa remembers the conversation well, however. "I had written an essay called 'Leonard Cohen: Black Romantic,'" she told me, "and had sent it to the journal *Canadian Literature*. In it, I had argued that Cohen was a 'black' romantic, and writing the essay had given me some sense of the questions to ask in the interview." Djwa added that during her conversation with the singer, "I sensed that he was a little spaced out but he was very helpful and spoke of his sense of 'wipe-out' while in Greece."

The interview was not Djwa's last encounter with Cohen. "He phoned me in the mideighties from California, regarding his friendship with Canadian poet, lawyer, and political activist F. R. Scott, whose biography, *The Politics of Imagination*, I was then writing," Djwa recalled. "He said he had attended law school at McGill for a time because it had been a good place for Scott, who was then McGill's dean of law. Scott gave Cohen permission to stay for a time at his summer cabin at North Hatley [*a village in Quebec, Canada—Ed.*], where he wrote much of [his first novel] *The Favorite Game*. Cohen was doubtful about leaving the family clothing business to become a writer, but he recalled that Scott 'gave me the courage to fail.'" —Ed.

Sandra Djwa: At one point, when reading *Spice-Box*, seeing all the poems that you simply call "song" and later, when you started singing on the TV show *Sunday*, I thought of you in connection with that Yiddish word "ngin." I think it means "singer of the people."

Leonard Cohen: Ngin, yes. That's close to the tradition. We have all somehow lost our minds in the last ten or fifteen years. Whatever we have been told about anything, although we remember it, and sometimes operate in those patterns, we have no deep abiding faith in anything we have been told, even in the hippest things, the newest things. Everybody has a sense that they are in their own capsule and the one that I have always been in, for want of a better word, is that of cantor—a priest of a catacomb religion that is underground, just beginning, and I am one of the many singers, one of the many, many priests, not by any means a high priest, but one of the creators of the liturgy that will create the church.

SD: Is that one of the reasons why the dominant personalities in most of your books are poet-priests? Even in *Beautiful Losers* the narrator-historian is a priest by election.

LC: Yes, and since this is the vocabulary we are using for this discussion, I would say that *Beautiful Losers* is a redemptive novel, an exercise to redeem the soul.

SD: I also thought it was a pop-apocalypse.

LC: Yeah, sure, that's good.

SD: But how do the two go together? That's what I don't understand.

LC: When there's a complete wipeout, there's a renewal. In that book I tried to wrestle with all the deities that are extant now—the idea of saintliness, purity, pop, McLuhanism, evil, the irrational—all the gods we set up for ourselves.

SD: But isn't there a kind of artistic dishonesty in setting up ideas to wrestle with and then trying to pin the structure of a book on it? It doesn't always work.

LC: If you could see the man who wrote that book. I have always said that my strength is that I have no ideas. I feel empty. I have never dazzled myself with thought, particularly my own thought—it is one of the processes that my heart doesn't leap out to.

When you said "a singer," that's it. A singer is one who embodies in his person the idea. I have never felt myself to be a man of letters. I've always felt that whatever there was, was me, and there was never any distance between myself and the reader. I've never had the feeling of writing a book but of going up and seizing somebody's lapel or hem.

I've always wanted to be created just like the priest creates the prayer for the mass for the congregation. It's not the idea of imposing a prayer but that he creates the finest part of themselves. It's that job more than anything else that I'm interested in.

SD: There seems to be a certain pattern in your work, that of creation, moving between aspiration and disintegration. It seems to me that your myth of art has two women figures, that of the beloved, the aspiring figure, and that of the mad-woman, the destructive. The whole structure seems to be that of the Orpheus myth.

LC: Absolutely. I've always honored both the wrathful deities and the blessed deities and I'm in this completely. There are no functions that I have in my daily life that give me any distance from what I do and I systematically cut all the things that might. I've burnt all my bridges. What you say is true and I acknowledge it as we sit here. As it comes out I just feel that I'm a child. There's a poem about this. I just wrote it yesterday and can't quote it exactly: "I have come to this green mountain / I am thirty-three / a child of the double trinity." One is dark and one light and the third that comes from it like a braid that takes its color from both, like a salamander. That seems to represent me to myself. That's the way it's always been and I don't think I have control over it myself. I can tell you honestly, I've tried a lot of disciplines—yoga, Hebraic discipline—in an effort to control my mind but I find that I have no control. It's not that a man chooses the gods that he worships—it's the gods who choose him. And it's only when we come closest to the gods that we engage in creation.

But I feel that these parts are unreachable parts of myself. There are times when I feel that I'll never do another thing. Creating a work is a lot of pain and that's all I'm trying to get across. And because of the pain you haven't got the opportunity to see the whole arena.

I'm not trying to dramatize or anything, but I vomit a lot at ideas. It's not that I put things in. It's just that certain things obsess me and I get nauseous. There are things I have to do. Of course you've got to watch yourself to see that you don't get addicted to pain and remember that there is another deity and that ecstasy is the other side. The one is the way to the other.

SD: Let's talk about Leonard Cohen, the folksinging personality.

LC: I wouldn't call myself a folksinging personality. I think this nation has a great case of schizophrenia. There's no contact, in a sense, between the people who watch me on TV and the other half. I really don't care what they call me. I'm not a particularly good painter but I'm doing a little painting now, putting together a collection. I have this feeling that if you liberate yourself, anything you lay your hand on can sparkle. Professionalism is the enemy of creativity and invention. There's a possibility for men to live in a way of continually changing their environment. It's a matter of whether or not you believe a man can change his environment. I believe he can. My painting and my singing are the same thing.

I don't care what people call me, whether you call it folksinging or some people call it a priestly function or some people see it as a revolutionary activity or acidheads see it as psychedelic revolution or poets see it as the popularization of poetry. I stand in with all these people. These are all the people who say we can change, get out of pain. That's why I'm interested in pop. In a way this is the first time that people have ever said, "This is our age and we exalt in it and we delight in it, it is ours." It's an assault on history and it's an assault on all these authoritarian voices who have always told us what was beautiful. I like to be created by pop because it's an ally in my own time. My time says it's beautiful and it's part of me and I want to be created by it.

SD: Is that why you choose an excerpt from a Ray Charles record—"Somebody said, lift that bale" [from "Ol' Man River"]—as an epigraph for *Beautiful Losers*?

LC: Yes, I think that's the real news on the streets today. Somebody saying it can be better . . . maybe it can't but somehow we can get closer to our center. Somebody saying whatever there is around that we don't like can be changed—the monolith has begun to dissolve.

SD: Are you suggesting the disintegration of personality when you quote from [Italian Jewish writer] Primo Levi at the beginning of *Flowers for Hitler*?

LC: That quotation is, "Take care not to let it happen in your own homes." He's saying, "What point is there to a political solution if in the homes these tortures and mutilations continue?" That's what *Flowers for Hitler* is all about. It's taking the mythology of the concentration camps and bringing it into the living room and saying, "This is what we do to each other." We outlaw genocide and concentration camps and gas and that, but if a man leaves his wife or they are cruel to each other, then that cruelty is going to find a manifestation if he has a political capacity and he has.

There's no point in refusing to acknowledge the wrathful deities. That's like putting pants on the legs of pianos like the Victorians did. The fact is that we all succumb to lustful thoughts, to evil thoughts, to thoughts of torture.

SD: In this admission you're suggesting that you're working in the same structure as are the contemporary writers—maybe it starts with [Louis-Ferdinand] Celine—[William] Burroughs, [Hugh] Selby, Gunter Grass, and for that matter, [Jean-Paul] Sartre in *Nausea*.

LC: The only thing that differs in those writers and myself is that I hold out the idea of ecstasy as the solution. If only people get high, they can face the evil part. If a man feels in his heart it's only going to be a mundane confrontation with feelings, and he has to recite to himself Norman Vincent Peale slogans—"Be better, be good"—he hasn't had a taste of that madness.

He's never soared, he's never let go of the silver thread and he doesn't know how it feels to be like a god. For him, all the stories about holiness and the temple of the body are meaningless.

SD: When Sartre talks about the salauds, the cowards who are us all, they're the ones who refuse the experience of nausea. There's some point at which you allow yourself to go or you don't. [D. H.] Lawrence talks about this too.

LC: The thing about Sartre is that he's never lost his mind. He represents a wonderful Talmudic sense of human possibility, but I know he's never going to say "and then the room turned to gold." He'll say, "The room turned to shit." But the room sometimes does turn to gold and unless you mention that, your philosophy is incomplete. Like Bertrand Russell, he hasn't flipped out. Anybody who has flipped and survived, who hasn't been broken by conformity or pure madness like an incapacity to operate, knows the ecstasy and the hallucination and the whole idea of the planets and of the music of the spheres and of endless force and life and god— enough to blow your head off. And Sartre never had his head blown off. The thing that people are interested in doing now is blowing their heads off and that's why the writing of schizophrenics like myself will be important.

COHEN CLIP

On Writing *Beautiful Losers*

"I wrote *Beautiful Losers* on [the Greek island of] Hydra, when I'd thought of myself as a loser. I was wiped out; I didn't like my life. I vowed I would just fill the pages with black or kill myself. After the book was over, I fasted for ten days and flipped out completely. It was my wildest trip. I hallucinated for a week. They took me to a hospital in Hydra. One afternoon, the whole sky was black with storks. They alighted on all the churches and left in the morning . . . and I was better. Then I decided to go to Nashville and become a songwriter."

—from "Beautiful Creep," by Richard Goldstein, the *Village Voice* (New York), December 28, 1967

COHEN CLIP
On Women

"When I see a woman transformed by the orgasm we have reached together, then I know we've met. Anything else is fiction. That's the vocabulary we speak in today. It's the only language left . . . I wish the women would hurry up and take over. It's going to happen so let's get it over with. Then we can finally recognize that women really are the minds and the force that holds everything together; and men really are gossips and artists. Then we could get about our childish work and they could keep the world going. I really am for the matriarchy."

—from "I've Been on the Outlaw Scene Since 15,"
by William Kloman, the *New York Times*, January 28, 1968

COHEN CLIP
On Revolution

"I have the feeling that every time you mention the word revolution you delay it twenty-five seconds. I've just found that abstract thought and talk about the revolution—and I see it in big red letters—doesn't really serve any purpose. Somehow each man has to determine what kind of life he's going to lead in terms of what he thinks a good life is. As for a political program, I'd have to leave that to the theoreticians. As for street action, I'd have to leave that to the tacticians. Wherever I happen to find myself I try to lead my life as decently as I can, generally falling along those lines. Somehow just to conduct your life as if the revolution had already taken place."

—from "Leonard Cohen," by P. Dingle,
Rat Subterranean News (New York), 1969

COHEN CLIP
On Buying Clothes

"I've had that raincoat for ten or twelve years now. That's *my* coat. I have one coat and one suit because, for one thing, I find it very difficult to buy clothes at a time like this. I somehow can't reconcile it with my visions of a human benefactor, to be buying clothes when people are in such bad shape elsewhere; so I wear out the old things I've got. Also, I can't find any clothes that represent me. And clothes are magical, a magical procedure, they really change the way you are in a day. Any woman knows this, and men have discovered it now. I mean, clothes are important to us and until I can discover in some clearer way what I am to myself I'll just keep on wearing my old clothes."

—from "An Interview with Leonard Cohen,"
by Michael Harris, *Duel* (Canada), Winter 1969

LADIES & GENTS, LEONARD COHEN

JACK HAFFERKAMP | Late 1970, interview | February 4, 1971, *Rolling Stone*

Cohen, who moved to the United States in 1967 to pursue a career in music, began to garner attention in the pop arena after the December 27 release that year of his debut album, *Songs of Leonard Cohen*. The record—which spent fourteen weeks on the charts, where it peaked at number eighty-three—featured such now-classic tunes as "Suzanne," "Sisters of Mercy, "So Long, Marianne," and "Hey, That's No Way to Say Goodbye."

A second album, *Songs from a Room*, followed on April 7, 1969. Though arguably just a bit weaker than its predecessor, it contained the highly popular "Bird on the Wire" (often referred to as "Bird on a Wire") plus such masterworks as "A Bunch of Lonesome Heroes" and "The Old Revolution." This disc charted for seventeen weeks and reached number sixty-three.

Perhaps one reason these albums didn't sell better is that Cohen granted few interviews to promote them and in fact performed only occasionally between 1967 and 1971. In late 1970, however, he did talk about *Songs from a Room* and an about-to-be-released third LP, *Songs of Love and Hate*, with *Rolling Stone* writer Jack Hafferkamp. The new album, which came out March 19, 1971, included such tours de force as "Joan of Arc" and "Famous Blue Raincoat," the latter a song/letter about a love triangle that ends "Sincerely, L. Cohen." Clearly the artist had reached a new creative peak.

Hafferkamp, whose article includes a description of one of Cohen's early concerts, conducted the interview in Berkeley, California. "At the time," he told me, "I was in a period of great turmoil: I'd recently been dumped by my young wife, was dodging the draft, and was wondering where and how I would find rent money. Cohen's studied craziness seemed like an island of sanity. Not much has changed since then." —Ed.

Leonard Cohen's fans are word people. They believe a song's lyrics are more important than its instrumentation, packaging, or the lead singer's crotch. It could even be that for most of them, words have become the first-aid station in the preventive detention camp of their feelings. Certainly they are all helpless romantics, trapped by rage in the age of efficiency.

Cohen, of course, is crazy, but he is cunning enough to keep on the loose. A mystery man with a big nose, he is a "beautiful creep." He wants to be handsome, but settles for looking better than he expected. And wishing to be slick, he succeeds just enough to keep on wishing. He has no desire to be a pop star, yet he wants to sell records.

Over the house phone at Berkeley's stately old Claremont Hotel, he agrees to a few questions only after I assure him that we will meet on equal terms. "I never do interviews," he says. "I prefer an interviewer to take the same risks that I do. In other words, not to make a question-and-answer kind of scene, because I'm interested in . . . like a description from your side . . . to practice the novelist's rather than the interviewer's art. Say, like what was the feeling of the interviewer and how does that relate to the work we all know. Rather than like . . . put me on the line for this or that type of question . . ."

Cohen ordered a scotch and soda for me from room service—at the time it seemed like the perfect drink. He introduced me to Charlie Daniels, a member of his touring band, the Army. Once an eighty-cigarette-a-day addict, Charlie is now down to five sticks of gum at once.

As I set up the tape recorder, Cohen turned down the sound from the TV. He left the picture tuned to *Lassie*. A definite feeling of uncertainty settled around us, the intruders. Cohen carefully scrutinized us. He repeated his insistence that our meeting be held on common ground. "I had to be reminded of other things I've said. It's just sheer fatigue which has allowed me to conduct this whole scene. I don't believe in it.

"One of the reasons I'm on tour is to meet people. I consider it a reconnaissance. I consider myself like in a military operation. I don't feel like a citizen. I feel like I know exactly what I have to do. Part of it is familiarizing myself with what people are thinking and doing. The kind of shape people are in is what I am interested in determining . . . because I want to lay out any information I have and I want to make it appropriate. So if I can find where people are at any particular moment, it makes it easier for me to discover if I have anything to say that is relevant to the situation."

A refugee from the men's garment industry (he pushed clothes racks for a time), he has *arrived* at thirty-six years of age. He is tastefully dressed in conservatively flared tan pants, black shirt, and bush jacket, but he carefully denies affluence by keeping himself particularly emaciated. He firmly believes that women are gaining control of the world, and that it is just. He empathizes, "Women are really strong. You notice how strong they are? Well, let them take over. Let us be what we're supposed to be— gossips, musicians, wrestlers. The premise being, there can be no free men unless there are free women."

His stories, poems, and songs are all quite personal, written to and about himself and the lifetimes he has drifted through. Sometimes nakedly, but just as often humorously, he looks down from the cross and decides that crucifixion may as well be holy. He answers cautiously, but once begun, his conversation glides easily from the writing of his books to the writing of his songs. "As I've said before, just because the lines don't come to the end of the page doesn't necessarily qualify it as poetry. Just because they do doesn't make it prose. Oh, I'm continually blackening pages . . .

"I've always played and sung. Ever since I was fifteen. I was in a barn dance group called the Buckskin Boys when I was about eighteen . . . seventeen. It was just at a certain moment that I felt that songs of a certain quality came to me that somehow demanded . . . or somehow engage a larger audience. Like when you write a good song, you feel like you can sing it to other people. When you write other songs that are not so good you just sing them to yourself. I don't know . . . I guess greed had something to do with it.

"And I forget, a lot had to do with poverty. I was writing books [two novels and four volumes of poetry] and they were being very well received . . . and that sort of thing, but I found it was very difficult to pay my grocery bill. I said, like it's really happening. I'm starving. I've got beautiful reviews for all my books, and I'm very well thought of in the tiny circles that know me, but like . . . I'm really starving. So then I started bringing some songs together. And it really changed my whole scene."

Bob Johnston, friend, producer, and keyboards, and Ron Cornelius, guitar and moustache for the Army, wandered in to tell of the arrival of the limousines. I asked about the picture on the jacket of his first LP, *Songs of Leonard Cohen*.

"The picture on the back is a Mexican religious picture called 'Anima Sola,' the lonely spirit or the lonely soul. It is the triumph of the spirit over matter. The spirit being that beautiful woman breaking out of the chains and the fire and prison.

"When the record came out . . . there was some difficulty between the producer [John Simon] and myself. I don't mean there was any malice. It was really like a misunderstanding. And I wasn't well enough versed in the whole recording procedure to be able to translate the ideas I had to him. So that he, naturally, took over and filled in the vacuum that was caused by my own ignorance and incompetence. . . . I like [the record] now. I think a lot of people have listened to it.

"The second one [*Songs from a Room*] was largely unloved as I can see it . . . from people's reactions. It was very bleak and wiped out. The voice in it has much despair and pain in the sound of the thing. And I think it's an accurate reflection of where the singer was . . . at the time. Too accurate for most people's taste. But as I believe that a general wipe-out is imminent and that many people will be undergoing the same kind of breakdown that the singer underwent, the record will become more meaningful as more people crack up.

"The third one [just released] is the way out. It is a return . . . or maybe not even a return—a claim, another kind of strength . . ."

Isn't that a kind of heavy responsibility? Aren't you making a claim to be some sort of guide or prophet? It seems that by releasing records you are making that sort of claim.

"Very true, very true," he said. "Look, I think the times are tough . . . these are hard times. I don't want in any way to set myself up as Timothy Leary or Abbie Hoffman. I'm not one of those guys. I have my feelings about how to move myself into areas that are not completely bordered with pain. And I've tried to lay out my chart as carefully as I can. I have come through something. I don't want to boast about it. I don't even want to talk about it. Look . . . the songs are inspired. I don't pretend to be a guide. I do pretend to be an instrument for certain kinds of information at certain moments. Not all moments, and it has nothing to do with me as a guy. I may be a perfect scoundrel. . . . As a matter of fact, I am . . . just like the guy on the scene. But there are moments when I am the instrument for certain kinds of information."

In the Canadian Film Board movie, *Ladies and Gentlemen, Mr. Leonard Cohen* [*A 1965 documentary. —Ed.*] you wrote something on the wall while you were sitting in the bathtub.

"'Caveat emptor,' or buyer beware. I think it's good advice. Especially these days. Not specifically from me, but . . . I let anybody judge me by the severest terms they choose . . . I simply think that on both sides of the underground railway there is a lot of occasion to exercise our skepticism."

As Cohen speaks it becomes readily apparent that meeting people is only one reason for the tour. Another, more important reason is that for him "tours are like bullfighting. They are a test of character every night." And that, as he says, "is something I am interested in examining."

One purposely unpublicized aspect of the current US–Canada tour has been the stops at various mental hospitals. Cohen has initiated these concerts, he insists, not from any sense of charity but because he enjoys them. There is none of that "sense of work, of showbiz, of turning people on." He does it because the people there are really in tune to the songs. "Those people are in the same landscape as the songs come out of. I feel that they understand them."

In his way, Cohen has explored many terrains, physical and psychic. Success as a songwriter and performer has allowed him to wander to many places: from Montreal, his home, to Cuba, Hydra, Paris, Nashville—and back to Montreal. He left Greece, he says, because "I was ready to leave. Whether the regime changed or not. As a matter of fact, Greece is a very peaceful place to be in now."

Carrying visions of the Spanish Civil War in his head, he went to Cuba to defend Havana during the Bay of Pigs. Slowly he came to realize that he "was exactly the kind of enemy the Fidelistos were describing: bourgeois, individualistic, a self-indulgent poet." He began hanging out with people who were out of work and on no side, "procurers, pushers, whores, and all-night-movie operators." Amid the Chinese and Czechoslovakian technicians, he found himself the only tourist in Havana.

In Paris during the O.A.S. riots and in Montreal during the so-called "occupation of the city" he felt the same stirrings. He is bothered by the fact that what he reads in other parts of the world about events he's seen usually has "very little correspondence with the actual ambiance of the place. None of those reports correspond at all to the reality that I perceive."

The Berkeley Community Theater was very nearly packed when Cohen came onstage fifteen minutes late. The audience was young but mixed. Streeties mingled with Cal frat men and their pin-mates. Only occasionally were they interrupted by a well-experienced face. He started "Suzanne," but stopped and walked offstage accompanied by much good-natured applause. The audience was his before he came to the theater. Smiling like an expectant mother, Cohen, the self-proclaimed arch-villain, returned to invite those in the back of the hall to fill up the empty seats and space in front of the stage. Naturally enough, very little encouragement was necessary. A large number of people scrambled forward. He called for the house lights. "We should all be able to see one another."

He began again with "The Stranger Song." His voice was surprisingly well defined and strong. After another song the Army appeared. Two more guitars, bass, keyboards, and two female voices, Elton Fowler, Susan Musmann, and, that night, Michelle Hopper, made up the rest of the group. They all started into "Bird on the Wire."

The association of Leonard Cohen with the Army was fortuitously arranged through the good offices of Bob Johnston. They provide just the right musical superstructure for his songs. Expertly but not overpoweringly they give his ideas a range and versatility his previous records have lacked. After the concert they would go back to Nashville with him to lay down the last track for the new album. If tonight's concert is a proper indication, several tracks will have a definite country sound.

Meanwhile, having found less space than bodies to fill it, the crowd began settling in the aisles. Aisles-sitting, though—as everyone knows—is illegal. An announcement was necessary. "I've had some crucial news from the authorities," he began facetiously, then broke into a spontaneous song:

> *It's forbidden to sit in the aisles / As for me I couldn't give a damn / I don't care where you sit / I don't care where you stand, either / Or recline in any position you wish / Nonetheless, I feel it is my civic duty / To tell you to get out of the aisles immediately / So come up on the stage instead / And they came up on the stage / And they won't go back again / And they came up on my stage / And they won't go back no more / Oh, I promise to do anything / But they won't go back no more / No, they won't go back anymore.*

And, clapping, laughing, and singing, the audience once again moved forward. The Army was engulfed. Only Cohen stood out as if people were afraid to get too close. A few murmurs of discontent were heard from the expensive seats, but they were to no avail. Not only was the stage filled, but the aisles remained jammed.

Another announcement of some seriousness was imperative: "It is with no regret that I bear the final tidings in this sordid drama. . . . They say we've got just one more song. . . . If the aisles aren't cleared by then the concert will end." Someone behind Cohen shouted, "Make it a long one." He replied, "I don't think they'll be taken in by our cunning. In a while they'll kill the power and then start on the rest of us. . . . I don't care what happens myself because I feel really good. . . . I can't concern myself with those details. I'm not in the business of clearing away people."

As the song began, something truly remarkable happened. Hesitantly, a few people began to filter back to their original seats. Appreciative applause from the seat-bound majority led even more people to reconsider the moral implications of being in the way. A general retreat commenced. And at that very moment, the police, who allegedly had been grouping for action, relented by giving permission for people to sit in the aisles. Cheers filled the house. Leonard Cohen was still grinning when he left the stage for intermission.

Intermission? He and the Army stepped into the wings, looked at one another, and wordlessly returned to the stage. "That was intermission.

This is so good, why stop now?" Although the concert was billed as an evening of songs and poetry, only two short poems were recited. Cohen sang several new numbers confidently. He was obviously pleased and his pleasure was returned by the audience.

The band couldn't leave without an encore. Tired, but game, Cohen returned to sing "Seems So Long Ago, Nancy." He explained that he wasn't sure if he could remember the song. Nancy's spirit was clear enough, but they hadn't done it in a long time. For help he invoked her memory by telling her story. They knew one another in Canada, long years ago. In 1961. Before there was a Woodstock Nation or hip newspapers. When to be strange was to be on your own. Nancy's father was an important judge, but she lived near the street. Her friends told her she was free. "She slept with everyone. Everyone. She had a child, but it was taken away. So she shot herself in the bathroom."

After that, the crowd wanted still more. But Cohen would only come back to bow. The concert was over. Backstage, road manager Bill Donovan searched everywhere for Cohen's already missing guitar. Leonard greeted some familiar faces and some he couldn't remember. Gracefully he edged from person to person toward the exit. Clumps of people stood around speaking low with much affirmative nodding of the head. The guitar was found to have been stuck in the wrong case.

Back at the hotel, exhausted, champagned, and groupied after (some intellectually, some in the usual way), Leonard Cohen sank wearily into the sofa. A bottle circulated. "Nancy was with us. Without her we wouldn't have been able to pull it off."

He slipped off his boots. People began arriving for a party. Partly from fatigue, partly from triumph, he spoke freely of the concert and bigger things. "I like that kind of situation where the public is involved. I happen to like it when things are questioned. When the very basis of the community is questioned. I enjoy those moments."

The cheerful détente he had achieved between the crowd and the police reinforced something he had said earlier. "I believe there is a lot of goodwill in society and in men . . . and it's just a matter of where you cast your energy. You can in some way place yourself at the disposal of the good will that does exist . . . or you can say there is no goodwill in society and what we must do is completely destroy the thing. I believe that in the most corrupt and reactionary circles there is goodwill. I believe that men are mutable and that things can change . . . It's a matter of how we want things to change."

More people arrived. Old friends, Ron Cornelius's relatives, and strangers hoping for a chance to talk to Cohen. Despite his exhaustion, Cohen was ready for them. "Man, you know what is best about having a good crowd and giving them everything you've got? The incoherence afterwards. That's what . . . Hey, where are the fourteen-year-old girls? This is California, isn't it? Where are the fourteen-year-old girls?"

COHEN CLIP

On the Sources for His Songs

"My songs have come to me. I've had to scrape them out of my heart. They come in pieces at a time and in showers and fragments and if I can put them together into a song and I have something at the end of the excavation I'm just grateful for having it. It tells me where I am and where I've been. I can't predispose the song to any situation or anything in the political realm, but I live in the political realm and I'm aware of what is going down and my songs come out of that awareness of ignorance. A lot of my songs come out of ignorance."

—from "Complexities and Mr. Cohen," by Billy
Walker, *Sounds* (UK), March 4, 1972

COHEN CLIP

On His Voice

"My voice just happens to be monotonous [and] I'm somewhat whiney, so they are called sad songs. But you could sing them joyfully too. It's a completely biological accident that my songs sound melancholy when I sing them."

—from "Behind the Enigma," by Tony Wilson,
New Musical Express (UK), March 25, 1972

FAMOUS LAST WORDS FROM LEONARD COHEN (THE POET'S FINAL INTERVIEW, HE HOPES)

PAUL SALTZMAN | June 1972, *Maclean's* (Canada)

About a year and a half after he talked with Hafferkamp, Cohen spoke in Toronto and Nashville with Paul Saltzman. Saying "I'm just reeling, man," the singer indicated that his upcoming concert tour might be his last—and that this interview might be his last as well. He would make similar comments some months later to British journalist Roy Hollingworth (*see page 40*).

Saltzman, who remains a fan today, is obviously glad that the singer changed his mind. "Meeting Leonard Cohen began with my producing four of his concerts in the early 1970s," he told me. "Taking Leonard on tour was a great honor for me as I'd read his poems and his novel *Beautiful Losers*, and was deeply impacted by them as a young man. Spending time only deepened how he influenced me: to be more circumspect, deeper, more conscious." —Ed.

Last fall I'd heard from a friend that Leonard was passing through Toronto. Which is generally the way people who know Leonard hear about him. A friend will whisper to another: "Leonard's in town y'know" or "Did you hear Leonard was in town last week?" and, as often as not, by the time you'd hear about it Leonard Cohen would be far away.

This time the rumor's true, he's still in town, and we meet in an elegant French restaurant where he and a writer friend are joyously immersed in a rare seafood celebration. When I arrive they have just had their way with wonderfully rich dishes of oysters and clams and shrimps and are elated by the discovery of a lobster pie on the dessert menu. Leonard looks healthier than ever. There was a time when he could describe himself as "a fat, slobby kid of twenty-five" but he is thirty-seven now and in fine shape, having discovered yoga, meditation, fasting, and the general effects of eating with consideration for the body.

He was here this time because the University of Toronto had just bought his papers and he was spending each day sifting through the material to see what kind of man he'd been in the early days. He was about to hit the road again, he said, to leave for Winnipeg to pick up his Toyota jeep and drive to the mountains near Los Angeles and spend a month in a Japanese monastery.

After that he's heading for Nashville, he adds, to rehearse with a new band for a concert tour of Europe. He's obliged to deliver two more albums to Columbia Records and has decided the best way to honor the contract is with two live albums produced on tour. I tell him that I'm trying to write about him and could I come down to see him. He pauses, peers over the lobster pie, and says, "OK, why not?" So, it's arranged. We'll get in touch and I'll go down to Nashville during the rehearsals.

I first met Leonard Cohen just before Christmas in 1970. He was doing a concert tour in the United States and I'd been asked to produce the four concerts here: Massey Hall in Toronto, Carleton University in Ottawa, Place des Arts in Montreal, and a free concert in a Montreal mental hospital. Leonard likes to play to mental patients, I was told; he admires the honesty of the audience. "If they don't like you they just get up and leave." By this time I was already haunted by him. Three years ago, I'd been touched, like so many others, by his music.

Later I'd read his poetry and the insane novel *Beautiful Losers* and had heard him say something on CBC-TV that comes to mind now whenever the temptation to make judgments about others arises. He said, "There's no story so fantastic that I cannot imagine myself the hero. And there's no story so evil that I cannot imagine myself the villain."

Just who was this obviously lost, half-crazy poet anyway? *Who was he?* I wanted to know. Such sensibilities were rare, to be sought out, to be near for a while.

We met at the Windsor Arms Hotel just off Bloor Street (the kind of place where Gloria Swanson stays when she's in town) and Leonard seemed more rested and healthier than he had on TV. He was trim and carried his body with a kind of refreshing precision and talked the way he walked, aware of his own speed. He was staying there with his group (two female singers, four musicians, a roadie, recording engineer, and equipment man).

The next day, after a very successful Massey Hall concert, we all flew off to Ottawa. The band had the kind of weariness that comes from six electrically intense weeks on the road. I was feeling very good and waiting anxiously for time to share with Leonard, when the moments weren't so frantic. There were so many things I wanted to find out.

In Ottawa the night was magical. During the second half of the concert, the roadie Billy Donovan and I moved from the dark side of the stage to the light near the piano. The space transformation, from dark to light, was shocking—like opposite electrical charges. The audience disappeared into an awesome black void in front of the stage. And powerful tension was growing between Leonard and the darkness. Immediately, I felt terrified for him; in front, the black entity, like some sort of energy monster, was sucking him in. I wanted to turn up the lights and release him. The hunger of the audience was frightening. There were signs of struggle on his face, fighting to keep control. Then suddenly he made an emotional connection with something out there and the night became his. Aldous Huxley's vision for mankind is to wake up, and Leonard woke the blackness up that night. The concert was over and the audience leaped to its feet, responding loudly and ecstatically. Leonard slipped the guitar strap from his shoulders, stood silent for a time, and said: "It's good to be back in Canada. This is coming home and I want to thank you for sharing this occasion."

Twenty minutes later, after the sound equipment was cleared and the gym empty, a girl approached us nervously and asked us to take her to Leonard's dressing room. She was reverential, entirely respectful. She followed quietly as we made our way outside to the dressing-room stairs. There, in front of us, were Leonard and the band laughing joyfully and throwing snowballs at each other. She was stunned. The girl obviously couldn't reconcile this scene with her fan's worship.

Later that night, Freddy of the sound crew and I were talking very confused, about the girl and the magic and the demanding quality of the audience, that strange energy, and I wondered how or why Leonard put up with this kind of exhausting tour. It was scary. We decided to go and talk to him about it. We knew he wouldn't be confused. It was 3 AM when we knocked on his hotel door. A weary voice asked who it was.

"It's Paul and Freddy . . . can we talk with you?" "Can it wait until morning, man?" We thought for a moment. "No, not really . . . "

The door opened and we all sat down at the open doorway on the rug and talked until dawn. Leonard explained that touring was "like an Italian wedding. You kind of know the bride and maybe you've met the groom once or twice, but you've never met anyone else that's there. And everyone gets too drunk and eats too much. The morning after you don't remember much about the wedding. As far as I can see, this is my last tour. But the will is frail and I may fall back and it might take ten more tours to finally quit, or this might be it."

Freddy and I were being familiar and intimate with Leonard, it was natural for both of us, and I'll never forget when he turned to us and said: "Listen, I like you boys, but don't think that because we're sitting here having a talk like this that we're close friends. When the ancient Japanese would meet they'd bow to each other for as much as half an hour, speaking words of greeting, gradually moving closer together, understanding the necessity of entering another's consciousness carefully."

He held his hands up, palms outward, and he pushed his hands toward us gently. He wanted us to be more aware of the distance between us.

Days later, when the tour was over and Leonard gone, I realized the significance of what he was saying. Friendships have been deeper for me since. *I wanted to see him again.*

It was ten below zero and Toronto was white when I left. The Delta jet is now dropping through pink cumulus clouds over Nashville and I can see the ripening greens and browns of the Tennessee countryside below. It is early March.

Billy and Ron, Leonard's lead guitarist, are waiting and it's good to see them again. We haven't seen each other since the Canadian tour. We all happily pile into a rented Capri and drive past the nearby palatial Southern estates surrounded by manicured acres that could only be kept up with "the right help," each property enclosed by similar stone walls built in the early days by black slaves. Later we pass through the section of town where the blacks live. The streets haven't been paved yet.

Studio A of Columbia Studios is a high room with sophisticated sound baffles, mixers, synthesizers, amplifiers, and all the hardware that's been good enough to create the sounds of Bob Dylan, Simon and Garfunkel, Pete Seeger, Mike Murphey; the list is legion. Inside Leonard's rehearsing with his band: Peter, from San Francisco, on acoustic and electric bass; David, from California, on acoustic guitar; and two lady singers, Lee from Toronto and Stephanie from England.

Leonard turns to me and says casually, "Hi, man." Ron takes his place on a stool with the rest of the group, puts his electric Gretch between his thighs, and off they go into "Joan of Arc." The rehearsal would go badly that afternoon. The voices of the girls were beautiful but they just didn't mesh with Leonard's. Eventually the girls would be told that it just wasn't working, that the chemistry hadn't happened, that they'd have to go home. They would be disappointed but relieved that the tension was over. Now you could see that Leonard and Bob Johnson, his record producer and organ player, were tired and frustrated. On his way out Leonard said he'd see me later at the YMCA where he goes for a workout every day. Twice a day if his body is feeling stiff and tense.

Physically relaxed after a workout at the Y, Leonard and I go over to his hotel for food and we settle down for our first talk. Leonard needs drawing out, he seems to be holding back, and finally he tells me about the Japanese monastery where he has just spent five weeks. The monastery was sparse but beautiful, high in the California mountains above the tree line, cold and exquisite. Remarkable vegetarian cuisine was prepared by a young monk. Leonard was up at four each morning and each day was spent in meditation and work. The experience had given him strength, he said, not aggressive physical strength, but a kind of power that comes from feeling directly connected inside. Now the tour, which is to take in twenty-three European cities in forty days, is a drag on his head, an unbelievable drain he must endure. He's tired of singing love songs that are seven years old and fed up with the music business. "I've been trying to get out of Nashville for three years," he says, "and now I must prepare to embrace a hundred thousand people on tour."

Later, up in his room with his lady, Suzanne, and Ron, I notice again this reluctance to initiate conversation. Mostly he listened, his attention happily on Suzanne's hand caressing his foot. They're so fine together. Warm and calm and loving. She's a lovely woman who, like Leonard, doesn't talk much. But when she does it's clear and rings true. She says to Leonard, "You've taught me most everything I know," and Ron adds, "He taught me more about how to take care of my guts than anyone."

During the next few days I slip easily into Leonard's ritual of work-outs in the morning and rehearsals in the afternoon. Leonard and I would occasionally take a drive in his Toyota jeep, fine times in the warm afternoon sun, but there was a tension growing between us. A number of times we made appointments to set up an interview for this article but he'd always put it off at the last minute.

On Sunday Suzanne left for Miami for a couple of days. Leonard came into the control room after the afternoon rehearsal and finally suggested we get the interview out of the way. Loading his guitar and my saddlebags into the back of his Toyota we headed for his hotel. I could see that the talk would be a chore for him.

We got to his room, both of us feeling pressured by the other and tense about talking. He didn't want to speak, to be asked questions about himself. And I didn't want to jeopardize our still-fledgling friendship by being the instrument of his discomfort. The moment was far too tense and I went out on the balcony.

The night air slowed me down and being alone in his room gradually made Leonard feel more at ease. When I went back in, he was sitting on his double bed and I sat down on the spare one.

It was about seven-thirty by now and we decided to set a time limit of one hour for the conversation. We ordered a cheese sandwich and milk for him and a tomato juice for me and while we waited I set up the cassette tape recorder I'd brought.

The food came and we continued to talk easily as I turned on the tape recorder:

"I lived a lot better when I had less money. A lot more luxuriously, and so it's very confusing, as you might imagine. My standard of living went down as my income increased." Leonard shifted onto his side, propping his head up with one hand and starting to eat his sandwich with the other. "Believe me, it's just the nature of money.

"Money in the hands of some people can only decrease their standard of living. I lived a lot better when I had no money. I was living in a beautiful big house on a Greek island. I was swimming every day, writing, working, meeting people from over the whole world, and moving around with tremendous mobility. You know, I can't imagine anyone living any better and I was living on about a thousand dollars a year. Now that I spend many times that, I find myself living in hotel rooms, breathing bad air, and very constrained as to movement."

He reached over the end of the bed, picked up his glass, and drank some milk as I asked him how he felt about Canada these days.

"It's my native land, my homeland, all the feelings one feels for one's homeland . . . very tender feelings about it. I don't like hearing it being criticized. I like to hear it praised. I return often and I live there part of every year. It's the last home I've had."

For several years, Leonard had been without a real home, constantly on the move. But now he'd just bought a house in Montreal for himself and Suzanne and his friend Mort [Rosengarten]; he was attempting to come home.

"And the next home, too. I think we're very lucky it's not a first-rate power and that it's . . . I don't know, it's my homeland, what can I say? And it's not even Canada, it's Montreal. Not even Montreal, it's a few streets: Belmont and Vendome. It was wonderful."

He looked warm and happy remembering his childhood and it brought to mind his saying, a few days earlier, that his only friends besides the people connected with his music were his childhood friends, Mort, Henry Zemel, Henry Moskowitz. Earlier in the evening, coming out of the bathroom, he'd stopped in front of the mirror. He looked at himself, running his fingers through his hair, a smile growing on his face, and said with a little bounce of energy: "I feel very boyish these days. Very boyish."

Now, sitting there seeing the traces of youthful joy on his face as he talked about Montreal, I remembered that his mother still keeps his room much as he left it. Leonard's father died when he was young, leaving him with a poet's sensitivity but with the premature burden of being the man of the house. He grew up with a certain fear of settling down, but also with the strength that comes from fulfilling such immediate and harsh demands.

I wondered if he was feeling as healthy as he seemed. He answered: "I'm just reeling, man. I'm just reeling. Sometimes in the midst of the thing I don't know how I do it. Like I manage to get my daily life together to get this tour together. But most of the time I'm staggering under the blows. It's no doubt that I contrive these blows for myself. I think everyone is responsible for their own condition. But I don't intend to stay here; I've run through a lot of programs to get myself out of here and this is one that I'm ending because it didn't work. And it's not a question of putting myself down. It's a question of being as accurate as possible."

"You know," he went on, "that's why I wouldn't like to intrude on anybody's life by trying to advise them. The real truth about my visions is that I don't have any special secret. I said it in a song: 'Please understand I never had a secret chart to get me to the heart of this or any other matter.'"

Leonard finished his sandwich and I dug into some cookies and the tomato juice. We were quiet for several minutes, feeling quite relaxed with the silence and with each other.

"Do you have a particular concept of what friendship is?"

"Well, not examining my friends' behavior but only examining my behavior in terms of my friends. I would say that your friends are among your worst enemies. I don't think I've been able to render my friends the kind of services that . . . you know, my intent isn't pure enough; I wouldn't say I'm a good friend."

"Are there any people who are good friends to you?"

"Yes, I have good friends, but I think they're among my worst enemies; they help me when they harm me, and they harm me when they help me. I mean a friendship is often a condition of mutual sympathy which reinforces weakness and does not do anybody any good."

"But is there a friendship that is not a mutual awakening process?" I ask.

"*That's* honesty."

"Well, then isn't that friendship?"

"Not for long, because it's hard to sustain. That's what I was trying to do with this conversation. If I would have been stronger, I would have said, 'Paul, the last thing you need is to sit around talking about these matters. Never mind the things I need, it's beyond the last thing I need, but the last thing that you need is to talk about high things. In another context at another age talking about it can have some value.'"

I wondered what Leonard felt his needs were and when I asked he said: "I like that line from the Hebrew liturgy for the dead which is: 'our needs are so manifold we dare not declare them.' Why do we dare not declare them? We all have a sinister preoccupation with descriptions of our discomfort and it's endless. It's endless. And it doesn't get you up. That's what's wrong with it, that's the only thing wrong with it. It doesn't get you to where you want to go. Period."

He tipped his glass, finishing the milk. "That's one of the reasons I don't like speaking about myself, because you forget what you really think. You begin to mistake the *description* for the feelings.

"But though I dislike talking, I'm still talking. It takes tremendous effort of will not to. Information is one thing and the application is another. Also, it's a matter of putting yourself into an environment where you are aided in doing the things you want to do and not tempted by the things you do not want to do. That's why cloistered societies are established, not because the cloister is in itself an end. But just because in a period of training you want to give yourself a chance. If I want to give myself a chance to develop certain strengths I don't put myself on a tour, or maybe I do to get the full negative imprint so that I don't have to do it again. Like this tour is the last time I will do this sort of thing."

He looked at the tape recorder, and then at me, and shifted to a more comfortable position lying on his bed:

"And this is the last time I'd do this sort of interview. I mean, this doesn't work for me as a viable way of self-improvement. It is forbidden . . . it is forbidden to talk about ways of getting high because we know that it is contrary to the goal. There is a Sufi story about a young man going on a journey to see a famous wise man and on his return his fellow student asked him: 'And what did he say about transmigration of the soul?' And his friend answered: 'I don't know. I didn't hear what he said.' 'And what did he say about transubstantiation of matter?' 'I don't know,' his friend answered. And his fellow student asked, slightly annoyed, 'Well then why did you go?' And his friend answered: 'To see how he ties his shoelace.'"

Leonard paused a moment and then continued: "Now that is like a real guide to good journalism. The essence of the man never comes out of this kind of conversation. Just because the density of the printed page does not transmit these essences."

Leonard had mentioned he was finishing a new book and when I noticed what looked like a manuscript, I asked him about it.

"I've just written a book called *The Energy of Slaves*, and in there I say that I'm in pain. I don't say it in those words because I don't like those words. They don't represent the real situation. It took eighty poems to represent the situation of where I am right now. That to me totally acquits me of any responsibility I have of keeping a record public. I put it in the book. It's carefully worked on. It's taken many years to write and it's there. It'll be between hard covers and it'll be there for as long as people want to keep it in circulation. It's careful and controlled and it's what we call art."

"Why have you put it out?" I asked.

"It's my work, that's all. And part of the nature of my work is to reach people. I mean, I'm not very interested in playing to empty halls. My work is to make songs and poems and I use whatever material I have at hand. I don't have the luxury of a vast range of material. I'm not entirely happy with the subject matter. I'd like to broaden my subject matter but as it is right now I only work with what is given."

He stood up and went over to the desk, picked up his brown leather pouch and held the thick sheaf of papers, each containing carefully handwritten poems, put them down on his bed and started looking through them. I remembered another time in Montreal when he had read some poems to me and had said that for years he had developed his craft so that he could write beautifully, but that now he was not interested in writing for beauty but only for truth.

"I am interested," he went on, "in this book's reception. I'm interested in how it will be received almost more than any other book, because I have the feeling that by making it public I may be making a mistake. I hope that I will find that this gnawing feeling is wrong or that I have mis-read it."

"Don't you think your work might bring people to a greater awareness?"

He thought about it for a moment, and looking at me spoke with sincere warmth: "Perhaps, but I don't think so. The most important thing I can say to you really is that you don't learn by talking. Those who know don't talk and those who talk don't know. There's some truth to that, you know. You don't find any of the great, enlightened masters sitting around rapping. *You just don't learn that way.*"

At that moment I went to turn off the tape machine and noticed that it had stopped, new batteries and all. We laughed about it and Leonard rolled onto his back saying, "It's very significant that probably the most important thing that we have said between us tonight was not recorded."

About ten-thirty, Suzanne phones from Miami. Although Leonard says love is for the birds, his face sure lit up when Suzanne was on the other end of the phone. He said, "Hello, Little One" with such intimacy that I felt drawn directly out of the room onto the balcony.

It's all coming down to the wire now. Home to roost. It's Tuesday night and this is the first rehearsal with Jenny [Warnes] and Donna [Washburn], the two new singers, who've just got in from L.A. The excitement is so strong in here you can touch it. The tour begins in two days. The lights are low and the garbage can is stuffed with ice, wine, and champagne. *These girls have got to work.*

Jenny is tall, with straight blond hair down to her shoulders. She stands holding her body straight but easy, a feeling of calm to her. She came from playing the lead in *Hair* in Los Angeles. Donna is a bit shorter, with a fuller, more sexual body, long light blond hair falling in natural curls over her shoulders. She's less calm than Jenny, more in need of reassurance.

The singing is going well. The first song. If it's going to come together, it's got to be now. Leonard is looking truly adolescent. Worn brown sneakers, favorite black slacks, old favorite gray sweater hanging loosely from his shoulders. He's listening to the girls and smiling as he sings. Standing at the mike, shoulders in their slight hunch, feet together, tapping, swaying slowly from side to side. "Oh you are really such a pretty little one / I see you've gone and changed your name again." Peter, on electric bass, is tapping away smiling, David looks happy, too. "Just as I've climbed this whole mountainside / To wash my eyelids in the rain."

The music takes off. Ron starts smiling, Bob too. "Oh so long Marianne / It's time that we began / To laugh and cry and cry and laugh / About it all again."

The new girls respond beautifully and they sing the last refrain again. The song finished, Leonard turns to the girls. He's smiling, delighted. "Fabulous . . . fabulous . . . just fabulous." He can't get over how well the song went. He's shaking the girls' hands saying, "Congratulations." He's just like a kid, he's so happy. People break to get some drink, but Leonard is too excited. "Com'on, let's keep going. Hey, seriously, that was fabulous. I'm so excited I've lost the capo from my guitar." He is stumbling around through the mike booms and chairs, looking on the floor and table and chairs for his capo. "Hey, anyone seen my capo?" The girls are giggling they're so happy it's come together. Leonard is still stumbling around: "Those sounds were so beautiful I couldn't sing, like music to my ears . . . . I'm so happy there are voices out there, the voices came." He's standing still now, overcome.

They get back together, Leonard saying, "Let's do 'Thin Green Candle' [*A reference to "One of Us Cannot Be Wrong." —Ed.*] . . . no, no, let's do 'Joan of Arc.'" They begin and suddenly in midverse Leonard stops: "I'm sorry. We might as well cool this right now. I can't sing. It's too beautiful." They look at each other. "The reason I need girls to sing with me is that my voice depresses me." Donna protests. "No . . . no," but Leonard goes on. "No, seriously, that's the truth. I need your voices to sweeten mine. No really, that's the truth. So please try to sing something simple in harmony with my voice." And they swing back into another song . . . *and it works.*

It's around midnight the next day and we're all packing up to leave the studio for the last time. What I've realized after this time with Leonard is that he's searching for the matter of which he is made. And I don't mean that in any sci-fi sense. It simply means that there are many parts of Leonard Cohen that Leonard doesn't like, even hates. Once when we were talking I asked him if he liked himself. He thought for a moment and said: "I like my true self." I took that to mean that like most of us he had made for himself a number of selves, public facades, heroic images, romantic possibilities but was now in the process of stripping them away to become his true self. Somewhere back there, perhaps in his twenties when he began replacing the slobby body with this one, he began a long uphill battle to bring himself together.

Quieting the internal strife frees the spirit. Leonard is constantly refining his techniques for getting high. Drugs don't work anymore. Neither does public acclaim or the music industry or Scientology (which he once was into), but yoga, fasting, and his writing help. So does Suzanne. The process is ongoing and more profound as the years pass. You can see it on his face. Refining. Always refining. And that's why I search out Leonard. Why I love the man. Leonard knows a lot about searching, and I'm trying to become better at it myself. He turned me onto it. My brother crystallized it when he took me aside one day and said: "You don't like yourself very much. That's why you run around. You're afraid if you slow down you'll find out there's nothing to you . . . but there is."

I say so long to everyone in the studio and walk over to Leonard. We shake hands and say a cool good-bye. Like the first time we ever said hello. Just recognition. Another encounter. Moments shared. Nothing promised.

COHEN CLIP

On Reaching for a Wider Audience

"There have been moments when I've felt that I've betrayed myself but I think I would have felt that from the other side too if I hadn't reached a wide audience. I would then have felt that I should have put more effort into reaching people. And sometimes, I feel I should have put more effort into reaching fewer people."

—from "The Strange, Sad, and Beautiful World of Leonard Cohen," by Andrew Furnival, *Petticoat* (UK), December 30, 1972

COHEN CLIP

On Ostensibly Leaving the Music Scene

"I'm leaving now . . . my interests are in other places now. At one time I really thought music had some sort of social import—now it's just music. . . . I like to listen to music myself, but, well, I don't feel I want to have the same involvement with it. It's over . . . I wish everybody well on the 'rock scene' . . . but I don't wanna be in it. . . . I've found myself not writing at all. I don't know whether I want to write. It's reached that state . . . so I've decided to screw it. And go. Maybe the other life won't have many good moments either . . . but I know this one, and I don't want it. . . . I just feel like I want to shut up. Just shut up."

—from "Cohen, Cohen, Gone," by Roy Hollingworth,
Melody Maker (UK), February 24, 1973

COHEN REGRETS

ALASTAIR PIRRIE | March 1973, interview | March 10, 1973, *New Musical Express* (UK)

On April 1, 1973, Columbia Records released *Live Songs*, a collection of tracks culled from Cohen's 1970 and 1972 concerts in London, Brussels, Paris, Berlin, the Isle of Wight, and Tennessee. Some of the tracks, including "Bird on the Wire" and "Story of Isaac," had appeared in studio versions; others, such as "Passing Through" and "Please Don't Pass Me By (A Disgrace)," had not.

Cohen probably hoped to promote the record when he met shortly before its release with fledgling journalist Alastair Pirrie. But Pirrie wanted to address some other topics—including the fact that Cohen had just told *Melody Maker*'s Roy Hollingworth that he was "leaving . . . the rock scene."

"I had briefly met Cohen before this interview," Pirrie told me. "It must have been a gig I was taken to. I spoke to him but he would never have remembered me. I was a face in a crowd, but I was mesmerized.

"Then suddenly I was fifteen or sixteen," Pirrie continued, "a freelance wannabe writer/ producer, and this piece turned out to be my first published sale. I was paid seven pounds for it, and I remember having to hang around the Royal Station Hotel in Newcastle upon Tyne for an age, all the time being told that Leonard Cohen was giving no interviews. I boldly booked a room at the hotel and luckily walked into an elevator to find Cohen chatting to a girl. She was pretty—beautiful, really. I was too polite to listen to their quiet argument, but they plainly knew each other.

"I had sneaked out of school and had a tape recorder held together with sticky tape," Pirrie recalled. "I had bought batteries for it, and that and the hotel room had consumed all my saved-up cash from some intern work I had done at the BBC. Spending every penny of my money was a triumph of hope over zero experience. Anyway, the lovely girl got out of the elevator and, as it continued to descend, I nervously asked Cohen for an interview. He gave me a look and then said, 'Sure' and led me into the public bar. He bought me wine and sat with me for a while, chatting to the tape recorder, reading me a new poem. . . .

"I rang the *New Musical Express* and told them I had the interview and they said it was impossible; Cohen was giving no interviews. I mailed them the piece on BBC stationery to earn a little credibility and the *NME* published it the same week. I was thrilled. That random act of kindness from Cohen to a nerdy kid got me some attention, and I went on to produce hundreds of hours of music TV in the United Kingdom and United States, and nowadays, I write for TV and film.

"It's weird which interviews and individuals you remember. I was a fan of Cohen before I met him, and I was more impressed after meeting him."

Pirrie concluded by thanking me for reminding him of his interview with Cohen "and of that clumsy piece in which I try so hard to sound like a grownup writer, and of those long-ago days of tea and oranges." —Ed.

If Leonard Cohen sticks to his announced decision to quit the music business, it will come as no surprise to those who know him well.

Among friends, he would often claim that he hated the business of selling his songs to people, and he hated the society that made this necessary.

One night recently, he told me why he wanted to quit. "I'm no longer a free man; I'm an exploited man. Once, long ago, my songs were not sold; they found their way to people anyway.

"Then people saw that profit could be made from them; then the profit interested me also. I have to fight too many people on too many levels to have to fight about money as well."

He paused and took a sip of his wine. "There is much to regret in the system of placing songs at the disposal of others.

"Now the record companies pressure me to force my songs because the stores want them to sell. I will not force my songs for them."

Cohen was born thirty-five years ago in Montreal, Canada. He started off his career studying arts at McGill University though later, interested in business, he switched to commerce.

Later still he tried law at Columbia University in New York and, on leaving, took a job in the family clothing factory. [*Actually, he studied law at McGill and attended the School of General Studies at Columbia. —Ed.*]

He had started writing at the age of fourteen—mostly prayers and poems to get women. Not long after he started in the family business, his first book of poems was published, and any plans he had to run the factory were forgotten.

At the end of the fifties Cohen took off with a woman called Marianne [Ihlen] and lived in virtual isolation on the Greek island of Hydra for nearly eight years.

When he left, he suffered a nervous breakdown and it was soon after this that he started putting his poetry to music.

He says that he has no concept of religion in his life but, strangely enough, he sings a song about Joan of Arc on his last LP, *Songs of Love and Hate*.

"It was a strange song indeed; it was out of myself and contained the notion of reverence. When I recorded that song I will admit to having a strong religious feeling. I don't think it'll happen again."

Cohen is a dark, sad man, and, at times, his deep, deadpan voice falters into a brooding silence.

He doesn't like Lennon-type protest songs. "I don't program the songs I write," he told me. "I just write what comes.

"If my passion was involved in those daily issues I would write about them. Anyway, I half feel that my songs do protest in their own way.

"I don't have to have a song called 'Give Peace a Chance.' I could write a song about conflict and, if I sang it in a peaceful way, then it would have the same message. I don't like these slogan writers."

All of his songs and poems are about people and situations that have come into his life.

"Suzanne" on his first LP, *Songs of Leonard Cohen*, is a description of a time spent with a girl of that name. It really did happen, and she did feed him tea and oranges that came all the way from China.

Another of his songs from that same LP was written when he was in Alberta and met two girls in a café.

"I was alone," he intoned gravely, "and I had nowhere to stay that evening. I went with them back to their room and we all slept together. When I awoke I wrote a song about them. I called it 'Sisters of Mercy.'"

Although Cohen was always dissatisfied with the record business, he didn't feel he was working in a void that isolated him from new experiences.

"It's been my experience that there is no situation which is artificial. There are responses that are artificial or untrue.

"But I mean, here we are sitting and drinking wine. You and I are together here. There is no room for a lie: we're just two men sitting talking."

If Cohen had to be remembered by only one of his songs, he would choose "Bird on a Wire." "The song is so important to me. It's that one verse where I say that 'I swear by this song, and by all that I have done wrong, I'll make it all up to thee.'

"In that verse it's a vow that I'll try and redeem everything that's gone wrong. I think I've made it too many times now, but I like to keep renewing it."

Cohen became more and more dissatisfied with each LP he produced, culminating in almost dejection over his last record, *Songs of Love and Hate*.

"I suppose you could call it gimmicky if you were feeling uncharitable toward me. I have certainly felt uncharitable toward me from time to time over that record, and regretted many things. It was overproduced and overelaborated . . . an experiment that failed."

During my last conversation with him, Cohen had changed. He smoked my cigarettes almost continuously and appeared much more withdrawn, answering questions vaguely and lapsing into silences much more frequently.

In his song "Bird on a Wire" there is a line in which he says, "I have tried in my way to be free." Perhaps he feels that this latest move will mean a new chance for him to be free. I think for a man as self-explorative as Leonard Cohen, freedom is a great deal further away.

COHEN CLIP
On a Dip in His Popularity

"I rarely hear praise anymore. I get the feeling that my songs have fallen out of favor. One hears an echo, and the echo I have been getting is not one of wholehearted appreciation. In England, my songs and person have been subject to satire. My person has been satirized as being suicidal, melancholy, and self-indulgent."

—from "I Have Been Satirized as Suicidal and Self-Indulgent," by Mike Jahn, *New York Times* Special Features Syndicate, June 1973

LEONARD COHEN

PAT HARBRON | Summer 1973, Interview | December 1973, *Beetle* (Canada)

Like Alastair Pirrie, Pat Harbron told me that he ranks his encounter with Cohen among the best moments from early in his own career. "My assignment to interview Leonard Cohen for *Beetle* magazine was quite a scoop for a twenty-year-old writer," recalled Harbron, who is now an acclaimed rock photographer. "It wasn't my first cover story but it was the best. Canada saw a number of homegrown rock-and-roll magazines come and go after the late sixties. *Beetle* was the biggest but not the longest lived.

"Cohen was as revered as a singer, poet, and songwriter forty years ago as he is today. I was familiar with his work, mostly his music, but the majority of my assignments had been about the rockers and counterculture comedians of the time. I'll bet Cohen was unaware of many of these artists and yet they very likely knew of him.

"The interview took place in Niagara-on-the-Lake, a Victorian-style town near the US border, about ninety minutes south of Toronto. Known for the Shaw Festival, NOTL as it was called, was always a hub for theatrical arts.

"There was a lot of buzz in the summer of 1973 for Leonard Cohen because the semiautobiographical play *Sisters of Mercy*, based on his songs and musings, was set to open at the new Shaw Festival Theatre before its off-Broadway run. Cohen was warm, confident, and gracious. Though he had an agenda to promote his play and thus sit for an interview, he appeared at ease, even enthusiastic.

"As a freelance writer and in the decades since as a photographer, I have worked with a great many artists and performers but I still think fondly of the afternoon spent with Leonard Cohen." —Ed.

Pat Harbron: How can you best classify your music? Some would have it as folk music.

Leonard Cohen: Let's hope it becomes folk music.

PH: Why?

LC: Well, it would be nice if it stuck around long enough to become folk music. But that's as good a term as any.

PH: Your music seems somber and laid-back, personality wise. Is there any reason for it?

LC: I don't know the reason for it. I think what you say is true.

PH: It is a reflection of your personality?

LC: That's just the way my voice comes out. I don't think too much about the way I do it. That's the way. That's the voice. That's the sound.

PH: "So Long, Marianne" came about as a commercial hit, in that it was very popular with a large number of people who, perhaps, were not aware that Leonard Cohen did it. It's just a song that they enjoyed. When you wrote that song, were you thinking in terms of commerciality?

LC: Well, one hopes that a song will find favor. But it wasn't planned. First of all, it's too long to really be considered a commercial song. It was written for the occasion itself, with the length that it ran . . . not with any plan. I never plan things that way. It's nice when it happens.

PH: Is there an aim that you're trying to stress to your audience through your music?

LC: None that I can speak about. You try to make the song as good as you can.

PH: Is the music an extension of your mood or a separate part of your thought?

LC: It takes in everything you know. And feel.

PH: How much of your music is imagination and how much of it is taken from real-life situations?

LC: I'd say it's all from real situations. The experience is real but one tries to treat the experience imaginatively.

PH: Does your environment influence your work?

LC: Oh yeah. It influences.

PH: In what way, in your case?

LC: It's hard to say exactly but the places I've lived in generally have a very strong presence and it finds its way into the music.

PH: Does the French and English culture difference make a difference to you?

LC: Well, although I've been to Toronto a lot of the time and traveled through Canada, I've never really lived anywhere but French Canada. My experience is quite limited. I know Montreal and that's about all.

PH: When you started to write did you have a culture in mind?

LC: No, I don't have any culture in mind.

PH: How important is the instrumental part of your music?

LC: I've tried different things, some of them more successful than others. Right now I'm thinking of something very much barer than my last couple of records. Just guitar and voice.

PH: On your latest album [*Live Songs*] the instrumentation is kept simple. Also, there is no percussion.

LC: I'd like to try using a drum. No, I haven't used it, except on one or two songs. That's because when I start to play guitar, my rhythm, my time, is very loose. And I like to keep it that way. And when you're working with a drummer, generally, you have to have something steady and driving behind you, whereas I want to keep the time very loose.

PH: How do you express feeling through a song?

LC: It's nothing you can command. You either express it or you don't. If you don't, you can throw the song away.

PH: Do you know, yourself, you have expressed yourself properly, without an audience?

LC: I can generally tell when it's any good. I like to deceive myself from time to time because one needs to throw away things. But, if I'm in an honest frame of mind I can generally tell.

PH: Do you try to reach an audience or let them come to you?

LC: I don't think you can pursue an audience any more than you can pursue a person.

PH: You have a choice of playing for yourself, just the audience, or both.

LC: Well, I don't like to exclude anyone, including myself or whoever's listening. But that's different from going after them. No, you can't.

PH: Do you think there's an age group that goes in for your material?

LC: I am not very aware of who buys the records, but I see at concerts there are people of all ages.

PH: Do you try to express more than one emotion in a song?

LC: Those are not really the considerations that you have when you're working. You know you're trying to manifest an experience. And experience, by its nature, is complex and involves many different kinds of things. So you don't stop with the idea of one or many. You start with the idea of manifesting an experience.

PH: Is there a reason for keeping your music as basic as it is?

LC: There are lots of reasons. One is that I don't really have the skill to make my music too complex. And two, my tastes are very simple. I like to keep it very elementary.

PH: Is music the most important medium you work with?

LC: I never think of it that way. I've always played the guitar and sang. It's just natural. I attempt to do the things mostly that only take one man. So I haven't worked in theater very much because it's a collective effort. I don't work in movies 'cause it's a collective effort. Same with television. The things I do alone, I do. That is writing and music.

PH: Is there any particular reason you work alone?

LC: It's just easier for me.

PH: Do you write with the intention of being successful?

LC: I think that I'm motivated by the same ambition—greed—as everybody else, and one likes to be successful. But on the other hand that's not the only factor. One likes to get one's work to the people.

PH: Is your idea of success simply financial?

LC: No. It's good to make a living. It's essential that a man makes a living, and I always like to get paid for what I do, but I don't like to do it for pay.

PH: What have you been trying to accomplish through your music?

LC: I'm unaware of any long-term goals. From the questions you ask, you feel that the whole activity is much more deliberate than it is for me. It's something I've always done and something that I will always do, as long as I have the capacity to do it. I don't have any places I'm aiming at, or any large long-term conspiracy in mind in terms of what to reach, where it's going, or what it has to do.

PH: But you have ambition?

LC: The only ambition I have is to survive and to keep alive and not to let the spirit die. [*Pauses.*] And to make a million dollars.

PH: Why do you do so few concerts?

LC: It's not really my field. I guess I could put together concerts and things but I don't like to have to go out when I have new songs or new treatments of songs. And I don't like the feeling that I'm on the boards and that it's just a career. I do it when I feel I'm ready for the road. I want to meet people and sing new songs. That only happens every couple of years.

PH: Do you prefer the music to your poetry?

LC: I don't have too many preferences.

PH: What is love by your description?

LC: Wow. I don't know. I don't really have an idea about it.

PH: Surely you must have thoughts on it.

LC: I don't think too much. I never think, to tell you the truth. My own personal life is chaotic. Anybody who looks at my own personal life will come to the conclusion, rapidly, that I don't think at all. There's a kind of interior urgency about all things, as I see it. And I respond to it. I generally respond to it, in real life, in exactly the wrong way of doing things. As a friend of mine once said, "Now Leonard, are you sure you're doing the wrong thing?" I hardly have a thought in my head. Something happens and I have to answer it with a poem or a song or my own work. I don't know a thing about love.

DEPRESSING? WHO? ME?

STEVE TURNER | June 29, 1974, *New Musical Express* (UK)

On August 11, 1974, Columbia Records released Cohen's *New Skin for the Old Ceremony*, his first album of all-new material since 1971's *Songs of Love and Hate*. The album did not sell as well as its predecessors but it featured such atmospheric tracks as "Who by Fire" and the classic "Chelsea Hotel No. 2." Over time, it helped to further cement Cohen's reputation as one of the musical greats of his generation.

Shortly before the album's release, he talked with British journalist Steve Turner, who had already been a fan for seven years. "I came across Leonard Cohen in early 1968, when tracks from *Songs of Leonard Cohen* began to be played in London boutiques and on the playlists of Britain's pirate radio ships," Turner told me. "He was of particular interest to me because he straddled the world of literature and popular music, of books and records. Uniquely, he was a published poet who'd turned to songs rather than a successful lyricist who fancied himself as a poet.

"I don't remember a lot about the interview," Turner continued, "except that the room was small and that I was accompanied by *NME* photographer Pennie Smith, who would go on to make her name during the punk era, especially with her dramatic photo of the Clash that later graced the cover of *London Calling*.

"In hindsight, I regret that I kept pushing him with questions about depression, heroism, and suicide, because I'm sure he had a lot to say about sunnier subjects. If I'd quizzed him about ecstatic moments, comedy, and the good things in life, this would have been a very different piece. But in 1974 Cohen was regarded as the poet of gloom and that was the line I pursued.

"The reason for the meeting was *Bird on a Wire*, the ninety-minute documentary by British filmmaker Tony Palmer that was due for its world premiere at the Rainbow Theatre in London in July. 'I would probably prefer it to represent me glamorously with all the shots calculated to make me seem attractive and good looking,' Cohen said at one point. 'I guess I would like it to advertise what a good fellow I am and what a sensitive artist. It doesn't do those things but it is accurate from a certain point of view as to the songs and some of the emotions.'"

The interview included a brief discussion about Canadian poet Irving Layton and Charisma Books. "This was pertinent to me because in 1972 the publisher had picked up my first poetry collection," Turner said. "Cohen was aware that I was about to become a Charisma author and seemed familiar with my book, but I was never quite sure why he loosened his attachment to the company. During the interview, he spoke to me of wanting to get Charisma to publish the work of Daphne Richardson—the girl whose prose was printed on the back of *Live Songs* and who had killed herself in 1972 by jumping off the roof of the BBC's headquarters in central London." —Ed.

Leonard Cohen doesn't give interviews. What he does do is to arrange for you to meet him in his hotel room where, over a period of up to two hours, he'll supply you with carefully worded statements on a number of matters.

He's a careful man. Careful that nothing too shallow or pretentious is attributed to his output. After all, we are dealing with a man of letters here and not merely a singer/songwriter. Words are this man's business. He has a past that already consists of two novels, five volumes of poetry, thirty-three recorded songs, and a play. And, what's more, the songs were the latest addition. Cohen is no rock star turned novelist, turned poet, turned playwright.

Also, there's all that trouble he had with the journalist [Roy Hollingworth] he confided in two years ago, the result of which was a headline story, "Cohen Quits?" As Cohen tells it, this wasn't the substance of an interview but more the reflection of a mood that happened to be upon him that day, and one that he was assured would be taken as "off the record."

"I didn't expect to see that casual conversation appear in a headline," he says. "I had been speaking as anybody who was tired at the moment would speak and said that I really wouldn't like to read an article in which this conversation was described as a manifesto or an ultimatum or anything like that. And then of course it did appear.

"It caused a lot of mischief in the actual mechanics of my life because people couldn't seriously consider continuing contracts and that sort of thing if I had quit. But I'd no more quit than I'd quit anything. I had a moment where I indulged myself in the luxury of feeling betrayed."

So, beware of the wicked journalist who appears to be unarmed but possesses a healthy memory or a notepad in the loo. Still, Cohen's attitude toward men of my profession doesn't seem to be a recent development. "I prefer interviewers to take the same risks that I do," he told Jack Hafferkamp, who was profiling him for the *New York Times* back in 1971. "In other words, not to make a question-and-answer type of scene." [*This quote actually appeared in Hafferkamp's* Rolling Stone *article. See page 18. —Ed.*]

I take the risk at four o'clock one Wednesday afternoon and visit him at his Chelsea hotel. His room is small, large-cupboard size, and most of the space is taken up with two single beds. Cohen also seems small and an accurate reproduction of what I'd expected to see after eight years of sullen photographs. In person, though, he laughs. It's a short, sharp schoolboy laugh full of suction and comes out of the left of his mouth. It's good to see that he laughs.

He is in London, it seems, to help in the promotion of the documentary film of his 1972 tour *Bird on a Wire*, and also to encourage the sales of *Collected Poems* by Irving Layton, a Canadian poet who has been a close friend of his for twenty-five years.

In fact, Charisma Books, which is publishing Layton's work, was set up as a result of a joint idea between Tony Stratton-Smith and Cohen, the main purpose of the company being to encourage young so-far-unpublished writers. However, for reasons that he doesn't care to divulge, Cohen is no longer playing a creative role in the project.

"We're close friends," he says of Layton, "and I have a tremendous admiration for him as a writer and as a man. I didn't sit at his feet or anything like that, but I've learned a tremendous amount from him because I've had the opportunity of a close friend who is a generation older than me, and so in a very effortless way I was able to see how he got through his years."

The film, though, is obviously the main purpose of Cohen's visit, and it's a film that over the past two years has come to cause him some grief. In his last British interview he seemed despondent about it ever coming out. He spoke of it being "totally unacceptable" and how it had put him in a "financial crisis" by absorbing $125,000 of his money. However, what consequently happened was that the whole film was reedited—there were over ninety hours of material to pull from—and it's this second version that will be premiered at the Rainbow on July 5.

"They shouldn't have showed it to me at all," says Cohen about version one. "I was close to the tour, I remembered all the good moments and I didn't think they were there." Version two he finds more pleasing, mainly because other people seem to like it. "I'll tell you what I think the strengths and weaknesses are," he says. "It has some music in it . . . and that's quite good. It also has some of the conditions under which the music was produced, which is quite good.

"Then it has one or two pieces which I think are a little pretentious—calculated to indicate the sensitivity of the chap. I'd say there are five or ten minutes of that here and there that I don't think are good and find embarrassing.

"There are certain extended sequences of concerts where real emotional intensity was captured and I think that eventually, taking it on the balance, the better parts prevail over the weaker parts and you are left with something that is quite interesting.

"I think it *is* quite a good study of someone on tour. In my secret heart of vanity, I would have liked it to be a really tremendous description of myself but it isn't that. It shows some grave weaknesses of character. That's nobody's fault—that's true."

Besides the activity surrounding the film, Cohen is also back at work in the studio, recording an album that he hopes will be released during September [New Skin for the Old Ceremony, *which as noted earlier, came out August 11, 1974. —Ed.*]. The songs have been written over the past two years and he feels that they're somewhat different from his past work. He can't say in what way because it lies in the song itself, not in the description.

Most people have come to regard Leonard Cohen as the poet of despair. He knows this and when I ask him about it he plays games with definitions. "You're asking me to make an evaluation about something which I can't compare to someone else's," he replies when I ask whether he has a depressing outlook on things. "I only have my own window to look out of."

So I tell him about Janie, a friend twice removed, who used to suffer from acute depression and who used a darkened room and his albums to plunge her even deeper into despair, until the pain could become almost enjoyable. Then I ask him about the reports that he'd played in various mental hospitals in Canada.

"Yes, I have played for mental . . . audiences," he replies. I ask him what the attraction was and he pauses for at least twenty seconds before giving his reason. "It was the feeling that . . . experience of a lot of people in mental hospitals would especially qualify them to be a receptive audience for my work."

"Well worded, Leonard," I thought, "but what do you mean?" The questions and answers go on for another five minutes without an explanation of any depth until I have to say: "You have a way of not really telling me what I want to know."

"Well, I'll tell you something," rejoinders Cohen, "and this is the truth—I'm not trying to obscure anything from you and I'm trying to answer as accurately and as sufficiently as I can."

And then, as if by accident, he spills his reasons out. "In a sense, when someone consents to go into a mental hospital or is committed, he has already acknowledged a tremendous defeat," he says. "To put it another way, he has already made a choice. And it was my feeling that the elements to this choice, and the elements of this choice, and the elements of this defeat, corresponded with certain elements that produced my songs, and that there would be an empathy between the people who had this experience and the experience as documented in my songs."

It appears that in the Cohen scenario of life there are the defeated and there are the heroes. The defeated, the truly defeated, inhabit the mental hospitals and graveyards. They either commit themselves or choose to quit living. The heroes struggle on with the business of living in the face of the meaningless.

"I see tremendous heroism all around me," Cohen says, "people getting up, doing their work and going to bed at night. When you use the word 'insanity' it seems to indicate that some people are beyond the pale, that they've stepped into an irredeemable world. But it is my experience of people who are called insane that they are not much different from us in this room, except that they've said 'Ah shit! I'm not going to continue to play these games anymore. I'm going to quit. Do what you want with me.'

"For many of them, I think that their perceptions are even wider than mine or yours, because they see things that are true that really do cause them to quit trying on the conventional plane. It's maybe because we don't see the things as clearly as they do that we continue to try to cope with the realities that are really overwhelming."

Cohen says that in the past he has considered suicide, but that he has always rejected it on the grounds of the effects upon those left living. "It's really an act of aggression against the people you leave behind," he says. "It's such a messy thing! You leave people with that taste for the rest of their lives. It's an act of such long and continuing implications that you have real control over. But I suspect that suicides really do care and really do understand the implications of their act—that it's not a thing that ends with themselves.

"You know, they leave their bodies around for one thing and they leave notes and incriminating evidence, but worst of all they leave all their closest friends with a sense of guilt, deserved or not. If I committed suicide Avril [his publicist] would wonder what she'd done wrong and . . . you might wonder whether you'd pushed me over the edge!"

Finally I ask him whether he finds a lot of joy in his life. He laughs a little to himself. "I don't know," he says. "I don't look at it in that way.

"I don't go around looking for joy. I don't go around looking for melancholy either. I don't have a program. I'm not on an archeological expedition."

INTERVIEW

ROBIN PIKE | September 15, 1974, interview | October 1974, *ZigZag* (UK)

Robin Pike talked with Cohen soon after Steve Turner did—and only weeks after *New Skin for the Old Ceremony* hit the stores. Like Turner, he was a longtime fan.

"I first met Leonard Cohen in about 1967 at the Institute of Contemporary Arts in London where he was giving a poetry reading," Pike told me. "What I particularly remember about our interview, which occurred seven years later, was his great courtesy towards me. I arrived at the hotel totally unannounced when he had just had a most stressful journey—his coach had broken down. Many artists would have refused to be interviewed under the circumstances, but Cohen wrote out a guest pass on the back of a laundry card so that we could meet in his dressing room.

"Strangely, on the way home, my car broke down on the same motorway Cohen had arrived on. I was far less relaxed about it than a certain Mr. Cohen would have been."

Pike covers a lot of interesting and often fresh ground in this interview, which touches on everything from Judaism and psychedelics to Fidel Castro and the Rolling Stones. —Ed.

September 15 this year was a Sunday. The day after Wembley. It was raining when we left Aylesbury and when we reached Bristol. We had been told that the tour party was staying at the Royal Hotel but they were not expecting us. At three fifteen in the afternoon we stood in the foyer of a deserted hotel and asked for Mr. Cohen. After a brief telephone call by the receptionist we were sent up to the second floor.

The door of the room was open and there on the bed, phone in hand, was Leonard Cohen. We were asked to wait in the next room and talked with John Miller, the bass player. The tour had opened at the CBS convention in Eastbourne the previous week. From there the band traveled to Paris to play at the Fête de l'Humanité, a gathering run by the French Communist Party, which was attended by three hundred thousand people and featured [Greek composer Mikis] Theodorakis, Cohen, and other literary figures.

The British tour had opened in Edinburgh and the previous night had played Liverpool. Everything had gone smoothly until the tour coach got within twenty miles of Bristol. At this point it broke down, its cooling system having totally failed. So they got out and hitched. Only nobody would stop—it was pouring rain, you may remember. Eventually Leonard and John were given a lift by a kindly man who happened himself to be a coach operator. The rest of the party didn't get in until much later. By this time they had missed lunch and the hotel had no food on a Sunday afternoon, so John went out to look for something to eat. He found a Wimpey Bar and returned with four hamburgers, four Cokes, some chips, and a piece of chocolate gateau. We ate and interviewed at the same time. John the bass player showed a lively interest in photography and proceeded to take shots of us from the most unlikely angles. He was particularly fond of one taken from inside the wardrobe.

The [Bristol] Hippodrome is a delightful theater, more like an opera house than a concert hall. There is a back street that runs past the stage door at the side of the theater. Almost opposite the stage door is a seedy snack bar. Five minutes before the performance was due to start, an observant passerby would have noticed a familiar figure seated at a table drinking a cup of coffee. It was Mr. Cohen. In the dressing room there was no alcohol and no cigarettes. Nothing. Just the artists waiting to go onstage. Only the tour manager appeared in the slightest way nervous. The theater was full, the audience warm and responsive, and at the end of the evening they could not leave. Audience and performers alike sang the words of the songs they all knew so well. "Hey, That's No Way to Say Goodbye."

Leonard Cohen was born in Montreal in 1934. He has a sister. His father died when he was nine years old. Leonard describes his upbringing as strict in a Victorian sense. The family was of a conservative Jewish tradition. It made full observance of Jewish faith and customs without the rigidity of the Orthodox tradition. Leonard's grandfather was a Hebrew scholar. An imposing figure with long uncut hair, Rabbi Solomon Klinitsky was greatly revered by his grandson. [*Cohen himself has spelled his grandfather's last name "Klinitsky" and "Klinitsky-Kline"; but the original spelling was apparently "Klonitzki-Kline." —Ed.*] Leonard was educated at a Christian school. These years are remembered but without feeling. School days were boring. He edited the school newspaper, played hockey, and was a cheerleader. At college he played guitar in what he describes as a "barnstorming" group. At the age of fifteen he left school to take a course in English literature at McGill University. At the same time he left home to live in a flat in downtown Montreal. The novel *The Favorite Game* deals with this period of his life.

Robin Pike: Nobody got thrown out or anything like that?

Leonard Cohen: The worst that could happen to you was that you'd fail a year and you'd start over again. The life was downtown—meeting the artists and the poets and discovering what café life was. I was young in those days. There was no oppressive tradition or anything so you were doing it yourself. It was fun. Just a few people around.

RP: I was wondering if you went through the business of reading all the Shakespeare plays—whether you read a lot of more stylized poetry.

LC: I read a lot of poetry—but not specifically connected with the course I was taking. There are some Shakespearean plays I haven't read. There are some I have read very, very thoroughly. I went out with a Shakespearean actress for a while so I used to have to learn all her plays so I could follow what they were about. But I didn't have a very thorough background in English literature at all.

RP: Do you have any favorite plays, particularly, say, Shakespearean plays?

LC: I like *Timon of Athens* very much. I think that's quite a late one.

RP: I'm thinking of the tragedies like [*King*] *Lear* or *Hamlet* or *Macbeth*.

LC: Well, to me it's like saying how do you feel about the high Himalayas or something. They're great, huge articulations of human experience, by the master poet of our race. It's hard for me sitting here, eating a hamburger, to say what I like or don't like. I stand in a certain reverence to these masters. Those people I don't take casually at all.

RP: Can I change the subject and ask you about your political involvement, particularly with, shall we say, revolutionary movements?

LC: I guess my interior connection with these movements approximates to Camus's experience, although of course I didn't take any of his risks. I went down to Cuba to observe and associate myself with that revolution just before the Bay of Pigs.

RP: Did you meet Castro?

LC: No, never on that level. Just as a foot soldier. It's hard for me to speak about those things. My feeling these days is very different. I don't think that armed revolution should be encouraged in industrial societies. I think it would be a disaster if such a thing ever happened. It really would be awful. What do you feel?

RP: Yes, I don't see revolution as achieving very much in those terms. More through infiltration than armed uprising. I believe you were involved with the Black Power movement at one time.

LC: Well, I knew some people in it. Michael X I knew very well. He's just waiting to be hung. I had many talks with him. For some races, there are men of imagination who are really oppressed and there is absolutely no other way. They have got to take up this position whether they really believe it in their hearts or not. They have to have a structure to which they can attach themselves. To wait and see, it just doesn't satisfy their hunger or their imagination. They can only see themselves extended through society with that kind of thrust behind them. There's no argument you can have with them. You can't say cool it out, or whatever is achieved by this or that except more violence? OK, let us be the ones who are making the violence on you guys, we're tired of being on the other side.

But he himself knew the limitations of this position. That's what we don't understand. The leaders of the Movement (to have that kind of power in the Movement means they're quite bright) understand perfectly the limitations of their position all the time. Michael said to me—he was completely against arming the blacks in America; he said it was crazy— they would never be able to resist that machine. They own the bullets and the armaments factories and the guns. So you give the blacks a few guns and have them against armies? He was even against knives. He said we should use our teeth. Something everybody has. That was his view of the thing. It was a different kind of subversion. The subversion of real life to implant black fear. He would invite me over to his place and he would serve me a drink, a delicious drink. I would say, "God, how do you make this?" He would say, "You don't expect me to tell you. If you know the secrets of our food, you know the secrets of our race and the secrets of our strength." You know, it was that kind of vision that he wanted to develop. Pretty good, too.

RP: How do you feel about your position as a Jew? Do you support, for instance, the movement to free Jewish prisoners in Soviet Russia? Particularly artists like the Panovs.

LC: Yes I do. Also Ukrania. I would like to see the breakup of the Russian empire. I think there are a lot of Russians who feel that way too. A lot of Russians are not really interested in the domination of Czechoslovakia, Bulgaria, Ukrania, and Latvia. It's a difficult position they've got themselves into. The Jews come under that kind of heading also.

RP: Do you actively work in this sort of area? Do you really lend your support?

LC: No. No, I give my name if anybody asks for it. I don't feel that my talents run in those directions. I've never disguised the fact that I'm Jewish and in any crisis in Israel I would be there. I was there in the last war and I would be there in another war. I am committed to the survival of the Jewish people. I have a lot of quarrels inside that camp with Jewish leadership and Jewish value and that sort of thing. I am committed to the survival of the Jewish people and I think that survival is threatened in places like the

Soviet Union. I think it's threatened in America on another level. It's just a tribal feeling. There's nothing enacted.

RP: You mentioned that you went back to Israel at the time of the last war and you sang. Can you say a bit more about that? How did you actually take part?

LC: I just attached myself to an air force entertainment group. We would just drop into little places, like a rocket site, and they would shine their flashlights at us and we would sing a few songs. Or they would give us a Jeep and we would go down the road toward the front and wherever we saw a few soldiers waiting for a helicopter or something like that we would sing a few songs. And maybe back at the airbase we would do a little concert, maybe with amplifiers. It was very informal and very intense. Wherever you saw soldiers you would just stop and sing.

RP: It strikes me as being rather dangerous. You didn't feel any personal anxiety about being killed?

LC: I did once or twice. But you get caught up in the thing. And the desert is beautiful and you think your life is meaningful for a moment or two. And war is wonderful. They'll never stamp it out. It's one of the few times people can act their best. It's so economical in terms of gesture and motion. Every single gesture is precise, every effort is at its maximum. Nobody goofs off. Everybody is responsible for his brother. The sense of community and kinship and brotherhood, devotion. There are opportunities to feel things that you simply cannot feel in modern city life. Very impressive.

RP: Obviously you found that stimulated you. Did you find it stimulated your writing at all?

LC: In a little way. But not really. I wrote a song there.

RP: Wars have in the past been times when people have written great things after or during.

LC: I didn't suffer enough. I didn't lose anyone I knew.

The conversation at this point turned to Leonard's experience of singing to patients in mental hospitals. He believes that it is good for a band to play free concerts and he has done a lot of this work in Canada.

RP: Do you see yourself then as an entertainer or as a therapist?

LC: I have a lot of admiration for the professional point of view. I think a therapist should be an entertainer. Whatever you are you should be an entertainer first. If you're going to present yourself to people they have to be entertained. Their imagination has to be engaged and they have to enter into the vortex of imagination and relaxation and suspense that is involved in entertainment.

RP: I'm thinking that if you go into a group of people and then you go away from it, perhaps without any measure of supervision, it might be difficult. Or would you expect the professional staff to take part in the entertainment as well and then to be able, perhaps to catch up anything that happened as a result of your work with them? It would be a very fleeting visit, wouldn't it?

LC: It just takes a tiny moment to receive a scar. It can be with you for the rest of your life. Similarly I think the things that touch us—I don't know, incidentally, if I'm one of these people, I'm just in a tradition—I'm probably just like a ninth-rate operator in a great tradition. I also have very clear ideas about where I stand in a great tradition. The kind of healing that goes with song or with art or whatever you care to mention is almost impossible to talk about because it happens to one person in an audience. Something out of the work touches them in some way. In any ordinary audience, also. Some connection is made. I don't think it's anything that all but the most sensitive doctor or worker could ever pick up on. And certainly, not guaranteed that it will happen to very many people. Mostly it's just entertainment for an evening. To get through the night.

RP: I just wondered whether possibly it might not be rather frightening and alarming if this particular spark did happen to strike and you were there, and then you'd gone and whatever had happened wouldn't have been supported by your presence again. And this is something that could really destroy what little bit of strength they had.

LC: I agree with you. This certainly happens outside of the hospitals, if you're dealing, as I do, with a certain kind of material. It happens to even the most casual of pop singers. You don't have to be dealing with very rarified or specialized material. Every singer has had this experience. Tom Jones has it. The people start to see the work as having a special kind of healing or visionary element and they assume that you are the master and the creator and the engineer of this balm, this unguent, this healing substance, and somehow that contact with you will guarantee the cure. They come forward in a certain kind of way through letter or through the person and, of course, they are doomed to disappointment and after all, of course, the artist himself can't function in the capacity of a healer, in a professional sense. So it does, as you say, often throw people into states of mind that are difficult. I had this happen just a couple of days ago. Did you see that girl, John? That black girl? Her manuscript, called "A Pyramid of Suffering," is a document of suffering.

John Miller [Cohen's bass player]: Where were you in it?

LC: All through it. References to my songs. She is a mental patient.

RP: How about Daphne Richardson, whose letter you had on the back of the *Live* [*Songs*] album? Could you say something about her? Because this seems possibly to tie in with this area.

LC: I knew her first of all through the mails. I try to read everything I get and I was struck by the power of her communications. She was at that time trying to get published a book of poems that were very experimental and were collage poems. And they weren't by any means inept. They were highly skilled. They were a collage of Dylan, myself, and her own work. And Dylan wouldn't give her permission to publish his work in scraps. And I did. I entered into this communication with her. I knew there was an edge to her letters that was so fanatic and so intense that she would experience great floods of disturbance. On the other hand, there was something about her mind that I found immensely attractive and delightful.

Then her story started to emerge. She sent me long, long letters and books that she'd written to me and of course there were these excessive kinds of letters that she would write to me that she wanted to come and stay with me or—you know. On the other hand, her doctors and the people in her hospitals that she would come in and out of—they didn't believe that she was in communication with me at all. They thought that this was a complete pipe dream.

So she was living a completely strange sort of life. They were strapping her down and that sort of thing and she would say, "Leonard Cohen, I'm going to be working on his book." I said, "I'd like you to illustrate my book"—she was a very fine draughtsman—and I had intended her to illustrate my last book, *The Energy of Slaves*. She'd be screaming at the doctors, "You've got to let me out! I'm illustrating Leonard Cohen's next book."

I did go over on my last tour and we arranged to meet and I met her for the first time and she was a very attractive girl in her thirties, and really nice and of a style and bearing that was very close to people that I know. I knew she had experience in mental hospitals. We arranged to do this book together and I looked at more of her drawings and I was very impressed. Then I went back to America. And it was just one period when I was out of touch with my correspondence and I came to this correspondence and I found telegrams and letters saying, "Please help. I've been put away again. They won't believe me. I need your help, please help." I got on the phone to my agent in London and I said, "Get ahold of Daphne right away, she's in trouble. I'm already late, it's a month since these telegrams had come." I said, "Tell her that the work on the book is on and I want her to start these illustrations. I'll get the manuscript to her."

And she'd just committed suicide three days before.

I was just too late.

Another three weeks or a week or anything. She was just holding on to this kind of activity.

RP: Yes, I can see that.

LC: She mentioned me in her suicide note. It was horrible.

RP: Why did you put it on the back of the record?

LC: Oh, she always wanted to be published. She couldn't get anyone to publish her. The letter was to me. There was a book she wrote to me from the mental hospital. I tell you, it was shattering. A testimony of pain. I've never read anything like it.

JM: What's the difference between that and the "Pyramid of Suffering"?

LC: Very close, but a suffering that is not enlightened. Daphne was like somebody sitting in this room. She was completely aware. There were no blank spots. She was not a compulsive or an obsessive kind of person. She went into pain that was so overwhelming that she couldn't function. But she always knew where she was and what she was doing. This girl is like under it—it's really a pyramid—that's a beautiful description of where she is. She's buried under a pyramid of suffering like there is no other. Daphne, however, had a sense of humor. She was attractive. She was a much more attractive figure. Warm. This girl was insane. The black girl was insane. There was no question about that. Daphne was . . . I really blew that. I felt bad about that.

But you're right, and it's made me much . . . the point that you just very delicately suggested that I ought not to meddle around with these things if I'm not going to be there day after day to really follow through. I really feel that way now.

RP: Yes, I think one thing one has to learn as a therapist is to be very careful to prepare one's patient for the time of parting if that is going to happen. It can be very painful.

Well, perhaps if I could change the subject again and ask you about one or two of your songs. About "Suzanne" and about Pearls Before Swine. Am I right in thinking they recorded that before you did?

LC: [*To Miller.*] Did you ever know that group?

JM: I never knew that. They recorded "Suzanne" before you?

LC: They recorded "Suzanne," yes.

JM: But not before you?

LC: Around the same time—very early.

JM: They were very interesting, Pearls Before Swine.

RP: Were they friends of yours? Or how did that come about?

LC: I think the song was just making its way through New York at the time. They just picked up on it. Are they still together? Is there such a group?

RP: I don't believe so. When I went to school there was a Buffy Sainte-Marie concert and I reviewed it for the paper and she sang "Suzanne." I wrote in my article that I swore she said, "I'm going to do a song now that *I* wrote." Was there any question as to who wrote "Suzanne"?

LC: Not really, no. The song was stolen from me in terms of legal copyright, but nobody has ever suggested I didn't write it. You may have got it wrong, but she is fantastic. I actually taught it to her mouth to mouth.

JM: She did it great.

LC: She is a greatly underestimated singer. I think she's one of the greatest.

RP: She has recorded one or two of your songs that you haven't recorded, is that right?

LC: She did a version of a long passage from *Beautiful Losers* called "God Is Alive." She did a beautiful job with that.

RP: And there is a song called "Bells," I think.

LC: She recorded "Bells." An early, early version, which we do. I just recorded that now. It's a version completely changed from the one I taught her.

RP: Could you say something about Nico?

LC: I hope I can see her when we get back to France. Or in London, if she's in town.

RP: She's been recording in London.

LC: She's incredible. She's a great singer and a great songwriter. Completely disregarded from what I can see. I don't think she sells fifty records, but I think she's one of the really original talents in the whole racket.

RP: Is it right that you wrote "Joan of Arc" particularly with her in mind?

LC: Oh, I wouldn't say that. How did you know that?

RP: It appeared in one of your recent interviews.

LC: Oh really? I don't remember if that's true. I know that I was after her—I was sniffing around. I was very taken by Nico in those days. I did write that song around that time.

RP: How about Lou Reed and the Velvet Underground?

LC: I knew those people in New York. When I first came to New York—I guess it was around 1966—Nico was singing at the Dom, which was an Andy Warhol club at the time on Eighth Street. I just stumbled in there one night and I didn't know any of these people. I saw this girl singing behind the bar. She was a sight to behold. I suppose the most beautiful woman I'd ever seen up to that moment. I just walked up and stood in front of her until people pushed me aside. I started writing songs for her then. She introduced me to Lou Reed at that time. And Lou Reed surprised me greatly because he had a book of my poems. I hadn't been published in America, and I had a very small audience even in Canada. So when Lou Reed asked me to sign *Flowers for Hitler*, I thought it was an extremely friendly gesture of his. The Velvet Underground had broken up at the time. He played me his songs. It was the first time I'd heard them. I thought they were excellent—really fine. I used to praise him.

RP: How well did you know him?

LC: I can't say I know him well at all. He was an early reader of *Beautiful Losers,* which he thought was a good book. In those days I guess he wasn't getting very many compliments on his work and I certainly wasn't. So we told each other how good we were. I liked him immediately because Nico liked him.

RP: Could I ask you about other people in the music business, like Van Morrison?

LC: I'm very fond of his work. I don't know him. I love his work, as a matter of fact. [*To Miller.*] Do you?

JM: Great. He's another one who's great and will never be a great star and possibly doesn't want to be.

RP: Could I ask you about the Rolling Stones? Whether you've ever had any contact with them, whether you think anything about their music?

LC: I met Mick Jagger once in the lobby of the Plaza Hotel and he said, "Are you in New York for a poetry reading?"

Some of their songs I like very much. I think it's wonderful, the phenomenon of the Rolling Stones—the figure of Mick Jagger. They are the bread and wine of the pop groups. I was a little bit older than other people when I came into contact with these figures, and I'd already had my mind blown by older and much more outrageous people that I'd met in my youth, so I wasn't about to succumb to the kind of fever that they produce in younger people. But I've always admired them from the slightly humorous point of view. I never did seriously ask myself if Mick Jagger was the Devil. But I think as figures they're quite interesting.

RP: You are in some senses rather an alien figure to a lot of people in the music business and I wonder to what extent you do consider yourself as quite separate from it.

LC: I feel totally separate from it. I love the phenomenon, but I don't live as one of those figures. My own personal style is very, very different. I don't perform in the same kind of field. My life is completely different and it developed on different grounds that came to my mind much earlier than the pop movement. My lifestyle was formulated in the middle fifties and has changed very little since then. The kinds of rooms that I could find myself in.

RP: Could I ask you about one or two more songs? "The Story of Isaac," for instance. Could you describe a little how you came to write that? It does include a reference to a father. Is this your father?

LC: It is hard to step outside the center of a song when you've written it and explain it to anyone, including yourself. All you know as a writer, as an artist, or as someone who deals and manipulates symbols is whether it has an interior integrity. I think this song does have that kind of interior integrity. It has fathers and sons in it and sacrifice and slaughter, and an extremely honest statement at the end. And that's all I can say about it.

The antiwar movement claims the song as its own and that's fine. The Fascist Party movement could also claim it as its own, and that's fine. I know that song is true. It does say something about fathers and sons and that curious place, generally over the slaughtering block where generations meet and have their intercourse. As to its meaning or anything else, I don't know, except that it exists as a psychic reality. That's about all I can say about it.

RP: There wasn't a particular circumstance at the time that you wrote it?

LC: I think probably that I did feel that one of the reasons that we have wars was so the older men can kill off the younger ones, so that there's no competition for the women. Or for their position. I do think that this is true. One of the reasons we do have wars periodically is so the older men can have the women. Also, completely remove the competition in terms of their own institutional positions. I also understand that the story of Isaac in the Bible has other significances, which have to do with faith and absurdity and what they used to call, in the fifties, existential religion.

Outside of all those cultural attachments, which the song has gathered to itself as it moves through society in its limping way, I just know that as an experience it's authentic psychically. It doesn't betray itself. That's all I mean. The song doesn't end with a plea for peace. It doesn't end with a plea for sanity between the generations. It ends saying, "I'll kill you if I can, I will help you if I must, I will kill you if I must, I will help you if I can." That's all I can say about it. My father died when I was nine, that's the reason I put that one of us had to go.

RP: Would you like to say anything about "The Butcher"?

LC: "The Butcher" is another one of those little songs that has that kind of psychic integrity. You could dignify it with a religious interpretation. I'm not interested in that, if people want to do that. If they want to dignify it or elaborate it on altars or dissecting tables or whatever it is—it's cool with me. Everybody's job should be protected. To me, when the energy is somehow generated within somebody to create something, the thing has to stand or fall by its own internal construction. To me that's another little song that has an internal authenticity or accuracy that allows it to exist.

RP: How about drugs?

LC: I don't use them myself. I think they're very bad for you. I think grass is terrible. I don't say this to anybody because nobody believes me. There's a great grass culture and far be it from me to intrude upon the pleasures of the young. I smoked grass for a long time. I know what it is, I know what it does, and I think we're a culture that is not yet wise enough to handle it. I've spoken to Moroccans who've observed Americans smoking and they think we're crazy. And they smoke a lot.

JM: Why?

LC: Because we smoke all the time.

JM: We smoke less than they?

LC: Much, much more. We smoke all the time.

JM: Am I wrong to think that in Morocco all they do is sit around with hash pipes?

LC: I am sure that there are those who do that. I could find those guys in Ireland who sit around the pubs drinking all day. But by and large we handle our alcohol. But American youth will smoke all the grass they have, all the time, until it's gone. I think there are other peoples who handle it better. I don't want to make a point about this. As far as I can see, they're not in such good shape either. The inscrutable Orientals are not that great in the handling of these problems either. Obviously people use grass and write beautiful things on it. I don't dispute any of the excellent and magnificent products that the thing has done. To me personally, I have seen the damage that it has done to myself and others. I don't think it's all that great. And that's the one [marijuana] that's supposed to be harmless.

RP: I asked you that after we were talking about "The Butcher" because of the line in "The Butcher."

LC: I have used drugs. I have used almost everything that I could ever get my hands on. I have taken them in every possible way. I think that drugs without a sacrament, without a ritual, without a really great understanding of their power are dangerous. I'm not talking about banning or not using drugs. I'm talking about the casual and indiscriminate and social use of drugs can be very, very dangerous. And is dangerous. I think that LSD is by far the most powerful substance in society. There's no question about that.

RP: Is it true that you were in a monastery?

LC: I have ties with certain monasteries that I visit from time to time.

RP: Do you visit as a retreat or do you visit as a novice, or would you consider taking vows?

LC: I visit them as a friend of the abbot rather than in any other capacity.

RP: What order is the monastery?

LC: There are one or two Trappist monasteries that I have visited and one or two Buddhist monasteries that I have visited. I don't like to speak too much about it—it tends to advertise myself as a virtuous person or something and my feeling has nothing to do with virtue. There are a couple of men who are very strong and interesting, whose company I enjoy tremendously. They happen to be in the religious industry or whatever you want to call it. They put you through changes, they make you work and you're not likely to sleep more than three or four hours a night.

RP: You observe their rules?

LC: Oh yes. I observe their rules. If you want to study with a very good professor at Heidelberg you'd have to learn German. It's just their vocabulary. I'm more than willing to learn their vocabulary in order to enjoy their company. It's just the way they operate. It's something they've inherited from their own tradition and are very good at it. Outside of that tradition is another situation. Within their tradition they really flower and they flourish. To get the benefits of their personalities you have to learn their vocabulary.

RP: We had a broadcast last Sunday—or was it the Sunday before?—in which Mick Jagger had to pick twelve records. They were really very interesting because he picked some classical Indian music which he liked to listen to, and as one can imagine a lot of black American music. But you probably couldn't do anything like that?

LC: I'm not too interested in music. I don't have a record player most of the time. I'm not that close to that side of things. If you asked me if there were some songs that I would like to remember, that I would like not to forget if the world was going to be overwhelmed by a vast amnesia, six songs that I would like to remember, I might be able to do that. But in terms of records and books—it would really be an effort to sit down and write an authentic and accurate list.

It is unlikely that we shall see Leonard Cohen touring in Britain again in the near future. He plans to reappear every few years to show us what he is doing. He believes that an entertainer is likely to develop an inflated idea of his own importance if he is constantly recording and touring. In any case, it takes him about three years to complete a song. He does not like the commercial hassles of the music business. In fact, he prefers his earlier film, *Ladies and Gentlemen, Mr. Leonard Cohen*, to his latest, *Bird on a Wire*.

The British tour ended at the Albert Hall on September 19th. He did not say good-bye. His last words to the audience were:

"Thank you for remembering the songs which I wrote, all those years ago, in a room."

INTERVIEW

JORDI SIERRA I FABRA | October 12–14, 1974, interview | 1978, *Leonard Cohen* (Spain)

In September and October of 1974, Cohen supported *New Skin for the Old Ceremony* with 29 concerts in Belgium, France, England, Denmark, Germany, Holland, Austria, and Spain. Two of the last of these gigs took place in Barcelona in mid-October, and famed Spanish journalist Jordi Sierra i Fabra used the occasion to have a wide-ranging, multiday conversation with the artist. The interview, which was translated to English by Jane Danko, appeared four years later in the Spanish book *Leonard Cohen*, which was edited by Alberto Manzano. —Ed.

"I don't think of myself as a singer, writer, or any other thing. The job of being a man is much more than any of that." —Leonard Cohen

Leonard Cohen performed in the Palau de la Música Catalana, in Barcelona, Spain, on Saturday, October 12, 1974. With the success of the first concert, a second concert was hurriedly scheduled as a matinee on Sunday, October 13. A man sparing with words, but exceedingly expressive with those he says, he agreed to meet with only three journalists, and each of these separately, in his dressing room at the Palau de la Música on the night of the first concert. The following morning, in brief moments at his hotel, he spoke freely with anyone who approached him or asked him a question.

The following is the result of a brief interview on October 12 and two other conversations with him during those days in which, for the first time, Leonard stood on Spanish soil.

Jordi Sierra i Fabra: After the announcement of your retirement from the world of music, why this tour and new album?

Leonard Cohen: I really never left. The announcement of my retirement was the result of a bit of sensationalism by a journalist who either took very lightly, or freely interpreted, something I said. There are times when one is facing a crisis, and the tone of what is said can be freely interpreted by anyone with a little imagination. In one of those good or bad moments of sincerity, when words come from the heart more than from the brain, that announcement was generated.

JF: Do you have many times of real depression?

LC: I wouldn't call it depression, rather a matter of conscience. One has to notice that we are immersed in a terrible and catastrophic age that is affecting many people. Each day, hundreds of nameless people die while I am singing and you are listening to music. It's a constant apocalypse, and in some people, that leaves its mark.

JF: Is it hard for you to leave your solitude to record an album or to go into the public light?

LC: It's hard from the very first, when I first start thinking of immersing myself again into the hecticness of constant travel, interviews, concerts. Today I sing here and tomorrow there, which means I never get to know people, the cities they live in, their problems, their circumstances. That makes me feel strange, as if I were not really me, only a person who is passing through, at whom people look, whom they hear, and nothing more. But I also do this to give myself some concrete answers at specific times in my life. I decided to make this tour, for example, as a way of reviewing my capabilities, as a profound analysis.

JF: What have you found out so far through this analysis?

LC: For the moment, that I want to present good music, out of respect for the people who are buying their tickets, and out of respect for myself. The rest I won't know until the tour is over and I have returned to my privacy.

JF: Are you really as sad as your songs? As pessimistic, and, at times, as bitter?

LC: My work is always autobiographical, and, I hope, objective. Of course, I am like my songs; but I don't consider myself sad, so I don't think my songs are sad.

JF: In any case, could one speak of a melancholy born of the heartbeat of that catastrophic world you spoke of before?

LC: It's possible that sincerity might be confused with many things, especially in the world of music, where so many commercial currents run. In any case, it's only a question of coloring. My music is a reflection of my personality, and my personality is a reflection of all that surrounds me. For me, seeing all of this as my work, the most important thing is to be worthy. So I treat this world that surrounds me with the integrity and dignity necessary to bring it, through me, to everyone else.

After that, it is the spiritual state of each person that determines how it will affect her or him. A person could think that I or my songs are sad because of that person's own spiritual state, because they are not affected by the chaotic emotions that surround us, because they are living in another state, and I don't mean to say that that state is more superficial or ordinary. On the contrary, it is the way of being forged by each individual, in which they live. But their power to understand will be affected by what they feel, and by the meaning they give to things. My songs are life and the facts of each day, and I am my songs.

JF: But it's obvious that, like you, many people think about and feel these things, because otherwise you never would have reached this great communion of ideas, or this link, between people and your expression as poet and singer. Do you think this is something good, a virtue that you have to offer?

LC: My songs have to be lived from the inside. No one will be able to see anything in them if they are on the outside. The fact that people buy my albums or are interested in me means that there are many people inside these songs. We can't talk about virtues, only about creating some relationships people can identify with.

JF: When you talk about people, do you see individual faces or is it a concept of the masses?

LC: People are a complex of everyday heroes, at least that's what I feel. There are millions of faces and personalities, but all together they form a people. Then, within each group, there emerges a value system that makes some into leaders and others into followers, that makes some into celebrities, and others into unknown people. All of them are heroes, but each with a different destiny.

JF: In spite of being Canadian, you have made the Mediterranean into something of a home. What do countries such as Greece and Spain mean to you?

LC: That they are two very pure vestiges in a technologized world. The folklore of both countries is something that is not found in many places, although it seems, from what I have seen since my arrival in Barcelona, that it is losing out in favor of Americanization. A country that has something such as flamenco, that has in its tradition poets like Lorca, shouldn't let itself be influenced, and certainly not governed, by a music made up by another mentality and put on it by strictly commercial interests.

JF: Is it true that you have a daughter named Lorca?

LC: Yes.

JF: Has coming to Spain, or the people here, made an impact on you?

LC: It isn't that I've found everything I had imagined, or that I've felt any special images or presences, if that is what you mean. But when the people have connected to my songs, and I have seen them happy, I have felt very connected to them, and that's why I very happily saluted Lorca, dedicating the success of the concert to his memory.

JF: What has Garcia Lorca meant in your life?

LC: I've talked about that from the stage. He has been a man of extraordinary influence on both my political and personal work. I admire him. At fourteen years of age, I realized that to define the words "purity" and "poetry," I could go to Lorca.

JF: Returning to the subject of Mediterranean influence, do you think of these concerts in Spain as having far-reaching effects on you?

LC: Yes, that above all, because I have been very influenced by the Mediterranean culture, since I live in the Mediterranean, and because Spain is a profoundly Mediterranean country. I have had a very well-known desire to come here, because of feelings I had, because of Lorca, and get to know the people.

JF: With this tour, and with the bad treatment you have received from the English and American critics, how are you feeling about this international exposure?

LC: I don't consider myself a great singer. I just play the guitar and interpret my lyrics. I do what I do because I have a need to do it, to express what I know, and to show people what I do. It's true that this tour has had some rough moments, especially in the US and England, but the unpleasant times have not come from the public, just from the critics, and I really don't pay attention to critics. Critics view things with a certain coldness. They focus on the sound, whether it's good or bad, whether one plays the guitar well, whether there is a large audience, and sometimes they can't see real success, because they don't look into the soul of the audience nor into the soul of the singer. I've seen the people applauding from their hearts, and that is what is truly important for me. And that's the way it was today, here in Barcelona. So this tour, in my opinion, has gone well indeed. I am content, happy.

JF: Today you played with a complete band, a keyboardist, saxophone, a bass viola, a cello, a guitar, and trumpet, and two girls playing the guitar and singing backup. Why don't you perform solo with just your guitar anymore?

LC: Because I realize that I could become tired, or perhaps I couldn't hold the attention of the audience if I were alone on the stage. So I surround myself with good musicians and sing with them. One has to evolve, but without losing one's identity, of course, and I can't do today what I did eight years ago.

JF: Why this severe attitude onstage, without ever moving around, without ever smiling, almost like you aren't really in the moment?

LC: There are those who sing laughing, who prance around and make a show. I sing serious songs, and I'm serious onstage because I couldn't do it any other way. I think that a bullfighter doesn't enter the ring laughing. Rather, he enters thinking that he is betting his life against the bull.

JF: Why did you end the concert with a military salute? Why do you do this after each concert you give?

LC: Because I don't consider myself a civilian. I consider myself a soldier, and that's the way soldiers salute.

JF: But . . . a soldier? On which side? In what sense?

LC: I will leave that to your imagination. I am a soldier. That's all. I don't want to speak of wars or sides.

JF: Nonetheless, "Lover Lover Lover" is dedicated to your "brothers" in the Arab–Israeli war, and besides, you were there, singing for them. This indicates you're taking a side, and in a way, fighting for it.

LC: Personal process is one thing. It's blood, it's the identification one feels with their roots and their origins. The militarism I practice as a person and a writer is another thing.

JF: But you worry about war, and for that reason it would be logical that you would be concerned about both sides.

LC: I don't want to talk about war.

JF: Do you feel commercialized when a million copies of your albums are sold?

LC: That isn't the problem. That feeling doesn't happen at the time a million albums are sold. It happens afterward, when I accept the fact that my songs are being recorded and entered into the commercial games. I feel neither guilty nor happy, but I could add that the system uses me as much as I use it, so we would have to speak in terms of collaboration. What concerns me is reaching the people, so I have to submit to the rules of the game, because this system is the only means I have to do what I have to do.

COHEN CLIP

On Cover Versions of His Songs

"I can't honestly say that I have heard my songs done in a way that totally satisfies me, I think, with the exception perhaps of 'Suzanne' by Judy Collins. And her treatments of the other songs are also very delicate and sensitive but I don't know if there are really versions of the songs that strike me the way I would like to be struck. Not that my own are that way, either . . ."

—from interview with Kathleen Kendall, WBAI-FM
(New York), December 4, 1974

LEONARD COHEN: THE ROMANTIC IN A RAGPICKER'S TRADE

PAUL WILLIAMS | March 1975, *Crawdaddy!* (US)

After touring Europe in September and October of 1974, Cohen performed in the United States and Canada from November of that year through March of 1975. Around this time, he had an illuminating encounter with Paul Williams, founder of the groundbreaking rock magazine *Crawdaddy!*. The interview appeared in that magazine two months after Columbia Records released *The Best of Leonard Cohen.* —Ed.

"I think marriage is the hottest furnace of the spirit today," Leonard Cohen said on the phone from Mexico. "Much more difficult than solitude, much more challenging for people who want to work on themselves. It's a situation in which there are no alibis, excruciating most of the time . . . but it's only in this situation that any kind of work can be done. Naturally I feel ambiguous about it."

The phone call—Leonard watching children running in and out of a telephone company office in Acapulco (once he saw a butterfly), me in a twelfth-floor record company cubicle in New York—was part two of a conversation that began in Leonard Cohen's lawyer's office, high above 42nd Street in Manhattan maybe three week earlier.

Leonard had just returned from a tour of Europe, thirty-eight concerts in forty-five days, including an outdoor performance in Paris in front of

130,000 people. He's a superstar in France ("If a girl in Paris has only one record, it's a Leonard Cohen album," my traveling friend informs me) and all over the continent. His latest album, *New Skin for the Old Ceremony*, sold 250,000 copies in Europe in its first six weeks.

In the US and in his native Canada, Cohen has not achieved the same kind of acceptance as a performer and recording artist. He is best known as a songwriter ("Suzanne," "Bird on a Wire"), poet, and novelist. *Beautiful Losers*, his second novel, is a steady seller on college campuses and is even taught in modern literature courses . . . though ten years ago it was considered almost too filthy to publish.

Talking with Leonard Cohen is like touching the earth unexpectedly after months of subway stations and supermarkets. There's a resiliency in the man and his sense of himself; he seems to know what he's doing. Most contemporary singer-songwriters are not mature artists: they're too young, or they tasted success too young and never got past its confusions. Cohen is an exception.

He's forty years old. When you meet him, whether or not you know his writing, you can't help but recognize immediately that he is his own creation. "I've been lucky," he says, in regard to his relationship with the music industry. "Nobody's ever twisted my arm. Perhaps because nobody ever saw any great profits to be made from my work." Perhaps. But more likely they saw right away that there is no way to push Leonard Cohen to release more product (he's made five albums in eight years) or tour more often (his recent appearances are his first in America in four years) or commercialize his sound. It's not that he resists—it's just that he's not malleable. He has to be bought and sold as what he is.

He is a son of wealthy Jewish parents in Montreal, Duddy Kravitz-era—"I had a very Messianic childhood," he told Richard Goldstein in 1967. "I was told I was a descendant of Aaron, the high priest." He was a published poet at age twenty, lived on an island in Greece for eight years, published a couple of novels, came to New York in 1966, and captured the attention of the pop music world with a song called "Suzanne," recorded by Judy Collins and Joshua Rifkin on their brilliant breakthrough album *In My Life*.

John Hammond signed him to Columbia Records, over the protests of many who thought it was the silliest thing he'd done since signing Bob Dylan. Cohen cut his first record in 1967. "Of course, it was terribly difficult," Hammond said in an interview in 1971. "You couldn't get Leonard to work with other musicians because he felt they were all laughing at him. And they mostly were." That album, *Songs of Leonard Cohen*, was followed by *Songs from a Room* in 1969, *Songs of Love and Hate* in 1971, *Live Songs* in 1972, and *New Skin* in 1974. His books of poems, already popular in Canada, were released here starting in 1967, and the attention he got as a songwriter also helped promote his novels into paperback form and popular acceptance.

He performed a few concerts—the Isle of Wright, Forest Hills in New York—three European tours in seven years, no tours at all in America until early 1975. He lived mostly in Montreal and on Hydra Island in Greece; spent a year in New York around 1969, spent almost two years living in a farm outside Franklin, Tennessee in 1971–1972. (His cabin was the former home of Boudleaux Bryant, author of "Bye Bye, Love.")

Sometime well after writing the song "Suzanne" he met his wife Suzanne [*In fact, they never married. —Ed.*]; they have two children, Adam and Lorca (the boy is two and a half years, the girl about six months old). "I live here with a woman and a child," he sings on his most recent album. "The situation makes me kind of nervous. Yes, I rise up from her arms, she says, 'I guess you call this love, I call it service.' Why don't you come on back to the war . . ."

Leonard Cohen is still as romantic—it's romantic (and accurate) to see the relationship between the sexes as a war—as he was when he first appeared on the American musical scene. But his romanticism has matured. It will be interesting to read his next novel.

Robert Altman made a movie, *McCabe & Mrs. Miller*, based (Altman has told Cohen) on songs from Leonard Cohen's first two albums. Sitting in Cohen's lawyer's office (plush and posh, it takes two elevators to get there; he was wearing a well-tailored suit, but he still stays in the historic, rundown Chelsea Hotel), I asked Leonard whether he had considered writing scores for other films.

"It's something that is in the mind from time to time," he told me, "but when it really comes down to it, the thing I like best is the song that stands by itself, that you can walk around, that just has its own life." He's soft-spoken but friendly, conscientious about answering questions, a warm person in a cool situation. "If people can use the material in other areas, I'm very happy."

He has a terrific face, a sure sign of maturity. "Were you consulted about the songs in *McCabe*?" I asked.

"I was living in Franklin, in Tennessee, and I'd come into Nashville just to see a movie—we'd been living out in the sticks for a long time. And I saw this movie called *Brewster McCloud*. Have you seen it? It's a very, very beautiful and I would say brilliant film. I sat through it twice. Maybe I just hadn't seen a movie in a long time, but it was really fine. I was in the studio that night, in Nashville, and I got this call from a chap called Robert Altman. And he says, 'Listen, I love those songs. I've built a film around them. Can I use them?' I said, 'Who are you?' He said, 'Well, I did *M*A*S*H*. That's my film.'

"I said, 'I know it was enormously successful, but I haven't seen it. Is there anything else that you've done that I might know?' 'Well, I did a picture that's been completely buried, that you wouldn't know about. It was called *Brewster McCloud*.'

"I said, 'Listen, I just came out of the theater, I saw it twice. You can have anything of mine you want!'

"I did do some additional music—only one thing that was used. I did a guitar background for a little soliloquy by Warren Beatty; it's just barely perceptible but that is one of the nicest things I ever did. I love that piece.

"Then I saw the picture, the finished picture without the music. The soundtrack hadn't been completed. And I said, 'Listen, man, I've got to tell you—if we ever work together again I want you to know you can get an honest opinion from me—I don't like it.' He was quite hurt, as I would be too, but . . .

"Then I went to the theater in Montreal, and I saw the picture with the music and everything, and it was great! I called Altman in London—it took me two days to track him down—and told him, 'Forget everything I said, it's really beautiful.'"

Cohen's life and his art seem to fit together very nicely. A sense of who and where he's been and what he's been doing began to emerge for me as our conversation ranged across different subjects:

About being a Canadian:

"The Canadians are like the Jews—they're continually examining their identity. We're on the edge of a great empire, and this throws the whole thing into a very special kind of relief. Canadians have always understood that we have to go along with the United States to a certain extent. But even though article after article [in the Canadian press] threatens us with the extinction of our identity, I don't think anybody in Canada seriously believes that we're going to become Americans. It's a curious kind of paranoia.

"I live in Montreal, which is a French city, in Quebec, which is a French country—especially now, it is a country. I live as a minority writer, almost in exile, because there is no English writing community where I live. These are very special Canadian problems, which to me form the Canadian character, because we're very much involved in this notion of what is minority and what is majority; and yet while these questions are in the air, it seems that everybody has space. Because we don't have the melting-pot notion at all in Canada, we have a federal system that runs right down into the psyche of the country.

"So in a sense I live like a foreigner in my own city, cut off by the fact that I don't speak French that well. I can get by, but it's not a tongue I could ever move around in in a way that would satisfy the appetites of the mind or the heart.

"And because I live in French Canada, we're estranged from the writers who live in Toronto and Winnipeg and Vancouver. So all these things are curious walls that either insulate or protect or exclude, depending on how you look at it.

"I don't think anybody knows me as a writer or as a singer in Montreal. Quebec has its own movie industry, its own music, its own theater; it's much more lively than Canada. And of course the language my books are translated into is not Quebecois, it's French, and the Quebecois have a certain superiority that their language is a little more vital. In any case, it is different. Certainly the rhythms are different. Michel Garnot, who lives up the street from me, has always said my stuff—my colloquial and often experimental English—should be translated into Quebecois, not into French.

"Montreal is a good base for me, my center in the world. We have a very little house, two or three rooms, in an immigrant section of town. It's mostly Portuguese and Greek immigrant workers, right in the middle of the city, the English to the west of us and the French to the east. Several friends of mine that I grew up with also live on that street. We bought a couple of houses that stand together.

"I spend time in Greece, in Tennessee, in Mexico, but I always go back to Montreal."

About the subject matter of the songs:

"A lot of people wonder if you are as depressed as your songs sound; and if so, why?" I asked. "It is the popular image. Where do these depths of despair come from?"

"I can't really answer that," Cohen said. "I think that when people hear a song, they hear it in a realm where these questions are irrelevant. It's only after they stop listening that the questions arise. The songs themselves don't partake of a description like elation or depression. It's like a sexual embrace—there are no questions until you step outside of the embrace, separate yourself from it."

I have to agree. I don't find Cohen's songs depressing. I once lived with a lady who played his songs on the guitar all the time when she was depressed. She could relate to them, but I assume she liked them because they gave her comfort; I don't think they depressed her further. The blues as an art form didn't come from the black man being more miserable than the white man, but rather from his being more honest with himself about it. I changed my approach.

"There's a real quality of intimacy, it seems to me," I began, "in everything you've written that I'm aware of—intimacy in terms of what you're saying about yourself or just in the nature of the situation you're describing. Is this something you feel art or writing should do, or something you find you have to do, or . . . ?"

"Of course, one is aware that there are different degrees, different styles of approaching, in other men and other works, but I've never had an aesthetic that commanded me to approach my material in a certain way. It *is* my style, it's the only way I know how to talk; it's not something I've planned or that I thought was better than a more general or more withdrawn or more objective approach.

"I always thought I was being objective. I always thought I was being clear. I always thought I was being factual. It's just a relative sense that it's intimate. In my own interior landscape it's not intimate enough, it's still much too far from the interior reality. That's what I'm working on.

"I have some songs now in the works that I think *are* intimate. I feel that these are getting there, but they still aren't . . . In a sense, intimacy has not been one of the qualities that I have consciously taken as a goal, or even as a guideline; it's more *accuracy* and authenticity of experience.

"I've always tried to make a documentary of the interior landscape. I say to myself, 'What *really* happened? What is really happening *now*, that you are thinking of this woman?' That's what I've tried to do, is make it authentic and accurate. And precise.

"That's where the language comes, of course—one word leads to the next, and as you know, when words happen to be your medium they have their own contagion and their own susceptibility and their own invitations and their own hospitality to other words. You move into the world of language, and it has its own rules and laws.

"But in terms of the subject matter and the approach, it's always been a documentary approach, an attempt to establish the authentic events."

About his early days:

"Before coming to New York, I'd performed now and then, in a very limited way; I'd gone around Canada, read and sang. My own early manhood, my early twenties, late teens, were all spent in song. There was no recording or anything like that going on, but that was the style of an evening; they were always musical. We would sit around and we would sing.

"There was also a very fine group of poets in the city, where I got my training. We'd put out our own books, our own magazines. There was no contract or deals made with any other part of the world. We did consider ourselves self-sufficient, and the training was quite rigorous."

"This was in Montreal?" I asked. "Did you travel to speak of in those early years?"

"I always thought that Montreal was one of the sacred cities of the mind, and I never felt any desire at all to travel out of Montreal. It was not until I was twenty-four, which is quite late in terms of traveling, that I left the city. I went to Europe. I'd gotten an award for a book I had written, *Let Us Compare Mythologies*, a very early book of poems.

"I went to London and then—I'm not a very good traveler—I went to Greece and I stayed there for the next eight years. I'd never been in a sunny place and I'd never known what the sun was; so I fell in love with the sun, and a blonde girl, and a white house."

"Were the novels written during that period?"

"Yeah, most of the work was written there; and even now, though the new songs were at least three or four or even five years in the making, it was in Greece last summer that those ten or twelve golden days came when I was able to see the end of the songs, see them to completion. My house in Greece, which I still have—I've heard it described in the European press as a 'villa,' which always amuses me, this little house up on a hill—it's always been a good place to work in."

"It's not difficult to maintain a house in Greece," I asked, "either politically or economically?"

"A lot of people criticized me, although I moved out of my house at the time of the coup in Greece and I stopped living there then—I can't acquire any virtue or merit from this act, because it wasn't political. There was something in the country that changed, and in myself, and I rarely went to Greece after that.

"But it had nothing to do with politics; I think the Greek people are in a sense above their own politics—that's a supercilious thing to say, but . . . the average guy there, he'll turn the picture over to the next leader, go down and wave his flag for the next governor, with a sense of, I think, profound contempt and sophistication about the whole process. Because they're very much in touch with their own existence."

"You never felt you were treated bad, as an American/Canadian?"

"No, I got there with the very first wave of foreigners, when there were only five or six of us, and we were a novelty. We were their entertainment, you know, our goings on with drinking and girls; we were their theater. They gave us credit and they were very nice to us, very helpful . . .

"I had a little record player that ran on batteries. I would work outside on my terrace, and if I would forget how fast the sun was moving and forget to move, the record would melt, right over the turntable. I used to play Ray Charles all the time and I lost a couple of Ray Charles records. I still have them; they're just like Dali watches, just dripped over the side of the turntable."

About being a novelist:

"To what extent," I wondered, "are you conscious of yourself as a novelist?"

"Well, I've never been intimidated by form. . . . What we call a novel, that is, a book of prose where there are characters and developments and changes and situations, that's always attracted me, because in a sense it is the heavyweight arena. I like it—it frightens me, from that point of view—because of the regime that is involved in novel writing. I can't be on the move. It needs a desk, it needs a room and a typewriter, a regime. And I like that very much."

"You haven't published a work of this sort since *Beautiful Losers*?"

"No, I haven't. This will be the first book of prose since then. The book is called *A Woman Being Born*—that's mostly what I'm working on now. I thought it was done but . . . it keeps suggesting a more and more massive form, so I go along with it. A lot of it is by dictation—I found that the early parts all start, 'Whatever you say . . . '"

About being more popular in Europe than America:

I mentioned a novelist friend who was experiencing the same thing, and Cohen responded: "I think this is the traditional path of gifted peo-ple in America. It's obvious. This is what happened to Faulkner, to Frost, to Miller, to a lot of jazz musicians. Americans are very, very provincial. They really are reluctant to accept new things. They are totally ignorant about what is going on in other countries. These countries in Europe are old, old cultures, with a tremendous sense of tolerance and curiosity built into them. So they're very interested in new American products. We're not at all interested in theirs, or in our own."

About critics:

"I seem to be caught in the critical establishment between two critical houses. On one side, the literary people are very resentful that I have made money in the rock world. This suggests to them somehow that I have sold out.

"And on the other side, a lot of people in the rock establishment, in their articles I notice that they always suggest that I don't know anything about music, that my tunes are very limited, as if I couldn't work in an augmented chord if I really thought it was needed. And that my voice is very thin, as if we were still in the days of Caruso or something. They apply standards to me that they've never applied to other singers in the field.

"Whereas in Europe this doesn't exist, there's no energy wasted on placing me, because the culture is wide enough to include a figure like myself, without any sense of abrasion."

"Does what's written about you have any kind of effect on you or, do you think, on the musician in general?" I wondered.

"At this point, yes, I am interested in the market journey of the product; but I'm very, very interested also in the mind of the reviewers, how they change over the decades, and how a man approaches new work. Whether he approaches it in a spirit of curiosity, charity, interest, or as a vehicle for his own self-aggrandizement, his own career. Whether he uses it as an opportunity to display humanism or cruelty . . . I mean, to me, the critic is on trial at this point."

(On Cohen's recent album he himself is put on trial in at least two songs; and he is judged harshly, in one case by the world—"The judge has no choice: a singer must die for the lie in his voice" ["A Singer Must Die"]—and in the other case by himself—"I never asked but I heard you cast your lot along with the poor. How come I overheard your prayer that you be this and nothing more than just some grateful, faithful woman's favorite singing millionaire, the patron saint of envy and the grocer of despair, working for the Yankee dollar" ["Field Commander Cohen"].

Clearly his own judgment is the harsher, albeit less permanent, of the two. Delightful threads of self-mockery and self-awareness run through the new songs, which are still primarily concerned with the theme of the intense active interrelatedness of male and female beings.)

About the singer's sensibility, 1966–1975:

"I was unaware of rock music when I first came with my songs to New York, I didn't really know what was happening. I was on my way to Nashville, which I knew a lot more about, because in Canada we listened to a lot of country and western music, and I used to be in a country and western group when I was quite young.

"So I thought I would head down to Nashville. I thought I could write some songs in that area. This was mostly an economic consideration; I'd published a lot of books but I'd never sold very many. Well, I hit New York and I found myself in the middle of this, what they called 'folksong' scene. . . . It was about 1966. There was Judy Collins, Phil Ochs—I met Mary Martin, a girl from Toronto, who knew me as a writer, and she was working at [folk musician manager Albert] Grossman's office and trying to get started on her own. She knew Judy Collins as a friend and I sang some songs for her . . .

"But I was really very moved when I came to New York by what was going on. There was a sensibility—not in any way new to me, because I was already thirty-two or thirty-three years old—but a sensibility that I thought I was quite alone in. It wasn't quite Kerouac, it wasn't quite Ginsberg, it was something after that. I had written books that I felt had that kind of sensibility. And I came to New York and there, five or ten years later, I found that or a compatible sensibility flourishing! So I was very happy. I felt very much at home.

"I felt the exhilaration of the moment, and I suppose I succumbed to the expectations of the moment, and subsequently to the disappointments of the moment. But I think those are things also that have to do with just the age of the man involved. You do learn a little bit about the world from twenty-five to thirty-five. It is the real educational period, I think, when you do enter into manhood and you do see that things tend to come and go, ideas, spiritual invitations, self-improvement rackets . . . and that there is another strain of human existence that continues, that is not to be despised. I mean just birth, marriage, death. And that these larger movements seem to be the sounds that really do orchestrate humanity.

"So at the same time where you indulge yourself with certain feelings of paranoia, disappointment, disillusion, on the other hand another kind of information establishes itself in the heart and the mind and you feel that this is the world and you're happy to know it.

"And then you maybe throw your weight behind other kinds of possibilities. You can begin to understand other kinds of human institutions—like marriage, like work, like order. You begin to withdraw . . . although part of the emotion will always be attached to anarchy, to chaos, to wild creativity, to notions like that. You begin to balance those concepts against other ones, like law and order. And I mean it in the real sense, not just a political slogan but the real law and the real order that seems to govern our existence."

About songs and poems and performing:

"Do the songs and poems," I asked, "clearly differentiate themselves for you?"

"Very rarely one crosses into the other realm. But the songs are by and large designed as songs, and the poems designed as poems." (Leonard gave me a hardcover copy of his recent—and largely ignored—book of poems, *The Energy of Slaves*. "Would you mind throwing the cover away?" he asked. I did so, and read the book with pleasure and much shock of recognition. The trouble with the cover was it made it look like a book by Leonard Nimoy.) "It could be read as one poem, one long poem, this book."

"Do you prefer to write songs or poems?"

"It depends on what part of the being is operative. Of course it's wonderful to write a song. I mean there is nothing like a song, and you sing it to your woman, or to your friend. People come to your house, and then you sing it in front of an audience and you record it. I mean it has an amazing thrust. And a poem, it waits on the page, and it moves in a much more secret way through the world. And that also is . . . Well, they each have their own way of travel."

"Is performing a natural extension of writing for you?"

"In a sense it's natural, but like every other thing that we call natural it takes a lot of work and practice."

"But what I mean is," I rephrased, "it's not a separate category of action?"

"No, it has the same terrors and pitfalls and possibilities for humiliation. For me, personally, it's a kind of dangerous work, but so is writing if you're really going to lay your life out."

"But performing has a more immediate danger?"

"Yeah, performing. I mean you can really be humiliated. There are other rewards and prizes that go with it—you can come out with a sense of glory, girls might fall in love with you, they might be paying you very well. All the possibilities of corruption and material gain and self-congratulation are present—but also at the same time there is this continual threat and presence of your own disgrace."

"You felt quite able to project the very personal, interior vision of your songs in front of 130,000 people?"

"When you're singing for that many people," Cohen explained, "it becomes private again.

"This last concert I gave in Paris, the stage was high, like the side of a building, and the audience was way, way, way down there, so you're really only dealing with the microphone. They're at an event, they're outside, the wind is howling; it's an event on a different order and you take your place in the moment.

"But an audience of two or three or four thousand is the real test, because you can really do all the wrong things. You can play to the crowd, you can play for laughs, you can play for self-pity, you can play for heroic aspect; there are so many ways of selling out in front of an audience. There's no such thing as a casual performance; one has an exact notion of what one is going to do out there."

"Forgive me for asking"—it may have seemed a significant question made banal, but it needed an answer—"what are you trying to achieve in your songs? What is your ambition?"

"To create a vapor and a mist," Cohen responded, "to make oneself attractive, to master it, to keep busy and avoid the poolroom and try to get good at what you're doing. Really, it's all an alibi for something nobody's ever been able to talk about.

"Mostly my idea of a song is, when you feel like singing and this is your song. It's not what songs *should* be, not choosing; this is the song you make because it's the only one you *can* make, this is the one that is yours. The fact is that you feel like singing, and this is the song that you know."

"As a rule," I asked, "does the music come first or the words?"

"Well," he said, "most of the time you're just scraping the bottom of the barrel to find any kind of voice at all. It could be a few words, a tone of voice, two chords together—it's a ragpicker's trade as I practice it; I don't stand on the mountain and receive tablets."

Leonard Cohen, when I met him in his lawyer's office, was unsure of his American audience, wondering whether they still existed. He was about to do three nights, six shows, at the Bottom Line in New York. "I'll be interested in seeing what happens in America. I haven't played any concerts here really for four years. You can completely die out . . . "

The third night at the Bottom Line was a cold, wet, nasty New York City day. I arrived shortly before the show was to start, wondering whether anyone would be there. It was standing room only. There was a line of people a city block long, huddling against the side of the building, fooling with broken umbrellas, waiting for a chance to buy tickets to get into the second show.

The crowd inside was terrific. So was Leonard and his group of musicians. The new stuff, arranged by Leonard's new producer and piano player ("John Lissauer is fantastic. People are going to know about him way beyond the contribution he makes to my scene"), is the best stuff musically that Cohen has ever done. Lyrically, it doesn't measure up to the astonishing, penetrating cleverness and word-trickiness of Cohen's earliest songs, but it appeals to me on a different level—the maturity of the vision, the appropriateness of the imagery and irony for our newly nonapocalyptic (but still struggle-filled) lives.

My favorite song on the new album, and they all run through my head, is "I Tried to Leave You," a disarmingly simply love song, *chanson*, that cuts to the heart of Cohen's dilemma: how to be a mature human male, with wife and children, and still stay alive. He pretends at irony:

"Goodnight my darling. I hope you're satisfied," he sings with a twist in his voice.

But the twist is that he really means it. He does so hope. "The years go by. You lose your pride. The baby's crying so you do not go outside." The melody is perfect. The empathy of the song bites the heart. The singer never drops either his own dignity or his lady's, not for the slightest moment. The pain and beauty of Cohen's vision is the perfect rejoinder to the pain and ugliness of Joseph Heller's portrait of the married North American career man. God bless our romantics; they give us strength to go on.

Leonard Cohen, reached after many complications (all lines to Mexico were busy and something about his lady taking the car keys) by phone in Acapulco, was very pleased and encouraged by the enthusiastic reception he got at the Bottom Line and at the Troubadour in Los Angeles. He was with his family, in a cottage outside the city, writing, relaxing, getting ready for several months of American concerts. At forty, he is the first of the rock generation of songwriters to reach maturity with his consciousness and courage and sense of humor intact.

COHEN CLIP

On Being a "Minor" Writer

"I consider myself a minor writer. That's not just an exercise in modesty, because I love the minor writers, like Robert Herrick. I'm not that kind of writer like Solzhenitsyn, a writer who has a great, great vision. I have a small corner. And I feel more like an inhabitant of that corner than any other kind of description, poet or writer or lyricist."

—from "Cohen Down the Road," by Karl Dallas,
Melody Maker (UK), May 22, 1976

SUFFERING FOR FAN AND PROFIT: THE RETURN OF LEONARD COHEN

MICK BROWN | May 24, 1976, interview | July 3, 1976, *Sounds* (UK)

In 1976, as in 1975, Cohen released no new material. He did, however, find time for a two-and-a-half-month, fifty-five-gig European tour. It was during this concert series that he met backstage after a show in Bristol, England, with journalist Mick Brown. "He was very cordial, gentlemanly, elegant," Brown told me. "The still, poised center of everything that was going on around him. I liked him." —Ed.

The poster outside the Colston Hall [in] Bristol announced the appearance that evening of "The Poet of Rock and Roll."

Inside, a girl takes photographs of the road crew setting up equipment onstage—for an art project, she explains. She really wanted to photograph the concert, so she'd scrimped, saved, begged, and borrowed enough to buy a couple of tickets. Now she can't make it on account of the revision she has to do for tomorrow's exams. She'd sold the tickets to friends in a matter of hours. She's all of sixteen years old.

Leonard Cohen is clearly bemused by it all. He sits back in his dressing room, issues a slight smile, and says isn't it amazing that some of these people were only eight years old when he wrote his first song? Cohen is forty-one.

Onstage, illuminated by the harsh glare of a single spotlight dividing his face into patches of darkness and light, he looks a curious cross between Lenny Bruce and an Old Testament prophet—the protruding, hawkish nose, the dark eyes, lines etched into his face and forehead.

Backstage he looks strangely vulnerable; a thin, slight figure dressed in pressed slacks and a brown leather jacket, a cigarette burning between his fingers. One has heard that Cohen can be reserved to the point of being difficult. In fact he's extraordinarily charming, polite, approachable.

It is a rule of the road that he never gives interviews or holds audience before a performance, using those couple of hours before going onstage to summon up reserves of energy and concentration for the task at hand.

After a performance he will talk, sign photographs and scraps of paper, receive gifts, kisses, handshakes. Gladly. He says he cherishes the attentions of his audience.

In Montreal he lives in an immigrant-worker neighborhood where he's known only as a guy who has two kids and a small house and who never seems to be around very much.

In the small village in Greece where he also spends his "sitting-down time" the people are similarly unconcerned with who he is or what he does. A little bit of attention on the road is, well, reassuring.

Outside his dressing room young matrons with glasses and wistful expressions hover in droves, thrusting programs at the road manager who brings them back signed. In the inner sanctum, Cohen holds court with a tribunal from a local college newspaper, hunched in a chair wreathed in cigarette smoke, ringed by earnest, inquiring faces; a scatter of papers on the floor—Cohen's poems, which one of his inquisitors has painstakingly copied by hand.

"What I'd really like to know is why your poetry is so stark, so incredibly blunt—a poem like, for instance . . ." Cohen takes the proffered sheet, glances at the writing. "Yeah—I like that poem. . . . If it didn't have the word 'cunt' in it I'd probably read it out loud onstage. But I'm not ready to say that word well enough yet. There are some things that are designed to rest on the page and not be spoken . . ."

"Do you use the same technique then for writing songs and poetry?"

"Yeah—just one word at a time . . ."

"To what extent then should poetry have relevance throughout time, or do you think it should sum up an episode, a moment, and preserve that on paper for forever?"

Cohen blinks at his questioner through the smoke-haze. "I don't know: forever is a long time . . ."

Leonard Cohen hasn't come back. He's never been away. While other performers tend to move, or even stand still, in a blaze of publicity, Cohen just keeps on toiling away quietly in what he calls his little corner—writing songs, sometimes; poems, sometimes; books, sometimes—all at his own pace.

Traveling . . . He's always been peripatetic—trace his career from Montreal to New York to Nashville to Greece—but more so in the last six or seven years, "since I could afford the airfares." He was in Ethiopia just before the revolution: "I just get to a place, check into a hotel, and hit the streets." The Wandering Jew.

"But to tell you the truth I'm getting a little tired of all that now. A tour'll cure that for you for a while." Not that he tours often; he says he needs the nourishment of a private life more than anything touring can give him. But, for whatever reasons, this year he's been back on the road— a brief round of club dates in the southern American states, and now Europe, where he seems to enjoy a larger and more loyal following than anywhere else.

So far it's been sold-out houses all the way, and Bristol is no exception—a lot of older faces in the audience, people for whom *Songs from a Room* was no doubt a soundtrack for sorrowful bedsit dramas all those years ago; a surprisingly large number of younger people who can't have been aware of Cohen first or second time around, but who've tuned into that finely honed angst somewhere along the way; and a man in elfin boots, long hair, and a cloak who stands up in one of those moments of pregnant, reverential silence that punctuate a Cohen performance and shouts out, "God bless you, Leonard" to crackle of sympathetic applause from the rest of the audience; an audience that, in short, substantiates the tag "The Poet" more than it does the description "Of Rock and Roll . . ."

The tour publicist says it's been like this everywhere Cohen has played, and it'll no doubt be the same tomorrow night when he plays the [Royal] Albert Hall, even though he's sure to get negative reviews.

This anticipation of the critical thumbs-down seems strange at first, but thinking about it Cohen has always been more popular with the paying customer than with the press, who perhaps find the disarming frankness and pessimism of his lyrics and the dark, confidential monotone of his voice too much of an invitation for cynicism to turn down. Actually, says his publicist, it's more of an inverted snobbery.

The first time Leonard played London the nationals loved him; it's since he became an institution that they changed their minds. And sure enough, the reviews of the Albert Hall concert are marked by a sort of reserve, dwelling on the despairing nature of Cohen's lyrics and the fact that much of his material was familiar from his albums, not to say previous visits.

Sure enough, it was, but familiarity is an intrinsic part of Cohen's appeal, and anyway he is hardly the most prolific writer of songs.

His last album, *New Skin for the Old Ceremony*, appeared almost two years ago, and free as he is from the normally pressurizing demands of a one-or-two-album-a-year record contract he tends to work at his own pace, which he admits is slow.

"Songs seem to take me a long time," he says. "I don't know why; they're not especially excellent for taking so long. I don't have any sense of urgency about any of my writing actually. I don't think mankind will be damaged if I don't put out a new album or a new book."

Nonetheless, he has put down five or six tracks for a new album, one of which, "Do I Have to Dance All Night," was hurriedly recorded at Musicland Studios in Munich for release as a single. [*Though frequently performed in concert and released in a concert version as a single in 1976, this song has never appeared on a Cohen album. —Ed.*]Cohen says it would be "amusing" to have a hit with it, and the song gets two airings at Bristol—once to close the first half of the show and again during one of the innumerable encores—to help make it happen.

It's unusually lively for a Cohen song, but it fits the mood of his backing band, who seem to relish the opportunity to rock out—a guitar and pedal-steel player, drums, bass, a keyboards player with a taste for synthesizer swirls, and two strong girl singers who sound mournfully ethereal in all the right places, and who also work slick Lambert/Hendricks/Ross type scat arrangement behind Leonard on "I Tried to Leave You."

Generally, there is not much levity to be found in a Cohen performance, and what there is comes not so much from his songs as his wry, self-mocking introductions and the bittersweet poems, which he reads over a loose, jazz-tinged instrumental backing.

But levity is not what Cohen's audience comes for. His concerts tend toward the atmosphere of a public confessional, a knowing, world-weary perambulation around the more painful areas of the human psyche.

Cohen is in the grand tradition of Jewish writers who wear their suffering on their sleeve. Maybe the English, generally tight-assed about their hang-ups, like living it vicariously.

There is certainly a reassurance of sorts to be found in listening to someone who can so clearly and painstakingly articulate the emotional crises we all go through at some time or another. If anybody's going to make your heart bleed for mankind in general, and for himself in particular, it's Leonard Cohen. But I for one am happy to thank him for it—at least some of the time.

Cohen agrees that his is very much a *relating* audience, often as prepared to share their confidence with him as he is with them. "There are some people who come to me for some illumination on their problems," he says. "I guess they feel I'm writing about some of the things they themselves are going through. But I don't usually have much help to give—there isn't much you can say to someone in the midst of their own crises."

Cohen, one senses, has enough trouble with his own. Not that his personal life is perpetually in shreds. Cohen gives every impression of being quite contented with—or at the very least philosophically resigned to—whatever life has brought his way.

He lives simply enough with his family; he says that because he didn't taste success until he was in his thirties he was already too set in his ways to develop expensive tastes. His friends are the guys he grew up with on the same street in Montreal. He smiles more often than you'd expect and seldom frowns.

You get the feeling Cohen has to do more than just wake up in the morning to find all that pathos that permeates his work, and that plumbing the more despondent depths of his soul is a struggle. Some people may say he struggles too hard and that his visions are intimate almost to the point of indecency.

Cohen says he abides by only one maxim in his writing: to always honor the difference between just a cry and a piece of work. "A cry of pain in itself is just that," he says. "It can affect you or you can turn away from it. But a piece of work that treats the experience that produced the cry of pain is a different matter altogether. The cry is transformed, alchemized, by the work by a certain objectivity, which doesn't surrender the emotion but gives it form. That's the difference between life and art."

His books are extensions of the same vision—the gospel of objective self-revelation, autobiographical "because I can only treat the things I know—and I just know a small corner. There are writers who are great visionaries, who can depict huge movements—things like that. They're the great writers. I'm just the other kind."

He supposes his writing is therapeutic in the way that any work is. "I feel better when I'm working than when I'm not, but I feel both things—a need to write and a need to quit. The need to write is greater—off and on. Sometimes you get tired of the whole thing, think you'll get an honest job. Sometimes you know you're just dealing with the pipes and you think you'd like to get out of the basement. But you recognize your limitations and try to work within them . . ."

He is a perfectionist—his own harshest critic. His first novel, *The Favorite Game*, went through four drafts before publication. He's spent the last two years working on another novel, but withdrew it from his publishers at the last moment. [*This reference is apparently to an attempted third novel. Cohen had already followed* The Favorite Game *with* Beautiful Losers, *his second novel, ten years before this interview. —Ed.*]

"It isn't any good," he says with a faint smile. "But somebody said it's as hard to write a bad book as it is to write a good one, so I guess it's kept me in shape doing it. In a way it's too personal; it treats people close to me in a way that is somehow inaccurate, one-sided."

A cry of pain rather than a piece of work? He laughs. "Yeah—it doesn't have that objectivity that I think it should have. I try to be truthful in whatever I do in some kind of way—not so much truthful to the fact as truthful to the quality of the experience. The book was true—but it wasn't *fair*."

His publishers wanted it just the same. "They think they can sell it," says Cohen.

It hasn't always been like that. Cohen spent his youth in lonely Montreal hotel rooms, struggling to write books that some people liked but nobody would buy. Eventually he started concentrating on writing songs instead, "to pay my grocery bills." He performed intermittently around Montreal and then moved to New York.

There he met Judy Collins and sang her some of his songs; she recorded one straight off. That led to a meeting with John Hammond—the legendary A&R man who discovered Dylan and Aretha Franklin—and a contract with Columbia Records.

On the way he managed to be duped out of the rights to "Suzanne" and a couple of other songs. "I didn't really understand American business practices," he says charitably, "but I heard someone singing 'Suzanne' in Corfu not so long ago and it seemed somehow fitting that I didn't own it."

It was around the time of his first album that he met Janis Joplin, an interlude in his life that prompted a song that is one of the highlights of his stage performance, "Chelsea Hotel No. 2." "I remember you well in the Chelsea Hotel / You were talking so brave and so sweet / Giving me head on the unmade bed / While the limousines wait in the street."

"I was saddened by her death," he says. "Not because someone dies—that in itself isn't terrible. But I liked her work so much; she was that good that you feel the body of work she left behind is just too brief.

"There are certain kinds of artists that blaze in a very bright light for a very brief time: the Rimbauds, the Shelleys, Tim Buckley—people like that; and Janis was one of them.

"Then there's the other kind, like Sartre or Bernard Shaw, who are careful about themselves and what the risks are. You can't get too safe, but as you get older you learn something about survival. The game is rough from a lot of points of view; because the prizes are big the defeats are big too.

"The life is rigorous, and the invitations to blowing it are numerous and frequent. Me? I'm careful as I can be without it getting too much of a drag. Anyway, I'm too old to die that kind of spectacular death. For me to commit suicide or O.D. would be . . ."—he pauses for the appropriate word—" . . . unbecoming. . . ."

LEONARD LATELY: A LEONARD COHEN INTERVIEW

BILL CONRAD | Fall 1976, interview | May 7, 2012, NoDepression.com

Bill Conrad spent time with Cohen a few months after Mick Brown did. He wrote about the Nashville encounter at the time for Texas's *Buddy* magazine, and again for NoDepression.com in 2012. The latter reminiscence follows. —Ed.

The release of Leonard Cohen's ten-song collection of new compositions, *Old Ideas*, motivated me to relive an afternoon and evening I shared with him in Nashville, Tennessee.

I was recently listening to k. d. lang's version of Cohen's now-classic "Hallelujah," and thought Leonard must love the irony of this tune's history. He first released it on his *Various Positions* album in 1984, after his label advised him it wasn't worth including. Almost two decades later, it has been recorded by more than 200 singers in multiple languages, and let us not forget its place on soundtracks from *Shrek* and TV's *Scrubs*. It has become the "White Christmas" of dark and moody songs. Even Cohen himself said, "I think it's a good song, but I think too many people sing it. Some have asked for a moratorium on 'Hallelujah.'"

Suzanne and Other Confessions

"Civilian life got impossible." Leonard Cohen, Canada's answer to Bob Dylan, was announcing in 1976, his return to road shows. His blue folksongs, contained in the *Songs from a Room* and *Songs of Love and Hate* albums, and his experimental dark novel *Beautiful Losers,* added so much gravity to the ponderous seventies decade.

For fifteen years he sailed between his native Montreal and his adopted escape hatch on the Greek isle of Hydra. When he ventured onto American soil, he enjoyed the hard contrast of life in New York City and the highest point in Los Angeles County, Mount Baldy. On the road, boundaries disappear for Leonard. He said, "It's not the country, but the hotel room."

When I met Leonard Cohen in that autumn of '76, he was lounging atop his queen-size bed in Room 418, enjoying the view of east Nashville from the fourth floor of Roger Miller's King of the Road Inn. A starstruck, up-and-coming singer named Michael Murphey was also in attendance. The clean-shaven, hair-trimmed-close Mr. Cohen was in Music City for a two-night stand at the cozy Exit-In, a club with fewer than 150 seats. That seventies version of Leonard was fashionably lean and cordially introverted—still juxtaposed with the moment.

While Cohen's shows and recordings kept him a central figure in Europe, Columbia Records stateside saw him as some sort of rare, sensitive creature who, in spite of his '67 success with *Songs of Leonard Cohen,* was a hard sell to the masses. His latest release, *New Skin for the Old Ceremony,* went gold across the Atlantic, but was hard to find in American shops.

He shouldn't have been surprised by corporate confusion. Leonard knew he was an odd mix of folk and blues, and blue singers do not sell rock-and-roll numbers. He accepted the media machine as a necessary distraction and agreed to visit with me, a roving journalist for *Buddy* magazine, a free music news publication out of Dallas, Texas.

When asked about another novel, he confessed his latest attempt was a failure. He had spent the previous two years, mostly on Hydra, a small Greek island, writing a book that in his opinion "wasn't any good." *How could this be?* He assured me, "It's true. I'm not being coy; as someone observed, it's just as hard to write a bad novel as a good one."

Leonard strongly advised aging the written word: "I think Horatio, the Roman poet, said you should put stuff away for nine years." After considering this time span, he added, "I don't think it has to be nine, but three or four years I think is a good idea, especially to take it on the road for a couple of years." This compressed maturation and life among civilians had him ready to "renew neurotic affiliations."

No stranger to Nashville and its hillbillies, Leonard lived in Franklin, just south of Music City, in '69–'70. During our time at the King of the Road, he recalled how much he enjoyed the company of his black neighbor, a whiskey-wise elder named Willie York. It was the time of psychedelics and Leonard decided to give Willie some LSD: "So he comes to me the next day, and I said, 'Willie, what'd you think of that?' He's a heavy drinker. He said, 'Leonard, that stuff makes ya awful nervous.'" Cohen loved recalling that moment in time. He concluded, "That's all he said, y'know; that's the only remark he cared to make about it." Leonard flashed a wry grin.

When it came to politics, Leonard said he voted for candidates who "look good and sound good, and who are least likely to embarrass the country." He had recently discovered a man with great potential: "I was watching television early on today, and there was one of those founders of the Dining Car Porters and Waiters Union—black guy, around sixty-five. He was talking and he sounded like Moses. It was something. It wasn't like hokey. It wasn't that kind of eloquence. It was classical. Obviously, the guy had been brought up on the Bible. I couldn't even hope to duplicate it. It was the most . . . I said, 'That man should be president!' You know? This guy was serving tables, eighty-five bucks a week!"

On with the show. Cohen's latest collection of players included a four-piece band, mostly acoustic, and a pair of sirens—slinky showgirls with angelic voices. One was brunette, the other blonde. The former exuded worldliness, while her partner came off as the innocent. Both were dressed in matching black. The blonde wore a floor-length, body-hugging dress, and the brunette, a pantsuit with white shirt and necktie. Were these Cohen's fabled "sisters of mercy," the two angels who saved him from an Alberta blizzard and inspired his classic ode from the '67 album? "Oh I hope you run into them / You who have been traveling so long."

Leonard's show was a soft-focus reflection of his somber side. Even his song introductions were sweet prose: "This examines betrayal from a point of view," and "This is a dialogue between you and your perfect lover . . . a song of unrelenting pessimism." His tender-cold lament for the late

Janis Joplin included her rejection of his advances: "I knew you well in the Chelsea Hotel . . . You told me again / You prefer handsome men / But for me you'd make an exception." Cohen's mastery of the facetious rhyme was woven throughout his melancholy. It was his recurring effort to "kinda wash the place out, change the air." He mused, "I like a place that serves liquor. You know, there's something happens to the audience when they're drinking." He really wanted to leave 'em laughing, and with lyrics like "You were Marlon Brando / And I was only Steve McQueen / You were that fancy K-Y Jelly / And I was ordinary Vaseline," he did not fail to please.

Leonard Cohen bowed from the waist—romantic theatrics—and opened his show with "Bird on a Wire," one of his many dark masterpieces. He told the audience he liked playing clubs because "people can talk to you, praise you, put you down." The stage became his farthest distance from his island retreat. It's where "every night is a problem, a challenge, a test just to get through without humiliating yourself." Cohen loved enduring, "browbeating an audience, subjecting people to all this intensity. I sometimes feel guilty about it, but you've got to make a living."

The Exit-In

With his back to just over a hundred fans who filled Nashville's Exit-In, Leonard paused for the third time to tune his guitar. A drunken voice blurted from the darkness, "Good enough for folk music!" A few patrons chuckled.

Leonard made a final adjustment, then casually turned to respond, "Yeah, but not good enough for eternity." He smiled his sardonic best and the adoring crowd filled the small room with laughter. Leonard was back, and we lucky few were there with him.

He left me with a final memory of life in Franklin and why he left Tennessee: "The girl I was with was what destroyed it, because she developed this obsession with Krystal burgers. I mean, it got to be a serious problem. She refused to cook, so we'd have to go in every day (twenty miles) to eat cheeseburgers, and it just destroyed the whole isolation." Before speaking her name, he silently reflected in nostalgic warmth. "Suzanne."

" . . . takes you down to a place by a river / She feeds you tea and oranges / That come all the way from China."

THE OBSCURE CASE OF LEONARD COHEN AND THE MYSTERIOUS MR. M.

BRUCE POLLOCK | Late 1976, interview | February 1977, *After Dark* (US)

Bruce Pollock has interviewed a lot of musicians, but he told me that his meeting with Leonard Cohen still ranks among his strangest such encounters. "Aside from Cohen," Pollock said, "the dramatic focal point was the previous interviewer, from *Creem* magazine, who refused to leave Cohen's apartment when I arrived, and who insisted on continuing his conversation with Cohen during my interview. And who then even refused to leave with me when both of our interviews were done.

"Perhaps due to some innate politeness—or dread fear—Cohen failed to acknowledge the inappropriate behavior of this third party," Pollock added. "Perhaps due to the sheer audacity of the situation—or dread fear—I put up with the intrusions of this increasingly drunken odd-ball. But the incident itself offered an eerie view of Cohen's ability to connect with his fans in personal relationships that, in Cohen's own words, always 'ended badly.' I often wonder whether I was in on the start of a beautiful friendship between Cohen and this deluded intruder—or whether Cohen eventually had to call the cops on him. Or at least call his publicist." —Ed.

As I hustled up Sixth Avenue toward the Algonquin Hotel for an interview with Columbia recording artist Leonard Cohen, writer of such heavyweight literary pop songs as "Suzanne," "Bird on a Wire," and "Dress Rehearsal Rag," I anticipated an epic conversation, a gargantuan verbal feast, an orgy of philosophical anecdote and analogy. After all, Cohen was far from being merely another songwriter; he was a published poet when he was fifteen, is a novelist twice over (*The Favorite Game, Beautiful Losers*), and I was about to be a published author myself. Cohen had read my book; I had read both of his. We'd be two authors talking shop. Before the afternoon was through, I was sure I'd have him begging me to send him one (if not all seven) of my unpublished novels. Perhaps a correspondence would result—the famous Cohen–Pollock letters, later to be collected in an expensive, coffee-table edition.

When I entered Cohen's room, I was rather surprised to find another interviewer in the process of finishing up his visit. How were Cohen and I to achieve any literary epiphanies with this eavesdropper, obviously a rock-and-roll degenerate, sitting on the couch drinking wine? Cohen sat in a chair at a table in the far corner, wearing the same gray pants and black shirt he'd worn during his concert the night before.

"If you'd rather be alone, M— will leave," Cohen said as I set up my tape recorder on the table.

"He can stay," I said, then after a pregnant pause, "another five minutes."

That settled, I commenced questioning Cohen about his first novel. How did he react to its publication and subsequent commercial failure? As he was fashioning a response, I began preparing myself to tell him about my first novel—still unpublished—my own expectations and fantasies. However, before I could verbalize them, he spoke.

"My training as a writer was not calculated to inflame the appetites," he said with ease. "In Montreal in the fifties, when I began to write, people didn't have the notion of superstars. The same prizes weren't in the air as there are today, so one had a kind of modest view of what a writing career was."

I couldn't have put it better myself. M—, still on the couch, showed no signs of leaving. Steadily swallowing wine, he ogled us with a slight smile with which he seemed to be transmitting signals to Cohen. "I just hope this doesn't get too boring for you," I told him. "I mean, for all I know, I may be asking him the same questions you did." Of course, I knew that wouldn't be the case. I'd be asking him insightful, prose-writer questions. Meaty stuff.

M— giggled. "Oh no," he slurred, "we didn't have that kind of interview. We were on a totally different wavelength."

Rattled, I immediately quoted from an obscure article Cohen had written eight years ago in an obscure publication called *Books*, about his first performance onstage as a singer and the beauty of his utter failure. Totally different wavelength, huh? I'd show the both of them wavelengths! In the light of his career since then, would he still say it was better to fail than succeed? I asked adroitly.

This was such an arcane reference that M— was awed back into silence, and Cohen himself was hard-pressed to recall it. However, when he did, I could see he was impressed. His answer came in the form of an allegory.

"A man visits a master who's living in a very pitiful terrain and the man says, 'How can you survive here?' The master says, 'If you think it's bad now, you should see what it's like in summer.' 'What happens in summer?' asks the man. The master says, 'In the summer I throw myself into a vat of boiling oil.' 'Isn't it worse then?' says the man. 'No,' says the master, 'pain cannot reach you there.'

"That's really the way things are," Cohen continued after acknowledging the chuckles from M—. "If you throw yourself into a kind of effort, it's not better or worse. Like a chameleon, you take the color of the experience if it's intense enough, and the pain cannot reach you there.

"Performing is definitely the boiling oil. You can't really develop an intellectual perspective on it—I mean, you're in it. You realize the next moment could bring total humiliation—or you could actually be lifted up into the emotion that began the song. But you're already in the boiling oil by the time you've gotten that far."

At this point M— burst in and asked Cohen if a character in *Beautiful Losers* was a real person. "Composite," Cohen answered. Then, before I could regain my balance, M— recited an entire paragraph from page 143 of the book—to Cohen's obvious delight. I too had read the book but had not thought to memorize it. Score one for M—. Retaliating, I brought up a moment from his concert, when he delivered a beautifully worded monologue about searching for the women who inspired "Sisters of Mercy." I asked him if he was, like the true romantic he set himself up to be, haunted by the past.

He seemed interested in the topic.

"I think everybody is involved in a kind of Count of Monte Cristo feeling. You somehow want the past to be vindicated. You want to evoke figures of the past. My own experience has been that almost everything you want happens. I meet people out of the past all the time. Not only that, I meet people that I wanted to create. It's like Nancy . . ." Cohen went on, referring to one of his songs, caught up in the idea. "The line is 'now you look around, you see her everywhere . . .'. This is just my own creation, but obviously there's a collective appetite for a certain kind of individual; that individual's created and you feel you had a certain tiny part in that creation."

Now that was a serious concept, something only two fiction writers could really get to the bottom of. But just as I was about to sink my teeth into it, M— hurled himself once again into the flow. "Does that song have anything to do with Marilyn Monroe?"

"No," said Cohen, "it was about a real Nancy."

By the time they'd finished discussing Marilyn Monroe, my momentum had been lost. Although it hadn't been in my original game plan, I pulled a surprise by asking Cohen about longevity in songwriters, why so few lasted past adolescence.

"I think there are a number of things that bear on that," said Cohen, fielding the hot shot and throwing me out by a good two feet. "You can burn yourself out, for one. The late teens and twenties are generally the lyric phase of a writer's career. If you achieve enough fame and women and money during that period, you quit, because that's generally the motivation. I didn't get enough money or women or fame for me to quit. I don't have enough yet, so I've got to keep on playing." He laughed. "I know it's rather unbecoming at forty to keep it all going, but I have to do it."

I couldn't decide whether he was putting me on or not. While my own train of thought stalled, M— roared in on the express. "Why do you in your songs, refer to yourself as ugly?" he asked.

Cohen smiled at him. "How do I look today?"

"You look handsome," said the now besotted M—, "energetic and alive."

"I need a haircut," parried Cohen.

"Maybe I will have some wine after all," I said, although no one had offered me any.

M— passed me the bottle while Cohen extemporized further on his looks.

"Actually, I've grown a lot better looking since I began calling myself ugly."

M— accused him of self-hatred.

"Maybe it's self-hatred," Cohen allowed, "maybe it's bending over backwards for accuracy."

"Cheese?" I said to no one in particular, "Why of course, thank you."

"In the sixties when I was writing the songs that come out of that experience," Cohen explained, "I saw really beautiful youths around. It's all a relative thing. If you're at a bar mitzvah, you may look pretty good; however, if you're with a bunch of lead guitarists at the Chelsea Hotel in 1966, and they're all beautiful, tall, blonde youths . . . "

"I don't think so," M— protested. "I think a lot of them just look very hairy. I think it's harder to look good at forty."

"Most of these lead guitarists don't make it to forty," I felt compelled to insert. They both ignored me. I drained the bottle.

"I feel OK these days, you know. I'm making a living. I managed to get away from my family. I've been through a war. I'm OK."

M— suddenly turned to me. "Go on," he said, motioning me back to my interview.

"Hah?"

"A friend of mine said about poetry," Cohen told M—, "that the two things necessary for a young poet are arrogance and inexperience."

M— seemed to identify.

"What about a prose writer?" I cried in panic. "Do you think it's the same thing, too?" However, M— was already reciting one of his poems to Cohen. Although I thought it a paltry work, Cohen seemed to like it. I cursed myself for not having had the sense to bring along one, if not all seven, of my unpublished novels for him to read. While M— recited another poem, I realized they were on the wavelength I had wanted to reach. M— was up there with Cohen, poet to poet, while I trailed a distant second, the interviewer, straight man, fink.

Finally M— got up to go to the john. Alone at last. Here was my big chance. With one sweeping question I could reestablish myself as an equal in Cohen's eyes. Instead I wound up asking him if he ever got letters from his fans and how he responded.

"You've got to play it by ear," he said. "You can involve yourself totally in the lives of your listeners, and it has got to be disaster. I put my work out the very best I can. It comes out of my life. It's a very large chunk of my life. I can understand if it becomes important in another life. But whether you involve yourself personally in these other lives is another matter.

"I'm not talking about somebody who has a fantasy of a singer. These are people who really relate to your own experience and vice versa. Now maybe they're living in some kind of milieu where they don't have people to relate to. You set yourself up as a kind of kin to these people and they see it and it's true. That's the fantastic thing about it. You meet them and immediately you see they are people who have your own experience. So over the years I have somehow fallen into some lives that my songs have led me into, and some of these lives have ended—rather violently, rather sadly . . ."

When M— emerged from the john, Cohen told us that he must leave for a recording session. M— asked whether he could tag along, but Cohen said no, which pleased me no end. I suggested to M— that if he were going downtown, I'd walk him part of the way. He said OK.

There's really a one-to-one relationship between Cohen and his songs, his books, of that much I was sure. Here were M— and I filling up yet another chapter—two seekers, neophytes, in a foot race to the door of the master. At least we'd be leaving together. Not only was I salvaging a tie out of the day's proceedings but I felt I was rescuing Cohen from a potentially maudlin evening with M—. In the next life Cohen might thank me.

However, as we neared the elevators, as if he'd forgotten something, M— wheeled around and headed back to Cohen's room, advising me to go on without him. What a move! I stood flatfooted in the hallway with no other choice but to leave, which I did. Score another one for M—.

WHAT HAPPENED WHEN PHIL SPECTOR MET LEONARD COHEN?

HARVEY KUBERNIK | January 1978, the *Los Angeles Phonograph* (Los Angeles)

More than three years passed from when Leonard Cohen issued *New Skin for the Old Ceremony* on August 11, 1974, until Columbia released his next collection of fresh material, *Death of a Ladies' Man*, which came out November 13, 1977. Unfortunately, the long wait ended with disappointment as the latter album is now widely regarded as Cohen's one serious misstep.

At the time of the LP's release, *Rolling Stone* critic Paul Nelson tried to be kind, describing the record as "either greatly flawed or great and flawed—and I'm betting on the latter." The consensus today, however, leans toward the former. *Rolling Stone* has called the record "a total waste," and Cohen himself seems to at least partly agree. There are hints of that dissatisfaction in this piece, which appeared shortly after the album and which takes us inside the sessions with Spector. —Ed.

Leonard Cohen—singer, songwriter, guitarist, poet, novelist, and sometime straight-faced spokesman of the hilarious ironies of the human condition—walks into the dimly lit recording studio control booth. The place is called Gold Star, and it is a shining capital of musical energy in the midst of a dying neighborhood in a particularly faded part of Hollywood.

Cohen lets a hint of a smile cross his face, but nothing more. He is not one to demonstrate elaborate emotional feeling in a personal situation. He sports a finely tailored dark blue blazer and well-cut grey slacks, and he radiates a poise uncommon to the environment at hand. His charm is substantial, and it isn't hard to fathom why at least some people find themselves so wholly taken with his art. It's not so much what he is about that is important, but what he seems to be about—not so much what he says, but what he implies.

As Cohen sits down in the booth, a voice screams out of the dark silence: "This isn't punk rock! This is ROCK PUNK!" Then the first notes of a rhythm track drive through the monitors.

The voice belongs to Phil Spector. Imposing, like a king bethroned [sic], he sits behind the mixing board, incessantly fondling an empty bottle, which once contained thirty-two ounces of pure Manischewitz concord grape wine. He wears a sharp, severe black suit, a green shirt, and a very expensive pair of shiny black leather boots—boots that are presumably made for rockin'.

In a year of unlikely artist/producer combinations—Reddy/Fowley, Flack/Ezrin, Grand Funk/Zappa, etc.—this is perhaps the most unlikely: Phil Spector, demon genius of the rock-and-roll production number, producing Leonard Cohen, ascetic prophet of acoustic disaffectedness, with the final product to be known as *Death of a Ladies' Man*.

"We've made some great fuckin' music on this album," Spector says, his voice assuming a high-pitched urgency, a blend of Arnold Stand and Jerry Mathers. With that, he leaps from his chair and hugs everyone in the room. He is very happy with his work, and he wants everyone to know it.

The seventies have been a strange decade for Spector. At the beginning of the period, he made two splendid albums with John Lennon. Then came interesting but generally disappointing projects with Harry Nilsson and Cher. When Spector produced a Dion LP for Warner Brothers at great cost last year, the company decided to not even release it in the US.

The worst blow came, in a sense, though, when Warner agreed to release a definitive Phil Spector anthology, an attractive, well-researched package, made with Spector's full cooperation. It was an incredible collection of music, and a beautifully presented one—but Phil Spector's greatest hits didn't even make *Billboard*'s Top 200 album list.

Insiders could probably explain away the LP's low sales: Warner probably didn't ship more than thirty thousand units at release, thereby marking the album as a sort of "labor-of-love" LP intended only for hardcore Spector fans or Spector supporters within the music industry. The record company didn't even allocate a complete disc-jockey service nationally. It certainly wasn't intended to be a major commercial release effort.

Nevertheless, there have been three albums since it was released—*Then I Kissed Her*, *Da Doo Ron Ron*, and *Be My Baby*. Michael Lloyd and Jimmy Ienner will no doubt continue to find it an insatiable source of future cover tunes for their boppers well into the eighties. Thus, while the album was hardly a moneymaker in terms of actual units sold, it has proven and will continue to prove to be a veritable gold mine of publishing royalties.

But that is hardly enough for Phil Spector, whose brilliance only *starts* with the songs he writes, but really gets to shining when he gets those songs into a studio. And so it is obvious that the Leonard Cohen sessions have been important to him, almost therapeutic. He certainly seems to be taking his work extremely seriously: he has been decidedly less theatrical in the studio of late; the usual Spector circus atmosphere seems to have been replaced at least in part by a rediscovered or new interest in the music itself. And that seems to be very good medicine, both for Spector and for Cohen.

Spector and Cohen, despite their obvious surface differences both in personal style and in musical direction, share one all-powerful element of musical taste—a love for rock and roll. It is deeply rooted in them, and it pervades the work they do together. It is their shared medium, their common ground. A mutual affection for rock's basic greatness has bound the two men together, and made their collaboration work.

"Working with Phil," says Cohen nonetheless, "I've found that some of his musical treatments are very . . . *foreign* to me. I've rarely worked in a live room that contains twenty-five musicians—including two drummers, three bassists, and *six* guitars."

The track Cohen and Spector are particularly interested in listening to right now is "Don't Go Home with Your Hard-On," the album's all-out stomper, with hosts of loud horns and pulsating beat that's hammered all the way home by dual drummers playing in perfect synch. Above it all comes Cohen's menacing, gritty vocal work, which holds center stage in a most unexpected but effective way. "I can really belt 'em out, you know," says the singer, as he takes a swig of Jose Cuervo from the bottle.

Cohen and Spector first met late in 1974, when Cohen was in Los Angeles for a rare club appearance—a two-night gig at the Troubadour. After the last show on the second night, Spector hosted an informal reception for Cohen at his home—a Spanish-style mansion in the grand, excessive southern California tradition.

Cohen was brought to Spector's attention, and vice versa, by Martin Machat, who had independently become lawyer and business manager for both men. Machat took Spector to see Cohen perform. Throughout Cohen's ninety-minute show, Spector sat quietly, very still, immediately impressed (he later said) by Cohen's mystery and his technique (or maybe the mystery of his technique . . . or the technique of his mystery . . .)

The two men got on well at the post-Troubadour reception, and kept in some sort of loose touch thereafter. Late in 1976, when Cohen visited Los Angeles again, Spector invited him to be his houseguest. The first night, the two worked out a new version of Patti Page's "I Went to Your Wedding"; by breakfast, they'd cowritten two new songs—Cohen the lyrics, Spector the music (picked out on the piano). The seed was sown for what ultimately became *Death of a Ladies' Man*.

Cohen is said to have remarked of Spector that "Phil is not a great songwriter, but he's a bold one. He's bold enough to employ the most pedestrian melodies, and yet somehow make them absolutely successful. That is why his compositions are brilliant." Cohen is especially impressed by Spector's early work—"To Know Him Is to Love Him," "(You've Lost That) Lovin' Feeling," etc. "In those songs, the storyline was as clear as clear could ever be. The images were very expressive—they spoke to us all. Spector's real greatness is his ability to induce those incredible little moments of poignant longing in us."

Cohen's own images are expressive, too, of course. On *Death of a Ladies' Man*, they seem particularly direct. "This is the most autobiographical album of my career," he says. "The words are in a tender, rather than a harsh setting, but there's still a lot of bitterness, negativity, and disappointment in them. I wish at times there was a little more space for the personality of the storyteller to emerge, but, in general, the tone of the album is very overt, totally open."

He goes on to say, "I was a little off-balance this year." Songs like "Iodine," "True Love Leaves No Traces," and the album's title track mirror his situation. All the usual Cohen concerns—lost love, personal chaos, doubt, romantic dilemma, alienation, lust, etc.—are present in strong force. "And don't forget humor," Cohen adds. He also says, "I worship women," and suspects that, with the release of this album, "Everybody will now know that within this serene Buddhistic interior, there beats an adolescent heart."

By 6 AM, Spector and Cohen are still listening to one rough mix after another. Bob Dylan appears somewhere in the midst of Spector's huge, complicated sounds. So do Hal Blaine, Jim Keltner, Nino Tempo, Jesse Ed Davis, Allen Ginsberg, Art Munson, Ray Pholman, and Dan and David Kessel—sons of jazz guitarist Barney Kessel. The music is hard and solid and soulful. There is, above all, nothing "El-lay" about it.

To this day, Spector meets people who can't believe that all his great hits were cut in Southern California. "They thought Gold Star was in New York," he says. "Of course, what I do is hardly typical California stuff. There are no four-part harmonies on *my* records . . . Maybe thirty-two-part harmonies . . ." He looks around the room. "Anyone here who plays Asylum records, please leave. Anybody laid-back in this room, get the fuck out of here!"

Cohen likes Los Angeles. A native of Montreal who has spent much of his time in recent years in the south of France and in other European hideaways, he has now moved to Southern California himself. "I like it," he says. "It's so desperate here that it's really not bad at all. And besides, this is the only city in the world where I've ever written a song while sitting in a driveway in a parked car."

Later in the morning, back at Spector's mansion, as the jukebox plays the psalms of Elvis, Dylan, Waylon, Otis, and the Drifters, Spector muses about his own life. "It didn't take extraordinary strength for me to change the way I was," he claims. "What I was doing just had to stop. It isn't hard to see that, especially after you've gone through a couple of windshields at high speeds.

"I have to admit that I did enjoy it to a certain extent—being rich, a millionaire in his mansion, and dressing up like Batman . . . But now I can see beyond that, and see just how unhealthy and unproductive it became.

"I'm ready for anything now. Nothing frightens me. I feel I can do more now than I could ever do before. I feel extremely ready musically. I'm more comfortable, more relaxed, more together. I understand what I want to do, and I'm going to do it. It's time to get serious again."

Then he says, "Come into the other room. I want to play you some more of the Leonard Cohen tracks."

And as he punches up "Don't Go Home with Your Hard-On" once again, and the tight, string, perfectly conceived production fills the air, he says, "Ain't none of us ready for the glue factory yet. I'll go one-on-one with any producer in the world, anytime." He smiles. "We can still kick ass!"

PART II

THE EIGHTIES

Cohen offers only two studio albums, but they feature such monumental works as "Hallelujah," "I Can't Forget," and "Tower of Song."

TV INTERVIEW

PATRICK WATSON | February I and 8, 1980, *Authors*, CBC (Canada)

By the beginning of 1980, Cohen had put the Spector project behind him and was promoting the considerably more satisfying *Recent Songs*, which Columbia had issued on September 27, 1979. In a pensive two-part television interview with the CBC's Patrick Watson, the singer talked about a wide variety of subjects, including *Death of a Lady's Man*, a book of poetry he'd issued in 1978 (not to be confused with the similarly named Spector-produced LP). —Ed.

Patrick Watson: It seems that Leonard Cohen has been trying to heal pain with his songs since he first began to write them at the age of sixteen. And by songs I mean all those volumes of delicate lyrical poetry and the two rowdy, frenzied novels as well as the haunting music that has made him renowned throughout the world.

Leonard Cohen rarely consents to television interviews but this week and next, on *Authors*, he speaks both about the pain and the healing. Now, some of the language you may find offensive, some of the ideas difficult and unorthodox. But the passage of Leonard Cohen through the highs and the hells of relationships and personal knowledge makes him a writer whose qualities transcend those of the work alone.

[*Speaking now to Cohen.*] Can I assume that when you're making a poem you are finding out where you are in the process of doing it? That it's not something you've thought about and you say, "Ah, right now I know I'll write it down," but rather that as you construct it you learn what you're seeing?

Leonard Cohen: That's one of the aspects of it.

PW: So in *Death of a Lady's Man*, I think I trace a growing yearning for certain kinds of stability and repose and unity of human relationships and unity of perception. Am I right in assuming that you found your way into that as you were doing this book or the work that led up to it?

LC: I think the longing exists on a conscious level but the deployment of the energies is somehow illuminated through the work. I know that I want to be in one place. I know that I don't really feel like moving around too much anymore. But I think that's because I want to try something big and I need stable surroundings to be able to really take flight.

PW: When I read the dedication to Masha Cohen—"to the memory of my mother"—and then came right through to the lines that end the book, saying, "I am satisfied and I give in. Long live the marriage of men and women, long live the one heart," I wondered if Masha Cohen, wherever she is now, is saying, "Leonard's on his way home."

LC: [*Smiles.*] I like that description.

PW: What was she saying either tacitly or explicitly to you in the period of roaming, reaching, very hungry Leonard Cohen? I mean hungry for experience—the man, it seemed to me in a lot of your early work, who wanted to know and have and test everything. Was she reacting to that in you?

LC: I think her reaction was twofold. I think she was critical of my life and the details of it she examined with not too much pleasure at certain points. But I always did feel that underneath it all there was a great support and somehow an affirmation of what I was doing.

PW: Thinking about you and her and the movement through *Death of a Lady's Man*, I remembered the story about Jack Kerouac and some young enthusiasts for his work coming to find him and there he was, forty, wearing a woolen knitted cardigan and living with his mom. And they were a little bit dismayed and turned away because he wasn't the Kerouac of *On the Road*. What happens to you now as you meet the fans, go on the road, meet the interviewers, and they're still looking for the Leonard of "Suzanne" or the earlier work? Or are they still looking for that? What are they asking you to be now?

LC: I find people very sympathetic and sensitive to where you are. I have no idea where I am or where they are, but I think both of us are willing to make those minute adjustments, moment to moment, to ourselves. I was really impressed with the people I met across the country and the kind of questions and just the kind of presence of people.

PW: You didn't feel you were being eaten then?

LC: Not at all.

PW: That's great. I'd like you to do a little reading while we talk and there's one that I found myself laughing out loud at yesterday, partly because of an image that came into my mind as I read it. I said, "You know what this is? This is T. S. Eliot writing a script for *All in the Family*." Do you know what I'm talking about?

LC: Well, I like *All in the Family* . . .

PW: This one. [*Points out poem in book.*]

LC: Oh, yeah.

PW: Can you read? Because the movement through the whole page is terrific.

LC: This is called "This Marriage." [*Cohen reads poem.*]

PW: You said a while ago you don't know where you are and you don't know where they are. When I read that for the first time yesterday, I put the book down with a very strong sense of having just run my fingers over a jewel that was very wonderfully crafted. Do you ever feel that when you go back over some of the better work? Are you ever able to say to yourself, "Good. OK. That's pretty damn good."

LC: Sometimes I do that but I don't really reflect on the work from that point of view too often. But sometimes you hear a song on the radio and it sounds OK or someone draws your attention to something that seems all right.

PW: Was there a time when it was of really vital importance for you to go on the road with the bands, sing to people, hear the reaction? And has that changed at all as your focus has gone toward a singular place and singular relationships?

LC: That process changed. I'm still interested in doing it and if I do finish another record I would like to tour behind it, but at the beginning it was rock and roll and that life and the unlimited range of possibilities that was offered you on the road.

PW: What kind of possibilities? Women? Companionship? Excitement? Drugs?

LC: Everything. All that. The life of the appetite. After a while, after the second and third tour, you begin to get very interested in the music and the performance and the test of character that the performance involves. And I think you get a more athlete's vision of the whole process. You just want to keep in the right kind of shape so you can deliver that concert every night. And the whole day focuses toward those three hours that you're in front of people.

PW: What role does instant response play? The difference between the time lag that's entailed when you labor over a book of poems for a year or two years and then it comes out and you wait and then you may get a review and you may get an interview and it slowly trickles back on the one side and then on the road, hit record, wham, everybody yelling and cheering on the other. Levels of importance in those two kinds of response for you?

LC: That instant response is gratifying, of course, but also you have the risk of the other thing going all the time, which is instant humiliation. But I've tried to design the work so that it can last beyond that immediate perception of it. The poems are designed to last at least until the next season and the songs too. So it's really time that I'm most interested in when it comes to a real evaluation of the work.

PW: How much time?

LC: Oh, I'm not greedy. I don't think of a thousand years or anything like that. But just if a song lasts for a few years or if a book keeps on turning up, people are still interested in it. Or if I myself can pick it up and not be totally embarrassed by it.

PW: So there is an important kind of satisfaction in that. A moment ago, when I talked about feeling the craft of "This Marriage" in *Death of a Lady's Man*, I may have misunderstood, [but] I thought you were saying, "That's not important to me, that expression of the craft." I thought I heard you saying, "I've done it, it's gone. If it brings some pleasure fine, but it doesn't matter to me." But it does matter.

LC: Well, it matters when you're in that role of evaluating your work but I myself take that role rarely. I don't think it's a role that one should dwell in. I am there from time to time, but it's not very often that I assume that viewpoint because then you'd just be looking back all the time and examining your career from a kind of stock-market point of view. I do do that from time to time but that isn't really where I dwell. Anyways, events rush in too quickly to allow you the luxury of that kind of reflection.

PW: *Death of a Lady's Man*, though, appears to be exactly that.

LC: Well, that kind of reflection is appropriate to the desk and to the meditations that go into the work but I think outside of that they're somehow inappropriate. The proper time to evaluate your life and the events in your life is when you're sitting in front of the table. Otherwise, you become a bore to others and a bore to yourself if every time you meet someone you say, "How am I doing?"

PW: Some of the motive in seeking a singular place and some kind of stability was to do something big. What's that mean?

LC: Just really to embrace that regime of a novel or a long prose work or a symphony or whatever it is. I just love that regime: getting up in the morning and having your coffee and playing guitar for half an hour or so, then going to the typewriter and doing a quota every day. It just locates your whole day.

PW: Are you doing that now?

LC: No.

PW: Or will you shortly?

LC: I hope so.

PW: Does that depend on having sorted out the personal messes to the point where you can get a physical space and a daily routine of bread, butter, and—

LC: I'm not so sure it involves sorting it out. I think you have to bite through. Maybe just establish yourself and begin the work and then let the mess gather around it in whatever way it does. I think that's what stops a lot of people from writing.

PW: Waiting to sort it out?

LC: Yeah. I don't think anything gets done that way.

PW: "If only I had the time, I would . . ."

LC: Yeah.

PW: Have you found that you can write well according to your own canons when you're in turmoil and driven and feeling a lot of pain?

LC: Well, I think there's a degree beyond which it becomes impossible to work.

PW: Oh, sure. When the noise level goes up.

LC: Yeah. I think it's just a matter of what grade of hair shirt you wear. I think some discomfort is necessary.

PW: I know that lots of people, through the history of poetry, through the history of literature, and to a very small extent some of my own experience, have resolved or at least found some illumination of the dark places they're in through the process of just writing about them.

LC: Well, I think you do a lot to affirm your worthiness by writing. I remember a prose poem by Baudelaire in which he says, "Today I betrayed three friends, I refused to give a recommendation to someone who deserves it, I gave one to someone who doesn't, I lied six or seven times. And now that I'm in my room and I've locked my door, let me do one thing that will justify myself to myself." I think that's a very accurate picture of the process with this particular racket.

PW: Leonard, during the hungry period—or what I'm arbitrarily calling the hungry period—the time when you were reaching out into everything, the mythology of a lot of our contemporaries and younger people about drugs was that they would take you into a new space where a lot of the horrors and the weight of the immediate physical world would vanish. Did you look for that through acid and other drugs and did you find it at all?

LC: Well, I'm not quite sure what the motivation was. I did try those drugs. The drugs and their effects are so different that it's hard to generalize about the experience, although I suppose you can in some way. I don't feel evangelical one way or the other. I think it's a dangerous process. I think it does break down a lot of the structures for better or for worse. In many individuals it's an unfortunate thing to have these landmarks dissolve. But there is something beyond that and I think it's appropriate for a certain period of experimentation, but it's certainly nothing to embrace as a lifelong enterprise.

PW: Can you point to anything in your work and say, "There's a door I stepped through that I might not have even seen the outlines of had it not been for some of that experience"?

LC: It's very hard to say what drugs do. LSD is a very, very powerful drug, which certainly does dissolve the foundations of your ordinary life and does afford a point of view that is usually not related to anything that is going on. But on the other hand, it binds you to a certain vision. It isn't really liberation; it really is another kind of bondage. But as a stage in our very rigid society, perhaps if a young person comes from a very rigid kind of background, it does blow the thing to pieces.

PW: So there's a chance of a fresh start . . .

LC: Yeah, as I say it's a dangerous process because many people are not really equipped to make fresh starts. Sometimes it's just a paralysis. You don't make a fresh start at all, you just stop what you're doing and don't do anything else. There are a lot of people burned out by acid.

PW: I find I'm laughing along in *Death of a Lady's Man*, and then starting back to see who it is I'm laughing at, who's being laughed at, and who's laughing. But reading quite a lot of your [other] poetry, I am aware of a kind of preoccupation with a multitude of depressing aspects in the world, really quite hideous, burdening aspects of the world that you have been grappling with in one way or another.

LC: Like what?

PW: Oh, the ones that get us all: messed-up human relationships . . .

LC: Oh yeah . . .

PW: Death, personal incapacity, inability to make it work, all of the both serious and joking things around failure that weave through *Death of a Lady's Man*. . . . Failure's I guess one of the depressing things but there may be much more intricate things that you find depressing, and I'd like to know about that and also if you're now finding ways to get your head and your heart into a way of seeing the world that isn't depressing.

LC: Well, I don't look at it that bleakly all the time. I don't think it's bleak at all. I feel totally responsible for my own condition and there are lots of good moments. I really don't know what to say about that. I'd like to tell you I've embarked on a program of transcendental meditation and I feel a lot better but I don't really—

PW: What do you mean, you'd like to tell me that? Have you and do you?

LC: No, I haven't. I mean to say there's no program that I've embraced. I think I have had some programs in the past that I've grasped at. I get two or three of 'em a day, but I just think that trying to get through is my program.

PW: But when you say, "trying to get through is my program," it sounds as if you're holding on with your fingernails and there's a great risk that you may not.

LC: Well . . . it's hard right now with your hospitality and the wine. . . . I really don't feel endangered at this particular moment.

■

PW: [*Watson introduces part two of the interview, which CBC broadcast the following week. —Ed.*] Leonard Cohen once told an interviewer [*CBC's Beryl Fox, in a conversation broadcast May 6, 1966. —Ed.*] that he was thinking of changing his name—to September. "Leonard September?" the incredulous interviewer asked. "No, September Cohen," Leonard said, with a twinkle. Submerged beneath the doleful songs and the mystical poems there is a mischievous impish inside to Leonard Cohen that sometimes surfaces in his poetry and the novels, but it's most apparent when he turns an absurdist eye toward the public side of his life—the fame, the reputation, the image, the excesses of the road tour work, and I suppose, most of all, the sadly beautiful vanity of man.

Last week on the *Authors* program, Leonard Cohen and I talked at length about the public side and he read from his new book, *Death of a Lady's Man*—a funny, bittersweet passage which seemed to me like a script from *All in the Family* as if it had been written by T. S. Eliot. But it was also a poem about the failure of a marriage, and while Cohen doesn't look at life bleakly all the time, I sensed in his wonderfully crafted words a deep yearning for stability and repose and unity. This seems to be a time for reflection in Leonard Cohen's life, for an evaluation of its sometimes-extreme events.

Well, this week our conversation turns away from the public aspects toward the more personal considerations of art, relationships, and the self. I asked him to begin with a reading of a poem entitled "The Rest Is Dross."

LC: [*Reads poem.*] Haven't read that for a long time.

PW: How is it?

LC: There are a number of flaws in it but I think it comes out as something authentic.

PW: What are the flaws?

LC: I think the last three lines, where I try the device of throwing the poem away, really mean to say to the reader, "I'm not throwing the poem away." I think I really did throw the poem away.

PW: Do you find yourself analyzing as you work in terms of devices, flaws . . . "Let's see how can I get this on to the next stage"? Is there a process of technical craft analysis like a diamond cutter looking at the lines of cleavage and saying, "this is the way I'll do it"?

LC: I think there is a technology and, to put it less charitably, a series of tricks as [Canadian poet Irving] Layton says that every poet learns sooner or later. But beyond that, there's something you can't fake, and I don't think that one's entirely successful. It's not bad right up to the last part. Maybe it's OK.

PW: I thought it was OK. I liked it a lot. Remember when Bob Dylan said that within three or five years or whatever time period he set himself he was going to be a star? Did you ever approach your craft as a public performer with that kind of intention?

LC: I don't think I really did, no. I always thought that my work was more eccentric and that if it touched the mainstream from time to time I would be lucky, but I never saw it as dominating a field as Dylan did. He was justifiable in feeling that way because he really did have his hand on all the kinds of music that really did lead to the mainstream and made a synthesis of them.

PW: But if you set out to do that, can you really be anything more ultimately than a kind of extremely sensitive reactor as differentiated from an initiator and inventor?

LC: I think in the case of a really good artist, you're doing both functions at the same time and it's an immediate, instantaneous reaction to the stimuli.

PW: So you're saying you've got to be to some extent in tune with the currents, whether or not you're swimming in the principal one.

LC: I think it's more than in tune. You really have to represent them. You have to be so open to the life around you that it isn't even a matter of translation or interpretation. You are manifesting the deepest feelings of people. I don't think it's anything you can plot. You either are one of those kinds of individuals or you aren't. There's nothing to be said for being one because it means a very tricky kind of existence.

PW: What's the source material for the work that lies ahead of you? I had a feeling that ten or fifteen years ago a lot of the source material was a population of girls that you'd known and your projection of yourself into them—your looking for some kinds of mystery and healing in them but to a large extent a projection of Leonard's persona on those girls. Is that right and how is that changing?

LC: Women did play a great part. We are meant to be here with each other and it's appropriate to treat that subject. But I think I had a quotation—I don't know if it was in my first book—from William Faulkner's *The Bear*. It goes like this:

> *"All right," he said. "Listen," and read again but only one stanza this time and closed the book and laid it on the table. "She cannot fade though thou has not thy bliss," McCaslin said. "Forever wilt thou love and she be fair."*
>
> *"He's talking about a girl," he said.*
>
> *"He had to talk about something," McCaslin said.*

I mean, you have to talk about something; otherwise you're writing theology or you're doing abstract mathematics, and I think we do have an appetite to worship and it's appropriate that we find each other, the mystery, men and women, and that some sacramental relationship has to be discovered between us.

PW: Was there a greater projection of yourself on the persons you encountered when you were younger that is disappearing now? There seems to be a motif of self-effacement, certainly in *Death of a Lady's Man*. I don't know whether you're playing with us there or whether that's your genuine investigation, but I'd like to know if there's been a movement from the real preoccupation with stating I am finding myself out there to a withdrawal of the self into some other kind of investigation.

LC: Yeah, I think I've exhausted the whole process of subject/object and seeing the world from that particular point of view for a little while. *Death of a Lady's Man* is a closing statement on a certain chapter. I do have a feeling that I would like to write a book or even live a life where the I is not so prevalent—

PW: The capital I—

LC: Yeah, I think that the only way out of suffering is to somewhat dissolve or attack that particular point of view.

PW: Do you think you would have come to that perception with the normal maturing of a middle-class Jewish Montrealer or has it had a lot to do with the travel, with the exposure to Eastern thinking—

LC: Well, I am a middle-class Jewish Montrealer—

PW: Yeah, but you're not a normal one. You haven't followed the patterns of your family.

LC: I think that every man who's growing up goes through those processes. This is one of those things that we're getting into bad shape about, regarding what an artist is.

PW: Who's the "we"? The Western world?

LC: Yeah, all of us, even the artists themselves, that our life is special.

PW: You don't think it is?

LC: It's special because it manifests itself in a durable form, but I think every man who works and raises a family is going to be up against these things and is going to have the same kind of process of maturing.

PW: It's said that you've said that having children is the only thing that really keeps you in contact with mankind and is an appropriate assault on the ego.

LC: I do feel that marriage and children are the only things that move you out of center stage. Otherwise it's just dating for the junior prom and exchanging identification bracelets and getting them back when the music is wrong.

PW: Leonard, are you surprised to find yourself viewing the partnership of men and women in this way and talking about it in language which now sounds very traditional and very square, very old-fashioned?

LC: No, I'm not surprised. It seems appropriate right now. On the other hand, I don't feel evangelical about it. I don't feel that everyone must get married and have children. I don't even know if it's right for me. I just feel like the institution is under such attack and there's something in me that comes to the aid of it. It is the foundation of human life, and whether one's marriage fails or not or one tries again or not is really irrelevant. This is the sacramental relationship, the foundation of human society, and it has to be affirmed.

PW: A businessman a few years older than you and me who knows you pretty well said to me once that you are the most saintly person that he knows. I don't know whether he was talking about the you now or the you that he's known over the years because he's known you a long time, but obviously he was perceiving a guy who has had some experience and has demonstrated a will to reduce the ego, reduce the I, to serve other people, to make his will transparent to the intentions of other people. Does that reflect the you that you know?

LC: That's a nice compliment.

PW: Is that an important thing to say about it, by the way, that it's a compliment? I was surprised that you said that.

LC: Well, if someone feels that someone is a saintly person, it means that there's been a special kind of transmission between those two people and rather than treat it heavily I chose to treat it lightly. I don't know who the guy is. It's obviously someone who has touched me and whom I have touched. But whether or not I am that thing . . . one never feels that way, anyways. But reducing the ego is the prudent thing to do as you grow older.

PW: "Prudent" has nothing in it of morality. Prudent is simply a strategy for getting on.

LC: Yeah, I think so. It's a pragmatic enterprise because you cannot hold onto the things that support the ego. Those things dissolve with time anyhow and our work is small and our bodies are fragile and our relationships are impermanent so to try to support an ego on those pillars is fruitless and just leads to suffering.

PW: When you said that we're in bad shape about our view of the artist, you were complaining in part about the terrific elevation of the ego within the artist community—I guess the whole world of media hype and puff about every artist, and that's a world that you inevitably get into when you go make records and [enter] the world of the performing artist. But you *have* enjoyed that. You have found that there is at least a transient satisfaction. You want to do it again.

LC: Oh yeah, I'd like to go on the road again with a band. I remember at Glasgow [Scotland] at the Apollo Theater . . . a few years ago, the stage manager pulling down the curtains and he said, "You've sent a lot of happy people home tonight, Mr. Cohen." Those are good feelings.

PW: If at the end looking back you were able to say, "Well, the poems were OK, but at some point I touched the life of one individual and healed or redirected or helped," would that latter really be a greater satisfaction? That's what I think I hear you say.

LC: If you really could help somebody, I guess it is. It would have to weigh pretty heavily. But there's something about putting a song into the world and just letting it take its path that is wonderful, too.

PW: But nobody puts a song into the world except individuals. It is an I who saw that particular way of putting together some sounds and words and experiences. It's not done by committees and institutions.

LC: It's when the I steps out of the way of that willing being and something from the world takes root or takes form and then is given back. It's the I, the self-importance, that really defeats the process. A poet can't feel important; he doesn't get anything if he feels important.

PW: When Will Shakespeare sits down at his desk with his dirty pen and [his friend, actor Richard] Burbage says, "You've got to have a play by this week Friday" and Shakespeare says, "Watch me, boy, I can do it," and he whips off *Macbeth*—

LC: That's because he's not thinking of himself as Will Shakespeare sitting at the desk and will he succeed or will he not succeed. He has the whole structure of craft and willingness to fall back on and he just lets it flow through him. By "flowing through him" I don't mean that in any light sense. It flows through him but doctored and modified by the great skills that he has. But he can't oppose himself to the world, which really is what self-importance is.

PW: Is there an example in your recollection of an artist or would-be artist who has opposed himself to the world and within that kind of glorying in his selfhood has screwed things up in a spectacular way. Dali?

LC: The persona that the guy develops to protect himself in the world is another question. What kind of image you really go into collusion with and encourage is another thing from the man sitting in front of a blank canvas.

PW: What's your inclination in that respect, at this point, at forty-four? To pull back and forget about persona and just be a very private person? Or to find some new social structures that can put you into contact with people?

LC: I don't really have a program. Events rush in too quickly for me to develop a real program about it. Songs come along and after a couple of years you have ten or twelve of them and you start to make a record, and then the demands of the technology and of the craft and of the career kind of carry it along.

PW: Is making contact with people an issue for you? A difficulty? A challenge?

LC: I like to make contact with people. It's nice to do it within a forum of work.

PW: A shared submission to the discipline.

LC: It's a wonderful thing. Writing a song of course is easy to talk about because it's so immediate and it's so easily used. It has such utilitarian value, songs. People do their washing up and make love and court, and a lot of the most mundane and important parts of their lives are enacted to music. And to be one of the people who score those activities . . . it's really very gratifying.

PW: As we finish, would you find something in *Death of a Lady's Man* that you feel would send people out of the theater feeling happy?

LC: I don't know if I can find one that will do that. [*Looks through book.*] Ah, there's a poem about marriage called "Slowly I Married Her."

PW: I don't know if it's going to make them happy but it's going to make them joyfully sad maybe. [*Cohen reads poem.*] I think I'll strike the word "sad." It made me sad when I first read it. Hearing you read it made me feel warm. That's a good poem, isn't it?

LC: Yeah, I think that one's a good one. Harry Belafonte's wife had been very suspicious about my presence because I had suggested that he change his show and stop singing calypso and start singing about himself. He's a very great singer, and we were drinking late into the night at the Four Seasons hotel. And I got out this poem. I thought he could set it to music. I don't know whether it was the vodka or not, but she wept a few tears that sealed the night very nicely.

PW: Thank you, Leonard. You never changed your name to September Cohen.

LC: No.

PW: You're stuck with Leonard.

LC: Too late now. Too late to change the name. Too late for suicide.

COHEN CLIP

On Becoming a Folksinger

"I thought I'd do just one album. I'd published *Beautiful Losers*, and I really couldn't meet any of my own bills. So I thought, I'm going to become a country-and-western singer. I was on my way to Nashville. I'd written some songs that I thought were country songs. That was the kind of music I'd grown up with. So on the way to Nashville, I came across some people in New York and somebody introduced me to Judy Collins, and I somehow got into the New York musical scene, which I knew nothing about at the time. I didn't know that there was Dylan and Phil Ochs and Judy Collins and Joan Baez."

—from "Conversations from a Room," by Tom Chaffin,
Canadian Forum, August/September 1983

A CONVERSATION WITH LEONARD COHEN

STEVE VENRIGHT | May 1983, interview | August 1983, *Shades* (Toronto)

The early 1980s was one of Cohen's quiet periods. He did not tour for four full years—from 1981 through 1984—and after he put out *Recent Songs* in 1979, he issued no records until 1984. Instead, he spent much of his time practicing Zen Buddhism. He did, however, offer the occasional interview, including one with a twenty-one-year-old waiter and aspiring journalist named Steve Venright.

In 2008, in the Toronto-based online magazine *Mondo*, Venright recalled the unusual circumstances that led to the conversation:

Twenty-five years ago, almost to the day, I sat in the bar of Toronto's King Edward Hotel asking Leonard Cohen questions about Art and Life, Truth and Beauty, the Sacred and the Profane. A week earlier, in a different establishment across town, I'd been asking him whether he wanted fries or salad with his chili dog. He'd just come down from the mountain—Mount Baldy near L.A., that is, where he'd been rigorously observing an ascetic lifestyle in a Zen monastery—and there he was, in my section, ordering a hot dog and Coke.

Fortunately, the restaurant happened to be empty apart from Mr. Cohen and his female companion (the distraction of serving my biggest idol might have doomed my other tables). Not so fortunately, as the chef tardily informed me, we'd run out of chili dogs. After working up the courage to break this news—which (must've been the Zen thing) he accepted with admirable composure—I worked up the courage to ask him for an interview.

I was a twenty-one-year-old waiter and would-be writer working in downtown Toronto (some things, apart from age, don't seem to change). The woman I was living with, in a dying relationship, was perhaps an even bigger Cohen fan than myself. When she heard that I'd met Leonard and would be interviewing him at the King Edward Hotel, where he was filming *I Am a Hotel*, and when it was quite clear that I would not be divulging his room number, she threatened to split up with me. It was one of those let-me-get-this-straight moments: if I refused to provide my girlfriend with the directions to another man's bedroom, I would be history. But such was the allure of Canada's "melancholy bard of popular music." (By the way, Suzie, it was Room 327.)

My real introduction to Leonard Cohen dates back to the end of a previous relationship, a couple years prior. It was a somewhat sweeter demise but, being my first serious breakup, painful beyond what I thought I could bear. And just when it seemed the moment couldn't get sadder, my soon-to-be-ex put the needle down on a record that was more soulfully dolorous than any music I'd ever heard. That voice and those words said with impossible beauty what my lover was trying her best to make me understand: it's over, but what we've been to each other will always be a part of us as we go our separate ways into the world.

The song was "Hey, That's No Way to Say Goodbye" and the voice belonged to a poet and novelist from Montreal who'd ventured into songwriting. I'd heard the name before, but from that moment on it would be imbued with a significance that's only grown deeper and stronger over the years: Leonard Cohen.

Someone once said that listening to Leonard Cohen's music made his life not worth living. Critics—and more recently bloggers intent on providing self-help advice—have called it "music to kill yourself by."

Thinking back to hearing that first song (actually considered to be one of the cheerier ditties among his early recordings), those sentiments, while not shared, are not hard for me to understand. I was young and my emotional spectrum was broad and intense. Hearing something that resonated so closely with my sorrow was almost, at first, devastating. How could anyone do that, I thought. Now I have to get through this too! But there was something in the voice—hypnotic, slightly frail, empathic, and oddly heroic—that compelled me to listen, that comforted me even as it tore at my heart, and that somehow helped me to feel that my life was, after all, very much worth living. Ever since that first transfixing exposure, the writings and music of Leonard Cohen have been an ongoing source of inspiration.

When it came time for the interview, I was nervous but well prepared with a list of questions that inquired as much into Cohen's work as an author as they did his career in music. Being accompanied by a wonderful photographer named Tom Robe, who was known for his live shots of musicians both famous and obscure, helped my confidence considerably. Tom got some terrific photos that day and his presence helped keep me from lapsing into the jitters. Leonard's warm demeanor, dry wit, and gracious attention to my very serious questions put me further at ease.

Still, it wasn't until a small chamber ensemble began playing dreamily as if on cue after the last topic had been addressed and Leonard said, "That was a really good interview," that I finally relaxed. Maybe it was the scotch talking, but Leonard proceeded to express his approval in a way that suggested our exchange had gone beyond the commonplace, and that he was pleased with the terrain we'd covered. Should he chance upon the fragments transcribed here, I hope he'll still find aspects of that long-ago conversation agreeable.

This week my son, an aspiring songwriter who's just a few months older than I was at the time of the interview, will see Leonard perform for the first time. His deep appreciation of Leonard's music began earlier than it had for me—Kerry was in the womb when his mother and I attended a concert on the tour for *Various Positions* (the album Leonard often cites as his favorite).

The tour that will bring Leonard back to Toronto (where it officially launches) has already received reverential reviews and awestruck ovations in other parts of the country. At seventy-three, he still refuses to perform with anything less than total commitment, playing for nearly three hours with multiple encores. For the shows in Toronto, where he and his nine-member band could easily sell out a stadium, he has chosen to play a more intimate venue, hitting the stage four nights when one or two might have sufficed.

This tour may have been prompted by financial concerns but it's clearly about more than money. It's even about more than music. It's about Art and Life, Truth and Beauty, the Sacred and the Profane, and it's about communing once again with the man who has evoked these in song with tremendous honesty, grace, and spirit for over four decades.

I really hope this isn't the last time Leonard Cohen brings his song to the world, but if it does turn out to be his farewell tour—well, it sure is some way to say good-bye.

Venright's 1983 conversation with Cohen began with some unpublished discussion of current projects, including a planned studio LP (apparently *Various Positions*) and a proposed spoken-word album based on the forthcoming *Book of Mercy*. The interviewer then turned the discussion to Zen. —Ed.

Steve Venright: Can you say what effect on your life Zen has had?

Leonard Cohen: It's just house cleaning. From time to time the dust and the dirty clothes accumulate in the corners and it's time to clean up.

SV: That reminds me of a poem of yours in *Death of a Lady's Man*—which I think is called "How to Speak Poetry"—where you're saying that [speaking poetry] is analogous to going over a laundry list.

LC: Yeah—nothing special.

SV: But does that apply to the songs, with your singing voice? I'd say there's so much emotion in your songs . . .

LC: Oh, I see what you mean—that's a good question. [*Ponders.*] I also go for natural expression, in singing.

SV: You seem to be placing some focus on Canada these days, as far as work goes. Are you involved in any projects at the moment abroad?

LC: No, I'm not. I've always been a bit of a patriot and I wanted to reconnect with Canada because I haven't really done anything here in a long time. I've lived here, but all my concert tours in the last seven or eight years have been in Europe.

SV: And I think you'd explain that as a matter of the audience already being there.

LC: Exactly.

SV: Whereas in Canada perhaps it would take more effort . . .

LC: It's also much more expensive because the space between the cities is so much farther. And another thing is, I think that because of what I've experienced in Quebec—that is, more or less an attack on the language I work in—I think that had something to do with me wanting to work in this country in English.

SV: Do you plan to tour with the album eventually?

LC: I would like to. I haven't toured for three years now, and I don't know if it has to do with the album, but sometimes you just get to miss the road and the kind of friendships that grow up when you're playing with people night after night.

SV: That's good to hear. How does the reception to your work in general differ from, say, in Europe?

LC: This city has always been very warm to my work, from the very beginning. From the very first book I put out there's been extremely generous attention to my work here.

SV: How does Toronto differ from Montreal in either respect for what you're doing or attention given to it?

LC: Well, Montreal to me is like Kyoto or Jerusalem.

SV: The Jerusalem of the north.

LC: Yes. It's a holy city, and they're properly not concerned with this sort of secular expression. They have heavier things on their mind, like the destiny of their blood and things like that. And Toronto is the cultural center of the country—I suppose they don't want to hear this in Edmonton—so it's appropriate that I work here.

SV: You were very involved in the pop culture of the sixties. How do you feel about the present pop culture that has been generated or engendered by punk rock and approaches like that?

LC: I feel there's been a general vulgarization of society—which I can't get too upset about one way or the other.

SV: You've probably been accused of it yourself at one point or another.

LC: Oh, I've been accused of selling out ever since I played a guitar chord in public.

SV: I guess by "vulgar" I was referring to responses you received to *Beautiful Losers* in particular. The sacred and the profane . . .

LC: That elegant book?

SV: That's going back a ways, I realize.

LC: It's still around. I guess "vulgar" is the wrong . . . things seem rather dull. I think we might *hope* for vulgarity. It seems rather dull and repetitive. But maybe that's just the observations of middle age.

SV: In what was intended as a private statement about your book *Flowers for Hitler* you once wrote, "All I ask is that you put it in the hands of my generation and it will be recognized." That was almost twenty years ago. Has your work attained the nature of recognition you would hope it to?

LC: Yes, and beyond. And beyond.

SV: It seems there was a change in either course or maybe sentiment when you came out with *Recent Songs*. There seems to be a peace in that album that maybe wasn't visible before.

LC: What was that?

SV: I just felt that either you were becoming a little more at peace with anxiety, or at least that there was a level to the album which was less aggressive. [*Cohen nods agreement.*] Do you feel this is sort of a natural course, or is there anything you attribute it to?

LC: I think I've stopped whining.

SV: [*Lengthy pause.*] How does that feel?

LC: A lot better! [*Laughter.*]

SV: I don't know if this is a heavy question or not, but I believe you said in the past that Beauty no longer mattered to you as much as Truth did. Do you find yourself ever sacrificing Beauty for the sake of Truth, or vice versa? Or is that impossible to discern?

LC: I feel the conversation flies in the face of Keats's famous observation that "Beauty is Truth and Truth Beauty is all you need know," or something like that—the end of "Grecian Urn." I don't know how I was ever tricked into talking about Truth and Beauty anyhow! [*Laughter.*]

SV: You've probably said as much on that subject through your work as anyone would need, in this lifetime, to know. Well, what's next? Do you see beyond December at this time with the album, the *Book of Psalms* [*Original title for what became* Book of Mercy. —*Ed.*], and the opera? Or are you going at that as it comes to you?

LC: More or less as it comes to you. And as you get older, with a certain gratitude that it's coming to you at all.

SV: Is it coming to you as strongly as ever?

LC: I meant just the time. You mean inspiration or work or the capacity to work.

SV: I'm thinking along the lines of the hunger, of the necessity to create.

LC: Yeah, I feel that very strong. And after a while you realize that when you're in good health, part of that good health is the song.

COHEN CLIP
On His Responsibility to Audiences

"I think about that a lot. . . . You think about whether you've failed . . . whether you've been a responsible voice or whether you've blown it or what you can do to set things right. It leads to all kinds of crises of feeling."

—from interview with Peter Gzowski, *Morningside*, CBC Radio, May 1, 1984

RADIO INTERVIEW

VICKI GABEREAU | May 1984 , interview | September 6, 1984, *Variety Tonight*, CBC (Canada)

Cohen still wasn't touring when he talked with Vicki Gabereau for a Canadian radio broadcast, but he was at work on *Various Positions*, which would be released in Canada on December 11, 1984, and would introduce such classics as "Hallelujah" and "If It Be Your Will." (As noted earlier, Columbia at the time declined to issue the album in the United States.) In this rambling conversation, Gabereau managed to coax Cohen into discussing everything from his kids to his exercise habits to his taste in clothes. —Ed.

Announcer: Leonard Cohen is probably a Canadian legend. Whether you see him as a soulful poet, a successful novelist, an habitué of Montreal bistros, or an expatriate on a Greek island, you probably know something about the man. He has eight albums out now and when Vicki spoke with him last May he was still working on his latest recording and he had just published his eighth book of poetry, *The Book of Memory*. [*Actually* The Book of Mercy. —*Ed.*] Vicki was pleased to meet him—finally.

Vicki Gabereau: I've often wondered if you really existed. I've seen you in performance but years ago and . . . you're so ethereal. You'd disappear all the time.

Leonard Cohen: Well, it takes a long time to prepare the work that I put out so I generally don't do anything for three or four years between anything I've done.

VG: Does it alarm your publishers when you don't appear for six years or something?

LC: No. Well . . . I bump into [publisher] Jack McLelland and have a drink with him from time to time so we know each other. We know that each of us exists.

VG: And eventually something will be produced.

LC: Hopefully.

VG: After each and every time that you do produce something, do you feel as if maybe this is the last one? Does that ever occur to you?

LC: You're always grateful for what you get and there's always anxiety that it's all used up.

VG: When did you start writing these fifty [poems in the book]?

LC: About two years ago. It took about a year to assemble. And they're the result of a certain kind of place that I found myself for three or four years when I felt the need to look into my own traditions and scriptures and roots.

VG: Do you make that decision one afternoon walking down the street?

LC: No, I don't think this is a book you can write on the basis of a decision. You either find yourself up against the wall in some kind of trouble and this is the only thing that can penetrate the silence that you find yourself in [or not].

VG: I would think that the order in which these are found now is not necessarily the order that they were written.

LC: It's more or less the order but there are things that had to be moved around.

VG: Do you remember which one you did first? I have a bet with myself but which one?

LC: No, I don't recall. It was one of the early ones.

VG: I thought it might be number thirty-three. Do you know them by heart, which one number thirty-three is? It's the one to your son, a prayer about your son.

LC: That one I remember very well. That wasn't the first, no, but I remember the circumstances of that one very much.

VG: Was there any great joy in preparing these? Did you feel relieved each time you would prepare one?

LC: I felt a certain release because they are prayers. It's difficult to talk about this but in the midst of the writing, the prayer is answered and that's when the psalm ends—when the deliverance comes.

VG: And you feel the release?

LC: You feel the release, yes.

VG: Where did you write these? In any particular place?

LC: I wrote these mostly in a little trailer. I was living in a trailer in the south of France in the countryside.

VG: Like a caravan?

LC: A caravan, yeah.

VG: In a camping ground?

LC: No, it was on a piece of property that was owned by someone I knew and they just let me park it at the corner. It was great.

VG: I've been in France quite a bit. I used to be married to a Frenchman so we would make the yearly trek to visit the mother and father and I would look at the camping grounds and I would think, "What a horror." They were cheek by jowl, these little caravans, and they would go from living cheek by jowl into the same situation, always dusty and—

LC: —and right on the edge of the road.

VG: Just a nightmare. I could never figure out how people could do that but I guess escape is escape, isn't it?

LC: Yeah.

VG: We were going to ask you to read some of these things but I think that it's not the right condition, sitting in the studio, to do this.

LC: I've tried once or twice on this book tour. Interviewers have asked me to read it but you really freeze because these are about as personal as you can get and it's very hard to pray in public.

VG: I must say, you've never been prone to secrecy about what you do and the way you have lived, but this really goes through the core. It is so personal. It is devastating.

LC: It is an attempt to speak from the deepest place.

VG: Do you think that that takes a certain kind of bravery? Reviewers have all said that it was extremely bold of you to do this.

LC: I sometimes worried about the indiscretion of the thing. I thought, first of all, there's a very good Book of Psalms that we already have and there's no urgency to produce another one. But it was the only thing I could say and that confers on it a certain legitimacy. And I know that they're true and I think that they could be useful to one or two people here and there.

VG: I would think so. I think they're quite uplifting.

LC: Well, one is driven into these kinds of words that are unfashionable but they saved me—

VG: From what?

LC: From despair. I don't think you approach this subject unless you're driven to it, unless all the other avenues of expression are blocked.

VG: You were going to call it the Book of Psalms, but you changed your mind, I take it.

LC: Yeah, because first of all, I wanted to avoid a reference to the great book that David wrote and all of them are not properly psalms, so I tried to stay away from that.

VG: When are they not properly psalms?

LC: Well, I think that psalms by their nature have to have an element of rejoicing and though that's not entirely absent, I think these are more conversations with the absolute. They find themselves in a certain kind of intimacy that involves doubt, involves anger, involves despair, and asks for help, where I think the psalms are more of a celebration.

VG: Yes. Were there more than fifty?

LC: There were a few more than fifty but some of them weren't as true. And on assembling them it became very, very clear—it wasn't a difficult choice. Some of them just didn't ring [true].

VG: Might they later, reworked?

LC: I don't think I would rework these. I was ready to stay in this land-scape as long as it was necessary. I don't think it's one you want to return to and as soon as the deliverance came, the inspiration went.

VG: Do you still go on your retreat?

LC: Well, I've been studying with an old Japanese gentleman for many years who's a friend.

VG: With whom you drink—

LC: With whom I drink cognac. He taught me how to drink. People ask me what did I learn from him: how to drink cognac.

VG: How do you drink it? A lot of it?

LC: A lot is one of the aspects. He's just become a close friend. It's nothing special outside of a friendship. I've been fortunate to have friendships with people of other generations up and down. It's just nice to have an older guy around to have—

VG: Yeah, they seem to know things.

LC: They know a bit more than you do.

VG: Yeah, they sure do. But what I don't understand is how one can sit—I have trouble with five minutes but I guess that's because I'm ill-skilled to sit for sixteen hours.

LC: Well, they say that the Zen people are the marines of the spiritual world. If you have that kind of nature that is attracted to the ordeal or to a certain vigorous kind of practice then that's a place for you but there's a saying in Zen, "Better not to begin."

VG: [*Laughs.*] Than to blow it?

LC: It's a severe practice and it's really not for everybody, and the fact that it's difficult is no guarantee of its effectiveness. There are many traditions around and it's a matter of finding one in which you can dissolve yourself for a little while.

VG: I think the first time you went you weren't convinced.

LC: The first time I went I couldn't believe it because there was this Japanese master and there was a German abbot and it was on the top of a mountain and we were marching around in the snow at three in the morning. I thought it was the revenge of World War II. I got out of it as fast as I could but something about it stayed in my mind and I started coming back more and more frequently until I began to understand what it was about.

VG: What is it about? Please—you tell me. Oh, Leonard, you must know. [*Laughs.*] What does it all mean?

LC: It's just a matter of getting straight with yourself from time to time. These decisions are not made out of luxury. There are times when you just feel that you have to do a little exercise.

VG: Do you do any physical exercise? You don't appear to be a tennis player.

LC: I'm pretty tough.

VG: Is that so? [*Laughs.*] In what area?

LC: Until very recently, when I messed up my knee, I used to work out every day and then when I messed up my knee, I took up light weightlifting. But then I messed up my back. My knee's in pretty good shape now so I'm going to try to get back—

VG: You can get new parts. I was watching television only this morning when they told me I could get new knees.

LC: I like [Canadian novelist] Mordy Richler's book about that. Did you ever read that book of his? It's about this millionaire that keeps a kind of harem of people whose livers and kidneys he uses. It's a wonderful book.

VG: Yeah, it's a good thought, too. Perhaps if we were born two hundred years hence, we could have everything replaced. I think that we've missed that boat.

LC: Yeah. I think whatever the span allotted us is sufficient. I wouldn't want—

VG: Sufficiently more for some than for others. [*There is a gap in the recording here. Apparently Julian Bream's recording of Rodrigo's* Concierto de Aranjuez *is played.* —Ed.] The Julian Bream thing, Rodrigo's *Concierto de Aranjuez*. Leonard Cohen, he chose that. That was great, wasn't it?

LC: Very beautiful.

VG: You may think that this is blasphemous to say but I remember when I was a kid my dad took me to the movie, the only movie he ever really took me to, and it was *El Cid*. You remember that movie?

LC: No.

VG: You weren't going to movies like that, I guess. Anyway, they played that thing all through the whole picture and I sobbed and carried on. It is a tearjerker, isn't it?

LC: Yeah, it's very, very emotional.

VG: Is that what you listen to? Do you listen to a lot of music?

LC: Well, I've been moving around a lot. I don't carry cassettes. But that is a piece I like to put on from time to time. A taxi driver was playing it in his car the other day and that's why I was thinking of it.

VG: That's nice for a change. Usually they've got the country-and-western music on, which I don't mind either but it must have been a relief.

LC: It was completely unexpected. A very tough New York taxi driver talking out of the side of his mouth with a cigar and he says, "Yeah, do you wanna hear the variations now?"

VG: [*Laughs.*] I love it. Tell me something: where are your papers? Where are all your things from all of the years gone by? Have you given them to the university?

LC: Actually, the University of Toronto bailed me out of poverty about twelve years ago by buying a bunch of my papers and laundry lists and old napkins and things—

VG: They really want things like that, don't they?

LC: That was a wonderful moment. I have a whole bunch of new stuff. Maybe I can sell it to them again. But a lot of them are in Montreal and Greece and various suitcases here and there where people are holding them for me.

VG: "Just keep this for me for a couple of years"? Are you a packrat type? Do you keep things?

LC: Yeah, I tend to keep everything. I keep all the letters I'm going to answer.

VG: Any minute now.

LC: Any minute now.

VG: I have boxes of them from years and years ago. Some never got answered. But as far as the papers are concerned, apart from bailing you out and giving you something tangible with which to pay the light bill, they've got to look at it in a sense of posterity. "This is a guy that is important to us and we need his stuff." But the point of all this rattling on is I just wonder how you consider yourself historically speaking, how the world will view you in some hundred years.

LC: You go from very inflated views of yourself to all the way down the other side. Sometimes I feel that those papers are more important than anything else I've put out—where they could be looked at not from the point of view of literature or of excellence but just of the point of view of somebody who's kept a very careful record of their thoughts and experiences. I think it might be useful from that point of view.

VG: Do you keep a diary?

LC: Well, in a sense it's one big diary set to guitar music.

VG: [*Laughs.*] Oh, God, you're such a poet. I'm always terrified of poets. I always think they know something I don't know, that I won't understand what they're writing. I get a book of poetry in the mail and I think, "Oh . . ."

LC: I feel the same way about poetry.

VG: Do you?

LC: The only thing that comforts me a bit is the thought that most poetry isn't any good and that the form is so seductive and so many people try it out and really there are only a few here and there who can master it. So with that sense of comfort I pick up a book and if I don't understand it, which is often the case, I just let it go down.

VG: Most often I get things that conjure up names of figures from the Grecian past about which I have no information until I don't know what the hell they're talking about and they could very well be making a great pun or a great observation and it just zooms right over my little head.

LC: Yes, it's unpleasant to find a poet that's better educated than you are.

VG: [*Laughs.*] Somehow they like to flaunt it.

LC: There is that. But that still resides in a lot of poetry, that aspect of elitism where there's an assumption that there's a vast common culture and that we all participate in it. Unfortunately, things are a little more fragmented now and most people know Mr. T and things like that.

VG: You are working on a new record or it's out?

LC: I'm just finishing it up now. It should be out in the fall. It's called *Various Positions* and it's coming out on CBS.

VG: Are you playing guitar?

LC: Playing guitar on quite a few of them, yeah.

VG: Do you have a tape with you? Could we play any of it?

LC: I have some rough mixes here.

VG: Carrying them around in your pocket? Your rough mixes?

LC: It's just a cassette of the rough mixes. I've been studying them on the road, because I'm going back to the studio to sweeten them up a bit.

VG: You carry them around in your pocket. Those are not the masters one would pray, no? Certainly not. Have you ever written anything for kids?

LC: No. I've made up quite a few stories to tell my own children.

VG: How old are they now?

LC: Nine and eleven.

VG: Young still. Do you see them? Do you live with them?

LC: I don't live with them but I manage to see them every day.

VG: Oh, well, that's lucky. But if you've been living in Greece . . .

LC: No, I've been living mostly in Montreal and New York. Now they're going to school in New York. They lived in the south of France for a long time. They went to school there. So that's why I got the trailer, to live nearby.

VG: Papa comes over for a story reading?

LC: Yeah, or they love to come over to the caravan.

VG: I'll bet they do. It's fun over there. And it probably rocks.

LC: Yeah, in the wind. Yeah it does.

VG: If you jump up and down lots it probably does too. Do you not live on Hydra anymore?

LC: I haven't been living in Greece for a while although I have taken the kids there for the summer now and then.

VG: What about concertizing? What was the last time you did that?

LC: The last time I went out was with my last record, which was '79–'80. I did about a hundred concerts in Europe and Australia. And I'll go out again with this new record in September. I'll do Europe in the fall and Australia in the winter and hopefully North America in the spring.

VG: Does that throw you, when you have such a long time in between performances? A weekend almost kills me to come back and try it again.

LC: I know what you mean. I think that's why I have a band. Otherwise I'd do the whole thing with my own guitar but the first two or three concerts my fingers won't work and I'm very nervous.

VG: Were you nervous when you worked with Phil Spector?

LC: I was very, very nervous that one of his guns would go off.

VG: Does he have guns?

LC: In the recording studio it looked like a small arsenal. He was carrying a gun and three or four bodyguards were carrying guns and there were bullets falling on the floor. And as the evening drew on and the Manischewitz wine was consumed—

VG: Oh God, how can you drink that stuff?

LC: I didn't drink it. And it got very loose. Yeah, things got a bit dangerous.

VG: This is a fair number of years ago. When was it—'77?

LC: Yeah, '77 I made that record.

VG: He has all but disappeared, as you know. He is a total recluse.

LC: Yes, he stays in this big house that he keeps at about thirty-two degrees.

VG: Fahrenheit?

LC: Yeah. It's very, very cold. After you get to know Phil a while, you take a fur coat when you go visit him. And he locks the door. He doesn't let you out.

VG: Oh how nice.

LC: It's hazardous.

VG: Did you ask, "How come it's so cold in here?"

LC: I don't know. He really is a magnificent eccentric. To work with him just by himself is really delightful. We wrote those songs together over a few months and when I visited him we'd have really good times and work until eight in the morning. But when he got into the studio, he moved into a different gear, and he became very exhibitionistic and very mad and I lost the handle on the record completely. He would take it away. He would take the tapes away every night under armed guard and then he mixed it in secret. He wouldn't let me in.

VG: Did you kick and scream? Beg?

LC: He disappeared. I couldn't find him. And I was stuck with the option, after a year's work, either to say no or just to let it go out as it was, and I thought it was good enough to go out but it wasn't at all what I thought it could have been. I thought the instinct was good for both of us to work with each other and I think the songs are very, very good but I think the voice is lost in the mix. It was just a matter of turning the right dials.

VG: Maybe he wanted you to disappear, who knows.

LC: I think he wanted me to disappear. One time he came over to me about four in the morning with half a bottle of Manischewitz in one hand and a .45 in the other and he put his arm around my shoulder and shoved the nozzle of the .45 into my neck and cocked it and said, "I love you, Leonard."

VG: Oh my God. Were there ever any moments in your life when you thought you could get that mad? Were you ever that much on the edge?

LC: Well, his madness has a kind of theatrical expression. Mine tends to get very silent.

VG: Oh, don't get silent yet. Five more minutes.

LC: [*Chuckles.*] OK.

VG: But have you ever thought you were going mad?

LC: I think you do have those feelings from time to time, yeah.

VG: I think you do. You never contemplated ending it all?

LC: No. I've been taught somehow or acquired a notion that it's not the right thing to do.

VG: Yes. I think you're right. Are you afraid to die?

LC: No.

VG: That may sound like an asinine question but—

LC: I think that [Canadian poet Irving] Layton put it very nicely. He has a poem addressed to Sir Mortimer, who is death, and he said, "I don't mind dying but it's the preliminaries that I'm worried about."

VG: [*Laughs.*] Do you see Layton a lot?

LC: I haven't seen him in the past year and I've missed him very much. I've tried to make contact but his former wife Betty died when he moved to Montreal, and when I came he was down at the funeral there. But I do want to see him in the next week or two.

VG: When did you first meet him?

LC: I was seventeen. I guess it was in my second or third year of college and I was writing poetry and he was one of the lights around the city.

VG: Did you take him your stuff?

LC: We never had a student–teacher association. We became friends right off and . . . we'd show each other poems. That was one of the aspects of his generosity even though he was and probably is a more accomplished writer than I am. There was never the sense that I was bringing my stuff to him.

VG: At university, were you considered a curiosity even at seventeen and eighteen?

LC: No, I don't know, maybe I was. But certainly among my friends and people I knew, there was no attempt of any of us to stand out in any special way. We thought we were sort of living *Brideshead Revisited* at McGill University.

VG: Is that so?

LC: This was before Sputnik. . . . It was before the university began to get anxious about what they were teaching. It was a very relaxed situation. I think we spent most of the time listening to that Rodrigo guitar concerto and drinking wine and writing poetry and chasing after girls.

VG: Which you almost could have made a living at. You had quite a reputation. Things have calmed down, I understand.

LC: I don't know if it was a living.

VG: But you have calmed down. You've cooled your jets, as youths will say today.

LC: I guess so.

VG: Have you?

LC: Not really.

VG: Have you not?

LC: In this respect, you mean? In the respect of womanizing?

VG: Yeah.

LC: I still am very excited by women but I guess the activity has declined somewhat.

VG: [*Laughs.*] Well, we won't carry on with that. When you were in university, what did you think you were gonna do with yourself? Did you think, "I'll make my living as a poet, as a writer" or "I'll drive a cab" or "I'll work in my family business" or what?

LC: I thought I would make it as a writer. There was really never anything else that I considered.

VG: Did you ever do any real job?

LC: Oh, yeah. I ran an elevator and I worked in factories and I did counseling at camps. I did a lot of odd jobs. I did radio journalism for a while.

VG: You did?

LC: I did just about anything. In the first five or six years, when I went to Greece, I went for a number of reasons. One of them was economic, and I'd come back to Canada and I'd put together six or seven hundred dollars and I'd go back to Greece and I could live for a year on that.

VG: No kidding.

LC: I was aiming for twelve hundred dollars a year. So I'd sell a story to *Cavalier* or something like that and get seven hundred dollars or do a piece for the CBC and get three or four hundred dollars, and that way I was able to live for a number of years and write.

VG: So you don't mind the Spartan existence?

LC: I have always been attracted to the voluptuousness of austerity. I never chose the style of my life because it hurt. It was on the contrary. I feel most comfortable and most abundant when things are very simple and I know where everything is and there's nothing around that I don't need.

VG: You're not interested in mirrored walls and plush carpets and that kind of thing.

LC: No, I don't feel comfortable in those. It's pleasant to visit a well-appointed house but for my own self I like to have it rather bare.

VG: What do you do today, for instance? This is work, what you and I are doing.

LC: Yes, sure.

VG: But will you work [on music] today? Will you write anything today?

LC: Maybe on the airplane—that's always a good time—because I'm going to Winnipeg tonight. That's quite a long trip.

VG: What happened to Edmonton and Calgary?

LC: Yeah, Winnipeg, Calgary, Edmonton. But I have my little Walkman and earphones and there are a couple of lyrics on my record that aren't finished so I'll probably work on those.

VG: You don't socialize on the plane and chat up everybody?

LC: No, I find it difficult to talk because of the noise.

VG: I like to concentrate fully on keeping the plane up.

LC: Yes, it's a very good idea.

VG: I went through quite a few clippings—old ones, new ones—and apart from the review kind of stories that they do about you, saying this is a work of bravery, this isn't, and all that garbage, people who do feature stories on you always want to say how you're dressed. Have you noticed that?

LC: They review my suit.

VG: Yes, they do. For instance, when you were staying at the King Eddy [Hotel in Toronto] and you were shooting *I Am a Hotel*, they instantly described what you were wearing and how dignified you were and how things had changed and your hair was cut and shaved and that you were communion-like and every time they saw you, you were different.

LC: I've been wearing the same suit for years.

VG: You look like you're from Marseilles, to tell you the truth. [*Laughs.*] But they like to know what you're wearing.

LC: Well, I usually wear a suit. I emerged before blue jeans and I was never very comfortable in that. And I like a slightly formal cast to things. A double-breasted suit I've always felt good in.

VG: You should be wearing a black shirt and a white tie and carrying a small violin case.

LC: I put on a gray shirt this morning but it didn't go with the rain.

VG: It's a lesson to be learned from living in British Columbia: You should never paint a room gray. Because the sky is gray, the room is gray, the carpet is gray, everything is gray. I made this mistake. [*Pauses.*] All right: *I Am a Hotel*. What has become of that?

LC: It was chosen as Canada's entry to the Montreux Television Festival. I don't think it's very good. I think it's respectable television but it was the first time I've gone into it, and I didn't really know what I was doing and I kind of lost the handle on the thing.

VG: That's the second time you've said that.

LC: Well, these handles are elusive.

VG: They fall off. You worked on a picture that was shot here, where you did the music for it, for [director Robert] Altman. Was it *McCabe & Mrs. Miller*?

LC: Yeah. Bob Altman wrote the film while listening to the record that a lot of those songs were on. He asked me if he could use the music. I was in a studio in Tennessee recording one of my albums and I got a call from Bob Altman. And that afternoon I'd gone to see *Brewster McCloud*. I'd sat through it twice. He said, "Can I use this music?" I said, "I don't know what you've done." He said, "Well I did *M*A*S*H*." I said, "I heard it was a grand success but I didn't see it. Is there anything else I might have seen?" He said, "I did another picture called *Brewster McCloud* but you wouldn't have seen it because nobody liked it." I said, "Take anything."

VG: [*Laughs.*] Take me, I'm yours.

LC: Yeah, and then I recorded a couple of extra guitar pieces for Warren Beatty's monologue and a few things like that. But mostly they were just lifted off the record.

VG: Do you go to movies? Did you when you were a kid? Obviously you're not a movie fanatic.

LC: I'm not a fanatic but there's a great song by Loudon Wainwright [III], "Movies Are a Mother to Me." It's a nice place to cool out in.

VG: It feels safe. Did you do the opera with Lewis Furey?

LC: Yeah, I wrote the lyrics to an idea that he had. He wrote the book and conceived of the thing and I was doing an experiment in Spenserian stanzas, which is an old form of very tight interlocking lines. So I wrote most of the lyrics in these Spenserian stanzas.

VG: What status has it now, the opera?

LC: It seems that it's going to be a Franco-Canadian television show. I think they're going to be filming at the end of the summer.

VG: Why don't you do a video? That's what somebody asked me. I was panicking all weekend long thinking of what in heaven's name I was going to ask you. I made notes on toilet paper, on martini blotters, everywhere, and then last night I thought I'll write 'em all down and figure out what I'm gonna do with this guy. Are you going to do a video or what? You'd be perfect.

LC: Well, this little show for the CBC was designed with that in mind. I wanted to make a long piece kind of video. It isn't too successful but with the new material I'd like to try it again.

VG: Some of my friends wanted to know [whether] you like Randy Newman.

LC: Oh he's very fine, yeah.

VG: He is, isn't he?

LC: Very fine writer and singer and arranger.

VG: Have you ever met him?

LC: I think we were recording at A&M studios in Los Angeles once and we shook each other's hand, but I don't know him as a man, no.

VG: He hasn't broken through to appeal to a great number of people.

LC: He did have a Top 40 hit—"Short People."

VG: Yes, he got in all kinds of hassle about that one, too. You ever got in any kind of trouble, where the public said you are really beyond the pale, you've just gone too far?

LC: No, I don't think so. During the great Maoist period in France where I have a fair audience I used to get accused of being a bourgeois individualist and that sort of thing. But nothing really directed to a song.

VG: New shoes will do that to a French communist. They'll accuse you of being bourgeois. Well, I will release you from this. I thank you very much for coming in.

LC: Well, thank you.

INTERVIEW

ROBERT SWARD | December 1984, interview | December 1986, *Malahat Review* (Canada)

A few months after he spoke with Vicki Gabereau, Cohen talked in Montreal with Robert Sward. The interview, which CBC Radio broadcast nationally in Canada, later appeared in edited form in the University of Victoria's *Malahat Review*. Cohen again discussed his new album, *Various Positions*, but Sward—himself a novelist and poet—appeared at least as interested in *Book of Mercy*, the artist's latest poetry collection. —Ed.

Robert Sward: Your latest album is called *Various Positions*. Why that title?

Leonard Cohen: When you're gathering songs together, the ones that you have and the ones that you can finish, they generally fall around a certain position, and this position seemed to me like walking, like walking around the circumference of the circle. It's the same area looked at from different positions. I like to have very neutral titles. My last album was called *Recent Songs* and that was the most perfect title I've ever come up with. But *Various Positions* is OK. My next one is going to be called *Songs in English*.

RS: What connections are there between *Various Positions* and *Book of Mercy*, your new book of poems?

LC: *Book of Mercy* is a secret book for me. It's something I never considered, although it has an organic place, I guess, among the things I've done.

It is a book of prayer and it is a sacred kind of conversation; the songs are related, of course. Everybody's work is all of one piece, but *Book of Mercy* is somehow to one side. For me personally it's just a document, an important document. But a popular song has to move more easily, lip to lip. Songs are addressed and constructed that way. *Book of Mercy* is a little book of prayer that is only valuable to someone who needs it at the time. It isn't aimed in the same way that a song is aimed.

RS: Yet I find it reads very much as if it were a love poem. It is a book of love without the kinds of tensions that are in your other love poems and songs. It's very much an I-thou relationship.

LC: Well, I hope it has those qualities, because if a thing doesn't have those qualities it doesn't go anywhere. It doesn't even touch yourself. But it is a particular kind of love poem. We always have someone looking over our shoulder when we write and we always have an idea of a public. But I think that in *Book of Mercy* that process was as rarefied as possible. The public almost evaporated in the construction of that book. It really was meant for people like myself who could use it at a particular time.

RS: Have you been surprised by the audience that it has found?

LC: I'm always happy that a thing finds any audience at all and I've gotten some very kind letters from people who are not readers of poetry. I've gotten letters from soldiers and people I ordinarily never hear from.

RS: In an early poem of yours, "Lines from My Grandfather's Journal," you write, "Even now prayer is my natural language." It strikes me that you may, to some extent, have found your natural language in *Book of Mercy*. And of course a psalm is also a song.

LC: I think that I was touched as a child by the music and the kind of charged speech that I heard in the synagogue, where everything was important. The absence of the casual has always attracted me. I've always considered the act of speaking in public to be very, very important and that's why I've never been terribly touched by the kind of work that is so deliberately casual, so deliberately colloquial. There are many great masters of that form, like Robert Creeley, but it isn't the sweetness for me. It isn't delicious. I always feel that the world was created through words, through speech in our tradition, and I've always seen the enormous light in charged speech, and that's what I've tried to get to. That's a hazardous position because you can get a kind of highfalutin' sound that doesn't really strike the ear very well, so it has its risks, that kind of attachment. But that is where I squarely stand.

RS: One sees the importance of naming in *Book of Mercy*, and you have just suggested that this is how the world came into being, through incantation, through saying and through naming.

LC: Yes, that's always touched me, the capacity to create the world through speech, and my world is created that way. It's only by naming the thing that it becomes a reality. A lot of people quarrel with that idea because that limits the direct perception of things. Everything is going through speech; everything is going through the idea, and a lot of people feel that things should be able to manifest before your awareness without the encumbrance of speech. I know it's a very old-fashioned idea and not popular today, but the kind of speech designed to last forever has always attracted me.

RS: You once said that "the angels of mercy are other people." What does that mean? And what is the relationship between angels and language?

LC: I don't know. One of the things I always liked about the early Beatnik poetry— Ginsberg and Kerouac and Corso—was the use of the word "angel." I never knew what they meant, except that it was a designation for a human being and that it affirmed the light in an individual. I don't know how I used the word "angel." I've forgotten exactly, but I don't think I ever got better than the way that Ginsberg and Kerouac used the word in the early fifties.

I always loved reading their poems where they talked about angels. I've read a lot of things about angels. I just wrote a song with Lewis Furey called "Angel Eyes." I like it as a term of endearment: "Darling, you're an angel." The fact that somebody can bring you the light, and you feel it, you feel healed or situated. And it's a migratory gift. We're all that for other people. Sometimes we are and sometimes we aren't.

I know that sometimes it's just the girl who sells you cigarettes saying, "have a good day" that changes the day. In that function she is an angel. An angel has no will of its own. An angel is only a messenger, only a channel. We have another kind of mythology that suggests angels act independently. But as I understand it from people who have gone into the matter, the angel actually has no will. The angel is merely a channel for the will.

RS: You speak about will in *Book of Mercy*. There's one psalm about the will and it seems to be a wall that prevents something happening or some opening of a channel.

LC: Well, we sense that there is a will that is behind all things, and we're also aware of our own will, and it's the distance between those two wills that creates the mystery that we call religion. It is the attempt to reconcile our will with another will that we can't quite put our finger on, but we feel is powerful and existent. It's the space between those two wills that creates our predicament.

RS: I am struck, in *Book of Mercy*, by the relative absence of will. One of course needs a thread of will to pray. One even needs a thread of will to write a psalm.

LC: Those are really ticklish questions. I think you put your finger on it. Somehow, in some way, we have to be a reflection of the will that is behind the whole mess. When you describe the outer husk of that will which is your own tiny will—in all things mostly to succeed, to dominate, to influence, to be king—when that will under certain conditions destroys itself, we come into contact with another will which seems to be much more authentic. But to reach that authentic will, our little will has to undergo a lot of battering. And it's not appropriate that our little will should be destroyed too often because we need it to interact with all the other little wills.

From time to time, things arrange themselves in such a way that that tiny will is annihilated, and then you're thrown back into a kind of silence until you can make contact with another authentic thrust of your being. And we call that prayer when we can affirm it. It happens rarely, but it happens in *Book of Mercy*, and that's why I feel it's kind of to one side, because I don't have any ambitions toward leading a religious life or a saintly life or a life of prayer. It's not my nature. I'm out on the street hustling with all the other wills. But from time to time you're thrown back to the point where you can't locate your tiny will, where it isn't functioning, and then you're invited to find another source of energy.

RS: You have to rediscover the little wills in order to take up various positions again.

LC: Yeah, that's right. The various positions are the positions of the little will.

RS: Has there been another time in your work where you have discovered the will, where you have abandoned the little wills?

LC: Well, I think that in writing, when you're cooking as a writer, it is a destruction of the little will . . . you are operating on some other fuel. But there are all kinds of writing. There are people like Charles Bukowski who make that tiny will glorious, and that's a kind of writing that I like very much: a writing in which there is no reference to anything beyond the individual's own predicament, his own mess, his own struggle. We don't really live in Sunday school, and *Book of Mercy* is Sunday school. It's a good little book and it's a good little Sunday school, but it isn't something that I could honestly stand behind all the time. I certainly wouldn't want to stand behind it publicly. It is that curious thing: a private book that has a public possibility. But it's not my intention to become known as a writer of prayers.

RS: What is it like going from *Book of Mercy* to a tour of forty European cities giving concerts, as you're about to do, singing songs from the new album?

LC: It's not very different. You definitely go into a concert with a prayer on your lips. There's no question about that. I think that anything risky that you do, anything that sets you up for the possibility of humiliation like a concert does . . . you have to lean on something that is a little better than yourself. I feel I'm always struggling with the material, whether it's a concert or a poem or a prayer or a conversation. It's very rarely that I find

I'm in a condition of grace where there's a kind of flow that is natural. I don't inhabit that landscape too often.

RS: Do you really feel as though you're experiencing humiliation when you're out there?

LC: I mean this in a kind of lighthearted way. When you walk on the stage and five thousand people have paid good money to hear you, there's definitely a sense that you can blow it. The possibilities for disgrace are enormous.

RS: Are your audiences in Europe, where you've done many, perhaps most of your concerts in the recent past, very different from your audiences in North America?

LC: Speaking technically, like a salesman about territories, there are real differences in audiences. For instance, a Berlin audience is very different from a Viennese audience. A Berlin audience is very tough, very critical and sharp, like the edge of a crystal. You have to demonstrate the capacity to master your material, yourself, the audience. There's a certain value placed on mastery. In Vienna, there's a certain value placed on vulnerability. They like to feel you struggling. They're warm, compassionate. Of course, it changes with seasons, whether you're playing in winter or summer, there's a thousand variables, but at the bottom, if you can find the door into the song . . . You're singing the same songs every night and it's necessary to find the entrance into the song, and that always changes, and sometimes you betray yourself in a song. You try to sing it the way you did the night before and people can feel it. People can feel that you haven't found your way into it. If you find your way into it, people respond to that. If you don't, you feel a certain frisson of alienation that you yourself have created. It's in the air.

RS: A resentment?

LC: It can go from a certain absence of warmth in the applause to things being thrown on the stage.

RS: Did that ever happen?

LC: I think I was shot at once at a big festival in Aix-en-Provence. That was when the Maoists were very powerful in France and they resented the fact that they actually had to buy a ticket. A lot of them broke down the fence and came into the concert and I did notice one of the lights on the stage go out after a kind of crack that sounded like a gunshot. I don't know. But they're tough critics, the Maoists.

RS: What about the French generally? You have said you are French. How do they respond to you?

LC: My work has been well received in France. One of the reasons is that they have a tradition that my work fits into. They like to hear that battle in the voice. They want to hear the real story. The well-known ones are Brassens and Brel, but they have hundreds of such singers. They don't have a preconception of what the voice should be. So my songs have struck home there.

RS: There was a lot of ferment in Montreal in the late 1940s and early fifties, a lot of excitement around poetry and figures like Irving Layton and Louis Dudek. Did that touch you at all?

LC: Oh, very much so. Both those men were very kind to me. I studied with Louis Dudek at McGill University and, as many people have mentioned, he is a really magnificent teacher. He gave a sort of dignity, an importance, to the whole enterprise of writing that enflamed young people. You wanted to write. You wanted to be a poet. And he looked at your poems and spoke about them and criticized them in a very accurate and compassionate way, which is his style. I never studied with Irving Layton. I never felt influenced by Irving or Louis as models, and there was never any attempt by Irving or Louis to influence their students toward a certain kind of writing. But they enlightened the whole process.

RS: I'm sure you're familiar with Irving's assessment of you as the high priest of poetry, himself [Irving Layton] as the prophet, and A. M. Klein as the archivist. How do you feel about that?

LC: I don't know what "archivist" means.

RS: Collector of the archives. Keeper of the scrolls. Keeper of the tradition.

LC: Well, I would never quarrel with that. That's a useful description. Irving, as the prophet, and probably the best writer we've ever produced in this country, does stand on a mountain. I inhabit a different kind of landscape.

RS: Is there any tension between your role as solitary poet, if one can call it that, and the role of public performer?

LC: I never think of myself as a solitary poet. I don't feel any conflicts in what I do. There are economic pressures, and there's a desire too, as a musician would say, to "keep your chops up," to keep singing and keep playing, just because that's the thing you know how to do. So between that and the need to make a living, you find yourself putting a tour together. What the real high calling behind any life is is very difficult for me to determine. It goes all the way from thinking that nothing any of us do is terribly important to feeling that every person has a divine spark and is here to fulfill a special mission. So between those two positions, there's lots of space. But I've put out a record and I know I have to go on a tour or nobody will know about the record, and if nobody knows about the record, it defeats the idea of the song moving from lip to lip, and it also makes it impossible for me to support my family. So all these things conspire to place me on a stage and hopefully be able to entertain people for an evening.

RS: So there are really very practical considerations as well.

LC: I don't think there is any other consideration but practical. I've never been able to disassociate the spiritual from the practical. I think that what we call the spirit or spirituality is the most intense form of the practical. I think you have to find those sources within yourself or there is no movement, there is no life to be led. Many people have different ways of locating that source. Some people avail themselves of the traditional ways, which we call religion or religious practice. There are many people who have absolutely no need of those particular references, but it doesn't mean that their lives are any less spiritual. On the contrary, it might mean that their lives are more spiritual. They are living spirits. And there's no distance.

RS: It strikes me that there's sometimes more irony in your songs than in your poems. I'm thinking of lines like, "He was just some Joseph looking for a manger" [*from "The Stranger Song" —Ed.*]. The inflections in your singing voice convey a variety of different attitudes, and in some instances an attitude like irony comes through more clearly in the songs.

LC: Yeah, I see what you mean. I think of Bob Dylan, who gets the inflections of street talk, the inflections of conversation, and does that with such mastery . . . where you can hear a little tough guy talking. You can hear somebody praying. You can hear somebody asking. You can hear somebody coming on to you. When you're composing that material and you know that it's going to occupy aural space, you can compose it with those inflections in mind. And of course it does invite irony because that irony can be conveyed with the voice alone whereas on the page you generally have to have a larger construction around the irony for it to come through. You can't just write, "What's it to ya?" If you sing, "What's it to ya?" to some nice chords it really does sound like, "Well, what's it to ya, baby?" But just to see it written, it would need a location.

RS: How much connection do you feel with Dylan's music, or with others, like Joni Mitchell, for example? Whose music is closest to you now?

LC: Well, like the Talmud says, there's good wine in every generation. We have a particular feeling for the music of our own generation and usually the songs we courted to are the songs that stay with us all our life as being the heavy ones. The singers of my own period, Joni Mitchell, Bob Dylan, Joan Baez, Ray Charles, all those singers have crossed over the generations. But we have a special kind of feeling for the singers that we use to make love to.

COHEN CLIP

On the "Great Judgment"

"I know that there is an eye that watches all of us. There is a judgment that weighs everything we do. And before this great force, which is greater than any government, I stand in awe and I kneel in respect. And it is to this great judgment that I dedicate this next song."

—from the introduction to "Hallelujah" at a Warsaw concert, 1985

INTERVIEW

KRISTINE McKENNA | January 1985, interview | 2001, *Book of Changes* (US)

In January 1985—a month after he talked with Sward and only weeks before he embarked on a two-month, forty-two-concert European tour—Cohen met with journalist Kristine McKenna at a house he owned in Los Angeles. Portions of the conversation appeared later that year in the *Los Angeles Times* and, in 1986, in *Another Room* magazine; the fuller version that follows comes from McKenna's 2001 interview collection, *Book of Changes.* —Ed.

Kristine McKenna: Do you prefer calm or chaos?

Leonard Cohen: I prefer calm, but it's not for human beings to have it their way. As to which is better for me creatively, I never have the sense of any deluxe position as an artist. I always feel I'm operating with very little and never feel I'm standing before a banquet table from which I can choose calm or chaos, one subject or another. Things seem to present themselves urgently and I don't really have much choice in the matter. I write very slowly, one word at a time, so I don't have any sense of a grand operation.

KM: Are you an easily enchanted person?

LC: I'm always being swept away. I've found that as you grow older you become crazier and more careful at the same time. It's like the base of a pyramid widening as the heights of folly deepen.

KM: What qualities do you find consistently compelling in people and in art?

LC: I don't have a list, but I find that when I'm feeling open and good about things, then people can get through to me. If I'm not, then everyone remains embedded in ice.

KM: You've been a regular contributor to popular culture for several decades. What's the most significant change you've observed in that arena?

LC: I don't see anything terribly different. The basic function of popular music is to create an environment for courting, lovemaking, and doing the dishes. It's useful because it addresses the heart in the midst of all these activities, and it will always be useful in this very important way. Sometimes the music business is hospitable to innovation and excellence, and sometimes it is not. At the moment it is not—the music business is in the icy grip of the dollar right now.

KM: What do you see as being your image?

LC: I get echoes back from different countries—it seems to be a kind of loner telling the truth, or something like that. As to how accurate that is, it's hard for me to say. Ultimately, one is simply happy that one's work is present enough that people even bother to attach an image to it.

KM: What are the recurring themes in your music?

LC: It's hard from the inside to say what something's about. I think you write it to find out what it's about. In terms of song, popular song has to move quickly from one lip to the next or it isn't popular song, and popular songs are usually about love and loss.

KM: Why is popular music obsessed with the theme of romantic love?

LC: Because the heart is a complex shish kebab in everybody's breast and nobody can tame or discipline it. We do live passionate, emotional lives somewhere inside, and that's really the most important thing to us. So nobody fools around with music because music is for the heart.

KM: Are you surprised at what you've achieved in life, or did you always feel you were destined to make yourself heard?

LC: I always had a compulsion to show off. I always had this notion of speaking simply about the things closest to me, and I thought I could do one or two things in writing. I had this idea of being a minor poet, because it was the minor poets who put one or two little poems in the anthologies that I liked. Those are the people who touched me, rather than the great writers like Shakespeare or Goethe.

KM: What do you feel to be your chief strength as an artist?

LC: With any artist who survives past his lyrical twenties, a central quality is perseverance. A lot of people decide not to go on when they realize exactly what is involved in the life of a writer. Many people, very legitimately, decide they don't want to lead this kind of life, so people drop away. And the people that remain, remain with their eyes wide open, realizing that it is a very specialized kind of existence that has enormous rewards, but involves you in a kind of daily life that leaves much to be desired.

KM: What's the biggest obstacle you've overcome in your life?

LC: They keep changing. The whole thing seems like an obstacle. Whether you're preparing dinner or trying to get across town, there seems to be a long line of insurmountable problems you must face. I find the whole production to be an ordeal and I don't know how other people do it.

KM: When you find your will and inspiration flagging, are there specific things you can do to revive them?

LC: That's a good question. You should try to keep yourself cheerful. Gossip, a good comedy, a joke, a glass of wine with a friend—all the conventional escapes are to be recommended.

KM: Willed cheerfulness often seems to be a mask that allows one to remain asleep.

LC: Depression and melancholy is the worst kind of sleep, and although we do have to have experiences with these kinds of emotions, they do cripple if they become chronic. So it's our responsibility to ease ourselves out of those conditions, and the conventional methods are indicated. Conversation, entertainment, a friend who flatters you—anything to break the gloom is valuable.

KM: What's the bitterest pill you've had to swallow?

LC: They've all seemed bitter, yet I don't feel bad. Things are tough, but I don't feel defeated. Things are as they should be, and it's never been any different. The fact that they're not putting us in concentration camps, that we can vote every four years—these things are to be celebrated. We have a certain modest liberty in this country—an extravagant liberty, compared with the rest of the world—that we should continually affirm. Outside of that, how to deal with one's own life and keep oneself straight with the people one knows and loves, and maintain some self-respect while looking at work you know is deeply imperfect—these are the things people confront constantly.

KM: It's a popular theory that artists produce better work when they're in a state of personal turmoil; do you think there's any truth to that?

LC: I think everyone is in turmoil and I'm suspicious of the tendency to isolate the artist from the rest of the world. I'm not quite sure why they've been separated out, but it seems that they have been. The artists probably want it that way because it gets them off the hook with their wives.

KM: Can one learn to avoid repeating the same mistakes, or does life always have the capacity to throw you back to the ignorance of point zero?

LC: The nature of writing is being thrown back to point zero. You look at the blank page in the morning and what next? In maintaining our associations with people, one never loses sight of point zero either, because human relations are fragile and the backlog they depend on can evaporate. A few bad moments with a friend and the whole backlog of experience can be annihilated. So we must be careful in our associations and continually review them. It's been my experience that things can be destroyed quite easily. It's like with virtue. You can work on virtue and it's like throwing a heavy stone to the top of a hill. You can roll it down in a second, but it takes a lot of work to get it up there.

TV INTERVIEW

RAY MARTIN | May 24, 1985, the *Midday Show with Ray Martin*, Nine Network (Sydney, Australia)

Cohen took a few weeks off after his European tour ended on March 24, 1985; then on April 30, he embarked on a thirty-five-concert series that lasted until July 21. This trip found him returning to Europe but also performing in the United States and Canada as well as in Australia, where on May 24 he appeared in concert and on Ray Martin's television program. On the TV show, Cohen and his band delivered "Coming Back to You" from *Various Positions*. Then Martin welcomed him to the program. —Ed.

Ray Martin: Great stuff. Leonard Cohen and the band. One of the living legends and we have got the pleasure of talking to Leonard. Please welcome back Leonard Cohen. Thank you.

Leonard Cohen: Thank you for having us over tonight.

RM: Well, it's all our pleasure. It was the Canadian country, wasn't it? That song had a country swing to it.

LC: Yeah, it had a country feel to it.

RM: Did you realize that today is Bob Dylan's forty-fourth birthday?

LC: Happy birthday, Bob.

RM: The reason I say that is that it seems like you have been in each other's shadow now for about twenty years, haven't you?

LC: I have known him for a long time. I bumped into him many years ago in Greenwich Village in New York and I have rejoiced in his genius over the years.

RM: It's not true, those reports that in fact he has modeled himself on you in terms of being the enigmatic figure?

LC: I taught him everything he knows. [*Laughter.*]

RM: I mentioned Canadian country and you are a Canadian. I am just wondering whether you have had to live with that, whether in fact had you been born in the United States, you would have had the focus of publicity, the sort of star attention, that Bob Dylan has been forced to live with.

LC: Maybe. I've lived in Canada most of my life and never felt a great desire to move south of the border. But it's true that we probably have the same kind of ambiguous feelings about the United States that you do down here.

RM: I think Pierre Trudeau referred to it as an inferiority complex.

LC: It's true. I was just talking to some people here in Sydney over the past few days. It seems that an artist or a sportsman or a scientist even has to have that stamp of approval from the US before we take him seriously. That's the sad thing.

RM: It is. Have you seen enough of Australia yet, Leonard, to really be able to see if we are like a South Pacific version of Canada?

LC: Well, I think in terms of this United States situation that we are talking about, that you have a better take on it here. We are just a few cities really arranged on the border of the United States, so our sense of identity is continually being threatened and a lot of people say what the hell, we will just go down there and work. Down here, you don't have that easy access to territorial United States. You got all the cultural stuff coming in on the television but I think it is an easier situation down here.

RM: Yes. I wonder too, in fact, [about] the sort of characters we have turned out, the Canadian character or the Australia character that we have. Small populations along one strip. In your case it's along the Saint Lawrence, in our case it's along the coast . . . British stock as I say, with a great alliance with America. [I wonder] whether you see Australians and Canadians somewhat the same?

LC: Well, I think we studied the same things in school and we looked at that map of the British Empire and we were both red. [*Laughter.*]

RM: Did that trouble you?

LC: No, no, and it's true that the world sees us as stereotypes. They see you as outbackers and kangaroo people and they see us as mounted police and snowmen. [*Laughter.*]

RM: Not true?

LC: It's true. [*Laughter.*]

RM: Can I make one of those sweeping generalizations and say that in my experience, and I have been to Canada many times, I find Canadians as a group perhaps more bland than Australians. They don't seem to be quite as outrageous and quite as upfront as Australians.

LC: No, I think that they are much more retiring, much more withdrawn than Australians. There's a real feeling down here of down to earth and it's an obscenity that keeps coming to my lips so I can't say it but there's an attitude down here like, so what, which is great . . . this country seems healthy. The body of this country seems to be completely intact and sunburnt and full of beans and Canada, we have that long winter and we are continually in this defensive position in regard to the United States so it is different.

RM: What about the criticism that often people make about Australia, that we are too hedonistic?

LC: I don't think you are hedonistic enough. To rejoice in your own landscape and your own bodies and your own families and your own good luck . . . I don't think there is anything wrong with that.

RM: Is it true that the real reason you have come down here is to taste Australian wine and Australian women? [*Laughter.*]

LC: Oh no, I- I- I- please, no.

RM: There's an ugly rumor doing the rounds.

LC: No, I would never want to have the reputation as someone who sweeps into a country on a raid. [*Laughter.*] No, I have tasted the wine.

RM: Is it true that it is in your contract that you must have red wine backstage?

LC: Who let that news out? [*Laughter.*]

RM: Do you feel very Jewish?

LC: I know that I am a Jew and I came from a good Jewish family, conservative and, yeah, I certainly feel that tradition deeply.

RM: Do you speak Hebrew?

LC: I can pray in Hebrew. I can speak to the Boss in Hebrew. [*Laughter.*]

RM: Did you feel especially Jewish when you went back to Poland? I read the story of your return there, which was quite an extraordinary trip, wasn't it?

LC: It was kind of an alarming and touching experience. One, because there had been a community there of three million Jews that was destroyed in a couple years during the war. So as a Jew I felt curious because there was a lot of cooperation to be able to do away with that many people. So I did have solidarity in that sense also, because the country is involved in some heroic struggle now. You do identify with their protest. I had no idea that I had any place in the Polish culture at all, so it was kind of alarming to find the crowds there and the kind of attention I got there.

RM: Now, your parents were Polish Jews?

LC: My mother was from Lithuania, which was a part of Poland, and my great-grandfather came over from Poland to Canada.

RM: I read as well you were very surprised to find that there was in fact a Leonard Cohen Festival of Music in—

LC: Yes, yeah. They have a festival of my songs at Krakow every year or so.

RM: Which is just near Auschwitz?

LC: Yeah. It's very hard to deal with. I was totally unequipped for the kind of pressures that were put on me. The national spokesman of Solidarity asked me to invite Lech Walesa to the Warsaw concert. He was under town confinement in Gdansk so I was invited to embarrass the government in some way, and I didn't have a chance to test my courage. Some of the guys in the band drew me aside and said, "Leonard, we don't know what weird missionary adventure [*laughter*] you're on but we are just getting paid by the week, so [*laughter*] don't say anything that is going to make it difficult to leave the country. Let's play the gig and get out of town."

RM: What was your inclination, though? Would you like to go back? You could go back on your own.

LC: Yeah, going back on my own. I might look into that sometime.

RM: What was the response? I have been to Poland a few times reporting and it seemed that any Western music that they weren't picking up on shortwave radio was at a premium, that in fact they were prepared to pay big money, many zlotys, for music. Did you find that there was a hunger there for your music?

LC: Not just for my music. There is a real appetite for the Western experience. I think they want to point west and they are being forced to point east. I think that they feel themselves part of the Western European culture and that really eats at the heart of a lot of people.

RM: We mentioned Bob Dylan, his birthday, but did you find going back there that it was at all an educational experience? You and Bob have both been somewhat critical of Western society. Was there any education in seeing the other side?

LC: Well . . . it is a difficult place to live. I think that people are really suffering under that regime. I think that probably the Polish people are difficult to govern anyhow . . .

RM: Yes.

LC: I know the Polish people because I come from that sort of family. They are independent and crazy.

RM: Yes, the most crazy romantics. I think they used to say the Irish were the crazy romantics but I think it is the Poles.

LC: But anybody who has ever seen a communist government, who has felt it for a moment, who has ever seen the public presence of a government . . . we don't know what it is to have the public intrusion into our private world. [*Silence.*] I hate it.

RM: Where will you spend your sixtieth birthday? Do you still see yourself doing gigs in places like Australia and drinking good red wine?

LC: Well, God willing I would like to keep on going. I listened to Alberta Hunter in New York a few years ago. She was eighty-two at the time and it was really wonderful to hear the experience in this woman's voice. You knew that she knew what she was talking about and when she said "God bless you" at the end of her set, you really did feel blessed.

RM: Yes. Despite the image of the prince of darkness and despair and the poet of melancholy, is it fun?

LC: There are a lot of good times on the road. You get very tight with the men and women that you are working with and you feel like you are part of the gang again.

RM: Yes, on the road. Marauding or raiding, but not raiding.

LC: No, no. [*Laughter.*]

RM: In fact, you can catch Leonard Cohen and the band in Sydney tonight at the Sydney Entertainment Center, on Saturday at the Melbourne State Theatre, on June 2nd at the Adelaide Festival Theatre, and June 5th in Perth at the Concert Hall. And it's your own fault if you don't take the opportunity to see Leonard Cohen and the band. Leonard, thank you very much indeed.

LC: Thank you very much.

SONGS AND THOUGHTS OF LEONARD COHEN

ROBERT O'BRIAN | January 1987, interview | September 1987, *RockBill* (US)

After performing for much of the first half of 1985, Cohen again largely disappeared from public life. There were no new albums that year or in the two years that followed, nor were there concerts or many interviews.

But there were a few, including one interesting discussion with journalist Robert O'Brian, who spoke with Cohen by phone in January 1987. "He was in Los Angeles," O'Brian told me. "When I said it was an honor to speak with him, he replied, 'I thank you for the opportunity.' So Old World. A gentleman. 'I thank you.' Throughout the interview, I could hear him taking pulls from his cigarette." —Ed.

Leonard Cohen, Montreal-born poet, novelist, and songwriter, became something of a cult figure when his novel, *Beautiful Losers*, appeared in the midsixties. The content was heady and dynamic, absorbed as it was in sexuality and salvation. In 1968 [*Actually, 1967. —Ed.*], at the tender age of thirty-four, Cohen released his first album, simply titled *Songs of Leonard Cohen*. This album is an indisputable classic among purveyors of the acoustic song form. Cohen's "singing" voice, a deep, solemn monotone, nearly devoid of melody, has become his trademark.

When asked about his future plans, Cohen repeats the Middle Eastern saying: "The devil laughs when we speak of tomorrow."

Robert O'Brian: You have a reputation for being a devout yet sensuous man. There are those who believe that spirituality involves the renunciation of sex.

Leonard Cohen: I don't have that view. I don't think it's appropriate for our Western culture. Perhaps, at a certain point, it was appropriate to Eastern cultures, but even now the Roman Catholic church is experiencing great revision on the celibacy of priests. I don't think it's essential for salvation, for the mercy and grace of God, to shun those activities. In the Jewish tradition, of course, one is encouraged to be fruitful and multiply and both the procreational and recreational aspects of sexual activity are affirmed.

RO: In "The Captain" [from *Various Positions*], you sing, "Complain, complain, that's all you do, ever since we lost. If it's not the crucifixion, then it's the Holocaust."

LC: What I mean to say is that there are many things about Christianity that attract me. The figure of Jesus is extremely attractive. It's difficult not to fall in love with that person. The notion of self-sacrifice, the notion that one has to be resurrected in oneself is a powerful idea that exists in most religions. There has to be an idea of rebirth, of being able to be born again. I think humanity needs that because you feel the sense of pain and moral destruction all the time. When we have this notion that there is no mechanism for resurrection, there is no redemption from sin, then we are forced to embrace evil and we get the kind of activity like genocide.

RO: But isn't resurrection written all over the Old Testament?

LC: The idea of redemption, of course, is in the Jewish tradition. But religion, when it becomes defensive and organized, gives its truth a sense of exclusivity. We find that in many religions: "We've got it and you don't." For many centuries, the Catholics had that papal doctrine—"Outside the church, there is no salvation." If Jesus was and is truly the Messiah and did die for our sins, as Christians often say, we are *all* saved. I think it's very inappropriate for one religious organization to exclude the rest of humanity from this aspect of redemption.

RO: What about the other extreme? Someone like Tolstoy who divided his land up among the peasants. You couldn't really do that here.

LC: Well, he [Tolstoy] couldn't do it, either. It leads you to some very absurd although poignant and touching situations. For instance, in his rather large house—I think it was in the living room with a salon—he set up a little shoemaking shop. His wife and daughter were wearing gowns from Paris, they were completely involved in opera and anything else they could manage at the time, and he was wearing peasant clothing and making sandals. So it leads you to some very conflicting stances. We don't love Tolstoy for his solutions; we love him for his appetite for justice.

RO: The best of art, even painting, has qualities that the eyes don't immediately apprehend. Like Chagall—peeking into heaven.

LC: I think—I can only speak of my own work—any great art has many harmonics, many resonances. The division of color art touches so wide a realm of the inner landscape. In my own work, I don't think I've ever suggested that the world isn't good, that a Messianic age should be brought about, or that we should all live in peace and harmony. What I'm trying to stress is the inner strength that will enable you to meet the inevitable and impossible moral choices that are going to confront you. What is the inner resource that you have to tap to be able to get through your life? In "The Captain" song, he says, "There is no decent place to stand in a massacre," but nevertheless, that does not absolve us from trying to be decent. I think it's important that we are aware that these choices are difficult, that we are humans and we live in a dualistic world, and we still have to take responsibilities for our decisions. We can't resign from them.

RO: So a thousand years from now, everything will be pretty much the same.

LC: From what I gather in reading ancient texts, right up to the present, human beings have always been confronted by the same kinds of problems. I think that this world is not a realm that admits to a solution. That isn't what this world is about. It's a different kind of activity that we have here. We have to deal with good and evil continually. With joy and despair, with all the antinomies, all the opposites and contraries. That's what our life is about. We can't abdicate that. I, myself, am not attracted to the easy solution, the dogmatic solution. I think that when you have large numbers of people attracted to the dogmatic solution, you get a very static, stolid kind of society that is quite unpleasant to live in. That's why I like our society. Nobody can quite dominate it.

RO: Your songs are so complete and mature. Not even Dylan maintains that continuity.

LC: A couple of years ago, Dylan and I met in a café in Paris to compare lyrics. Let me preface what I'm going to say by saying that there's no guarantee of anything, but my songs take a really long time. They come one word at a time. It's real sweat. Dylan and I were exchanging lyrics that day. I admired a lyric from *Slow Train Coming*. I said, "That's really beautiful," and he said, "Yeah and I wrote it in fifteen minutes." He was admiring "Hallelujah" and I told him, "It took me a year to do that!" Some people write lyrics in the back of a taxicab. For me, it's always been one word at a time.

RO: How do you find women friends who can tolerate your roaming ways?

LC: It depends on what the commitment is. If the commitment is fragile, then people cannot surround each other with freedom. If the commitment is profound, then other solutions are set up and that becomes the activity of the marriage or the relationship. In other words, there's nothing fixed. It has to be explored day by day, but the exploration takes place on the foundation of the commitment. It's only when we hold onto this fixed idea of the self that we get into trouble. But when you relinquish the fixed idea of the self, and lean on the commitment, then at least you have a chance to move around and explore.

RO: "Story of Isaac" and "The Night Comes On" hint at the Middle East.

LC: Well, I'm gonna tell you a little story I just heard. There was this scorpion that was trying to get across the stream. He was too small to get across and he came to a camel and said, "Will you carry me across the stream?" The camel said, "Of course I'm not going to carry you across the stream. You're a scorpion and you're gonna sting me." Well, after many hours of persuasion, the camel was finally convinced to take the scorpion across the stream. Midway across the stream, the scorpion stung the camel. They're both going down. They're both being swept away and the camel says, "Why did you sting me?" and the scorpion says, "Because this is the Middle East."

[*The following exchanges from Robert O'Brian's interview with Cohen did not make it into the article published in* RockBill. —*Ed.*]

RO: How do you keep the Sabbath?

LC: I light a candle every Friday.

RO: If there is true justice, where is Hitler today?

LC: Oh, probably drinking tea somewhere with Franklin Roosevelt. We have to embrace a kind of modesty when we discuss these things.

RO: According to *Edie*, the book about Edie Sedgwick, you could tell beforehand that there'd be a fire in her room at the Chelsea Hotel. How?

LC: It was nothing supernatural. I just noticed that her candles were situated too close to the curtains.

RO: The painting featured on your first album jacket is beautiful. What does it mean? Beauty in chains?

LC: These things cannot be explained; they must be embraced.

LEN

JON WILDE | December 1987, interview | February 1988, *Blitz* (UK)

"Few names in music have more cool cachet than that of Leonard Cohen," journalist Jon Wilde wrote in the online magazine *Sabotage Times* in 2012. "Back in early 1988 it was all very different. Cohen hadn't delivered an album in more than four years. *Various Positions*, his 1984 release, was (wrongly) deemed so substandard that his US record company chose not to release it. By 1988, Cohen's music-biz stock was at its very lowest. To the post-punk generation he was, in the words of [rock artist] Paul Weller, 'the bloke who makes music to slit your wrists to.' Somehow, during those post-post years the ocean had rolled over Leonard Norman Cohen, leaving him so out of fashion as to be almost forgotten.

"He was about to release his comeback album, *I'm Your Man*," Wilde continued. "The press weren't exactly queuing up to interview him. I'd have happily queued up for six months in the cold to spend five minutes in his company, not least because I'd recently had the best sex of my life to the accompaniment of his debut album, 1967's *Songs of Leonard Cohen*.

"I spent an invigorating two hours in his company. He had a reputation of being reserved to the point of impossibility, but I've never met a funnier or more graceful man. We met in the restaurant of a Covent Garden hotel. The next table consisted of a gaggle of blue-rinsed old ladies on a Women's Institute outing. My abiding memory is Laughing Len congratulating me on lowering my voice when I used the word 'cunt,' quoting from one of his poems. 'Jon,' he said, gently taking my hand, 'the word "cunt" should always be whispered.' Spoken like a true poet."

Wilde conducted this thoughtful interview in December 1987, two months before it appeared in print and two months before Columbia released *I'm Your Man*. In the conversation, Cohen spent almost no time doing what his record company undoubtedly wanted him to do—promoting the new album—and much time talking about love, pain, sex, beauty, and the other factors that clearly rule his life. —Ed.

For over twenty years, Leonard Cohen's anguished, monotone ballads have echoed inside gloomy bedsits the world over. The list of Cohen classics is long—"Suzanne," "Famous Blue Raincoat," "Bird on the Wire," "Avalanche," "Sisters of Mercy," to name a few—and his work inspires heated devotion in his legions of followers. His latest album, *I'm Your Man*, shows Cohen attempting to come up to date by dallying with dance music.

Bing Crosby's "That's What Life Is All About" quietly saturates the hotel lounge. Len Cohen, the poet, is whispering, as you might expect, in that deep, trembling, hurt way of his.

"It's good, that sandwich. How's yours? OK? Is yours cheese? It looks like chopped egg from here."

I always have a cheese one. There's something about cheese . . .

"Yeah, you're right about that."

Len orders a big roast beef one with salad. Then it starts. I ask him if he thinks his serenity is always on the verge of collapsing into something else—manic laughter, irresponsibility, repugnance even. I say, sorry it's such a big one to start. Then he smiles.

"That's OK. I've been 'round the block a couple of times today. I think I can handle it. Basically, I feel that everything is changing into something else. Serenity is not a condition I find myself in too often. When it comes, I tend to wallow in it for as long as it lasts. It's an excellent thing. We should have more of it. It doesn't matter whether you need it or not. It comes."

Jon Wilde: In the poem "To a Teacher" you write of "a long pain ending without a song to prove it." Have you been attempting to conquer pain by facing it?

Leonard Cohen: I think that activity is natural to us. Then there's the question of one's work and making one's living. These things don't really occur in the metaphysical realm. These are just things that anybody's got to do. It's what we've got to do between meals. That line is taken from a poem that was written to a specific person, a Montreal poet who went over the edge. Up to a certain point, he'd been able to document his condition very accurately. Then he just went too far. Tried to kill his wife. Was put in a loony bin. Died some time after that.

JW: Has it been a case of getting to know your sorrow, trying to reach the end of your sorrow?

LC: I don't really think you have a luxury in these matters. I don't think you can regard whatever condition you are in as an experiment. When you're in it, you are in it and our duty is to transcend sorrow. Nobody wants to stick around in these places. If you've got ways of getting out of them, I think it's your responsibility to do so. As far as joy is concerned, the more the better. At the moment? I have a few laughs.

JW: What is desperation? Queues? Crowds? Decisions?

LC: I guess that the source of all suffering is a sense of separation between you and everything else. That separation is always fictitious but that fiction is always very powerful. Sometimes, you kneel before it. It is a fiction, though, and it has to be dissolved like all other fictions. There are all kinds of distances. There's distance that is needed for perspective but there's also a sinister distance in which you feel totally separate from everything around you. That's the same as suffering.

JW: Is love something of a delusion? Julian Barnes talks about the delusion in imagining that other people could possibly find our condition as thrilling and eye-watering as we do ourselves. That makes sense.

LC: I see everything as a delusion. Love is the reality. [*Laughs.*]

JW: Dorothy Parker once remarked, "Love is like quicksilver in the hand. Leave the fingers open and it stays. Clutch it and it darts away." This also seems to make sense.

LC: Yeah, I think Blake said something similar. "He who binds himself to a joy doth the winged thing destroy. He who kisses the joy as it flies lives forever in Eternity's sunrise." Everybody, in a certain way, approaches things with a dissecting scalpel. It's a good idea to leave that on the shelf for a while if you can.

JW: Maybe it's better to be in love than to be in most things, though. I mean . . . it's better to be in love than to be in Cardiff. Or in trouble with the police.

LC: That's probably true. I think that we have a natural affinity for each other and we are all deeply connected but we get into this illusion that we are separate, alone, abandoned. This also produces suffering.

JW: In "There Is a War" you sing of the war between a man and a woman along with the other kinds of warfare. Getting even. As though the same rules apply . . .

LC: A lot of people ask me about that song but a lot of people forget that the last line of every verse is, "Let's get back to the war." Of course, there are all kinds of conflicts between men and women, rich and poor, all kinds of castes and classes. I talk of getting back to the war meaning that we have to throw ourselves into the predicament. If we are willing to get into it, to confront it, that's one of the ways through it.

JW: Is there anything greater in life than the sight of a naked beautiful woman?

LC: Not too many.

JW: Like in "Came So Far for Beauty," you seem, at times, to be completely under the spell of beauty, almost submissive to it. Could you give up everything for beauty?

LC: Again, I don't think these things are decisions one makes. If you have the kind of nature where you are ready to go the whole way, then you're stuck with that kind of nature and you just go the whole way.

JW: Does it transform the world?

LC: I don't know about the world. Beauty certainly does something for me. [*Laughs.*] I'm a sucker for it. This is bigger than the both of us.

JW: What are the sacred things? Sex most of all? Love. Intimacy. The Eyes. The Intensity. The secret? The first kiss. Anything else?

LC: Well, in all these things, you stand the risk of being rejected. I think that's mostly what constitutes danger for people, the sense that it's not going to work. Outside of famine, war, torture, sickness, and death, that's probably the thing on a daily level that we worry about the most. Is sex the most sacred? I dunno. I forget. [*Laughs.*]

JW: You have to be as clear as possible.

LC: Clarity is one of the things I like to go for. I don't think we're ever free from this mysterious mechanism, though. Mystery can go all the way from not knowing what to do with yourself to standing in awe at the vast activity of the cosmos which no man can penetrate. I don't think we're ever free from any of that. On the other hand, you can't go around continually expressing your awe before these celestial mechanics. These are things that maybe we should keep to ourselves. I think that we're surrounded by, infused with, and operate on a mysterious landscape, every one of us. It's something to keep your mouth shut about if it really is a mystery.

Len Cohen comes from Montreal's moneyed Westmont district. His father died when he was nine but he doesn't talk about that. One day, he was sitting down at a card table on a porch when he decided to quit his job. He started writing a poem instead. He graduated from McGill University in 1955 and turned himself over to writing. He was barely out of his teens when he published his first collections of poems, *Let Us Compare Mythologies* and *The Spice-Box of Earth*. Two novels, *The Favorite Game* (1963) and *Beautiful Losers* (1966), followed. His first LP, *Songs of Leonard Cohen*, arrived in 1967, with dark, brooding masterpieces like "Suzanne," "Sisters of Mercy," "So Long, Marianne," and "Hey, That's No Way to Say Goodbye." They were full of beauty; tender, acute perceptions on the vagaries of falling in and out of love. The voice was a gentle, baying monotone. It never rose. It was plaintive and consuming.

It was to remain so, through twenty years of heavyhearted lamenting. Some dissenters saw Cohen as a lugubrious folk minstrel with nothing but misery and self-pity to offer. His followers adored him. There was something in the man and the voice that inspired heated devotion. The songs poured out. "Bird on the Wire," "Famous Blue Raincoat," "Chelsea Hotel No. 2," "Who by Fire," "Take This Longing," "The Guests," "If It Be Your Will" . . . all of them haunted by that black, somber wash of a voice. Best of all were 1971's *Songs of Love and Hate* (which featured the almighty "Avalanche") and 1979's *Recent Songs*. Strangest and, perhaps, most intense of all was 1977's Phil Spector collaboration, *Death of a Ladies' Man*, of which more later.

Through all this time, Cohen has endured as the supreme stylist of the anguished ballad, of the dark romance, of the melancholic state. Fusing sexuality with spirituality, most of his work (from records to poems) has sidestepped the risk of damp self-indulgence. Cohen, believe me, is rarely, very rarely funereal. There is a massive sense of joy glistening in these songs. Len Cohen's broken voice sounds like its owner has seen and felt it all but it never sounds like its owner wants to give up and get out. This romantic comes to tell how it is. It is not without suffering. It is not without splendor or wild rejoicing. It comes to worship or abandon itself. Sometimes to warn or to weep. But never to wilt, and lick dust.

Barry Manilow's "If I Should Love Again" saturates the hotel lounge.

JW: Do you simply aim to cause ripples?

LC: I don't think anybody really knows what they're doing at any point.

JW: I must say, Len, that's an admirable thing to say.

LC: [*Laughs.*] How did I ever get into this racket? I dunno! What am I exactly doing in it? I don't know. I haven't got a clue. I think it just comes down to nudging the guy next to you and saying, "That's the way, isn't it?" They can either agree or not agree. One is continually trying to affirm something with the man in the next seat. I don't think it's like a buffet table where you choose what you're gonna eat. Somehow things are given and they are given powerfully. You're stuck with them. Your own nature is one of those things. You don't wake up in the morning and choose the sort of guy you're gonna be. Maybe you can in a really superficial way. Like in Rhinehart's *Dice Man*. I loved that book very much, as a wonderful escapist idea. I think you're kind of stuck with who you are and that's what you're dealing with. That's the hand that you've been dealt. To escape from the burden of decision is a delightful notion . . . but nothing more.

JW: The darkness in your songs almost sounds like a sense of menace at times . . .

LC: There's certainly a dark side to it. I also think there's a couple of laughs in there, which people miss.

JW: When you sing, "Giving me head on the unmade bed, while the limos wait in the street" in "Chelsea Hotel No. 2," that always makes me laugh.

LC: That's not a bad line, is it?

JW: Why are there two limos, though?

LC: One for each of us. We're both waiting to leave. We're both killing time or something!

JW: You've always written about emotional pain, never physical pain.

LC: I don't think I've written about that and I don't know too much about it. I've had the occasional toothache, y'know.

JW: You once walked out on the stage to five hundred people and remarked, "The person here in the most pain is me." Could you ever have said something like that and not laughed out loud?

LC: Well, I can't even remember saying it! It is a hilarious line, though. I think Steve Martin could have delivered that line better than me. If I ever said anything like that, I hope I was laughing.

JW: Your new LP is completely off the beam, nothing like you've tried before. An emphasis on dance. It sounds almost too willing to come up to date.

LC: You think it works?

JW: I think it's an interesting failure.

LC: OK. Well . . . it wasn't a curious effort to come up to date but I don't think you can stand apart from what's going on. You say it's erratic, uneven. Mmmm. I'm interested in stretching out a bit. I think my sound has always been a little different to whatever else has been happening, though. Out of time or something.

JW: You're a man out of time, Len?

LC: Well, let's just say I hear a different drum. Like that poem I wrote that went, "When it comes to lamentations, I prefer Aretha Franklin to Leonard Cohen, let us say he hears a different drum." I never thought I had a voice in the sense of a singer's voice. I can hardly carry a tune but I think it's a true voice in the sense that it's not a lie. It presents the singer and the story he's telling.

JW: Going back to *Death of a Ladies' Man*, you said at that time, "Sometimes the heart must roast on the fire like a shish kebab." That seems to have been a messy time for you. The making of the LP now seems dominated by all that surrounded it. There's that story that it was virtually recorded at gunpoint.

LC: Well, Phil [Spector] had a lot of guns all over the place. You'd always be tripping over bullets that had fallen out of guns. Once I challenged one of Phil's bodyguards to draw on me. It got that tense. My state of mind was only slightly less demented than Spector's at the time.

JW: Wasn't this a time of great personal tragedy for you?

LC: I don't know if I'd dignify my condition by the use of the word tragedy. When I was writing the album with Phil, it was all very agreeable. He is a very charming and hospitable man. Though he did lock the doors when you visited him so you couldn't leave without his permission. Outside of that, he was a very sweet guy. As far as the actual record went, it was definitely the most painful to make because I lost control of it. Phil would confiscate the tapes every night under armed guard. There was a lot of love in the air though, curiously enough. Phil is a very affectionate person if you manage to penetrate the extremities of his expression. At one time, at three o'clock in the morning, he came over to my place with a bottle of red wine in one hand and a .45 in the other. He put his arm around my shoulder, shoved the .45 into my neck and said, "Leonard, I love you." I said, "Phil, I sincerely hope you do!" I had the notion of hiring my own private army and fighting it out with them on Sunset Boulevard, but I was a coward in those days.

JW: Didn't you also have some weird scene with [Norman] Mailer over the poem "Dear Mailer"? ("Dear Mailer, don't ever fuck with me, or . . . I will kill you and your entire family.")

LC: I actually recited the poem to Mailer with a smile, at some reading where we met up. He didn't punch me out but he was alarmed. He said, "God, don't publish that. You don't know that some loony isn't going to be excited by it and do what you threatened to do." It really scared him. I then had second thoughts about the poem because suddenly I saw it from his point of view. Earlier, I saw it as a humorous response to the position he was taking at the time, coming on like a bully. I had a real laugh when I originally wrote it. I then tried to stop its publication but it had already gone to press.

JW: Perhaps your most famous line is, "For you've touched her perfect body with your mind" from "Suzanne." Is it special to you?

LC: People have quoted that a lot. It's one of those lines where you either say, "Yeah, that's the way it is," or you puke.

JW: Perhaps your most interesting lines come from a poem in *The Energy of Slaves*, where you write, "My own music is not merely naked, it is open-legged, it is like a cunt, and like a cunt, must needs be house-proud." Now, that's quite a line, Len.

LC: [*Laughs.*] Well, people should have a kind of nervous reaction to that word. It is one of the sacred words and it deserves to be whispered. I'm glad you whispered it when you said it.

JW: Could you just as easily have said that your work was like a prick?

LC: Not myself, no. I guess a woman could have said that. [*Laughs.*] I'm starting to remember the line now. It takes a while for it to return. I guess, at the time I wrote that [around 1969], I felt in a grieved state where I somehow felt that everything I was coming across in writing and everything around me was false. I was hungry for a kind of expression that was a lot more raw than what I was getting. I wanted to read something that was on the frontline, that comes from real, undiluted experience and I wasn't defending anything. Now that word belongs to the woman and to her nakedness and that is still the prerogative of the woman to uncover and that power is still not diminished.

JW: I assume that the words pour out of you.

LC: Not at all. I always feel I'm scraping the bottom of the barrel when I write and it takes a long time to bring anything to completion. I don't get any sense of luxury or excitement. I always hope I'm going to come up with something, anything. The hunger to speak is there but the capacity is seldom there. [*A tall man in a black suit suddenly approaches our table and hands Len a small black travel bag. Len lets out a huge sigh of relief. The man bows and disappears.*]

JW: What's that then, Len?

LC: I left it in the car last night. It's got everything. My tattoo.

JW: You've got your tattoo in your bag?

LC: It's one of those stick-on ones, a big snake, a present for my daughter. Here are my airplane tickets. Checkbooks. A picture of my girlfriend.

JW: Can I have a gander, Len?

LC: Sure. I took it myself.

JW: Very beautiful. What's that bit of paper there?

LC: That's my AIDS test result. Negative. It's good to carry that around. "Hi, I'm Leonard, here's my card!" It's like being let out of prison, getting one of those.

JW: Do you feel like the spokesman for the human condition? That's a big job.

LC: If I was sure I had the job, I'd probably feel pretty good.

JW: Do you always see emptiness coming? Can you always avoid it?

LC: I think loneliness or emptiness is a fearful condition and I've certainly felt it throughout my life. I think you have to learn to live with it. You have to get used to being married to your hand.

JW: A solitary man?

LC: I tend to spend a lot of time alone but it's usually because I've gone to the wrong city or lost my phonebook. We're always moving between those poles.

JW: What makes you shy or vulnerable?

LC: I'm always on the edge of helplessness, though that's not the edge I like. I prefer the other edge, the one that gives you the notion that you're on top of things.

JW: Do you ever wish you could be a virgin again?

LC: I'm completely innocent. Absolutely. I am an innocent man.

JW: Do you ever feel that your own feelings are not like anyone else's?

LC: On the contrary. I feel that my feelings are like everybody else's. I don't think a writer knows his feelings, though. That's why he writes. I would say that he probably knows them less than anyone else. Generally speaking, a writer is more confused, more bewildered, than other people who aren't writers. One of the absolute qualifications for a writer is not knowing his arse from his elbow. I think that's where it starts. With a lack of knowledge. The sense of not knowing what is happening and the need to organize experience on the page or in the song is one of the motivations of a writer.

JW: You seem to completely trust the emotions. The emotional response. Does this imply that you distrust the intellectual response?

LC: I don't want to present myself as some kind of anti-intellectual fascist. There's a lot of that going on today and it's a very fashionable position. I think we should row with both oars. There's the intellect and the emotions.

JW: You seem to have been through some weird times. I recall you saying at some point in the midseventies, "It may turn out that the records still keep coming and the books keep coming but I won't be there." What did that mean?

LC: What did I mean by what? Search me! I've never been very attached to my opinions. I'm not flippant about them but, whenever I hear myself say something, I recognize my own unwillingness to stand behind it.

JW: Is communication terrifying?

LC: It's the easiest thing and the hardest thing.

JW: What do you remember?

LC: My mother crying. My father dying. My childhood was very ordinary. I always seemed to be living exactly the same childhood as all my friends. There were never any special stresses. Nothing extraordinary about it. I can't even say that it's extraordinary now. One's own life is mysterious. The predicaments one finds oneself in at particular moments are the result of a web of inextricable circumstances that I certainly can't penetrate. As you get older, you begin to accept the circumstances.

JW: You have a strong purpose of mind?

LC: [*Laughs.*] To do anything . . . bullfighting, boxing, motorcar racing, singing, or even getting to work every morning. I don't know what I'm doing most of the time. There's a certain humor in realizing that. I can never figure out the kind of tie to put on in the morning. I don't have any strategy or plan to get through the day. It is literally a problem for me to decide which side of the bed to get out on. These are staggering problems. I remember talking to this Trappist monk in a monastery. He's been there twelve years. A pretty severe regime. I expressed my admiration for him and he said "Leonard, I've been here twelve years and every morning, I have to decide whether I'm going to stay or not." I knew exactly what he was talking about.

JW: How would you like to be seen?

LC: I would like the word stylist. I'd like to think of myself that way. You want your work to have certain qualities. To be stylish in the way that any designer of an aircraft or automobile would want their machine to move well.

JW: Would you like to come back as something else . . . a scorpion or a bullfrog or any of those things?

LC: As long as it isn't Leonard Cohen, I'll settle for anything.

JW: What happens next?

LC: I pick up my black bag and get on a plane.

INTERVIEW

KRISTINE MCKENNA | March 1988, interview | May 6, 1988, *L.A. Weekly* (Los Angeles)

In 1988, after three years without a tour or a new album, Cohen moved into high gear, releasing *I'm Your Man* on February 2 and supporting it with one of his most ambitious tours ever. He performed fifty-nine concerts between April and July in seventeen European countries, then did another twenty-five gigs in the United States and Canada in July, October, and November.

And he was talking as much as he was singing. In the first of six 1988 interviews included in this book, he chatted with Kristine McKenna, whose 1985 interview with Cohen appears earlier in this volume. This conversation took place at the artist's Los Angeles home. —Ed.

Kristine McKenna: What is your earliest memory?

Leonard Cohen: Pissing on a doctor who was examining me when I was three. I remember it as a sparkling moment because I wasn't punished for it, yet it produced a sense of alarm in the atmosphere that I found exciting.

KM: Is memory the mechanism that gives memory to the present, or does it obstruct our ability to enjoy it?

LC: Memory is like the soundtrack to a film. You don't want it operating all the time, but there are occasions when it can interact with the action and produce powerful effects. It's important that we have our soundtrack appropriately tuned to our activity.

KM: What's the first piece of music that made an impact on you?

LC: Synagogue music was the first music that addressed a part of my soul that was hungry. I still love that music, but many permutations of it have been lost to history. So many beautiful Hebrew traditions were wiped out in a single afternoon of the Second World War.

KM: Did that episode in history play a role in shaping what's widely perceived as your dark cast of mind?

LC: Yes, I think so. I don't think any Jew who grew up during the war and had European parents could be untouched by that. I don't think I have a dark cast of mind, by the way—realistic is how I'd describe it. Look at what humans do to one another. And all that was learned from the Holocaust is that people can get away with such acts. Yes, war criminals are still being prosecuted, but this is mere nail polish on the claws. Human beings have a deeply homicidal appetite—I see it in myself, and in everyone else. Acknowledging it is a first step towards controlling it, and it's best not to provoke it by having people starve, and giving people an excuse to devour one another. It's best to establish a system where people get a square deal.

KM: What do you do on your record, *I'm Your Man*, that you've never done before?

LC: This record broke down three or four times in the making of it, and the sense of struggle was more pronounced for a number of reasons. For one thing, I came to the end of a period I'd roughly describe as a religious inquiry, and many of the songs for this record began as purely religious songs. For instance, "I Can't Forget" began as a song about the exodus of the Hebrew children from Egypt, which was intended as a metaphor for the freeing of the soul from bondage. When I went in to record the vocal for the track, however, I found I couldn't get the words out of my throat. I couldn't sing the words because I wasn't entitled to speak of the emancipation of the spirit.

KM: Who is entitled to speak about it, if not you and everyone else?

LC: Anybody who has emancipated their spirit is entitled to speak about it, but at that point I was in the process of breaking down. What I mean by breaking down is that you can't get out of bed, you can't move.

KM: How did you pull yourself out of that?

LC: Somebody told me a story that turned things around.

KM: Must've been an amazing story.

LC: I don't think so, but I'll tell you if you like. It concerns realms I value deeply, and a kind of conversation I've always avoided. I was in a condition of acute distress, couldn't move, couldn't answer the telephone, but an old friend got through to me and told me she wanted to tell me about some dreams. I said that's the last thing I want to hear. I know you're into crystal healing and I really don't want to hear about your dreams, especially now. She came over anyhow and told me two dreams, which I listened to reluctantly.

First she said, "I dreamed I was you, and the pain was so intense that I woke up because I couldn't stand it." The second dream was a dream her father had. He'd always been a very active guy and was experiencing profound depression over the dropping of the body that comes with age. One morning he woke up in an unusually good mood, refreshed after a deep sleep. She said, "It's good to see you like this, Papa," and he replied, "I had a dream about your friend Leonard Cohen. I don't have to worry because Leonard is picking up the stones." For some reason, something turned in my heart when she said that to me. I greeted the change of heart reluctantly because I didn't want to indulge this idea that suffering has real mechanical value, but perhaps I was doing something useful in my immobilized state. Maybe I was visiting people in their dreams and making myself useful. I don't know what any of this means, but her telling me this story changed my mood.

KM: Is creativity rooted in a drive to alleviate pain?

LC: The problem we have here on the crust of this star is physical and mental anguish. A teacher I once had told me that the older you get, the lonelier you become and the deeper the love you need. Loneliness creates an appetite for deeper love, and the entire predicament deepens. And as a result of suffering, your capacity to love deeply increases.

KM: Have you experienced pivotal episodes and explosions of insight, or does your understanding of the human condition remain essentially shrouded in a fog that waxes and wanes?

LC: I've had moments of shattering illumination. The things you see in those moments never leave you, but those kinds of illumination are rare and unbidden. In fact, they're so unbidden that they only come when you're not poised to receive them.

KM: If you were asked to compile a list of things you know to be true, would there be anything on it? Or, is what is "true" always relative and in a state of flux?

LC: There is an absolute, but it's nothing you can speak about or objectify. We have an appetite for objectification of the absolute so we'll have someone to hurl our prayers at, but in order to experience the absolute, we must dissolve this subject/object relationship with it. We have to stop seeing the absolute—truth, beauty, God—as outside of ourselves.

KM: Your image is that of a ladies' man. How do you feel about that?

LC: As I get older, I value the reputation.

KM: Do you feel particularly knowledgeable about courtship and romance?

LC: Nobody masters the heart, but we all learn a few social tricks to deodorize ourselves for those initial encounters.

KM: How would you define glamour?

LC: Glamour is a certain coincidence of style and power, and is very much rooted in a particular moment—which is why the glamour of yesterday strikes us as quaint today. Many people who are considered glamorous don't seem that way to me, though there are certain moods where I find everyone glamorous, and I'll buy the cover story of anyone who's out there, whether it's Michael Jackson or Elizabeth Taylor. Mostly I tend to see them as hard-working people.

KM: What three things never fail to bring you pleasure?

LC: Good weather, a woman's body, and the moon.

KM: What's your idea of an important achievement?

LC: There is only one achievement, and that's the acceptance of your lot.

KM: You once commented that every artist—painter, musician, writer—has one piece that he does over and over again. Describe yours.

LC: I did one for a long time, and I'm about to begin a sketch for another one. The beautiful thing about this endeavor is that you don't think you're doing the same song repeatedly but in fact, the thing keeps returning to you in the original blue gown, and that's what gives you the energy to do it. With me, it really is the same song from "So Long, Marianne" to "The Gypsy's Wife" to "Coming Back to You." That song is rooted in some kind of inspired confusion of womanhood, godliness, beauty, and darkness. It was the world I lived in, and it was true. I think of my songs as more or less true because I paid the full price for every one of them.

KM: You've said that a singer is basically a storyteller; what's essential to a good story?

LC: Something in the story must correspond to your own experience. A good storyteller is talking about you and telling your story, and thus, succeeds in illuminating your own dismal problem. A singer is a storyteller comparable to somebody you meet in a bar, or the kind of conversation you have with a new romantic friend. It's not so much that their story has a beginning, middle, and an end—it's that you want to hear the telling. With singers, I know their story, rather than a story they tell. For instance, you hear a story in Sinatra's voice. He may be singing about love, lost or found, but he's telling his own story.

KM: You recently commented that you find your work growing more refined with the years. Do you feel in command of your creative vocabulary now?

LC: I don't have a sense of mastery—I don't think anyone ever does—but you do get a sense of what the landscape is. And even after weeks of hammering away at something that refuses to yield, you don't give up because experience has indicated that it may take a year. You become less willing to abandon things and begin to cultivate old-fashioned virtues like patience and perseverance. But the process never gets any easier—in fact, it gets harder. I've found myself in my underwear on a carpet in a hotel, banging my head on the floor, trying to find a rhyme for the word "orange." I know there's an ordinary, rational world all around me and that this enterprise has no deep significance, yet one is on the floor. No, it doesn't get easier.

KM: How do you explain the fact that after twenty years of operating as an essentially underground artist, you've suddenly become palatable to the mainstream audience?

LC: There's been a change in the marketplace—I don't think there's anything profound about this change, either, because it's simply a manifestation of the cyclical nature of business. For instance, in the sixties people discovered they had minds and they wanted music that addressed their minds. Then, because their minds were addressed with so much nonsense, they quite justifiably decided music should address their bodies and people danced for the next fifteen years. People have been jogging and jostling themselves about for a long time and they're tired now, so they'd like their minds addressed again. Record companies respond to these market expressions, and that's part of whatever modest hospitality my work is presently enjoying.

Beyond that, I recently spoke to a journalist who was talking about how dismal things are, what with friends dying of AIDS, and the sense of claustrophobia and general uselessness of the whole cultural enterprise. He said my new record might do well in America because the themes I've been elaborating for a long time are apparent to people now. These are the final days, this is the darkness, this is the flood. The catastrophe has already happened and the question we now face is: What is the appropriate behavior in a catastrophe?

KM: When was the last time you surprised yourself?

LC: My mood has changed radically and I'm so grateful for the change. I'm surprised to be able to say that I'm happy.

KM: How did you pull that off?

LC: I was allowed to change my mind.

LEONARD COHEN: THE PROFITS OF DOOM

STEVE TURNER | April 1988, *Q* (UK)

"What I mostly remember about this interview was that Leonard Cohen was funnier than I'd remembered him being in 1974," said Steve Turner, whose previous conversation with the singer appears earlier in this book. "Also, after it was over, he took off straight for Heathrow Airport in a chauffeur-driven car and asked me to join him, as the apartment I was then living in was en route."

Turner and Cohen covered a lot of turf in their conversation. "Some of what we discussed I couldn't include in the final version of the article," Turner recalled. "We started talking about prayer (he'd not long before published *Book of Mercy*) and then about Judaism. 'I follow some of the Jewish practices,' he said, 'but I could in no way describe myself as an observant Jew.' Did he pray? 'I think every man prays in his heart.' But did he? 'Oh, prayers spring from my heart. Certainly.'

"I was curious about the fact that religious images had always percolated through his songs, many of them from the Bible," Turner told me. "Cohen said, 'Those images come to me naturally because I was brought up in Montreal where there are a lot of symbols of the different religions. I guess my reading of the Bible has contributed but there has always been that kind of imagery in my world.'

"We briefly talked about 'Hallelujah,' a praise song if ever there was one," Turner recalled. "Cohen said, 'I say it doesn't matter which hallelujah you utter, the profane or the sacred one. It doesn't matter. It's just saying amen to what is.'

"We ended up talking in general about the language of his songs," Turner said. "I wondered whether he ever threw in images just because the words sounded nice, rather than because they embodied an idea.

"'What about the "burning violin" in "Dance Me to the End of Love," for example?' I asked. Said Cohen: 'Although I don't think anyone needs to know what gave me that image, there were these little orchestras the Germans put together in concentration camps. They played while people were being incinerated or gassed. If you want to read the song from that point of view, it becomes something quite different.'

"I asked about the 'heroes in the seaweed' in 'Suzanne.'

"'I was meaning that there's heroism in the most unexpected and lowly places,' Cohen said. So he never used words simply for their effect? 'I think that if a group of words has that kind of resonance it means that it is striking a certain truth. What you like about your favorite writers is that they're able to put things together that weren't together before and to touch you with that new combination of images or ideas.

"'I think that's what we call writing and that's what we call poetry,' Cohen concluded. 'The first guy who said, "My love is like a red, red rose"—you could say, "Well, what do you mean? In what way?" A botanist may really take exception to the image. A lot of images we really love don't stand up to that kind of scalpel work.'"

Interesting—but no more so than the published interview, which follows. —Ed.

His singing voice is only slightly more tuneful than the low rumble of his speaking voice. His melancholy outlook attracts the special attention of the lonely, depressed, and jilted and he once claimed that although he used only three musical chords he in fact knew five.

Yet Leonard Cohen, whose debut album was released in 1967, has sold around ten million records worldwide and continues to exert an influence on contemporary songwriters such as Morrissey, Suzanne Vega, Ian McCulloch, and Nick Cave.

"I guess there's something about my position they relate to," says the singer. "I have this kind of outsider position. I haven't deliberately taken it, but it's where I've somehow found myself. Maybe these people see some kind of fidelity in my career.

"Suzanne Vega has mentioned me in a few interviews, Nick Cave covered 'Avalanche,' and when I last toured Britain, in 1985, Ian McCulloch came to a couple of concerts and talked to me afterwards on the bus. I can see a certain kind of rapport between my work and the work of these people."

Back in 1967, *Songs of Leonard Cohen*, the album that showcased such classic Cohen as "Suzanne," "So Long, Marianne," "Hey, That's No Way to Say Goodbye," and "Sisters of Mercy," was something of an oddity. Just as everyone was going psychedelic, a sepia-tinted Cohen glared gloomily out from a black-bordered record cover looking like Franz Kafka on a bad day. Hadn't anyone offered him a flower or blown him a bubble?

Just as everyone was getting hooked on the *Sgt. Pepper* wonderland of phasing, backward taping, and electronic sound, the Canadian song-writer turned up with nothing more than an acoustic guitar and a bunch of poems about women. Just as everyone was learning to get high, Cohen was plumbing the depths of depression, contemplating the desperation at the other end of love, and coining such memorable lines as "I lean from my windowsill in this hotel I chose / One hand on my suicide, one hand on the rose" ("Stories of the Street" [from *Songs of Leonard Cohen*]).

He rapidly became staple late-night listening in student halls of residence, the perfect soundtrack to go along with a couple of candles and a bottle of wine. Almost a generation older than his main audience, he displayed a rich lived-in voice and religiously tinged love lyrics that suggested a mixture of romance, seduction, mystery, and wisdom.

His life story added to the impression. He enjoyed a Bohemian existence between a home in Montreal, a room at the Chelsea Hotel in New York, and a cottage on the island of Hydra. His name was romantically linked with many of the female singers of the day including Judy Collins, Joni Mitchell, and Janis Joplin.

Whereas many songwriters yearned to be authors, thereby gaining the artistic respect not afforded at the time to rock stars, Cohen was an established literary figure seeking to broaden his audience through the music business.

He'd published five volumes of poetry as well as the novels *The Favorite Game* (1963) and *Beautiful Losers* (1966). At a time when Lennon and McCartney were being compared to Schubert and Dylan to Homer, this counted for a lot. The *New York Times* in 1968 saw him as on the verge of becoming a "major spokesman" for his generation, describing him as "a man-child of our time."

Today, at fifty-three, he's definitely more man than child. He wears a dark pinstriped suit over a khaki shirt and blue tie, has grey flecks in his dark cropped hair, and is spending time in Paris in order to be close to his two teenage children who are at school in the city.

He's a serious man, but not too serious. He can afford to laugh at his image as a suicidal Lothario or at his limited vocal range. "You're stuck with your voice," he admits. "You're stuck with your vision and you're stuck with your skill." What voice is he stuck with? "The one you hear." Could he sing another way? "No. That's what I mean." To prove the point he sings the chorus of "I Wanna Hold Your Hand" and immediately turns the jaunty pop tune into a Cohen dirge.

How does he feel about being defined principally for songs about women delivered with all the excitement of a prisoner awaiting execution? "I wouldn't argue with it although I don't think it's that accurate," he says. "I don't think it's unique to write about women. Most men write songs to women. It's hard to say exactly what you're doing. You just have this appetite to sing. I do think, though, that there are a couple of laughs here and there in my work.

"I think a little depression is valuable for writing, though, and sometimes it comes on me very strong. Freud said that, but then he had cocaine! There are moments when the crisis becomes too intense to be able to dissolve through writing. That's when activities like meditation and manual labor become helpful."

It was in Paris that he produced *I'm Your Man*, his ninth album and the first that's been heard from him since *Various Positions* was released exactly three years ago. "It just seems to take me a long time to bring things to completion," he explains. "I generally do a book between albums."

He now lives a more settled life in the old part of Montreal, writing books at his word processor, composing songs in his music room, hanging out with friends like Canadian poet Irving Layton, and occasionally flying to Los Angeles. He hasn't visited his Greek cottage in four years.

"I live alone on a little street where a lot of the friends I grew up with live," he says. "One is a sculptor, another a photographer, and one friend I even roomed with back in my college days. I don't really like traveling anymore. I've done so much touring that it's a real pleasure to stay in one place for a long time.

"But I will be touring with this album because I consider it a part of making a record. I'll do about fifty concerts in Europe, thirty in the United States and Canada, then about twenty in Australia and Japan."

Since 1969 he's made regular visits to a Buddhist meditation center in New Mexico where besides meditating for between four and fourteen hours a day he puts in work as gardener, cleaner, painter, builder, and carpenter. Last year he spent a total of four months there.

"It keeps the mind fit," he says. "It cools me out and gets me closer to myself. I cut right down on smoking and start eating right. I could go to a health farm, I suppose, but there you wouldn't get a chance to bang nails and carry boulders. Buddhist meditation frees you from God and frees you from religion. You can experience complete at-homeness in this world."

Although the world hasn't heard from Cohen since February 1985, last year's *Famous Blue Raincoat* by Jennifer Warnes, an album of Cohen covers, brought fresh attention to his material. Two of the songs—"First We Take Manhattan" and "Ain't No Cure for Love"—turn up on *I'm Your Man*.

Explains Cohen, "I was writing for my new record and Jennifer, who is an old friend and musical collaborator [she sang on his 1973 recording *Live Songs*, although her credit is misspelt on the sleeve: "Jennifer Warren"], said she wanted to do an album of my songs. She'd been saying this for a long time and I always thought it was just an expression of friendship. I never thought she'd actually do it.

"While she was preparing to record she heard 'First We Take Manhattan' and wanted to do it. I was also writing 'Ain't No Cure for Love' at the time so I gave that to her as well."

For someone stuck with a particular voice and vision, Cohen has done remarkably well. On albums such as *New Skin for the Old Ceremony* (1974) and the Phil Spector collaboration *Death of a Ladies' Man* (1977), he introduced a new musical complexity while retaining the same somber sentiment that was by now his trademark. *I'm Your Man* has enough familiar Cohenisms to please the faithful (tales of yearning and impending doom) and enough experimentation to assure his critics that he's not through yet.

"I think the thing we like about a singer," says Cohen, "is that he's really singing with his own voice. He's not putting you on. That's why people like me can get away with making records. There are certain times when I feel that my voice is absolutely appropriate for the song, like in 'Tower of Song' on the new album, for example.

"That curious thing we call a song is satisfying. I remember during one of my first appearances at the Newport Folk Festival admitting to someone that I was scared because I realized I didn't know how to sing. This friend said to me, 'None of you guys knows how to sing. When I want to hear singers I go to the Metropolitan Opera.'

"A lot of us don't know how to sing according to certain standards but there is a whole tradition of music where you just want to hear the man telling a story as accurately and as authentically as you can. That is why there is a place for singers like me."

It's strange to consider that many of the women who populate his earlier songs, whose names still evoke a fancy-free youth, are now middle-aged mothers. Marianne, who shared life with him on Hydra and was pictured on the back cover of *Songs from a Room*, is a fifty-year-old married woman living in Oslo. Suzanne [Verdal, inspiration for the song], who once lived on the waterfront in Montreal, is in her midforties and Cohen still sees her when she returns.

"I don't know exactly what Suzanne's doing now and I've never asked her what the song meant to her," he says. "People touch off songs. They give you a seed and the song that develops may not eventually be specifically about them although there is something of them in it. There was a girl called Suzanne who did invite me down to her place by the river and did feed me tea and oranges."

Cohen has never married although he's rarely been without a woman beside him. "I think a delight in women is not something you want to lose," he says. For much of the seventies he was living with a French woman [*Actually, Suzanne Elrod, who, according to Cohen biographer Sylvie Simmons, was from Miami, Florida. He didn't meet his French girlfriend, Dominique Isserman, until 1982. —Ed.*] who bore him his two children (but failed to be immortalized in any of his song titles). [*As noted above, the song that bears her first name was inspired by a different Suzanne. —Ed.*] When the relationship broke up around the time of *Death of a Ladies' Man*, he says, it was exactly like getting divorced. He remains very close to his son and daughter, whose musical criticisms he appreciates.

He claims not to know why he's never made it to the altar. Surprisingly, he's not antimarriage as such. "Not at all. I think marriage is the foundation stone of the whole enterprise." Yet he's remained a notorious bachelor? "Something like that. Stuck in my ways!"

I suggest that his songs betray a fascination with the adventure of a falling both in and out of love and that permanence is not really what he's seeking. "Probably not," he says with a smirk. "Something like that. I don't know whether I ever liked the adventure but I got into it now and again. In and then out!"

So he really hasn't changed much in twenty-one years? "I used to be a restless young man but now I'm a restless middle-aged man," he says. "You can't help but change, though I'd be hard pressed to say exactly in what way."

At fifty-three he still carries the image of being a ladies' man, falling in love for the poetry it evokes within him. I tell him that I can best imagine him late at night in a Parisian pavement café, a Turkish cigarette in his fingers, staring into the eyes of a long-haired woman of romantic European extraction, perhaps recounting a literary tale.

"Sometimes it's that way," he admits with a smile, "but to keep the thing going you have to write a dozen or so books and a couple of hundred songs as well." Does he like being a ladies' man? "I'm no ladies' man," he says. "I don't have any particular facility in the matter."

Maybe the mood he creates is more depressing than the actual content of the songs?

"It might be. Some people might find it comforting. Some people might find it depressing. Some people might find it boring. I think these are all legitimate perceptions."

It would be legitimate to call his songs "boring"?

"If you're not into it. I can be bored by Wagner if I'm not into it. They're just songs and they're meant to do what songs are meant to do. To get you through a moment. Something to listen to while you're washing up. Something to set the mood while you're reaching for a lady's hand. Something just to fill the air when the air is too empty."

Does he ever feel, "Here I am, I'm fifty-three and I'm *still* chasing girls and writing songs about them?"

"Yeah. Really. I hope it never stops."

I'M YOUR MAN

ALBERTO MANZANO | May 1988, *Rockdelux* (Spain)

Cohen's 1988 tour included a stop in Spain. That's where he talked with his Spanish translator, Alberto Manzano, who had been invited to the Madrid launch of *I'm Your Man*.

"He was with his French companion, [photographer] Dominique Issermann, who I had the honor of meeting during the dinner sponsored by CBS Spain following the reception," Manzano told me. "The day after, we agreed to meet up to talk about the album in his room at the Palace Hotel, where, as usual, he was staying.

"After more than an hour of conversation," continued Manzano, "we went out for a stroll in the Old Quarter. During our walk, Leonard could not resist the temptation of buying some chocolate, which he was prohibited from having, and then he stopped at an old clothes shop in the Atocha neighborhood, where he bought himself a grey shirt." —Ed.

Alberto Manzano: Perhaps the most immediate surprise when listening to *I'm Your Man* is the use of the synthesizer. I have heard that in recent years you have been composing with a small synthesizer that you take with you everywhere instead of your guitar. Why this change in your manner of working and in your music?

Leonard Cohen: It's true I have been working with these toy synthesizers for these past few years because I have been wanting to make songs with rhythms that I can't play on the guitar. I don't know how to play some of these rhythms although I like them in other people's songs. It plays with 4/4 rhythm. But with my little machine you can press a button and you can get a sound of a tango or a slow rock or fast rock or a waltz or a two step or a polka or a reggae, and with all these advantages it makes the instrument very lovable, and you feel very loving and attached and intimate with your toy synthesizer.

AM: After the initial surprise, I remember being perplexed when listening to the record, a feeling similar to the one I had when I first heard *Death of a Ladies' Man*. But *Death of a Ladies' Man* was recorded almost at gunpoint, and you lost control of the album. I think Phil Spector got to the point of confiscating the tapes and taking them home to do the mixing secretly. I understand that you have made *I'm Your Man* totally at your leisure; you are even the producer of some of the songs. What I wanted to ask you was if the music on this album has come out naturally or whether it is the result of some sort of marketing strategy?

LC: It's really interesting that you mention Phil Spector because I love Phil and I think the songs we wrote were very good. I did lose control of the recording. All the vocals are scratch vocals; I didn't even learn how to sing any of those songs. They were Phil Spector's tunes and I never mastered them. I only did them once or twice and he mixed the record in secret, but there was something about the recording process that touched me. I think there is some quality of Phil Spector that has finally surfaced in my work in a way that I can affirm. I think the song "Ain't No Cure for Love" owes a lot to Phil. So I always loved Phil and I feel that now I have an opportunity to express my gratitude to him.

AM: So there was no strategy?

LC: People have asked me if I used these synthesizers and these rhythms because I wanted to enter the eighties marketplace. Well, of course, I am aware of the marketplace but there was no market strategy with this record. I experimented with many ways of doing the songs. I failed many times in the studio and I ruined four or five of these songs I couldn't bring to completion. The only way these songs could survive at all is in the form that they have. And if I hadn't bumped into [keyboardist] Jeff Fisher in Montreal, who was introduced to me by Lewis Furey, and if I hadn't given my own tapes of "Manhattan" to Jeff Fisher, I doubt if I would ever have been able to record these songs 'cause I didn't seem to be able to do it myself.

I had many ideas for this song but when I heard Jeff Fisher's arrangement it had just that quality of Clint Eastwood and Sergio Leone's spaghetti westerns that I think was needed to give an ironic or humorous dimension to the song. Because it is a song that invites people to allow me to control the world and to gather behind me in this effort. It's a mad declaration and if I had made it with a certain kind of "serious Leonard Cohen music" I do not think that I could have tolerated it. I needed the synthesizer, I needed that ironic quasi disco, quasi Clint Eastwood feel, to be able to deliver the song at all. But I think it maintains its sense of menace because of the very poppy kind of rhythms that it has. Also, in my opinion, it's a very beautiful piece of synthesizer music that Jeff Fisher came up with.

AM: But there is a big change between your previous album, *Various Positions*, and *I'm Your Man*. I think it is quite evident.

LC: It's true with every record, because every record the critics have said that the one before was better. I know you're not saying that, but there has been some perception here of someone who has been failing consistently and embarrassingly since my very first record, that it's been downhill ever since. In a certain way it's true: the first record did have an authentic and intimate quality that maybe none of the other records have had.

But there's no conscious effort to gather my old audience or to solicit a new audience. I have the feeling that all of the people that heard my first album are dead, and I notice that in the audience there always seem to be a lot of people who weren't born when I wrote my first song. I think that I always sensed that I was in this for the long haul, so it isn't a specific audience that one is aiming one's work at, the young or the old. You make your work for the people that are in your own predicament and these people are of any age.

AM: I have the impression that the entire album is a kind of joke. You yourself seem to be having quite a good time. The banana that you are eating on the front cover . . . you are heard laughing after that line: "And I thank you for those items that you sent me," and you write "I was born with the gift of a golden voice." You have always been ironical, but here you are laughing about it all, starting with yourself. Are you laughing with pleasure?

LC: I love this question and I can say yes to every single part of this question. For me, this record has the energy of joy, of self-laughter. It has the joy of being able to rest at the surface. And there are actually a couple of lines like "that golden voice" that have made me laugh as I was writing so I knew it was a good joke and it was true. It's a laugh that comes with the release of truth.

AM: Every depth has its surface . . .

LC: It's true, and in "Ain't No Cure for Love," for example, the whole idea is funny, even though it's very true. There's a surface to the song. You don't have to go beneath the surface. You're not invited to penetrate the song and analyze it but if you should be so foolish as to want to penetrate the song and analyze it you'd find that it is correct even theologically. Jesus appears in the last verse and whispers to me that you can't get away from this; even the angelic host understands. Well, Christ who gave himself a lot, who knew that the only way to love was to sacrifice, he knows that if you love, your love will take a wound, so those parts of the world that are inhabited are still there, but nobody's invited to look at them if they don't want to. So the song just exists as a song that reaches your ear, but if there's something else going on all the better. But it's better to say those things as a joke than to rub somebody's nose in it.

AM: The harmony part of Jennifer Warnes in this song is really beautiful. Maybe it is because she knew it pretty well after she had recorded it in her album *Famous Blue Raincoat*. Both records, hers and yours, have been released almost at the same time.

LC: That's true although there's no overall strategy to produce these two records together, but Jennifer, [bassist] Roscoe Beck, and I are close friends and very much interested in each other's musical life also. I would say that both these records are the collaboration of various elements and, yes, they did grow out of the friendship between these three individuals. Roscoe played hundreds of concerts with me, we all live in Los Angeles, and Roscoe is helping me organize my band right now, and he's also working on a project with Jennifer.

AM: I have heard that you are preparing an album for Jennifer with songs of Edith Piaf, which you will translate. Can you tell me about that project?

LC: Oh yeah, that's somewhere down the road, though I don't know when I'll get around to it. It takes me years to finish what I'm writing. I started to translate a song for Jennifer. In fact, the three of us—Roscoe Beck, Jennifer, and I—were talking about what Jennifer should do next. . . . I suggested that she should do an Edith Piaf album and I'd do the translation for her. She loved the idea, and then we started thinking about the song "C'est l'amour" . . . "C'est l'amour qui fait qu'on s'aime," I couldn't even translate the first line. Is it love that makes us love each other? I don't know what it means, so the problem is how I'm going to get these translations done.

AM: But you translated Lorca's poem, "Take This Waltz," very well.

LC: The Lorca poem took me 150 hours to translate and a nervous breakdown, so it's a very high price you have to pay for doing a translation, as you very well know.

AM: I think it even manages to clarify some images of the original poem.

LC: I can't tell. There's no way that I can judge. I can just remember the feelings that I got when I read Lorca in translations when I was a boy, so I tried to make that kind of song. I'll never know what Lorca sounds like to a Spanish ear. I just imagine. But you translated my poem of Lorca into Spanish. I find that very interesting. It could be something like a great translation by Borges. Then I should translate your Spanish poem into another English poem and we can keep on going.

AM: Yeah. That's a good idea . . .

LC: This is no church and I think we should do something crazier, more surrealist. That's what Lorca brought to us, the surrealism.

AM: "Jazz Police" is really wild and the craziest song in your album . . .

LC: Jeff [Fisher] wrote the mad choir part: "Jazz Police, I hear you calling . . ." and the original idea was to make a rap song and something quite wild and irresponsible, something that had its own inner contradictions that would break down by themselves and every verse I started with a very serious proposition and it just breaks down into a joke or a little absurdity. . . .

I'd shown Jeff some of the lyrics and he wrote the rhythm to go with it. I tried it as a laugh but it didn't work so then I tried it as a kind of chant with Anjani Thomas. Then it seemed to work better and Jeff came in after that and changed some of the chords to go with the harmonies that Anjani and I had created. So it was a real collaboration in that sense too.

I'm sorry that I did something to that track that I regret now. The track was much more adventurous and crazy than it is even now. I wasn't ready to take the whole risk so I became the jazz police in my own song and limited it and took out some stuff that was really wild. The song was wonderful and it could have been more wonderful and more crazy.

AM: So "Jazz Police" was produced by Jeff Fisher. He also produced "Manhattan." Who is he?

LC: It was my friend Lewis Furey who introduced me to Jeff Fisher. In fact, Lewis is living in Paris and he's married to the French actress Carole Laure and they are living right beside me. So Lewis has introduced me in one way or another to three very important people in my life. He introduced me to John Lissauer back in Montreal, and he introduced me to Jeff Fisher, and his wife introduced me to Dominique Issermann, who has had a curious catalytic whirl in my life.

AM: The songs "Ain't No Cure for Love" and "I'm Your Man" seem to be addressed to Dominique. And it returns to your image of romantic hero.

LC: I see it more like some divine balance at work—that if you experience love, you take a wound, that love and sacrifice are involved somehow one with the other, that the condition that most elevates us is the condition that most annihilates us, that somehow the destruction of the ego is involved with love. But once you submit yourself to this experience, you can never again feel at the center of your own drama, that somehow the heroic position has to fail here with love. But I didn't want to discuss it in those terms because I think that everybody understands what "ain't no cure for love" means, especially if you're in it.

So although there was some kind of theological or philosophical position behind the statement, it wasn't written from that point of view. It was written from the point of view of a man who could not shake the feeling that he had lost the woman of his life and that there was no solution to this problem and that even time was not a solution—that there are certain wounds that time does not heal. So I even found myself arguing from the theological point of view that if the wound of Jesus comes to express his love for mankind then it will never heal. And even the angels confirm it. They say even the angels know that there ain't no cure for love.

AM: In the song "I'm Your Man," you say that you would do anything that your lover asked you to. Are you her slave? Do you really think that one should accept all the terms imposed by love, whatever they are?

LC: That was a song in which I said to myself, "What would I do to be accepted by the woman and what does the woman want? What does a woman want from a man?" Many men have addressed this problem: what kind of a man does she want me to be? And it's only the hunger for the woman, the necessity to live in her presence, whether this is love or not.

We can't fool ourselves. We can't think that we can escape each other's presence. Whatever the relationships between men and women are—how good, how bad, clear, unclear, modern, postmodern, whatever, chauvinistic, emancipated—the fact is we are each other's content: the woman is the man's content and the man is the woman's content. We cannot live without each other.

So accepting that as one of the aspects of being in love, or dying of love, a man dying of love writes this song: Whatever you want me to be I'll be. I don't know what it's all about. If you've got to be angry at me, be angry at me. I stand here as the object of your anger, 'cause that's what it takes to live in your presence. If you've got to take me for a ride, if that's what it takes to live in your presence, take me for a ride. The only thing I know is that I cannot exist outside of your love.

AM: In all your records, there have always been songs with some reference to war, although they have been short notes like in "Stories of the Street," "The Old Revolution," or "Joan of Arc," and more extensively in "There Is a War," "The Traitor," or "The Captain." What difference is there between "First We Take Manhattan" and these other songs?

LC: I think "First We Take Manhattan" is crazier and a more honest song. The other songs, I don't want to judge or value or even analyze but I think they're more analytical, intellectual, or cerebral pieces. "First We Take

Manhattan" is a direct response to the boredom, to the anxiety, to the sense of weightlessness, that I feel in my daily life. I don't know whether anybody else feels this way. I suspect some people do feel this way—that the world has disappeared, that the catastrophe has already taken place, that the flood has already come, that we don't have to wait for the nuclear holocaust, that the world has been destroyed somehow.

But you can't take these ideas out with you on the street. You can't operate with them, you can't wear them like a parrot on your shoulder and go up the street and say, "I've got the truth, and this is the way it is." But I got some sense that the thing has been destroyed and is lost and that this world doesn't exist, and this is the shadow of something, this is the fallout, the residue, the dust of some catastrophe, and there's nothing to grasp onto.

AM: Then why to take Manhattan and Berlin?

LC: Most of us are living in cities that only exist as traffic jams. Athens, New York, Paris, Barcelona, they all are cities that nobody has defined yet. All of us are thinking that we live in that small area which surrounds the cathedral, but this is only a tourist attraction now. So in this mythical sense these cities don't exist anymore. There are few people living in their own time. Most are living in a mythological period that is the legacy of literature and political manipulation. We are not living in our own time. People don't look at what is around them, and I am one of them, one of those who don't look around. But from time to time you have the desire to embrace reality. So this is what the song is really about.

AM: And "First We Take Manhattan" is your response to this new situation?

LC: Yeah, it's coming out of the hard sense that the world has been destroyed and that somehow an effort has to be made and a response has to be made and so it's not addressed to any power that exists. I'm not sure they are just the agents of paranoia. They are just a projection of the paranoia that everybody contributes to, that everybody feeds, so in a certain sense I was also attracted by the extremist position, by the fundamentalist Islamist position, fundamental Orthodox Jewish position, fundamental newborn Christian position, PLO, Terrorist Red Army, Direct Action, new fascist groups. All these people seem to be operating in a beautiful world of certainty of action, action being the response to this dispersion of the moral universe, direct action.

It's nothing that I can support, any of these movements, although I'm very attracted to the freedom that this certainty gives you. So I wanted to create a movement of my own that I could inhabit, that was just a response to this landscape that I'm trying to describe. I offer myself as a point of irritation around which some kind of gathering can take place, like a pearl.

AM: Listening to "Everybody Knows," I can imagine skeletons dancing. The music is cheerful, but the text is apocalyptic. You write: "Everybody knows it's coming apart. . . . The Plague is coming. . . . The deal is rotten [like Gurdjieff used to say]. . . . The boat is sinking. . . . The Captain lied." I mean, it's a strange funeral, with that cheerful tone.

LC: Yes, without the music "Everybody Knows" would be pretty hard to take and without, as you say, that kind of skeletonic funeral dance that comes out of the Great Plague, the Black Plague Death . . . and also the language rhymes, like "everybody talking to their pockets, everybody wants a box of chocolate." Those kinds of rhymes have got to also modify the funeral quality of the message. The language is not serious language; it's street language, it's nonsense rhymes.

It also pushes things very, very far just to get a laugh and that makes it amusing. It gives a jingle effect that as I say modifies and mitigates the heaviness of the vision. I think that everybody does know these things. . . . These ideas were started a long time ago in my work, but the romantic world is over just as Lorca said in that poem "Take This Waltz." These romantic images that he's using . . . he knows they're rotten, he knows they're old, he knows they're finished. That's why it's such a modern poem. He's using the conventions of popular song, that kind of puppy love which in a way is the most beautiful love—the innocent love, love that has not been defeated yet—to take these images from that experience and graft them on this world where huge women smile down from these billboards and everybody knows that the thing is rotten.

AM: They remain old ideas. . . . You have been repeating these apocalyptic ideas like a parrot, through your books and songs. It has always been a reiterative subject, with the spirit of the prophet Isaiah always in the background.

LC: There seems to be some appetite to say those words: "Everybody knows it's coming apart." Maybe I'm wrong, maybe it's because I'm middle-aged and maybe nothing's coming apart and I'm quite aware of that too. I say in "Tower of Song" that "there's a mighty judgment coming but I may be wrong / You hear these funny voices in the Tower of Song." I may be just hearing some funny voices but for me it's coming apart. To me those images, those romantic expectations, those religious expectations, the political vocabulary, are obsolete. I've never felt so much difference between the private life and the public life. There doesn't seem to be a public life and there's nobody speaking in a way that seems to address me.

I go to the movies, I watch the political drama with interest. It's educating, but I don't get a sense that anybody's speaking to me. That gap between the private world and the public world is very, very wide now. And we got to criticize that when it gets wide, and in the sixties it was close. I guess that's why we call it the sixties, because the public life and the private life seemed to have some rapport and some response to one another. There doesn't seem to be a public life that addresses me today. I don't know why. Maybe I'm just getting old, maybe not, maybe I'm right, so I wrote a song like "Everybody Knows" to close that gap and the only way to close it is by speaking of it humorously, speaking of it as a joke, and saying the things that we all know.

AM: After *Book of Mercy* and *Various Positions*, two works markedly devotional, I even began to think that you had become a monk. . . . But here you are again in the world with *I'm Your Man*, a much more social and political album . . .

LC: I thought I couldn't make any relationships, with a woman, with a friend, or with the public, even in terms of a career or a profession. I thought I was breaking down, but why was I breaking down? There was something I had to protect, some image of myself that I had to protect, and what was the image? A nice guy, a decent guy, a religious guy, a compassionate guy, a smart guy, a beautiful guy? Whatever the images of myself that I had to protect, to defend, they were making me unhappy, and the unhappier I got the more withdrawn I got.

So I was a singer, and a voice was telling me, "OK, if that's what you are, if you want to be a singer, write some songs that people like and be a singer." I had grandiose ideas that I couldn't realize, I couldn't live. So I was very seriously withdrawing and going to a monastery, although that is not a solution. I even knew that at the time, because life in a monastery is very abrasive.

In fact, it's the same in the Zen tradition. Like pebbles in a bag, the monks polish each other. If you're very close, if you're getting your rough edges knocked out by the other guys that you're living so close to, there's no refuge in a monastery, but we keep this mythology alive that you know somehow it's solitude and pure and holy and you can speak to God in the wilderness. But that isn't what a monastery's about—it's just the opposite. You've got to be ready to speak to God, lying next to somebody in the dormitory, washing next to a guy in the shower, working next to a guy, eating next to a guy, and you're never gonna be alone; there's no solitude.

So anyway, I was somehow defending all these images of myself and the effort became too great and I broke down. I couldn't keep these things going and as I started breaking down little by little, the songs started getting clearer and clearer. I don't want to give the impression that it just sort of came, that expressions came, but the work started. I started bringing up to completion, the language, I started getting the ideas, started getting simpler and yeah, I was able to stand in the frontline of my own life again and thinking of myself as a songwriter, thinking of myself as having work, as having friends, as having a lover. And I put all those ideas into the albums.

COHEN CLIP

On Growing Older

"I like it. On the other hand, a friend of mine [Irving Layton], who's probably the best poet alive, wrote a [piece], 'The Inescapable Lousiness of Growing Old.' [I] don't want to make a case for it. But my own experience is that you just start to get a handle [on] things, you get to see how [things] work. You observe a couple of generations. Dylan says, 'Those phony false alarms' [and you] begin to penetrate those things. It's the most [interesting] thing around, to see yourself and your friends [and your] children getting older. It really is the most fascinating activity."

—from interview with Kris Kirk, *Poetry Commotion* (Canada), June 18, 1988

DINNER WITH LEONARD

ELIZABETH BOLEMAN-HERRING | June 18, 1988 , interview | September 1988,
the *Athenian* (Athens, Greece)

After talking with Albert Manzano and performing in Madrid, Cohen moved on to give concerts in about two dozen other cities throughout Europe, including Athens, Greece, which is where he encountered author Elizabeth Boleman-Herring. Her interview with the singer first appeared there in an English-language monthly called the *Athenian* and in a different version in a Greek-language magazine called *Periodiko*. Both publications are now defunct.

In a 2012 article for HuffingtonPost.com, Boleman-Herring recalled how her conversation with the artist came about:

> Alone among the clamoring journalists in Leonard Cohen's second home-of-the-heart, Greece, I was granted an interview with the poet-troubadour whose fan I had been, at that time, for some twenty years. He was in medias res of his *I'm Your Man* world tour and, upon arriving in the city, granted a press conference at Athens's Ledra-Marriott Hotel.
>
> Wearing a brand-new charcoal-grey suit (Armani, I believe) and a just-off-the-rack white shirt of quite some cost, he was jetlagged and unprepared for the feeding frenzy of Greek arts reporters.
>
> Cohen is very, very big in Greece, and in Europe, in general, where poetry still has a passionate following.
>
> Alone among the hacks there that day, I was a native speaker. Alone among them, I had two degrees in American lit; had all Cohen's books and records; had been a student of poet Coleman Barks, the great translator of Rumi; and was a published poet myself. Alone among them, I could quote Leonard's lyrics back to him . . . and make sense of them. I could parse him.

But that's not what got me my exclusive, three-day-long interview with Leonard Cohen. Instead, it was the fact that, alone among those talking-all-over-one-another scribes, I had a needle and thread in my purse . . . and Leonard's brand-new suit pants were split (they'd never been sewn, in fact) right up the seat. After he spoke to the crowd, I made my way through the throng, needle and black thread proffered.

"You're going to want to talk to me."

"Oh?"

"Mr. Cohen, your pants are split right up the back seam."

"Can you come up to my room? Now?"

"Of course. With my tape recorder? And, I know you: no hanky-panky?"

A weary smile.

And so, it began. The interview that went on for three days and certain innocent intervals of three nights. Plus one megaconcert at Athens's Lycabettus Theater.

I sewed up his pants expertly, handed out to me from a crack in the bathroom door. We talked at length. We sang a duet of "Molly Malone," which I still have on tape. For a few years after, we wrote. He was in love, at the time, with French photographer Dominique Issermann, which I just guessed at (from a cryptic inscription on his latest album). He thought I was psychic: I opined that he must be interviewed primarily by morons.

Now, listening to the tracks on one of his more recent CDs, *Ten New Songs*, I realize that something I asked him about, something we spoke of, in that long-ago interview (and the column I wrote framing it) might have, must have, stuck, somewhere in that fertile, magpie's mind of his.

I asked him about a favorite poet, a favorite poem, of mine, "The God Abandons Antony," by Constantine Cavafys, as translated by my friend and mentor, Edmund "Mike" Keeley. He knew it by heart. I knew it by heart. In Mike's English translation.

Now, in *Ten New Songs'* "Alexandra Leaving," Cohen has "transposed" Cavafys's great lyric about courageous resignation, dignity in defeat, from Marc Antony, on the eve of his and Cleopatra's death in Alexandria, to a contemporary lover facing the end of a *tutoiment*. The Roman emperor about to lose absolutely everything becomes—in a stroke of Cohen-genius—Alexandra's lover; Alexandra having left him now, in spirit if not in the flesh, for another:

> *Suddenly the night has grown colder / The god of love preparing to depart / Alexandra hoisted on his shoulder / They slip between the sentries of the heart.*
>
> *As someone long prepared for this to happen* [That line, and one other, taken directly from Cavafys] / *Go firmly to the window, drink it in*

/ Exquisite music / Alexandra laughing / Your firm commitments tangible
again / And you who had the honor of her evening / And by the honor had
your own restored / Say good-bye to Alexandra leaving / Alexandra leaving
with her lord.

Sweet God, it's a magnificent song! And, if you know your Plutarch, know your Cavafys, know your Cohen, it is even so much the richer. The Greeks will all "get" this song; the Greeks now being crushed by The Crisis, being crushed by the great powers of the European Union. And they will thank, are thanking, Leonard Cohen now for writing this song, an anthem that encapsulates their sorrow, their strength, their wistful acknowledgment of complicity in their own defeat.

There are other songs on this CD that will "live and breathe" as well, long after their author no longer lives and breathes: "In My Secret Life," "A Thousand Kisses Deep," "You Have Loved Enough," and "The Land of Plenty," in my opinion. Leonard told me, twenty years ago, that only one of his compositions would "endure." I believe, strongly, that he was wrong, and this compilation, released as the poet regards a world, and even himself, being "abandoned by the god," contains many lasting gifts to future, unborn audiences.

And so, it is now 2012, and Leonard Cohen is yet again going out on tour. I have not again seen him, in the flesh, since that last day, in 1988, in Athens, but I know he remains very much the same man I met, and hung out with, for three days so very long ago, when we were both so very much younger.

And, wherever you're singing tonight, Mr. Cohen, I pray that there are many, many more members of your audience now who "get" you, and stand up to applaud long and hard at the end of each song; audience members both cerebral and big-hearted. For "You have loved enough / Now let [us] be your lovers."

Here's Boleman-Herring's 1988 interview. —Ed.

Sometimes, I feel I was really born in 1967, the year I entered university. I was sixteen, the Vietnam War was going great guns, and I felt like a purblind, newborn kitten whose eyes were just opening. What the kitten saw was ugly.

Time and *Newsweek* covers featured such people as North Vietnam's General Giap and the US's [General William] Westmoreland and, in uniform, the young and moribund.

We were all learning catchphrases such as M-16 and MIG; the Ho Chi Minh Trail and the DMZ. (In 1967, Oh Best Beloved, there were still DMZs in our world.) But an October cover of *Time*, featuring Dana Stone's photograph of a fallen marine, ran with a banner reading: "Rising Doubt About the War."

That year of this purblind kitten, Leonard Cohen's first album, *Songs of Leonard Cohen,* came out around Christmastime, and the poems written and scored and sung by the rabbi's grandson from Montreal became part of her vocabulary as well.

I was seventeen when I first heard Leonard Cohen sing. The songs, for that first album, weren't as political as those that came later. "Suzanne" and "Sisters of Mercy" and "Hey, That's No Way to Say Goodbye" were love songs tied up with ribbons of spirituality and cynicism, despair and compromise. (Love in our ruins.)

The sixties "litters" believed they'd—we'd—end the war, that love would conquer all. Really.

The older cats of the seventies—remember that AP photo of the little Vietnamese girl, naked, napalmed, fleeing the firestorm?—were giving up. Leonard Cohen went political.

Back from an idyll in his "First Mate's House" on the Greek island of Hydra, and the arms of a Norwegian blonde he'd immortalize in "[So Long] Marianne"—ah, the man *has* loved women—he came out with *Songs from a Room.*

The lyrics were more bitter. One song, "Story of Isaac," was a sermon on the sacrifice of purblind kittens. It was also, as are all of Cohen's songs, more personal than that. (Isaac is nine in the song; Cohen lost his father and composed his first poem at nine.)

You who build the altars now / To sacrifice these children / You must not do it anymore / A scheme is not a vision / And you have not been tempted / By a demon or a god / You who stand above them now/ Your hatchets blunt and bloody / You were not there before / When I lay upon the mountain / And my father's hand was trembling / With the beauty of the Word.

So I and my peers teethed on a distant war and the bittersweet Eucharist of Cohen. Twenty years have passed, as I write here. Cohen is middle-aged and visits Hydra seldom now. But his 1988 world tour, introducing an album titled *I'm Your Man,* has brought him to Athens, and the Lycabettus Theater.

Twenty years have passed, and I'm no longer a longhaired hippie literature and journalism major with a peace sign on the seat of my purple bellbottoms. I may—in that interval—have become a fairly pushy woman-scribbler, because I somehow managed to pull off dinner, dinners, alone with Leonard Cohen.

It was June 18th, and Cohen, wearing a suit tailored in Milan, looked for all the world like a cross between Dustin Hoffman and Al Pacino, impersonating a flat-bellied Mafioso. He enjoyed his *fassolada* and spaghetti that first evening, and he talked for some five hours about everything from the Talmud, his Lithuanian mother, Greece in 1959, Bruce Springsteen, and the unnamed woman (I finally guessed her identity) he intended to marry to journalism. Cohen claims to be not a lyricist, not a poet, not a singer, but a journalist now. The shoe fits: the songs are still reports from the militarized zone(s).

Part of the interview I taped and can share. Much of it, however, was sung or conducted on elevators or behind the piano in the Ledra-Marriott Hotel bar. But "dinner with Leonard" I got on tape: a dream come true.

Elizabeth Boleman-Herring: Why didn't you carry on your family tradition?

Leonard Cohen: I did.

EBH: You became a "priest"?

LC: I became a bad priest.

EBH: There's no such thing as a bad priest.

LC: That's what Graham Greene thought . . .

EBH: What comes first for you, lyrics or melody?

LC: They're usually born together, like twins. Maybe one comes out a little ahead of the other, but they're close. Maybe one line comes and then just a chord change in a certain key: C to F—always a beautiful change; one of the most beautiful there is. Just a chord change will suggest a line or two. I'll work like that until maybe the first verse is done. Then, I have a musical form. Then, there's the bridge.

EBH: At nine, you understood—

LC: —the connection. Instinctively made the connection, between language and deep feeling.

EBH: Who gave you the raw material at home? My own mother read Shakespeare to me in my cradle in 1952.

LC: Nobody was ever that mean to me! They read me fairytales, nursery rhymes . . . lullabies. [*Waiter appears with huge platter.*] Oh boy, am I ever lucky: spaghetti Bolognese!

EBH: Leonard, that's the only thing I can cook . . .

LC: . . . so, can you get a divorce?

EBH: There's no death in your lyrics.

LC: No death . . .

EBH: No death in your lyrics or no death, period?

LC: Well, something between the two.

EBH: How long have you known that?

LC: I've always known that.

EBH: Do you put other people's poetry to music often?

LC: Lorca's poem, I translated. I translated a good poem, "Take This Waltz," and I put it in a nice musical setting, and I know it will live forever.

EBH: Come on: Which of your songs will survive?

LC: "Take This Waltz": about twenty-three years, and then it will be completely forgotten. They'll all be forgotten: everything I ever wrote.

EBH: Does that bother you?

LC: Not in the least. I couldn't care less.

EBH: Why do you keep singing?

LC: Who knows? There were other things I was interested in.

EBH: Such as?

LC: World domination!

EBH: [*Willing to have my leg pulled, again and again, throughout this and following evenings.*] You like Cavafys, you said.

LC: "The God Abandons Antony." [*Declaiming.*] "Like a man long-prepared . . ." That poem is good.

EBH: It's pretty close to your worldview.

LC: You're there by the window. You see them going by. The ghostly clamor. The high-pitched voices. The atmosphere of abandon and ecstasy . . . [*Pauses.*]

EBH: . . . and?

LC: . . . you don't say to yourself: "Am I imagining this? Is it really happening?" It's really happening.

EBH: And do you try to hold onto it?

LC: [*Grins.*] For a second or two, why not? And you see that that fails . . .

EBH: . . . like relationships?

LC: . . . like relationships and *all* things.

EBH: Have you ever written anything mean, cruel?

LC: Never.

EBH: No, not the man who wrote "The Guests." Where did that one come from?

LC: "The Guests" was the nicest song that ever happened to me. The music I'd had for a long time, unusually, but I didn't know what it was for. And then there was this girl who went to Persia to study with the Sufi order of the Whirling Dervishes. She became entitled to teach the dance and went back to America and began to teach. To be "entitled" to teach the dance, you must not only have mastered it, you must have mastered its implications.

So, I'd written my song, and this girl had begun to form Sufi groups and, when she was in the Middle East, she'd formed an association with a Sheikh who was interested in her personally. After she'd been teaching for a couple of years, this man came to America to review the progress of the various Sufi groups and he told her his own were dancing to a song written by a Westerner. And she asked what song. And he said, "The Guests"—it has the spirit of Rumi in it. Rumi, who lived in the thirteenth century, was the founder of the Dervishes. He was probably the greatest ascetic religious poet—in the same league as King David.

EBH: Do you aspire to dance naked, like David, in the streets? [*Forgive me, dear readers, but I was then a jejune thirty-six to his fifty-three.*]

LC: I have no aspirations. My mind doesn't work that way. I think more like . . . a dog, a TV set, and a woman by my side when I think of the really wonderful things.

EBH: You've got that in alphabetical order . . .

LC: Well, in those moments when those things can be appreciated, they all have the same value, the same weight. That's what brings the peace. . . . Those are the really lovely moments.

EBH: Few and far between?

LC: No—going on all the time.

EBH: . . . but there's your deep sadness. It permeates your songs.

LC: "The sad thing" that has the same weight as "the happy thing" and "the indifferent thing," "the beautiful thing," and "the thing." *Boy, is this fasolada good!* I'm eating your dinner, too. [*And, he did just that: everyone does, as I talk so damned much.*]

EBH: How readily do you answer personal questions?

LC: There's a certain type of question that has the appearance of a personal question that you can take a position on and speak about with a certain amount of intimacy. But I don't think anybody can answer really personal questions. I think we're all too shy.

EBH: How many times have you been in love? You've never married, but you have two children . . .

LC: Well, I started in love, but people finally weaned me away from it . . .

EBH: [*Shouting.*] Did you have to say that?

LC: But they were not successful! [*The room fell silent around us: we were really shouting.*]

EBH: But you've never married.

LC: No. [*Singing.*] I never really fell in love, so I never saw the point. If I understood what "they" were trying to tell me, I was in love, but they all said that wasn't good enough: I had to "fall."

EBH: And that's never happened?

LC: It's finally happened . . . if by falling in love they mean that life becomes impossible to live and you hardly know how to get from one moment to another, and that you cannot entertain the idea of living without the approval and love of "the object." If that's what falling in love is, I know what it's like.

EBH: When did this happen?

LC: A few months ago.

EBH: Where is she?

LC: [*Singing.*] "Where, where, where is my gypsy wife tonight?" Not far. Just a heartbeat away.

EBH: Will you stay fallen?

LC: Well, that really awful feeling has gone. I took a lot of antidepressants and spent several months in a monastery [*grins*] and that finally went. I never fell in love till I was a man of fifty-two. And this new album is for her.

EBH: "For D.I.," wherever she is. Have you gone from sad to tortured, then?

LC: Oh, no! Nietzsche called love "the gay science."

EBH: Well, here's the scholar who wrote "O tangle of matter and ghost . . ."

LC: I *was* a superb lyricist.

EBH: Was?

LC: . . . and completely unrecognized. And that's the beautiful thing about it . . .

EBH: "Humbled in love"?

LC: I wrote for years and years and people laughed. They thought it was the funniest stuff in the world. I sang my heart out. Everything I felt, I wrote down.

EBH: Why?

LC: Be free from "why."

EBH: Well, I've got past "should." Maybe "why" will take a few more years.

LC: You've got a great big heart, Elizabeth, but you're very, very cerebral.

EBH: A lobotomy might help, but, then, I couldn't make sense of: "Do you remember the pledges / That we pledged in the passionate night? / They're soiled now and torn at the edges / Like moths on a stale yellow light."

LC: Cerebral is OK. That's Raja Yoga, the path of the mind.

EBH: I would have preferred a different path.

LC: Well, we never get what we prefer.

COHEN CLIP

On Breaking Down

"When I finished *Beautiful Losers* I was living on Hydra. I went to another island and when I wanted to come back I hired a boatman to get me to another, bigger boat that was headed that way. It was about 110 degrees, very hot sun. The fisherman said to me, 'You'd better come in under the tarp.' I said no. He said, 'Sea Wolf, huh?' When I got back to Hydra I couldn't get up the stairs to my house. They got a donkey and took me up. I went to bed and I couldn't eat for ten or fifteen days. They finally called a doctor and I was hallucinating and going crazy and went down to 116 pounds and, you know, a breakdown of some kind. But that seemed right: I'd been working pretty hard and taking speed. I'd had a sunstroke, obviously. And I'd just finished this book."

—from interview with Mark Rowland, *Musician* (US), July 1988

RADIO INTERVIEW

TOM SCHNABEL | July 13, 1988, *Morning Becomes Eclectic*, KCRW-FM (Santa Monica, California)

Tom Schnabel interviewed Cohen live on the radio. "I stayed up late the night before," he later wrote, "preparing for my conversation with the gravelly voiced poet who always seemed to keep his knife sharpened in his lyrics. I hoped he wouldn't turn that knife on me.

"When he walked in, I was struck by how good-looking he was. My anxiety was disarmed somewhat by his gentle handshake and the kindness in his eyes. I had no doubt, after repeated listenings, that his new LP, *I'm Your Man*, was a masterpiece: dramatic, caustic, comic. Thirty minutes was little time to explore twenty years of work, but I jumped at the chance to talk with this gracious and fascinating man." —Ed.

Tom Schnabel: Did it surprise you that this new album has been so successful?

Leonard Cohen: Well, you hope but you never expect.

TS: Do you take it as a compliment that you're more popular in Europe than in America?

LC: I'm grateful to have an audience anywhere. The audience in Europe is wide. I seem to have struck deep into some of the countries. I have small pockets of listeners in America. I like singing in the United States because my language comes out of this language and people can follow the real meaning of the songs. I use the cadences and rhythms of the American language. I know that in Norway, for instance, or in Scandinavia where

English is a second language, there still is some kind of translation process going on.

TS: Do you identify more with a European cultural tradition of songwriters—Jacques Brel, Mikis Theodorakis, Georges Moustaki, [Georges] Brassens?

LC: Of course these singers and songwriters have meant a good deal to me. But so does Chuck Berry.

TS: Did growing up as a Jew in Montreal during World War II affect your songwriting?

LC: I suppose everything is part of the composite. It was a very privileged position that I grew up in, so it was only toward the end of the war that I really understood what was going on during it. The only deprivations we suffered was that we couldn't get American bubble gum, and the comics weren't in color. We were very protected from the reality.

TS: You were brought up in a traditional Jewish home?

LC: Yes, and a family very involved in the community, in establishing hospitals and synagogues, a free loan association. My grandfather founded the first Anglo-Jewish newspaper in North America.

TS: I was wondering how your songs reflect your own view of yourself, as a songwriter and a musician.

LC: It's very hard for me to locate a view of myself. It's one of the things I'm least interested in. I'm reminded of that story I read in *Dalva*, a novel by Jim Harrison, who is speaking of certain tribes where the white man tried to introduce the mirror, and certain native American tribes refused to accept the mirror. The reason was, they said, that your face is for others to look at.

TS: Is songwriting for you a lonely craft?

LC: That hardly begins to describe it. It's a desperate kind of activity. I don't know why it should be that way, but it is. It seems to take an enormous effort to bring work to completion.

TS: Do the words come first, or do you hear the music?

LC: It's generally some uneasy marriage of those two elements. A phrase will come, or a chord change. Then you'll get maybe the first verse with music and words, but then as the words change the musical form has to change. It usually takes a couple of years to bring a song to completion.

TS: Do you get tired of hearing "Suzanne"? Would you listen to it if it came on the radio when you were driving your car?

LC: I think that would be the only occasion that I'd listen to it. Well, I don't listen to any of my work. I don't even have a player. I have a little Walkman. I usually have to buy them every couple of months. I leave them in hotel rooms.

TS: Is it more important for you to be recognized as a poet or as a musician?

LC: Well, depending on how isolated you feel, any kind of recognition is welcome.

TS: In reading your bio, I was wondering what motivated you to leave your Greek island of Hydra and head for Nashville, Tennessee. Was it to gain wider exposure of your poetry, or just to make money?

LC: There was certainly an economic aspect. I'd been living on an island on the Mediterranean for some time. Never completely—I'd always have to come back to Canada to put money together—but I was living for a thousand dollars a year there. I'd come back to make a thousand dollars and my boat or plane fare, then go back for as long as that would last. I wrote a lot of books there and a lot of songs.

At a certain point I just felt like changing. When I moved back to Canada, I published a novel, *Beautiful Losers*, which got a lot of stunning reviews, but I couldn't even pay the rent. In hindsight, it seems like the height of folly—I'll take care of my financial problems by becoming a singer. But I got ambushed in New York by the so-called folksong renaissance that was going on there. It did take care of the financial problem, actually.

TS: How did [record producer] John Hammond hear about you?

LC: John Hammond was an extremely gracious man. Someone arranged an introduction. I was living at the Chelsea [Hotel] and he said, "Would you like to play me some songs?" We went back to my room and I played him seven or eight songs and he said, "You got it."

TS: People have been talking about your voice ever since your early songs. Is it the voice that God gave you or did you work in a certain way to develop your . . . golden voice?

LC: I think in my first record I had a voice that was appropriate to the songs. Then I think I got lost for a long time. I think that now in the last two records I've begun to find the voice that represents me. But it's not a strategy. I think it's cigarettes and whiskey.

TS: I remember reading in an interview that you said that rather than having a dark cast of mind you were merely realistic. Do you think reality is dark?

LC: I think it participates in all the shades. But I think that people have an appetite for seriousness. And seriousness is neither light nor dark. It's just the way it is, and there's a great nourishment when you just name the thing as it is. I think there are certain occasions where cynicism is appropriate. One should be cautious.

TS: Has your view of romance changed over the past twenty years, since you embarked on your songwriting career?

LC: Well, I think that it changes naturally, but I think that the position I took in some of those early songs is not so far from the position I take now.

TS: Which is?

LC: That the kind of surrender that is involved with love means that you have to take a wound also.

TS: Do you think that it's a typical growth process, or that it's more your own?

LC: I can't believe that my predicament is unique.

RADIO INTERVIEW

KRISTINE MCKENNA | October 1988, *Eight Hours to Harry*, KCRW-FM (Santa Monica, California)

Leonard Cohen returned to KCRW a few months after his conversation with Tom Schnabel. This time he spoke with Kristine McKenna, whose two other interviews with Cohen appear earlier in this book. —Ed.

Kristine McKenna: The first group you were in was a country outfit called the Buckskin Boys. How are your roots in country music manifest in the music you're making now?

Leonard Cohen: I've always liked country music and there's always some kind of reference to it in my work. The Buckskin Boys were a trio and we were basically a square-dance group who played in church basements and auditoriums. I played rhythm guitar, and the only singing I did was to join in on the occasional chorus.

KM: What were your feelings about a career in music then? Were you already committed to the idea?

LC: I never had an idea of a career in music or a career in anything else, and I always wondered what people were talking about when they used the word "career." It seemed to come up a lot amongst the people who worked hard at university, but I mostly found myself sitting around coffee shops with other people who felt that the word "career" had ominous overtones. I always knew, however, that I was in this for the long haul, and the kind of models I had when I was training as a young writer in what later became known as the Montreal school of poetry were men who were accustomed to not being popularly received. So when my so-called career evaporated in the world, in the seventies, I was never really aware of the evaporation. I knew I was going to continue doing my work, regardless of the response.

KM: You never waver in your faith in your ability to do the work, or the value of it?

LC: It's not that I don't waver—I live in a condition of wavering and accept that that's part of the job description. The condition of this kind of work is continually dealing with doubt, with the breakdown, and with the possibility that you've deceived yourself and others all of your life. Those are the challenges and you learn to live with them.

KM: What serves to dispel doubt for you?

LC: You learn a few things over the years. One of the things I learned was that if I stick with something long enough it's going to yield. In other words, if I've been working on a song for a month and have been unable to bring it to completion, usually I would abandon it—and I've abandoned very good material over the years. But lately I've begun to wrestle with things because I don't have the resources and the raw material is growing more scarce. So, when there's an indication that a song might exist, I'm ready to wrestle with it for a long time, and I find that it yields. It's an approach that works in every aspect of life.

KM: When you got your first taste of international success, did it cause you to lose your balance?

LC: No, because when I was a young man my friends and I thought we were famous and believed that every time we met for a beer it was a historic event. I grew up before television so it was easier to create one's own mythology, but we truly believed that Montreal was a holy city, all of us were sainted, gifted beings, our love affairs were important, our songs immortal, our poems deathless, and we would lead lives of delicious self-sacrifice to art or God. It was a curious mythology because we lived in a provincial town, yet the messianic idea was strong in the collective psyche there.

KM: Women are usually presented in your songs as agents of change, and as catalysts that launch you on a quest for self-knowledge. Do you see it that way?

LC: I don't have that kind of perspective on my own work. One writes about one's own experience, and certainly the experience with a woman for a man is critical. If you're going to lead your life seriously then you're going to be changed by the people you meet. I know I've been described as a romantic, but I've never felt that way. I think a careful analysis of my songs would indicate that it's not a romantic position, but rather a realistic view that has striven for accuracy in terms of description.

KM: Several critics have made the observation that one of the central themes in your work is defeat. Do you think that's accurate?

LC: Anybody who's been wiped out—and that includes most people—understands this theme. And the wipeout specific to our particular culture is of the self. We exist in a continual process of establishing a personality that works for a while, then finally disintegrates under the abrasive activity of maintaining it. When it falls we're resurrected through the creation of a new self. Don't forget that the central myth of our culture, the crucifixion, also involves a resurrection, and that is what we're continually doing; the personality we create gets crucified because it isn't any good. It doesn't work, it's inappropriate, it's fictitious, so it gets crucified and hung up there for everybody to see. We call that failure and it goes on right to the end, until finally you don't have to do it anymore.

KM: So there's no such thing as a personality that works?

LC: It's not supposed to work and you're not supposed to hang onto it. It works for a while, and when it stops working you're the first one to know because you start making a lot of mistakes based on this fixed image you have about yourself that you have to guard and protect. When the burden of maintenance becomes too excessive you have to let it fall, and when it falls it's painful.

KM: All these issues seem to come to a head in the romantic relationship. Why does it happen there?

LC: They come to a head in any relationship because a relationship has to be based on something authentic if it's going to survive the initial thrill of first encounter. Once the encounters become frequent, the authenticity of the personality is called upon to reveal itself because people can't rest together if they're lying to each other. So eventually, some kind of mutual confession takes place, and usually we're so appalled by what is revealed that we immediately scurry off to find the new thrill of a first encounter. So relationship is the arena where personality has to die.

KM: Do we all know whether or not we're lying? Is it possible to live a lie and remain unaware of it?

LC: You can't remain unaware of it for long because it hurts too much—unless, of course, you have a pathological personality that's nourished by its manipulations and lies.

KM: Would you agree that one of the great catch-22s of love is that you must lose it in order to know its value?

LC: That certainly seems to be one of the scenarios. We continually wrestle with these items. You lose your love, then find that the thing you discarded is the thing you want, so you attach yourself to it in an addictive way, which pretty well precludes your ever getting it back. But we have to live with these defeated scenarios in order to repair ourselves. I think you do learn by experience, and that if the pain is sufficiently acute, you will avoid returning there.

KM: Much of the imagery in your music has biblical associations. Is that intentional?

LC: I've always regarded the Bible as a collection of stories we all know, and it's important to tap into a common reservoir. Our Bible was written during one of the great periods of the language, and most of the great orators of recent memory—Jesse Jackson or Martin Luther King Jr., for instance—are based in that tradition. That's where the richness of our language resides.

KM: As far as using biblical references in your work, you seem to operate on the assumption that there's an audience out there with a shared vocabulary and mythology. Do you think contemporary audiences are familiar with these stories?

LC: I don't think so anymore, no. We seem to be in the process of evaporating our culture pretty thoroughly, but something else will happen. We also seem to be in one of those periods where there's a great gap between public expression and private experience, and where almost anything that manifests itself on the public level has an air of artificiality and irrelevance. You listen to politicians speaking and you can't believe they live in the same country as you because they seem to be speaking from some position that's fictional. It's not their fault, it's just that the public style today has gotten tired and is in a process of collapsing, and it takes a courageous person to speak with the language that already exists in the private sphere. I don't want to offer a wholesale condemnation, but I've found hardly anything that speaks to my private experience.

KM: In talking about your album *I'm Your Man*, you've said that it was shaped by an emotional crisis you were experiencing that caused the record to change direction radically as you were making it. Could you talk about that?

LC: The record did change directions many times, and once quite dramatically. "Everybody Knows" began as a song called "Waiting for the Miracle," which wasn't a bad song. Nonetheless, I found I couldn't sing it because I questioned whether I was really waiting for the miracle. That's the question I ask myself about all my material at a certain point: is it really true? It doesn't matter whether or not it's a successful metaphor; what matters is whether it honestly reflects my predicament.

When I first went into the studio with the songs for the record I found myself choking on the words. I was in a state where I couldn't speak and didn't want to answer the telephone, and as people who've experienced this sort of thing can tell you, it's a condition that can deepen into quite a serious predicament. The personality I'd been maintaining was in the process of collapsing, so I had to revise my work until it became the only possible song I could sing. My own situation was so disagreeable that most forms of failure hardly touched me. That allowed me to take a lot of chances.

KM: So how did you liberate yourself from the dark place you'd wandered into?

LC: I don't know if I'm out of it. I remember there was one moment, I was just lying in bed saying I can't take this anymore, and a little voice said, "You don't have to take it anymore." It is that precious, miraculous moment when you realize you can change your mind, you can abandon your predicament and nothing's going to happen to you.

KM: Are these predicaments—which are also called depressions—the result of carelessness and not paying attention, or is it more a case of when the universe decides it's your turn to cry, you're gonna feel like crying regardless of how you've been living?

LC: Accident is the name we give to a pattern we don't allow to penetrate our conscious mind, but I think what happens is, we use up our disguises. You just wear them until the mask wears thin, and you find you've got this thing strapped across your face that everybody can see through. You can't feel the water on your face because you're wearing this old mask, and the soul longs for refreshment so deeply that it eventually arranges for you to feel so bad that you're forced to rip off your mask.

KM: You once told me that "there's only one achievement in life, and that's the acceptance of your lot." Can you elaborate?

LC: I don't like the tone of that declaration—it seems to be somewhat of an oversimplification. All the old holy books say that it's important to be happy with your lot, but to achieve it is a mysterious and difficult task. I can't penetrate the mystery of suffering, and the kind of suffering we have here, without natural catastrophe, without war, is a very privileged kind of suffering. We're very lucky to be able to suffer this way because we're not being tortured. Nonetheless, it's no joke, the kind of suffering I've observed in myself and in friends, and I've seen people working bravely to correct the profound imbalances that cast them into this mode of suffering. I really don't want to speak casually or superficially about it at this moment.

KM: Is the kind of suffering you're referring to essentially spiritual crisis?

LC: It's religious in that a lot of information in our religious systems has been discarded, and people find themselves in predicaments that have the potential of being addressed from a religious point of view, but they lack the religious vocabulary to address it. This is unfortunate because although the secular approach to personality and the destruction of the self is valuable, it's one-sided. The fact is we do feel a connection with the divine and sense the presence of a deep meaning that the mind cannot penetrate. The notion that we're divine beings is one that's been largely discarded by society, yet there is a crucial kind of nourishment that belief can supply. So yes, in that sense the crisis we're discussing is a religious one.

COHEN CLIP

On Artistic Credibility

"Artistic credibility, for me, is not determined by how I'm perceived or embraced by the marketplace. I can't imagine *anything* that the marketplace would put me through that would be more intense or severe or dangerous than the things I put myself through. It doesn't pose a threat that is any different or any more serious than the continual cunning, diabolical intrigues that one is already involved in."

—from "Leonard Cohen's Impeccable Chop,"
by Mark Dery, *Frets* (US), November 1988

COHEN CLIP

On Pop Music

"When I was thirteen, I knew every jukebox in town; I used to escape from my house and steal quarters. So it's not as though I am some scholar investigating this pop phenomenon. I helped create this pop phenomenon, and I am also a manifestation of it. I don't feel I have to justify myself."

—from "Leonard Cohen," by Mark Dery, *Keyboard* (US), September 1989

PART III

THE NINETIES

Cohen issues The Future *and a book of poems and songs, then climbs Mount Baldy to try out the life of a monk.*

LEONARD COHEN AND THE DEATH OF COOL

DEBORAH SPRAGUE | November 1991, interview | Spring 1992, *Your Flesh* (US)

After 1988's flurry of activity, Cohen again stepped away from the spotlight. A tribute album, *I'm Your Fan*, appeared in 1991 and, that same year, the Canadian Music Hall of Fame inducted the singer. But he embarked on no concert tours from 1989 through 1992, gave few interviews, and released no new music for nearly five years.

The musical drought ended with the November 24, 1992, appearance of the well-received *The Future*, and in the year leading up to its release, Cohen began talking with the press again.

One such conversation was with Deborah Sprague, who compared the prospect of interviewing Cohen to scaling Everest or Kilimanjaro. "It's at once compelling and foreboding, and seemingly impossible to go into without rigorous preparation," she told me. "Imagine my surprise when I was given the chance to sit down with the man in a less-than-welcoming office-building setting, only to be confronted with one of the kindest, most welcoming, and genuinely involved musicians I'd encountered over the course of hundreds of such meetings.

"Cohen was honest about his perceptions of the world and his impressions of himself and utterly without guile in pondering his place in the universe—both as a human being and an artist," Sprague continued. "The abundant charm was clearly not a veneer, the interest in things outside his own skin—including those about this writer's life—quite genuine. When his then-publicist phoned later that day to say, 'Mr. Cohen wanted me to tell you he enjoyed your time together—and that you are a gentle soul,' I felt affirmed to the nth degree, paychecks and awards be damned." —Ed.

He was the first next Bob Dylan, the first to bring to "rock" the idea that impressionable young girls will flock to a dumpy, middle-aged shlub, providing he's got a good enough line in smooth talk, the man who made monotone semimarketable (thereby setting the stage for lessers from Bob Smith to Barry White). Yep. Leonard Cohen's cut quite a swath through rock's rich tapestry for a guy who's released just eight albums over the course of the past quarter century.

As a depressive poet, Cohen is still peerless, as proven by the lyrics he recites from a due-in-'90, but still forthcoming, LP. His work even holds up in the hands of the new-wave losers that burdened *I'm Your Fan*, last year's Cohen entry in the tribute album stakes. OK, folks like John Cale, Nick Cave, and, oddly enough, Kiwi loungesters Dead Famous People seemed to "get it," but for the most part, the musos in question had little clue as to the formality, dignity, and self-surrender that makes a Cohen tick: then again, asking 'em to do so is like asking a prep schooler to "interpret" Bukowski.

From his days as a Montreal beat poet (his first book, *Let Us Compare Mythologies,* was issued in 1956) with a country music fetish until the 1967 release of *Songs of Leonard Cohen,* he wandered across Europe, returning from his travels with (for better or worse) the concept of the beautiful loser—which became the title of his bestselling crank epic. The past two-and-a-half decades have seen him alternate periods of total isolation with periods of, well, moderate isolation. Highlighted by a collaboration with Phil Spector—who kidnapped the tapes of 1977's *Death of a Ladies' Man* at gunpoint—and a religious awakening that, like few others in popular music, produced works (like *Various Positions*) that might actually win a few converts, it's been a career that Cohen characterizes as "modest." Don't believe it for a minute.

Deborah Sprague: How did the tribute project come about?

Leonard Cohen: I had nothing at all to do with it. I didn't know when it began and I didn't know when it ended. It was the brainchild of Christian Fevret, who is the editor of a rock magazine in Paris whose name no one can pronounce. It's a magazine that holds up the flaming torch of rock and roll.

DS: Do you find it easy to let go of your songs?

LC: I'm one of those parents that's happy to let go; I'd be happy if it was made into Muzak. I don't have a sense of proprietorship, which probably stems from coming up as a folksinger where it was understood that songs develop a patina through interpretation. I feel that's the mark of excellence. I was struck with the respect the singers paid to the arrangement or to my own delivery, which was very gratifying.

DS: Do you prefer that people abide by a strict interpretation of your work?

LC: I've never gotten over the pleasure of someone covering one of my songs. My career has really been quite modest in the world and not many people have done so. Somehow my critical faculties go into a state of suspended animation when I hear someone's covered one of my tunes. I'm not there to judge it, just to say thank you.

DS: You're known as a pretty fair interpreter yourself, given your handling of [poet Federico Garcia] Lorca. Is it difficult for you?

LC: Unfortunately, all my efforts are painstaking. I'd prefer it if I were gifted and spontaneous and swift, but my work requires a great deal of painstaking. That's no guarantee of its quality, but it does. With the Lorca poem, the translation took 150 hours, just to get it into English that resembled—I would never presume to say duplicated—the greatness of Lorca's poem. It was a long, drawn-out affair, and the only reason I would even attempt it is my love for Lorca. I loved him as a kid; I named my daughter Lorca, so you can see this is not a casual figure in my life. She wears the same name beautifully; she is a very strange and eccentric soul. . . .

DS: That same amount of effort must go into your own songs; let's face it, you're not exactly prolific.

LC: I wish I knew. If I knew where good songs came from, I'd go there more often. Dylan gave a concert in Paris I happened to be at, and we met the next day and got into a lot of shoptalk about writing. He was doing a song of mine called "Hallelujah" and he liked the song and asked how long it took. I was embarrassed to tell him. [I thought], "I'm lying about this, but I'll say it took two years" 'cause it was more than that. The conversation went on and I praised a song of his called "I and I" and I asked him how long that took and he said, "fifteen minutes" and I believe him. I wish I was in that tribe. Hank Williams could write songs in half an hour, or so the story goes.

DS: Did you benefit from growing up before making your public debut?

LC: I don't know if we ever grow up, but I was trained in a school of writing that no one will remember called the Montreal school of poetry. We were a bunch of poverty-stricken writers who cared a lot about poetry and nothing else since in those days there were no grants or prizes . . . there weren't even many women. We put out little magazines or books and read to one another and it was probably the most savage and most discerning panel of critics you could ever face. I think that's where most of my notions developed.

DS: Would it have been different if you had been forced to go to the masses from day one?

LC: We were so naive and so out of it and so far from the mainstream that we thought we were writing for the masses. There was never a sense of elitism in the groups I was in. On the contrary, a very radical sensibility informed the whole thing. In effect, we were in revolt against a literary establishment that spoke with an English accent and declared you couldn't really write great poetry unless you came out of Oxford. They didn't think people who spoke like us could write English verse. It was designed to be read by everybody. It wasn't; it was read by about four hundred people.

DS: Did your concerns change when it became four hundred thousand?

LC: Well, my bank account changed, but I don't think my concerns did. I had songs like "Suzanne" ripped off, stolen from me. I didn't make as much money as I should have, but it was still a degree I never dreamed of.

DS: The early songs were so unrelievedly sad.

LC: There is a great deal of sadness.

DS: Yet over the years you've developed a wonderful sense of humor, mostly about yourself.

LC: It's refreshing to hear you say that. I was reading the reviews of this in England, and there they were calling me Laughing Len and saying they oughta sell razor blades with this record. . . . you get into the computer with this image and whenever they punch up your name, there it is.

DS: Was there a change for the better that affected your writing, making you less desperate?

LC: When things get truly desperate, you start laughing. . . . You experience what it really means to crack up. . . . I remember what [seventeenth-century playwright and poet] Ben Jonson said: "I've studied all the philosophies and all the theologies but cheerfulness keeps breaking through." [*Laughs.*] I've read that as you approach middle age, the brain cells associated with anxiety start to die—so it doesn't matter whether you go to church every Sunday or do your yoga or whatever, you'll start to feel better about yourself.

DS: There's no nastiness; do you see chinks in your armor?

LC: It's not so much armor, as it is threads, Band-Aids, and chicken wire. Some kind of triumphant cheerfulness starts to arise. I dunno where it comes from, maybe up above, but you become able to lean on it and to laugh. Not at others, there's no point.

DS: Do you feel responsible for perpetuating, or even inventing, the myth of the beautiful loser?

LC: I do think there's a difference, but it's hard to judge. There's a blessing in traditional Judaism that I always found quite profound: it's called the blessing on hearing bad news. When you hear bad news, when you see what appears to be a loser, and before you make the determination about whether this is a guy who deserves to lose, it's good to remember that blessing. When you deal with suffering, it's appropriate to be reluctant about making a judgment. In the realms of pain, it's best to keep quiet and lend a helping hand. And if you can't lend a helping hand, at least offer a silent blessing. If you can't do that, it's best to do nothing at all.

DS: You don't get hamstrung by nostalgia, do you?

LC: That's a very interesting observation and I appreciate it very much; I'm not nostalgic. There are people I know who have a very finely developed sense of nostalgia and they can draw me into moods where I look at the past in a way that's uncharacteristic. I don't look at the sixties as the good old days; people ask me, "Isn't it terrible what happened to the ideals of the sixties?" and I have to say I don't know. Maybe it is, but during the sixties I never thought it was so great either, with the amount of charlatanism and hustling that went on—there's really nothing to regret about its passing.

When you reach a certain level of disintegration, the degree to which you can put yourself on is greatly diminished. Since you're writing to recover your self-respect in some way, to discover some sort of significance to your own life, then you find you can lie less and less. The style then takes on a certain bluntness, a certain honesty. It's no virtue. It's just that it hurts more to put yourself on.

DS: Does that sense become more acute?

LC: I think so. These paradoxes are popular, but that doesn't mean they're not true: you get more vulnerable and stronger at the same time.

DS: Do you have to detach yourself or not?

LC: To really home in, you have to detach yourself from your own cowardice, your own laziness, your own doubt. Then you take the plunge into the material and get ready to drown . . . or swim.

The thing that we're hungry for cannot be described by a political position right now. There is some kind of moral resurrection that people from all positions on the spectrum can participate in. I don't want my songs to be slogans for the right, left, or middle. I want it to be a cry defined in very concrete images.

DS: That runs contrary to today's sound-bite mentality.

LC: I don't have the chops to comment sociologically. Maybe I'm just getting cranky and old, but there's very little in the public realm that's not gibberish to me. There's very little real commitment—the artists are doing exactly what the politicians are doing: staying right at the surface, not really committing to anything, just taking easy party positions. They may be on the right side, but they're offering slogans, not commitments.

DS: And they elevate "Cool" above everything else.

LC: Cool. The notion of cool has been destroying the heart for years. I remember when I came to New York for the first time in the early fifties, when Cool was starting to be developed as an important position. I remember sitting in a coffee shop in the Village, and I'd heard about a new spirit, a sweet spirit, and I remember sitting there, taking my paper placemat, and writing in big letters "KILL COOL!"

Something has crossed the threshold that we never thought would. It's inside, in us. The wind isn't howling out there anymore, it's howling within us, and everyone understands the beast has been unleashed. Extreme caution is advised.

COHEN CLIP

On Personal Lyrics

"I don't think my writing has got personal enough yet. . . . When it's really personal everybody understands it. There's a middle ground, which is just unzipping and self-indulgence, but when you really tell the truth people immediately perceive that. Like when I wrote the lyrics for 'I Can't Forget,' it went through so many transformations to get it really personal. It started off as a kind of hymn and I ended up stuck sitting at this very kitchen table thinking, 'Where am I really? What can I really tell anyone about anything?' So I thought, 'I've got to start from scratch. How am I living this day? What am I doing now?' So I wrote, 'I stumbled out of bed / Got ready for the struggle / I smoked a cigarette / And I tightened up my gut / I said, This can't be me, must be my double / I can't forget [but] I don't remember what.'"

—from "Porridge? Lozenge? Syringe?" by Adrian Deevoy, *Q* (UK) 1991

COHEN CLIP

On His Family and Childhood

"My mother's presence is very strong in my heart, particularly since she died. One thing that I owe to my family is that it exposed me to a form of culture and thought but always in moderation. There were none of the fanatical elements that I see in many other similar families. I am grateful to my family. . . . [My father] died at the age of fifty-two. . . . My father and I would be very close today. . . . It would have been difficult for him to see me walking around Montreal with a guitar. That wasn't what he had in mind for his son. But he was a gentleman. . . . I don't think about my childhood much. I don't think that it's a legitimate explanation of one's life. I think that in order to survive one must be reborn, one must overcome one's childhood, the injustices, and recognize the privileges. You can't use your past as an alibi."   —from "Come On Gorilla," by Christian Fevret, *Les Inrockuptibles* (France), c. 1992

COHEN CLIP

On Songs He Doesn't Understand

"I can't understand half the songs in the center, which is supposed to be the pop world. Either they've moved into a new stage of cryptology that I've been unable to follow and penetrate or it's just lazy or it's gotten slack or people just aren't workin' hard enough on the craft. I don't understand what they're saying most of the time. A lot of the stuff is, I think, just . . . lazy; but because of the social urgencies that produce rap—and because of the demands of rhyme and rhythm—you get coherent statements and you get the impression of a mind . . . that has formed and gathered around a topic and is ready to manifest it. Another thing is that we've had twenty years or so of dance music, which I think we deserved because the self-indulgences of the sixties got pretty intense. I mean, there were a few geniuses like Dylan or Phil Ochs who are writing great, complex songs with lots of words in them. But lots of people scrambled and scratched up the bandwagon and, you know, we got a kind of language in our popular music that was intolerable after a while. You really couldn't figure out what they were saying."

—from "Leonard Cohen's *The Future*," by Bob Mackowitz, Sony Music radio special (Canada), 1992

THE SMOKY LIFE

JENNIE PUNTER | January 1992, *Music Express* (North America)

Jennie Punter moved to Toronto in the spring of 1991 to become associate editor at *Music Express*, a large-format monthly published in Canada and distributed in the United States through now-defunct record retail chains. "That job marked a turning point for me on all fronts," she told me. "And Leonard Cohen played a memorable role in what followed."

At the time, said Punter, her music collection was rapidly expanding, but Leonard Cohen was barely in the mix. So when *Music Express* was offered a chance to interview Cohen in conjunction with the release of the tribute album *I'm Your Fan*, she was not the resident expert.

Still, many of the artists on *I'm Your Fan* were bands or songwriters that Punter had been writing about and listening to "so I had that sonic background," she said. "I finished reading *Beautiful Losers*. I borrowed some records and Cohen's subtle artistry started to sink in.

"When I got on the phone with Cohen, there was no time limit," Punter recalled. "We talked for almost an hour. He talked a lot about his creative process, past and present. At one point, Cohen told me he had just started working with a Mac computer drawing tool and asked whether I wanted to see what he was currently working on. He stayed on the phone as I went to the office fax machine to retrieve a copy of a recent drawing: the back of a naked woman, lounging on her side, etched in black-and-white. My colleagues teased me about this for weeks: 'What did you really talk about?' 'Are you his new girlfriend?' Et cetera, et cetera.

"Death of a Ladies' Man? I don't think so."

A few months later, said Punter, Cohen arrived in Toronto for the launch of *The Future*, the collection of new work hinted at when they had discussed the tribute disc. "His girlfriend Rebecca De Mornay was by his side in the Cabana Room, then a hip grungy spot for local indie bands," Punter said. "The Sony Music label guy introduced us, and Cohen politely recalled our phone conversation. I'm not the only old Toronto music hack who remembers that night fondly, seeing this suave legend with a movie star on his arm mixing it up at the Cabana, the sight of so many raucous shows for now-legendary local bands. I only now understand that Sony's tactic of choosing this location was a deliberate move to build a new audience for Cohen's work.

"I met Cohen again in 1995 at a party at MuchMusic headquarters, following a listening event for Michael Jackson's *HIStory: Past, Present and Future Book I*," Punter added. "Cohen asked me what I thought about the Michael Jackson album I'd just heard. I stumbled. I was there just for the free wine and conversation and I loved Jackson's music in the 1970s and *Bad* and so on. Cohen stopped me in my tracks. His exact words: 'Well, did you tap your toe?' Uh, yes, I guess I did." —Ed.

He was born like this, he had no choice; he was born with the gift of the charcoal voice. Leonard Cohen answers the phone, with a low smoky hello. It's morning in Los Angeles, and I imagine a cup of warm coffee sits close to his synthesizer, from which he coaxes a few chords during our conversation.

Poet, prophet, loner, singer, father, scribbler: what can one begin to say about a man whose life and works have been examined by everyone from the fickle music media to ivory tower scholars? Here and now at least, Leonard Cohen is laboring over words and music and recordings that will be released sometime next year. And when the songs are finally out there? "I'll feel . . ." Cohen pauses, "I can't give you any analogy . . . excremental!"

Montreal born and bred, Cohen is often referred to as a poet and novelist who "turned" to music in the sixties. But the music was always there, and the poetry is still written, or regrouped and published. Before his troubadour days, Cohen tooted the clarinet in his high school band. Later he played square dances with the Buckskin Boys, a country-and-western trio (he still listens to country music in his car). His first collection of poetry, *Let Us Compare Mythologies*, was published in 1955 [*Actually, 1956. —Ed.*] (there are about a dozen books of his poetry out). He also wrote two novels in the sixties, including *Beautiful Losers* (1966). Cohen's recording career began in 1968, with *Songs of Leonard Cohen* [*Released December 26, 1967. —Ed.*], and roughly a dozen albums have followed (mostly on CBS/Sony).

"When it comes down to it, they are different things," Cohen says when asked to compare the arts of songwriting and poetry writing. "It's the same in that you have to sweat over both of them—at least I do. It doesn't mean they're good. A poem requires solitude, you stop as you're reading and go back over it, the language is very dense and you can move any way you want. A song has a very fast, forward motion."

Cohen moves between L.A. and Montreal, and occasionally finds time to visit an old haunt, a Grecian isle where he owns "a house with a lot of rooms" he bought for fifteen hundred dollars in 1960. "People welcomed me, let me live on credit for a long time. The materials are very beautiful, everywhere you look. Nothing insults you, and I think we get used to being insulted and after a while, you tend to go numb." Cohen has also taken to the road many times, staging brilliant, often lengthy, and much-celebrated concert tours in North America, Australia, and Europe.

"It's something I really enjoy doing, I mean, if it's going well," he says with characteristic modesty. "If your band is good, and your technical crew is good, then it is a really great way to live . . . on the road . . . kind of like a motorcycle gang going from town to town. It is my life, and somebody said you learn about life in three major arenas—love, money, and war—and that takes in all three."

Musicians have been interpreting Cohen's songs almost as long as he's been writing them—artists from Judy Collins to Aaron Neville to Suzanne Vega. And the songwriter also finds himself behind the mic, night after night, crooning about "Suzanne" and "So Long, Marianne." "If a song has lasted twenty or thirty years, there's something there. The real challenge is to find the gate to the song and to open it and to explore it again," he explains, adding, "but if you've got a good band that really helps."

Well, early last year, several bands and a number of Cohen-esque singers were invited by Christian Fevret (editor of France's top rock magazine) to cover their favorite Leonard Cohen song. Appropriately titled *I'm Your Fan*, the resulting tribute album includes acts like R.E.M. ("First We Take Manhattan"), House of Love ("Who by Fire"), Dead Famous People ("True Love"), and Nick Cave & the Bad Seeds (a very quirky "Tower of Song"). Of the seventeen artists on the album, most stay pretty faithful to the Cohen originals in terms of mood and even delivery—further proof of the man's influence on modern rock and roll.

Cohen found the tribute fascinating on many levels. "I like to hear the things that are different and the things that defer to my own arrangement or interpretation," he says. "Mostly I got an emotional hit from the thing. That's all you really look for when you look at your own work. You look at it from the point of durability. Will the language still have meaning—the lyrical material—the music . . . will it stand up? Has it been designed to stand up?"

Cohen tells me that an English publisher wants to reissue *Beautiful Losers*, which is still in print in several countries. "You write a lot of bad songs . . . you never start out to write a bad song. You can pretty well tell if a thing will last. I think some of the weaker material quite legitimately dies away," he says. "You never expect great sales from this . . . I never did have them. But it's been able to give me a life that's very free. It's not luxurious, but it's free."

But free doesn't necessarily mean easy. "The whole operation is about as graceful and smooth as a bear trying to get honey out of a highly populated bee hive," Cohen says with a low chuckle. "I mean, you're sort of scraping and swiping. . . . It's really in my case very difficult, lots of mistakes, starting over. Each of those four things—the writing, then the recording of the songs, then the rehearsal and then touring—all are done with difficulty. And as I say, that doesn't simply guarantee excellence. It's just the way I get things together."

While it has often been stuck into the folksinger-songwriter vein, Cohen's music—including the versions on *I'm Your Fan*—does resonate with echoes of some of his favorite sounds. "Everything from George Jones and country music to the great cantorial songs of my own Jewish heritage," he muses. "Gregorian chants, R&B."

And today's task, the new album, will it sound . . . like Leonard Cohen? "Well, you'll hear this cigarette smoke voice droning away," he says, "so people will be able to tell whose record it is. The songs I've recorded I'm happy with. The nature of work is repetition . . . that's why they call it work. But as long as they give me the time, I'm happy with this life."

LEONARD COHEN: INSIDE THE TOWER OF SONG

PAUL ZOLLO | February 1992, interview | April 1993, *SongTalk* (US)

Unlike nearly all of the other conversations in this book, the one that follows focuses almost entirely on songwriting. As such, it provides a valuable window into Cohen's craft.

"As a songwriter, Leonard Cohen has always been a God among men to me," said interviewer Paul Zollo, who is a senior editor of *American Songwriter* and a songwriter himself. "Just to recognize that he does dwell, after all, in our normal realm—specifically in the Mid-Wilshire district of Los Angeles, was remarkable. Here was his fabled tower of song. And here was the great man himself—dapper, dressed in a black suit, attended to then by a small group of young lovely women who worked there.

"Cohen's home was stark and clean; no clutter at all, the seeming effect of a focused, dedicated mind," Zollo told me. "He showed me it was all about enabling himself to write good songs, a process about which he's about as wise as any human, but also funnier.

"I looked in his closet, and it was filled with a rack of black suits, all identical. His countenance was very peaceful, reflective of his time up at the summit of Mount Baldy, where he'd become a monk among monks, although one who admittedly would be playing with metaphors and rhymes while his fellow monks meditated on worlds beyond song.

"To Leonard the song was and remains everything, and his allegiance to the fullness of the form was proudly displayed as we sat on the floor of his upstairs office and pored over notebooks of songs and their revisions. As he told me in this interview, he cut out verses other songwriters would rejoice at creating—and always with specific, detailed reason. He is as completely open to whatever might simply arrive as he is careful to control the content of what gets in, and what doesn't. But all of it is done with great humility, respect for the potential of the song itself, and love of music.

261

"His status elevated quite a lot since I did this interview," Zollo concluded. "It was prior to his world tour and recent global triumphs. It was even before the status of his miracle song 'Hallelujah' was elevated to standard level, a rare occurrence in today's musical world, given that it was never a hit for Leonard. It's a song that is famous simply because it's truly great—and as such, has been recorded by a wide range of singers who have introduced it into our culture in a lasting way. It's a great sign for songwriters that a song still matters so much. It's because of how much it matters to him." —Ed.

We are sitting Indian-style on the second floor of Leonard Cohen's home in Los Angeles. On his bookshelf are many books that he's written, including two novels and several volumes of poetry. An unearthly rain is exploding outside as he scans countless notebooks of song, endless revisions that span decades and fill thousands of pages within hundreds of notebooks. For every verse that he keeps, there are untold dozens that he discards. When I mention that a lesser writer would have been happy with simply two of the six verses that he wrote for the stunning "Democracy" from his album *The Future*, he answers, "I've got about sixty."

His tower of song isn't really that tall, only two floors that I can see anyway, but to him it's both a fortress of solitude and a factory, a place where, he says, "I summon every version of myself that I can to join this workforce, this team, this legion." It's here that he gives songs the kind of respect bottles of fine wine receive, the knowledge that years—decades even—are needed for them to ripen to full maturity. Quoting from the Talmud he says, "There's good wine in every generation," referring to the new songwriters who crop up every few years. But his own work has extended across generations and decades; he packed as much brilliance into 1992's *The Future* as he instilled into his first album in 1967. "I always knew I was in this for the long haul," he says, "but somewhere along the line the work just got harder."

Like Dylan, Simon, and few others, Leonard Cohen has expanded the vocabulary of the popular song into the domain of poetry. And like both Simon and Dylan, Cohen will work and rework his songs until he achieves a kind of impossible perfection. He didn't need Dylan's influence, however, to inspire his poetic approach to songwriting. He'd already written much poetry and two highly acclaimed novels by the time Dylan emerged, leading the poet Allen Ginsberg to comment, "Dylan blew everybody's mind, except Leonard's."

In the beginning, Cohen was both a member of a Canadian country group called the Buckskins and a member of what is now known as the Montreal School of Poetry. When he wasn't playing folksongs on his guitar, he was lyrically chanting his poetry. It was only a matter of time until the words and the music came together and Cohen became a songwriter.

Songwriting was for him then, as it remains today, a labor of love. Few thoughts of making it a career entered his thoughts for many years. "We used to play music for fun. Much more than now. Now nobody picks up a guitar unless they're paid for it. Now every kid who picks up a guitar is invited to dream."

The first song he ever wrote was aptly called "Chant," a poem he loosely set to music: "Hold me heartlight, soft light hold me, moonlight in your mouth . . ." When John Hammond, the same guy who discovered Dylan, Springsteen, and Billie Holiday, heard some of Leonard's early songs, he told him, "You've got it," and signed him to Columbia Records.

His first album, *Songs of Leonard Cohen*, was an extraordinary debut for any songwriter and recording artist. Like later debuts by artists such as John Prine and Rickie Lee Jones, his first record evidenced a level of writing, a resounding maturity, and musical grace seldom found on a first album. In songs such as "Suzanne" and "Sisters of Mercy," Cohen moved beyond the realm of the popular song to reach into places previously untouched with words and music.

His following albums continued to resound with beautiful, intimate poetry while stretching the boundaries of songwriting, in such classic songs as "Chelsea Hotel No. 2," "Joan of Arc," and "Famous Blue Raincoat." So moved was Kris Kristofferson by the simple valor of Cohen's "Bird on the Wire" that he requested its opening be inscribed on his tombstone: "Like a bird on a wire, like a drunk in a midnight choir, I have tried in my way to be free." Bob Dylan made the accurate comment that Cohen's songs had become almost like prayers. It's true: a certain sanctity connects all of Cohen's work, a timeless devotional beauty that runs entirely opposite to almost everything that is modern.

He was born on September 21, 1934, in Montreal. His father died when he was nine. At seventeen he went to McGill University, where he formed the Buckskin Boys and wrote his first book of poetry, *Let Us Compare Mythologies*. His second volume, published in 1961 and entitled *The Spice-Box of Earth*, was acclaimed around the world. But as it's always been with his careers, the extreme acclaim that his work received never equaled extreme amounts of money. "I couldn't make a living," he said.

For seven years he lived on the island of Hydra in Greece with Marianne Jensen and her son Axel. [*Marianne was known by her maiden name, Ihlen, after she split from her husband, whose first name, like the son's, was Axel. —Ed.*] While there he wrote another book of poems, *Flowers for Hitler*, and two novels, *The Favorite Game* and *Beautiful Losers*.

Again the praise was vast and forthcoming but the financial rewards were scarce. The *Boston Globe* wrote, "James Joyce is not dead. He is living in Montreal under the name of Cohen." But he was frustrated by the inequality between the praise and the money, and rejected the novelist's life to move to America and become a songwriter.

Contradicting the old adage that the devil is in the details, Cohen has shown many times that the divine can be discovered there. As he once said to Jennifer Warnes, "Your most particular answer will be your most universal one." It is the unique specificity of his songs that enables one not only to envision them but to enter them. The miraculous "Suzanne," for example, is a song toward which many songwriters have aspired, and it is Cohen's descriptive use of details, along with one of his most haunting melodies, that distinguishes this astonishing song.

When I mentioned to him that to this day it seems miraculous to me that someone could have written it, he agreed, not egotistically but with a kind of hushed reverence. "It is miraculous," he said softly.

In conversation he is often Whitmanesque, speaking in evocative and inspired lists of specific human activity similar to the touching human details found in all of his songs. For example, when asked if he felt that many meaningful songs were still being written, he beautifully expounded on the meaning of meaningful songs:

"There are always meaningful songs for somebody. People are doing their courting, people are finding their wives, people are making babies, people are washing their dishes, people are getting through the day, with songs that we may find insignificant. But their significance is affirmed by others. There's always someone affirming the significance of a song by taking a woman into his arms or by getting through the night. That's what dignifies the song.

"Songs don't dignify human activity. Human activity dignifies the song."

Paul Zollo: Are you always working on songs or do you write only for specific projects?

Leonard Cohen: No, I'm writing all the time. And as the songs begin to coalesce, I'm not doing anything else but writing. I wish I were one of those people who wrote songs quickly. But I'm not. So it takes me a great deal of time to find out what the song is. So I am working most of the time.

PZ: When you say, "what the song is," do you mean that in terms of meaning—where the meaning is leading you?

LC: Yes. I find that easy versions of the song arrive first. Although they might be able to stand as songs, they can't stand as songs that I can sing. So to find a song that I can sing, to engage my interest, to penetrate my boredom with myself and my disinterest in my own opinions, to penetrate those barriers, the song has to speak to me with a certain urgency. To be able to find that song that I can be interested in takes many versions and it takes a lot of uncovering.

PZ: Do you mean that you're trying to reach something that is outside of your immediate realm of thought?

LC: My immediate realm of thought is bureaucratic and like a traffic jam. My ordinary state of mind is very much like the waiting room at the DMV [Department of Motor Vehicles]. Or, as I put it in a quatrain, "The voices in my head, they don't care what I do, they just want to argue the matter through and through."

So to penetrate this chattering and this meaningless debate that is occupying most of my attention, I have to come up with something that really speaks to my deepest interest. Otherwise I just nod off in one way or another. So to find that song, that urgent song, takes a lot of versions and a lot of work and a lot of sweat.

But why shouldn't my work be hard? Almost everybody's work is hard. One is distracted by this notion that there is such a thing as inspiration, that it comes fast and easy. And some people are graced by that style. I'm not. So I have to work as hard as any stiff, to come up with the payload.

PZ: So you're not a writer for whom ideas simply appear?

LC: I haven't had an idea in a long, long time. And I'm not sure I ever had one.

Now my friend Irving Layton, the great Canadian writer, said, "Leonard's mind is unpolluted by a single idea." And he meant it as a kind of compliment. He's a close friend and he knows me, and it's true. I don't have ideas. I don't really speculate on things. I get opinions but I'm not really attached to them. Most of them are tiresome. I have to trot them out in conversations from time to time just to cooperate in the social adventure. But I have a kind of amnesia and my ideas just kind of float above this profound disinterest in myself and other people. So to find something that really touches and addresses my attention, I have to do a lot of hard, manual work.

PZ: What does that work consist of?

LC: Just versions. I will drag you upstairs after the vacuuming stops and I will show you version after version after version of some of the tunes on this new album.

PZ: You do have whole notebooks of songs?

LC: Whole notebooks. I'm very happy to be able to speak this way to fellow craftsmen. Some people may find it encouraging to see how slow and dismal and painstaking is the process.

For instance, a song like "Closing Time" began in 3/4 time with a really strong, nostalgic, melancholy country feel. Entirely different words. It began:

The parking lot is empty / They switch off the Budweiser sign / It's dark from here to San Jobete / It's dark all down the line / They ought to hand the night a ticket / For speeding, it's a crime / I had so much to tell you / Yeah, but now it's closing time.

And I recorded the song and I sang it. And I choked over it. Even though another singer could have done it perfectly well. It's a perfectly reasonable song. And a good one, I might say. A respectable song. But I choked over it.

There wasn't anything that really addressed my attention. The finishing of it was agreeable because it's always an agreeable feeling. But when I tried to sing it I realized it came from my boredom and not from my attention. It came from my desire to finish the song and not from the *urgency* to locate a construction that would engross me.

So I went to work again. Then I filled *another notebook* from beginning to end with the lyric, or the attempts at the lyric, which eventually made it onto the album. So most of [my songs] have a dismal history, like the one I've just accounted.

PZ: Generally, do you finish the melody and then work on the lyrics for a long time?

LC: They're born together, they struggle together, and they influence one another. When the lyric begins to be revised, of course, the line can't carry it with its new nuance or its new meaning. And generally the musical line has to change, which involves changing the next musical line, which involves changing the next lyrical line, so the process is mutual and painstaking and slow.

PZ: Do you generally begin a song with a lyrical idea?

LC: It begins with an appetite to discover my self-respect. To redeem the day. So the day does not go down in debt. It begins with that kind of appetite.

PZ: Do you work on guitar?

LC: It usually was guitar but now I have been working with keyboards.

PZ: Does the instrument affect the song you are writing?

LC: They have certainly affected my songs. I only have one chop. All guitar players have chops. Especially professional ones. But I have only one chop. It's a chop that very few guitarists can emulate. Hence, I have a certain kind of backhanded respect from guitar players because they know that I have a chop that they can't master. And that chop was the basis of a lot of my good songs.

But on the keyboard, because you can set up patterns and rhythms, I can mock up songs in a way that I couldn't do with my guitar. There were these rhythms that I heard but I couldn't really duplicate with my own instrument. So it's changed the writing quite a bit.

PZ: Writing in that way could be either more freeing or more restrictive. You have a rhythm that is set but you are free from playing the guitar.

LC: "Freedom" and "restriction" are just luxurious terms to one who is locked in a dungeon in the tower of song. These are just . . . ideas. I don't have the sense of restriction or freedom. I just have the sense of work. I have the sense of hard labor.

PZ: Is this hard labor ever enjoyable for you?

LC: It has a certain nourishment. The mental physique is muscular. That gives you a certain stride as you walk along the dismal landscape of your inner thoughts. You have a certain kind of tone to your activity. But most of the time it doesn't help. It's just hard work.

But I think unemployment is the great affliction of man. Even people with jobs are unemployed. In fact, most people with jobs are unemployed. I can say, happily and gratefully, that I am fully employed. Maybe all hard work means is fully employed. We have a sense here that it's smart not to work. The hustle, the con, these have been elevated to a very high position in our morality. And probably if I could mount a con or a hustle in terms of my own work I would probably embrace the same philosophy. But I am a working stiff. It takes me months and months of full employment to break the code of the song. To find out if there can be a song there.

PZ: When you're working to break that code, is it a process of actively thinking about what the song should say?

LC: Anything that I can bring to it. Thought, meditation, drinking, disillusion, insomnia, vacations . . .

Because once the song enters the mill, it's worked on by everything that I can summon. And I need everything. I try everything. I try to ignore it, try to repress it, try to get high, try to get intoxicated, try to get sober. All the versions of myself that I can summon are summoned to participate in this project, this work force.

PZ: In your experience, do any of these things work better than others?

LC: Nothing works. After a while, if you stick with a song long enough it will yield. But long enough is way beyond any reasonable estimation of what you think long enough may be. In fact, long enough is way beyond. It's abandoning that idea of what you think long enough may be.

Because if you think it's a week, that's not long enough. If you think it's a month, it's not long enough. If you think it's a *year*, it's not long enough. If you think it's a decade, it's not long enough.

"Anthem" took a decade to write. And I've recorded it three times. More. I had a version prepared for my last album with strings and voices and overdubs. The whole thing completely finished. I listened to it. There was something wrong with the lyric, there was something wrong with the tune, there was something wrong with the tempo. There was a lie somewhere in there. There was a disclosure that I was refusing to make.

There was a solemnity that I hadn't achieved. There was something wrong with the damn thing. All I knew is that I couldn't sing it. You could hear it in the vocal, that the guy was putting you on.

PZ: Is "Anthem" in any way an answer to Dylan's song "Everything Is Broken"?

LC: I had a line in "Democracy" that referred specifically to that Dylan song, "Everything Is Broken," which was, "The singer says it's broken and the painter says it's gray . . ." But, no, "Anthem" was written a long time before that Dylan song. I'd say 1982 but it was actually earlier than that that that song began to form.

PZ: Including the part about the crack in everything?

LC: That's very old. That has been the background of much of my work. I had those lines in the works for a long time. I've been recycling them in many songs. I must not be able to nail it.

PZ: You said earlier that you had no ideas, but that certainly is an idea.

LC: Yeah. When I say that I don't have any ideas, it doesn't come to me in the form of an idea. It comes in the form of an image. I didn't start with a philosophical position that human activity is not perfectable. And that all human activity is flawed. And it is by intimacy with the flaw that we discern our real humanity and our real connection with divine inspiration. I didn't come up with it that way. I saw something broken. It's a different form of cognition.

PZ: Do images usually come to you in that way?

LC: Well, things come so damn slow. Things come and it's a tollgate, and they're particularly asking for something that you can't manage.

They say, "We got the goods here. What do you got to pay?" Well, I've got my intelligence, I've got a mind. "No, we don't want that." I've got my whole training as a poet. "No, we don't want that." I've got some licks, I've got some skills with my fingers on the guitar. "No, we don't want that either." Well, I've got a broken heart. "No, we don't want that." I've got a pretty girlfriend. "No, we don't want that." I've got sexual desire. "No, we don't want that." I've got a whole lot of things and the tollgate keeper says, "That's not going to get it. We want you in a condition that you are not accustomed to. And that you yourself cannot name. We want you in a condition of receptivity that you cannot produce by yourself." How are you going to come up with that?

PZ: What's the answer?

LC: [*Laughs.*] I don't know. But I've been lucky over the years. I've been willing to pay the price.

PZ: How much does it cost?

LC: [*Pause.*] It's hard to name. It's hard to name because it keeps changing.

PZ: Is it a sense that you are reaching outside of yourself to write these songs?

LC: If I knew where the good songs came from, I'd go there more often. It's a mysterious condition. It's much like the life of a Catholic nun. You're married to a mystery.

PZ: Do you consider the tower of song to be a place of exile or of retreat?

LC: I think you can use it as a retreat but it doesn't work. It's best thought of as a factory. It's some combination between a factory and a bordello. But it's just the tower of song.

PZ: You've spoken about the hard labor that goes into your songs, and part of that must be due to the fact that your verses are so rich, and that you write long songs with many verses. I think other songwriters might have come up with two of the verses in "Democracy" and stopped.

LC: I've got about sixty. There are about three or four parallel songs in the material that I've got. I saw that the song could develop in about three or four ways and there actually exist about three or four versions of "Democracy." The one I chose seemed to be the one that I could sing at that moment. I addressed almost everything that was going on in America.

This was when the Berlin Wall came down and everyone was saying democracy is coming to the East. And I was like that gloomy fellow who always turns up at a party to ruin the orgy. And I said, "I don't think it's going to happen that way. I don't think this is such a good idea. I think a lot of suffering will be the consequence of this wall coming down." But then I asked myself, "Where is democracy really coming?" And it was the USA. But I had verses:

> It ain't coming to us European style / Concentration camp behind a smile / It ain't coming from the East / With its temporary feast / As Count Dracula comes strolling down the aisle . . .

So while everyone was rejoicing, I thought it wasn't going to be like that, euphoric, the honeymoon.

So it was these world events that occasioned the song. And also the love of America. Because I think the irony of America is transcendent in the song.

It's not an ironic song. It's a song of deep intimacy and affirmation of the experiment of democracy in this country. That this is really where the experiment is unfolding. This is really where the races confront one another, where the classes, where the genders, where even the sexual orientations confront one another. This is the real laboratory of democracy. So I wanted to have that feeling in the song too. But I treated the relationship between the blacks and the Jews.

For instance, I had:

First we killed the Lord and then we stole the blues / This gutter people always in the news / But who really gets to laugh behind the black man's back / When he makes his little crack about the Jews? / Who really gets to profit and who really gets to pay? / Who really rides the slavery ship right into Charleston Bay? / Democracy is coming to the USA.

Verses like that.

PZ: Why did you take that out?

LC: I didn't want to compromise the anthemic, hymn-like quality. I didn't want it to get too punchy. I didn't want to start a fight in the song. I wanted a revelation in the heart rather than a confrontation or a call-to-arms or a defense.

There were a lot of verses like that, and this was long before the riots. There was:

From the church where the outcasts can hide / Or the mosque where the blood is dignified / Like the fingers on your hand, like the hourglass of sand / We can separate but not divide from the eye above the pyramid / And the dollar's cruel display / From the law behind the law / Behind the law we still obey / Democracy is coming to the USA.

There were a lot of verses like that. Good ones.

PZ: It's hard to believe you'd write a verse like that and discard it.

LC: The thing is that before I can discard the verse, I have to write it. Even if it's bad—those two happen to be good, I'm presenting the best of my discarded work—but even the bad ones took as long to write as the good ones. As someone once observed, it's just as hard to write a bad novel as a good novel. It's just as hard to write a bad verse as a good verse. I can't discard a verse before it is written because it is the writing of the verse that produces whatever delights or interests or facets that are going to catch the light. The cutting of the gem has to be finished before you can see whether it shines.

You can't discover that in the raw.

PZ: I love the verse that has "I'm stubborn as the garbage bags that refuse to decay / I'm junk but I'm still holding up this little wild bouquet."

LC: Most of us from the middle class, we have a kind of old, nineteenth-century idea of what democracy is, which is, more or less, to oversimplify it, that the masses are going to love Shakespeare and Beethoven. That's more or less our idea of what democracy is. But that ain't it. It's going to come up in unexpected ways from the stuff that we think is junk: the people we think are junk, the ideas we think are junk, the television we think is junk.

PZ: You also have the line "The maestro says it's Mozart, but it sounds like bubblegum." That junk is sometimes promoted as great art.

LC: Some stuff is being promoted as junk and it is great art. Remember the way that a lot of rock and roll was greeted by the authorities and the musicologists and even the hip people. And when people were putting me down as being one thing or another, it wasn't the guy in the subway. He didn't know about me. It was the hip people, writing the columns in the hip newspapers, college papers, music papers.

So it's very difficult to see what the verdict is going to be about a piece of work. And the thing that makes it an interesting game is that each generation revises the game, and decides on what is poetry and song for itself. Often rejecting the very carefully considered verdicts of the previous generations. I mean, did the hippies ever think that they would be the objects of ridicule by a generation? Self-righteous and prideful for the really bold and courageous steps they had taken to find themselves imbued in the face of an unmovable society; the risks, the chances, the dope they smoked, the acid they dropped? Did they ever think they would be held up as figures of derision, like cartoon characters? No.

And so it is with every generation. There's that remark: "He who marries the spirit of his own generation is a widower in the next."

PZ: You've written novels and books of poetry. And you once made a comment about having a calm, domestic life as a novelist before becoming a songwriter. Is the life of a songwriter entirely different from that of the poet or novelist?

LC: It used to be. Because I used to be able to write songs on the run. I used to work hard but I didn't really begin slaving over them till 1983. I always used to work hard. But I had no idea what hard work was until something changed in my mind.

PZ: Do you know what that was?

LC: I don't really know what it was. Maybe some sense that this whole enterprise is limited, that there was an end in sight.

PZ: An end to your songwriting?

LC: No, an end to your life. That you were really truly mortal. I don't know what it was exactly, I'm just speculating. But at a certain moment I found myself engaged in songwriting in the same way that I had been engaged in novel writing when I was very young. In other words, it's something you do every day and you can't get too far from it, otherwise you forget *what it's about.*

PZ: It wasn't that way for you prior to that time?

LC: It was, but I'm speaking of degree. I always thought that I sweated over the stuff. But I had no idea what sweating over the stuff meant until I found myself in my underwear crawling along the carpet in a shabby room at the Royalton Hotel unable to nail a verse. And knowing that I had a recording session and knowing that I could get by with what I had but that I'm not going to be able to do it.

That kind of change I knew gradually was there and I knew that I had to work in a certain way that was nothing I had ever known anything about.

PZ: In the early days, did a song such as "Suzanne" come easy to you?

LC: No, no, I worked months and months on "Suzanne." It's just a matter of intensity. I was still able to juggle stuff: a life, a woman, a dream, other ambitions, other tangents. At a certain point I realized I only had one ball in my hand, and that was The Song. Everything else had been wrecked or compromised and I couldn't go back, and I was a one-ball juggler. I'd do incredible things with that ball to justify the absurdity of the presentation.

Because what are you going to do with that ball? You don't have three anymore. You've just got one. And maybe only one arm. What are you going to do? You can flip it off your wrist, or bounce it off your head. You have to come up with some pretty good moves. You have to learn them from scratch. And that's what I learned, that you have to learn them from scratch.

There is some continuity between "Suzanne" and "Waiting for a Miracle" [*sic*]. Of course there is; it's the same guy. Maybe it's like you lose your arm, you're a shoemaker. You're a pretty good shoemaker, maybe not the best but one of the top ten. You lose your arm and nobody knows. All they know is that your shoes keep on being pretty good. But in your workshop, you're holding onto the edge of the shoe with your teeth, you're holding it down and hammering with your other hand. It's quite an acrobatic presentation to get that shoe together. It may be the same shoe, it's just a lot harder to come by and you don't want to complain about it.

So maybe that's all that happened, is that I got wiped out in some kind of way and that just meant that I had to work harder to get the same results. I don't have any estimation or evaluation. I just know that the work got really hard.

PZ: Why did you move from writing novels and poems to songwriting?

LC: I never saw the difference. There was a certain point that I saw that I couldn't make a living [as a poet or novelist]. But to become a songwriter or a singer, to address an economic problem, is the height of folly, especially in your early thirties. So I don't know why I did it or why I do anything. I never had a strategy. I just play it by ear.

I just know that I had written what I thought was a pretty good novel, *Beautiful Losers*. It had been hailed by all the authorities as being a work of significance. Whether it is or not, who knows. But I had the credentials. But I couldn't pay my bills. It had only sold a couple thousand copies. So it was folly to begin another novel. I didn't want to teach; it just wasn't my cup of tea.

I didn't have the personal style for that. I was too dissolute. I had to stay up too late, I had to move too fast. It wasn't a good place for me.

PZ: Have you ever had the desire to write another novel?

LC: You toy with it but it's the regime that I like very much, writing a novel. I like that you really can't do anything else. You've got to be in one place. That's the way it is now with songwriting. I've got to have my synthesizer and my Mac. I can't really entertain a lot of distractions. [Otherwise] you forget what it's about very easily.

PZ: Is it more satisfying for you to write a song, something that you can enter again after writing and perform?

LC: The performance of songs is a wonderful opportunity. It is a great privilege. It is a great way to test your courage. And to test the song. And even to test the audience.

PZ: Earlier you said that you could only write something that you would be able to sing, that—

LC: I'm not trying to suggest that this has any dimension or hierarchy of better, worse. It's just a shape that it's got to have. Otherwise I can't wrap my voice around it.

There are songs like "Dress Rehearsal Rag" that I recorded once and I will never sing. Judy Collins did a very beautiful version of it, better than mine. I would never do that song in concert; I can't get behind it.

But it's not a matter of excellence or anything but just the appropriate shape of my voice and psyche.

PZ: Earlier you said that you couldn't sing an early version of "Anthem" because it had a lie in it. Does this mean that the songs have to resonate in truth for you to be able to sing them?

LC: They have to resonate with the kind of truth that I can recognize. They have to have the kind of balance of truth and lies, light and dark.

PZ: Jennifer Warnes said that you once told her that the most particular answer is the most universal one.

LC: I think so. I think that's advice that a lot of good writers have given me and the world. You don't really want to say "the tree," you want to say "the sycamore."

PZ: Why is that?

LC: I don't know. And it's not even true. But there is a certain truth to it. We seem to be able to relate to detail. We seem to have an appetite for it. It seems that your days are made of details, and if you can't get the sense of another person's day of details, your own day of details is summoned in your mind in some way rather than just a general line like "the days went by." It's better to say "watching *Captain Kangaroo*." Not "watching TV." Sitting in my room "with that hopeless little screen." Not just "TV," but "the hopeless, little screen."

I think those are the details that delight us. They delight us because we can share a life then. It's our sense of insignificance and isolation that produces a great deal of suffering.

PZ: It's one of the great things about your work, your rich use of details. So many songs we hear are empty, and have no details at all.

LC: I love to hear the details. I was just working on a line this morning for a song called "I Was Never Any Good at Loving You." And the line was—I don't think I've nailed it yet—"I was running from the law, I thought you knew, forgiveness was the way it felt with you" or "forgiven was the way I felt with you." Then I got a metaphysical line, about the old law and the new law, the Old Testament and the New Testament: "I was running from the law, the old and the new, forgiven was the way I felt with you." No, I thought, it's too intellectual. Then I thought I got it: "I was running from the cops and the robbers too, forgiven was the way I felt with you." You got cops and robbers, it dignifies the line by making it available, making it commonplace.

PZ: Each of those three versions works well. And so many of your lines—though I understand how hard you work on them and revise them—have the feeling of being inevitable. They don't feel forced; they just feel like the perfect line.

LC: I appreciate that. Somebody said that art is the concealment of art.

PZ: Is there much concealing?

LC: Unless you want to present the piece with the axe-marks on it, which is legitimate, [to show] where the construction or the carving is. I like the polished stuff too.

At a certain point, when the Jews were first commanded to raise an altar, the commandment was on unhewn stone. Apparently the god that wanted that particular altar didn't want slick, didn't want smooth. He wanted an unhewn stone placed on another unhewn stone. Maybe then you go looking for stones that fit. Maybe that was the process that God wanted the makers of this altar to undergo.

Now I think Dylan has lines, hundreds of great lines that have the feel of unhewn stone. But they really fit in there. But they're not smoothed out. It's inspired but not polished.

That is not to say that he doesn't have lyrics of great polish. That kind of genius can manifest all the forms and all the styles.

PZ: When you're working on lines such as those that you mentioned, is that a process of working just with words, separate from music?

LC: No. I don't remember the chicken or the egg. I know the song began. But I keep moving them back and forth between the notebook and the keyboard. Trying to find where the song is. I had it as a shuffle. I had it as a kind of 6/8 song like "Blueberry Hill."

PZ: So when working on a lyric, there's always a melody in your mind that accompanies the lyric?

LC: Usually, yes, the line will have a kind of rhythm that will indicate, at the very least, where the voice will go up and where the voice will go down. I guess that's the rudimentary beginnings of what they call melody.

PZ: I asked that because your songs, unlike most, are always in perfect meter and perfect rhyme schemes. It seems it would be possible to work on them just as lyrics, without music.

LC: It doesn't seem to work that way. Because the line of music is very influential in determining the length of a line or the density, the syllabic density.

PZ: You mentioned working on a Mac. Is that musical work as well as lyrical work?

LC: I like to set them up. They usually go from the napkin to the notebook to the Mac. And back and forth. And there's a certain moment when there's enough. I like to see it.

They say that the Torah was written with black fire on white fire. So I get that feeling from the computer, the bright black against the bright background. It gives it a certain theatrical dignity to see it on the screen. And also word processing enables you to cut and paste. But I generally have to go back to the napkin and the notebook. But at certain periods during the making of the song, I'll mock it up as a song just to be able to study it in a certain way.

PZ: You mentioned that whole verse about the Jews in "Democracy" that you took out, and in "The Future" there is that line, "I'm the little Jew who wrote the Bible." There are so many great Jewish songwriters, yet it's so rare that any of them mention being Jewish in a song—

LC: [*Laughs.*] I smiled to myself when that line came. A friend of mine said, "I dare you to leave that line in."

PZ: You were tempted to remove it?

LC: I'm tempted to remove everything. At any time. I guess I've got a kind of alcoholic courage. Most people are reluctant to remove things. My sin is on the other side. I'm ready to discard the whole song at any time and start over.

And I think it's just as grave a defect because probably, at some point down the line, I've thrown away some songs that were pretty good. And they're buried out there somewhere.

PZ: Do you ever construct songs from things you've discarded?

LC: I continually recycle.

PZ: Do you think being Jewish affects your writing?

LC: I have no idea. I've never been anything else. So I don't know what it would be like not to have this reference. This reference that you can reject or embrace. You can have a million attitudes to this reference but you can't change the reference.

PZ: You've studied the Torah and the Talmud?

LC: Yeah, yeah, in a modest way.

PZ: When you're writing a song like "The Future," for example, which is in A minor, do you choose a key that will match the tone of the song?

LC: Yeah. I choose a key not so much as Garth Hudson [of the Band] would—he has a whole philosophy of music based on keys and colors and what moods different keys produce. I think that's quite valuable, I just don't have the chops to be able to do that because I can't play in all the keys. So I can't really examine the effects of all the keys. With the synthesizer I could play in all of them but I don't try that.

PZ: Do you think that there are colors that coincide with each key?

LC: I think there are but mostly for me it's range. Some keys will place the voice a little deeper than others. My voice has gotten very, very deep over the years and seems even to be deepening. I thought it was because of fifty thousand cigarettes and several swimming pools of whiskey that my voice has gotten low. But I gave up smoking a couple of years ago and it's still getting deeper.

PZ: You actually do sound like a different person on the earlier records.

LC: Sounds like a different person. Something happened to me too. I know what it was. My voice really started to change around 1982. It started to deepen and I started to cop to the fact that it was deepening.

PZ: That very low voice is such a resonant sound. Are you happy with how it has evolved?

LC: I'm surprised that I can even, with fear and trembling, describe myself to myself as a singer. I'm beginning to be able to do that. I never thought I would but there is something in the voice that is quite acceptable. I never thought I would be able to develop a voice that had any kind of character.

PZ: In terms of keys again, do you ever change keys while writing?

LC: Oh, yeah. It's funny, today I was thinking about modulating in a tune, which I have never done. I've never modulated a song in midstream.

PZ: Key changes can be quite corny. I can't think of a song of yours where you would want one.

LC: No, I don't know. I think it could be nice. I've never tried it. I might find a way to do it—maybe in the middle of a line except in the beginning of a verse. There might be some sneaky ways to do it.

I did it in a certain kind of way in "Anthem." When I went up to the B-flat from the F. It threw it into another key. So in a sense, that chorus is in another key and then it comes back through suspended chords and into the original key.

So I have looked into them.

PZ: Do you feel that minor keys are more expressive than major keys?

LC: I think the juxtaposition of a major chord with no seventh going into a minor chord is a nice feel. I like that feel.

PZ: In "Famous Blue Raincoat," which is A minor, the chorus shifts into C major, which is very beautiful.

LC: Yeah. That's nice. I guess I got that from Spanish music, which has that.

PZ: You mentioned how much you discard of what you write. Is your critical voice at play while writing, or do you try to write something first and then bring in the critic?

LC: I bring all the people in to the team, the workforce, the legion. There's a lot of voices that these things run through.

PZ: Do they ever get in the way?

LC: Get in the way hardly begins to describe it. [*Laughter.*] It's mayhem. It's mayhem and people are walking over each other's hands. It's panic. It's fire in the theater. People are being trampled and they're bullies and cowards. All the versions of yourself that you can summon are there. And some you didn't even know were around.

PZ: When you finally finish a song, is there a sense of triumph?

LC: Oh, yes. There's a wonderful sense of done-ness. That's the thing I like best. That sense of finish-ness.

PZ: How long does that last?

LC: A long time. I'm still invigorated by having finished this last record and I finished it six months ago and I still feel, "God, I finished this record. Isn't it great?" You have to keep it to yourself after a while. Your friends are ready to rejoice with you for a day or a week. But they're not ready to rejoice after six months of "Hey, let's go get a drink. I finished my record six months ago!" It's an invitation people find easy to resist.

PZ: Does drinking ever help you write?

LC: No. Nothing helps. But drinking helps performing. Sometimes. Of course you've got to be judicious.

PZ: Would it be OK with you if I named some of your songs to see what response you have to them?

LC: Sure.

PZ: "Sisters of Mercy."

LC: That's the only song I wrote in one sitting. The melody I had worked on for some time. I didn't really know what the song was. I remember that my mother had liked it.

Then I was in Edmonton, which is one of our largest northern cities, and there was a snowstorm and I found myself in a vestibule with two young hitchhiking women who didn't have a place to stay. I invited them back to my little hotel room and there was a big double bed and they went to sleep in it immediately.

They were exhausted by the storm and the cold. And I sat in this stuffed chair inside the window beside the Saskatchewan River. And while they were sleeping I wrote the lyrics. And that never happened to me before. And I think it must be wonderful to be that kind of writer.

Because I just wrote the lines with a few revisions and when they awakened I sang it to them. And it has never happened to me like that before. Or since.

PZ: "Hey, That's No Way to Say Goodbye."

LC: The first band I sang that for was a group called the Stormy Clovers, a Canadian group out of Toronto. I wrote it in two hotels. One was the Chelsea and the other was the Penn Terminal Hotel. I remember Marianne looking at my notebook, seeing this song, and asking, "Who'd you write this for?"

PZ: "Chelsea Hotel No. 2."

LC: [*Pauses.*] I came to New York and I was living at other hotels and I had heard about the Chelsea Hotel as being a place where I might meet people of my own kind. And I did. [*Laughs.*] It was a grand, mad place. Much has been written about it.

PZ: That song was written for Janis Joplin?

LC: It was very indiscreet of me to let that news out. I don't know when I did. Looking back I'm sorry I did because there are some lines in it that are extremely intimate. And since I let the cat out of the bag, yes, it was written for her.

PZ: "Hallelujah."

LC: That was a song that took me a long time to write. Dylan and I were having coffee the day after his concert in Paris a few years ago and he was doing that song in concert. And he asked me how long it took to write it. And I told him a couple of years. I lied actually. It was more than a couple of years.

Then I praised a song of his, "I and I," and asked him how long it had taken and he said, "Fifteen minutes." [*Laughs.*]

PZ: Dylan said, around the time that "Hallelujah" came out, that your songs were almost like prayers.

LC: I didn't hear that but I know he does take some interest in my songs. We have a mutual interest. Everybody's interested in Dylan but it's pleasant to have Dylan interested in me.

PZ: It seems that his comment is true. Songs like "Hallelujah" or "If It Be Your Will" have a sanctity to them.

LC: "If It Be Your Will" really is a prayer. And "Hallelujah" has that feeling. A lot of them do. "Dance Me to the End of Love." "Suzanne." I love church music and synagogue music. Mosque music.

PZ: It's especially resonant in this time because so few songs that we hear have any sense of holiness.

LC: Well, there's a line in "The Future": "When they said repent, I wonder what they meant." I understand that they forgot how to build the arch for several hundred years. Masons forgot how to do certain kinds of arches; it was lost.

So it is in our time that certain spiritual mechanisms that were very useful have been abandoned and forgot. Redemption, repentance, resurrection. All those ideas are thrown out with the bathwater. People became suspicious of religion plus all these redemptive mechanisms that are very useful.

PZ: "Famous Blue Raincoat."

LC: That was one I thought was never finished. And I thought that Jennifer Warnes's version in a sense was better because I worked on a different version for her, and I thought it was somewhat more coherent. But I always thought that that was a song you could see the carpentry in a bit. Although there are some images in it that I am very pleased with. And the tune is real good. But I'm willing to defend it, saying it was impressionistic. It's stylistically coherent.

And I can defend it if I have to. But secretly I always felt that there was a certain incoherence that prevented it from being a great song.

PZ: I'd have to disagree.

LC: Well, I'm glad to hear it. Please disagree with any of this.

PZ: I think the greatness of that song lies in the fact that you're alluding to a story without coming out and giving all the facts, yet the story is more powerful because of what you don't say, or can't say.

LC: Yes. It may be. When I was at school there was a book that was very popular called *Seven Types of Ambiguity*. One of the things it criticized was something called "The Author's Intention." You've got to discard the author's intention. It doesn't matter what the author's intention in the piece is, or what his interpretation of the piece is, or what his evaluation or estimation of the piece is. It exists independently of his opinions about it. So maybe it is a good song, after all. I'm ready to buy your version.

This is all part of this make-believe mind that one has to present socially and professionally if you care about these matters. It's like asking somebody in a burning building if they care about architecture. [*Laughs.*] Where's the fire escape? That's all I care about in terms of architecture. Can I open the window?

PZ: "First We Take Manhattan."

LC: I felt for some time that the motivating energy, or the captivating energy, or the engrossing energy available to us today is the energy coming from the extremes. That's why we have Malcolm X. And somehow it's only these extremist positions that can compel our attention. And I find in my own mind that I have to resist these extremist positions when I find myself drifting into a mystical fascism in regards to myself. [*Laughs.*] So this song, "First We Take Manhattan," what is it? Is he serious? And who is "we"? And what is this constituency that he's addressing? Well, it's that constituency that shares this sense of titillation with extremist positions.

I'd rather do that with an appetite for extremism than blow up a bus full of schoolchildren.

PZ: When I first started playing guitar and writing songs, one of the first songs I ever learned was "Suzanne." And I remember thinking, "How does anyone write a song this beautiful?" And to this day, it's a miracle.

LC: It is a miracle. I don't know where the good songs come from or else I'd go there more often. I knew that I was on top of something.

I developed the picking pattern first. I was spending a lot of time on the waterfront and the harbor area of Montreal. It hadn't been reconstructed yet.

It's now called Old Montreal and a lot of the buildings have been restored. It wasn't at that time. And there was that sailor's church that has the statue of the Virgin. Gilded so that the sun comes down on her. And I knew there was a song there.

Then I met Suzanne [Verdal], who was the wife of Armand Vaillancourt, a friend of mine. She was a dancer and she took me down to a place near the river.

She was one of the first people to have a loft on the Saint Lawrence. I knew that it was about that church and I knew that it was about the river. I didn't know I had anything to crystallize the song. And then her name entered into the song and then it was a matter of reportage, of really just being as accurate as I could about what she did.

PZ: It took you a long time to finish?

LC: Yes, I had many work sheets. Nothing compared to the work sheets I have now. But it took me several months.

PZ: Did she feed you tea and oranges, as in the song?

LC: She fed me a tea called Constant Comment, which has small pieces of orange rind in it, which gave birth to the image.

PZ: I always loved the line, "And she shows you where to look among the garbage and the flowers, there are heroes in the seaweed." They're hopeful lines.

LC: Yes. It is hopeful. I'm very grateful for those lines and for that song.

PZ: "Bird on a Wire."

LC: It was begun in Greece because there were no wires on the island where I was living to a certain moment. There were no telephone wires. There were no telephones. There was no electricity. So at a certain point they put in these telephone poles, and you wouldn't notice them now, but when they first went up, it was about all I did—stare out the window at these telephone wires and think how civilization had caught up with me and I wasn't going to be able to escape after all. I wasn't going to be able to live this eleventh-century life that I thought I had found for myself. So that was the beginning.

Then, of course, I noticed that birds came to the wires and that was how that song began. "Like a drunk in a midnight choir," that's also set on the island. Where drinkers, me included, would come up the stairs. There was great tolerance among the people for that because it could be in the middle of the night. You'd see three guys with their arms around each other, stumbling up the stairs and singing these impeccable thirds. So that image came from the island: "Like a drunk in a midnight choir."

PZ: You wrote that you "finished it in Hollywood in a motel in 1969 along with everything else." What did you mean?

LC: Everything was being finished. The sixties were being finished. Maybe that's what I meant. But I felt the sixties were finished a long time before that.

I don't think the sixties ever began. I think the whole sixties lasted maybe fifteen or twenty minutes in somebody's mind. I saw it move very, very quickly into the marketplace. I don't think there were any sixties.

PZ: "I'm Your Man."

LC: I sweated over that one. I really sweated over it. I can show you the notebook for that. It started off as a song called "I Cried Enough for You." It was related to a version of "Waiting for a Miracle" [*sic*] that I recorded.

The rhyme scheme was developed by toeing the line with that musical version that I put down. But it didn't work.

PZ: You quoted Dylan once when you said, "I know my song well before I start singing." Do you always have the song completely finished before you begin recording?

LC: Yeah. Sometimes there's a rude awakening. As there have been several times in the past. As with "Anthem." Several times I thought I had sung that song well and then when I heard it I realized I hadn't.

PZ: What do you think of songwriters who write in the studio?

LC: I think they're amazing. I have tremendous admiration for that kind of courage and that kind of belief in one's own inspiration. That the gods are going to be favorable to you. That you're going to go in there with nothing but the will and the skill, and the thing is going to emerge. And great stuff has been done that way. It's not like this never works. There are masters of that style. Dylan is one of them. I think he's gone in with nothing and come up with great things. That is to say that my impression about Dylan is that he's used all the approaches: the spontaneous, the polished, the unhewn, the deliberate. He masters all those forms.

PZ: There aren't many songwriters of your generation who have been able to maintain the quality of their past work the way you have been able to.

LC: First of all, you get tired. There aren't that many bullfighters in their forties. You do your great work as a bullfighter in your twenties and your thirties.

There is a certain age that is appropriate to this tremendous expenditure of energy and the tremendous bravery and courage that you need to go into the fray. It often is a young man's game, or as Browning said, "The first fine careless frenzy." That is what the lyric poem is based on, the song is based on. But there are some old guys who hang in there and come up with some very interesting work.

PZ: In your work you've shown that a songwriter can go beyond that early frenzy and come to a new place and do new things that haven't been done.

LC: I certainly felt the need to find that place. I always thought I was in it for the long haul, touch wood.

PZ: Does it have to do with interest, that you're still interested with the process?

LC: It was to do with two things. One is economic urgency. I just never made enough money to say, "Oh, man, I think I'm gonna get a yacht now and scuba-dive." I never had those kinds of funds available to me to make radical decisions about what I might do in life. Besides that, I was trained in what later became known as the Montreal School of Poetry. Before there were prizes, before there were grants, before there were even girls who cared about what I did. We would meet, a loosely defined group of people. There were no prizes, as I said, no rewards other than the work itself. We would read each other poems. We were *passionately* involved with poems and our *lives* were involved with this occupation. And we'd have to defend every line. We'd read poems to each other and you were attacked! With a kind of savagery that defangs rock criticism completely. There ain't anybody that I've ever read who can come up with anything like the savagery, and I might say the accuracy, that we laid on each other.

We had in our minds the examples of poets who continued to work their whole lives. There was never any sense of a raid on the marketplace, that you should come up with a hit and get out. That kind of sensibility simply did not take root in my mind until very recently. [*Laughs.*] I think maybe it's a nice idea but it's not going to happen when you write seven-minute songs.

So I always had the sense of being in this for *keeps*, if your health lasts you. And you're fortunate enough to have the days at your disposal so you can keep on doing this. I never had the sense that there was an end. That there was a retirement or that there was a *jackpot*.

PZ: You mentioned the early frenzy of youth. Do you find you need frenzy or conflict in your life to write great songs or can you create from a place of calm?

LC: I certainly think so and I'm looking forward to achieving that interior condition so that I can write from it. But I haven't yet. I've come a long way compared to the kind of trouble I was in when I was younger. Compared to that kind of trouble, this kind of trouble sounds like peace to me. But of course one is still involved in this struggle and while you're involved in this struggle you know peace is just a momentary thing, but you can't claim it. I'm a lot more comfortable with myself than I was a while ago. I'm still writing out of the conflicts and I don't know if they'll ever resolve.

PZ: Do you find the song to be a more powerful art form than others?

LC: I love it. As a mode of employment. I don't even think about art forms. I'm very grateful to have stumbled into this line of work. It's tough but I like it.

PZ: Do you have the sense that some of your songs are lasting and timeless?

LC: Sometimes I have a feeling that, as I'm fond of saying, a lot of my songs have lasted as long as the Volvo.

PZ: They're sturdy.

LC: They seem to be sturdy. This last album [*The Future*] I think is very, very sturdy. If it has any faults it's that it's a little too well armored. It seems to have a kind of resilience like a little Sherman Tank, that it can go over any landscape. I don't know whether that's something you want parking in your garage, but it seems to have a kind of armored energy. I've tried to make the songs sturdy over the years.

PZ: Is it your feeling that songs will continue to evolve, that there are new places to go with them?

LC: I think they will. It's a very good question and it summons the whole aesthetic. I think it's not important that they change or that anybody has a strategy for changing them. Or anyone has to monkey with them experimentally. Because I think that songs primarily are for courting, for finding your mate. For deep things. For summoning love, for healing broken nights, and for the central accompaniment to life's tasks. Which is no mean or small thing.

I think it's important that they address those needs rather than they look into themselves in terms of experimenting with form or with matter. But I think that they will, of course, change. I think that, although there's got to be songs about making love and losing and finding love, the fact that you're on the edge of a burning city, this definitely is going to affect the thing. But it affects it in surprising ways that you don't have to worry about.

Like [German love song] "Lili Marlene" came out of the war. [*It was written during World War I and became popular during World War II. —Ed.*] It's a very conventional song. A very beautiful song. It touched the troops on both sides. People who had undergone the baptism of fire sang "Lili Marlene," though they thought it was the corniest song in the world. So I don't think it's necessary to tinker with the form. It's just necessary to let the world speak to you.

PZ: Do you have a discipline for writing? Do you write at the same time every day?

LC: I get up very early. I like to fill those early hours with that effort.

PZ: Most of your writing is done in the morning?

LC: Yes. I find it clearer. The mind is very clear in those early hours.

PZ: Is that a daily thing?

LC: Usually. I blow it and fall into disillusion and disrepair. Where the mind and the body and the writing and the relationships and everything else goes to hell. I start drinking too much or eating too much or talking too much or vacationing too much. And then I start recovering the boundaries and putting back the fences and trimming the hedges. But when the thing is working, I find early in the morning best.

I get up at four thirty. My alarm is set for four thirty. Sometimes I sleep through it. But when I'm being good to myself, I get up at four thirty, get dressed, go down to a zendo [meditation hall] not far from here. And while the others, I suppose, are moving toward enlightenment, I'm working on a song while I'm sitting there. At a certain moment I can bring what I've learned at the zendo, the capacity to concentrate, I can bring it to bear on the lines that are eluding me.

Then I come back to the house after two hours. It's about six thirty now, quarter to seven. I brew an enormous pot of coffee and sit down in a very deliberate way, at the kitchen table or at the computer, and begin, first of all, to put down the lines that have come to me so that I don't forget them. And then play the song over and over again, try to find some form.

Those are wonderful hours. Before the phone starts ringing, before your civilian life returns to you with all its bewildering complexities. It's a simple time in the morning. A *wonderful*, invigorating time.

PZ: Do you find that your mind is always working on songs, even when you're not actively working?

LC: Yes. But I'm actively working on songs most of the time. Which is why my personal life has collapsed. Mostly I'm working on songs.

TV INTERVIEW

BARBARA GOWDY | November 19, 1992, TVOntario (Ontario, Canada)

In one of his last interviews of 1992, Cohen talked for TVOntario with writer Barbara Gowdy. "This was both the easiest and the most exciting interview I have ever done," she later wrote. "Exciting because Leonard Cohen's 'Suzanne' was an anthem to me and for thousands of other teenaged girls in the late sixties. When you mention that song, people tend to go on about the lyric about how 'she feeds you tea and oranges that come all the way from China,' but it was the line 'And you know that she's half crazy but that's why you want to be there' that I went for, exonerating, as it seemed to, my behavior then and over the next fifteen years.

"The fact that the interview went off so smoothly—that came as a surprise," Gowdy continued. "I had only a few hours to prepare for it, I had nothing to wear, I forgot my shoes. But from the minute he entered the room, Leonard was relaxed and gracious. And once the interview started he was remarkably open. It was as if he didn't know how famous he was, despite all the women lined up in the hallway outside the hotel room where the interview took place. It was as if getting close to the truth was much more important than giving an impression of cleverness or mystery."

Gowdy's interview aired on November 19—just five days before the release of *The Future*. —Ed.

Barbara Gowdy: In the title song of your new recording, *The Future*, it says, "There'll be the breaking of the ancient Western code / Your private life will suddenly explode / There'll be fires on the road . . . / I've seen the future, baby, it is murder." How are we to take this?

Leonard Cohen: With a grain of salt, I guess. "There'll be the breaking of the ancient Western code, I mean your private life will suddenly explode." That is this whole investment in private space that the West has painfully established over the centuries. That is specifically what is going to collapse. "There will be phantoms, there'll be fires on the road"—a return to suspicion, superstition, return to the tribal paranoia and the white man dancing. It evokes a scene of the end of things but with certain variations.

BG: That's kind of bleak, isn't it, even for you?

LC: It would be bleak if it wasn't set to a hot dance track.

BG: Yeah, there's an upbeat rhythm behind it.

LC: If I'd just nailed that onto the church door like Martin Luther, it would be a very grim prophecy. But the track on the album has a certain buoyancy that allows the lyric to survive in a happier landscape.

BG: I read an interview years ago in which you said that on a personal level your lyrics tend to be prophetic.

LC: They really are prophetic but, unfortunately, the songs take so long to finish that my prophecy business is collapsing. My song on the unification of Germany is just finished, a long time after the event. My song called "Democracy" was used and people identified it with the victory of the Democratic Party. I'd written it long before that. It just didn't come out until very recently.

BG: That song, the lyrics—I couldn't get you to sing some of the lyrics for me?

LC: [*Surprised.*] Which one? "Democracy"? [*Recites.*]

> It's coming through a hole in the air, from those nights in Tiananmen Square / It's coming from the feel that it's not exactly real, or it's real, but it's not exactly there / From the wars against disorder, from the sirens night and day, from the fires of the homeless, from the ashes of the gay / Democracy is coming to the USA.

BG: Not bad. So what is the future—is it murder or is it democracy?

LC: I think it is murder . . . myself. I think that the possibilities—the appetite for homicide grows in every heart. The extremist positions begin to sound more and more attractive. I find myself perking up my ears when

I hear someone from the Ku Klux Klan talking or the Black American Nationalists, even though I am not welcome in either of those parties. I find the rhetoric has a certain edge, pizzazz, attraction. I think everybody feels more hospitable to the extremist position as it is articulated now.

BG: How will that fit into democracy?

LC: Democracy's the flip side of the future. Democracy is the alternative and I believe that growing with this sense of ambiguity about our lives, about our jobs, about our marriages, about our loves, about our affiliations and loyalties—in the background is the faith we call democracy, which is the greatest religion the West has produced. It is the first religion that affirms other religions, the first culture that affirms other cultures and that designates it as great. [G. K.] Chesterton said about religion, "It's a great idea, too bad nobody's tried it." We are at the edge of this experiment; it's just begun. Democracy's a very, very recent idea as it's applied to the masses.

I think America's the great laboratory. Regardless of how ironic we've trained ourselves to be about America—we in Canada and in Europe—in a certain way our blessings can be summoned for America; somehow we understand that it is there the great experiment is taking place. The races are confronting each other, the classes live side by side, the rich and the poor watch the same screen every night—so something is going on there that's going to affect us all. And I don't think anyone with goodwill cannot wish it well.

BG: That sounds optimistic.

LC: I think there's an optimistic note there.

BG: There's more optimism in this album. The song called "Anthem." Can you sing the refrain for me?

LC: "Ring the bells that still can ring, forget your perfect offering / There is a crack in everything, that's how the light gets in."

BG: What is the light?

LC: The light is the capacity to reconcile your experience, your sorrow, with every day that dawns. It is that understanding, which is beyond significance or meaning, that allows you to live a life and embrace the disasters and sorrows and joys that are our common lot. But it's only with the recognition that there is a crack in everything. I think all other visions are doomed to irretrievable gloom. And whenever anyone asks us to accept a perfect solution, that should immediately alert us to the flaws in that presentation.

BG: I thought you were going to say the light was love. There's a lot of talk of love on this album. In fact, the 1925 Irving Berlin song, the song "Always" . . .

LC: A grand song, very popular in our house when I was growing up. My mother loved the song, and we used to play it when I was playing clarinet in dance bands around Montreal. It had the prestige of "Stardust" as one of the songs you played toward the end of the dance. I always loved the song. It's a very gentle song: "I'll be loving you, always, with a love that's true . . ."

I changed the tempo from 3/4 to 4/4 and it allows a lot of space to arise when it's turned into an R&B song.

BG: Why is it on this album after all this time?

LC: I think it's on this album because the track survived. I wouldn't have put it on the album unless the track had a certain exuberance. I prepared a lot of Red Needles. That's a cocktail I invented in Needles, California, in 1976. It consists of tequila and cranberry juice and Sprite and fresh-cut fruit. I prepared pitchers of this cocktail for the musicians and we couldn't stop playing; most of the takes are twenty-five minutes long, and we kept this one because it's eight minutes long. I did fall down in it; that's where the guitar solo occurs. It was a very exuberant, passionate evening, and several musicians told me it was the happiest time they ever spent in a recording studio.

BG: Has the way you feel about romantic love changed over the years?

LC: I'm not sure how I felt about it. I've never considered myself a romantic person. I find it very difficult to locate sentimentality or nostalgia or that kind of warm passion or potato feeling in myself, so I'm not sure what is meant by romantic love.

BG: I would say, it's being able to say, "I'll be loving you always."

LC: Well, again, just as I'm able to say, "I've seen the future, brother, it is murder" with an upbeat dance tune, I can say, "I'll be loving you always" with a lot of drunken musicians hammering out the tune around me. If you can find the proper landscape in which you can summon these deep feelings, then I think you're very privileged. I don't know, given just the man and woman in the room, would I be able to come up with that kind of pledge—"I'll be loving you always, with a love that's true always, not for just an hour, not for just a day, not for just a year, but always"? I think we're all familiar at least with the appetite for that kind of pledge, that commitment.

BG: The reason I ask is it seems in your earlier work, when you talked about romantic love, that it was in contention with the creative process. In order to commune with the angels, you had to leave the woman. There doesn't seem so much of that in this work.

LC: Well, there certainly was a quarrel of some kind but I think that in many songs, many poems, it was resolved by the presence of the woman. She allowed you—freed you—to pray and I think it's more that than separation. One hand on her shoulder allowed you to summon other powers with the other hand. The close presence of the woman has always been an element even if it's in terms of tension or debate or as you say, contention, just as I like to use a woman's voice in my recording of song. My voice, such as it is, needs all the help it can get. Besides that, the presence of the female voice allows my voice to speak more clearly.

BG: What do you think you say to women—it might be an unfair question—in your lyrics, in your poems?

LC: I think I've been saying the same thing from the very beginning. We're all in the same boat, we've entered into this quarrel, into this cage, union, and extremely ambiguous circumstance together and we're going to sort it out together. That is why I never thought of myself as a romantic poet because I always was very clear from the beginning that this confrontation involves some serious risks to the versions of oneself.

BG: You mean the confrontation between men and women?

LC: Yeah. And it's always been confrontational. Not in an aggressive sense but in an acknowledging sense that there are some profound differences and it involves serious risks and that these risks are really best acknowledged. And I think that's the tone of most of the stuff and if the love and passion can transgress that mutual acknowledgment then you do have something that takes off. Either it's a song or a poem or the moment. But without that, you've got the moon-in-June school of writing—though my stuff gets close to the moon-in-June school of writing, but I think it's that acknowledgment of the risk that rescues it every time.

BG: There's a song called "Light as the Breeze" in which the woman gives the man in the song a warning where she says, "Drink deeply, pilgrim" . . .

LC: ". . . but don't forget there's still a woman beneath this resplendent chemise."

BG: It seems to me that in your earlier lyrics and poems, the women often were too saintly or they were angels of mercy or compassion. To come right out with that kind of almost feminist warning . . . it seemed like a new voice.

LC: [*Contemplating and then beginning slowly.*] Perhaps I'm suffering from convenient amnesia as to lines from previous songs. . . . I know that in this one I say, "You can drink it or you can nurse it, it doesn't matter how you worship, as long as you're down on your knees." I think that's been my position more or less over the years, and creakily standing up and regretting it and getting down again.

BG: Is it the man who should be down on his knees?

LC: Maybe this is some kind of alibi I'm about to spin, but I've never felt that distant from the woman's position. She's not outside of my intimate experience. I've never felt the woman was an alien creature from my point of view that I had to either overwhelm or glorify. I think that if you've experienced yourself as neither man nor woman—think that anyone who sings about these matters has to have that experience and I think everyone has had the experience, in an embrace you're neither man nor woman—you forget who you are. Once you have experienced yourself as neither man nor woman, when you are reborn into the predetermined form, which you inhabit, you come back with the residue of experience or the residue of wisdom, which enables you to recognize in the other extremely familiar traits.

BG: I'd like to talk about writing here. Especially your novel writing, because you wrote two wildly successful novels that sold over eight hundred thousand copies each, but it's been twenty-six years now since *Beautiful Losers* was published, and I wonder why you never returned to the fiction form.

LC: I got lost in the song. I got very involved in the life of music and the lyric and I went to some quite remote places—at a certain point I was only writing Spenserian stanzas to be set to music. I don't think there's anyone else in the Western world writing Spenserian stanzas with that very intricate verse form. So I got very interested in the whole lyrical form.

BG: Would you consider yourself a writer of songs before a poet?

LC: Yes, I'm a songwriter.

BG: A lot of people who are interested in the word and rhyme and poetry reject rhyme because it feels like an armature and the perfect word to express what you mean might not rhyme. Do you find that?

LC: No. But I don't feel any sense of evangelism about the matter. I think that much of the work that is done today in music and songwriting and verse suffers from this unwillingness to submit yourself to the anvil of rhythm and rhyme. It makes it too easy. When you are compelled to find rhymes and to satisfy rhythms, it makes you run through everything you know about the language. It makes you run through word after word after word and test every idea.

BG: In "Waiting for the Miracle," the miracle is that there is that word, isn't it?

LC: That's right. Young songwriters often ask me for advice and all I know is that if you stick with a song long enough, it will yield, but long enough is way beyond any reasonable estimation of what long enough might be.

I'm not advising this as a *modus operandi* for anybody, but I know that the reason I write is to discover the newness of my mind and the newness of my thought. And that can only be discovered when you submit yourself to this process in which you have to defend the words and the lines and the new ideas. Nothing new arises if you're just allowed to unfold your thought with no tension.

BG: You live in L.A. part of the year, don't you?

LC: Well, I find myself down there a lot and I've been unable to develop a strategy of habitation. Sometimes I'm down there, sometimes I'm in Montreal.

BG: When we up here in Canada think of being a writer in L.A., it seems as if there would be too many distractions, the glamour and the drive-by shootings. Does that affect your work?

LC: I think that L.A. has a very appropriate landscape for my work. It is really, truly an apocalyptic landscape. Geologically, the place is about to fly apart. Socially and politically, we know that it's erupting every two years, there is real social unrest, and many of the writers who've worked there have perceived that this is the place where the destruction of the American psyche is going on in a very discernible manner. I find it a very hospitable place to work.

BG: Stimulating.

LC: It seems to be true. The social contract is fraying. People are not quite certain how to behave with one another. It is up for grabs. I don't like that part of it. Especially since my daughter's been living with me, I really have felt that I'd like to get back to Canada.

BG: That's good. [*Considers for a moment.*] You seem less world-weary than you did thirty years ago.

LC: I'm in better shape now, too. [*Laughs.*]

BG: Whatever else you are, you're undeniably successful. Your albums and your books sell in the hundreds of thousands.

LC: But it often hasn't been that way, and I'm very grateful now, especially that my songs are being revived by very young bands. That's always agreeable to see. Especially the song. You don't mind the book going into the dusty corner, but the song really has an urgency and if it isn't sung, it's nowhere.

BG: To what extent do you think the melancholy image of you, true or not, as the tortured spiritual lover and troubadour has added to or detracted from your success?

LC: I don't know. You live on the front line of your life and as I say, you're kind of dodging the shrapnel and the missiles most of the time. It's very difficult to develop an overall strategy about things or a perspective on your life. I have been tortured, I am tortured, we all are tortured. People are living with a kind of intolerable ambiguity about their lives. When you hear politicians speak, you say to yourself, "They don't seem to have heard the bad news." It develops a terrible schizophrenia in society between the public utterance and private experience. You just give up thinking anybody's going to talk to you again from that public realm. That causes the social contract to fray—you don't know where people stand. Somehow, I felt that part of my job was to own up to this intolerable sense of ambiguity that seems to inform all my activities.

BG: So would you say as much as you can that you are what you write? That you stand by your songs?

LC: I would stand by them. But I've been presenting this rap for a long time, which is a catastrophe has taken place, there's no point in waiting for it, and somehow in the interior plane or the interior landscape a catastrophe has taken place, there is a flood going on.

BG: It's been going on for thirty years?

LC: It's been going on a long time—I don't know when the wave broke the wall. But I do believe we are in this torrent, that the landmarks are down and the lights have gone out and you're holding on to your orange crate in the torrent and somebody goes by holding on to his broken flagstaff. What is the appropriate behavior in this circumstance? Is it to declare yourself a conservative or a liberal or for abortion or against abortion? Those kinds of descriptions seem to be totally irrelevant to the situation. I prefer my descriptions of myself as they have developed over the years in my songs and books. I think that those descriptions are much more appropriate and, yes, I would stand by them.

THE LONELINESS OF THE LONG-SUFFERING FOLKIE

WAYNE ROBINS | November 22, 1992, *Newsday* (Long Island, New York)

Wayne Robins interviewed Cohen in New York City, at Le Parker Meridien Hotel on West 57th Street. "It was a well-focused, totally engaging conversation," he told me. "I hadn't really been a Cohen fan until *The Future*, which is the project we were discussing, so I was very interested in talking about its beguiling combination of pessimism, nihilism, and hope, as well as its full-bodied musical arrangements." —Ed.

On his new album, *The Future*, Leonard Cohen views history's changing currents with more than a little bit of wariness. "Give me back the Berlin Wall / Give me Stalin and St. Paul / I've seen the future, brother, it is murder," he sings in the title song.

While others assumed that the end of the Cold War would signal the triumph of democracy in Eastern Europe, Cohen wasn't so sure. There is a song called "Democracy" in which he sees it coming, all right, "through a hole in the air / From those nights in Tiananmen Square . . . From the fires of the homeless / From the ashes of the gay: Democracy is coming / To the USA."

"I began to write it when the events in Eastern Europe began to indicate there was a democratic resurrection, and the Berlin Wall came down and people were saying, democracy is coming to the East," Cohen said last week in a Midtown [New York] hotel suite. "I was one of those people who weren't entirely convinced that this was going to happen, and that it wasn't going to come about without a tremendous amount of suffering."

From the genocidal Civil War in what was once Yugoslavia to the neo-Nazi-tinged violence against foreigners in Germany, events have proven Cohen's suspicions to be regrettably on the mark. But mixed with caution is the Canadian writer and musician's optimism about America.

"I was not unaware of the ironic impact of saying, 'Democracy is coming to the USA,' but the song is affirmative," he said. "I just can't keep my tongue in my cheek that long. I'm Canadian, and we watch America very carefully. Everybody in the world watches America. And regardless of the skepticism and irony, [wise guy] superiority that most intellectual circles have about America, it is acknowledged that this is where the experiment is taking place, where the races are confronting one another, where the rich and poor are confronting one another, where men and women, the classes . . . this is the great laboratory of democracy."

Cohen's interests are only partly external. The fifty-eight-year-old writer, who divides his time between Montreal and Los Angeles, wrestles with shifting emotional states in "Waiting for the Miracle." "You wouldn't like it baby, you wouldn't like it here / There's not much entertainment, and the critics are severe," he sings in his husky, seductive growl over a spare but lushly melodic musical track.

"[There are] people who are bitten by this particular bug, where meaning has evaporated and significance has dissolved," Cohen said. "Many people now confess to me that they inhabit this kind of landscape, where nothing has much taste. I mean, they're not selling fifty million Prozac pills a week for nothing; we are undergoing some kind of nervous breakdown. And it's from the point of that nervous breakdown and beyond that the song is written. . . . I've been talking about this catastrophe, this interior catastrophe, for a long time. I find a lot more hospitality to this idea now. So all the songs are about that position, but I think treated vigorously, and if I may say so, cheerfully."

The courtly Cohen is dressed so impeccably in a designer suit that he makes the typical *GQ* model look frumpy. Despite his calm bearing and consummate manners, he is no stranger to the apocalyptic emotional struggles his songs describe. *The Future* took four years to finish.

"I tend to get shattered as I bring a project to completion," Cohen said. "I have to discard versions of myself, and versions of the songs, until I can get to a situation where I can defend every word, every line. But that place often involves a real shattering of equanimity, or of balance . . . I have to go to this naked and raw place. And it usually involves the breakdown of my personality, and I flip out. . . . I can't go into crowds, I don't want to leave my house, I don't want to leave my room, I don't want to answer the phone, all my relationships collapse."

When the work is over, Cohen climbs back. "You try slowly to repair your relationships or support system, so you try the Prozac or Deseryl [another antidepressant], or you go to synagogue or the meditation hall, you go back to yoga or start running, whatever repair mode is accessible, you embrace."

Cohen has been the laureate of creative agony since the 1960s, when he was a celebrated triple threat as poet (*The Spice-Box of Earth*), novelist (*Beautiful Losers* and *The Favorite Game*), and singer-songwriter. His songs such as "Suzanne," "Hey, That's No Way to Say Goodbye," and "Bird on the Wire" are folk-pop standards.

Though his recording career went through something of an eclipse in the 1970s, he has come back strong in the last decade. Singer Jennifer Warnes had a surprise bestseller in 1986 with the critically acclaimed *Famous Blue Raincoat*, an album of Cohen material; the often-wry songs of his 1988 album *I'm Your Man* helped generated a renaissance of Cohen's own career. Last year, a number of left-of-center rockers released a tribute album of Cohen songs called *I'm Your Fan*, with appearances by the Pixies, Nick Cave, House of Love, John Cale, and R.E.M., the latter of which contributed a stunning version of "First We Take Manhattan."

Cohen is philosophical about the attention he's receiving from a new generation. "You live with wild dreams of yourself and your own importance that are chronically disappointed, and when some of them aren't you're pleased," he said.

Cohen has never married ("I was able to find ideological justification for my fright, which was developed quite extensively in my young manhood," he said), but has two children. His daughter, eighteen, lives with him in Los Angeles; his son, twenty, attends Syracuse University.

Back in the 1960s, Cohen's sensitive, passionate writing made him a figure of romantic obsession to young educated women, and he is still, to some, an intellectual sex symbol. In retrospect, he finds it amusing that he was the object of such lust.

"It's so curious, because I couldn't get a date," he said. "I couldn't find anybody to have dinner with. By the time that first record came out, which rescued me, I was already in such a shattered situation that I found myself living at the Henry Hudson Hotel on West 57th Street, going to the Morningstar Cafe on Eighth Avenue, trying to find some way to approach the waitress and ask her out. I would get letters of longing from around the world, and I would find myself walking the streets of New York at three in the morning, trying to strike up conversations with the women selling cigarettes in hotels. I think it's always like that. It's never delivered to you."

COHEN CLIP
On His Hydra Home

"I still have my house there that I bought for fifteen hundred dollars in 1960. My kids still use it. But it's a long way to go to find yourself not very far from the place you've left. When I got there, there was no electricity or running water. It was a very different kind of place. Not that I fault anyone for wanting to have linoleum and electricity as opposed to rough stone floors and chopping firewood. But it's not that far away anymore."
—from a sidebar to Wayne Robins's article, *Newsday*, November 22, 1992

GROWING OLD PASSIONATELY

ALAN JACKSON | November 22, 1992, the *Observer* (London)

"I was excited to meet Leonard Cohen," Alan Jackson told me, "as I'd had his albums with me through my teenage years and through university and I'd even read a novel of his. What I wasn't prepared for was just what a naturally charming man he is, in the purest and most positive sense of the term.

"He was doing a full day of press and promotion in a London hotel suite, so time for individual interviews was limited," Jackson recalled. "Mine lasted just half an hour. He was dressed formally in a well-cut dark suit, dark shirt, and tie and had impeccable, almost formal manners—something you don't often encounter in celebrities or public figures.

"What I particularly recall was how intense the encounter was. He invited me to sit in a chair very close to his and he maintained eye contact throughout, concentrating on the questions, deliberating over the answers, and giving me for those thirty minutes the impression that the interview was of real importance to him—and that I was also. It was a feeling you don't often get from interviewees, and I've been talking to famous people for a living for over twenty-five years now. He really was charm personified.

"It was a time in his life when he was involved romantically with the actress Rebecca De Mornay. Cohen has often been dubbed 'Laughing Len' in the British media and there had been some expressions of mystification in the press here about how 'Laughing Len' (an ironic take on the fact that a lot of people consider him the epitome of misery and melancholy) had managed to attract this much younger and beautiful woman. After meeting him, it made perfect sense to me. I could completely see how he could work his magic on anyone that he chose." —Ed.

Leonard Cohen recently walked along a street crowded with college students while in the company of a writer friend, a man in his midseventies.

"We passed a café. Outside were a number of lovely young women, and suddenly he grabbed my arm and said with an urgency, 'Leonard, don't believe anyone who tells you you're not going to feel something about this matter when you're older.'"

A still handsome and charismatic fifty-eight himself, Cohen smiles at the memory and notes wryly, "How you adjust yourself to that fact is something else, of course, and certainly we would hope that we civilize ourselves as we grow older. But the idea that your creative impetus is over by thirty, that you immolate yourself on this pyre of energy and sexuality and can then go back to cleaning up and doing the dishes . . . it just ain't so. The fire continues to burn fiercely as you get older. It's passionate."

Although evidence of this enduring life force is everywhere in his lyrics, non-devotees remain unfamiliar with Cohen the Sensualist. Instead there is the lingering stereotype of Cohen the Miserablist, a hangdog, beat-generation character forever intoning depressive lyrics in some twilight zone. But the man himself, soberly suited and hunched over strong coffee in a Mayfair hotel suite, proves a conversational delight: funny, sage, generous, and warm.

No wonder, then, that he remains the muse of folk-rock princesses such as Suzanne Vega and Jennifer Warnes, whose superior LP of Cohen interpretations, *Famous Blue Raincoat*, released in 1986, helped to refocus attention on his then-neglected catalog of songs. He deflects the idea that he is king of a court of gifted women admirers, however ("What a lovely idea . . ."), and will confirm reports that he is romantically involved with the actress Rebecca De Mornay, to whom his new LP, *The Future*, is dedicated, only in the most decorous of tones—"There is a formal arrangement between us, yes."

Appropriately enough, the album—his first for four years—reads and sounds like the work of a man in love. Its concerns are more than merely romantic and interpersonal, however. "Democracy," the centerpiece, is a six-verse epic on the changing political mood of America, and was distilled from an original eighty verses. "It ain't coming to us European-style, a concentration camp behind the smile," says Cohen, snatching a discarded segment from memory. "It ain't coming from the East, with its temporary feast, as Count Dracula comes strolling down the aisle . . ."

Even in its truncated, recorded form, the song is an intense piece of work, and one that would have been seen as highly prophetic had it been released immediately after it was written in late 1988. At that point, Cohen stopped work on the album to help nurse his teenage son back from a near-fatal road accident, then found it hard to reengage with the project. "There was the normal, dismal process of assembling and rejecting, medication, heavy drinking, giving up smoking, changing girlfriends, y'know . . . all the stuff that goes into these things," he says of the ensuing hiatus.

Reading the lyrics of "Democracy" before playing the song, it is impossible not to be struck by Cohen's still-developing talent as a writer—each word and line is perfectly weighted to give a momentum independent of any melody or arrangement, each image makes its point with astonishing precision. "You've no idea how that is music to my ears," says Cohen of the observation.

"I don't do anything else—this is the front line for me. I try and keep my human associations going, but this is my pledge and my consecration. And though it's not necessary to talk about it in such highfalutin' terms, it's all that's going on for me. I'm a miniaturist. I'm trying to do what the microchip has done—find a form in which deep experience can be manifested with brevity, so that a six-minute song can have the qualities of a novel, can really take you on a trip. And I think I'm on the edge of doing it."

The audience for Cohen's current experimentation may well be his biggest for twenty years. He admits that he felt shut out by the music industry between the years 1972 and 1985, and says that it felt like a near-religious experience when record companies began to return his calls. He is sincerely grateful too for all the signs of interest in his work by other artists, not only last year's hip *I'm Your Fan*, on which R.E.M., the Pixies, John Cale, and Ian McCulloch covered classics from his songbook, but also such ponderous if well-meant tributes as Neil Diamond's doleful "Suzanne."

"Although I kept working, I was effectively out of the business and a kind of joke for quite a long time, so my critical faculties still go into immediate but grateful suspension the minute anyone covers one of my songs," he says. "It's only recently that things have turned around for me, so I'm still not interested in if it's any good or not—I'm just thrilled. But out of everything I would have to single out Jennifer's album. It's such a perfect and dedicated interpretation of my songs that there's nothing for me to do but tip my head in awe."

With perfect manners and a still-passionate spirit, Cohen is committed to continuing his quest to refine his songwriting skills further. "There is a wisdom appropriate to each age of man, and the early wisdoms all embrace notions of glorious finality, of burning beautifully—not a bad idea.

"But after a certain point in life, the allure of all that fades," he says. "Now that I'm in advanced middleage I've discovered a certain buoyancy. Life weighs heavily upon one's shoulders, but then you find that, with a certain kind of shrug, it will just lift off for a moment or two."

He drinks deeply from his coffee cup and then admonishes himself for such relative optimism. "Having spoken in such a cavalier fashion I will, of course, be smitten with an acute clinical depression very shortly," he says, with a short, sharp smile.

LEONARD COHEN: THE LORD BYRON OF ROCK AND ROLL

KAREN SCHOEMER | November 29, 1992, the *New York Times* (New York)

"I was trying to play a part," recalled Karen Schoemer of her interview with Cohen. "I'd listened to a lot of his albums and was wallowing in the Byronic romanticism I thought he represented. It was method journalism. He was charming and played his own part well.

"My connection with him was learned—it was secondhand," Schoemer told me. "I had older friends whose lives had been affected by him so I was going on their experiences rather than my own. He represented an idea to me, a post-Dylan hippie intellectualism, and that's what I was trying to investigate. I wanted to bring it to life, coax it out of the past. He was cooperative, a great sport." —Ed.

Leonard Cohen has stopped to smell a rose. He was in the middle of a train of thought, sitting at a table in a piano lounge of a ritzy hotel in midtown Manhattan. But the lure of blood red petals, the possible prick of thorn and the whiff of romance have proven irresistible. He leans forward, bends the stem toward him, and breathes. The fragile petals contrast sharply with the chiseled age of his face. The strong reds and greens accentuate his iron-gray hair and tailored charcoal suit.

Mr. Cohen is a man made for such poetic moments. Songwriter, icon of sixties folk, sometime novelist, and perennial sage, he is in town to talk about his new album, *The Future*, his first record since the critically lauded *I'm Your Man* in 1988. He says he enjoys doing interviews, but he says it with a bit more flourish: "I'm very happy to cooperate with the convention of promoting the record."

Mr. Cohen speaks like a poet. He culls a phrase like "blacken pages" where lesser mortals might simply say "write"; he has a store of aphorisms at his beck and call. "If I knew where songs came from I would go there more often," he says at one point. He is prone to quoting poetry at will, although the poet he most likes to quote is himself. "Sail on, sail on, oh mighty ship of state / To the shores of need, past the reefs of greed, through the squalls of hate," he rejoinders on the general topic of America's post-election political climate, borrowing lyrics from his song "Democracy."

And Mr. Cohen, who is fifty-eight years old, has lived the life of a poet, full of deeds and escapades that qualify for the realm of the extraordinary. Born in Montreal, he played in a country band called the Buckskin Boys when he was a teenager. He was already embroiled in the bohemian life by the midfifties, when he published his first volume of poetry, *Let Us Compare Mythologies*. He spent several years living on the Greek island Hydra, and in the midsixties, he became part of the Greenwich Village folk scene, hanging out with Bob Dylan and Joni Mitchell and releasing dark and voluptuous albums like *Songs of Leonard Cohen* and *Songs from a Room*. His lyrics chronicled affairs with women both mysterious and infamous. "Suzanne" contained the consummate line "You've touched her perfect body with your mind." "Chelsea Hotel No. 2," from the 1974 album *New Skin for the Old Ceremony,* was about Janis Joplin.

He has even more anecdotes up his sleeve. Out of the blue, Mr. Cohen is liable to begin a tale by saying, "You know, I was a close friend of Michael X, who was the leader of the black Muslims in England. . . ."

After New York, Mr. Cohen lived for a year on a fifteen-hundred-acre homestead in Franklin, Tennessee, rented for seventy-five dollars a month. "Ah, that was a very pleasant period of my life," he says wistfully. "There was a shack—a well-equipped shack, but not much more than that—beside a stream. There were peacocks and peahens. They used to come to my cabin every morning. I'd feed them. I had one of those centennial rifles that Remington put out, I think, in '67." He pauses. "When was this country founded? Seventy-six?" He seems somewhat dismayed that mathematics could interfere with a colorful detail of his story. "Anyway, I had some kind of centennial rifle. I would amuse myself by shooting icicles on the far side of the creek."

In the midseventies, a volatile partnership with the legendary producer Phil Spector resulted in the album *Death of a Ladies' Man*. Since the eighties, Mr. Cohen has matured into a hero of the disaffected musical intelligentsia. Last year, younger fringe artists like Nick Cave, Lloyd Cole, and Ian McCulloch contributed to a Leonard Cohen tribute album, *I'm Your Fan*, released by Atlantic. Like a handful of his peers—Tom Waits, Marianne Faithfull—Mr. Cohen is revered to a level that renders his modest commercial success irrelevant. He is a singular entity: a kind of rock-and-roll Lord Byron, a cultural scholar in the unlikely medium of pop.

Mr. Cohen has been working consistently on *The Future* since the release of *I'm Your Man*. "Some people write good songs in the back of taxicabs," he remarks. "I wish I were in that tribe." Throughout the album, the time he spent is evident. Never has Mr. Cohen's low, groaning voice sounded quite so world-weary and edged with disgust. Never has his outlook seemed quite so grim. The song "The Future" pledges that whatever lies ahead is unquestionably uglier than the dismal state of things today; "Democracy" is an iconoclast's lament on contemporary politics.

These songs, Mr. Cohen says, were "occasioned by the collapse of the Berlin Wall, which all my friends rejoiced about. I was the only dour person at the party, saying, 'This isn't that good news. This is going to produce a great deal of suffering. You're going to settle for the Berlin Wall when you see what's coming next.'" The tension in his voice rises. "You're going to settle for a hole in the ozone layer. You'll settle for crack. You'll settle for social unrest. You'll settle for the L.A. riots. This is kindergarten stuff compared to the homicidal impulse that is developing in every breast!"

Mr. Cohen stops short, catching himself being carried away on the waves of despair. "Oh, forgive me for going on like that," he sighs. "I have these gloomy visions of things."

He finds the subject of America's new president [Bill Clinton] somewhat more calming. "I'm a Canadian," he says, "and Canadians are educated to watch America very closely—just as women are educated to watch men very closely—because what America does affects us. My song 'Democracy,' which was begun in '88 or '89, was certainly not designed as promotional material for the Democratic Party. I believe my songs last as long as the Volvo, which is about thirty years. So I don't want to identify this song with this administration, which may last eight years. I've still got twenty-two years.

"But of course, as a Canadian, I wish the administration well," he continues. "I can summon many blessings for the man, and especially for his wife, whom I find immensely attractive."

As the evening wears on, the lights in the hotel lounge are brought down a notch, and Mr. Cohen's reflection turns inward. "I find that more and more I inhabit the front line of my own life, with missiles and shrapnel flying through the air," he says. "You really don't have the opportunity to develop much of a strategy about things. Certainly not about your career, and not even about your loves or dreams. So there's a certain urgency to the moment, and how to negotiate from one instance to the next."

A blonde woman in a close-fitting gold dress sits down at the piano and begins to sing. "They say that falling in love is wonderful / It's wonderful, so they say . . ." Mr. Cohen falls silent, listening. Gently and abstractly, he fingers the rose.

COHEN CLIP
On His State of Mind

"A pessimist is somebody who is waiting for the rain. Me, I'm already wet. I don't wait for the rain to fall. We are in the catastrophe. There's no point in waiting for the catastrophe. Everybody knows it. You know it's the flood. I mean it's not 'when I'm gone, I don't care what happens.' It's 'the deluge is here and I care what happens.'"

—from interview with Michel Field, *Le Cercle de Minuit*, France 2 TV, December 1992

COHEN CLIP
On Surviving Amid Desolation

"My songs are about issues that appear to be widespread but are in fact all funneled down into songs about how I can survive amid the desolation. It's about me. How am I going to make it through? How can I fortify those close to me? Look, there's this flood I've been talking about for twenty years now, and it's wiped away everything moral, spiritual, political, every damn thing. All I'm asking is, 'What is the appropriate behavior in these circumstances?' When you're hanging onto a piece of orange crate and people are floating away and going under all around you, are you really gonna give a fuck about the conservative/liberal divide? No! Are you really gonna talk about Communist vs. capitalist? No! Are you really gonna waste time debating Shiite vs. Sunni? Only if you're stupid! And as for the rainforests, is that really what's important? I think not. We're missing the point."

—from "Heavy Cohen," by Cliff Jones, *Rock CD*, December 1992

COHEN CLIP
On What He Is

"I'm not even a novelist. I'm not even a poet. I'm a songwriter. Eventually, you realize you're not going to be doing anything else. You're not going to be leading the social movement. You're not going to be the light of your generation. You're not going to be many of the things you thought you might be. You're this guy sitting in front of the table in the good parts of the day, and crawling around on the carpet in the bad parts. That's what you're doing. You're writing songs for the popular market. . . . Maybe you have a dream that they last for a while."

—from "Life of a Lady's Man," by Brian D. Johnson,
Maclean's (Canada), December 7, 1992

COHEN CLIP
On Happiness

"I think it would be very incautious to declare yourself a happy man. There are a lot of forces that immediately are animated when someone makes that statement and you usually get creamed within seconds. So I'll refrain from that kind of proclamation. But I can't complain. I find the whole thing very workable."

—from "Rebirth of a Ladies' Man," by Brendan Kelly,
Financial Post (Toronto), December 12, 1992

COHEN CLIP

On His Favorite Song

"When people ask me, 'What's your favorite song?' I say [Fats Domino's] 'Blueberry Hill.' 'I found my thrill on Blueberry Hill / The moon stood still on Blueberry Hill.' That's as good as it gets, as far as I know. You know everything about that moment. You know, you're continually seesawing back and forth between the secular and the spiritual until from time to time you hit it right. It's there on 'Blueberry Hill,' or 'Ol' Man River' from Ray Charles."

—from "Sincerely, L. Cohen," by Brian Cullman,
Details for Men (US), January 1993

COHEN CLIP

On Songwriting

"I've only learned one thing writing songs, and that is, if you stay with it long enough, the song will yield. But 'long enough' is beyond any reasonable length of what long enough might suggest to you. You might think it's a few months—it might be a year or two. . . . The work of it seems to be involved with rejecting every version of the song that is too easy. And then you read it, and it is kind of a surprise, because it's a position you couldn't have come to through any other process. It doesn't involve a slogan; you even transcend your own politics. You burn away those versions of yourself, your courage, and your modesty until you get something irreducible, that lowest guy on the food chain shouting, 'They're gonna hear from me.'"

—from "Painstaking Effort Pays Off in Leonard Cohen's *Future*," by Tom Moon, *Philadelphia Inquirer*, January 4, 1993

COHEN CLIP

On His Son's Car Accident

"A lot of things happened during the recording of this album [*The Future*]. My son had a very serious car smash and I spent four months beside him in the hospital. That upset the process. A child being hurt like that is the parent's nightmare. It calls on resources you never knew you had. He was badly hurt and when he perceived how badly hurt he was it represented a real assault on his morale. You're ready to deal with your own disasters but not someone else's. When I saw his courage that's where I drew my courage from."

—from "Hello, I Must Be Cohen," by Gavin Martin, *New Musical Express* (UK), January 9, 1993

COHEN CLIP

On Having Children

"I never wanted them, to tell you the truth, at the beginning. For a long time, I felt I'd been maneuvered into it and probably had been. I didn't like the idea. First of all, kids are the only event that moves you out of center stage. I'm not just talking for a performer, I mean in your own life. It's the only thing that ever happens to you where you stop thinking of yourself as the star of the whole play. The demand and the urgency that kids present is unavoidable. It's the only time in your life that you stop thinking about yourself, so I didn't like it. I didn't like that at all. Of course, you love the kids, goo-goo and everything else, but I really didn't like the maintenance. But I'm sure glad I had them because they are about the best company I have in my life."

—from "The D-Files: Leonard Cohen," radio interview by David Fanning, RTE (Ireland), January 21, 1993

COHEN CLIP

On His Musical Resurrection

"I started to get the news that I was being resurrected from my daughter, who was about fourteen at the time. She was telling me: 'You know, Dad, a lot of garage bands are playing your stuff.'"

—from "Leonard Cohen . . . What's Your Problem? Doom and Gloom," by Patrick Humphries, *Vox*, February 1993

COHEN CLIP

On His One Extravagance

"As one's family grows and one's sense of responsibility grows, yes, you need more money, but I've always been drawn by the voluptuousness of austerity. I would say that the sole extravagance that I indulge myself in is caviar. Unfortunately, I have developed I won't say a need, but a taste for caviar."

—from "The Joking Troubadour of Gloom," by Tim Rostron, the *Daily Telegraph* (London), April 26, I993

THE FUTURE

ALBERTO MANZANO | May 1993, Interview | Spring 1993, *El Europeo* (Spain)

Though a 1997 best-of package included two new songs, 1992's *The Future* turned out to be the last collection of fresh material that Cohen would release for nine years. But that doesn't mean he disappeared from public view—at least not right away. In 1993, in fact, he conducted at least as many interviews as he had in the previous year.

"Leonard had arrived in Madrid to promote his new album, *The Future*," Alberto Manzano told me. "I took the opportunity to call the Spanish singer Enrique Morente, with whom I was preparing a record of versions of Leonard's songs in flamenco style called *Omega*. Enrique didn't hesitate in rushing out to meet him and I introduced them to each other. We talked at length in the bar at the Palace Hotel, where the poet Federico Garcia Lorca used to have a few drinks when he was in Madrid. Leonard's eyes had a special shine as he smiled faintly. He was delighted with it all.

"The next day," Manzano continued, "we went to the Spanish TV studios to record a play-back of the song 'Closing Time.' I didn't like it very much. It was too long and rushed. I told Leonard that it was not a song that was representative of the album. 'Marketing stuff, Alberto,' he replied." —Ed.

Alberto Manzano: The hummingbird appears on the front cover of your new album, *The Future*, but it had already appeared in that other album of 1979, *Recent Songs*. What has the hummingbird been doing all these years?

Leonard Cohen: When I was writing these songs, the hummingbird would come every morning outside my window, so it came here to rescue the heart from the handcuffs. You've been the only one that's noticed it was on my other album.

AM: Is the idea of the cover that of the spirit setting the heart free of its chains?

LC: Something like that. I'm not quite sure what it means. These three symbols, the bird, the heart, and the handcuffs . . . I worked with them in different ways and finally I gave them to an artist in Los Angeles— Michael Petit—and we developed this symbol for the record. Something to do with liberation, something to do with imprisonment.

AM: The song that serves as the title for the album shows a terrible apocalyptic vision of the future. It takes up, once again, the spirit of Isaiah and the message of earlier songs like "First We Take Manhattan" and "Everybody Knows."

LC: I don't have any biblical ambitions and I know that whatever life I'm leading is beyond the control of my personality, beyond the direction of my intentions. I think as you get older you understand that you're in the grip of forces that are greater than the ones you believe you are commanding. Whatever role you tend to be living is fuelled, it's running on its own, an energy with its own motion. So I don't pretend to emulate a prophet and I don't pretend to emulate one that's not a prophet. I just go to where the energy is in my own landscape.

You're just living your own life and where do you go when you want to speak? Where do you go when you want to sing? You have to find where the well is, or where the food is, and when I'm hungry or thirsty I try to find where to go so that I can eat and I can drink. And I often go to places where the landscape is burning, where the city is burning, where the sea is coming over the shore. That's where I go to eat and where I go to sing. I don't know if it has any meaning for anybody else. But the rest of the landscape is very quiet and very dull, very boring. And I feel chained there and imprisoned there. I feel I cannot speak there. Maybe I should stay there and not speak, and not sing. But when I want to sing I have to go to where the sea is flooding, where the city is burning.

AM: In "Democracy," your other political song on the album, you convert the "Sermon on the Mount" into a good example for the democratic movement.

LC: It's a good example in the sense that it's a mystery. Just like democracy is a mystery. Democracy is the great religion of the West. Probably the greatest religion because it affirms other religions; probably the greatest culture because it affirms other cultures. But it's based on faith, it's based on appetite for fraternity, it's based on love, and therefore it shares the characteristics of a religious movement. It's also like a religion in that it's never really been tried.

Nobody is ready to surrender to a democratic heart. Nobody is willing to affirm the equality of all phenomena. Nobody is willing to say the night is the same as the day, and they both rest on zero. Nobody is willing to say that the black is the same as the white when it rests on zero, or the good is the same as the bad when it rests on zero. Nobody is willing to really embrace a democratic vision, but the vision is there and we move towards it.

The Sermon on the Mount has the same mysterious quality. The words resonate in our hearts and in our minds but it's impossible to really grasp it: "Blessed are the meek for they shall inherit the Earth." "Blessed are the poor in spirit for they shall see God." These words resonate with possibility, with potential in our minds, but nobody can grasp the meaning of that because we see that the meek are crushed underfoot, they don't inherit the Earth; we see that the poor in spirit are going to mental hospitals, they don't see God, or if they do, they see terrible versions of God. So like democracy, fraternity, equality, liberty, they resonate in the heart. But when it comes down to individual choices, we're very unwilling to surrender our status, to surrender our position in regard to the others. And we're frightened by the notion that we might have to share our room with strangers; we might have to share our heart with strangers, to share our life with strangers, with those poorer than us.

So we have this resonance where the basis of our religious teaching [is]—"blessed are the poor," "blessed are the meek." But where are they? Do we want them with us? Do we really want the poor in our restaurants? Do we want to share our jackets with the beggars? They resonate in our minds, and they create this notion, this tension, this direction towards this possibility that we call Christianity, this possibility that we call democracy . . .

AM: Do you think there is hope for this utopian human democracy?

LC: I think we are on the edge of a democratic experiment. I think it has begun. I think that the idea has escaped into the world. It becomes a kind of necessity that is stronger than hope, and it will result in a tremendous amount of human suffering like all other ideas that get into the air like an infection. I don't know whether there's an absolute quality to democracy, or to Islam or to Christianity, but it's like fuel—it makes people act, whether it's for the good or the bad, I couldn't possibly decide. But we see that the populations of the world are no longer content with their previous positions in regard to authority. Democracy makes everybody nervous.

AM: Up till now some of the implications of the American democracy in the world have not been very attractive. What's your opinion of this "soft revolution" which [President Bill] Clinton is leading?

LC: A lot of people feel very hopeful about the victory of the Democratic candidate. People have said to me that he's listened to the music, he's smoked the grass, he's had the long hair, he was born after World War II, he has the social credentials, the cultural credentials, to manifest this vision. Whether he will or nor depends on a whole number of variables that nobody can predict, but he has produced hope in people's hearts.

I, of course, as you know, am not given to hope. It is not one of the emotions that I embrace very enthusiastically, but you can summon your blessings for the administration. Of course you hope that things will turn out. There are so many social problems in America that have to be addressed. One of the wonderful things about America is that democracy is being tested in a way it's not being tested in other parts of the world.

AM: You say love is one of the foundations of democracy, but how does one feed it and eliminate all the garbage that covers it?

LC: Love is the foundation of democracy, but it's very important for people to have a certain kind of education. Which we're not getting. Democracy affirms the equality of phenomena. It affirms the equality of the white and the black, and the poor and the rich. It's filled with affirmations, with validations for the fragment of society, but unless the fragments of society can experience themselves as a something other than the fragments, then democracy will fail.

It is important to experience yourself as a man, but also it's important to experience yourself as neither a man nor a woman. It's important to experience yourself as a black or as a white, but it's important to experience yourself as neither black nor white. So while democracy affirms black and white and man and woman, it hasn't yet matured to a position where it affirms a position that is neither black nor white, that is neither man nor woman.

It hints at this wisdom. That's what we love about it. It hints that there is a transcendent category that is neither black nor white nor man nor woman, nor rich nor poor, that there's a transcendent category. But it hasn't yet developed the educational institutions for people to experience themselves as neither man nor woman, as neither black nor white, as neither East nor West, as neither Christian nor Islam nor Jew. It hasn't developed the educational institutions to mature the wisdom of zero. But we hope it will. And we work towards that goal, each in our own way.

AM: I remember that poem of yours which said, "Any system you contrive without us will be brought down." It was published in the early seventies in the book *The Energy of Slaves*, although then it seemed to have been written by an anarchist.

LC: Anarchism represents a faith that human beings can develop their own contracts with each other without having these contracts imposed from above, and that relates to this position that I was speaking about that affirms, that validates the man, the woman, the black, the white—that affirms the wisdom that understands that the black and the white, the man and the woman, the Christian, the Jew, the Muslim; that the basis of this expression is zero, that there's a fundamental experience that's neither black nor white, nor man nor woman. Anarchism affirms or hints or points or believes or hopes that there is a position that everyone instinctively understands, that allows them to make contracts with each other on a personal and rational and loving basis that does not need to be ordered from above. So it's always an attractive position, especially to the young.

AM: You definitely seem to be thrown into a sort of political crusade in your latest albums. Why this obsessive and urgent return to revolutionary formalities?

LC: Well, when I feel the fascist arise in my own heart, I say, "Ah, the fascist is here again." In me. The fascist can deal with the situation, the situation is chaotic and the fascist arises, and I like him; he looks good. "First we take Manhattan, then we take Berlin." The extremist arises, the terrorist, who's unwilling to deal on the democratic plane, on the parliamentary plane, unwilling to enter into the debate with all his voices. The leader arises with his black shirt and silver buckle and his revolver on his belt and he says, "I'm going to take charge. I don't want to hear what everybody is saying. I don't want to listen to any more arguments. I don't want to hear any more positions."

And that fascist, that hero, arises and I find him attractive and I also find him menacing, and I deal with him. And then the other terrorist arises from the left, who says, "None of your institutions are worth protecting. Don't talk to me about order, don't talk to me about family, don't talk to me about your beautiful monuments and your works of art and your museums and your restaurants and your hotels. I don't want to hear about those things—they're all going down. There may be something good. I'm sorry about it. If a child is going to be burnt, forgive me. The thing produces only suffering, the whole affair deserves to be blown up, and I'm going to blow it up." And he stands up, and he's young and he's beautiful and his shirt is open, and he's wearing rags and he has a bomb in his hand, and he throws it. And I have to deal with him. So in periods like the ones we're in, all of those figures arise, and they arise very powerfully and I deal with them, and that's how this record was written, in dealing with those figures that spoke so powerfully to me during this period.

AM: So the album seems to move between those two poles, represented by "Democracy" and "The Future." That is, the vision of democracy coming "in amorous array," as you say in that song, and on the other hand, a maddened futuristic panorama.

LC: Yeah, I think it does, although there is no strategy. These are the songs that were saved out of the shipwreck. There were lots of songs I was working on. One was called "Blue Alert," one was called "My Secret Life."

None of them survived. [*In fact, "In My Secret Life" surfaced on 2001's* Ten New Songs *while "Blue Alert" became the title track of a Cohen-pro-*

duced 2006 album by Anjani Thomas, who was by then his lover. —Ed.]
These were the ones that survived, and at the end of three, four years you
say, "What have I got? How have I wasted this time? What have I been
working on?" And you see what you have, and it generally has some kind
of truth, some kind of coherence, but it doesn't begin with a strategy. But
yes, you either have "The Future" or you have "Democracy." Somehow
these two possibilities set up a tension, or you have a kind of philosophical background, a compassionate background like the song "Anthem,"
which says it doesn't matter whether you have "The Future" or whether
you have "Democracy," "there is a crack in everything," this world is not
perfect. The central myth of our culture is the expulsion from the Garden
of Eden.

Nobody wants to believe the central myth of our culture is that we've
been expelled from the Garden of Eden, and this world is the manifestation of a fall. We fall from birth into death, from dream into failure, from
health into sickness. This is the situation. We're not in Paradise. Nobody
wants to accept that. There's a great black blues verse that goes like this:
"Everybody wants to laugh, nobody wants to cry / Everybody wants to go
to heaven, nobody wants to die."

So this culture refuses to affirm death. And it is the central myth of
our culture, both the Crucifixion and the expulsion from Paradise, but
we refuse to affirm that we have been expelled from Paradise, and we
develop utopian theories—socialism, fascism, democracy—to bring us
back to Paradise. But there is a crack in everything, because this is the
realm of the crack, the realm of failure, the realm of death, and unless
we affirm failure and death, we're going to be very unhappy. The more
we affirm death, the happier we get. The more we affirm failure, the more
successful we get.

AM: On this album I miss finding a formally religious song, which you
usually include in your recordings—songs like "Hallelujah" or "The
Guests." Is this because your spiritual thirst has been quenched?

LC: I suppose my thirst has been satisfied. It's not a thirst, but . . . I know
what you mean. I miss that in this record also, but that's the only record I
could produce at the time and I think it's . . . an old soldier putting on his

uniform and his medals and his cane and walking across the battlefield with as much strengthened dignity as he can gather just before he falls down. I feel there's something brave about the record, something poignant. I think it's a record that I can forgive myself for having produced.

AM: I'm also missing some more personal songs on this album . . .

LC: Yes, I think I should write some very personal songs now. My song "My Secret Life" was really about my secret life, but I couldn't manifest it. I couldn't finish it. I'll try to go back to work on that song. My song "Blue Alert" also examines the intoxication of love, of sexual love. I hope my next record will have that very personal feeling to it.

AM: Still referring to that kind of spiritual song in your work, one would say that they exude a certain "saintly" quality. What do you think about that?

LC: I don't know what to say to that. I always loved the music that is called holy, the cantorial music of the church and of the synagogue, I always loved that music. I don't know what the quality of it is, but I think it's the word we use—holy—to describe the quality, but . . . I don't know what to say about it. I think maybe they take place in a moral landscape where there's something to be won and something to be lost. I think that gives the impression of some kind of spiritual struggle going on.

AM: Your last book, *Book of Mercy*, seems to be a book of prayer in essence. Is prayer a way of finding silence and peace for you?

LC: Prayer is a good way. Swimming is a good way. Making love is a good way. Dancing is a good way. But the real prayer is when none is praying. Every religion has a technology to produce the silent one in which the father and the mother have dissolved, in which the man and the woman have dissolved, in which night and day have dissolved, and the silent one arises, the silent sage arises. Every religion has a technology that arises to produce this experience. After this experience, when the ordinary self is reborn, it's born with the residue of this experience and can deal more compassionately and more sensitively and more intelligently with the other elements that arise with him, that are born with him. When the silent one arises in the heart, he embraces the whole world. He embraces God, he embraces the Devil, and not one ant is left out of this embrace; not one atom is left out of this embrace when the silent one arises.

AM: For many years you have practiced Zen meditation. Do you think that path has manifested itself in your songs?

LC: That's right. I don't know any other form of meditation because I've never studied any other form. I met a man twenty-five years ago and I liked what he said, and I liked who he was and I began to study with him. His name was Roshi Sasaki. He was a roshi; that is a teacher in the Rinzai tradition of Zen. And I suppose if he had been a professor of physics in Heidelberg I would have learned German and studied physics, but he happened to be an old monk, so I began to study with him in his own terms.

And that was in a meditation hall on a mountain near Los Angeles, Mount Baldy. And I don't know if I've made any progress and I don't know if there's any progress to be made. I know that I like to go there often and sit there, especially in the mornings with the other monks. I like the smell of the incense. I like the quiet, the smell of ozone in the air. I like the fraternity of the other monks and nuns. For the past few years I've stopped trying to place my mind anywhere in the meditation hall. I merely work on my songs, so I'm probably doing something inappropriate. I just follow my songs and I work on the rhymes and the lines when I sit there in the morning and the evening.

AM: From what you say, it seems to have to do more with the person than the doctrine. Knowing your close relationship with Roshi, one could come to the conclusion that he has taken on the figure of your father. You have always had friends older than yourself . . .

LC: I don't know anymore. I've forgotten who he is. I've forgotten what he's teaching. We became friends. But I think you could look at things that way. That's a popular style of thinking of things today, a psychological style. Sometimes I take care of Roshi; he seems like my child, not like my father. So yes, he's an older man, and I've always had older friends, but I've always had younger friends. So it's difficult to apply these explanations, but I wouldn't resist it. The guide, your spiritual friend, sometimes mother, sometimes brother, sometimes child. The spiritual guide does not take on a specific persona. In fact, the whole essence of a spiritual guide is to present to you a self that is not fixed. A good spiritual guide will never become solid in your life; he will present the other possibility of a relationship that is not solid, is not fixed.

AM: On one occasion you said that Roshi was the only person from whom you could learn something.

LC: Well, maybe I said that but it isn't true. You can learn from many people. You of course are continually learning from your friends. And if they're good friends, they are always calling you on something. They stop you from going too far and they stop you from not going far enough. If you've got good friends, you can depend on them to tell you what your situation is at any time, but also with a friend you forget who they are. It's just someone you're very comfortable with. And it's more on the level of friendship now that I see Roshi. Of course, I know that he's a great teacher but I've given up learning from Roshi and I think he's given up teaching me, so now we just eat together.

AM: I've heard you have been helping Roshi to open some meditation centers in the States.

LC: I'm now one of the older people around, so it's natural that I participate in a small way in helping the community keep going.

AM: When you began meditating in the seventies, you recorded two of your most dramatic and desolate albums, *Songs from a Room* and *Songs of Love and Hate*. At that time, you even became known as "the most powerful nonchemical depressive in the world." In your case, the depression, the sadness, seemed to be a great source of creativity.

LC: You live with it like a friend, and you know that if you make too many mistakes this friend is going to sit on your head. So it's not something that is objective. It is like a shadow that you live with, and it never goes away, and you just begin to conduct yourself in a certain manner so that it does not overwhelm you. It's like living with eczema, a skin disease: if you eat the wrong things, your skin will become red and swollen, and you won't be able to move, you won't be able to sit, and you won't be able to lie down. That's the way it is with depression. If you absorb the wrong thing, you'll become too uncomfortable to continue.

AM: There is a certain opinion about you that says that the more you suffer, the better you are, creatively speaking.

LC: It's a curious process. I don't pretend to understand it. I know that when I begin seriously working on some song, I become very uncomfortable with myself, and I have to start discarding versions of myself that make me uncomfortable. . . . When I hear [one of these versions] speaking to me, I say, "That's a lie, you have to go," but he doesn't want to go. I have to make him go. And then the next one arrives and says, "I am you and this is what I think." "No, you're not me and you'll have to go too." So each one of these figures arises and they have to be killed, or they're dying when they speak to me, and that's uncomfortable. You come to the place where you get the language you can accept, and you can become comfortable. It seems to be a long way, and a very stupid way of doing things. But that's my way.

AM: People used to say, "When you feel really bad, there's nothing better than Leonard Cohen."

LC: I appreciate that connection, and I think that is very valid. The slaves have always come to a moment where they can no longer be slaves, and they rise up. The blacks come to a certain point where they can no longer be treated as blacks, and they rise up. The women come to a point where they can no longer be treated as women and they insist that their situation must be revised. They ask for new versions of themselves; they ask it from themselves and they ask it from others.

I think the next category of slaves to arise will be those who suffer from depression. And I think this is a real, universal constituency that transcends borders and cultures, and the next great uprising, and perhaps the one we're waiting for, is when the depressed—to call them by a term that does not really describe them—the hungry ones will arise.

We don't have the luxury yet to arise, because we know that our condition is not yet as urgent as the condition of those who are really hungry, the condition of the ones who are hungry in the body. But somewhere along the line the next hungry ones will arise and demand a revision of their predicament, from themselves and from the others. And in some way I hint at this possibility.

AM: Going back to the terrain of spiritual teachings . . . What do you think has been the reason for the failure of the majority of spiritual teachers who have arrived in the West to teach a spirituality supposedly richer than ours?

LC: Oh yes, they all got wrecked in the West. I don't want to name their names, but many Zen masters became alcoholic or began sleeping with their students or the wives of their students. Many Indian masters fell into the spell of American women and practices. American sexuality is powerful, American women are powerful. There are very few spiritual masters who have achieved the power of an American woman. They're like children in the hands of an American woman.

The East has a lot to learn from America. It's a popular position that America is an infant, a country with little to teach and the masters come from the East with the ancient wisdom, but they all shipwreck in America. None of them can survive America. They all have to get down on their knees and begin studying America. America is the great spiritual experiment. Roshi often turned to me and said, "I studied women with you, Cohen."

AM: But East needs West, a soul needs a body . . .

LC: Of course we need each other like the fingers on the hand. The little finger needs the thumb to hold onto something.

AM: After the shipwreck of your marriage [*As noted earlier, Cohen never actually married. —Ed.*], have you found a shore?

LC: I've been rescued many times, but I don't have any . . . It's very kind of you to address me like I might know something, but I really am that guy who's shattered. I'm not someone who speaks about this shattering as a literary device. I do get shattered by this world, and it's really being shattered, and I'm just speaking to you from holding onto an orange crate in the flood.

AM: You have ruined your knees meditating and have spent your life kneeling before women. Do you think you will be able to get up?

LC: Oh yes, I can stand. I'm sick of pretending I'm broken from bending. I've been too long on my knees. I'm going to get up now. [*Cohen gets up.*]

AM: Oh, it wasn't something literal . . . Only a few questions more and we're finished. Recently, they have named you Doctor Honoris Causa at the McGill University in Montreal, where you studied. How did you find that experience?

LC: It's very touching to be recognized by your old university, to go there and wear a red cap and gown and be called a doctor. [But] there's a menacing side to those moments. You really think you're finished . . . it sounds like a funeral service. I think when Dylan was honored by Yale [*Actually Princeton. —Ed.*] he wrote a song called "Day of [the] Locusts" about all those grasshoppers that come and eat everything up, and leave nothing behind. There's a feeling like you've made some terrible mistake to be at this moment when they're honoring you for your poems and your songs. But also it's a great feeling. It's your old university. You're standing in your old hall.

AM: And what do you think of the homage album which the French magazine *Les Inrockuptibles* has devoted to you, with a new collection of bands doing versions of your songs?

LC: Those are my young brothers who were singing my songs. It's a good feeling, but . . . there's something very final about these kind of honors. There's something funeral about it. When some guys do your songs, when your younger brothers do your songs, it's really a nice feeling.

AM: Why were you not part of the concert in homage to Dylan?

LC: I think I was invited, but I made a joke. Don Ienner, who's the president of Columbia, mentioned this concert to me and I made a joke. He said that there would be a Dylan tribute. I said, "Bob Dylan, that commie. He singlehandedly destroyed society." I said, "My daughter wrote on the edge of her book: 'Your sons and your daughters are beyond your control.' Thanks a lot, Bob." And I don't know if they thought I was serious or not. Then I was never asked again.

AM: What do you think of the rejection of the Irish singer Sinéad O'Connor by Dylan's fans?

LC: I don't know. I wasn't there. They say that some people were laughing, were clapping, some people were booing . . . The industrial democracy of America is not the same as a society like Ireland. Basically Americans feel that all religions should be affirmed, and that they should not be attacked, because America was formed by a lot of people whose religion was being attacked. That's why they came to America. So an attack on religion, although it's tolerated in America, isn't really enjoyed because the foundation of America was people escaping from religious persecution. . . . :

AM: What do you think should be the true role of a singer, of a poet, in this society?

LC: What we want our artists to tell us is the truth, and as we get older we produce a wide variety of speakers, of artists, of painters, because our appetites are very wide. We want the modest poet, the arrogant poet, the alcoholic poet, the ascetic poet, the sad singer, the happy singer, the austere singer. We want the singer who has retreated, the singer who is hiding, the singer who is dancing. We need to produce a whole variety of artists to address our own situation, which is so vast that we can hardly locate it. There's a line from a Hebrew prayer: "Our needs are so manifold we dare not declare them." Our needs are so vast that we cannot even begin to locate them. So we produce a whole number of figures to speak to us and nobody speaks to us clearly enough or perfectly enough. So we all have work to do.

AM: Once you said that an artist must shatter his ego to produce a masterpiece.

LC: It's very important for an artist to cultivate a very strong ego. Without the strong ego, the artist cannot survive, because the world is always saying to the artist, "Shut up and go home." . . . Without a really strong ego he really will shut up and go home. But within his work, if he holds onto this position of himself, he can't create his work. . . . He has to dissolve his ego into the work. And that's what I mean by "the ego must be shattered." If he comes to the work, if he comes to the prayer, and says, "I am the artist" and "I am praying to God" and "I am creating a masterpiece" and "the music is me," then of course we are justified in laughing at him, and then he becomes a comedian.

The comedian is the one who does not dissolve his ego and he holds the ego up to us as something that is laughable. The comedian never loses his ego; that's why he's funny. He's always holding onto his own version of himself in the midst of catastrophe. That's the difference between the comedian and the artist—that in the midst of the catastrophe that we all know we're in, the artist shatters his ego in front of the catastrophe and enters into it. The comedian holds onto it and we think it's funny, and when the artist dissolves his ego into the catastrophe we think it's art.

AM: What do you think of the ego trip of the majority of pop stars?

LC: We seem to support the notion that our singers and poets have strong personalities in public. . . . We seem to be amused when they break their guitars onstage or trash hotel rooms or speak impolitely to their elders or develop arrogant and extravagant personalities. We seem to like it, to encourage it. And I think for the young, these positions are completely understandable and necessary.

The young feel impotent. The young feel that they cannot penetrate into society. They feel they cannot operate the levers in the mechanisms of society, that they will not be noticed. So they produce representatives that have a contemptuous point of view towards these mechanisms the adult world represents. So they produce their guerrilla artists and that's what I think the rock-and-roll artists are. They're representatives of the youth that threaten the order and break down the walls and produce openings into the world. The young will always produce these leaders that disdain or disrespect the elder world. In that way the gates are broken and the young can enter into the elder world. So I think this kind of artist that the young produce is necessary and appropriate as things are constituted now.

What we want as we get older is something different. As we get older, we know that this world was not worth penetrating, that it was not worth breaking down the doors to enter this world. Because when you find yourself in that world as you grow older you see that it's nothing special, that there's no need to resist the world. But from the point of view of the young there seems to be this mysterious world of the adults who seem to have all the power and so we produce these representatives to challenge that power.

Once you're an adult you realize that there is no power in this world, that it's all weakness, sickness, and suffering, that it is all failure. So what were the young trying to get from us? That's what we look at when we see the young criticizing us and the young trying to take away our authority. Our lives are failures and our days are filled with suffering and envy and disaster, so that's why we shrug our shoulders when we see the young trying to take our world away. We would be happy to give them our world.

AM: "Soldier of life," "prophet of the heart." With which of these two titles do you feel more comfortable?

LC: My friend Irving Layton says that all these archetypes are finished. He says the poet is finished. There is no poet, there is no warrior, there is no priest. These descriptions are helpful to the young, because the young are trying to find out who to be. The young are looking for a job—unemployment is a very serious question—but as you get older these categories no longer have the charm or the urgency. You have to develop original strategies and original identifications to survive. Even these categories are not useful.

AM: Why have you included two songs that are not yours on this album? I can't recall you have ever done that.

LC: I thought they were successful enough to be kept. For instance, "Always" was a wonderful recording session. I prepared my cocktail of Red Needle—tequila, cranberry juice, and fruit—and I gave it to all the musicians and we couldn't stop playing this song, and the version that I have on the record just happens to be the shortest version. All the other ones were twenty-five minutes, and nobody would stop playing, and several of the musicians told me afterward that it was the happiest recording session they'd ever been to. And the point where the solo guitar comes in, in the second verse, that's where I fell down; I couldn't sing anymore, and I had to lie down beside the microphone for a few moments, so it was an extravagant, wonderful occasion and I kept the song because I felt it had that good quality to it. I thought "Be for Real" was a really good song that I discovered. People didn't know about it and I started playing it over and over. I think that both those songs will gather resonances around them in the future. I think in five or ten years those songs will really sound good.

AM: Who is Frederick Knight?

LC: Frederick Knight was a black singer and composer who had some hits around the middle seventies. His version of the song is the definitive version. It's falsetto. Very, very beautiful.

AM: Why didn't you play yourself the instrumental piece "Tacoma Trailer" on the album?

LC: I played it with my synthesizer and my expander string section, and I played the whole thing just like that, and then I couldn't play it again. So I asked Bill Ginn to transcribe it and play it because I thought it had something great, very sweet, to it. I couldn't possibly play it again. I just played it once. I played all those parts at once. I was setting up different kinds of rhythms and pulses and string movements.

AM: Some of the lines in the text of "Anthem" have been taken from the song "The Bells," which you wrote as the finishing touch for Lewis Furey's film, *Night Magic*, but the music is different.

LC: Some lines, yes. Some lines were taken. It was originally my own song. I had written the lyrics and the tune. But, yes, Lewis needed something to end *Night Magic*. It was a point of contention between Lewis and I, because I had originally given him some Spenserian stanzas for a song cycle that he wanted to do for a record, and he liked the stuff I gave him so much that he first of all decided to turn it into a ballet, which I thought was OK, and then he expanded this very modest song cycle into a movie, which I thought was not successful at all. And he started needing all kinds of material once he had gotten into this huge form of the movie. So I was raping my work and pillaging through things just to finish the movie for him; so I gave him this incomplete lyric, and I didn't give him my melody because he was doing the music. But I'd always been trying to record this song. I've been trying to record that song for *Various Positions*—several versions that didn't work. I prepared a version for *I'm Your Man*, complete with overdubs and strings and choirs, that I couldn't use in the end because some words were wrong, the feeling was wrong, the time was wrong. Finally in this record I tried it several times. I tried one with Don Was, I tried one with Steve Lindsay, I did one myself. Finally I played it myself and then substituted strings for the parts that I had played.

AM: There is another old song on the album, "Waiting for the Miracle," cowritten with Sharon Robinson. On one occasion you told me it was a mix between "Everybody Knows" and another unedited song, "I've Cried Enough for You."

LC: I've been writing that song since the early eighties, maybe late seventies. I have versions of "Waiting for the Miracle" way before *Various Positions*. I recorded a full version with Sharon. Then I tried one with Don Was, I tried one with Steve Lindsay . . . and then finally I played it myself on the synthesizer and added strings and drums, changed some chords. I hope Sharon likes it because I've changed it some. But Sharon and I have been writing songs together for a long time. We wrote our first song together actually on tour. It was a song called "Summertime" and it was just recorded by Diana Ross. So eight years later we recorded what we'd written on the '80 tour. We wrote another song called "Lucky" and we've written a few other songs together.

AM: What was your collaboration on the homage record to Charles Mingus like?

LC: Hal Willner was the producer. I'd met him when he was producing a television show called *Night Music*. When he put me together with Sonny Rollins and he asked me to read a poem of Charlie Mingus's, I couldn't understand it. So I just read the first line for Hal Willner and a few other lines too. Long poem. But I just did it because Hal Willner asked me to do it. The Harry Partch instruments are wonderful. I'm very interested in him too, [composer] Harry Partch. I'm trying to find his early recordings. He invented these instruments. They're incredible. Have you seen any pictures of them?

AM: I saw some photos of those instruments in an encyclopaedia of the history of rock. They are colorful, beautiful.

LC: They are fantastic.

AM: And what about your participation in the record of *Are You Okay?*, by Was (Not Was)?

LC: At that television show that Hal Willner produced I met Don Was and David Was and Sweet Pea and Lord Harry, the singers, and his band and we became friendly. So it became a personal thing and Don Was asked me to read this poem about Elvis that David had created. I gave it a try and they liked it. I really don't like collaborating with anybody else, but I force myself to from time to time.

AM: What do you think of this project in which I am working with Enrique Morente, to bring flamenco to some of your songs?

LC: I would love to be involved with a flamenco song once in my life. I would love just to have some connection with that expression because I love the music. If I could find some way of collaborating with a great artist like Morente it would be wonderful. I hope I can find the right song for it. To me it would be like Ray Charles would sing one of my songs. Or Aaron Neville—he's one of my favorite singers—he's doing two more of my songs. He's doing "If It Be Your Will" and maybe "Anthem" on his next record. To hear my songs translated into this genre is a wonderful thing for me. If my songs were to be translated into the flamenco genre I would be really touched.

RADIO INTERVIEW

VIN SCELSA | June 13, 1993, *Idiot's Delight*, WXRK-FM (New York)

Vin Scelsa, a longtime fixture on New York–area radio and a pioneer of freeform FM program-ming, is known for his eclectic and frequently surprising playlists but also for his incisive inter-views. This conversation with Cohen—whose music Scelsa has loved since his teen years—helps to explain why. Some of the turf it covers has been addressed elsewhere, but there are lots of fascinating little details that you're not likely to read in other interviews. Stay tuned to find out, for example, Cohen's choice for the most underrated pop singer as well as how he met Jack Kerouac and why he got into a fight with Joan Baez. —Ed.

Vin Scelsa: Leonard Cohen is my guest here on *Idiot's Delight* tonight . . . and I've always wanted to ask you, Leonard Cohen, about that song "First We Take Manhattan," about the sort of guerrilla military attack thing that's going on there. What is that all about?

Leonard Cohen: Well, it became clear a while ago that all the energy had moved out of the center, that the center could no longer hold, that the rational positions were losing a sense of justification and that all the energy, all the fun, was going to the edges. So you are in a period now where the extremist position, the oversimplified position, is the one that captures hearts. And this was a kind of geopolitical investigation into that frame of mind, which I felt was about to manifest and which has mani-fested so stridently over the past few years. I think you're quite right—it is the guerrilla sensibility. That is, there's no justice so that things have to be overturned in our own terms. We have to crack the mold and fashion one closer to our hearts. It's a very dangerous situation. I meant to indicate that kind of mad, logical, extremist, terrorist, guerrilla position that has seized the hearts and minds of most of the activists in the world today.

VS: And there's an element of revenge in there as well.

LC: Everybody feels that they've been wronged, everybody has become an injustice collector, everybody wants their situation to be corrected as deliciously and as viciously as possible.

VS: What do we do with that, if everybody wants that and everybody's got their own selfish thing?

LC: The advice I give now, especially when young people ask me what to do . . . I say, "Duck!" [*Scelsa laughs.*] The excrement is about to hit the ventilator.

VC: Really. Well, that's what *The Future* is all about really, isn't it? The new album of yours.

LC: That's what it's about. Also, the terrorist position is so seductive that everybody has embraced it. The governments have embraced it, the lovers have embraced it. The same politics of the bedroom and the living room and of the legislative assemblies of the world . . . it is the terrorist position. Reduce everything to confrontation, to revenge.

VS: Do you think the media plays a big part in all that?

LC: It's way beyond that. It's all lost. My friend [Irving] Layton described it as nail polish. Our culture, our civilization, all this beautiful stuff from Mozart to [writer Charles] Bukowski, as exalted or as funky as it gets, it's just nail polish on the claws and the nail polish has begun to crack and flake and the claws are showing through. And that's what we're living with—a world in which the claws have been exposed. And it's only been a tiny brief moment when they were covered with nail polish and now the nail polish is coming off.

VS: The future looks pretty grim.

LC: It is grim. It always has been grim. But if I'd just nailed this up as a manifesto on the church door, it would be quite a grim document but it's married to a happy little dance track.

VS: Yeah! And there is an element of humor that runs through it as well.

LC: It's quite funny. "I am the little Jew who wrote the Bible . . . all the poets trying to sound like Charlie Manson." There are a couple of laughs in it. But the lyric in any case melts into the music and the music melts into the lyric and you get a kind of refreshment, a kind of breath of fresh air. To hear these matters examined in this kind of way I think produces oxygen.

VS: You write a lot of lyrics for your songs and will frequently change the song in performance. Why is that?

LC: I don't know. It just takes me a long time to figure out what a song is about and all the easy versions come first: the alibis, the slogans, the correct positions—even if they're not, even if they're adventurous. The quick fix comes first. And we live our life on that basis and we're not expected to dredge up the most profound things in conversation. There is a kind of lightness to our ordinary life.

But I find I don't want that feel in the song. I want to know what's really underneath my opinions. I find my opinions *incredibly* boring. My mind, my heart, my life is so far ahead of my opinions. The opinions, you refine them, you trot them out at the appropriate moments and you can even get behind them sometimes and argue them but basically they are *incredibly* dull and boring—mine and almost everybody else's I come across.

So there's something else that's sitting under the opinions and that's what I like to get to in the song. And that's a line: What is the position of the guy in the future? Is he left? Is he right? Is he a lunatic? Is he sane? Has he turned his back on it? Has he embraced it? It is the real inner life that I'm trying to manifest in the songs.

VS: So you'll literally live with these songs for a long period of time.

LC: Yeah, and keep peeling them away. But before I can throw a verse away, I have to write it with exactly the kind of diligence and care and effort that it would take to write the one that I'm going to keep. Because it's in the putting your ass on the line in the writing of it, in the commitment to the rhyme, to the rhythm . . . it's exactly that process that produces the material that is not boring, that is not the slogan, that is not the alibi. So before you can discard the verse, you have to write it with the same kind of effort as the one you would keep.

VS: When John Cale visited us nine, ten, eleven months ago, when he put out a live performance album that has your song on it, "Hallelujah"—

LC: Oh, yes. Wonderful performance.

VS: Cale talked about how he had to gather together several people here in New York to track down all the lyrics to the song including "Ratso," Larry Sloman, because there are so many lyrics and while you had recorded a version, there are verses and verses and verses extant that were not on your recorded version. I think you must be unique in that regard.

LC: I don't know. It just seems to me that . . . as [poet Robert] Browning said, "the first fine careless frenzy." There is something wonderful about just laying it out and it being beautiful and limpid and lying there or hanging there or twisting there. You know that first-thought, best-thought promotional activity of the writing Jewish Buddhists. This idea that it's all just there, just say it. That's never worked for me. My first thoughts are dull, are prejudiced, are poisonous. I find last thought, best thought.

VS: Is it because those first thoughts are so spontaneous and visceral and the last thought is the deep?

LC: I suppose they are spontaneous and visceral if you are a spontaneous and visceral kind of chap. I'm not. I'm very formal, uptight, and agonized most of the time. It takes me a long time to get to the spontaneous, visceral quality that is every human's heritage. I have to do a lot of undressing, a lot of stripping, a lot of sweating. I have to go into the sauna to really sweat it out and then it gets spontaneous and visceral, like six months down the road. At the beginning it's just formal. I can fake visceral and spontaneous. In fact, most of the things that go down for visceral and spontaneous are fake. You can hear when you hear it. But very few things that you love are spontaneous and visceral. First thought, best thought and spontaneous and visceral are highly overrated qualities. I think right now what the age seems to demand is a much more modest approach to our psyches. Let us not assume that everything we come up with, just 'cause it's fast, is good.

VS: So you wouldn't have necessarily gotten along with Jack Kerouac on a literary level.

LC: I did get along with him.

VS: But do you appreciate his work?

LC: I appreciate his work very much. And he was a certain kind of genius who was able to spin it out that way, like some great glistening spider. Everything that he produced had this silver shining quality that was connected, one thing to the other. The sense of connection in Kerouac, the way that he can unify his own vision moment after moment so things don't just hang. His embrace is so wide that he does not need these Roman nails. I'm not so generous an individual. I don't have that kind of gift. That kind of gift destroys the generation of writers that comes after him. Just like Dylan's did. That kind of gift is wonderful in the genius that comes up with it. Then you have everybody not writing but typing, as one of our other writers observed.

VS: Truman Capote said that.

LC: "That's not writing, it's typing." Well, it wasn't typing with Kerouac, it was really spinning the great tale of America.

VS: When and where did your paths cross?

LC: I think the first time I saw Jack Kerouac was at the [Village] Vanguard [in New York].

VS: Saw him reading? With like a jazz group or a pianist behind him?

LC: Yeah. I think that was the first time. And then I bumped into him at a party that I think Ginsberg kindly invited me to. I saw him a couple of times thereafter.

VS: Now, when you were coming of age in Montreal, there was a community of artists, writers, musicians who were in a way similar to what was happening in New York and San Francisco in the Beat era. Or were they different?

LC: There were a group of poets, some of whom have distinguished themselves in Canada. There were really just a half a dozen or a dozen of us who had a very high investment in this activity. And there were no prizes or grants or awards. There weren't even any girls. There was just the work. And we Xeroxed—not even Xeroxed, we mimeographed—those first books and put them out. But the thing that distinguished that activity was a savage integrity. We would gather several times a week in cafés or in rented rooms and we would read each other our verses. And you had to defend your verse, your poem, because every word was scrutinized and attacked by the others.

VS: I would imagine the group was so small because you immediately got rid of the pretenders. Because that sounds really frightening—"defend."

LC: It was. You had to defend your poem. You had to defend your writing. I saw grown men cry under those circumstances. But generally it was filled with good humor and drink and a sense of fraternity that seems to have passed from any of the other literary communities I've bumped into before or since.

VS: Who were your prime influences as a writer, first starting out writing poetry?

LC: It's hard to say. I was very much encouraged by a friend of mine by the name of Irving Layton. Not influenced by his work but by the man himself, by his manner, by his generosity. We became friends and we remain friends. He is, I think, without any argument the greatest poet that English Canada ever produced. And maybe the best poet for my money writing in English today. He lives in Montreal. He's not known here.

VS: I don't know him. It's a shame if you describe him that way.

LC: You might quarrel is he the Mississippi or the Himalayas? These are just matters of personal taste but it's indisputable that there is a sense of greatness about his work. The man is eighty now. He's published over sixty volumes of work. He deserves to be read throughout the world. He's finding an audience in Italy now. For some odd reason the Italians have begun to translate him.

VS: When you started performing, you were performing as a poet. You were on a circuit where you became a kind of pop rock star before you began playing music.

LC: Well, in a very, very minor capacity because we're talking about a country where an edition of poetry that did gloriously well meant that you sold two or three hundred copies.

VS: Gloriously well? So *The Spice-Box of Earth*, a book like that, would sell only a few hundred copies?

LC: My first book sold four hundred copies. It was called *Let Us Compare Mythologies*, and that was considered a stunning success and it was reviewed in all these mimeographed journals that no one read—there's a readership of a few hundred people in the country. Well, very much due to the work of Irving Layton and Frank Scott, Phyllis Webb, Raymond Souster . . . certain people that started promoting the idea of poetry and then our nationalist energies were tapped and we started to feel like we had to produce a culture and protect it and so laws started to be passed and that sort of thing but in those days . . . when you're talking about stardom, you're talking about a very, very tiny landscape.

VS: But you were performing at that time.

LC: We didn't think of it as performing although I think you're quite right. We were showing off. We were trying to be loved in whatever terms were available. But those were tiny poetry readings of twenty, twenty-five people at the most.

VS: But have you always felt that the spoken tradition in poetry is important to your work? Is it important to have it read out loud?

LC: You know, you were trying to get ahead in some way and you were ready to accept any invitation to publish a poem in a mimeographed magazine or to read in a tiny bookstore on a Thursday night. Our commitment to the enterprise was absolute. We didn't want to be or do anything else. None of us wanted to teach in university. I don't know what the other alternatives were but the commitment was really very impressive now that I look back on it. My own and my friends'. What we brought to it then, because there were no rewards, there was nothing else going on.

VS: It was pure.

LC: It had a certain purity that I think produced some very good work.

VS: As I've said many times on the air, I have avoided on a couple of occasions accepting an invitation to have you come up. Record company people have said, "We know how much you love Leonard Cohen." I've said, "Ah, I don't know, I'm a little nervous, I think I'm intimidated by him." Plus, I respect the man so much and you're such an important part of my life that I didn't want to see the man behind my image, my myth, that I had created for you.

LC: I think that there's a certain wisdom in that position. Because I think that people do get in the way of their work, their own personalities, their own moods, their own daily moment that you might find them in. I think there are exceptions, of course, but I don't know why one would really want to meet someone whose work is . . . would you really like to meet Isaiah or King David? Not necessary.

VS: [*Laughs.*] Yeah, right. I'm one of those people who spent countless hours in my attic bedroom in my parents' home devouring *Beautiful Losers*, the novel, devouring your poems, listening to that first album when it was on vinyl and ruining it because I played it so many times that I had to go out and buy another copy of it. So for me you've always been a real important figure. And something has changed in me, I guess, over the last couple years, because this time I went to them and said, "Please, if Leonard is in town on a Sunday night, could he come by?" So something happens in our own ability to deal with our heroes.

LC: I think when you make your treasures your own and you really claim them, you can use that strength to sell out into the world. I think that's what we're all doing with our work is pitching in at this point. These are very grave times and they're not times to stand on ceremony. We've all got to pitch in. I know that sounds like a fatuous observation but I mean from moment to moment, whoever you're talking to. This is not a moment for false modesty or pretentions or attitudes. I remember when I came down to New York by myself in the fifties, I'd heard that there was a kind of generous community of artists and writers and people and that they lived in Greenwich Village. And I came down and I felt such a cold shoulder from everybody and everywhere. A naive reaction, of course, but I remember sitting in some café in the Village at that time and writing on my placemat, "kill cool" and holding it up for the patrons to see. And that's what I feel right now. Kill attitude! What a drag. It's about time that we started pitching in. I mean, moment to moment in the conversation with whoever you happen to be with. *Help out* because these are times that try the souls of men.

VS: And there's no room for that attitude.

LC: I think that that attitude is very poor advice in terms of an emergency. I don't think that attitude has any place at all. Everybody thinks that that's where the edge is, that's where the sex is, that's where the fun is, that's where the thrust is, that's where it's happening. But it ain't. It's just getting worse and worse.

VS: So where it's happening is within you and how you deal from moment to moment—

LC: Whoever you're with, whether you're buying cigarettes or having an interview, there's no need for you to pull this shit of attitude. What could it possibly serve? We've got our professional attitudinists and we should cherish them. But there is such a thing as courtesy.

VS: Who's a professional attitudinist? Dylan?

VS: Oh, I think he's long ago abdicated. I think he was a grand and shining and probably immortal example of that position and, like any great one, the imitators that come after are very tedious. The man who develops that is, of course, cherished. But Dylan long ago has abdicated that. Dylan is a working musician who goes from town to town singing his songs.

VS: Constantly.

VS: And for whatever reasons, and they're his own, he has completely left the scene of fashion and influence. And my hat's off to him. He's just a working stiff. The pay is good but it's still rough to go from town to town singing your songs on whatever level you do it.

VS: Well, you've been out now for what? A couple of months? And more to come?

LC: Mmm hmm.

VS: Do you like performing?

LC: I like it when it goes well. I like it when I don't humiliate myself. I like it when I'm not ashamed of myself at the end of the evening. But you set yourself up for those disgraces and when you can avoid them, you think that you still know how to do the step or you can still pull it off.

VS: But when you go out onstage, do you feel comfortable or do you feel alien somehow up there?

LC: I feel that if I'm in the right kind of shape, I can deliver. If I haven't sold myself some bill of goods about who I am. If you can overlook the version of yourself that you've bought and that people have helped you buy, especially when you've had a little success. In a sense it was easier in those years when I was more or less a kind of joke, and the records weren't selling and the whole deal was not considered terribly important. Then, when I could get out on the stage and I could sing a song like, "A singer must die for the lie in his voice, I thank you, I thank you for doing your duty, you keepers of truth, you guardians of beauty, your vision is right, my vision is wrong, I'm sorry for smudging the air with my song" [from "A Singer Must Die," on *New Skin for the Old Ceremony*].

That's hard to sing when you're more popular. People have been very kind to me over the past couple of years and I've enjoyed a resurrection and I'm very pleased about it. But it invites you to buy versions of yourself that stand in the way of delivering the song in the best way possible and I fall for it sometimes.

VS: That's human to fall for that. It's very easy to get caught up in that. And I suppose with age and, hopefully, with the wisdom that you get from just living longer you learn how to deal with that—or not. Are you saying that maybe you don't learn how to deal with that?

LC: I don't think it's written anywhere that you get wiser as you get older. I find that you get a certain kind of vulnerability, a certain fragility also. Or maybe just the range gets wider. You get more strong and more weak. You get more generous and somehow more miserly at the same time. Yeah, as Layton says, the tricks that every poet learns eventually . . . you do find a way through it but I'm not so sure it gets easier or better.

VS: I said before that I wanted to take you back to that moment where you decided to sing your songs rather than write them as poems. What was the impulse to pick up a guitar and start to create songs?

LC: Well, it started with the guitar and I'd always played guitar. When I was about seventeen or eighteen, a couple of us formed a group called the Buckskin Boys in Montreal. So it preceded my formal writing. I didn't know about formal writing. I wasn't terribly interested in it. I was interested in country music and what they called folk music in those days. We sang all those songs and we sang at barn dances, at square dances, in school auditoriums and church basements. That was my first paying job and that was really the first time I ever stood up in front of people, was to play rhythm guitar in the Buckskin Boys.

I then got really interested in the lyric. I thought, "Jesus, these are beautiful." As I started researching songs, I went down to the Harvard Library of folk music and spent a summer there just listening to all the songs, all these incredible lyrics, and I got really deeply into it.

VS: You mean like the mountain ballads and those things, all that John Jacob Niles stuff that he compiled?

LC: Oh yeah. And you'd sit there in that library at Harvard and you could listen to everything that was recorded. And then the whole [Alan] Lomax and *People's Songbook* and the Almanac Singers . . . that whole tradition touched me very deeply. Their passionate concern. These kinds of attitudes now that are so belittled and so scorned. Where people actually would dare to sing songs about brotherhood. Those songs touched me very deeply in the lyrics. Also as a way to approach young women. I was shy. I didn't exactly know how to do it, so there was something about the words on the page, that I could arrange it in some way to get some kind of attention. So all those streams combined to give me a passionate interest in blackening the page in a certain kind of way, where the lines don't come to the end of the page.

VS: Can you tell how you got to know Judy Collins and she came to record "Suzanne"? I know it wasn't the first recorded version of the song but it was the one that really introduced you—

LC: Judy Collins was *extremely* generous to me, *extremely* kind. She was there long before I was there and we had a mutual friend and I'd borrowed some money to come to New York. I had some songs. Must have been about '65. And we had a mutual friend and I went over to her house and you know who was there? One of the writers of "Ballad for Americans"—I think Earl Robinson.

VS: Part of that tradition that you were just talking about.

LC: I knew his work. I sang her a couple of songs and she received them very kindly, very compassionately. I can't even think of these things happening today, it's become so tough. I mean, you really don't want to help anybody out anymore. Those impulses seem to have been blunted.

VS: Too much competition?

LC: Yeah. Not in her case. And she said, I really like these songs but there isn't anything . . . please keep in touch," but in the kindest way possible. And then I went back to Montreal and I knew that I was on top of a good song. I had the fingerpicking worked out and I knew that it was connected to the harbor in Montreal and then I started writing verse after verse and finally when I came upon a version that I liked I called Judy and I sang it to her over the phone. And she said, "I want to record that immediately." That was "Suzanne." [*This account differs from the one given by Collins in*

At home in Montreal, 1972. BIRGIT REINKE

At the airport in
Paris, 1976.

Paris concert, September 7, 1974.

Toulouse, France, November 19, 1980. ALBERTO MANZANO

Hydra, January 1981.
ALBERTO MANZANO

With daughter Lorca, Hydra, January 1981. ALBERTO MANZANO

Barcelona, Spain, May 15, 1993. IVAN GIESEN

With singer Jennifer Warnes at Jackson Browne's 50th birthday party, Los Angeles, October 1998. ALBERTO MANZANO

With the late Spanish singer Enrique Morente, FIB Festival, Benicassim, Spain, July 2008. ANGEL SANCHEZ / ALBERTO MANZANO ARCHIVES

In concert, Ghent, Belgium, August 12, 2012. ALBERT MANZANO ARCHIVES (THANKS TO RIA)

Barcelona, Spain, September 21, 2009. IVAN GIESEN

I'm Your Man, Sylvie Simmons's Cohen biography. Collins told Simmons that she decided to record both "Suzanne" and "Dress Rehearsal Rag" on the day Cohen first played them for her, not after a subsequent phone call. —Ed.]

VS: It has been said by many—sometimes in a joking fashion, sometimes quite seriously—that Leonard Cohen's albums and songs are the soundtracks for depressed, suicidal people. The songs can be very bleak, very sad, but is that you? Are you a depressed, suicidal person? Have you been at times in your life?

LC: I've never been suicidal. It doesn't come to me, that version of the bleakness but, yes, I have known real depression and a lot of the songs come out of that experience and I think people are beginning to understand how this is not the blues—this is a different kind of experience. I think William Styron wrote about it recently. That kind of experience I'm not unfamiliar with. So it is a landscape that I know about and a lot of those songs have come from that place. . . . Music is a matter of taste and a lot of people just don't want to hear that kind of sound in a man's voice or music. It's quite fine. The curious thing is that people who know that kind of landscape have written me and said it gets them out of it. That it gets them through it.

VS: Yes. Well, in much the same way that blues music gets people out of the blues. Blues is an exuberant music and there is a great deal of hope and love in your songs. I've always had to argue with people. They say, "Leonard Cohen's music is to slit your wrists by." No it's not!

LC: It is if you're not familiar with that landscape. Why should people be invited into a place that is uncomfortable and the value of the piece is that it's going to get you out of it? But if you are familiar with it, it does help to get you out of it.

VS: What has allowed you to get out of those moods?

LC: The work itself is an element. Studying the mood very carefully in a very concentrated way has been helpful. And I've tried everything.

VS: Have you been in analysis?

LC: No, I was never drawn to analysis. I'd read a great deal of Freud and of other analysts and the approach never seemed to invite me. What did invite me was the kind of empty self-examination of the Zendo, of Zen meditation. And that helped me very, very much.

VS: Who taught you that?

LC: I bumped into a man who was about my age at the time he came to America. He's now eighty-six. I bumped into him about twenty years ago and I began to study with him and drink with him. And as he said to me two or three years ago, "Leonard, I never tried to give you my religion. I just poured you saki." And it's true.

VS: A potent combination, I guess, the study and the saki.

LC: If he'd been a professor of physics at the University of Heidelberg, I probably would have learned German and studied at Heidelberg. There was something about the man that touched me deeply. I've been very fortunate to have very close men friends in different generations. So the example of Layton in relation to his work, the diligence and the passion that he's brought to his work, with this other man whose name is Sasaki Roshi, his huge embrace of the disparate elements in which we operate, his very wide humorous and compassionate embrace of all things, has touched me very much. So to drink with him is a great honor and I've been drinking with him for a long, long time now.

VS: Let's go back to the Chelsea Hotel. You spent some time in the Chelsea Hotel.

LC: That was a dangerous place. I don't know what it's like these days. After a while, you got very wary about accepting a potato chip from anyone.

VS: You didn't know what was going to be on it.

LC: I went on a lot of involuntary trips, just accepting the hospitality of fellow lodgers.

VS: Joan Baez talks jokingly . . . she says she was the only straight person at the party. She was the only one who didn't take drugs.

LC: It's true. And I had an argument with her that was based on her investment in her own straightness.

VS: [*Laughs.*] Really?

LC: It concerns Mahatma Gandhi, whom she revered. And this argument took place in the Chelsea Hotel. She had formed this nonviolent group and I had just finished a biography of Gandhi in which it was mentioned as a footnote that he chewed rauwolfia, which is a weed that grows by the side of Indian country paths and is the active ingredient in Valium or whatever the popular tranquilizer was at the time. So I suddenly had a different version of the whole nonviolent movement in India, where everybody's chewing rauwolfia and sitting down and the British troops are coming at them and they're not exactly Nazis, the British, so [the Indians] did get beat up and pushed around and suffered terribly but they didn't get put into ovens. But they're sitting there on the road and they are feeling very, very relaxed—way beyond the normal capacity for relaxation.

So I brought this up to Joan Baez. And she was very, very annoyed that I suggested that drugs were a part of the nonviolent movement because she had this deep investment in being the straight girl around. Well, she was, and she did it magnificently. Now she also had a certain antipathy to the idea of mysticism and she didn't like the last line of "Suzanne"—"She's touched your perfect body with her mind." She felt that this was succumbing to the dark forces of religion and mysticism, which she also felt [determined] to defend society against. Which I cherish in her. So she had another line that she would sing when she sang it. I don't know what it was . . . "She touched your perfect body with her thumb [or] with her hand."

VS: Something a bit more natural.

LC: Yes, because we know that you cannot touch things with your mind in any tangible sense and believing that you can leads you into the darkness of mystical speculation, which we want to avoid at all costs. That was her position. But in the Rolling Thunder Review, when she came to Montreal with Dylan and much water had gone under many bridges, she sang the song and when I saw her in the catacombs of the Forum in Montreal, she said, "I finally got it right." Very generous of her.

VS: She was able to grow into it and accept it. Back to the Chelsea Hotel. Another question I've always wanted to ask you: The song which is called "Chelsea Hotel No. 2"—why "No. 2"? Is there another . . .

LC: There were many "Chelsea Hotels" but I was singing a different "Chelsea Hotel" during a tour of 1972 and Ron Cornelius, the San Francisco guitarist, was playing with me, and we developed the song, he gave me a chord for it. And we sang it. It was excruciatingly slow. Well, I was on Mandrax at the time. They used to call me Captain Mandrax.

VS: Mandrax? That's one I don't even know.

LC: I think it was like a Quaalude. I think it was the English version of it. And my performances started getting slower and slower. I was in the Mahatma Gandhi stage of my performance. I was relaxed beyond any reasonable state.

VS: No fear of British soldiers or the audience! [*Laughs.*]

LC: No. I was ready to embrace the world with a great sense of relaxation. There's a very bad movie that was made about that tour called *Bird on the Wire*, a documentary, and I think we can be seen singing "Chelsea Hotel No. 1." [*The film, directed by Tony Palmer, is actually called* Bird on a Wire. —*Ed.*] It takes about half an hour to sing the song. Anyways, I had to rewrite the song. There were different lyrics, of course. So I finished that "Chelsea Hotel No. 2" in the Imperial Hotel in Asmara, Ethiopia.

VS: Rather far from the Chelsea Hotel.

LC: Yeah, but I finally got it together. I was very indiscrete in an interview somewhere and I let it be known that I wrote the song for Janis Joplin. I think it was very ungentlemanly of me to let that news out and thereafter, once it was out, I used her name in the introduction to the song in concerts but I wish I hadn't.

VS: I'm not surprised that you wish you hadn't. The song stands by itself, for one thing and, for another, it's nobody's business, really.

LC: It's nobody's business. I think since the cat is out of the bag I'm quite willing to talk about it but I do feel it's one of the few times where I feel I did something cheap. I attached the name of a great singer to this song in some way to promote the song. I was indiscrete about what had happened. These things went down and I had no business talking about them or at least identifying the actors . . .

VS: As long as we've brought it up, though, can you tell the story that you sometimes tell in introducing the song about the elevator in the Chelsea hotel?

LC: Do you mind if I don't?

VS: OK, sure, sure . . . There is this fall going to be published a volume of your collected works. Is that not correct?

LC: A selection of poems and songs from the past twenty or thirty years.

VS: Some of the books are constantly reprinted but you haven't done anything for print per se in quite a while.

LC: No, I think the last collection was in 1968. Then I put out a couple of books that made no impression at all, especially in this country. *Death of a Lady's Man* and *Book of Mercy*. *Energy of Slaves.*

VS: Is novel writing something you're still interested in?

LC: I like the regime that goes with writing of the novel. Maybe I could get back to that sometime. I have now some kind of romantic idea of just going to the desk a few hours a day and living in a bright place with a good woman.

VS: That bright place is California these days, isn't it?

LC: Yeah, I've been living there for a while now.

VS: But you go back and forth between that and Montreal?

LC: Yes, about half and half.

VS: Can you talk a little bit about Jennifer Warnes?

LC: Jennifer Warnes is a very important figure in my life. Her voice is like the California weather. It seems very, very sunny and up but there's an earthquake behind it, there's a tidal flood, there's another element that produces one of the most compelling sounds in popular music. I think she's the most underrated pop singer around. I think she has the best pipes around. A lot of people have ripped off her style. I just wish that she could make the kind of living that she deserves to make out of recording.

VS: That element of sunshine hiding the earthquake underneath would make it seem very appropriate for your songs.

LC: I chose Jennifer Warnes out of an audition in 1972. I was looking for a backup singer and she came in. I didn't know that she already had a career, that she'd appeared with the Smothers Brothers, that she had been a lead in *Hair*, or that she'd put out her own . . . I didn't know who she was.

VS: You can see her in reruns now. The Smothers Brothers are running all those old episodes again. It's odd to see her cast back in that light. So she auditioned for you for backup vocal?

LC: Right. And I chose her and went on tour and we became very close friends over the years and as my star fell, she would always say to me, "I really want to do an album of your songs," and I thought this was just an expression of friendship. Because there was nothing in the marketplace that indicated a growing appetite for such a record. And we became musical friends as well as personal friends and we would show each other our work. She's a wonderful writer of prose, not just of songs. A really impressive creative imagination. I just like her take on things. She's one of the few people that I will ever show a song in progress to. Because she knows exactly where the song is and she doesn't exert any leverage on the song to make it go the way she wants. You can show her a song just as it is. There are very few people I would ever think of doing that with. She does the same thing.

VS: You can trust the honesty of her feedback, knowing that she's gonna give it to you straight.

LC: Yeah. Her instincts are impeccable in music.

VS: So she recorded *Famous Blue Raincoat,* an album of the songs of Leonard Cohen.

LC: Yeah, and she went from office to office of the record labels and she was kind of laughed out of the place in each and every one until she went to this new outfit called Cypress Records and they gave her some money to do it and actually the record did very well and was very much responsible for a kind of new take on what I was about.

VS: Well, that record and then a couple of years later the *I'm Your Fan* album where a bunch of musicians in Europe and here in the States got together and recorded their versions of your songs, taking its title from *I'm Your Man.* That also helped to introduce you to a whole new audience that hadn't known you before. [Can you talk about] a song on her most recent album that you are a cowriter of called "Way Down Deep"? This is the only version of the song at this point, right? You have not recorded this song.

LC: I have an entirely different version of this song, which I tried to prepare for this new record. I just couldn't finish it in time.

VS: You cowrote the song with Jennifer and someone named Amy La Television.

LC: Amy La Television wrote a song called "Way Down Deep" and . . . I thought it [had] a wonderful hook. And Jennifer phoned me and said, "Would you work on this song?" I don't lightly commit myself to that because that's a long, long period.

VS: We know what that means for you. [*Laughs.*] This could be years.

LC: I said, "Count me out. Let me off the hook on this one, Jennifer, because I'm in the middle of trying to write *The Future* and I can't get into this song."

VS: What an odd statement that is: "I'm in the middle of trying to write the future." The poet as God. [*Laughs.*]

LC: I meant the record.

VS: Yes, I know. [*Laughs.*]

LC: Anyway, she said it's going to be the most important song on the album. I'm going to begin with it and end with it and it's going to unfold and it's going to examine everything from the creation of the world to the women's movement and we're going to have everything in this song called "Way Down Deep." So I started writing verses to it. I heard Amy's version and I couldn't quite penetrate it except for the hook. So I started writing and it went through a lot of changes. Jennifer's using some of my verses and curiously enough, some of Amy's verses started making sense to Jennifer and she started using them. . . . Anyway, the thing became completely Jennifer's song. Jorge Calderon played bass on her version of "Bird on the Wire" and he's with me now.

VS: David Mansfield's on steel guitar and fiddle on the track. Have you ever played with Mansfield?

LC: No, I haven't.

VS: He's one of the great wonders on the violin. But you usually have a violinist in your bands, don't you?

LC: Yes, I have a wonderful violinist by the name of Bobby Furgo playing with me. [*Scelsa plays "Way Down Deep," then "Tower of Song." —Ed.*] When Jennifer came up with that part [in "Tower of Song"], I knew we'd nailed the song.

VS: The "da-doo-dum-dum" part. That's perfect.

LC: That really gave the song the perspective of real humor. Real lightness.

VS: Sure. But there was enough humor in it to start out with. "I ache in the places where I used to play" and "I was born with this golden voice." I mean, for people who say that there is no sense of humor in Leonard

Cohen's work, there's a perfect example of its existence. Does that "Tower [of Song]" exist anyplace, do you think?

LC: A lot of people I know are in it.

VS: Hank Williams is up very high in the tower.

LC: Yeah, different floor.

VS: [You'll] be in town tomorrow night performing with a big band, right? A lot of pieces in the band?

LC: Well, we're nine onstage. There are two singers and six musicians.

VS: Has your method of composing changed over the years with the changes in technology? Have you embraced computers?

LC: I love computers. Most of my last album was written with the Mac Performa program. I played into the Mac from my keyboard and then changed in the Mac and then replayed and then dumped onto a twenty-four-track.

VS: For those of us who don't know, you have a keyboard, like a piano keyboard, in front of you?

LC: That's right, I have a keyboard that has an output that enables it to transmit signals to a computer, which then enables you to change those signals in the computer and then replay them out through the keyboard so there are endless variations and changes that you can make on it.

VS: So you can write the arrangements as well.

LC: Yes. Most of the arrangements were done that way on this new record.

VS: Now why does it seem to me that Leonard Cohen and computer technology shouldn't go hand in hand?

LC: I don't know. There was something about the computer. I was given one. I felt the same way and Macintosh had some kind of promotional program in Canada and they gave a computer to half a dozen writers and I said, "Look this is just a waste of money, chaps . . ."

VS: Prior to this, would you write in longhand or on the typewriter?

LC: Typewriter. I always liked typewriters.

VS: And you'd compose with a guitar?

LC: That's right. Very rarely the keyboard but usually the guitar. But when they showed me how to work this thing and I also began drawing on it with a freestanding stylus that works on a digitized tablet and by pressure on the stylus you can widen or narrow the line itself so you can brush paint . . . there are many programs available now that are much more sophisticated than the ones I use but I loved it. It seemed magic to me. And while I could never really repair toasters or cars, I have a feeling for the computer.

VS: Is there a kind of a relationship to poetry in the computer do you think or am I going too far? There's a mystery about them . . .

LC: There are computer mystics around. The philosophy and theory of the computer . . . that's a little too deep for me. All I know is that I can do things with them. They seem like very friendly devices. First of all, you can change the typography on a lyric and that often changes the way you're looking at it. You can put the whole thing out in old English type so you have a very modern line like "Give it to me, baby." When you see that written in Gothic type it has a different meaning. And you can move things around that way and it refreshes the mind and it invites you to think about things different ways. It's a very friendly kind of activity.

VS: Do you write every day?

LC: I do.

VS: And do you have a set ritual? Do you have a discipline?

LC: The record starts in fits and starts. You first of all gather the songs that didn't make it onto the previous record because I'm always operating from a position of poverty. It's not like I have thousands of songs like Prince to choose between. There are only a few things going. So you take the ones that didn't make it onto the last record and you start messing around with them and you're documenting your life and the whole dismal thing starts to unfold and as you approach the later stages of the thing, you're in it all the time. I've developed a very pleasant life based around this obsessive activity.

VS: Between albums will you remove yourself from that activity?

LC: Well, between albums I have the tour. I tour every four years because that's usually what it takes to put the album out. I go on this tour that is a completely changed kind of activity. I'm singing and dancing and talking to people and the other parts of the time are really quite solitary.

VS: Does that solitary aspect of touring generate its own creativity or not?

LC: I've never been able to write on the road but it's so great to get out of your room, to be able to talk to people. Of course you're tired a lot of the time. And the possibilities of disgrace are abundant. There are many obvious things about touring that are dangerous and fatiguing but it's really great to get out of your house and get behind the songs and to gamble every night that you're going to have the purity of spirit or the enthusiasm or the care . . . you're gonna be able to summon your best self and present the songs.

VS: It's something that I've always wondered about with performers—with actors, for instance, who do the same play every night—how they can summon that freshness. If you sing the same song with the same group of musicians night after night after night, doesn't it become rote after a while?

LC: I've never found it to be that. I guess the thing is so risky moment by moment, certainly with the kind of show that we do. There are not too many guarantees. If anybody plays a wrong note, it's gonna blow the song in some kind of way. It's very precise. We're all worried about blowing it. It isn't like strolling in, this wandering troubadour, and playing a few chords. The songs are very carefully arranged and presented. Also, the red wine helps. I tend to drink a bit of red wine.

VS: While you're performing?

LC: No, not while. A few glasses, sometimes many glasses, with a meal that we take in common, all of us, the technicians, the crew, and the musicians. We generally eat together and some of us will drink together. And I must pay my debt publicly to the red wine. It's a wonderful thing. But I only drink professionally. I never drink after intermission. And I try to invite the people I work with not to drink after intermission also. I think it's a sacramental activity. We drink together and we play and the wine speaks with the song. If you start drinking after the concert, then you're really gong to get into trouble.

VS: . . . Now in a sense, [the song "Closing Time"] brings you back to those first musical performances of yours when you were playing country music in Montreal.

LC: That's the full circle.

VS: Setting the apocalypse or something like it in a country and western bar.

LC: I was in this little town in Ontario. We were playing a concert there and I got a note from someone in the audience. It was Mike Doddman's brother. [Mike was] my buddy in the Buckskin Boys. He sent me a note saying Mike had died. I'd lost contact with these boys. They were from my street; we grew up together. And [Mike's brother] came backstage and showed me a picture of Mike, who was the harmonica player for the Buckskin Boys. He'd become a Trappist monk in his last years. And I now have a picture of him celebrating the mass. Anyway, let's not get dismal. Yeah, it was, it's back to the Buckskin Boys.

VS: Tell me about "Waiting for the Miracle." What is the miracle for you?

LC: The miracle is to move to the other side of the miracle where you cop to the fact that you're waiting for it and that it may or may not come. But free from waiting, free from the miracle, so let's do something crazy, something absolutely wrong, while we're waiting for the miracle to come. Once you have embraced this notion that you're waiting for the miracle, that this thing is not going to work out, that there is a crack in everything, that this landscape is treacherous, and we don't get what we want but we must wait but to go to the other side of waiting where you're free from waiting . . . that gives you this madness. "Baby, let's get married, we've been alone too long, let's be alone together, let's see if we're that strong."

VS: This is very much akin to the Zen philosophy that you were talking about before, isn't it?

LC: I never figured out what the Zen philosophy was because this teacher of mine couldn't speak English.

VS: Wait a minute! You didn't mention that before, Leonard. It was just the saki that you used to communicate . . .

LC: Mostly. Actually it was cognac. He taught me to be able to distinguish by taste between the different kinds of cognac. He would say, "Remy Martin, slightly feminine taste. Courvoisier, a slightly masculine taste." After you've drunk a bottle or so, these possibilities become very rich.

VS: I see. So "Waiting for the Miracle" is not necessarily a Zen sort of—

LC: Even when he's got a translator, nobody can quite figure out what he's saying.

VS: [*Laughs.*] I thank you for being my guest on *Idiot's Delight* tonight.

LC: I thank you for inviting me.

COHEN CLIP
On His Musical Forebears

"The kind of training I had as a young writer, a young composer, made me very much aware of where I stood in a long line of singers or poets: musicians from the Troubadours; even before that, from Homer; and even before that, from Isaiah and King David; coming all the way down through the various strains into English literature; into poetry; into folk poetry like Robbie Burns; into folksingers like Pete Seeger, Allan Lomax, and Woody Guthrie; and down to my own generation. I've always been aware of that tradition, and to be one of the figures that allows the tradition to continue is very gratifying."

—from interview with Jim O'Brien, *B-Side Magazine* (UK),
August/September 1993

THE PROPHET OF LOVE LOOKS INTO THE ABYSS: A CONVERSATION WITH LEONARD COHEN

THOM JUREK | August 18, 1993, *Metro Times* (Detroit)

What Thom Jurek remembers most about his Cohen interview is how excited the singer was to be performing in Detroit. "While he'd played Ann Arbor a few years before," Jurek told me, "he hadn't played in Detroit for more than a decade at that point and he was clearly looking forward to it—he kept talking about its landmarks and Motown. The [June 19] show had sold out long in advance, and he was quite thrilled to be playing in a proper rock club—the State Theater (now the Fillmore), which held a few thousand people. The reason, he said, was knowing people could walk around or sit, could mingle and talk with one another as well as enjoy the music. That it could be a community event rather than just a concert."

Jurek also recalled that during the interview, Cohen had on his lap a then recently published collection of all of Hank Williams's lyrics. "He would stop speaking for a moment and sing the tunes, or quote from them often, especially when it was apropos in our discussion," Jurek remembered. "He commented on Williams's humanity, that he was both quite strong to be that fearless in showing his vulnerability, especially during that time in country music. He called Williams's lyrics the epitome of poetry and compassion, because it was clear that the experiences Williams sang about were not only ones people could relate to but ones that the country singer had lived through.

"The interview was supposed to be for twenty minutes," Jurek added. "It lasted nearly two hours. I still have the tape somewhere. This was before he went to live on Mount Baldy, when he was still with Rebecca De Mornay."

Jurek recalled asking Cohen why it had taken so long after the release of *The Future* for him to tour. "He explained that it was because backing vocalist Julie Christensen had borne a child; it was important to hold off on the tour to give that new family time to bond." What about finding another singer? Cohen said he hadn't even considered that. "The reason, he said—and I am pretty sure I remember this by heart—was: 'She shouldn't be punished for bringing life into the world.'" —Ed.

For more than thirty years, Leonard Cohen has hungrily pursued the truth in both his poetry and his music. Since his first collection of poems, *Let Us Compare Mythologies*, appeared in 1956 in his native Montreal, Cohen has publicly chronicled standing on the edge of an emotional abyss. He accepts and even celebrates carnality, despair, apocalypse, hope, holiness, and disintegration as equal and necessary parts of the human journey.

At fifty-eight, Cohen is considered by many to be Western culture's prophet of love and the elder statesman of the bedroom, due to his uncanny ability to chart the commonality of the unspeakable—the joy, ecstasy, guilt, panic, and regret that take place in the recesses of the human soul when expressing its desire for another.

His oeuvre is impressive, if not prolific. It includes two published (and many unpublished) novels, among them *Beautiful Losers*, which has to date sold more than eight hundred thousand copies; eight collections of poems; eleven records, including a live album and a "best of" collection; and a film. He recorded the soundtrack to Robert Altman's *McCabe & Mrs. Miller*. His songs have been recorded by everyone from Judy Collins (who in 1966 brought Cohen's songwriting to international attention) to Joan Baez to Nick Cave; he has been the subject of a number of film documentaries; his music and poetry have been used in a Broadway production and ballet; two tribute recordings have been done in his honor— Jennifer Warnes's phenomenal *Famous Blue Raincoat: The Songs of Leonard Cohen*, released in 1985, and last year's *I'm Your Fan*, which included such artists as R.E.M. and John Cale. He has also edited *Stranger Music*, a collection of his lyrics and poems, for publication by Knopf later this year. The publisher is also reprinting Cohen's novels.

While Cohen's infrequent recordings regularly reach the Top 10 in Canada and throughout Europe, in America he remains a cult figure whose records sell steadily, but not in great numbers. But that is changing. His 1988 release, *I'm Your Man*, was universally acclaimed and went gold within months of its release, and his latest album, *The Future*, may even surpass that achievement. This most recent collection of sharp art songs may be his finest recorded moment. He examines the apocalyptic course the world is on with both moral authority and empathy, calling himself on the title track, "the little Jew who wrote the Bible." The album examines amorous relationships as if they too were at the end of time, calling for trust and emotional risk in proportions that have never before been witnessed. As with all of his records, it is at once pastoral, shocking, seductive, vulnerable, and direct—qualities that have guaranteed Cohen's endurance in the pop marketplace.

Cohen spoke to me from Montreal, where he lives half the year (the rest is spent in Los Angeles). In interview, Cohen was gracious and intense, listening carefully to questions, attempting to put as much information in his answers as possible. His smoky voice never quavered, but he sounded insistent and sure of himself.

Thom Jurek: To what do you attribute your longevity? It's as if you're in your prime right now, and a whole new generation of young people is getting hip to your work and claiming it as having relevance to them.

Leonard Cohen: From the very beginning, I was in it for the long haul. And the long haul for all of us is a lifetime. At fifty-eight, if I'm in my prime, I believe that's how it should be. Any artist should get better with time; there's more experience, more maturity, hopefully more vision, perhaps one even looks death a little squarer in the eye. As far as continuing relevance, I feel blessed to be part of a continuum that includes both Bob Dylan and Nick Cave. I'm gratified that I can speak to someone who is twenty-five as well—though I believe differently—as to someone who is fifty-five.

TJ: Although you've been recording for twenty-six years, your output hasn't been exactly prolific—nine studio records in all that time. Is there a reason you work so slowly?

LC: The process of songwriting for me is arduous and painful because I have to go to the place where the song is. I have to inhabit it and allow it to have its way with me. I have to write perfectly many verses that get thrown away because they are imperfect for a particular song; and it takes time and patience and tears to get there. I have to get ripped apart in the process.

TJ: Did this happen to you on *The Future*?

LC: Yes. This record was every minute of the four years it took to get it out. Some of the songs were ten years in the making; in fact, many of them were old songs that weren't finished for one reason or another until now. I'm speaking to you after the struggle. It's easy to talk about now, but in the process of making that record, just like all the ones that came before it, I get wrecked. I wish I could say to you, "I write my songs in fifteen minutes in a taxi, or in a hotel lounge," but, unfortunately, it isn't true.

TJ: Perhaps this is why your records last: What you put into them is possibly evident to the listener?

LC: I don't know if it is or not. I don't have any sense of that, but it would be agreeable if that were the reason. *The Future* as a record is here and will stay here because there's flesh and blood in it.

TJ: The title track has such an apocalyptic feel to it. There seems to be a nostalgia for the conflicts of old: "Give me crack and anal sex. . . . Give me Stalin and Saint Paul. . . ."

LC: I think the future is already here. I think that there is a collective despair that everything has collapsed, that the world has been destroyed. People are saying to each other that they can't take the reality they're living in anymore; they're actually admitting it to one another. The evidence that everything is still running is in place—the mail, garbage pickup, going to work—but there's a panic that everything isn't what it seems.

TJ: And that's essentially what the song says. That's a real trait with you—you speak elegantly, but so accessibly. It's easy for people to understand the things you say. You never try to cover them in alliteration or specialized language. Even your metaphors are spare and to the point.

LC: Because I have no secrets. A lot of writers have secrets that they spend their whole lives getting to, hinting at in their work, that there is something there that they're not revealing. I am completely open and transparent, and therefore it's easy for anyone to grasp the emotion that's there. I'm the person who tries everything, and experience myself as falling apart. I try drugs, Jung, Zen meditation, love and it all falls apart at every moment. And the place where it all comes out is in the critical examination of those things—the songs. And because of this, I'm vulnerable. There's the line in "Anthem" that says, "There's a crack in everything / That's how the light gets in." That sums it up; it is as close to a credo as I've come.

TJ: Perhaps that's why the critics who have derided you used the adage about "Leonard Cohen has continually rewritten the same song, he never has any new ideas."

LC: And they're absolutely right. I have explored the same territory—in many different ways—because I have no answers to the problems and because I keep going to the same sources because they are timeless. And as I get older, I hope I can explore them more deeply, and with more courage and honesty rather than just urgency. Irving Layton, the great Canadian poet, once wrote about me that "Leonard Cohen has been blessed with never having had an original idea," and I take that as a compliment because these things are what everybody goes through.

Everybody lives the life of the heart, and we all know what it's like to feel and break down, and I think we cherish that in our musicians and singers when they reveal that.

TJ: These themes you explore so often: sex, religion, contact, disintegration, war, and apocalypse—you were far from being P.C. in the sixties and seventies—all seem connected in your songs and poems. Do you look at life and art that way?

LC: They are all connected. If you leave God out of sex, it becomes pornographic; if you leave sex out of God, it becomes self-righteous. Religion and war are obviously connected, and all of it is connected to the person who has to live through it; I am living through it, trying to make sense out of it, or not or let it go. Those themes are timeless in themselves. One of the reasons I use biblical references continually is because even though the culture has changed in terms of where it gets its information—from television, mostly—the images contained in the Bible have remained.

TJ: So how does it feel to be a "commercial success" in the US?

LC: I have never shunned success. I have always tried to write hits that people would find enjoyable. My record company and I have an agreeable relationship; I sell enough records to keep them happy but few enough so that they don't worry about the next one. If anything, I would have liked for them to treat me more as a commodity than an artist because I worry about the artist part enough for both of us. At the times when commercial defeats and setbacks happened, I wasn't too troubled, because I knew the worth of the work, and I look back on a lot of my songs and poems and feel good about them because a lot of them have lasted. But it's an agreeable thing. Even my books, which haven't been in print in America for a while, are being reprinted. I have always been able to provide for my children and make a decent living, so I haven't much to complain about.

TJ: Sounds like a nice life.

LC: It is, but it's a fragile one, too.

COHEN CLIP

On Music He Admires

"If I hear George Jones singing 'Grand Tour,' it can blow me away. If I hear Otis Redding singing 'These Arms.' But your interest in music diminishes dramatically when you're on the road. In fact, we've created a 'music crime' on the bus, which is, y'know, if you play music . . . The first time was the night before last, when we actually listened to some bebop, some jazz, some Miles, Bud Powell. It's been a long time since anybody dared to play a note of prerecorded music on the bus." [*Laughs.*]

—interview with Dev Sherlock, *Musician*, November 1993

COHEN CLIP

On His Inner Life

"I find as you get older the range of your inner life widens. It's not that you get any better or worse. It's that you're more sad and you're more happy. You're more competent and you're more out of it. You're more attentive and you're more withdrawn. The polarities seem to get very, very strong and they seem to get wider and wider apart. And the extremes seem to be more and more acute, more and more emphasized. So the range just gets bigger and bigger until finally it gets so big that it embraces the whole cosmos and you dissolve and that's called death."

—interview with Laurie Brown, *Prime Time News*,
CBC (Canada), December 3, 1993

"I AM THE LITTLE JEW WHO WROTE THE BIBLE"

ARTHUR KURZWEIL | November 23, 1993, interview | January 1994, the *Jewish Book News* (US)

The following conversation took place in conjunction with the publication of Cohen's book, *Stranger Music: Selected Poems and Songs.* It occurred in a conference room of the New York office of Random House, which published the collection. At the time, interviewer Arthur Kurzweil was editor-in-chief of the Jewish Book Club, and he had selected Cohen's anthology as an offering to the club's more than twenty thousand members. An abbreviated version of the interview appeared in the *Jewish Book News.* This is the complete conversation, which includes more discussion of Cohen's Jewish roots and thinking than any other interview I've seen. —Ed.

Arthur Kurzweil: I want to tell you at the outset that I'm a big fan and have been for years.

Leonard Cohen: Oh, thank you very much. That's very kind of you.

AK: I have more memorabilia about you than I'm willing to admit to most people. For example, this particular book [*indicates a copy of* The Favorite Game]: there was a time when I wouldn't let anyone else touch it. [*Cohen laughs.*] It was just a crazy thing. But I just wouldn't let anybody touch it.

LC: Oh, so you know my background?

AK: I know . . . lots about you, I think, or at least, I know what they say. And I also want to let you know I saw you in concert in New York not long ago.

LC: Thank you very much for coming.

AK: It was a great night. I'm interested in your grandfather who I understand wrote some books.

LC: Both my grandfathers were distinguished. My mother's father—"Rabbi Solomon Klonitsky-Kline" is the way that they transcribed his name in the publications that were printed here—was known as Sar HaDikduki, the Prince of Grammarians. And he wrote a thesaurus of Talmudic interpretation and a dictionary of synonyms and homonyms. They were used in institutions of higher learning until Israel took over the grammatical institution.

He was a wonderful man, and my mother always used to tell me that "people came from a hundred miles" to hear him speak. My grandfather was the principal of a yeshiva in Kovno [*now Kaunas, Lithuania's second-largest city*]. He was a disciple of Rabbi Yitzchak Elchanan and, in fact, my grandfather closed his teacher's eyes when his teacher died.

He had a very strong secular side to him. He liked to ride horses, for instance. He was a kind of confrontational teacher, especially when he got to New York, where he ended up. He came first to Atlanta, where his daughter married into the Alexander family of Georgia, who were Jews who arrived in 1708, and he originally moved to Atlanta. But there was nothing there for him, so he moved to New York and he became part of the *Forward* and that group of Yiddish writers, although I don't think he contributed to any of the newspapers. But he kept on with his grammatical and Talmudic studies.

AK: And your other grandfather?

LC: My other grandfather, Rabbi Lyon Cohen, was also a very distinguished man who helped found many of the institutions that defined Jewish life in Canada. He was a vice president of the first Zionist organization in Canada. He made a trip to the Holy Land.

AK: A trip to the Holy Land at that point would have been a pretty interesting journey.

LC: Yes, a very interesting journey. He met Baron de Hirsch and he planned and helped establish, for Canada, the Jewish Colonization Association, which was to settle Jewish refugees in the prairie provinces and on farms. He was the founder of the first Anglo Jewish newspaper in North America. It was called the *Jewish Times*, published in Montreal. He was also one of the founders of Congregation Shaar Hashomayim in Montreal.

AK: Was he involved in the Jewish Public Library in Montreal?

LC: Yes, he was involved in that, although that was a different branch, a different expression of Montreal Jewry.

I remember reading speeches of his where he spoke with great pride that the Jewish community of Montreal had absorbed its refugees from Kishinev without ever asking the municipality or the government for a single cent. [*In 1903 in Kishinev, which is now the largest municipality in Moldovia, an anti-Jewish riot resulted in death or severe injury for hundreds of Jews and the destruction of hundreds of Jewish homes and businesses. —Ed.*] Montreal Jewry was very well organized.

And I am proud to say that he was one of the organizers of these institutions. Baron de Hirsch Fund was one of his undertakings. Also B'nai B'rith and the Jewish General Hospital. And the [philanthropic] Hebrew Free Loan Association was a very special interest of his. And of course all the institutions connected with Shaar Hashomayim.

AK: Both grandfathers were immigrants?

LC: They were both born in Europe; I think my grandfather came here when he was three. His father, who was also a very interesting man, Lazarus Cohen, came in 1860.

AK: To Canada?

LC: Yes, with his son.

AK: Are you named after him?

LC: Oh there's a tradition of L's. Lazarus, Lyon, Leonard.

AK: One of the reasons I'm asking you about your grandparents is that Jewish family history and genealogy is an interest of mine. In fact, there's a book on the shelf behind you that I wrote called *From Generation to Generation* . . .

LC: Oh, yes?!

AK: . . . which is a guidebook for people who want to learn how to do Jewish genealogical research.

LC: Ah, that's interesting!

AK: So I did a lot of genealogical research in my own family. I went to Eastern Europe a number of times to the towns where my grandparents had come from. A couple of my trips to Eastern Europe had a connection with you. I'd like to tell you about both of them.

LC: Yes?

AK: I researched my mother's family and discovered she had a first cousin she thought was killed during the Holocaust, who was living in Budapest with his wife, children, and grandchildren. So not that long ago I discovered . . .

LC: Family!

AK: Yes, family in Budapest, and it was wonderful. I have a second cousin, Zsuzsa, who lived in Budapest. She's now in Australia, but she grew up in Budapest. I met her for the first time in Budapest. We were speaking in English and I said to her, "Where did you learn English?" and she said to me "Cohen."

LC: Ah! [*Laughs.*]

AK: I said, "What do you mean 'Cohen'?" and she showed me your albums and she said, "This is how I learned English."

LC: Ah, that's very nice! Thank you!

AK: Extraordinary.

LC: Yes! Thank you! Thank you for telling me that!

AK: That was in Budapest. Then I went to Warsaw, Poland, where I also discovered a cousin of my father, who I also didn't know existed, who also survived the Holocaust and is living in Warsaw with his wife and daughter. One afternoon they introduced me to an actress, a young woman, who was a friend of theirs, with whom we spent the day. As we were walking through the streets that were once the Warsaw Ghetto, I said to her, "What music do you like?" She said, "Cohen." [*Cohen laughs with pleasure.*] So my question is this: Why do you think it is that you have this following in Eastern Europe?

LC: I did a tour of Poland before the government changed, before the Solidarity government was established, and I discovered—I had known, but without a great deal of data—that Poland was probably my largest audience in the world. Unfortunately, they paid me in zlotys, which, as you know, are nontransferable.

But I discovered a huge audience there, and at times, when my so-called career in the West almost evaporated in most places, there was always this following in Eastern Europe generally, but Poland specifically. I don't know why.

My great-grandfather came from Vilkaviskis, which was part of Poland at the time [*and is now in southwest Lithuania*], and I was very pleased to be able to say that I came from Poland, although they didn't really think of me as Polish. But it was very interesting.

I don't know. Of course, I grew up out of that world in some way. It was not hidden from me. Actually when I arrived in Greece, in '59 or '60, I really did feel that I had come home. I felt the architecture was familiar, I felt the village life was familiar, although I had no experience with village life.

AK: Some of the articles I've read about you over the years have indicated that you dabbled or more than dabbled in various kinds of spiritual paths.

Can you tell me if I'm right in thinking the line "Did you ever go 'clear'?" from "Famous Blue Raincoat" [from the album *Songs of Love and Hate*] was a Scientology reference?

LC: It was. I did look into Scientology. I looked into a lot of things when I was a young man. Scientology was one of them. It didn't last for long.

But it was very interesting, as I continued my studies in these matters, to see, really, how good Scientology was from the viewpoint of their data, of their information, of their actual knowledge, their wisdom writings, so to speak. It was not bad at all. I know it's scorned. I don't know what the organization is today, but it seems to have the political residue of any large, growing organization. But I was surprised to see how well organized the studies were. Yeah, I did look into that.

AK: There were others?

LC: Well, from the Communist party to the Republican Party. From Scientology to delusions of myself as the High Priest rebuilding the Temple.

AK: How do Jewish things fit into all of that?

LC: Well, I became a very serious student of a Zen monk. Although, I think "dabble" can describe anybody's activity in these matters, because who of us can say that we have fully embraced this material? But I remember Allen Ginsberg saying to me at a certain point, "How do you reconcile this with Judaism?" because he was a student of Chogyam Trungpa [a Tibetan Buddhist master, author, and founder of Naropa Institute who died in 1987]. I said that I find no conflict myself. But the organization, or the man that I was in contact with, was a very different order than Trungpa. Much less organized.

As you know, there are Jewish practitioners in the Zen movement— very serious ones. In fact, there is a succession holder, there's a dharma teacher, an actual successor to a roshi [a spiritual guide], in Los Angeles, who I think is married to the daughter of an Orthodox rabbi. And he maintains a Jewish practice in the midst of the zendo [Buddhist meditation hall] regime, very much the way some [Roman Catholic] Trappist monks maintained a zendo in the midst of their monastic discipline. I don't think these are necessarily mutually exclusive, depending on your position. In Japan itself, Shinto, the family religion, and Zen, are often practiced side by side. The fact is that Zen was often not accorded the status of a religion in various periods in the East. And as I've received it from my teacher, there is no conflict because there is no prayerful worship and there is no discussion of a deity.

AK: So there's room for it?

LC: It's not even that there's room for it. One of the patriarchs, when asked, "What is the essence of Zen?" replied, "Vast emptiness and nothing special." So there's not only room for it, there's boundless space available for whatever mental constructions you happen to wish to establish.

I've inherited an extremely good religion. I have no need to change it. For instance, in the *Hollywood Reporter* recently [October 12, 1993] there was a notice that I was going to narrate a film of the National Film Board of Canada on the *Tibetan Book of the Dead*. And they said something like, "We had expected that Richard Gere would have been asked, but Cohen, a Buddhist, was . . ."

And I wrote them. I don't know if the letter has been published yet, because this appeared a couple weeks ago. I said, "My mother and father, of blessed memory, would be very disturbed to hear me described as a Buddhist." I said, "I am a Jew," and I said, "Some time ago I became intrigued with the incoherent ramblings of an old Zen monk [Roshi Sasaki, founder of the Mount Baldy Zen Center in California], who just recently said to me, 'Leonard, I've known you for twenty-five years, and I've never tried to give you my religion, I've just poured you sake.' And I lifted my glass to him and I said 'Rabbi, you are indeed the light of your generation.'"

And that's the way I feel. I've met some very impressive young Jewish men around him. For instance, the leader of the Ithaca Zen Center comes from seven generations of rabbis. And his feeling is that he's found a real rabbi. That's my feeling also.

In other words, there's something that is not negotiable about the absolute, some refusal to name qualities about the absolute that fits in with my most rigorous, deepest appetites, about the matters of which I was taught or were indicated to me.

So this young man's idea is that this old man is the real thing, that this is the purest expression of that reality that is expressed in the Shema [a central part of Jewish prayer]: there is only one thing going on, and don't even suggest that there is something else going on. There is an absolute unity that is manifesting on this plane, and on all planes, and nothing can compromise this understanding.

Zen, or at least the lineage of this particular teacher, seems to be able to provide a landscape where Jewish practitioners can manifest their deepest appetites concerning the absolute.

There is a story—it may be apocryphal, but the facts are not; some of the details would need to be checked: when this same young man was at Cornell, he began to study with this old teacher. The leader, or whoever it was, of the Chabad house, said to one of the other Jewish students, "Now that you know your studies and are progressing well, and your understanding has matured, go up to the mountain and bring David back." David was the errant student who had embraced these other teachings and was living a life of what you might call "biblical purity." He was very passionate, a very passionate heart.

So, the other David—they are both called David—prepares himself and goes up to the mountain and sits with him and says, "What's going on here? Enough is enough. You've taken enough acid, you've eaten enough mushrooms, you whored after enough false gods. Now, come back and take up your burden."

So the first David says, "Stay with me for a little while."

Well, the upshot of the story was that the second David abandoned Chabad and began to study with the first David, feeling that this was indeed the real thing.

We're in a period when a radical approach to these matters, if not affirmed, is at least tolerated. And I think we are in a period when these relationships will be redefined radically.

AK: I grew up in a Jewish household with parents who were quite respectful toward Judaism, and I attended a Conservative Hebrew School for a few years before my bar mitzvah. But it was not until I stumbled across [spiritual teacher and Timothy Leary associate] Ram Dass . . .

LC: So you understand the trip completely.

AK: I always felt that stuff opened me up to Judaism.

LC: I understand that.

AK: Now, "There's a crack in everything; that's how the light gets in." [from "Anthem," on *The Future*] This, to me, is such a Jewish idea. . . .

LC: I think so too.

AK: Is it also a Zen idea?

LC: I can't even *locate* a Zen idea. [*Kurzweil laughs.*] As I said, I don't really know that much about Zen or Buddhism because I was never really interested in a new religion. When I was young, I investigated various forms around, because they were there. You met a girl or you met somebody, you went on the trip. I had a good Jewish education. I remember sitting with my grandfather, studying the Book of Isaiah. He was already well along in his years, and he'd read a passage, and he'd speak about it and nod off, and his finger would go back to the beginning of the passage as he moved his body, and he'd start fresh, with that same verse again and read it again and expound it again, and sometimes the whole evening was spent on the exposition of one verse.

So I had a clear idea of the implications of what a Jewish life was. I saw my family was deeply involved in the organization of a community. It was no joke.

AK: Yes!

LC: This was not like a theoretical thing. The Hebrew Free Loan Society— people could borrow money free! That's a translation of a Jewish idea into action. I saw this all the time, all around me. And also found my family's businesses conducted at a level of ethics and honor that you couldn't help but be impressed by.

So I saw the thing. So as I say, the ideas in Zen, I'm not sure what they are, because I've only known one old man. I don't know how authentically he represents his tradition. I just know that he's provided a space for me to kind of dance with the Lord that I couldn't find in a lot of the other places I went to.

AK: Why do you think that so many of us young Jews went to the East? Since you observed Jewish communal life and organizational life up close, what was it about it that was bankrupt or that was a turnoff in some way?

LC: I was brought up in the Conservative tradition, which I have the deepest respect for. I'm a member of my synagogue. I light the candles Friday night. And I feel very close to the whole trip. I don't think we were able to develop a meditational system that could seize and address the deep appetites of our best young people, the people who really had to have an experience with the Absolute. We didn't take that seriously.

I think our faith is full of atheists and agnostics. I think that there are lots of nominal Jews around. But I think there are people who really believe, who have really had an experience, who have really been embraced, who have felt this embrace, who have felt themselves dissolve in the midst of a prayer. And felt that the prayer was praying them.

I think these things exist in our literature; we pick up a book by [Jewish philosopher Martin] Buber, a Chassidic tale, or something, and these things are hinted at. But in the mainstream, these things had the status of superstition. So I think that was a very unsatisfactory condition and many of our brightest and best looked into it, looked for it, but simply couldn't find it.

Also, I think there is the prophetic element in Judaism, the prophets, that world vision articulated, let's say, by Isaiah. I think that's also not taken seriously. It was only after studying with my old Zen teacher for many years, when I broke my knees, and I couldn't practice in the meditation hall—I began practicing a Judaism that I had never practiced. Laying tefillin every morning, and going through the Shemoneh Esreh [the central prayer of Jewish liturgy], and really understanding that there were these eighteen steps, and that they were a ladder, and that these were a way of preparing yourself for the day, if you really penetrated each of those paragraphs.

While starting from a very low place, you could put your chin up over the windowsill and actually see a world that you could affirm.

Nobody had ever talked to me that way about anything. The actual use of the liturgy, of our wisdom books, the actual use of them as a real thing, as a thing that is written with white fire on black fire or black fire on white fire, which is the way they say the Torah was written—that idea, of something passionate and not negotiable, that atmosphere, did not touch me at all in my education. And it *has* to.

Now it does touch other groups, but those other groups seem to have forgotten the messianic implication, which is that we all are part of a brotherhood under the Almighty. And the exclusive elements, the nominal elements, seemed to be emphasized and a kind of scorn for the nations, for the goyim. A kind of exclusivity that I found wholly unacceptable, and many people I know find wholly unacceptable. That has also precluded a number of our best from affirming their connection with groups that at least have the fire going. I don't want to get specific, because I don't want to mount criticism against any group that is passionately involved in that kind of destiny.

But you ask why some of our brightest and best have not been able to embrace the tradition. It's because the tradition has betrayed itself, because the messianic unfolding has not been affirmed. And the meditational systems have not been affirmed. And we don't have teachers who are warm in their invitation.

There's something punitive about the invitation. "Do this or else." The Mercy of the Lord is not affirmed, one side of the tree is affirmed, justice or judgment is affirmed, very, very strongly, but the other side is not affirmed and I don't think it's known. I don't think it's experienced. So we need a system that will provide experience in these matters, an experience that is not within the confines of an exclusive vision, that affirms one element in humanity and scorns the rest.

AK: Do you know the work of Rabbi Adin Steinsaltz? He's been translating the Talmud into English.

LC: Yes. I love it. I love it. I've only looked at a few of the volumes, but I've studied them. When I couldn't practice in the zendo, I began to study these things. I had a Jewish education, but it didn't have the real taste and the real juice. Yes, English! It says we can pray in seventy languages, we can study in seventy languages!

AK: One of Rabbi Steinsaltz's mottos is "Let my people know."

LC: Wonderful.

AK: You're echoing what the rabbi often says, that we shouldn't take somebody else's word for what Judaism is. We should find out for ourselves. And we discover we didn't know the treasures that we have.

LC: Wonderful.

AK: You made a comment earlier that reminded me of one of my trips to Eastern Europe. I visited Eastern Europe a number of times. On one of my trips all I did was go to old Jewish cemeteries. I went from town to town, from Jewish cemetery to Jewish cemetery to Jewish cemetery, for weeks. I couldn't get enough of them. At a certain point, in the cemetery of the town where my great-grandfather was born, I had this experience of feeling, as vividly as can be, that I had been killed as a child in the Holocaust.

LC: Uh-huh.

AK: In my dabbling with books on Eastern religions, reincarnation was always a given. Without it, nothing made sense, and with it, everything started to make some sense. I later learned that many of the most illustrious Jewish sages throughout our history taught about the reincarnation of the soul. I then learned that a lot of people have had these similar kinds of experiences that I had. What do you think about reincarnation? Does it make sense to you?

LC: I don't really think about these things very deeply. It seems to be part of a conceptual point of view that you can develop, and develop a very legitimate argument. When I say "conceptual," I don't mean that scornfully. I mean that it involves the mind and an idea and an experience. And I can get into a whole number of very fascinating conceptual propositions, and reincarnation is one of them.

It doesn't have the urgency of the present demand—that we get right with ourselves and with our Maker. The absolute demand, from moment to moment, that we not violate the birthright and the position that we have as human beings.

These Tibetans, this book that I'm supposed to be narrating, *The Tibetan Book of the Dead*, is a very, very careful examination of these various states. And in Chasidism it is, for example, very, very clear how long the spirit hovers above the body. There are people who are very sensitive.

The same people who said, "you shall not kill" also talked about shellfish, and I think we have to accord a certain respect for these matters. If somebody can pick up very clear ideas about human behavior, and also mention shellfish and cooking the lamb in the milk of its mother, I think we should take these things a lot more seriously than we might, because the same minds are perceiving the absolute importance of both of these possibilities. Very delicate and subtle minds tell us the spirit of the individual is hovering over the body, so I don't think there's any reason to discard that notion.

When I say, "What about reincarnation?" my old teacher says, "Tibetan fairytale." That's his point of view. It's not that he wishes to denigrate or degrade that position. It's more like, "Don't you have anything better to think about? Your position in the cosmos is at stake at this moment. How do you want to deal with it? How would you like to be with me in this room?" I tend to feel that way.

AK: A moment ago, we were talking about how they spoiled Judaism for many of us. They also spoiled poetry for many of us.

LC: I have to exclude myself from this "us," because they didn't spoil Judaism for me.

AK: Nor for me either.

LC: There was something in it. Yes, I had to go whoring after false gods, and maybe I'm still in the bed of one. But, there was something about what I saw . . . people have their stories: I grew up in a Catholic city and my Catholic friends have horror stories about what Catholicism was, and my Jewish friends have horror stories about what Judaism was. I never had them. I never rebelled against my parents, even when I was taking acid and living in the Chelsea Hotel. It never occurred to me once to blame my family, my city, my religion, my tribe, my destiny, my position, on who they were. I always thought it was great! I always thought my family practice was great, and I've tried to keep it up—in my half-ass way.

But poetry . . .

AK: Yes, poetry. I run the Jewish Book Club. We sell books of Jewish interest to twenty-two thousand households. We sell a lot of books. But poetry never sells, no matter who it is. And, as you can see I am ignoring that data by offering your new book. [*Cohen laughs.*] Why do you think that is? I know my own horror stories in high school, the murdering of poetry! What are your thoughts on this?

LC: I don't think it's for everybody in its pure form. It's like bee pollen. It's nice to have honey in your cakes, but there are purists who like the pollen and the propolis. There are bee cultists.

I feel that way about poetry. The honey of poetry is all over the place. It's in the writing in the *National Geographic*, when the thing is absolutely clear and beautiful. It's in movies. It's all over. The taste of significance is what we call poetry. And when something resonates with a particular kind of significance, we might not call it poetry, but we've experienced poetry.

It's got something to do with truth and rhythm and authority and music. It's all over the place. For the few cultists and purists who like to look at a page where the words don't come to the end of the line, I think that's a very specific kind of interest and a very specific kind of appetite, and I really don't think it's for everybody.

So I've never been dismayed. My feeling is, I was completely hooked on this stuff as a kid. I loved it when I first came across it—in the songs my mother sang, in the liturgy, in the pop music. There was a certain resonance when something was said in a certain kind of way. It seemed to embrace the cosmos. Not just my heart but every heart was involved, and loneliness was dissolved, and you felt like you were this aching creature in the midst of the aching cosmos and the ache was OK. Not only was it OK but it was the way that you embraced the sun and the moon.

I went into pop music. I felt that that's where I could manifest it. Just on the page wasn't going to do it for me. Because I wanted to live it! And I didn't want to live it in poetry readings, although there's nothing wrong with that. I just felt that there was a lute behind it, there was a ten-stringed instrument behind it. That was the way that I got the stuff. So I naturally moved into this kind of expression that I got lost in.

AK: So there's no difference between a poem and a lyric?

LC: It's the life that you want to lead. You can be the subject and poetry can be the object, and you can keep the subject/object relationship and that's completely legitimate. It is the point of view of the scholar.

But I wanted to *live* this world. When I read the Psalms or when they lift up the Torah, "Etz chayim hi l'mah chazikim bah." [*Literally, "It is a tree of life for those who grasp it." This verse is sung as part of the response from a congregation upon seeing the raised Torah scroll.*] That kind of thing sent a chill down my back. I wanted to be that one who lifted up the Torah. I wanted to say that. I wanted to be in that position. When they told me I was a Kohayn, I believed it. [*"Kohayn" is Hebrew for "priest" and the source of the name "Cohen."*] I didn't think this was some auxiliary information. I believed. I wanted to wear white clothes, and to go into the Holy of Holies, and to negotiate with the deepest resources of my soul.

So I took the whole thing seriously. I was this little kid, and whatever they told me in these matters, it resonated. I wanted to be that figure who sang, "This is a Tree of Life; all that you hold on to." So I tried to be that. I tried to become that. That world seemed open to me. And I was able to become that.

In my own modest way, I became that little figure to myself. So that was poetry to me. And I think it's available to everybody.

AK: Were you making the point before that there was some connection between your breaking your knees and your adopting of Torah observance? How did you break your knees?

LC: I fell. I was running across a mountain at night and I ran into a wall. A low stone wall. I tripped over it and I badly damaged my knees and I had to have microsurgery. Fortunately, I just tore the meniscus in both knees. It was painful but not catastrophic.

And so I couldn't practice. I was used to sitting straight, in silence, with my knees crossed and my back straight, which were the instructions of that teacher called Shakyamuni or the Buddha. He didn't say that much about anything except to sit, fold your legs carefully under you, and sit with your back straight. And that's it. Then figure it out for yourself. That's basically the instructions he gave.

AK: And suddenly you were in a situation where you couldn't do that?

LC: Yes. I had some friends who were rabbis, and one particular friend, Simcha, was the head of the Chabad at McGill. [*Chabad is an acronym for the Hebrew Kabbalistic terms "chochma," "bina," and "da'at," meaning wisdom, understanding and knowledge, In general use, it refers to the Chasidic group known as Lubavitch.*] And we used to meet and talk—and drink actually. And I had been interested, but I never really led a formal Orthodox life. And I felt the appetite. I felt, "What is this tefillin?" [*Tefillin refers to a set of two small black leather boxes containing verses from the Torah.*] I inherited my grandfather's tefillin. I had the bag. And I wondered, "What is this thing? What are these morning prayers?" And I began to look into them, and to study them, and to say them and to try to penetrate them. And to try to make sense of them, in the deepest way.

And it was my studies with this old Zen monk, it was my experience in the zendo, that opened it for me for the first time. I saw I really could use this material, and I saw how exquisite and skillful these prayers were, how they had been designed by minds that you have to incline your heads toward. These minds who designed these prayers or received the inspiration to design these prayers—these are incredibly subtle and exquisite prayers for lifting the soul.

So I began to practice this form that was such a happy homecoming. I wrote *Book of Mercy* out of that period. I tried to make my tiny homage to a tradition that had somehow been withheld, not deliberately withheld, but had been lost to me, let's say, and lost to my own family practice.

AK: I keep thinking, as you're talking, of that image of your grandfather going back to that verse, and again, back to that verse. Somehow he saw something and achieved something.

LC: Oh yes! Well, he was a wonderful spirit. He swam in it. It wasn't that he could ever leave it.

He happened to be in a confrontational, belligerent stance regarding the rabbinical vision. There was something about it that he didn't like. But he was in it, and there was no way that he could be anything else but Rabbi Solomon Klonitsky-Klein.

Incidentally, when he died, he was writing a dictionary without reference books. He was a little gone, but nevertheless he felt confident enough to sit: A . . . B . . . C . . . He was really one of those people who could put the pin through a page and know the letter it touched on the other side. You know what I mean! He was one of those minds. [*In 1917, in the journal* Psychological Review, *psychologist George Stratton documented a group of Talmudic scholars from Poland who memorized all 5,422 pages of the Talmud so when a pin was stuck through any page they could tell you what word was stuck on the other side. Rabbi Solomon Schechter, founder of the Conservative movement in America, claimed to have witnessed this amazing feat.*]

AK: Is it true that your father gave you a leather-bound book of poetry that made an impact on you?

LC: My father left me a library of poetry. When it was his bar mitzvah, which was around 1907, it must have been the custom in Montreal to give these leather-bound books of English poetry. When he died I inherited his library. And I don't even know if I made this up now, because it seems highly unlikely, but he gave me a book called *The Romance of the King's Army.* [*The book, by A. B. Tucker, actually appeared in 1908. —Ed.*] He was an army man, a patriarch, an Edwardian kind of gentleman.

He wore a monocle. He had spats and a cane. He would go out with his service medals on his tuxedo. That kind of thing. A very distinguished, wonderful figure. Very disciplinarian.

So he gave me this book before he died, and the quotation in the beginning of the book—and that was what really struck me—was, "You would be surprised, my son, with how little wisdom the world is governed." The quintessential religious position is that this world, the world that is governed without God, is a world of folly. "You would be surprised, my son, with how little wisdom the world is governed." To give that to a kid of eight . . . it was a very, very strong message from someone. And he died shortly afterward.

But that seemed to undermine the whole secular position. That there was no wisdom in the world. You had to turn elsewhere.

[*Kurzweil and Cohen sit in silence for a long moment.*]

AK: Why the monocle? Was that a style?

LC: I think they were designed to peer at your inferiors. [*Cohen and Kurzweil laugh.*]

AK: Your Hebrew name is Eliezer?

LC: Eliezer.

AK: And your father's Hebrew name?

LC: Nissan.

AK: So, Eliezer ben Nissan.

LC: Nissan, Nathan. Natan it would be today, isn't it?

AK: Nissan is Natan, which is Nathan. Yes, Natan. As we are talking about these things, I keep on thinking about that line, "I'm the little Jew who wrote the Bible" [*from Cohen's song "The Future," from the album of the same name*].

LC: Exactly. That line was spontaneous, and I asked myself whether I wanted to keep it there. But it is the way I feel. I do feel that this is my position. *This is where I am situated.*

AK: I have to admit that I wondered, when I thought about inviting you to have this conversation and I chose your book to be a selection of the Jewish Book Club, not knowing you personally, if you want to be "the little Jew who wrote the Bible" or "the Jewish poet." But, obviously, I am hearing something very different.

LC: Oh, I *am* the little Jew who wrote the Bible. *I am the little Jew who wrote the Bible.* "You don't know me from the wind. You never will, you never did." I'm saying this to the nations. "I'm the little Jew who wrote the Bible." I'm that *little one*. "I've seen the nations rise and fall, I've heard their stories . . ."

AK: ". . . heard them all . . ."

LC: ". . . heard them all. But love's the only engine of survival."

I *know* what it takes to survive. I *know* what a people needs to survive and as I get older I feel less modest about taking these positions because I realized we *are* the ones who wrote the Bible. And, at our best, we inhabit a biblical landscape, and this is where we should situate ourselves without apology.

For these things, for the burning bush, for those experiences. Those are the experiences that we have the obligation to manifest. That biblical landscape is our urgent invitation, and we have to be there. Otherwise it's really not worth saving or manifesting or redeeming or anything, unless we really take up that invitation to walk onto that biblical landscape. That's where we are.

Now what *is* the biblical landscape? It is the victory of experience. That's what the Bible celebrates. The victory of experience. So the experience of these things is absolutely necessary, as well as a teaching that enables the student to manifest, to experience these episodes that are burning through the Bible, that are now relegated to the realm of miracles or superstition, or something that can't happen to you.

AK: The story of Isaac. We read it every morning.

LC: Yes, that binding! So that's what I learnt from my old teacher, my old rabbi. And when I brought that writer Leon Wieseltier up Mount Baldy— he wrote about it in the *New Yorker ["The Prince of Bummers" by Leon Wieseltier, the* New Yorker, *July 26, 1993]*—I said to him, "I'm going to shul, do you want to come with me?" I meant it.

Harry Rasky—a wonderful Canadian filmmaker, did a wonderful movie on the Holocaust—when he got in trouble I said, "Come to shul. I'll bring you here."

He came, and he sat, and he studied with my old teacher.

That's what it's like. That's how I imagined what a Chassidic court would be. That's what it's like to me.

I think that we can bring this experience back to our traditions. I see these like training centers. It used to happen. There were Jews who used to study with Sufi masters, at a certain great period in our history, and bring it back, and the opposite.

But this kind of exclusivity! A confident people is not exclusive. A great religion *affirms* other religions. A great culture *affirms* other cultures. A great nation *affirms* other nations. A great individual *affirms* other individuals, validates the being-ness of others and the vitality. That's the way I feel about this thing.

AK: Yes! By the way, another uplifting line of yours, "I haven't been this happy since the end of World War Two" [from "Waiting for the Miracle," on Cohen's *The Future*] . . .

LC: Right! [*Laughs.*] I know. As I've said before, if I knew where those lines come from, I'd go there more often.

AK: I have so many things I've collected, just to give you an indication of the extent to which I've gotten involved with your work. I have so many things. I even once sent for this stuff . . .

LC: Oh, yeah!

AK: . . . I don't think I ever read it. But there was something just so intriguing to me about it. [*Shows Cohen literature about Kateri Tekakwitha (1656–1680), a Native American who converted to Roman Catholicism and who is referred to frequently in Cohen's novel* Beautiful Losers.]

LC: Yes, well she's buried just outside of Montreal. They've changed their name now, to Kahnawake from Caughnwaga. [*Kahnawake Mohawk Territory is a reserve of the Iroquoian-speaking Mohawk nation. It is on the Saint Lawrence River, across from Montreal, on its south shore.*]

AK: How do you pronounce her name?

LC: Tee-kahk-wee-tah. She's wonderful. She's in the soil around Montreal. It's not remote. I always loved her, and I always loved the Indians. My father used to take me to this reservation.

AK: Oh, really?

LC: All the time. Before I ever heard of Kateri Tekakwitha. I used to go with him Sunday afternoons and we'd watch the dances of the Indians. Strange that I found out later that Kateri's remains are buried there. I'm sorry. I forgot what you asked.

AK: I wasn't really asking. I was just confessing about sending for these pamphlets about Kateri Tekakwitha!

LC: It's amazing, it's amazing. Well, you're absolved. You know there's a statue of her on the doors of Saint Patrick's Cathedral here in New York.

AK: I'll have to go over there.

LC: Sometimes when I've been in New York, there's a flower store nearby, and I'd go and buy a lily and I'd put it with a rubber band on her braid because the braids come out of the door. It's a very beautiful statue of Kateri Tekakwitha.

[*Without missing a beat, Cohen changes the subject.*] So, when the second David came up the mountain to the first David, he came into the zendo and sat down with the first David and said to him, "Look, this is wonderful. I feel this is the real thing. But there's a statue of the Buddha. This is really intolerable. To have an idol!"

So the first David said, "Really?" And then he picked up the statue and threw it out. [*Cohen and Kurzweil laugh.*]

AK: That's great. I think we've done it! Thank you very much for this conversation!

LC: Thank *you* so much for coming. It's very, very kind of you.

AK: Well it's my pleasure. When I graduated from college, in 1971, I bought a one-way ticket to Europe and traveled around. I had my guitar with me, and I figured I only had room for one songbook. This [*Songs of Leonard Cohen*] was the songbook that traveled with me in Europe.

LC: Ah, great. That's very kind!

AK: It's been to Spain and to Yugoslavia and to Morocco and to Italy and to Israel. All over the place.

LC: Tell me, if you have a moment or two, what was your story? So you heard Baba Ram Dass, and then what was your trip? Where were you at the time? Just tell me a little about your own trip.

AK: I was in high school and college in the sixties.

LC: What college? What high school?

AK: I went to East Meadow High School on Long Island, a suburban public high school. I went to Hofstra University, and then I got a master's degree in library science from Florida State in Tallahassee. I was busy, for a number of years, trying to end the war in Vietnam. Then I graduated college and went to Europe and it was at that time when I was beginning to discover Jewish stuff. And when I got back from Europe I discovered Ram Dass. I knew he was originally Dr. Richard Alpert and was at Harvard University, with Timothy Leary. Then Ram Dass went to India, and he met his guru, and then came back to the States. I started hearing him on WBAI. And then I went to hear him lecture and bought his tapes and just sat for hours. I must have a hundred recordings of his talks. I bought myself a printing press, setting the type by hand, and I sat, like a monk, I suppose, in my apartment, for months, printing little poetry cards. I'd find a poem and I'd set it in hand type and I'd just print them . . .

LC: Ah, it's an old tradition. Beautiful!

AK: . . . and listen to Ram Dass tapes. My studio apartment on 101st Street in New York City was a little monastery for me. And at a certain point I realized that Ram Dass, a Jew steeped in Hinduism, was opening me up to Jewish things. And slowly but surely I became more interested in trying some of these things on and realizing, like you were saying, that the Shemoneh Esreh [central part of the Jewish prayer] is not just a bunch of words, that it's a spiritual ladder.

LC: Right!

AK: Then there is Rabbi Adin Steinsaltz, who we were talking about before: he's a brilliant, profound, wise rabbi in Jerusalem, who comes to New York three or four times a year, and who is trying to be a bridge between worlds.

LC: And you began studying with him?

AK: Yes, I began to study his books and study with him. And I looked for every opportunity to go sit with him and bring him my problems, to ask him my questions. And he became a very important person for me. And my genealogical research was very important to me, too. I was interested in my family tree, and I started tracing. I discovered that I had more in common with my dead ancestors than my living relatives. And, as I have often said, they are sometimes much easier to get along with.

LC: Right.

AK: So I hung around with my dead ancestors and went to old Jewish cemeteries in Poland and Hungary and Russia, and I did research and discovered who they were—and not only how they died but how they lived.

LC: Is your book available?

AK: I just finished a second edition. [From Generation to Generation: How to Trace Your Jewish Genealogy and Family History *originally appeared in 1980. Revised editions were issued in 1994 and 2004.*]

LC: I'd like to see this. Can you send me one?

AK: I would love to. I also wrote a book on Jewish genealogy for children that has a picture in it of my second cousin, Zsuzsa Barta, who learned English from your records in Budapest. So I'll send it to you, and mark it, so you can see it.

LC: Great. Have you written a lot of books?

AK: I wrote three books on Jewish genealogy and family history.

LC: Incredible! That's wonderful.

AK: So when I saw the names of the towns that your family came from, I knew them all. I knew them from maps.

LC: Well, now listen. Let me ask you something. The synagogue in Vilkaviskis, which is also known as Vilkavisk, was wooden. Is it true that it was octagonal?

AK: Have you seen the book *Wooden Synagogues*?

LC: No.

AK: Well, I have an album. It's out of print. It was published in Poland right after the Holocaust [actually 1959] called *Wooden Synagogues*. I'll look it up and see if there is a picture of it.

LC: Would you? I heard something in my family that it was like that.

AK: That it was octagonal? Some of them were absolutely exquisite. This book is extraordinary: pictures, drawings, and floor plans of wooden synagogues in Poland, of which none exist any longer. There is not a single one that stands. I'll look and see.

LC: Because I have letters from my great-grandfather to my grandfather.

AK: Really? From the old country?

LC: Yes, yes. They are beautiful letters. They formally started off, "May the Almighty in His divine wisdom grant you and your family the blessings . . ." I mean beautiful salutations. And he says, "Thank you for your gift of thirty rubles. I had to ride twenty miles to the post office. And, thank God, I go to the synagogue every morning and every evening." It was really an evocation of a life there. Wonderful letters.

AK: Well, I'll do a little checking. It would be fun if I found something for you.

LC: That's very kind of you. There were a couple of books written, kind of privately, about the family, by a Montreal genealogist.

AK: Is this somebody who is related to you?

LC: No, just because the family was a strong . . .

AK: A kind of illustrious family in the town.

LC: Well, it was illustrious only in the sense that they served. They were not particularly illustrious.

AK: Their reputation as community people . . .

LC: Yes, they were community people, exactly.

AK: Could I ask you to sign my items?

LC: Of course. I'll even stamp it with my little colophon [printer's mark] I developed. I'll show it to you. Maybe you're the man to ask about this. This is my colophon. The two hearts are intertwined in the same way two triangles are intertwined in a Magen David. [*Literally "Shield of David," it is a hexagram made from two equilateral triangles. A Magen David has been known, since at least the seventeenth century, to represent the Jewish people. It also appears on the flag of Israel.*] I never knew this existed until I designed it. When I was reading a book by Gershom Scholem [*often described as the founder of the modern, academic study of Kabbalah*], he curiously enough happened to describe a synagogue, I think eighth century in Asia Minor. And he just happened to mention that there were two hearts interlocked on one of the walls. So I don't know.

AK: I know an essay that Scholem wrote about the Star of David. I have the book at home with that essay in it.

LC: It's wonderful that you're a scholar, among other things. It's wonderful that you have this stuff down like that.

AK: Well, it would be nice to find something.

RADIO INTERVIEW

CHRIS DOURIDAS | December 1993, *Morning Becomes Eclectic*, KCRW-FM (Santa Monica, California)

As 1993 came to a close, Cohen sat down with veteran disc jockey Chris Douridas for a live radio interview. The singer talked about his creative process and also about his frustrations with the American music business and his failed attempts to have his videos shown on television.

"I remember Leonard brought me a gift that day," Douridas told me. "A set of worry beads from Greece, a traditional strand of beads a person uses to pass the time in Greek and Cypriot cultures. It was reflective of his love of Greece and also of my Greek heritage.

"Leonard has made many appearances at KCRW over the years," Douridas added, "and along the way we've become friends. I love him dearly." —Ed.

Chris Douridas: It's great to have you here. Thanks for joining us in the rain this morning.

Leonard Cohen: Oh, thank you for having me down.

CD: When you release a collection of songs, I wonder if there's a pain of separation for you or is it a kind of freedom, a joyous sort of release for you?

LC: I'm always happiest when an album is finished. The quality I like most about an album is its doneness.

CD: So there's no trepidation when you finally release it?

LC: No, I haven't had a sense of trepidation about almost anything for a long, long time and when I finish an album it is such a sense of having completed a task that I can barely contain myself. Also, there's a possibility of substantial income, which is always delightful to speculate upon.

CD: So it's kind of like a lottery. You're putting something out there and waiting to see what comes back.

LC: Well, I take the work very seriously and it's a rigorous activity and it's done with, as my confrere put it, blood on the tracks. One deserves the right to be comic about it after it's over. But the work is rigorous.

CD: The creative process, as you said, can be grueling. There's a Hebrew term for it that I've heard you refer to in the Book of Genesis.

LC: Well, God referred to it; it wasn't actually me. But it's in the first lines of Genesis. That notion has been used as an explanation of the creative process, since the process that God himself used in creating the cosmos involved tohu and bohu—chaos and desolation. The spirit of the Lord moved over the chaos and desolation. So lest anybody think that the making of anything is some kind of glamorous activity involved with bricks that are already baked it's not at all that way. You're dealing with the mud and the water. Those are the ingredients of anything that is beautiful—chaos and desolation.

CD: Diving into the creative process like that and surrendering yourself to this raw-material creation. . . . What must that be like to live with?

LC: It's a bitch. I would advise anybody to avoid this enterprise like the plague. It's not a really suitable profession except for a very few people. And even the ones that have the credentials of talent and application often don't have the right spirit or psychology for it and self-destruct early on in the game. So I'm very reluctant to invite anybody into this guild.

CD: But I suspect that when you're putting together an album, you have to invite people into these lower depths with you to help interpret the songs.

LC: You invite them but nobody really wants to come when they see it up close. And if you have any respect for your family or those you love, you allow them to bow out. And you make the occasion as graceful as possible. Nobody can follow you where you've got to go to do good work. Now, there are people who write great songs in the back of taxicabs and they are of an especially blessed tribe. But there is another tribe that doesn't do it that way. And I'd much prefer to be in the former but I am in the latter. Nobody can follow you there and nobody wants to come and friends drop away and people turn aside and you can't expect anybody to go the distance with you [*pause*] except for maybe one person in your life. Maybe one person can do it. One intimate soul.

CD: Was there one for you on this project?

LC: Yes there was. God has been good to me and usually someone has arisen in my life at these junctures and provided some kind of perspective and comfort, some kind of cheerfulness and help.

CD: And I suppose that can be found in the dedication to the album.

LC: Usually I dedicate these albums to the one who allowed the record to exist.

CD: When you listen to the album, there seems to be two emerging visions of the future. Kind of a positive and negative vision. It makes me think of something a mentor of yours, a poet in Canada, Irving Layton, said of you: "One eye was filled with joy and the other with pain." Aside from being a beautiful line, do you think that still holds true for you?

LC: I don't know, but I love Irving Layton. He's an old friend and an old teacher of mine. He said one of the most penetrating things I've ever heard about the qualities a young poet needs. He said the most essential qualities for a young poet are arrogance and inexperience. And I had plenty of those qualities when I was very young. Layton has been a great example to me. He's about eighty-five now and at the height of his powers. He's produced maybe seventy books of verse and he goes from strength to strength. He has a wife of thirty. He goes on and on and on. I hope to be able to limp in his footsteps.

CD: Being from Canada and having spent a lot of time in Greece and the United States . . . I'm interested in your perspective of America and what it is for you. You once referred to the United States as a great experiment.

LC: Well, I'm a guest in your country and I don't think it's appropriate for me to shoot my mouth off about it. But I find myself defending America in many parts of the world. Not so much recently, but until quite recently . . . there was some kind of superiority, especially among the Europeans and the Canadians, about America. But America is the great experiment in democracy and it's in America that the real confrontation between the rich and the poor, between the black and the white, between cultures, [occurs]. . . . It's here that this experiment is unfolding. In Europe, which is beginning to have its own cultural problems with its own confrontations, they look a little less scornfully over here now than they did because America's been dealing with these problems for a long, long time. And I think the outcome in America is very important for the rest of the world too.

CD: What's the life of a song for you? Do the words come first? I suspect they do, being a poet.

LC: When you asked me the life of a song, I thought . . . they last about as long as a Volvo. Thirty years.

CD: What happens in thirty years?

LC: I don't know but the ones I wrote thirty years ago are still moving around and I have high hopes that the new ones will also be around for a while.

CD: In terms of putting the songs together, do the words come first and then the melody?

LC: They're born together.

CD: How do you know that words need to become a song? How do you know that it's not done once it's just the words there?

LC: One of the main motivations is like the bill from your kid's college and that produces a sense of panic that makes you want to express yourself in some way. It's a vice. It's just a habit. One finds at a certain point that one doesn't know how to do anything else. For instance, if you have a sense that you have another life ahead of you, that this sophisticated work that you're doing now with music is just to pass the time before you get to your real profession, beware: you'll find one moment that you really are a disc jockey living in L.A. That's what I found out about myself, that I was a songwriter living in L.A. That's why I write songs, because I don't know how to do anything else.

CD: Say you've finished a song like "Democracy." Do you immediately want to get it in a demo form to record it or do you wait till you're about to get to an album and do it all at once?

LC: I have an intensely private and personal feeling about my work that I really do keep to myself, and I got that covered—whether the songs are any good or they mean anything or I've worked hard enough on them or they're gonna live or they're gonna die. But beyond that, there's the relationship with the record company and with the marketplace that you have to deal with. You can't deal with it of course unless you're feeling strong and confident and cheerful about the work you've done. But mostly if you're gonna survive as a songwriter living in L.A., you've really got to deal with the record company and with the marketplace. So most of the things you do with the songs themselves and what comes out after the record is really determined by the severe iron laws of the marketplace.

CD: And now there's that added area of video.

LC: If only there were. I make videos but they're not shown in America.

CD: Why do you think that is?

LC: I don't know. I would really like to have people speculate on this matter.

CD: There is actually one video completed for *The Future*, right?

LC: There's a video for every record I've put out ever since there's been videos. But none of them is ever shown in America.

CD: I guess there's a video for "Closing Time."

LC: It's a wonderful video. Too bad nobody will ever see it here.

CD: Do you think you'll compile them at one point and—

LC: For what? I mean, they're compiled right now on the shelves of my library. For some odd reason, I can't be shown. I thought at least I could be shown on the old people's home of music channels—VH1—but I'm not even permitted to be shown on VH1. I don't know what it is. I would honestly love to have it explained to me. Because there's no way to sell records in this country, no way to have a career in this country, without video.

CD: I heard a rumor that you were going to be working with David Lynch on a new video for the album.

LC: He's always spreading rumors like that around.

CD: [*Laughs.*] If it were to be true, what song might it be?

LC: "The Future." But now that I thoroughly and profoundly have grasped this concept that I cannot get a video on a music channel in America, to put the kind of effort that is necessary into making a second video is very much less of an attractive idea than it was when I was filled with the heady intoxication of my record company's speculations on the success of this record.

CD: Much of your material seems to come out of spiritual and sexual experiences and I wonder if you might speak to that tension between spiritual and sexual.

LC: There's no tension for me. Everybody else seems to find some tension in this thing but for me, it's just business as usual.

CD: You just came back from a rather successful European tour—

LC: Promotional tour, yeah.

CD: So you weren't actually performing in concert over there?

LC: No, I was doing a lot of television work.

CD: Your career is really sustained by the support you're getting in Europe and in Canada.

LC: It always has been.

CD: Something you said really troubled me. . . . [You seem to have] given up on developing a career in the United States.

LC: There's a kind of rapport that one keeps with a small audience here or there in the larger cities but once you've been designated as out of the mainstream, it's very, very difficult . . . one can't penetrate that description of oneself. It's there and it stands. I can do a concert tour and I can fill modest halls in the larger cities of this country but in the sense of reaching an audience and sustaining that rapport, it's impossible.

CD: Will you be taking a tour across the United States soon?

LC: I will do that.

CD: We're getting a lot of calls—people saying, "When is he going to play in town?"

LC: That's very kind. I really appreciate the interest. I don't think it'll be before the early summer.

CD: How about boxed sets? Everybody seems to be getting a box set these days. Is that something you could do? Put your songs together like that?

LC: Of course you can suggest these things. These marketing tools are available and there is a modest interest in these matters in Sony in regard to me.

CD: I can't thank you enough for coming by. It's been a pleasure having you here at the station and I wish you the best of luck on the future, in the future, with *The Future*.

LC: Thank you very much. And I appreciate the support of this station. It's touching.

INTERVIEW

RICHARD GUILLIATT | December 12, 1993, the *Sunday Times Magazine* (London)

This final 1993 conversation leaves little doubt that Cohen was wrestling with demons at the time. Though claiming to have "no complaints," he sounded troubled—not to mention intoxicated. And it wasn't long after this talk that he moved to the Zen Buddhist retreat on California's Mount Baldy that he had been visiting for years. He would be ordained as a monk there in 1996. —Ed.

Night in Los Angeles, and the city is on fire, its outskirts put to the torch by anonymous pyromaniacs. After the riots and the floods, the entire city seems unnerved by this latest visitation of disaster. Yet here is Leonard Cohen—the poet laureate of pessimism, the world heavyweight champion of existential despair—getting cheerfully drunk in a Chinese restaurant on Wilshire Boulevard.

"All life agrees with me," says Cohen, exuding the woozy bonhomie of a man being caressed by the effects of three strong bloody Marys. "I have no complaints." Having just that afternoon finished mixing a live recording, Cohen had brought us here an hour ago with the stated intention of eating a brief dinner before continuing on to his nearby apartment to conduct an interview. But the vodka is flowing and Cohen's train of thought is getting so expansive that it frequently disappears over the horizon.

"Who are you, anyway?" he inquires jovially. "Why did you come here? You haven't had enough to drink, I can see that."

Considering that Cohen's poems, novels, and songs constitute a forty-year exploration of life's murkiest emotional depths, this display of cheerfulness would seem grossly out of character, not to mention bad for his image. But the truth is Leonard Cohen's career is going so well these days that even Leonard Cohen couldn't complain. His last two albums, *I'm Your Man* and *The Future*, reestablished him as the most literate songwriter in popular music, his 1966 novel *Beautiful Losers* has just been reissued in paperback, and his best writings are now preserved between the covers of *Stranger Music*, a 400-page collection just published by Cape.

In the process of being rediscovered, Cohen has also undergone yet another of his periodic image transformations. In the 1950s he was a literary Young Lion in Canada, in the 1960s he was a folksinger, and in the 1970s he crafted a series of albums so irredeemably bleak that by the 1980s he didn't have much of a career left. Now, as he approaches sixty, he finds himself cast as some venerable philosopher of the heart, a wordsmith whose perennial obsessions—sex, death, and spiritual yearning—are once again tuned in to the zeitgeist.

"You know," he says with droll gravity, "it really is very, very nice to be resurrected in one's autumnal years." The role of world-weary Don Juan is one that Cohen, a never-married romantic with a worldwide coterie of female admirers, is clearly not averse to playing. With his double-breasted grey suit, black crew-neck sweater, close-cropped grey hair, and prescription aviator shades, he looks like some aging gangster sitting here on a pink leather banquette at the back of the deserted restaurant. The effect is capped off by his dolorous baritone voice, which is perfectly modulated for his deadpan bons mots.

Earlier, on the drive over to the restaurant, Cohen had pulled up at a red light and studied the face of a young brunette woman talking on a cellular telephone in a dark Mercedes next to us. "I should get that girl's number," he murmured, fishing around in his suit pocket to produce his own cellular phone as if preparing to try out an in-transit seduction routine. As the Mercedes sped off, he watched its tail lights recede and sighed.

Cohen's cellular telephone was actually a gift from Rebecca De Mornay, the thirty-one-year-old actress who has been his companion for the past five years and who lives just a few miles north of him in Hollywood. *The Future* was dedicated to De Mornay with a biblical inscription and she also helped him compile *Stranger Music*. But tonight she is in Atlanta making a movie, and Cohen is being strangely noncommittal about their relationship, claiming at regular intervals to be looking for a companion for the night, but in the next breath describing De Mornay as "the light of my life."

Has their relationship ended? "Oh, I wouldn't say that," Cohen demurs. "I certainly wouldn't say that to you." He feigns elaborate interest in his wristwatch and his drink, then adds: "Leave Rebecca out of it, OK? Rebecca is a dear, dear creature and I don't want to bring her into this drunken talk."

It's the kind of enigmatic routine Cohen has perfected over the years. As far back as 1968, he shocked Canada's literary establishment by refusing to accept the country's most prestigious literary award, telexing an archly worded statement which read simply: "No, the poems themselves forbid it absolutely." By then his public persona had already taken shape; the coolly self-mocking bard swathed in a dark suit and a veil of irony.

Cohen is equally hard to pigeonhole today. Although he gets up in the predawn hours every day to meditate at a Buddhist temple near his home, he claims not to be a Buddhist and describes the temple priest as his "drinking partner." He has been signed to the same record company for twenty-seven years, yet jokes constantly about its consistent failure to promote his records. He eschews religion, yet his work is shot through with biblical imagery.

Despite his contradictions, evasions, and occasional lapses into Leonard Cohen Schtick, it's impossible not to be charmed by the man. His gracious, old-world manners are genuine and there is nothing frivolous about his work, which strives to lay bare what Cohen once described as "the life of the heart."

"I've always been struggling with the sense that it's pretty tricky to negotiate the day and the night," he says. "The calling in my life has been to struggle with that predicament. But," he adds with a smile, "I've had a couple good laughs now and then, too."

As Cohen's career has wandered from poetry to prose to the pop charts, he has sometimes struggled to find both the audience and the musical format that could support the heavy burdens of his intentions. For much of the 1970s he found himself pigeonholed as a one-note depressive, a reputation not helped by his frequent and sometimes public disintegrations. But he came back swinging in 1988 with *I'm Your Man*, an album that modernized his sound and highlighted the scabrous humor that is often overlooked in his work. Since then he has been on a roll, staging arresting performances and releasing a strong 1992 album, *The Future*, on which he shifted his gaze to the social calamities shaking Europe and the US.

Cohen's "modest enterprise" can now support a full-time staff of three, which administers his publishing and other affairs while he divides his time between two modest apartments, one in his hometown of Montreal and the other in Los Angeles. *The Future* is approaching sales of one million copies, and Cohen appears to have found an audience that crosses all generational lines. He was particularly gratified by the 1991 album *I'm Your Fan*, on which a bevy of twentysomething alternative rock bands paid tribute by recording a collection of his songs.

"I've always felt a kinship," says Cohen. "I felt it to the beats, to the beatniks, to the hipsters, to the hippies. I've always been able to make connections."

Indeed, when Cohen signed to Columbia Records in 1967 he had already spent a decade in the literary limelight of his native Canada. Born into an affluent family in Montreal in 1934, he published his first chapbook of poems at the age of twenty-two while studying at McGill University, and by 1963 he was living an archetypal bohemian existence amid a cadre of writers on the Greek island of Hydra. He wrote a semiautobiographical novel called *The Favorite Game*, and followed that in 1966 with *Beautiful Losers*. Cohen was heavily influenced by the feverish romanticism of the Spanish poet Federico García Lorca, and by the beats. *Beautiful Losers* was an ambitious book that leapt from long stretches of bisexual carnality to historical ruminations on the fate of the Canadian Indians to hilarious parodies of experimental writing.

Asked about his literary influences at the time, Cohen smiles. "Well, there was a lot of amphetamine around," he responds. These days Cohen prefers the more controlled comfort of a few drinks. "I think it's impossible to get through this vale of tears entirely sober," he says. "I'm more like Baudelaire: let me be drunk with wine, with women, with poetry—whatever the thing is."

Although *Beautiful Losers* was widely hailed by the US critics, Cohen was barely eking out a living, and in 1966 he moved to New York to check out the city's exploding folk scene. He had been writing songs and busking since he was a teenager, and when the singer Judy Collins recorded his song "Suzanne," he was signed to Columbia as a recording artist. The move shocked Cohen's peers back in Montreal, and when *Songs of Leonard Cohen* was released in 1967 some of New York's rock critics were not exactly flattering either. "I'm cold as a new razor blade," sang Cohen on "So Long, Marianne," his elegiac farewell to the first great love of his life. It wasn't really a welcome sentiment in the Summer of Love, and the violins and icy backing singers owed more to European art songs than American pop. In retrospect, Cohen sounds almost exuberant compared with the gravelly dirges that would soon follow, but not for the first time he found himself accused of being the worst singer in the known universe.

Living in a room at the Chelsea Hotel, Cohen was enjoying most of the pleasures that bohemian New York offered in 1967, although as a performer he was prone to fleeing the stage in panic. "There was a lot of money involved," he recalls, "there was a career, there were prizes, there were rewards. The kind of life I had led in Montreal, there were no prizes, no rewards—you mimeographed your poems and circulated them among your friends. There was nothing at stake. But yeah, when there was big money and beautiful girls and heavy competition and vicious critics—New York City, in other words—of course I got nervous. Even now I drink heavily on tour."

Cohen's first big performance was an antiwar rally in New York, and by 1968 the *New York Times* was hailing him as "a major spokesman" of his generation. In reality, he was ten years older than most of his musical peers and felt ill at ease with the anti-American rhetoric he heard. Cohen's mother had fled Russia as a teenager and her stories about communism had eradicated whatever nascent leftist ideas young Leonard ever harbored. Hence, he remained resolutely self-absorbed even as the music around him became increasingly politicized. His albums appeared every couple of years—*Songs from a Room*, *Songs of Love and Hate*, *New Skin for the Old Ceremony*—chipping away at familiar themes of loss and yearning and receiving generally laudatory reviews. He moved to a fifteen-hundred-acre ranch in Kentucky for a couple of years, fulfilling a long-held desire to get close to the country music he had loved since childhood. He began attending a Buddhist temple in 1970 and started a long-term relationship with Suzanne Elrod, with whom he had a son, Adam, in 1973 and a daughter, Lorca, a year later. [*Actually, Adam was born in September 1972 and Lorca in September 1974. —Ed.*]

None of these events did anything to lighten the lyrical melancholy of Cohen's music, or broaden its musical palette. His depressions were periodic and he once broke down onstage in Israel. He was so dissatisfied with the sound of his records that he attempted a collaboration with the legendary pop producer Phil Spector in 1976, but Spector was in the midst of cocaine-induced dementia and Cohen had just broken up with Elrod. The resulting album, *Death of a Ladies' Man*, was a disaster that Cohen

tower of song . . ."

"I don't know why, but something happened to me ten years ago," muses Cohen. "When things got really desperate, I started to cheer up."

It would be stretching things to say Cohen has become whimsical in his advancing years. His love songs still have titles like "Ain't No Cure for Love" and the passion in them is still a poignant quest for some brief escape. Desire and disgust, the sacred and the sacrilegious all collide between the sheets in his songs: one wonders whether he believes faithfulness is even possible between men and women.

"If you're in the midst of a relationship, you should honor the terms of the relationship," he responds. "I've always believed that. I've never been able to follow it, but I've always believed it. . . . Monogamous marriage and commitment, all those ferocious ideas, are the very highest expression of a male possibility." He pauses a beat. "I'm not good enough for that. It's a great idea, though."

By 9 PM the restaurant is still deserted and Cohen is munching on a fortune cookie. "I'm feeling lonely tonight," he says with mock melodrama. "I don't know who to call. It's going to be a long night and my nights don't last that long because I have to get up at three thirty."

What will happen at three thirty is that Cohen will rise from his bed and drive into South Central, the poor black neighborhood south of his home, to meditate for several hours at a Buddhist temple. While it might seem characteristically weird of Cohen to pick one of the most violent neighborhoods in America as his place of spiritual contemplation, the Zen monk who opened the temple twenty years ago chose the location because of its cheap rent. Cohen has been going there ever since and bought his apartment because of its proximity to the temple, which he visits every day. Zen meditation is usually perceived as a path to blissful equanimity, but Cohen takes a more idiosyncratic view. "It's usually misery that drives you there," he says. "I mean, who really wants to get up at three thirty in the morning, as I am going to do tomorrow morning, and drive down into a dangerous neighborhood, cross your legs in a very unnatural way, and sit motionless for a couple of hours? I don't think happiness is the motivation for this kind of activity. It's just the opposite. It's confusion and suffering that leads you to these kind of stern measures."

It's the temple that keeps Cohen in his current apartment, against the advice of friends who were spooked by last year's riots. Driving home after dinner, he points to some of the destruction in his local neighborhood—a Tandy store that was leveled, an incinerated gas station. The riots confirmed a certain apocalyptic view he has long harbored, and which became explicit on his recent album *The Future*. Its two central songs, "The Future" and "Democracy," depict the political turmoil of Europe and the US as flip sides of the same coin, the agonies of societies trying to transform themselves or perish. "We're going to have the same kind of revolution here," he says, "and it's just a matter of who's going to run it, whether it's going to be Democrats with a compassionate position or people with a chip on their shoulder about race." Unlike many Canadians, Cohen is a passionate defender of the American ideal, but the solutions he sees to the country's present problems are surprisingly authoritarian—more police on the streets, the censoring of violent television, the application of force.

"At certain times of crisis, like in every other society, extraordinary gency measures have to be invoked. . . . The fact is that the pred-
vels, whether it's Wall Street or the streets—are about to
arkly. "And they're laughing at our laws."

A. pad, a duplex on a quiet tree-lined street in an
antly black neighborhood. Cohen lives on the
at five-room apartment with polished wood
e that denotes a life devoid of unnecessary
e furniture wooden; there are a few rugs,
taining a ghetto blaster and some CDs
ards and album sleeves that usually
to of Cohen with Roshi, his Zen
an improvement on the more
as lived with little more than a

f at home," he offers, ushering me into
ke any office—a couple of high-backed grey
ing a large wooden desk, on top of which are a
macintosh computer, and a printer. The one thing that denotes Cohen's profession is the black Technics synthesizer that occupies the center of the desk like an oblong spaceship. Nearby is a glass-doored stained cabinet that contains Cohen's notebooks and sketches. It's a disarmingly modest setup, the kind of place one would expect to find a struggling writer with a day job toiling in obscurity. Cohen's earlier description of his modus operandi suddenly seemed very apt: "I'm always

scratching away, y'know, I'm always working. I'm a very hard-working fellow. But I don't have any luxury in the matter. I don't have any choice. There's no virtue involved. Unless I keep working at it diligently, I tend to begin suffering very acutely."

Sitting cross-legged on the floor in his grey suit, Cohen is now leafing through a notebook filled with his scribblings, reciting lines from a new song he has half written. The notebooks are filled with pencil sketches and computer-graphic renderings of a voluptuous black woman who visits regularly to pose nude for him. He holds aloft one sketch, a back view of her naked in the bath. "Beautiful ass," he murmurs appreciatively.

Cohen's life suddenly seems like it would have its salutary moments. When the telephone rings, he lifts his head expectantly. "I wonder," he intones gravely, "if that's someone who wants to spend the night with me?"

COHEN CLIP

On His Typewriter

"I once had drawn a bath and I put pine oil in it and I noticed the pine oil stained the water the same color as my Olivetti. I was in a mood of some extravagance and I put the typewriter in the bathtub and tried to type underwater. Then I threw my manuscript for *Flowers for Hitler* in the bath and tried to scrub it with a nailbrush. This was during a particularly tense period one winter in Montreal. Then I took the typewriter out of the bathtub and in a rage over some imagined injustices a woman had done to me, flung it across the room. . . . The Olivetti cracked. I thought it was finished and I just stowed it in a corner of the house. About a year later I went to the Olivetti factory on Nun's Island and brought the thing to the front desk. The man there just looked at it and said 'not a chance.' Then—I don't know why—when the fellow's back was turned I walked in the factory proper, toward a workbench where an elderly man was working on some typewriters. I approached him and I said I really needed this typewriter. He told me to come back in a few weeks, and when I did he had repaired it meticulously."

—from interview with Scott Cohen in the book *Yakety Yak*, 1994

COHEN CLIP

On Whether Zen Stops Him from Thinking

"Nothing can stop you from thinking. The human mind is designed to think continually. Something I wrote quite a few years ago was, 'The voices in my head, they don't care what I do, they just want to argue the matter through and through.' It is a common mistake, to think you're going to go into some kind of spiritual practice and you're going to be relieved of the human burdens, from human crosses like thought, jealousy, despair—in fact, if anything, these feelings are amplified."

—from interview with Anjelica Huston, *Interview*, November 1995

TV INTERVIEW

STINA LUNDBERG DABROWSKI | September 1997 | Swedish National Television (Scandinavia)

Leonard Cohen didn't do a lot of talking, at least to outsiders, during his years with the Buddhists on Mount Baldy. In 1997, however, he met there with Swedish journalist Stina Lundberg Dabrowski. Her obvious rapport with the artist produced a revealing conversation.

The year before, on August 9, 1996, Cohen had been ordained as a Zen Buddhist monk. Dabrowski found him dressed in robes, with a shaved head, and with ostensibly no interest in commercial pursuits. At the time, Columbia was about to issue *More Best of Leonard Cohen*, which came out October 7 and included two previously unreleased songs. But Cohen wasn't exactly pushing the record: it was Dabrowski who brought it up, near the end of the interview. And when she did, Cohen responded that he had no plans to promote it. —Ed.

Leonard Cohen: Come on in. Seriously speaking, if you would like to rest, there's a little bed in there. I've got whiskey.

Stina Lundberg Dabrowski: Whiskey, please.

LC: Now you're talking. [*They move to a meditation room.*] So this is the room we come to in the very early morning after we have our tea.

SLD: So how many hours do you spend in here?

LC: There's close to an hour in the morning and then during the sesshin [days of intense practice] an hour in the afternoon and then another hour listening to the old master. So during the retreats close to three hours a day.

Meditation in most people's minds has a goal. You want to get somewhere. This kind of meditation, the assumption is that you're already there and you just want to manifest that reality that you already embody. So you're not trying to get free or go someplace. You're just trying to be what you really are.

SLD: How do you sit when you do your meditation?

LC: We sit on a cushion like this [*demonstrates*] or we sit on a bench. But the idea is to find a position that supports the back. So generally you make a kind of tripod out of your body where your knees will be two feet of that tripod and your butt will be the other. Some people sit in different ways. A good full lotus is considered the best kind of position.

SLD: I have my skirt. Otherwise I would do it myself.

LC: Go on, do it. Please do it.

SLD: Well, I have the skirt.

LC: Pull your skirt up. We'll give you a robe.

SLD: [*Laughs.*] So why did you flee from this place the first time you came here?

LC: Well, first time I came here I was in real trouble. The head monk was German and they were waking me up very, very early in the morning. We were building this dining hall over there and repairing it and there were no windows and the snow would come in over your rice and you'd be walking through the ice in sandals and they'd be beating you in the zendo and I thought—

SLD: Why beating you?

LC: It appeared to be beating at that time. When you fall asleep or you doze and your posture would decay, they'd come over with a stick. I'll show you that stick. They'd come over with the stick and they'd strike you very sharply twice on either shoulder. It felt like getting beaten to me. It all seemed like the revenge of World War II. They'd gotten a bunch of American kids up here and were torturing them to death. I didn't want any part of it so one day when they were filing out for breakfast I just dropped out of the line and when they were sitting down here I sneaked below window level, down to the parking lot, got in my car, and drove down to Mexico.

SLD: What made you come back again?

LC: A sense of something unfinished, a sense of something vital, something that would keep me alive. You have to have an experience that is not of the world in order to enjoy the world.

SLD: So you couldn't enjoy what you had?

LC: I can now.

SLD: But you could not enjoy—

LC: I don't have it all now. [*Cohen and Dabrowski laugh.*]

SLD: So when you had it you couldn't enjoy it and now you can enjoy it and you don't have it.

LC: I don't have it.

SLD: So which is worse?

LC: Both are pretty good.

SLD: But you seem happier now.

LC: Yes, I feel OK these days. I like being up here. It's a good life. It's a rigorous life. It's a severe life. But if I didn't have these kinds of rules and regulations I'd be lying in bed watching television, scratching myself. I need a lot of order, a lot of form.

SLD: Why do you need that hard discipline?

LC: I don't know. I'm just lazy and self-indulgent and full of self-pity. I need a lot of fences and hedges and regulations and rules. Otherwise I'd just collapse into some kind of relentless form of useless self-examination.

SLD: You were experiencing discomfort all the time?

LC: Yeah. Discomfort from anguish, through deep paralyzing anguish for no reason at all, one thought. Red wine was pretty good . . .

SLD: Red wine?

LC: Yeah, red wine was pretty good in addressing this problem. But you can't stay drunk forever, although I did try. But it really doesn't work. It's just another kind of medication that doesn't work. It works for some people. I know some people who have managed to stay drunk their whole life and they really do it well.

SLD: You took a lot of drugs, too.

LC: Yeah, they work pretty good temporarily. The problem is that they don't work on any ongoing basis so they just wreck you, make you feel worse. That was my experience with it. So it's experience like that that brings you to this kind of hospital up here in the mountains, which is a place where you start again at the beginning. You learn how to sit, you learn how to walk, you learn how to eat, you learn how to be quiet, you learn how to sit still. And you have the opportunity for self-reform. Put the thing back together again.

A lot of people who think that I've changed my religion look very suspiciously or even scornfully or even express great disappointment that I've abandoned my own culture, that I've abandoned Judaism. Well, I was never looking for a new religion. I have a very good religion, which is called Judaism. I have no interest in acquiring another religion.

[*Cohen walks with Dabrowski in the rain.*] This is very sweet and soft. We don't get this very often.

SLD: It's very nice. Do you watch TV?

LC: We don't have any TV up here. But I love TV. [*Cohen and Dabrowski arrive at his cabin and sit at a table with drinks.*] Now, let's get down to business, kid.

SLD: By the way, in the monastery I was a bit surprised to . . . [*Holds up drink.*]

LC: I know, this is terrible. I don't know why I've let you Swedes corrupt me. I knew you'd get me to drink.

SLD: What does your master say about this?

LC: It's very good to drink on a cold day.

SLD: It's cold today?

LC: Yeah, well, a rainy day. When one isn't working and one is entertaining, it's entirely appropriate to drink. In fact, it would be a great breach of hospitality if I didn't offer you something to drink. If you want to keep a bottle of Scotch in your room and take a nip now and then and still follow the regime, letter by letter, you can do that. If you want to keep a chocolate bar in the corner of your room and eat something besides our very, very good vegetarian . . . fine. If you want to fall in love with a beautiful young nun and somehow you can incorporate this into your practice, go ahead. It usually doesn't happen that way. Usually that bottle stays for a year.

SLD: Even in your—

LC: Even in my cabin. People are worried that I'm not working hard enough or suffering enough, I know. Or that I'm not following the regime as strictly as I should. But let them rest assured I am. Even though I smile from time to time and raise my glass, I am suffering sufficiently and I am following all the rules.

SLD: OK. So tell me about your suffering, please.

LC: I can't. I'm not permitted while I'm being a host. It would again violate the rules of hospitality to tell you how bad I feel.

SLD: But you had it all. You had what a lot of men are striving, struggling, trying so hard to get. You had the success, you had the money, you had the fame, you had the women—

LC: Not enough.

SLD: Not enough? Is that the reason you're suffering?

LC: The cover story looked very good. I think people could legitimately say, "What's he complaining about?" Yes, it's true.

SLD: But why were you complaining?

LC: I don't think I was complaining. I was just saying "ouch!" because it hurt. I tried everything they had.

SLD: Like?

LC: Well, the things that you mentioned. Wine, women, song, money, career, drugs, art, every kind of extravagance, every kind of restraint.

SLD: And what helped?

LC: Everything helped in its way in the sense that it said, "This doesn't work." I think that's the greatest help you can get from anything is to find out that it doesn't work. Because nothing works. Nothing in this human realm is meant to work. So once you can deeply appreciate that, for one thing the mind of compassion grows if you understand that everybody's up against it. I remember reading some works of Simone Veil, a French woman who lived in France during the war and she said there's only one question worth asking anybody and that question is, "What are you going through?"

SLD: What are you going through?

LC: "What are you going through?"

SLD: What *are* you going through?

LC: Well, when I look back at my life, I see that it was very contracted. Now maybe in relation to other people it was expansive and it was free and it was admirable and maybe it really was that. But a lot of the time from the inside it felt . . . it didn't have anything to do with ambition . . . it wasn't that I wanted to make it. It wasn't to do with money, it wasn't to do with fame, it wasn't even to do with love. It was just some fundamental sense that this was not flowing with the authentic motion. There was something stopping everything. I had that feeling very, very deeply until recently.

Now of course it changed and often at a concert—I laugh about this but it doesn't make it any less true—with a couple of bottles of red wine under my belt and a good band and good songs, the good songs that I wrote, they're not bad songs, they're good songs . . . I know all that. And sometimes with the love of the audience, the interest, and looking at the faces of people that are looking at me as I'm singing and everything is working, I've felt completely at home and completely at the center of something that was creating love. The very source of things. I felt very, very good. That's what kept me touring.

SLD: Wasn't it enough?

LC: It was too dependent on things.

SLD: On success, on that things went well?

LC: Things had to go well. It's a terrible feeling that I never took a concert casually and I don't think any musician or singer I've ever worked with has taken one of our concerts with anything but real seriousness so if it doesn't go well you do feel that you've betrayed yourself and you've betrayed people and you've wasted their time and you've wasted their money. It's a very bad feeling. On the other hand, when it goes well, it is as I've described it. But besides all that you're dependent. You're dependent on the wine, dependent on the applause, dependent on the song, dependent on the love.

SLD: [*They walk in the rain again and arrive at a dining room.*] This is a dining room?

LC: This is our dining room, yes.

SLD: [*Addressing a chef.*] But now you're cooking for everybody here?

Chef: At the moment yes, but there's only nine people, ten people here. It's a small group.

LC: The last group was about forty.

Chef: Yeah, there were more then, but then I had a lot of help.

LC: How many was it we had?

Chef: I think forty-three last time.

LC: Forty-three. Three meals a day and cookies at night. That was a lot of work. So can we eat?

Chef: Please.

[*Cohen and Dabrowski are shown eating, then back in his room.*]

SLD: But why did you decide to go into a monastery? A lot of people experience this anguish that you went through . . .

LC: Well, I consider myself extremely fortunate in that I bumped into this practice a long time ago and I was able to taste it. I was able to experience something that I had experienced nowhere else. It was clean. It didn't have any dogmatic information. Nobody told you anything. You were invited to work this out by yourself. You were given some guidelines and more importantly you were given the living example of a very human guy and an old man who had already experienced and resolved these questions at the fundamental level of consciousness.

SLD: But you never believed in therapy . . .

LC: I don't say I never believed in it. There didn't seem to be the moment when I wanted to go into it. . . . There seemed to be some flaw in the reasoning. Now I know therapists will say, "He's in denial, he's trying to delay the moment when he comes to us."

[*After an interlude that includes a snippet from "Tower of Song" and some old photos of Cohen, the conversation resumes.*]

LC: There was quite a lively group of Scandinavian writers when I first arrived in Hydra . . . Johan Tengstrom and I started writing our first books together at the same table in my house.

SLD: But he's still a writer. You've passed through a lot of stages.

LC: Oh, terrible. I'm a traitor to the craft. Johan Tengstrom polished his talent until he stands on the brink of a Nobel Prize, where I became just a vulgar popular singer.

SLD: Are you really a writer who failed his—

LC: Completely. I'm a writer who failed his promise.

SLD: So what are you?

LC: But I have a new book over there. You see that?

SLD: Yeah.

LC: I think I might be able to redeem myself.

SLD: Is it true?

LC: Yes.

SLD: So you are writing now.

LC: I don't know. I'm blackening pages but I don't know if it's writing.

SLD: You're very humble.

LC: As I think Gore Vidal [*Actually, it was Truman Capote. —Ed.*] said about Jack Kerouac, "That isn't writing, that's typing."

SLD: In what ways have you experienced love in your life?

LC: Oh, wonderful love . . . I had wonderful love but I did not give back wonderful love. There were people who loved me very, very deeply and very genuinely and I was unable to reply to their love.

SLD: Why?

LC: Because I was obsessed with some fictional sense of separation that I couldn't reach across the table for it. I couldn't reach across the bed. I couldn't reach across the moon. I couldn't reach across my song. I couldn't reach and touch the thing that was being offered me. It was being offered me everywhere and it is always being offered everyone. It is offered at all times, at all moments, and we create a fictional barrier, we succumb to a fictional disease, and we buy into a fictional separation from the thing we want the most, which is a sense of ourselves and a sense of being at home with ourselves.

SLD: Do you get that feeling now?

LC: Yes. A lot. But that's God's world in which there is no separation between you and anything else. As my old teacher says, you can't live in God's world—there's no restaurants or toilets. So you have to leave God's world and be in a human world.

SLD: What is love to you?

LC: Love is that activity that makes the power of man and woman . . . that incorporates it into your own heart, where you can embody man and woman, when you can embody hell and heaven, when you can reconcile and . . . when man and woman becomes your content. In other words, when your woman becomes your own content and you become her content, that's love. That as I understand is love—that's the mechanics.

SLD: What does that mean, that she becomes your content?

LC: She becomes what fills you and you become what fills her and you recognize the full equality of that exchange because if she's smaller than you, she can't fill you and if you're larger than her, you can't fill her. So there has to be an understanding that there really is an absolute equality of power, different kinds of power, obviously different kinds of magic, different kinds of strength, different kinds of movement and as different as night and day. And it is the night and day and it is the moon and the sun and it is the land and the sea and it is plus and minus and it is heaven and hell. It is all those antinomies. But they're all fundamentally equal. So you cannot have a woman as your content, she can't fill up every space in you where she must be unless you understand that she occupies the same cosmic space as you do and you occupy the same cosmic space as she does. Then there can be an exchange and then there can be love.

SLD: Did you experience this?

LC: Yes, I have experienced it. But those are the experiences that make me want to start again, back when I grow up and go to college and—

SLD: Do it all over again but in another way.

LC: [*Laughs.*] Because it's very sweet when you see it done right. You don't have to change the world. There don't have to be any revolutions. It doesn't really matter what is going on around you.

SLD: Do you still have a longing to live the old-fashioned kind of life?

LC: Yes, I do. But it's crazy. And sometimes I think about what career should I take. Sometimes you forget that you're living in this sixty-three-year-old body. I find myself speculating more and more as I find myself more and more healthy and experience more and more energy and the world looks brighter and brighter in some sense, on some days—some days it doesn't. But because I feel those currents running through me, I start to forget that this mental activity is enclosed in this body that is not at all appropriate. I think, find some nice girl and marry her, some nice twenty-two-year-old girl and find a nice little house.

I know I could really enjoy that now. A nice little house with a lovely tablecloth and some nice crystal. And a little money coming in. And I'd know how to treat a woman now. And if we had children, I'd really enjoy them. Not like the first time around where I really had to push myself into some mold that I didn't feel I was naturally in. I did my best and thank God they turned out OK but now I think, yes, I'll find that wonderful young girl and we'll have that tablecloth and we don't need a big house because I know now that riches and big houses and all those things mean nothing. I know that the only thing that counts is to express love and respect and to bend your knee before the object of your love so that she can bend her knee to you. I know that now. I didn't know then.

SLD: So why don't you do it?

LC: Well, I feel that it's not quite the right moment. Maybe next time around. [*Laughs.*]

SLD: You're not quite ready yet?

LC: I don't feel it's really appropriate now. Because I'm *not* twenty-five years old. Sometimes I feel I'm twenty-five years old and that's what I should be doing—and that I should choose a job, not a job like a singer or a writer, not one of those jobs in the arts where the competition is ferocious and the whole situation is scornful and it's dicey and it involves you in investigations of yourself that don't lead anywhere except into sorrow. I don't want to be one of those people, I know what they're like. I wouldn't go near that. There are lots of good jobs.

SLD: Like?

LC: Simple jobs. You could work in a bookstore. You could be a librarian. There's lots of stuff.

SLD: Your relations to your kids and to your ex-wives [*sic*] or women . . . have they changed after your entering the monastery?

LC: That's hard to say. I don't know if anything changes, especially relationships that are really screwed up. It's pretty hard to straighten them out but, yeah, something does change. It's hard to put your finger on it.

SLD: Do your children ever come here?

LC: Sure, on visiting day they sometimes come up. My son [*Adam, by now a singer/songwriter. —Ed.*] called me up a few weeks ago. He never asks me for any help. He said, "There's just one line, Dad. One line in a song I can't get. Could you help me with it?" He said, "I've really been sweating over it." How wonderful, and what a wonderful afternoon we spent. He came up with a sandwich from down below and I had my second lunch with him and we sat outside . . . it was good weather.

SLD: Could you help him?

LC: Yeah, I gave him a couple of words. He just needed a word or two. [*Smiles.*] And that's what we're both doing . . .

SLD: He was close to death a couple of years ago.

LC: Yes, he had a very serious car accident. He was running around with a black band in Guadalupe.

SLD: But he survived but you stayed with him for a couple of months when he was in hospital. How did that change you?

LC: About four months.

SLD: What happened to you during this time?

LC: The thing that happened to both of us is that we were able to get very tight. And those kinds of experiences, they resonate very deep in everybody's heart. It's hard to say exactly what they change but you do find out something about the human body and frailty and you find out something about courage. Not just love between you and the other person but what human beings are capable of.

I saw this kid who was smashed completely and there was a very strong psychic element in his recovery, both involved with my love, his understanding of my unconditional love, my understanding of his incredible courage and his incredible effort. So there were very deep and mysterious human mechanics of the love and of the heart going on which I wouldn't even presume to describe but they certainly had a part in the healing.

SLD: Attachment . . . is that something you're thinking about?

LC: Oh, there's one funny moment I just remembered when my son was in intensive care and he was very smashed and they didn't really know what to do yet. They were just examining him and wondering what approach to take to the damage. And he was on large amounts of morphine and he was in and out of consciousness. And I was reading the Bible out loud to him. I was sitting by his bed reading the Bible and he came to at one time and he turned to me and he recognized me and he said, "Dad, can you read something else?" [*Cohen and Dabrowski laugh.*]

SLD: I guess that was a happy moment in your life. Did you [read something else]?

[*Cohen nods.*]

SLD: A very long time ago you said that women were the salvation for mankind, that they had the brains and the power and the men were playing or artists or joking around—

LC: Gossips.

SLD: Gossips, exactly. And the sooner the women took over the better.

LC: Right. Well, now that they've taken over we can judge whether it's better or not. [*Laughs.*] I may have been wrong.

SLD: But do you mean that women have equal strength to men or do you mean that they are stronger?

LC: Men and women have exactly equal strength but it really wasn't acknowledged that way. Lip service was paid to it and everybody would say that men and women are equal but now in men's hearts they really understand that they are dealing with power *at least* as great as their own.

SLD: Are you happy with this?

LC: Yes. I'm very happy with it.

SLD: You have given so much to so many people. If you are now feeling so fine and you are not interested in creating any more of this stuff, isn't this very sad for the rest of the world?

LC: I don't think it's too sad 'cause you and I know that the stuff's already been created so there's no danger of it being uncreated.

SLD: But the source is still there, the well is still giving water . . .

LC: I think that those poems and songs I wrote then have a certain value. And the poems and songs I'm singing for you right now have another kind of value.

SLD: But does it mean anything to you, what kind of impact you have on the world?

LC: It's hard to discuss the very serious things but, yes, it does mean something to me. Because I get mail, just a little mail, but I get it from people who tell me that my songs are useful. Someone will say that they played my song "If It Be Your Will" at their friend's funeral. Or they played "Dance Me to the End of Love" at their wedding or "Hallelujah" got them through the night or their mother listened to my records as she lay dying of cancer right to the last moment. I see that they [the songs] moved into the world and were able to be useful and helpful and it makes me feel good because it's important that you feel useful. And I do—I do feel that the things have been useful.

SLD: But now you are releasing a new best-of album.

LC: Yeah.

SLD: Are you not going out to—

LC: Tour with it? No, no.

SLD: Why not?

LC: Well, I can't interrupt these studies here.

SLD: I was very surprised when I came here and you said, "Well, they're doing this record but I don't give a shit." I never heard an artist say that.

LC: It's not that I don't give a shit. Because there are people who are spending their time and their money and their energy to do it. I don't in any sense want to convey the fact that I'm scornful of the activity. It's just that I'm involved in an activity now that cannot be interrupted. It's too important for me to interrupt it and it's too important for whatever future work I might do. It's too important for the health of my soul. And the time is limited. Old Roshi, his time is limited—he's ninety.

My body is going to decay naturally over the years and I'm not going to be able to do this kind of practice. I'll be able to do another kind of practice but this one here on this mountain with these kinds of rules and regulations—which I understand so intimately and which I understand the value of so intimately—I won't be able to do that very long. So time is like an arrow. The thing is moving very, very quickly. And it's like the Hebrew saying, "If I am not for myself, who will be? And if not now, when? But if I am only for myself, what am I?"

So all those questions are answered. But I don't think it's a moment for me to climb down the mountain, abandon this investigation, put a band together and go out on tour. No, I don't think that's the moment right now. And please forgive me. And I say this to my listeners: please forgive me for not going out with a band at this moment but I am trying to learn some things and trying to get myself into a shape which I hope will result in songs that are deeper and better and maybe on that basis I'll be forgiven.

SLD: I'm sure.

[Cohen laughs, then he and Dabrowski are seen outside his cabin.]

SLD: So what do you want to say to the Swedish people?

LC: You can speak for me, OK?

SLD: No, you can speak for yourself very well. Thank you very much.

LC: Put it there, kid. [*Shakes Dabrowski's hand.*]

SLD: Nice talking to you.

LC: It was a pleasure.

SLD: Bye bye.

LC: Please come again. I hate to see you go. This is terrible. This is a terrible moment.

SLD: Separation.

LC: The moment of separation. OK, so let me take you to your car. See you later.

SLD: Bye bye.

LC: Bye. Are you driving? [*Cohen waves to Dabrowski and walks back toward his cabin.*]

COHEN CLIP
On Hearing His Old Songs

"I hardly ever get a chance to hear my old songs. Sometimes I hear one on some generous retrospective radio station when I'm in town, but I don't feel like that person anymore. I stand in awe. People say the very early songs were the most important. I listen to them like I'm listening to someone else. I have a lot of respect for the young heart who produced those visions."

—from "A Life in the Day of Leonard Cohen," by Nigel Williamson, the *Sunday Times Magazine* (London), 1997

COHEN CLIP
On His Buddhist Monastery Retreat

"There is no one here who is not, in a certain sense, broken down, who has not found that he doesn't know how to deal with the things you have to face in ordinary life. So they come here. It's not at all an isolated situation. In ordinary life down the mountain sometimes you finish your day's work, you go home, you shut your door, you watch the TV . . . and you're really alone. Here you're never alone. There's little private space, very little time to yourself. There's a saying in Zen, like pebbles in a bag, they polish one another. We're doing that all the time here. So one doesn't have the sense of isolation here . . ."

—from interview with Jean-Luc Esse on *Synergie*
(French radio show), October 6, 1997

TV INTERVIEW

VALERIE PRINGLE | October 28, 1997, *W5*, CTV (Canada)

Like Stina Dabrowski, veteran Canadian broadcaster Valerie Pringle spoke with Cohen in 1997. He was still on Mount Baldy, where he would remain until 1999, but he came down from the mountain to meet Pringle at Shutters on the Beach, a luxury hotel in Santa Monica, California. Their discussion included some of the singer's most forthright comments to date about his struggles with depression.

"I had interviewed him before but this was the best conversation," Pringle told me. "We ran in the waves by the hotel for b-roll. He was fabulous. I have quoted from that interview quite often." —Ed.

Valerie Pringle: Leonard Cohen was born to a well-to-do family in Montreal. He was a latecomer to the pop-music scene. He didn't begin making records until he was in his thirties. Classics like "Suzanne" and "Sisters of Mercy" made Leonard Cohen an international success. His songs are rich with metaphor and melancholy. For more than thirty years, those weighty themes of love, death, and salvation have made him an anomaly in the world of light pop music.

Now this musician with a touch of the mystic is exploring a new path. For the past four years, Leonard Cohen has lived in an austere Zen Buddhist monastery atop Mount Baldy in California. He is a friend and follower of Roshi, a ninety-year-old monk who leads the center. Last year, Cohen himself was ordained as a Buddhist monk. He gets up every morning at two thirty after only four hours' sleep. It's a rigorous lifestyle but one that he has chosen to help him cope with a burden that he's struggled with most of his life. I talked to Leonard Cohen in Los Angeles.

Leonard Cohen: I bumped into this old man. He seemed to be old when I met him although he's younger than I am [*sic*], Roshi. And he seemed to know a thing or two that I was interested in looking into.

VP: But what was it that you were looking for? What did he know that you needed?

LC: I don't think anybody goes into this kind of activity unless their personal level of distress reaches a certain unendurable point. To be serious about it, nobody gets into a very rigorous activity unless they're suffering.

VP: What were you suffering from—depression?

LC: Depression is one thing but just a general sense of confusion, bewilderment, a sense of shipwreck—that you've screwed up badly.

VP: When you talk about being in distress, do you mean depression? Has mental illness been a strong factor in your life?

LC: Yes. I feel like I'm coming out of the closet, but depression has certainly been an element that I've had to deal with all through my life. And my cover story looked wonderful.

VP: That you were just this bummed-out artist and you had success writing songs about it.

LC: No, the guys would say, "What's he got to complain about?" Nobody dealt me any bad cards.

VP: But if you're manic-depressive, that's a bad card.

LC: I think it just goes with the territory. Everybody's got something that they gotta deal with that is rough.

VP: And the solutions you sought included what? Travel, drugs, scotch, Prozac . . .

LC: Well, yeah, I still do. What happened was that somewhere along the line I understood that this question had to be addressed on the fundamental level of consciousness.

VP: You say that your cover story dealing with depression was that you were an artist and had success with your songs, particularly some of the more depressing songs. Did you ever worry that if you dealt with the depression, that if you actually got better, you would lose touch with your artistic side that understood that kind of pain and expressed it so well?

LC: No. That's a popular notion—that it is exclusively suffering that produces good work or insightful work. I don't think that's the case. I think in a certain sense it's a trigger or a lever but I think that good work is produced in spite of suffering and as a response, as a victory over suffering.

VP: That's an interesting concept—a victory over suffering.

LC: Yeah, because if the degree of intensity of anybody's distress is sufficiently high, you can't move, and for people who've experienced acute clinical depression . . . the problem is getting to the next moment—the room tilts, you lose your balance and you're incapable of coherent thought.

VP: Have you been that bad?

LC: Yeah. I've been there.

VP: You said one thing about Roshi—that he said you knew how to work but you didn't know how to play.

LC: Yeah, when I first came there . . . usually people are pressed into the rigorous activities of maintenance and meditation. He sent me down the hill to learn tennis, to take tennis lessons.

VP: [*Laughs.*] "Leonard, have a little fun, lighten up, have a laugh."

LC: Lighten up—that's what enlightenment means: that you've lightened up.

VP: So you played tennis?

LC: I never learned. I did take a number of lessons. I think the thing that scared me away was that automatic machine that hurls balls at you at about ninety miles an hour. [*Cohen and Pringle laugh.*]

VP: Tell me about women.

LC: You're a much better authority on the matter than I am.

VP: I don't know. Do you feel that you ever really connected with women? That maybe there were separate relationships but there was no lifelong connection?

LC: Sometimes you get lonely and you embrace some scenario of self-pity or loneliness but no, most of the time I don't because I have had long-lasting attachments. Also, I think having children takes the edge off that fundamental loneliness that people who don't have children might feel. Having been close to my kids all through my life—and, in fact, they're living here now—and watching them grow up and being part of their lives . . . I think that undermines that fundamental sense of loneliness.

VP: So you're a good dad?

LC: I'm probably a lousy dad but I think that everybody concerned understood that I did the best I could. Yeah, I think OK.

VP: And Adam [Cohen, his son] is gonna be an artist, a songwriter like you?

LC: He's the real thing. I kind of have croaked my way through the whole enterprise. I was interested in presenting some kind of curious voice and keeping some kind of record of my own activities but Adam is the real thing. He's got a beautiful voice, he's got perfect pitch, he dances, he's beautiful.

VP: He was born with a "golden voice" [quoting Cohen's "Tower of Song"] . . .

LC: He really does have it.

VP: So he's living in the "Tower of Song." How far above you is he?

LC: Oh, I think he's floating above the structure. He's got some very unusual gifts.

VP: And Lorca [Cohen's daughter]?

LC: Lorca . . . she just finished a course at the Cordon Bleu in Paris, a special pastry course, and she's finishing up at the Southern California School of Culinary Arts. She'll have a cooking diploma. She's got a good job at a trendy restaurant in town. She has to accumulate a certain amount of apprentice hours.

VP: Are there any women in your life now?

LC: I have a number of close women friends but romantic sexual activities are really inappropriate to this particular life.

VP: Because you're a monk? Do you have to be celibate?

LC: No, no. If you've got the strength after one of those days to lie down with someone or if you can find someone your own age that is willing to lie down with you go for it. But it's not the appropriate place.

VP: Is that OK with you? Because women and sex seemed like such an important part of your life. There was a great line by [novelist] Tom Robbins who said, "Nobody says the word 'naked' as nakedly as Leonard Cohen." And they still call you a "chick magnet" into your sixties.

LC: [Laughs.] Nothing is forever. I don't know how things are going to unfold up there [on Mount Baldy] but right now it doesn't seem to be . . . when you're really studying something and you want to avoid distractions . . . but I have very close relationships with a number of people in my life, men and women. It's not really going up the mountain and cutting off a life. That's not the view of Zen practice.

VP: The only line I'd heard about [actress and former lover] Rebecca De Mornay and the end of that relationship was "she got wise to me."

LC: I think it's true. I had brunch with her several months ago. I said to her, "I want to thank you for letting me off the hook so gracefully and allowing our friendship to resume on its original basis." And she said, "Oh yeah . . ." And I said, "I know why you let me off the hook so gracefully." And she said, "Why?" I said, "Because you knew that I gave it my best shot." And she said, "Yes, I know you gave it your best shot."

VP: Did you write the song "Suzanne" before you met Suzanne Elrod, the mother of your kids?

LC: Yes, but there are a lot of Suzannes around. This was written for— or at least the narrative concerned—the wife of the Quebecois sculptor Armand Vaillancourt. Her name was Suzanne Verdal. And she did live down by the river, by the Saint Lawrence.

VP: Did she feed you tea and oranges?

LC: She served me that tea called Constant Comment, which has little bits of dried orange in it. So I elaborated on that.

VP: You said you beware of charismatic mystics. You could see the power of your own charisma in your performing career.

LC: That's why I completely understand that it has nothing to do with content. Some people—headhunters, cannibals—have the gift of gathering people around their particular fiercely burning spark of life. A lot of people have that and there are good ones and bad ones.

VP: You gotta get people who write to you or come to you and look to you for wisdom. They think you're wise, they think you've seen the future, baby . . .

LC: Yeah, sure. That's why I know how susceptible one is.

VP: But when people say that do you just think, "I don't know, I'm still looking"?

LC: Well, I think that there is an oracular function in any artist. In other words, generally if he's good, he's working on a level that is better than he knows and better than himself.

VP: Do you have one or two lines—'cause I know you kill yourself writing, it's a huge amount of work—that you think, "That's a great line . . ."

LC: Occasionally I think "ring the bells that still can ring, forget your perfect offering, there is a crack in everything, that's how the light gets in" . . . sometimes I feel that I nailed it. It's more like I nailed it for myself.

VP: The crack is interesting, given we just were talking about your depression and how you coped with life.

LC: That defined my character and I could either have gone under with it or luckily fallen upon certain solutions for it that I have. One was that curious activity called art. And again, that curious activity called religion.

VP: Quite a life you've had.

LC: I've been lucky. Kids come to me and ask me for advice. Usually I say I've got good advice but it's one word: duck!

VP: [*Laughs.*] But you didn't take it.

LC: I tried to. I got hit by a little shrapnel here and there.

VP: And you're fit and strong?

LC: I'm in good shape. I could probably take you at arm wrestling and you're twenty years younger than me. Yeah, I feel fine. Thank God.

VP: Two quick questions about the [two] new songs [on *More Best of Leonard Cohen*]. "The Great Event."

LC: Did you hear that yet?

VP: It's a little weird . . .

LC: It's a little odd, yes.

VP: "Never Any Good"?

LC: [*Recites the lyrics, which end with, "I was never any good, never any good, never any good at loving you."*]

VP: Yes you were!

LC: Thank you. [*Laughs.*]

COHEN CLIP

On Being Produced by John Hammond

"He got the basic tracks of 'Suzanne,' 'The Stranger Song,' and 'Master Song,' which were powerful songs on that particular [first] album. He allowed me leeway. I asked for a full-length mirror to be brought in. All my life, I'd practiced in front of a mirror so I could see my hands. So I could see myself and gather some kind of presentable image both to myself and the world. And he brought in a beautiful full-length mirror."

—from "The *Billboard* Interview: Leonard Cohen," by Susan Nunziata, *Billboard*, November 26, 1998

PART IV

THE NEW MILLENNIUM

Down from the mountain, Cohen enjoys a fresh outlook on life—and the biggest successes of his half-century career.

TV INTERVIEW

STINA LUNDBERG DABROWSKI | Early 2001, Swedish National Television (Scandinavia)

In the late 1990s, Cohen appeared to be making good on his decades-old promise to withdraw from the music business. Living with the Buddhists on Mount Baldy, he offered no concerts, no records, and few interviews. But the situation changed with the new decade. On February 20, 2001, Columbia Records issued *Field Commander Cohen: Tour of 1979*, a collection of vintage concert performances that arguably ranks as the best of his first three live albums; and then, on October 9, came *Ten New Songs*—the first collection of fresh material in nine years—which included such gems as "In My Secret Life," "A Thousand Kisses Deep," "Love Itself," and "Boogie Street."

Now down from the mountain and living in Los Angeles, meanwhile, Cohen began to perform and give more interviews. One of the most memorable ones from this period took place in Paris with Stina Lundberg Dabrowski, whose 1997 conversation with the singer appears earlier in this book. Cohen spoke frankly with her about his decision to leave the monastery.

"I have a rule of not interviewing a person more than once," Dabrowski told me, "as I think you create a relationship at the first encounter and therefore you are not as willing to pose critical questions the second or third time. I made an exception with Leonard Cohen because I think he was so uniquely interesting." This from a woman who has also interviewed everyone from Nelson Mandela to Norman Mailer to Mikhail Gorbachev.

"I put a very embarrassing question [to Cohen] in the Paris interview," Dabrowski added. "Something about my friends wanting to make love with him. I wanted to cut it away but thought his reaction was so nice I couldn't do it, even though I hate myself every time I have seen it."

A heavily edited version of the interview aired in Scandinavia in early 2001. Here is a more expanded version, transcribed from the raw footage. —Ed.

Stina Lundberg Dabrowski: It was a nice trip [to California to visit Cohen at Mount Baldy in 1997]. The luggage people weren't on strike either.

Leonard Cohen: We'll go back.

SLD: Yeah? Are you going back?

LC: Oh sure, one day I'll go back.

SLD: When were you there last time?

LC: Well, I haven't been there since I left but [Cohen's Zen teacher] Roshi's been down in Los Angeles a lot. I always meet with him when he's in town.

SLD: But you haven't been there since '99.

LC: No. I think I left in '99.

[*There is a break in the videotape, after which Cohen begins talking about his collaboration with singer/songwriter Sharon Robinson. —Ed.*]

LC: We wrote "Waiting for the Miracle" together. We also wrote several other songs together. And I'm the godfather of her son. So our families are close.

SLD: Oh, are you? And how old is her son?

LC: Her son's twelve. And a very accomplished pianist. And Sharon is classically trained also. So our families have been close. And [recording engineer] Leanne [Ungar] also. We've worked together for many, many years. She's engineered six or seven of my records.

SLD: But that must be very unusual . . . a female technician in the music business . . .

LC: I never thought of it that way but—

SLD: I never met one.

LC: It's true there aren't many and especially when she started there were very, very few. But she never presents herself as somebody who's overcome anything.

SLD: [*To technician.*] Does he need powder?

Technician: No, he looks great. Great haircut, too.

LC: It's my own hair.

SLD: Last time you didn't have any hair at all.

LC: But it's with the same razor. But with a comb on it.

SLD: You do it yourself?

LC: Yeah, of course. I'll do yours if you like.

SLD: I'm not quite ready for it. I have a daughter, though, who shaved all her hair off recently.

LC: So as I say, Leanne never presents herself as someone who's overcome anything. She's terribly modest. Also her husband was the guitar player for the band, so everybody is very connected. So it's a very intimate feeling.

SLD: And some of the songs you wrote together were Sharon's songs?

LC: Yes, all these songs. In fact, it's actually Sharon's record in a certain way. She did all the synthesizer work and all the background singing and the melodies and of course there was a little change.

SLD: You even changed the words together with her . . .

LC: No, no.

SLD: I read the original and then I read the newest version that's on the record and I thought you had changed it together with her.

LC: Not together with her. I keep changing them. They get stopped at one point or another.

SLD: And they get kind of simpler and simpler.

LC: I try to figure out what they mean myself.

SLD: And more and more meaningful.

LC: I try to get down there.

SLD: There are very many good songs. Are you happy with the record?

LC: I like it. It's very relaxed. Even with the anxiety we have when we're listening to it to detect technical problems, we always find ourselves at the end of each song more or less relaxed. [*To waiter:*] Merci, monsieur.

SLD: It's funny, but you don't speak French?

LC: Plus ou moins, oui. [More or less, yes.]

SLD: Oui? C'est vrai? [Yes? Really?]

LC: Oui, c'est vrai. [Yes, really.] Would you have some milk?

SLD: Yes please. Et pourquoi vous ne parlez pas français tout le temps? [And why don't you speak French all the time?]

LC: Oh, c'est plus comfortable en anglais. Je parle français mais il y a long-temps que je n'ai pas parlais, et même lá-bas je n'ai pas parlais du ventre, vraiment. [Oh, I'm more comfortable in English. I speak French, but it's a long time since I spoke it, and even over there I didn't speak from the gut, really.]

SLD: Non? [No?]

LC: Je connais la langue, mais pas comme ma langue maternelle. [I know the language, but not like my mother tongue.]

SLD: I didn't know that. But I was thinking—

LC: Je viens de Montréal, non? I come from Montreal—

SLD: I know, I know.

LC: —mais de la minorité anglaise assez détesté maintenant. Mais oui, mes amis sont français [—but from the English minority, pretty detested these days. But yes, my friends are French]—it's been my world.

SLD: So it's funny—you never wrote any song or any poem in French. [*Dabrowski is correct, but it's worth noting that Cohen has sung in the language, in such tunes as "The Partisan" and "The Lost Canadian (Un Canadien Errant)," neither of which he wrote. —Ed.*]

LC: I don't have it from the gut. Even French poetry I have trouble with because I don't really feel the language. I know it, I can speak it, I can make myself understood and I can understand everything. But a song, poetry, has got to come from the deepest places. I don't have that in French. [*Raises glass.*] Good to see you.

SLD: Nice to see you too. So . . . but I was amazed. I remember when I visited you in the monastery and you had this schedule. [*Shows him the paper.*] Do you recognize?

LC: Oh yeah. Yeah, that's a good schedule.

SLD: That's a very good schedule. And the schedule you have today is a bit different.

LC: It's a bit different . . . but not so different.

SLD: Look at this schedule. [*Shows him another paper.*]

LC: Oh, this schedule here. Yeah, there's a lot of stuff here, huh? Well, this is my social life. I meet lots of people.

SLD: When I saw your schedule for this trip, I was overwhelmed by the amount of things you are doing in a very short time.

LC: Yeah. Good training at Mount Baldy. Sets you up for this sort of thing.

SLD: So you feel ready to meet the world in this way.

LC: Well, I think if I had my preferences, I might do something else but I have a small constituency in many countries so it's important for me to alert them that there's a record so I participate in the convention of promotions.

SLD: "I've closed the *Book of Longing* and do what I gotta do."

LC: Yeah.

SLD: Is that what you are doing?

LC: I guess so.

SLD: You've closed your book of poetry and you are promoting a record that people want you to—

LC: "I've closed the *Book of Longing*, I do what I am told." That's right. But I haven't quite finished that book yet so I'll open it when I go back. I've got about 250 poems there now and these songs come from that book. I'd like to finish it.

SLD: Who's telling you what to do?

LC: You hear these voices. Everybody has them.

SLD: But from within or from without?

LC: Both.

SLD: Was it a hard decision to leave the monastery?

LC: It was hard in the sense that I left a lot of close friends, brothers and sisters, and Roshi, who is an old, old friend of mine, and I'd been cooking for him and we were kind of dependent on one another. So in that sense it was hard. I asked his permission to leave.

SLD: Why did you leave?

LC: For a couple of reasons. One, I felt something had come to a conclusion. I'd been there five or six years. My association with the community, of course, doesn't end. I see Roshi a lot. In fact, he was down in Los Angeles. He wasn't feeling well so I made him the chicken soup that he likes.

SLD: A Jewish kind of chicken soup?

LC: Yeah, my mother's recipe. I guess the only difference is that I skin the chicken first before I boil it to remove a bit of the fat but more or less the same. And Roshi doesn't really like garlic.

SLD: No?

LC: No, he doesn't like garlic.

SLD: What a pity.

LC: Well, nobody's perfect. So of course the association with that community continues.

SLD: But *why* did you leave? You say you'd come to a conclusion but what was it?

LC: Well, it's difficult to speak of the reasons why you do anything. I'm never sure exactly why I'm doing anything. But one of the wonderful things that happened to me up on Mount Baldy is that I discovered I had no religious aptitude, that I wasn't really a religious man. That I didn't have that gift, that I didn't have the gift for that kind of life, although I love it in many ways. I love the structure and I love the sense of solidarity with the students and the monks.

SLD: But was it something that you lacked or something that you couldn't live without?

LC: Well, I'd always been associated with Roshi. When I finished my last tour it was in '93, I was in my late fifties, Roshi was close to ninety. So I thought that if I'm ever going to intensify my studies with him, that this was the moment to do it, that there wasn't an endless amount of time. That was one of the reasons I wanted to move closer to him. The other was just a sense of chaos in my life, a sense of disorder. I'd been drinking a lot—on tour I tend to drink and sing, which is a nice part of the whole process. But I'd gone overboard a bit and I was at loose ends and I needed some kind of form. And [at Mount Baldy] they've got that in spades. [*Laughs.*] But I'd always spent a week or two and then as the years unfolded a month or two, then sometimes half a year or so. I was very familiar with the schedule.

SLD: But finally you found that you're not the religious type, so to speak.

LC: I have no real gift for it.

SLD: What is the gift you need?

LC: I don't know. I feel I have a small gift: with a lot of work I can rhyme words. I feel I have some gift there. With the comprehension of religious concepts, I was barely able to get them intellectually. It's very hard for me to follow a philosophical model. I don't have that kind of mind. I just felt that at that moment it had ended. And it was a great revelation, and a great sense of relaxation accompanied this revelation.

SLD: Were you afraid to tell Roshi that you were going to leave the monastery?

LC: I wasn't afraid but I was concerned.

SLD: Did you think that he was going to get disappointed?

LC: Well, he granted me permission very reluctantly. I went to India for four or five months and when I came back he invited me up to the mountain and we had a formal dinner. All the senior monks were there. And after they left, he said to me, "Jikan, when you left, half of me died." I just winked at him and he winked at me back. Because these are just words. [*Laughs.*] Nothing really changes between us.

SLD: But you have a very, very deep and close relation[ship].

LC: I love him.

SLD: Is there anyone that you love more than him?

LC: It's easier to love, having had that relationship with Roshi because that's what he's all about. It's not a sentimental love. It's a kind of impersonal love.

SLD: Without attachment?

LC: Of course there's a human element of attachment and friendship and loneliness but it has a fundamental quality of the impersonal. What Roshi loves in you is not necessarily who you think you are but what you really are. He loves that and allows you through that love to locate it. I think that's the most selfless kind of love. He loves what you really are.

SLD: Can *you* love somebody for who she or he really is?

LC: Well, it's not really in your hands. That understanding deepens slowly as you get older . . .

SLD: You're still young in these matters?

LC: Yeah, and I think love is all overlooking. I think to love you have to overlook everything. You have to forget about most things.

SLD: And forgive.

LC: And forgive, yeah.

SLD: You've written some poems in the monastery. One of my favorites is very short. I don't know if you would like to read it. [*Dabrowski hands him a paper with the poem "The Sweetest Little Song." Cohen puts on a pair of prescription sunglasses and reads.*]

LC: "The Sweetest Little Song." But I like the drawing. [*Cohen's own illustration of a naked woman in a bathtub.*] It's nice in the way it's [presented] . . . where'd you get this from, the Internet?

SLD: Yeah, from the Internet. You can get everything from the Internet.

LC: I know, I know.

SLD: I almost looked into your pockets in the Internet. [*Laughs.*] So what's your comment on that one? It's funny, I made a test. I said this first line to at least twenty people. I said, "You go your way" and everybody [said], "And I'll go mine."

LC: [*Laughs.*] Yeah.

SLD: And you changed it.

LC: Yeah, I think that is the kernel of a love poem. That is the sweetest thing you can hear from someone. Roshi told me . . . I don't know if it's a Japanese thing, but he has a saying: "Husband and wife drinking tea. Your smile, my smile. Your tears, my tears." I guess it's the description of a real union.

SLD: You said before [in their prior interview] that you received so much love but you weren't able to give back.

LC: I think that's true. I wouldn't put it that way now but it's true. I remember Roshi saying—I think I said it to you last time—the older we get, the lonelier we become and the deeper the love we need.

SLD: But are you a better lover today?

LC: I'm a very intermittent lover. I'm very grateful because some kind of relaxation overtook me when I realized I was no longer a religious seeker. It's not so much that I got what I was looking for but the search itself dissolved and with that came the sense of relaxation. I don't mean I don't get bummed out and frustrated but the background is somehow relaxed now. So in that condition you can sense other people. That certainly must be the beginning of a deep relationship. It's just to sense the predicament of someone else.

SLD: So in a way you can say that you failed as a monk?

LC: Yeah. Thank God. Well, I think one of the qualities of that kind of life is to recognize that you fail. Young monks, young students, come with very sublime religious aspirations and those are quickly overthrown. I tried to put that idea in that song "A Thousand Kisses Deep." It says, "Summon now to deal with your invincible defeat, you live your life as if it's real but a thousand kisses deep." I think everybody has that experience, both young and old, of an uncomfortable quality to one's life, a sense of defeat that can either embitter you as it does to some or it can open your heart as it does to other, more fortunate people, and I'm lucky to be one of those people. To be able to at least from time to time live a thousand kisses deep. You can't do it all the time.

SLD: But you lived this kind of life before. You were a singer, a public person, you went on tours, you made promotion, and you did a lot of other things, too. And then you went to this very different kind of life in the monastery. And now you're back again, and you write a lot about "I'm on Boogie Street."

LC: "Back on Boogie Street."

SLD: And "Babylon." [*A reference to "By the Rivers Dark." —Ed.*] Is that how you see this world?

LC: Yeah, but . . . this is the place where we are. Of course, the Zen monasteries are not apart from the world. There's a Zen saying, "The lotus that blooms in the garden is swept away at the first fire. The lotus that blooms in the fire endures forever." There's always a feeling in Roshi's school that you've got to be in the world, you've got to be in the midst of the world, and you've got to be able to make a living. All his monks are getting married now. We've had three births, three children born.

SLD: In the monastery?

LC: Yeah. So he's marrying off his monks now.

SLD: That's pretty unusual.

LC: It's pretty interesting.

SLD: I was amazed when I visited you and you were drinking whiskey and you said if I fall in love with a young nun you never know what happens.

LC: In my dreams. [*Laughs.*]

SLD: But is this Roshi's kind of monastery?

LC: The regime is very severe and the distractions are also intense. I remember many mornings when I'd be giving Roshi breakfast . . . and he'd pull down the bottle of cognac and say, "You need a drink, Jikan." And he'd say, "Who's that outside?" There'd be some monk shoveling the snow. He'd say, "Get him in here." And we'd all start drinking at four in the morning. And then Roshi would say, "Now it's over," and the bell would ring and you'd go to the next work period. So there was drinking and at the appropriate moment. Roshi's hospitality has always been impeccable.

SLD: But it seems to be a very special kind of Zen that you have been taught that includes these things. Very nice kind, it seems to me, but different . . .

LC: Yeah, probably. I've visited other monasteries. Roshi established a system here that resembles a Japanese monastery but is not actually a duplication. I don't know what goes on over there and he's adapted his Zen.

SLD: Is the American a more liberal way?

LC: Well, it has this very interesting amalgamation of a very severe schedule with, as I say, very intense distractions. It seems to work. Although it's hard when you're drunk to go back to shoveling the snow.

SLD: At five in the morning.

LC: Yeah.

SLD: Why were you called Jikan? The silent one it means.

LC: Well, it doesn't really mean that. I never really figured out what it means because Roshi never wanted his students to get proud of the names that he gave them. People would say, "Roshi's given me the name Solitary Cliff or Penetrating Pine Tree" or something and they'd get very proud of the whole thing. [*Laughs.*] I'm not sure what Jikan means. It has something to do with silence. As Roshi explained, he said it's normal silence, ordinary silence.

SLD: So nothing to boast about.

LC: No nothing to . . . no.

SLD: But this life that you lived before and this life that you are living now again after the stay in the monastery . . . how do you experience it now compared to before—being here, promoting your record, being surrounded by journalists who are at you all the time?

LC: This has the same taste as life up on Mount Baldy, to tell you the truth, because this is very intense and you've got to show up for every interview, just like you have to show up every time the bell rings or the clapper sounds.

SLD: No matter how you feel.

LC: No matter how you feel, so it's not terribly different.

SLD: I was amazed that you didn't even give yourself one day to adjust to the time [zone change to Paris].

LC: Well, I like to throw myself into it.

SLD: Yeah? And you can keep yourself awake during the day with the jetlag?

LC: I haven't been sleeping much. You must experience that yourself all the time, the places you go. It's all so easy to overlook.

SLD: So being back on Boogie Street . . .

LC: It's very nice here on Boogie Street. But up there [on Mount Baldy] is Boogie Street, too. A monastery, of the kind Roshi runs in any case, it's more like a hospital.

SLD: And he's the doctor.

LC: And he's the doctor.

SLD: What does he cure?

LC: He cures the illusion that you're sick. [*Pause.*] And he was successful in my case. He cured the illusion that I needed his teachings.

SLD: So what were the sicknesses that you thought you had?

LC: I guess the same sicknesses everybody has—that you don't get what you want, and if you do get it, it isn't what you wanted. The objects of your desire continually escape you. There's some wisdom, some path that if you could only embrace it, you could extract yourself from distress and suffering. All these aspirations that all of us nourish. That there's another life that would be better, that another way would be better, another lover would be better, another métier would be better . . . this idea that there's something to grasp.

SLD: And you were a victim of that illusion before?

LC: I was a specialist.

SLD: You were a specialist! Even better than most of us. [*Cohen laughs.*] Because you had more of it. You had more of the fame, of the money, of the women.

LC: Maybe that's so. I think that everybody experiences the same kind of longing and dissatisfaction.

SLD: No matter how much you have?

LC: No matter how much you have. I don't know if it's any more bitter when you have a lot than when you have little. I don't think we have a standard to be able to judge who's suffering more. But I think we can take it for granted that everybody suffers a sense of something left undone, unfelt, unexperienced, and mostly it's in the West where we don't experience famine and other kinds of natural disasters as often. It usually is on the level of the heart. We don't feel we love enough or have enough love.

SLD: I know myself that the heaviest burden to carry is that of fame and riches.

LC: Yes, Jesus said that too. He said it's easier for a camel to pass through the eye of a needle than for a rich man to enter the kingdom of heaven. But he also said a little later on in that passage that all things are possible with God.

SLD: Do you agree?

LC: [*Laughs.*] I wouldn't dare disagree. It's not my place to disagree with Jesus Christ.

SLD: You're feeling happy with being back in business?

LC: Yeah, I feel grateful that I was able to bring this record to completion. I feel grateful that I bumped into Sharon again and renewed our association, both our friendship and our collaboration, and to be working with Leanne. I always think that the greatest distress is unemployment both on the level of society and the individual and to be fully employed is a privilege and I'm very happy about that.

SLD: But making a record is one thing and people appreciating it but all the things that come with it . . .

LC: Well, that's part of the deal.

SLD: It's part of the deal but you can enjoy it more or less.

LC: I'd be a fool to resent it. It doesn't happen to me very often because it's generally a number of years between records or books. So I don't get out that often. It isn't a life I lead regularly. So I choose to think of it as an aspect of my social life. I meet people and I talk. You come to a city like Paris and we don't have much time to get around but speaking to journalists, for instance, from Paris, journalists who really know what's going on, you can kind of get the sense of the city and of what's going on just talking to people. So I choose to see it as a social opportunity rather than as an onerous task.

SLD: So you can really experience a big difference in how you tackle things now compared to earlier?

LC: Well, I read somewhere that, as you get older, the brain cells associated with anxiety begin to die.

SLD: Oh, so that's why I feel so much better. [*Laughs.*]

LC: In my case, it seems to be true. You can just take it all a little more lightly.

SLD: It's also very common that when you grow a little older you start thinking more about your childhood and a lot of people want to get back to their roots. And you were born a Jew. Did you at all experience this?

LC: Well, when I began to study with Roshi, it wasn't because I wanted a new religion. I was always happy with the religion I was born into and it satisfied all the religious questions. I was more interested in the technical questions and the questions of a structure of a life. So there was never any point that I abandoned Judaism.

SLD: No, I know, but did you experience this need to go back to . . .

LC: I don't have those feelings. I think you get very interested in your children as you get older, and very touched by their lives.

SLD: Are you a grandfather?

LC: No, my children are very lazy. They won't produce any children, any grandchildren for me. Maybe one day. [*Cohen's son, Adam, had a child in 2007 with a woman he's no longer with. His daughter, Lorca, had a child in 2011; the father is gay singer Rufus Wainwright. —Ed.*]

SLD: But you're very close to them.

LC: Yes, I live in a duplex in Los Angeles and my daughter lives in the flat underneath mine and my son lives a very short distance away also. So that's been a very agreeable feature of coming back to the city.

SLD: I just heard that he [son Adam] went to Hydra and there he met a young woman that he became very fond of and it happened to be the daughter of Marianne.

LC: I don't think it's so. I think he did meet a Scandinavian woman but I don't think they were connected. He spoke to me of it. I forget what the explanation was but it wasn't so.

SLD: OK, it was just a rumor.

LC: Yeah.

SLD: It's dangerous, the Internet, because a little rumor can become news for the world in a couple of seconds.

LC: He's going back to Hydra in August. We were having lunch the other day and he said, "You know, Dad, I dream of Hydra three or four times a week. My dream takes place in Hydra." He spent a lot of his childhood there. I love the place but he really knows every little corner and byway as a child knows.

SLD: It is a beautiful island.

LC: Yeah, it is. It is a nice place.

SLD: But you're not going back?

LC: I went for the first time in many years two summers ago on my way back from India. And it is marvelous and my house is wonderful. Yeah, it's a good place.

SLD: And next year they're gonna celebrate your birthday there. People gather from all over the world the twenty-first of September, 2002.

LC: Yes, that's another outcome of the Internet.

SLD: What do you think about that?

LC: I don't know what to think about it. I don't think I'm going to be there.

SLD: No?

LC: I don't think so but I'm very gratified that there are people for whom my songs and poems are important enough to gather around.

SLD: Are you afraid or worried about how this new record is going to be received?

LC: No, I'm not.

SLD: Are you not sensitive for criticism?

LC: No, I'm not.

SLD: Were you earlier?

LC: Maybe at the beginning but after thirty or forty years in this racket, you get a pretty thick skin.

SLD: Yeah? Do you really?

LC: I have. Of course, one likes to be praised and one likes to be loved and appreciated. It's always gratifying but generally when I read a review, I am the reviewer. I read the person's writing. I see how they express themselves. I don't read many [reviews] but when I do, I read from the point of view of a critic of the review. That's in self-defense.

SLD: Are you going out on tour?

LC: I don't think so.

SLD: I have a special order from Stockholm to beg you to come and read your poems at a poem cinema or now it's called a people cinema. I guess you've been asked this before.

LC: I think it was mentioned but I need eight musicians behind me to get the courage to go up onstage.

SLD: Why don't you bring them then?

LC: If I do go out on tour, I have a good band. But I don't know, I hope I don't fall over tomorrow but I'm going to be sixty-seven in a few weeks and naturally a sense of limitation begins to arise that is quite tangible.

SLD: Physically?

LC: Not physical, no. Fortunately, because of the training at Mount Baldy, I'm in pretty good shape. No, it's not from the point of view of stamina; it's about the point of view of time.

SLD: What is it that you've got to do?

LC: I'd like to do another record and I'd like to finish this book.

SLD: The *Book of Longing.*

LC: The *Book of Longing.* And maybe after that I'd go out. But it seems to me that's a priority. Because when you go out on the road, it involves at least a year of work and you can't really do anything else while you're doing it.

SLD: How do you cope without the discipline, the rules and the regulations of the monastery?

LC: Well, it's lovely to sleep in past three o'clock in the morning. It's a delicious feeling, although I often get up at three just out of habit. But that kind of discipline I never lacked. I was always disciplined in regard to my work. It was the wider sense of a life and I put on a pretty good show. My cover story was pretty good. It looked like my life was orderly because it revolved around writing and recording. But the interior sense I had was of deep disorder and that's one of the reasons I went up to Mount Baldy and why for thirty years I would spend a part of each year up there, just to depend on the routine so that I could stop having to improvise. It was the improvisation of the life that finally got me. But we began to work almost immediately after I came down. So the days have been very, very structured.

SLD: But when I was there, you said that if I didn't follow these rules and regulations, I would be lying in bed watching TV and scratching my back all day long.

LC: Oh, yeah. Well, these girls won't let me do it.

SLD: Is it just a coincidence that they happen to be women, the people you are working with?

LC: Well, it's certainly a delightful coincidence that they're women and they're women I've known for a long time and they happen to be beautiful but their stunning competence is what deeply attracts me to them. Sharon is a prodigious talent and Leanne is to my mind the best engineer around. So the fact that they happen to be women is a wonderful bonus.

SLD: What about the *Book of Longing*?

LC: Yeah, there are about 250 poems there now and these songs come mostly from that period of the past ten years.

SLD: But will you publish the book actually?

LC: I don't have any deep sense of urgency about publishing. I'd like to keep it around for a while.

SLD: You can actually read some of the poems on your homepage. "The Moon" . . . this one I like very much, too.

LC: Oh, "The Moon." That I wrote up at Mount Baldy. Yeah, that's from Jarkko [Arjatsalo]'s site [leonardcohenfiles.com]. It comes out of Helsinki [Finland].

SLD: He sent you his regards, too.

LC: Oh, thank you so much.

SLD: And this. [*Hands him another poem.*] As you're not coming to Stockholm, we can have the poetry reading here.

LC: "Sorrows of the Elderly." [*Reads poem, then laughs.*]

SLD: Can you explain it?

LC: Oh, it's just a joke . . . on us.

SLD: On the elderly?

LC: On the elderly. [*Laughs.*] I shouldn't include you.

SLD: Yes you should. [*Laughs.*] You know you should.

LC: [*Points to a page on the table with one of his drawings.*] Where's that picture from?

SLD: This is from a German magazine.

LC: Oh yeah.

SLD: I must say, I don't like complimenting people that I interview but you are a fantastic artist as well.

LC: Oh, thank you.

SLD: Did you never have an exhibition?

LC: No, the great pleasure of drawing and painting for me is that it has absolutely no professional application. It's not at all connected with anything. So I do it freely and with a great deal of pleasure.

SLD: And the fact that a lot of people would love to buy these paintings for huge amounts of money . . .

LC: I'll put them on the Internet. They can download them.

SLD: No, but does that not mean anything to you?

LC: I wouldn't like to think of it that way. It's one of those private matters. I love people to see it and I give drawings to anybody who wants one or I'll make a copy. A lot of them are done on the computer so I can just email them to people. Whoever wants one is welcome. But for it to enter that world of commerce and anxiety and presentation . . . it is just too intimate a pleasure. I love to sketch.

SLD: So you don't look upon yourself as an artist? You look upon yourself as a musician and a songwriter and a singer.

LC: Yeah, I think of myself as a songwriter.

SLD: And what about the author?

LC: Yeah, I write books and people have given me the title poet. But I always think that poetry is a verdict given by others, by the next generation. If your work has a certain kind of intensity and a capacity to endure, after twenty-five or thirty or fifty or a hundred years, I think it's legitimate to call it poetry. The fact that you describe it as poetry means very little. The fact that the lines don't come to the end of the page doesn't mean it's poetry. So I never think of myself that way. I think of myself as a writer, as a journalist, someone who is describing a small corner of the universe.

SLD: But you're not a journalist, because a journalist describes reality but you describe the essence of reality.

LC: Well, that's my reality. This is the only interior predicament that I have any access to and I try to describe it as accurately as I can. In that sense, I think of myself as a journalist and that's why I feel a certain solidarity with journalists.

SLD: Yeah?

LC: Yeah. My arena, my landscape, is very, very small. But it's the same kind of activity to report as precisely as I can the conditions that pertain.

SLD: I think you said or wrote somewhere that you wanted to keep a diary of your life. You wanted to report.

LC: It seems to be the nature of the work . . . a kind of diary keeper, a kind of journal keeper.

SLD: But aren't you too shy to keep an honest diary?

LC: I may be too dishonest to keep an honest diary but I'm not too shy. [*Laughs.*]

SLD: Are you dishonest?

LC: One is struggling with that all the time, especially in this kind of work. Every writer learns certain tricks, so that's OK. There are certain techniques and tricks that you have and maybe you can fool others but you can't fool yourself in these matters. And you don't want to fool yourself so you keep digging for the authentic tone. Of course it's unfair to present yourself socially with brutal honesty. It's like if someone asks you, "How are you?" and you tell them, they don't want [to hear it] . . . It's unfair to tell people how you are. That's what poetry or writing a song is for.

SLD: I think your sense of humor has developed a lot. A lot of the new poems are very—

LC: Some of them are funny, yeah.

SLD: They're *very* funny.

LC: My friends always thought I had a sense of humor. I got the reputation [for being humorless] and I think it's not altogether illegitimate because my songs were about stressful conditions, sometimes with no resolution. I think a lot of them had a dark feeling. I hope that the writing of the song penetrated the darkness somehow, but for a lot of people it didn't, so I understand that I got labeled as a depressed, pessimistic sort of guy.

SLD: But you were not?

LC: No, I wasn't, no.

SLD: But you have managed now to put down your sense of humor in words.

LC: Well, a lot of that book, the *Book of Longing*, is a kind of sendup of the monks' life, an ironic reflection on the religious vocation.

SLD: Almost every one is very funny.

LC: Yeah, 'cause they're not poems. They're really jokes.

SLD: [*Laughs.*] So the *Book of Longing* is a book of jokes?

LC: The whole thing is a joke. [*She hands him a poem.*] Ah, yeah, what is that?

SLD: You don't know them by heart?

LC: This doesn't look like it's finished . . . yeah, maybe it is. It's called "The Correct Attitude." [*Reads poem.*] Haven't read that since I wrote it.

SLD: Is that true or is it—

LC: It's just a joke. It's all just a joke.

SLD: But do you have the correct attitude? Do you care if it ends or if it goes on?

LC: [*Pauses.*] Not really. [*Long pause.*] You?

SLD: Sometimes I don't, sometimes I do.

LC: Well, that's it. I think your answer is better.

SLD: [*Laughs.*] But it's not interesting.

LC: Yeah, it is. It takes two people to answer that question.

SLD: So when you were little, were you more known as this funny little bloke or were you this serious little chap?

LC: I don't know. In the time that I grew up, psychological profiles were not fashionable. You just followed orders more or less and whatever you could do on the sly you did but it was a pretty disciplined kind of existence when I was a kid. There wasn't the kind of youth rebellion that we see today and authority and parental control were very strong and nobody cared what your inner condition was, as long as your shoes were underneath your bed in the right way. We weren't close with our parents. We didn't really discuss our inner condition with our parents. It was a very wise kind of upbringing. It didn't invite self-indulgence.

SLD: But you learned discipline.

LC: You learnt good manners, which is better than discipline.

SLD: And your dog?

LC: My dog? I'm very happy these days because my daughter who lives in the same house as I do has dogs. I love dogs and she's brought two dogs into my life. It's really wonderful. And I play with them every day and teach them tricks.

SLD: What kind of dogs?

LC: Mutts. Just street dogs. She got them from the pound.

SLD: Did you have a dog when you were little?

LC: Yes, I had a Scottish terrier. My mother named him Tovarich—comrade. We called him Tinky. Yes, I guess the closest being to me during childhood. The dog would sleep under my bed and follow me to school and wait for me so that was a great sense of companionship.

SLD: Because you sometimes write about a dog.

LC: Well, I have his picture on my dresser in Los Angeles. We loved that dog. My sister gave me his picture framed, as a present.

SLD: And what happened when he died?

LC: He died when he was about thirteen, which is quite old for a dog. He just asked to go out one night. You know how a dog will go and stand beside the door? So we opened the door, it was a winter night, and he walked out, and we never saw him again. And it was very distressing. I put ads in the newspaper and people would say, "Yes, we have found a Scottie" and you'd drive fifty miles and it wouldn't be your Scottie. And we only found him in the springtime when the snow melted and the smell came from under the neighbor's porch. He had just gone outside and gone under the neighbor's porch to die. Some kind of charity to his owners. But we loved that little dog.

SLD: And after that you didn't have any other dog?

LC: No, then I finished university and I started living a kind of vagabond life and never living anywhere for [long]. When I lived on Hydra, there was a dog named Flopsy who kind of belonged to a lot of people, and sometimes she'd stay at my house.

SLD: But now . . .

LC: Now my daughter has these dogs.

[*The cameraman changes tapes. When the video resumes, Cohen has moved on to a new subject. —Ed.*]

LC: How else would you dare to get married if you weren't confused?

SLD: [*Laughs.*] Are you confused?

LC: I don't think so.

SLD: You're not getting married.

LC: No.

SLD: You were never married.

LC: No, I was never married.

SLD: Why?

LC: [*Pause.*] Coward. Cowardice. I had these children, fortunately, but I never ... I also grew up in a period where there was a great deal of antiauthoritarian feeling, so some of the people of my generation never felt they had to consult an authority or have the affirmation of a church or a state to seal their union. I guess I participated in that kind of ...

SLD: So you're a child of your time?

LC: Of course.

SLD: I asked a couple of my female friends for help with questions to you.

LC: How'd they do?

SLD: They did fine but they all had the same question.

LC: What is the question?

SLD: Ask him if he wants to make love to me.

LC: [*Laughs.*] I'm not so active in this front anymore. But I suppose I could make an exception.

SLD: So I'll tell them that. I was a bit surprised actually because since '93 you've been so much into the spiritual world and when I talked to you last, we talked about very serious spiritual matters. But it seems that you still come across as the ladies' man.

LC: [*Laughs.*] Yeah, it's a curious reputation—very inaccurate. There are a lot of women in my life certainly. Somehow I appreciate the competence of women. I like the way women work, so I find myself working with a woman engineer and a woman cowriter, my manager is a woman . . .

SLD: In what way are they different from men [in] their way of working?

LC: More selfless.

SLD: Less ego?

LC: Less ego, not so much on the line. Or a more skillful negotiation with the ego. And also very quick. Very, very quick, which I appreciate.

SLD: But you tried to kill the ladies' man in the seventies already. *Death of a Ladies' Man.*

LC: Well, women took care of that.

SLD: How do you mean?

LC: I didn't try to kill anyone. I felt I got creamed in a certain way. But everybody has that feeling of the disaster of the heart because nobody masters the heart. And nobody's a real ladies' man or a love gangster. Nobody really gets a handle on that. Your heart just cooks like shish kabob in your breast and it's sizzling and crackling and too hot for the body. So those descriptions of course are easy and a kind of joke, a kind of simple description. I've known some men who had real reputations as ladies' men, who are real lady killers, and they don't have any handle on it, either. I don't think anybody feels very confident in that realm at whatever level you're operating.

SLD: So how did you feel?

LC: Well, the reputation was completely undeserved, for one thing. I don't think my concerns about women and about sex were any deeper or more elaborate than any other guy that I met. Women are the content of men and men are the content of women so everybody's involved in this enterprise with everything they've got, and most are hanging on by the skin of their teeth and, as I say, nobody masters the situation, especially if it really touches the heart. Then one is in a condition of anxiety most of the time. And even the great ladies' men that I've bumped into, and I've met some real ones—and I'm not in their league—the sense of anxiety about the conquest is still very much there. Because in any case, the woman chooses.

SLD: How?

LC: I think the woman chooses. It's been told to me that the woman chooses, and she decides within seconds of meeting the man whether or not she's going to give herself to him. In any case, I think in most cases the woman is running the show in these matters, and I'm happy to let them have it.

SLD: But in the *Book of Longing* there is a long poem, and I probably don't remember the lines right, but it was something like, "My dick is the horse and my life is the chart . . . "

LC: Is the cart.

SLD: "Is the cart." Sorry.

LC: Yeah, very vulgar line, I wish I hadn't written it. In fact, I've changed it.

SLD: To what?

LC: I don't remember what I changed it to now, because I've had a growing sense of dissatisfaction with that poem. I must remove it from the site [*chuckles*] or at least it needs more work. It came out of a time when I'd just come down from Mount Baldy and I was writing very, very quickly and with a kind of wild sense of freedom from the schedule, and I was blackening a lot of pages and sending them off to the website, and that's one I have to look at.

SLD: Why? It's very direct.

LC: It's very direct but I think the language [could be] a little bit more musical. Try for a different music.

SLD: But what did it mean? What was the content?

LC: I think the content is that that's where a man's brain is. And when I watch the young, as I do because I have two young . . . well, they're not children, they're young adults. I remember going to a party that my son invited me to, and I sat there just thanking my lucky stars that I wasn't twenty-five, because . . . the level of suffering at one of these events was overwhelming. The mutual displays of attraction, the effort that had gone into each personal presentation, the expectations, the disappointments. It seemed to be one of the circles of hell that I was pleased not to be in.

SLD: So where are you now?

LC: Well, I'm not in that inner circle, in any case. Nothing's over till it's over but I find myself in a graceful moment, a more or less relaxed situation, and the whole background of the record was a sense of relaxation. The work was very hard and intense and sometimes frustrating but it didn't have the background of anxiety. It had a background of . . . I won't go so far as to say peace but relaxation. And fortunately, that seems to have continued. But there's no guarantee. You can slip off the path at any time.

SLD: But do you have this feeling that you can be more satisfied and happy in the moment now?

LC: I do, and I'm very grateful to Roshi and to the periods of training I've gone through with him and to his friendship, an unconditional acceptance, for that feeling of relaxation.

SLD: Is there an easier way to reach that stage or do you have to go through this hard Roshi school?

LC: I think it just happens. I don't even think it's because of Roshi. He's the instrument somehow, which makes these things possible sometimes. I don't think it's anything he does. I don't think it's anything you do. I think that this anxiety dissolves from time to time and it may return. But for the moment somehow it's dissolved and I was able to do good work.

SLD: So the depressions that you suffered from very much in your earlier days—

LC: They've lifted. They've lifted completely.

SLD: So aging is quite nice?

LC: In my case, it's been a great blessing.

SLD: But there must be some hard part of it.

LC: Well, I think the collapse of the body is an aspect to it. I'm not in old age. I think I'm in my good period before the onset of the diseases that eventually kill you. I think it was Tennessee Williams who said, "Life is a fairly well-written play, except for the third act." It's a very bad third act. [*Chuckles.*]

SLD: But for you it was the best so far.

LC: Well, just beginning the third act is fine. I don't know how the third act will unfold, but it doesn't unfold very well for anybody. So I'm probably in the most graceful period that I've ever experienced before the onset of the unpleasant destruction of the body, which is inevitable. I'm very lucky to be in that period.

SLD: Do you see there is a big difference between aging for a man and for a woman?

LC: Women say it is. Most of the women I talk to about it say, "You're lucky, we're finished at whatever-it-is." But I know a lot of women my age who are also dealing with it very gracefully—and very gratefully. A lot of people, men and women, are just relieved that a certain aspect of the struggle is over.

SLD: Which aspect is this?

LC: Mating, courting, marriage. Or the ceaseless search for a companion. Finally, one senses that one is alone and that it's not that bad—in fact, it even may be sweet. My sister's in that situation also. She lost her husband a few years ago. They were married for thirty or forty years. And it was difficult at the beginning for her. But she's a very active person. She's five years my elder. And I see that she's settled into a life without criticism, without commentary, no one to review her activities or her thought or her speech, and she seems to be experiencing a great deal of contentment from that.

SLD: But don't you miss a companion?

LC: But I have companionship.

SLD: But don't you miss a woman in your life?

LC: Oh, there are women in my life, but . . .

SLD: *A* woman? *The* woman.

LC: The woman. I don't as yet. I don't know what it will be like tomorrow or next week, but at the moment I have very close friends. There's not the woman. But I don't have a sense of unbearable loneliness or any sense of anxiety about it. And sometimes women are kind enough to sleep over in a less-intense capacity than I may have chosen before. So it's not as though I don't have the intimacy of women from time to time.

SLD: Do you miss those intense experiences?

LC: I was never very good at enjoying it. I was drawn to those intense experiences, and obsessed with those intense experiences for much of my life, but I can't say that I really enjoyed them.

SLD: How did you feel about them?

LC: Well, I generally gave myself a bad review.

SLD: So . . . you had to perform?

LC: I think there was an aspect of performance and a severe review of the episode. And a sense that the performance had not really been stunning. But more accurately than that, there was a sense of anxiety that was the background of the whole enterprise, and that sense of anxiety seems to have lifted. So I find I can enjoy both men and women, because even when you meet men there is a kind of war dance going on; there's a kind of sexual dance going on with women and a kind of war dance going on with men. And it's very agreeable to have those dances confined to one or two steps rather than the acrobatics that usually attended them.

SLD: You wrote once that a man never gets over the first sight of a naked woman.

LC: I think that's true and certainly our Western art confirms that. And I love doing nudes also . . . drawings. Yes, and I marvel at the insistence of that mechanism that is placed in us because it never disappears and one is always shocked, stunned, surprised, delighted by that apparition of "the other," especially at the height of her reproductive capacities, that youth, that promise, that vitality. That is the great sustaining energy in the human situation. So no, we're designed not to grow tired. We don't get a chance to see it that often as we get older, but when we do . . . And of course the culture completely understands that, so it's continually presenting us with pictures, whether they actually occur in the flesh in our lives it's really not important anymore, because there are so many opportunities to see beauty, to see beautiful people. They're on the screen, they're on the billboards, they're everywhere. I don't see that as some sort of indication of the degeneration of our civilization. I see it as the affirmation of that mechanism that is in all of us.

SLD: You're talking about actors, actresses, everything . . .

LC: Yes, it's there.

SLD: I'm thinking of one of the poems again that you wrote. I don't know it by heart but . . . "Because of a Few Songs."

LC: Oh yeah. I like that poem.

SLD: Could you read that please? It's about what we are talking about now.

LC: [*Reads poem.*] I was happy with that little poem.

SLD: Why?

LC: I wanted to thank everybody. I wanted to thank the women who had bent over the bed and covered me up like a baby that is shivering.

SLD: But why do you think women have been so kind to you? Why do women want to show themselves naked?

LC: Well, I'm not the only guy that has this experience. This is what goes on between men and women. I don't want to break this news to you, Stina. [*Laughs.*]

SLD: [*Laughs.*] . . . but it is not news either that you have a special gift, that there are an abundance of women who will happily do that for you . . .

LC: Where are they now that we need them?

SLD: Well, I have a bunch of friends at home . . .

LC: You get stuck with a certain kind of reputation that, like all reputations, have some truth to them but mostly are deeply inaccurate and I certainly don't feel any mastery in this enterprise.

SLD: But you're not unhappy with the reputation either?

LC: Well, I've met a number of women in my life who refused to come close to me because of that reputation. There are a lot of women—I'm talking over the years when I say a lot of women; there's not bevies of women that are waiting for me outside of every door. But there have been a number of women who have refused any kind of intimacy—I'm not talking about sexual intimacy—because they just didn't want to be a name on a list. And there never really was a list. But there were women, modest women, who had a certain sense of themselves, who simply didn't want to be numbered among the women that I was supposed to have enjoyed. So it's not always been a benefit. On the other hand, having had the reputation as a poet or a writer or a singer, I often was not obliged to have to present my credentials to everybody. So that was agreeable.

SLD: When you write about Marianne and the time you spent a very long time ago on Hydra with her and you present her as a woman who gave you a lot of nice warmth and order and flowers on the table, a sandwich when you needed it—

LC: Yes, she did.

SLD: Is that a kind of romantic era in your life?

LC: I don't think my characterization of it is romantic; I think it's accurate.

Marianne happened to be on the island the last time I was on Hydra, which was just two years ago. I hadn't been there for many years and she happened to be visiting the island at the same time and we spent a very pleasant evening together. I made dinner for her and we talked and it was a very sweet moment. But she was very, very helpful to me. Helpful hardly begins to describe it. She created the atmosphere in which I could work. And for that, of course, she has my gratitude.

SLD: But you don't feel sad that you couldn't stay within this . . .

LC: I was constitutionally unable to stay with anybody at that time. We had a long association. The periods of absence began to get longer and longer until we realized we weren't really living together. But we did live together for some years and that was a period of great enrichment.

SLD: Can you give your son advice or would you like to teach him how to avoid the most difficult mistakes?

LC: I listen to him for advice. He seems to have a better handle on it than I do. He's very competent in these matters.

What I do enjoy in my relationship with my son is that we have the same work. That's really a wonderful thing to have with one's child. I've been going to his concerts around town. He's been playing in small clubs. I have a drink with him or a cigarette backstage and I see he's nervous and he knows that I understand that feeling. And I watch him play his songs. They're wonderful. And we have that in common. And it creates a real bond above and beyond just the filial relationship—the fact that we know the work of the other.

SLD: He's brave because it must be very difficult to be in the same trade as a very . . . his father had so much fame . . .

LC: I know, I know. He is. He has a lot of courage. But I was speaking to a journalist yesterday who had interviewed Adam when he came here for a concert. And she asked him that question. She said, "Isn't it hard to have Leonard Cohen as your father and begin in the music business?"

SLD: He will have that question many times.

LC: And he said, "He's my dad." Which I thought was a very sweet answer to my ears.

SLD: Why do you think that you had such a hard time reaching to the state of mind that you're in now?

LC: I don't think anybody determines it or understands it. I don't think we can really penetrate into these matters.

SLD: You're not so interested in the psychological explanation?

LC: No, I don't trust them. As I say in that song, "I know that I'm forgiven but I don't know how I know / I don't trust my inner feelings, inner feelings come and go." I think that psychological explanations can be valuable and psychotherapy can be valuable for some people. But the fundamental question of how and why people are as they are is something that we can't penetrate and is part of a plan that we simply cannot grasp and the feelings that arise we don't determine. What we're going to see next we don't determine, what we're going to hear next, taste next, feel next, or think next we don't determine.

And yet we have this sense that we're running the show. So if anything is relaxed in my mind it's the sense of control or the quest for meaning. I say in that song "Alexandra Leaving," "You who were bewildered by a meaning, whose code was broken, crucifix uncrossed, say good-bye to Alexandra leaving, say good-bye to Alexandra lost." Though I wouldn't claim it as my own, I've had that temporary relaxation of concern for the meaning. It's none of my business.

SLD: Yeah, I like those lines very much: "I don't trust my inner feelings, inner feelings come and go." [*Laughs.*]

LC: Yes, and it seems to me that the psychological establishment today has placed a great deal of emphasis on getting in touch with your inner feelings. Of course, it has some kind of value. But my experience is that there is no fixed self. There's no one whom I can locate as the real me and dissolving the search for the real me *is* relaxation, *is* the content of peace. But these recognitions are temporary and fleeting. Then we go back to thinking that we really know who we are.

SLD: And who are you today?

LC: [*Laughs.*] I'm your guest.

SLD: Your "secret life" that you sing about—

LC: I love that song. I loved it the moment Sharon brought it to me. I had been working on that lyric for years and I had about fifty verses and I pared them down and that was the first song we wrote together. I was *so* happy with that song when Sharon brought it to me with the melody.

SLD: It's wonderful, it's really wonderful. You told me about honesty, being honest . . .

LC: I say, "I smile when I'm angry, I cheat and I lie, I do what I have to do to get by / But I know what is wrong and I know what is right and I die for the truth in my secret life."

SLD: Is the truth important for you?

LC: No, I've never been a great seeker after the truth. I wasn't aware of any lies. I wasn't aware that anybody was putting anything over on me or that God or the universe was trying to trick me. So I never had a sense of a quest for the truth.

SLD: Did you have a quest for being honest?

LC: I didn't have a quest. I think that's the background of any writer's work is trying to be honest. Except for the typing, which is labor of itself, that's what the work is: trying to approach some ideal of honesty. And you never really get there and you never really should. Because you don't know the truth of this whole enterprise. No one knows the truth. I tried to say that in that song "Boogie Street": "Though all the maps of blood and flesh are posted on the door there's no one who has told us yet what Boogie Street is for." You may have the maps of Boogie Street and the genetic code and all the mechanics may be displayed but what the whole enterprise is about . . . no one has a handle on that.

SLD: Do you look back upon your life a lot?

LC: No, I don't.

SLD: One always views you as a part not of the sixties movements but of your certain generation but you were always older than the generation you kind of belonged to.

LC: Yes, in a sense that's true. I was always at least ten years older than the great figures of the sixties.

SLD: And you wore a suit.

LC: I always wore a suit. I grew up in a family that manufactured clothing and my teenage years were spent before the popularity of blue jeans. So those were clothes that were never really natural to me.

SLD: Did you take a bar mitzvah?

LC: Oh, of course. I grew up in a world that has almost passed away. In a little corner of North America, the Jewish community of Montreal, which still is a very strong community with a very integrated sense of responsibility and hospitals and charity and—

SLD: You have a poem about this too. "The one who says he's not a Jew is not a Jew."

LC: Oh yeah. I said, "Anyone who says I am not a Jew is not a Jew. I'm sorry but this decision is final." Because when I went up to Mount Baldy, there was criticism from certain circles that I'd abandoned my religion, that I'd converted to something. So I just wrote that joke.

SLD: And you added that you were voted the most well-dressed man in Montreal or was it in Canada?

LC: There was a list of credentials at the bottom of that poem. I think I removed them but maybe I'll put them back because people seemed to think they were funny. I just listed a number of the most absurd credentials that I could come up with. Somebody sent me a clipping from a

Montreal newspaper. It was determined that I was one of the best-dressed men in Montreal.

SLD: *The* best-dressed man.

LC: I may have said that. I may have exaggerated in the poem.

SLD: So what do you think of what you see in Paris? Here you see a lot of very well-dressed people, very beautiful people, very rich—

LC: Yeah, I'm not in their league.

SLD: But what do you think of the way of life?

LC: I don't think I really know the way of life, although I've lived in Paris. I don't think there is a way of life. There are certain styles and traditions in these great cities. But people are just trying to get by.

SLD: And do you have a feeling that you are helping them to get by, that you are helping people?

LC: Well, I'm pitching in. Like you are, like everybody is. Doing my tiny part. But I think one learns early in this kind of activity that the part one plays is very, very limited.

SLD: But now the part you play is going to be very much more exposed.

LC: But even so, even with a great hit song, which I probably won't have, but even with that . . . there are so many other activities and influences and forces at work on a human psyche that it would be supremely ignorant to believe that your effect has any precedence, or even prominence or even reality.

SLD: But the fact that you are now releasing a new album . . . is that because you felt the need to publish your new songs and sing your new songs, or have you responded to a demand?

LC: It's part of the work, just like promoting it is part of the work. It's my work, it's my job. I've always felt that unemployment is a great distress, both in society and in the individual. So I'm very happy to be totally and fully employed, with the same intensity as the life I lived at Mount Baldy, so this is just the fruits of that work.

SLD: Are you nervous?

LC: No.

SLD: Are you going back home to write the new album?

LC: I'd like to. I don't think of it as the new album but I would like to continue writing. I also have a record I'm working on, which is just my own songs but I would like to continue working with Sharon. We've got into the habit of working together now, the three of us every day, and we don't seem to want to let each other go now. They came here just as a kind of treat. The record company offered them [the chance] to spend a week in Paris but I've involved them now in the interviews and they were supposed to go back after Paris while I continue on to Spain and Germany and Italy. But I asked them if they wanted to come and they've agreed. So we're going to spend yet another two or three weeks together. We've spent the better part of the last two years together.

SLD: And so it will hopefully continue then?

LC: I hope so. Because it's wonderful having friends like this.

SLD: And what about the writer who failed his trade?

LC: I still scribble away. I think everybody fails their trade. When you look at the tradition and who you're up against, it's hard to come away with a sense of real accomplishment. You're happy that you can do your work. But you can't fool yourself about where you stand in the great tradition. Ultimately, you're up against Shakespeare and Homer and King David . . .

SLD: Yes, but I remember reading that James Joyce is not dead—he's living in Montreal and his name is Leonard Cohen.

LC: I don't think they're gonna put that on my tombstone. One knows very well . . . [The late French singer, songwriter, poet, composer, artist, actor, and director] Serge Gainsbourg, who used to drink at this bar here, when he was . . . described as a poet, he said, "I'm not a poet" and they asked him, "Well, what are you?" He said, "I am a kind of pseudo poet," and I think that's a good description. I always think of myself as a minor poet. That's not some kind of artificial modesty. That's an accurate assessment of my work in relationship to the work that has been done.

SLD: So are you writing what's going to be on your tombstone?

LC: No. Listen, it's hard for me to write and that's one writing job that I can ignore.

SLD: Do you care what will be on it?

LC: [*Laughs.*] No. I don't care. It's not for me.

SLD: So what is most important for you now?

LC: [*Long pause.*] It's a good question but it doesn't seem to register on my dial. I don't know what's most important. I guess the health and welfare of one's children is the most important thing. After that comes one's own health and one's own work. And then playing with the dogs has a big importance in my life.

COHEN CLIP

On "A Thousand Kisses Deep" and Life in General

"We don't write the play, we don't produce it, we don't direct it, and we're not even actors in it. Everybody eventually comes to the conclusion that things are not unfolding exactly the way they wanted, and that the whole enterprise has a basis that you can't penetrate. Nevertheless, you live your life as if it's real. But with the understanding: it's only a thousand kisses deep, that is, with that deep intuitive understanding that this is unfolding according to a pattern that you simply cannot discern."

—from "State of Grace," by Doug Saunders,
the *Globe and Mail*, September 1, 2001

COHEN CLIP

On Antidepressants

"I was involved in early medication, like Desipramine. And the MAOs [monoamine oxidase inhibitors], and the new generation—Paxil, Zoloft, and Wellbutrin. I even tried experimental antiseizure drugs, ones that had some small successes in treating depression. I was told they all give you a 'bottom,' a floor beneath which you are not expected to plunge. I plunged. And all were disagreeable, in subtly different ways. . . . On Prozac, I thought I had attained some kind of higher plateau because my interest in women had dissolved. Then I realized it was just a side effect. That stuff crushes your libido. . . . A few years ago . . . I threw out all the drugs I had. I said, 'These things really don't even begin to confront my predicament.' I figured, if I am going to go down I would rather go down with my eyes wide open."

—from "A Happy Man," by Mireille Silcott, *Saturday Night* (Canada), September 15, 2001

COHEN CLIP

On Depression

"Memories were not the cause of that depression. During the course of my life, there have been some wonderful women. And it was not that I could not find love, but that I could not accept love, because I did not know how. Perhaps the breakup [with Marianne] was an element in that depression, but I really never knew where my depressive condition came from, but it had to do with an isolation of myself. It has been the force, the determinant mechanism that made me adapt this attitude in life. I lived trying to avoid it, to escape it, to understand it, to handle it. It made me turn to drink, it pushed me to drugs, and it led me to Zen."

—from "An Intimate Conversation with Leonard Cohen," by Elena Pita, *El Mundo* (Spain), September 26, 2001

COHEN CLIP
On Rap Music

"In the case of Eminem and some of the other rappers, the lyrics are impressive. I think it's great. I studied and was formed in this tradition that honored the ancient idea of music being declaimed or chanted, of lyrics being declaimed or chanted to a rhythmic background. So I feel this is not at all a threat to Western civilization. . . . If it is in bad taste, you know, much of what we cherish today was once considered in bad taste. I have no idea where these things are going to go, but if it endures, it's not going to be because someone affirmed to the good taste or the bad taste of it."

—from "Cohen on Wry," by Michael Krugman, *Flaunt* (US), October 2001

COHEN CLIP
On Being Signed to Columbia Records

"I wasn't deeply aware of an impending explosion. But there was a sense of freedom and opportunity in the air. I was heard by a very great A&R man called John Hammond, who signed everybody from Billie Holiday to Bruce Springsteen. He was a very kind man, he had heard Judy [Collins's] version of 'Suzanne' and he invited me out to lunch near the Chelsea Hotel. Afterward, he asked me if I would mind playing some tunes. So I did, very nervously, and he said just three words to me: 'You got it.' About the best words I ever heard."

—from "Leonard Cohen: Love's Hard Man," by Alan Franks, the *Times Magazine* (London), October 13, 2001

COHEN CLIP
On Life in the Monastery

"A strange thing happened when I was liberated from everyday communication. I didn't want to, but I found myself thinking in terms of songs again. I was amused by it at first, like I was being taunted. . . . A lot of the time in the meditation hall, when I was expected to have my mind on other matters, I was instead concentrating deeply on the problem of finding rhymes for words like 'orange.'"

—from "Cohen Emerges from Monastery with New CD," by Tom Moon, *Philadelphia Inquirer*, October 24, 2001

COHEN CLIP

On Playing a Heroic Role

"Heroism is very high maintenance. After a while, when tremendous energy is devoted to maintaining this hero as the center figure of the drama, the evidence accumulates that this hero is relentlessly defeated. So at a certain point the modest wisdom arises that it would be best to let this hero die and get on with your life."

—from "Leonard Cohen: Down from the Mountain, Singing with More Serenity," by Ann Powers, the *New York Times*, October 28, 2001

HAPPY AT LAST: THE POET RETURNS FROM HIS ZEN RETREAT WITH A NEW ALBUM AND A SUNNIER DISPOSITION

J. POET | **November 2001, *Pulse!* (US)**

"I met Leonard Cohen at his home in Los Angeles, a modest, sparsely furnished cottage in a middle-class neighborhood," recalled the journalist who goes by the pen name j. poet. "There were no trappings of stardom, no gold records or photos of himself on the wall. He'd just returned from a few years meditating and studying Zen in semi-seclusion and he radiated a calm, serene aura. He greeted me warmly, and as we conversed, he recalled meeting me once before, many years earlier, which I found flattering. He answered all my questions slowly and deliberately, showing off flashes of ironic wit.

"After the interview," poet told me, "Cohen showed me his garden, home studio, and bedroom. As I was leaving, he mentioned a still-untitled book of poems and drawings he was working on, *Book of Longing*, which was published in 2006. He printed out a caricature of himself that made me laugh out loud. He gave it to me as a parting gift and I still treasure it." —Ed.

"Welcome to my public relations crisis," Leonard Cohen says, as he opens the door to his apartment. His speaking voice and his singing voice share the same qualities, a low, measured rumble that's both world weary and comforting, but his somber tone is undercut by the warm smile that often punctuates his conversation.

It's a hot summer day in L.A., but Cohen is dressed almost formally—a black fedora, black and white hound's tooth jacket, gray T-shirt, black slacks, and black Chinese meditation slippers.

"A few weeks after I turned in this record, the company told me I was going to have a promo emergency if I didn't get busy, so they've had me on the phone for the last two months talking to people about it," he said, walking through his sparsely furnished, two-bedroom unit. There's a small electric keyboard in the guest room, and his classical guitar leans against the wall of his own bedroom. "Would you like a drink? Water? Alcohol? A cigarette?" He's a considerate host and sets up the sunny kitchen for the interview with precise, efficient movements.

The work that caused the emergency is *Ten New Songs*, his first album of new material since *The Future*, released nine years ago. It's an unexpected pleasure, in light of rumors that Cohen had retired to a monastery to shun the public life and meditate. "I did spend five or six years on Mount Baldy with Kyozan Joshu Sasaki, Roshi," Cohen said. "But a Zen Center is a very social place, so it's hardly withdrawing from the world. There's a Zen saying: 'Like the pebbles in a bag, the monks polish one another.' I've been involved in this community for almost thirty years now."

Like Zen, Cohen's work has an economy of line and an attention to detail that is missing from most popular music. His work takes us deep into the recesses of the romantic soul, a place where love, sex, death, and redemption spin together in a slow melancholy waltz, occasionally highlighted by a sizzling laser burst of ironic humor.

"I'd like to think that there may be a chuckle or two in the songs," Cohen said, that sly half smile coming again to his lips, "but it seems to evade my critics, who haven't always been kind. I've been called everything over the years. [*"The Prince of Bummers"* and *"Duke of Doom"* are just two of the colorful, and facile, epithets that have been hung around the poet's neck.] One writer even suggested the record company include a packet of razor blades with the albums, and market them as a do-it-yourself suicide kit."

Cohen is an unusually deliberate artist, known for the protracted effort he puts into his work. "I was reading *Billboard* magazine a few months ago, and learned that my first album, *Songs of Leonard Cohen*, had just gone gold." He smiled, considering the patterns his cigarette smoke traced in the air. "That's what, thirty-three years? That's a pace I'm comfortable with."

In the past, Cohen has characterized the songwriting process as a holy ordeal, like wrestling with angels. "These songs were written up on Mount Baldy, part of a larger body of work, and I wouldn't dramatize the process quite so extravagantly," the singer said. "Not to say it didn't take a lot of work, but it's gotten easier since I've accepted the fact that I sweat over every word. I'm not of the school that can write a song in a taxicab or jot down a tune on the back of a napkin. Which is not to say that laboring over them is any guarantee of excellence."

One thing that may have made the process easier this time is Cohen's collaboration with his longtime friend and fellow Zen student Sharon Robinson, the Grammy-winning (Patti Labelle's "New Attitude") singer, composer, and musician who contributed her considerable composing and arranging skills to the album. They'd collaborated before on songs for Cohen—"Everybody Knows" (on *I'm Your Man*) and "Waiting for the Miracle" (on *The Future*)—and Diana Ross ("Summertime") but this is the first complete record they've done together.

"I had melodies in progress for some of these songs when I ran into Sharon and decided to revisit our collaboration. I wound up liking her take on the songs better than mine and kept inviting her to make more and more contributions. She'd pick out a verse and turn it into a chorus and reshape the music. In terms of the writing and performance it became a duo, and in terms of production it was a trio." (Cohen's longtime engineer, Leanne Ungar, helped supervise the mix.)

The album was recorded at Still Life, the name Cohen has given to his small backyard studio, and the performances have a warm, underproduced sound. "The conventional wisdom was, and still is, that you have to drop the tracks onto analog tape before you mix, to recover the warmth and presence you lose in the digital format. We found that we lost the warmth we had in digital, so we boldly mixed it using Pro Tools [audio software]."

The only minor problem was the fact that Cohen's home studio wasn't soundproofed, but since he gets up early to meditate, he was able to do the vocal tracks before dawn, or late at night, when ambient sound was at a minimum. "It was a luxury to be able to try different readings of a song, and I did innumerable takes on most of them."

The melodies on *Ten New Songs* are still low key, but Robinson's rhythm tracks have hints of country, R&B, and, on "Boogie Street," even a bit of hip-hop. "We had several models in the back of our minds when we were working on the music—a slow R&B song might be referred to for 'In My Secret Life,' a country song might be referred to for 'That Don't Make It Junk,' the model of a protest folksong might be referred to in 'Land of Plenty.' The temptation is that [digital music programs] offer you so many possibilities. You can get lost for months trying to explore them all. I kept in mind what the beats used to say: 'First thought, best thought.'"

One of the most striking, and Zen-like, tunes on *Ten New Songs* is "Love Itself," which draws its inspiration from the motes of dust dancing in a sunbeam. Every poet has played with this universal phenomenon, but few as successfully as Cohen. "The song does have a pedestrian genesis. I was sitting in a sunny room, watching the motes of dust, and accepted their graceful invitation to join in their activity and forget who I was, or remember who I was. It's that rare experience of dissolution of self, not the careful examination of self that I usually work with. I played it for a couple of brother monks and sister nuns and they said it was better than sesshin—a seven-day session of intense meditation."

Cohen also designs the cover art for his albums and singles and his desk was littered with various treatments for the single Columbia is releasing of "In My Secret Life," mostly for the European market, where he is more commercially successful. He also shot a video for the tune with the Canadian visual artist Floria Sigsmondi. "MTV doesn't want anything to do with me," Cohen said, "but they have content laws in Canada. A certain percentage of everything on TV has to be Canadian, and they show the videos there."

As he moved with his guest to the door, Cohen suddenly grinned. "I've been really happy for the past three years," he said, in an almost confessional tone. "I read somewhere that in some people, the brain cells that cause anxiety die as you get older. I don't know if it's that, or the discipline [of sitting Zazen], but life does seem to be getting easier. And I'm not touring for this album. I'm taking the next month off to finish a book I've been working on. I have about 250 poems and a bunch of goofy little drawings that I want to put together and get out. [*He goes to the computer and boots up a hilariously self-effacing self-portrait.*]

"And I have a couple of songs I did with Sharon that didn't make it onto *Ten New Songs*. The process went so smoothly that I'm looking forward to starting a new record."

EXILE ON MAIN STREET

BRETT GRAINGER | **November 2001,** *Elm Street* **(Canada)**

Another of Cohen's late 2001 conversations was with journalist Brett Grainger, who got a green light for his meeting with the artist while on his honeymoon. "I more or less went straight from my honeymoon to the interview in Montreal," Grainger told me. "The first thing that struck me was that he answered the door wearing sunglasses. This despite the fact that he'd been alone in a hotel room that didn't appear to have any windows. I thought, 'This is the real deal.'"

Grainger also concluded that Cohen was "exactly the gentleman I thought he would be—patient, reflective, genuinely engaged with the questions. A rarity for anyone in entertainment, at least my experience of it. It was certainly the highlight of my career as an entertainment journalist.

"The one thing I regret not asking was what it was like growing up in Catholic Montreal," Grainger continued. "While Cohen is Jewish and has engaged in Buddhist practice, his work has always been permeated by a Christian—and specifically Roman Catholic—sensibility. I'd have loved to hear his thoughts about that, what it is about Catholicism he finds or found interesting and compelling, especially at a time when anti-Semitism was still very much alive and well in Catholic Quebec."

One thing Grainger doesn't regret is including a paragraph about hearing Cohen urinate through a wall. "I debated about whether to mention that because I feared the detail was too intrusive and indiscreet," he said. "But in the end I felt it made him seem more like a man, an elderly man at that. It brought him a little bit off the pedestal, which is what Buddhists say one should do with all idols. Including the Buddha. So I suspected he would have approved.

"All the same," Grainger concluded, "the article is definitely the work of a young man. I wish I could have that hour with him again at age thirty-nine." —Ed.

I'm on Sainte-Catherine Street in downtown Montreal. It's my first visit in a few years, and the strip is looking decidedly less seedy than I've ever seen it. A minor economic recovery has given the old lady a major lift—signs for shoe stores and reputable eateries now easily outnumber those for danseuses nues.

After lunch at Reuben's, I head to the corner of Rue de la Montagne and turn right, continuing north with the mountain in my sights until I arrive at the entrance to the Hotel Vogue, ready for my appointment with the city's favorite son, Leonard Cohen. Right off the top, I'm not crazy about the location. I dislike the anonymous, controlled environments that hotels offer a person in my profession. Interviewing a celebrity in a hotel room is like sun tanning with your clothes on: it's safe, but it won't give you much color.

No need to worry. Even against the vacuous decor, Cohen has more individuality than a thumbprint. "How are you, man?" he says, opening the door, then turning around to search the room for a match to relight his pipe. In profile, he reveals clues to his age. The well-tailored clothes hang loosely on him; at sixty-seven, he's also acquired a noticeable stoop. The long facial creases arcing downward from either side of his nose have grown into dark parentheses that contain a soft, enigmatic smile. He's dressed in his familiar uniform: dark double-breasted suit, grey shirt with dark striped tie, black slip-on shoes. The hair is more salt than pepper and cut short. But it's not the military buzz he was sporting during his six years at a Zen monastery on Mount Baldy, just outside of Los Angeles, where he engaged in what he calls "a study of friendship" with an aging monk, Joshu Sasaki Roshi.

Cohen secures a match and lights up. The dense aroma of pipe tobacco hangs like incense in the room. I feel a little as if I've come to the mountaintop to visit the guru. He is wearing sunglasses—big, graded-tint aviator lenses in plastic frames—even though he's in a windowless hotel room, and until quite recently alone.

Suddenly, it occurs to me that a hotel is the perfect place to interview Leonard Cohen. After all, this is the man who starred in a film called *I*

Am a Hotel and penned a Byronic ode to Janis Joplin and an unmade bed in a room at New York's Chelsea. Hotels are the other mountains in his life. He might just feel more at home here in the Hotel Vogue than in his own house.

Puffing away, Cohen doffs the shades and we sit down at a table where he tells me about the challenges of conducting a recent European press tour—giving more than one hundred interviews—while mastering the final tracks on his latest album, *Ten New Songs*.

Cohen may have come down from the mountain, but the mountain is still in the music. Starting with the very Zen title, there's a spareness to the entire project, as if he were trying to starve his songs down to a bare skeleton of notes and broken syllables. "I smile when I'm angry," he sings on "In My Secret Life." "I cheat and I lie / I do what I have to do to get by." The austere production of *Various Positions* and *I'm Your Man*—Euro-disco synths, drum machine, and an angelic chorus of backing vocals—is back, as is the voice ravaged by a fierce regimen of excess, really no more these days than a gruff whisper from the basement (or as he likes to say, "almost an octave more serious").

Not that he needs to worry about the pop charts. Call it the Woody Allen factor. In an industry of one-hit wonders, Leonard Cohen is more than an oddity. He's a miracle: a senior citizen with carte blanche to record just about anything he wants and release it to an adoring and loyal fan base scattered around the world. (More than three hundred people have registered for a conference dedicated to Cohen next summer on the Greek island of Hydra, which the poet himself is unlikely to attend.) Sharon Robinson, Cohen's producer and musical collaborator on the new album, puts it this way, "There was no input at all from the record company. Leonard has a lot of autonomy when it comes to his career."

How to explain his good fortune? It's certainly not his prolific pace. To update an observation made by the literary critic Stephen Scobie, Leonard Cohen is a singer who hasn't issued a new studio album for nine years, a poet who hasn't published a new collection for seventeen years, and a novelist who hasn't written a new novel for thirty-six years. Part of the reason is that he's damn picky. It is well known that Cohen went through five hundred revisions of the words to "Take This Waltz" (from *I'm Your Man*) before finally recording it; he has been working for years on many of the lyrics for *Ten New Songs* (a process he calls "blackening pages"). A single line can tie him up in knots for weeks. Given this kind of monkish devotion, it isn't shocking that Cohen's lyrics attain the exalted status of poetry. What perhaps should be more surprising is that they also succeed as great love songs, the kind you might find yourself humming along with on the radio.

My tape recorder isn't working.

Engaging in some light banter about the weather, I try to look casual as I whack the machine against the table. The combination of a late summer heat wave and the lack of air-conditioning in Cohen's Montreal residence made it necessary to meet at the hotel. "You're a citizen of Mountain Street once again," I say, slipping in a reference to his second novel, *Beautiful Losers*.

"I used to live at the top of Mountain Street," says Cohen. (I whack the machine again.)

"By Sherbrooke?" (Whack.) I'm starting to get some idea of how hot it must be at Cohen's place.

"No, no," he says. (Whack. Whack.) "Above Sherbrooke."

"Oh, on the actual mountain," I say, breaking into a cold sweat. Air-conditioning be damned, I'm dying in here. So is my machine. I blurt out an apology and bumble through the standard idiot's checklist: switch batteries, examine the tape, wiggle moving parts.

"That's OK, man," says Cohen. "Check it out. Take your time." He gets up to pour another coffee, then sits down and relights his pipe. My machine is back together; I take a breath and hit "rec."

Cohen leans forward slightly. "Let's test it," he says. "One, two." Then it dawns on me: somehow the voice-activated recording switch has been turned on. The mike isn't picking up Cohen's whispery bass. I flip off the switch. "One of my recurring nightmares," I say, "is that I get through an interview, then find out later that the machine wasn't working."

"I had a similar experience a long time ago," says Cohen, "when I was interviewing Glenn Gould for *Esquire* magazine. This was before the days of tape recorders. Gould was famously reluctant to do interviews, but he accepted me as an interviewer. He had his gloves on and he was very, very courteous, and we began to talk.

"The conversation got heated," he continues, "and I put my pen down. I thought, 'I'm going to remember everything he says because it's really fascinating.' We talked for a couple of hours and I thought, I've really got this nailed. Then I went back to my apartment on Mountain Street and I couldn't remember a thing. *Esquire* phoned me a few days later and said, 'How did it go?'" I said, 'I'm working on it.' Then they started phoning me every second day. Then every day. And then I stopped answering the phone. I think I had to return the advance."

We laugh, then Cohen crosses the room to pour himself another coffee. I seize the moment to bring up an observation attributed to Irving Layton, his longtime avuncular drinking buddy. Once at a dinner party in Montreal, I say, Layton asked, "Do you know what the problem with Leonard Cohen is?" His answer? "Leonard Cohen is a narcissist who hates himself." Cohen laughs at the bon mot. "That's good," he says. "But I think Irving may have been talking about himself there."

It was Saint Augustine who wrote, "I am a problem to myself," but it might as well have been Cohen. In interviews, he often defines the human condition as "a gathering around a perplexity." Accordingly, the subject matter and primary concern of each of his fourteen albums, nine books of poetry, and two novels is always the same: Leonard Cohen. His art can be read as the transcript of an extended interview with himself, a kind of spiritual journalism in which the poet addresses his attention to the confrontation with love and its loss.

It's gotten him a bit of a reputation along the way. "Prince of bummers," "poet of pessimism," "troubadour of travail," "the Dr. Kevorkian of song"—journalists can't seem to get enough of the cliché of the dark knight, the tortured soul spinning his suffering into gold. But the gloomy picture does not match the man today—if it ever did. Increasingly, Cohen's depression and the inner conflicts that marked his earlier days are being replaced by a sense of ease with the world and with himself; the dystopic prophet who recorded *The Future* has finally come to terms with his exile on main street. Recently, Cohen allowed one of his self-portraits to be posted on his unofficial Web site, leonardcohenfiles.com. It depicts the aging poet in a mournful, ironic pose above the words "happy at last."

Are the anxious days behind? "For the moment," he answers. "You never write the end. But yes, I'm in a graceful period now. My kids are well [son Adam, twenty-nine, and daughter Lorca, twenty-seven], my work's going well, my friends seem to be OK for the moment." Cohen's close collaboration on the new album with Sharon Robinson, who wrote all of the music—a first for Cohen—suggests that the notorious perfectionist is at a place where he is ready to relinquish some control over his creative process. Lyrically, Robinson says, there's a sense of reconciliation and peace in his songs that wasn't there before. On "Here It Is," he sings, "May everyone live, and may everyone die. Hello, my love, and my love, good-bye."

"I had a lovely moment with Irving recently," says Cohen. (Good moments are few these days with Layton, who is suffering from Alzheimer's disease.) "We were having a smoke and he said, 'Leonard, have you noticed that you have declined in your sexual interests?' He's eighty-nine. So I said, 'I have, Irving.' He said, 'I'm relieved to hear that.' I said, 'So I take it, Irving, that you also have observed some decline in your own sexual interests.' He said, 'Yes, Leonard, I have.' I said, 'When did you first begin to notice this decline in your sexual interests?' He said, 'Oh, about the age of sixteen or seventeen.'"

In interviews, Cohen has the frustrating habit of repeating stories verbatim, and this one has been getting regular rotation. But it illustrates an important shift in the poet's concerns: as Cohen's sexual interests begin to wane, they have been replaced by another love, a desire to live closer to the deep, silent waters that feed a love "a thousand kisses deep," as he sings on one of the new tunes. The monk known on Mount Baldy as Jikan, "Silent One," is singing love songs to the silence, "the common and current stillness that resides at the center of all things."

I ask him if he has a favorite book of the Bible. "I like Isaiah," he says, "especially the first chapters. I love the Psalms." Cohen explains that one of his new songs, "By the Rivers Dark," was inspired by Psalm 137, the one that begins, "By the rivers of Babylon." Suddenly, the poet of pleasure is quoting the scriptures of exile: "'If I forget thee, O Jerusalem, may my right arm forget its cunning and my tongue cleave to the roof of my mouth if I set not Jerusalem above my deepest joy.' But I say the opposite," he continues. "Be the truth unsaid and the blessings gone, if I forget my Babylon."

It's all very heretical. Can you be a good Jew and love Babylon? "Well," he says, "the Talmud was written in Babylon. A lot of good Jews lived and wrote and thought and prayed there. And that's where we are—we're on Boogie Street. We're in Babylon. I think it's appropriate to live completely where you are and not reserve some mythical or spiritual refuge as an alternative. That can produce a kind of dangerous spiritual schizophrenia. We have to make it here; we have to make Jerusalem in Babylon."

He leans back a little in his chair. "Something like that," he says, raising his hand to wave away the air of seriousness that has filled the room like the smoke curling up from his pipe. "I say it better in the song: 'Kiss my lips and then it's done, I'm back on Boogie Street.' As Roshi says, you can't live in paradise. No restaurants or toilets."

That's a good thing, because Cohen has drained a carafe of coffee in under an hour. "Just gonna take a leak," he says, sprinting to the bathroom. The slow, labored sounds coming from behind the door punctuate the longer stretches of silence, and I'm reminded of an old Cohen tune, "Paper Thin Hotel," from *Death of a Ladies' Man*. Cohen reemerges, and we make our way out of the room and into the elevator. The doors close, then open, and we spill out into the anonymous, profane cacophony of the hotel lobby to say our good-byes. He shakes my hand and then it's done, I'm back on Mountain Street.

THE PRINCE OF PRURIENCE AND LOSS

JOHN LELAND | November 2001, *GQ* (US)

John Leland's Cohen profile includes evidence of the singer's penchant for retelling stories: You've already heard the Irving Layton joke that opens this piece, as well as a few of the other anecdotes. But keep reading. Leland offers some fresh insights, and so does his subject. —Ed.

Two O.G.'s were talking about sex, and one of them was Leonard Cohen. It was October of last year, and Cohen had paid a call on his old friend, the writer Irving Layton. Layton, who is now eighty-nine and in poor health, is Canada's most celebrated poet and until recently its alpha rake—earthy, literary, Jewish, horny, a beacon for younger writers and obsessives of the flesh such as Cohen. Leonard, Layton asked, have you noticed a decline in your sexual activity?

In the kitchen of his house in Montreal, Cohen smiles now to recount the conversation. His own amatory legend, which he likes to downplay, includes liaisons with Joni Mitchell, Janis Joplin, and Rebecca De Mornay, among others, and verses that do not flinch at naming body parts or private acts. His eyes are serious, his voice playfully light. This is Leonard Cohen, poet of the sad song, telling a joke. "I said, 'Well, I have, Layton. And I take it that you also have observed some decline in your sexual interest?' Yes, the elder poet had as well. So Cohen asked him when he first noticed the decline. "He said, 'Oh, maybe when I was sixteen or seventeen.'"

Strictly speaking, this is the punch line, but Cohen does not leave it alone. "I think with all human creatures it's downhill," he continues, descending into darker, more familiar territory of bummer and rue. "One is seized by the rage for a number of years, and then the rest of the world begins to intrude and assert itself."

For thirty-five years, since Judy Collins recorded his mournful ballad "Suzanne," Leonard Cohen has cut a worldly, burdened figure through the literary quadrants of pop music, engaging the big questions—sex, salvation, worth—in plainspoken rhyme that has earned him admirers as distant as Nick Cave and Neil Diamond. He is a badass of dark verse. He has come to Montreal, from his main home on the outskirts of South Central Los Angeles, to talk about his new album, titled, with typical austerity, *Ten New Songs*, and about the journey that produced it.

He wears his gray hair short and pushed forward. A striped tie hangs loosely around a gray silk shirt already damp in the unseasonable heat. The album, which came out October 9, is his first since he checked into a mountain Zen monastery in 1994, emerging, with little explanation, five years later. Like his previous twelve recordings, the new one is filled with finely wrought lyrics of obsession and incompletion. He has also published two novels and nine books of poetry that are even more unflinching than his music. Scattered across forty-five years, these works have brought him pockets of adulation, comparisons to the Spanish poet Federico García Lorca, and tribute albums from alternative rockers and Slovakian girl bands—and, above all, a haphazard path that by now qualifies as a long and sustaining career.

Over a breakfast of strong coffee and cigarettes, he shows me a poem he wrote in the monastery, around the time he was thinking about coming down. It begins, "I've become thin and beautiful again . . ."

We are in for a long talk.

The home in Montreal is a modest row house in the old immigrant quarter, sparsely genteel, next door to a Zen center Cohen helped found, with photographs of his son, Adam, twenty-nine, who is a singer-songwriter, and daughter, Lorca, twenty-six, a painter and sculptor, on display. The house is comfortable but underused. When Cohen first left this city, at twenty-two, he did so as a celebrated Canadian poet, hoping to storm the Beat poetry and folk music scenes developing in downtown New York. After a couple of fizzled starts, he remembers landing in Max's Kansas City, where a young man named Lou Reed introduced him to the luminaries of the Warhol crowd. Cohen had just published his prodigiously bleak 1966 novel, *Beautiful Losers*, which was a commercial failure at the time, though it has since gone on to sell a million copies. The gamesmanship at Max's got heated; Cohen felt cut. Finally, Reed said to him, "You don't have to take anything from these assholes, you wrote *Beautiful Losers*." Though he never fully abandoned Montreal, he keeps the house mainly so his children will have a connection with the city where they grew up. He has never mentioned Montreal in a song. (In a telling contrast, according to the Web site leonardcohenfiles.com, he has used the word "naked" seventeen times.)

Two portraits in the house could serve as guideposts to Cohen's sojourn from the city's tight Jewish community—which produced the late Mordecai Richler, Layton, and A. M. Klein, among others—to his unlikely status, in late middle age, as a part-time pop star and full-time soul man. The first is of a seventeenth-century Mohawk girl named [Kateri and baptised as] Catherine Tekakwitha, whose oppressive virginity and bid for sainthood figure in *Beautiful Losers*. The other portrait is of an elderly Zen teacher named Joshu Sasaki Roshi, who has been Leonard's spiritual advisor since the 1970s. From different sides, the two pictures address the idea of carnal quiet toward which Cohen's writings have steadfastly groped. Tekakwitha shines with chaste incandescence; Roshi grins in slurry satisfaction beside a half-empty bottle of wine.

A little more than seven years ago, Cohen decided he needed a change of place, not just physical but spiritual. He was ending a tour in support of an album called *The Future*, a corrosive look at decline on a broad scale, and ending a love affair with Rebecca De Mornay. (A rhyme from the album's title track ran, "Destroy another fetus now / We don't like children anyhow.") He removed himself to a Buddhist monastery sixty-five hundred feet up on Mount Baldy, in the San Gabriel Mountains outside Los Angeles, and to the teachings of Roshi. Cohen had been to the monastery before, for short periods, but this trip was different. Though he makes little of the circumstances, he says that even at the time, he knew he would be there for years. "It sounds dramatic, and I suppose I could put a dramatic spin on it if I were interested in self-dramatization," he says, "but it was a very natural unfolding. I was close to sixty, my old teacher was close to ninety, and I thought it would be appropriate to spend some time with him."

Roshi, who came to the United States from Japan in 1962 ("I came to have a good time," he once said), has been a comfort to and an influence on Cohen in his life and in his music. Some years ago, the two men were in New York, and Cohen felt pelted by criticisms that his music was too gloomy and indulgent. At the time, he was recording his 1984 album, *Various Positions*. The two men had fortified themselves with a very strong Chinese liqueur called Ng-Ka-Fy, and Roshi was nodding off. "I didn't think he was paying any attention," Cohen says. "The next morning, I said, 'What did you think, Roshi?' He said, 'Leonard, you should sing more sad.' That was a very good piece of advice."

I ask: Leonard, why so many sad songs?

"I never thought of it that way, as morbidity or sadness," he says. "We never say of a blues singer that he sounds sad. Of course he sounds sad. If the song is authentically an expression of the person's suffering, then the suffering is transcended and you don't get the whine, you don't get the complaint, even though it may be all about a whine and a complaint. It's experienced as relief, as comfort, as pleasure."

Nick Cave, who has turned a dark line or two himself, remembers discovering the pleasures of Cohen at the age of fourteen, in a country town in Australia where he used to drink pilfered beer and listen to Cohen's *Songs of Love and Hate*, an album his friend's mother considered unhealthily depressing. "It just changed me," Cave says. "How sexy his whole way of writing was. It's been decried as depressing, but he's one of the funniest writers we have. I can't think of a lyric that doesn't have a smile hidden in the lines. There are two things going on all the time: warmth and a wicked wit. I wish I had that."

It should be said that Leonard Cohen does not write his songs from depression but from conflict, from what he calls "the opposing movements in the mind that produce the need for resolving the chaos and observing order." There was a time when he felt the curtain of depression, and he sought relief in Prozac, Desyrel, MAO inhibitors, and other armaments of the modern medicine cabinet. "They all made me feel a lot worse," he says. Then around 1998 or 1999, without warning, his depression lifted on its own, and to the betterment of his writing. The despair never provided him with material, he says. "I didn't feel it was necessarily the engine of the activity. It's anguish. It's a pain in the ass. On the contrary, I find my capacity to concentrate enhanced without that background of horror."

Pilgrims who have trekked up to Mount Baldy, seeking either enlightenment or Cohen, describe the monastery as Spartan, beautiful, and cold. Cohen occupied a wooden cabin with a narrow bed, dirty carpet, and few amenities, apart from his synthesizer and laptop computer. Mornings began at 2:30 or 3 AM, with chores and meditation; on Friday evenings, Cohen, the grandson of a prominent Canadian rabbi, lit candles to observe the Sabbath. He is not a man of simple faith nor eager to foreclose his options. At any rate, his Judaism did not clash with the Zen teachings at the center. In August 1996, he was ordained as a monk and Roshi gave him the name Jikan, which has been roughly translated as "silent one." "Since his English is very poor, I never really found out what that means," Cohen says. "It's got something to do with silence, but normal silence, not special, holy, righteous, renunciated silence. Just ordinary silence. Or the silence out of which everything evolves, the silence at the center of things." He told one interviewer on the mountain that Roshi had recommended the ordainment for tax purposes.

He was not, Cohen insists, trying to retire or retreat from the world. "It's the wrong place to go to if you want to retire, because it's a very busy kind of place, as monasteries or Zen centers are," he says. The center had phones and also a steady onus of snow to shovel, dishes to wash. He served as a cook for Roshi and gave occasional interviews. The Rinzai Zen discipline of the center sought rigorous, sweaty engagement with the world, not pious withdrawal.

In his work, Cohen has been scrupulously direct in engaging the world. For all the gloom in his writing, fans are as likely to be drawn to the humor and bite of his boudoir reportage. In other words, the dirty stuff: the bawdy swash of a song like "Don't Go Home with Your Hard-On," which featured Bob Dylan and Allen Ginsberg singing sloppy backup, or the well-mannered vitriol of "Everybody Knows": "Everybody knows that you've been discreet / But there were so many people you just had to meet / Without your clothes / And everybody knows."

Leonard Cohen is less willing to speak so directly in conversation. After three decades of interviews, he knows how to give a little taste and then eloquently retreat, covering his tracks by professing a lack of eloquence. For years he has expressed regret at revealing that his song "Chelsea Hotel," with its line "Giving me head on the unmade bed," referred to an affair with Janis Joplin. The lyric, which borders on cruelty, was fine, he says, but he should have let it remain anonymous. Relationships with God, with women, with the world, "are appropriately addressed in one's work," he says. "Otherwise it's just gossip, which is not a particularly exalted activity. A great deal of time and attention has gone into producing the language. To speak casually about the matter is taking the name in vain. There's a commandment against it."

That said, he offers me some unpublished writings, which he hopes will answer some of my questions. The descriptive poems from Mount Baldy add meat to the dry bones of the pilgrims' accounts of the monastery. Besides the meditating and the chores, the robes and the shaved pate, the poems recount three-hundred-dollar bottles of Ballantine's scotch and the pleasures of lower altitudes. Cohen writes:

> *I'm loose in the belt and tight in the jowl / Crazy young beauties still covered with the grime / Of shrines and ashrams / Want to examine their imagination / In an old man's room*

He did not go up the mountain to discover the scalding virtues of self-denial.

In the house in Montreal, he taps at his laptop like an archaeologist reconstructing an elusive event. The directories in the computer are labyrinthine inventories of Cohen's consciousness. Entries for a single song lyric pile up: "Final version #1," which innocently offers itself as conclusive, is really just a speed bump along the way to "Final version #20" and beyond.

"That's good," he says, pulling up a poem called "Lovesick Monk" and offering a window on his life on Mount Baldy. It begins, not burying the lead, "It's dismal here." Later, a line of verse stretches across a drawing of a woman's bare backside, offering up a typical mix of portent and self-mockery. Across her ass it reads, "This is the perfection of the great way."

There is something alluringly incomplete about Leonard Cohen, and I think this is one of the traits that make him so seductive to women. His songs pick repeatedly at the same themes of unfulfillment, circling back over a few gnawing aches. He is not afraid to seek company in his ruin. His best lyrics are reductive, distilling a single yearning to metallic purity, often in language hewed down to monosyllables. He shows me a passage from a song in progress, an embryonic draft that has been through just sixteen revisions but is pure brutal Cohen: "You came to me this morning / And you handled me like meat / You've got to be a man to know / How good that feels, how sweet."

His filmic biographer, Harry Rasky, who directed a documentary called *The Song of Leonard Cohen*, once described him as "the first great vaginal poet," a line that means nothing to me or Cohen, except maybe this: His verses, like his conversation, create hollow spaces rather than eager projections. There is room to come inside; there are bruises to handle roughly.

Cohen's revelation on Mount Baldy, when it came, was the opposite of an epiphany. Instead it was a recognition that there would be no epiphany. It came upon him like medicine, harsh but healing. "One has a sense of a gift," he explains. "I have a gift for rhyme. I found with a sense of relief that I had no gift for the spiritual life." What this meant, he says, was that he was free to abandon the quest, without the aroma of disappointment or failure, nor a rejection of the cause. "I didn't have to seek for anything. And with the search, the anxieties attendant on that search ended. I don't know if 'happiness' is the word to describe the feeling; maybe 'applied indifference.'"

When he came down from the mountain in 1999, a few months before his sixty-fifth birthday, he brought a laptop full of songs, ten of which he deemed worthy of use. For a typical song, Cohen might write thirty or forty verses before arriving at five or six he can live with: "Unfortunately, I have to write a whole verse before I can discard it. I'm not sure that it's not any good until I finish it. Some people write great songs in the backs of taxicabs. I'm not like that." He ran across a sometime collaborator named Sharon Robinson, who helped him set the songs to music and record them in a backyard studio outside his Los Angeles home. They recorded their vocals late at night and in the early mornings, so as not to pick up the chirping of birds. In the spirit of incompletion, they used Robinson's demo tracks as the final accompaniment.

The songs are among the gentlest of his career, melancholy but not broken. The images are tautly visual, creating big vistas from a few little words: "The ponies run, the girls are young / The odds are there to beat."

Lust, which has been a lacerating force in Cohen's life and consequently in his work, is for the moment diminished. Instead the songs all refer, however obliquely, to the resolution of the time on Mount Baldy. His was not a break with faith; he continues to pursue meaning through Buddhism and Judaism. But this compulsive inquiry, as ever, will require labor-intensive immersion in his work, not deliverance. The new album reflects this acceptance. "As my old teacher says, 'You can't live in paradise: there are no toilets or restaurants.' Regardless of whatever descriptions you have of yourself, you have to keep coming back," Cohen says, to what he calls, somewhat infelicitously, Boogie Street, "the ordinary landscape of work and desire."

On a street outside the house in Montreal, the conversation circles inevitably around to work and sex. For a brief period of time, before his musical career took off, Cohen worked as a reporter. He got an assignment to interview the Canadian pianist Glenn Gould and was so impressed with the clarity of Gould's ideas that he did not bother to take notes; the words, he was sure, were burned into his mind. It was the last assignment he ever took. But the experience stayed with him, and even now, he says, "I think of myself as a journalist and my songs as reportage. I draw something as accurately as I can with the evidence available."

At his courtly insistence, we are on a mission to find Montreal bagels, the slender, heavy ones of which the city is justly proud. Sex and seduction have been recurring causes in his work and life, and so in interviews. I ask if he ever instigated the romantic turmoil in his life to have something to write about. This is not the first time he has considered the question. He says, "Layton once suggested that the poet does it for the poem, screws things up to have something to write about. I don't know if that's so. All that speculation suggests that we're in control, that we're doing things according to a plan. That runs counter to my understanding of how things work."

What Cohen will say for his career is that it has largely left him free to work. At an awards ceremony, he once thanked the executives of his record company for not paying too much attention to his work. His brief tastes of celebrity—he was once, for example, mobbed in Norway, where he fleetingly enjoyed a profile to rival that of Britney Spears—relieved any envy of greater stardom. At the same time, the fidelity of his fans has allowed him a working life more literary than pop, neither enslaved by his fans' needs nor oppressing them with his.

He protests amusement at his rep as a swordsman. "It's amazingly inaccurate, but it's interesting to read about," he says. And it has allowed him into the fraternity, access to the players' lore. "Because of this fictitious reputation, I have the credentials that permit me to enter into conversation with the Great Ones," he says. "From what I gather, when it comes to the objects of love that they desire—not the ones that come easily, but the women they want—then the background is anxiety. It has a physical resonance. Nobody masters it."

So he will continue to plumb the contours of this anxiety, unquenched by either Prozac or Zen, by the examples of Catherine or Roshi. Perhaps because Cohen was always older than the rock crowd, his work has sought deeper purchase in life's conflict, rather than the rock-and-roll joys of release. This is a key both to his longevity and to his next move. The conflict still beckons. As he sang a decade and a half ago, in bittersweet acknowledgment, there ain't no cure for love. But for Cohen, at least, there are the annealing self-examinations of the laptop. And for the rest of us, there is the work of Leonard Cohen.

BROTHER OF MERCY

MIKAL GILMORE | Late 2001, interview | March 2002, *Spin* (US)

Mikal Gilmore—for decades one of America's leading music journalists—delivers a typically insightful report in the following feature, which describes a meeting with Cohen in 2001 and, as a bonus, also limns a memorable encounter with the singer thirteen years earlier. —Ed.

In 1994, Leonard Cohen disappeared from public life. Cohen happens to be one of the most underappreciated artists in rock-and-roll history. But in the early 1990s, with works like *I'm Your Man* and *The Future*, he was enjoying the most successful period of his long career. Younger artists (including Jeff Buckley, Nick Cave, Tori Amos, and R.E.M.) were covering his songs, and filmmakers such as Oliver Stone and Atom Egoyan were featuring his work in their movies. At age fifty-nine, Leonard Cohen seemed, somewhat improbably, at the top of his game.

Then he simply walked away. He left behind his legendary love affairs (affectionately and notoriously documented in many songs), his two-story home in Los Angeles, and, it seemed, his artistic career as well. He took up full-time residence at a retreat led by his longtime Zen master and elderly friend, Kyozan Joshu Sasaki, sixty-five hundred feet up Mount Baldy, about an hour northeast of L.A. No one expected to hear anything more of him.

Then, just as quietly, Cohen left the center in 1999 and returned to his previous life. He's released a new album, *Ten New Songs*, that is, in many ways, unlike anything he has recorded before. In contrast to the acerbic themes of *I'm Your Man* and *The Future*, Cohen's new album is about the acceptance that comes after suffering and aging. It is not about a fearsome future; rather, it's about a tolerant present. Like Cohen's best work, it follows its own rhythms, shapes, and passions. And it hints at answers to two overriding questions. Why did he leave the world behind when the world finally seemed ready for him? And why has he returned with what might be called his bravest vision since his brilliant 1966 novel, *Beautiful Losers*?

The answer to both is: something happened to Leonard Cohen while he was gone, something he'll say only so much about. More on that later. Right now, there's some catching up to do.

1988. It is a pleasant summer evening in Los Angeles, and I am meeting Cohen, currently touring in support of *I'm Your Man*, at his mid-Wilshire-area home. I have spoken with him on various occasions since 1979. I remember one telephone interview in which we were talking about romantic and sexual love—subjects that have always saturated Cohen's work.

"People are lonely," he commented then, "and their attempts at love, in whatever terms they've made those attempts, they've failed. And so people don't want to get ripped off again; they get defensive and hard and cunning and suspicious. And of course they can never fall in love under those circumstances. By falling in love, just to be able to surrender, for a moment, your particular point of view, the trance of your own subjectivity, and to accommodate someone else." He paused. "The situation between men and women," he declared, "is *irredeemable*."

He paused again, then laughed. "Drunk," he chortled. "Drunk again."

This evening in 1988, though, drinks aren't on the menu. Instead, Cohen is making chicken soup. Around the kitchen are a few small religious icons and portraits—some symbols of Cohen's own religion, Judaism, a few bits of Hindu and Buddhist statuary, and a picture of Kateri Tekakwitha, the famed Iroquois Indian who looks over the narrative heart of *Beautiful Losers*.

Leonard Cohen was born in Montreal in 1934 into a family prominent in the Jewish community. But Cohen also found himself fascinated by Catholicism. "I didn't experience any of the oppressive qualities of it," he says, salting the soup. "I just saw the child, the mother, the sacrifice, the beauty of the ritual. And when I began to read the New Testament, I found a radical model that touched me very much. Love your enemy: 'Blessed are the meek, for they shall inherit the Earth.'"

His sense of Jewish identity and interest in Christian iconography and redemption would figure prominently in Cohen's work. "Like the families of many of my friends, my family gave me encouragement to be noble and good. When I was [at Montreal's McGill University] and I started to write poetry and meet other writers, we had the sense that what we were doing was very important. We weren't in London or New York—we didn't have the weight of the literary establishment around to say what was and was not possible. It was completely open-ended. We had the sense of an historic occasion every time we gathered and had a glass of beer."

Cohen also credits his summer camp experience—where the director was a socialist and a folksinger—as decisive. "He played good guitar," says Cohen of the director, "and he introduced me to folksinging via unionism and leftwing thought. I found out about a whole leftist position, a resistance position. I'd never known there was anything to resist. I got a guitar, and after the camp season was finished, I started learning songs. I went down to the folksong library at Harvard and listened. I didn't see much difference between songs and poems, so I didn't have to make any great leap between writing and singing."

In 1956, Cohen self-published his first poetry collection, *Let Us Compare Mythologies*. It met with praise, and his next, *The Spice-Box of Earth*, in 1961, fixed his position as Canada's major new literary voice. By then, however, Cohen was living on the Greek island of Hydra with a fetching Norwegian woman named Marianne Ihlen and her son. The relationship began a pattern: Like many before and after him, Cohen would find himself drawn in by the assurances of domestic and sexual commitment but also confined by the realities of the same. Although he lived in what seemed like paradise, he remained restless.

Cohen kept writing, publishing the semiautobiographical *The Favorite Game* in 1963, and then, in 1966, *Beautiful Losers*. It is a formally daring and startlingly sexual work about a man's search for transcendence amid romantic and historical betrayals, and many still cite it as a major event in postwar literature. It makes plain that if Cohen had desired, he could easily have reached for the sort of literary standing accorded authors such as Norman Mailer, Thomas Pynchon, and Henry Miller.

But Cohen's ambitions were changing. "I'd get some very good reviews for *Beautiful Losers*," he says, "but it only sold a few thousand books. It was like facing a hard truth. I really worked at this; I'd produced two novels, three books of poems, and I couldn't pay my rent. This was serious, because I had people who depended on me."

By the late 1960s, Cohen had drifted to New York City, where he realized that the ambitions of literature and the effects of popular music were not antithetical. "I bumped into Lou Reed at Max's Kansas City," he recalled, "and he said, 'You're the guy who wrote *Beautiful Losers*. Sit down.' I was surprised that I had some credentials on the scene. Lou Reed, Bob Dylan, Phil Ochs: all those guys knew what I'd written. I realized I hadn't really missed the boat."

His songwriting caught the right ears, and Columbia released *Songs of Leonard Cohen* in 1968. [*Actually, December 27, 1967. —Ed.*] With classics like "Suzanne" (already popularized by Judy Collins) and "Sisters of Mercy," it established Cohen as a spokesman for lost souls.

But despite his new reputation, Cohen was increasingly forlorn, and his relationship with Ihlen was fading. "After my record came out, I theoretically had access to interesting people. But I still found myself walking the streets, trying to find someone to have a cup of coffee with. I began to develop this idea that some catastrophe was taking place. I couldn't see why I couldn't make contact."

In 1969, Cohen met twenty-four-year-old Suzanne Elrod, the woman with whom he would share his longest and most tempestuous relationship. (She was not the legendary "Suzanne" of his most famous song, though Cohen admits her name was part of the attraction.) The two formed what Cohen describes as a marriage, though it was never formalized. In the coming years, Cohen's recordings (including *Songs of Love and Hate* and *Death of a Ladies' Man*) were often-stark portrayals of the struggle for romantic faith amid sexual warfare and of hope in the face of cultural dissolution. Much of the work was about his stormy relationship with

Elrod. (She "outwitted me at every turn," he says.) They had two children together and separated in the midseventies.

Although Cohen's music was growing more imaginative, his records sold modestly in the US. Legend has it that when Cohen first played 1984's *Various Positions* for Columbia pooh-bah Walter Yetnikoff, Yetnikoff said, "Leonard, we know you're great. We just don't know if you're any good." Columbia declined to release the album stateside.

By 1988, however, things are looking up. *I'm Your Man*, a grimly catchy record with moody electronic orchestration, is doing better than any other album Cohen has released in the US and is even a bona-fide hit in parts of Europe. When a newly enthusiastic Columbia grants Cohen an award for the album's successful international sales, he replies, "Thank you. I have always been touched by the modesty of your interest in my work."

After our talk over chicken soup, I travel to New York City to see Cohen perform a sold-out concert at Carnegie Hall. It is a powerful show, and the song that seems to stir the audience most is "First We Take Manhattan"—a sinister tale of a terrorist's revenge from *I'm Your Man*. Live, at the heart of a show full of songs about acquiescence and grief, it's like a call to battle. (And thirteen years later, when Jeff Buckley's version of Cohen's "Hallelujah" becomes VH1's chosen requiem in the wake of the attacks on New York's World Trade Center, "Manhattan" will sound like rueful prophecy.)

After the show, I visit Cohen in his room at the Mayfair hotel, just off Central Park. It is a hot, sticky afternoon, yet Cohen is dressed obliviously and impeccably in a dark, double-breasted pinstripe suit, with a crisp white shirt and a smart tie. Cohen insists that I take the most comfortable chair in the room, then calls room service to order me an ice-cold drink.

"These are extreme times," he begins, after a few moments. As he talks, he stands up from his chair, unzips his slacks, removes them, and folds them carefully over the back of another chair. Cohen keeps his jacket and tie on as he sits back down. "I think we are now living amidst a plague of biblical proportions. I think our order, our manners, our political systems, are breaking down. And I think that redemptive love may be breaking down as well."

I've heard this sort of thing from him before. But is it depression or enlightened realism? He continues: "There is no point in trying to forestall the apocalypse. The bomb has already gone off. We are now living in the midst of its aftermath. The question is: how can we live with this knowledge with grace and kindness? That's how I arrived at 'First We Take Manhattan.' We can no longer buy the version of reality that is presented to us. There's hardly any public expression that means anything to anybody. There's not a politician speaking who touches you. There's hardly a song you hear—"

There is a knock at the door. "Excuse me," says Cohen. He stands up and carefully pulls his pinstripe slacks back on, opens the door, and signs the bill for my cold soda. He closes the door, hands me the drink, takes his pants back off, sits down, and smiles warmly. There is nothing coy or ironic here—it's a truly gentle and compassionate expression. I realize then that Leonard Cohen is demonstrating how one behaves with grace and etiquette, even though he's consumed with the dreadful knowledge that we are all living on borrowed time.

On 1992's *The Future*, Cohen would traverse emotional lines he had not crossed before. "Things are going to slide in all directions," he sings on the title track. "The blizzard of the world / Has crossed the threshold / . . . Get ready for the future: it is murder."

I have always liked songs and art that are both honest and merciless, but I have to admit that "The Future" scared the fuck out of me. I decide that first chance I get, I will catch up with Cohen again and see how he is holding up. But by then, he is gone—moved on to a place where questions about his art would seem to have no further usefulness.

2001. I am knocking on the same door to the same house in Los Angeles. The man who answers again wears a beautiful suit and again insists I take the most comfortable seat. Of course, Leonard Cohen has also changed a bit. He is sixty-six now, and he wears his pepper gray hair in a shaven crop.

Cohen left the Mount Baldy center in 1999, after a five-year residency. We are meeting now to discuss *Ten New Songs*. The record begins in reverence for things past and ends with a prayer:

For the millions in the prison / That wealth has set apart / For the Christ who has not risen / From the caverns of the heart . . . / May the lights in the Land of Plenty / Shine on the truth some day.

Conceptually, it seems miles apart from *The Future*'s fearful fatalism. "*The Future* came out of suffering," Cohen says simply. "This came out of celebration."

When he first returned from the Zen center, Cohen had no immediate plans for recording. Then, one night at the Beverly Center mall, he ran into Sharon Robinson, a good friend who had done backup vocals on some of Cohen's earlier work (Cohen is godfather to her son, Michael). Before long, the two began swapping tunes. As it happened, *Ten New Songs* was written and performed almost entirely by Robinson and Cohen. "I think it's a fine piece of work, and Sharon did most of it," he says. "Occasionally I would make some adjustments. I'd say, 'Sharon, does this tune have more than four notes? You know the limitations I have.'"

Cohen picks up a pack of Vantage cigarettes and lights one. He smokes them almost nonstop throughout our conversations. "I started smoking again about a year ago," he says apologetically. "Got to quit again."

I ask Cohen the obvious: Why did he withdraw from his career? He studies his cigarette. "The whole market application felt remote to me," he says. "I was fifty-eight; I had the respect of my peers and another generation or two. But my daily predicament was such that there wasn't much nourishment from that kind of retrospection. I went up to the monastery in 1993, after my last tour, with the feeling of, 'If this works, I'll stay.' I didn't put a limit on it, but I knew I was going to be there for a while.

"Also, I was there because I had the good fortune to study with Roshi [as Cohen refers to Sasaki, his Zen master]. He's the real thing, man. He is a hell-raiser—there's not an ounce of piety about him. This guy is smart enough to be rich, and yet he lives in a little shack up there in the snow. He's a very exalted figure."

The phone in the hallway rings. Cohen pauses to hear who might be calling, but the caller hangs up when the machine answers. Cohen smiles. "I offer a prayer of gratitude when no one leaves a message."

Cohen begins to tell the story of the time he told Roshi that he wanted to leave the monastery and return to his life. "We are very close friends, Roshi and I. We were the two oldest guys up there, even though there were many years separating us. I had been cooking for him and looking after him for some time. So when I asked his permission to leave . .

. disappointment is not the right word. He was sad—just like you would be if a close friend went away. He asked me why I wanted to leave. I said, 'I don't know why.' He said, 'How long?' I said, 'I don't know, Roshi.' He said, 'Don't know. OK.'"

Cohen stubs out his cigarette and sits quietly. After a few moments, he offers to fix me lunch. (I learned long ago that it is impossible not to partake of food when you visit Leonard Cohen's home.) Afterward, Cohen takes me to his recording studio, built above his garage. He lights up again and settles into a sofa.

"I can't talk about what really happened to me up there, because it's personal. I don't want to see it all in print," he says. "The truth is I went up there to address the relentless depression that I'd had all my life. I'd say that everything I've done—wine, women, song, religion, meditation— was involved in a struggle to somehow penetrate this depression, which was the background of all my activities. But by imperceptible degrees, something happened at Mount Baldy, and my depression lifted. It hasn't come back for two and a half years.

"Roshi said something nice to me one time," he continues. "He said that the older you get, the lonelier you become, and the deeper the love you need. Which means that this hero that you're trying to maintain as the central figure in the drama of your life—this hero is not enjoying the life of a hero. You're exerting a tremendous maintenance to keep this heroic stance available to you, and the hero is suffering defeat after defeat. And they're not heroic defeats: they're ignoble defeats. Finally, one day you say, 'Let him die—I can't invest any more in this heroic position.' From there, you just live your life as if it's real—as if you have to make decisions even though you have absolutely no guarantee of any of the consequences of your decisions."

It's now late in the afternoon. Cohen trades one cigarette for another and pauses to admire the shadows cast by the lowering sun. "I'd like to continue working," he says. "I hope I don't fall over tomorrow. I have a whole new set of songs I'm working on, and I've returned to writing on guitar. Also, I'd like to publish my writings from Mount Baldy. It isn't that in my life I had some inner vision that I've been trying to present—I just had the appetite to work. I felt that this was my work and that it was the only work I could do."

Cohen puts on his suit jacket and walks me outside. "I'm in my mid-sixties now," he says. He looks up at the sun, which beats down hard. "I don't pretend to have salvation or the answers or anything like that. I'm not saved." He smiles. "But on the other hand, I'm not spent."

COHEN CLIP

On Lyrics

"It's just how they resonate. You know they resonate with a truth that is hard to locate but which is operating with some force in your life. I often feel that about a Dylan song or a song even with Edith Piaf . . . the words are going too fast for me to really understand them in French but you feel that they are talking about something that is true, that you can't locate by yourself and someone has located it for you and you just feel like you've put in the last piece in the jigsaw puzzle for that moment. That that moment has been clarified. The moment that you're in at the moment that you're listening to it. Yeah, the pieces fit . . . Isn't that wonderful when all the pieces fit?"

—response to Lian Lunson, director of *I'm Your Man* (2005), who had said "The Traitor" was one of her favorite songs in the film but "I can't get my hands around what it's about"

COHEN CLIP

On Embezzlement of His Money by a Former Manager

"What can I do? I had to go to work. I have no money left. I'm not saying it's bad; I have enough of an understanding of the way the world works to understand that these things happen. . . . I said, 'I can walk away with nothing.' I said, 'Let me start again. Let me start fresh at seventy. I can cobble together a little nest egg again.'"

—from "A 'Devastated' Leonard Cohen," by Kathleen Macklem, Macleans.ca, August 17, 2005

COHEN CLIP

On His Lover, Marianne Ihlen

"There wasn't a man that wasn't interested in Marianne. There was no one who wasn't interested in approaching that beauty and that generosity. . . . She was a traditional Nordic beauty; that was indisputable. But she was also very kind, and she was one of the most modest people about her beauty. You know, looking at her from a distance of forty, forty-five years almost, I see how very rare those qualities are. And she just knew things about the moment, about graciousness, about service, about hospitality, about generosity. And she had that other side too, where she drank wine and danced and became wild and beautiful and threatening and dangerous, you know, if you were a man with her. . . . We had to catch the boat back to Hydra. And we got up and got a taxi. And I've never forgotten this. Nothing happened, just sitting in the back of the taxi with Marianne, lit a cigarette, and thinking: 'I'm an adult. I'm with this beautiful woman, we have a little money in our pocket.' That feeling . . . I think I've tried to re-create it hundreds of times unsuccessfully. Just that feeling of being grown up, with somebody beautiful that you're happy to be beside, and all the world is in front of you. Your body is suntanned, and you're going to get on a boat."

—from *If It Be Your Will*, NRK (Norway) radio documentary
by Kari Hesthamar, 2006

COHEN CLIP

On Why He Left Mount Baldy

"I don't know if I could tell you the whole story because it's very private. I'd gone to see [Zen master] Roshi and had become a monk. . . . But the life is very rigorous. It's designed to overthrow a twenty-one-year-old. I was already in my late sixties. So there was that part of it but I had the feeling that it wasn't doing any good and it wasn't really addressing this real problem of distress, which seemed to be the background of all my feelings and activities and thoughts. So I began to feel that this is a lot of work for very little return. . . . There were other feelings that are ambiguous or too difficult to describe. They probably should be described in song or poetry rather than conversation."

—from interview with Terry Gross, *Fresh Air*,
National Public Radio (US), 2006

RADIO INTERVIEW

SHELAGH ROGERS | February 7, 2006, *Sounds Like Canada*, CBC (Canada)

Cohen must have felt talked out after all his 2001 interviews, because another long period of relative silence followed. He did release an album, *Dear Heather*, on October 26, 2004, but he talked little to the press until late 2005, when he alleged (*see page xvi*) that his former manager Kelley Lynch had misappropriated more than $5 million of his money, leaving him with a nest egg of just $150,000.

The following year brought better news. On February 3, 2006, the Canadian Songwriters Hall of Fame inducted Cohen and five of his songs—"Ain't No Cure for Love," "Bird on the Wire," "Everybody Knows," "Hallelujah," and "Suzanne." That same month, Cohen won a $9.5 million civil suit against Lynch. And in May, he published *Book of Longing*, a new collection of poetry. That month also witnessed the release of *Blue Alert*, an album by his then-girlfriend, Anjani Thomas, that he had produced. When Cohen and Thomas showed up at a Toronto bookstore on May 13 to promote both releases, the event marked Cohen's first public appearance in thirteen years.

A few days after the Hall of Fame induction, Cohen talked about that honor—and the forthcoming poetry book and Anjani CD—with the CBC's Shelagh Rogers. —Ed.

Shelagh Rogers: Let me ask you about "Everybody Knows," because this is another inductee [into the Songwriters Hall of Fame]. "Everybody knows that the dice are loaded / Everybody rolls with their fingers crossed." What kind of song is this?

Leonard Cohen: I guess I was trying to write a tough song, a song that indicated to myself and the world that I really knew the score about something or other. We all have these archetypes floating around in our minds and we become them from moment to moment. That guy [in the song] was a kind of know-it-all who'd been there and done that and seen it all. I think that was how it began but then under the tyranny of rhyme, other lines emerged that I could never possibly come up with. There were good lines there: "a long-stemmed rose" and "without your clothes." Things like that are wonderful gifts and I don't know how they arrive.

It's not that I don't sweat over it because I do. I sweat over every word. And it takes me a long time to bring these songs to completion. But when these little gifts appear, you're still wonderfully surprised and grateful. That song has a particular number of them and then it began to allow me to explore my own feelings about the way things were rather than become active in some cause, which is not really my nature. I could activate impulses that somehow coincide with a sense or a need or an appetite for reform. I think Yeats's father said that poetry is the social act of a solitary man.

SR: Another song being inducted is "Ain't No Cure for Love."

LC: "Ain't No Cure for Love" . . . that song I hardly remember. Can you sing it? I forget how it goes.

SR: [*Sings.*] "There ain't no cure, ain't no cure . . ."

LC: Well, that's for sure.

SR: [*Laughs.*] OK. I can't believe I sang for Leonard Cohen. Hello, John Hammond.

LC: It hints at something. Sometimes you don't really know what a song is about. "Ain't No Cure for Love," I just know it's true. And it suggests that love is an ailment. It's not an original idea that love is a fever or a disease but in another sense it's the same landscape as "There is a crack in everything." That our impulses and our motivations . . . they're hopeless.

First of all, we don't determine them. We receive them. We act on them. And we fall in love with things and with ideas and with people and we can't help ourselves. We're just programmed that way, constructed that way. In the same way that we're bloodthirsty, homicidal predators, in the same way we're tender creatures filled with the highest ideals and the profoundest aspirations and the widest appetite for love. And regardless of all the evidence—and there are mountains of it—to the contrary, we simply cannot help falling in love. Not just with each other, but that's certainly part of it. But with principles and ideals and a dream of virtue.

SR: Do you know more about love now than you did when you wrote—

LC: I was never good at it. This I can say with real certainty.

SR: Has it been a good dance?

LC: It's been a good dance. I just wrote a song with Anjani Thomas called "Thanks for the Dance" and it goes, "Thanks for the dance, it was hell, it was swell, it was fun / Thanks for all the dances, one-two-three, one-two-three-one."

SR: [*Laughs.*] Beautiful. Will that show up on the new CD with Anjani?

LC: Yes, that's the final song of that album called *Blue Alert*.

SR: You go back a ways with her.

LC: Anjani played keyboard and sang backup for me on a 1984 tour. So I've known Anjani for a long, long time. I've known her professionally and now we're neighbors of the deepest kind.

SR: You have a new album coming out and a new book of poetry?

LC: Yes I do. I have a book of poetry called *Book of Longing*. And it's poems and drawings and it has a wonderful cover.

SR: What's on it?

LC: It's a bird. What I like about it is that it was a drawing I discarded and had no use for. But I endlessly recycle my scribbles and sketches and it's really wonderful when something reappears. You should never throw anything away, including people and ideas. It's really true that you should never give up on anyone. Everything can be used.

SR: So there's a book, there's a CD, there's this lovely induction into the Canadian—

LC: It's so very kind to have this happen to a number of songs, because to have songs go into the hearts of your countrymen and women is really a wonderful thing. I heard an interview with [filmmaker] Oliver Stone once and he said [he] had a hit with I think it was *Platoon*. He said every artist should experience this. He said if he could decree something he would have every artist experience a hit because he said there's nothing like it. He said it's unstoppable and you just have the sense that the whole world is expressing this unspeakable hospitality to your soul.

I've never had a huge hit. But my songs, a few of them, have made their way, and I've had that feeling, like you go into a café someplace and a song of yours is playing or you pass by a park and some kid is playing one of your songs. It's really great and this is the kind of symbolic culmination. There is no hall of fame. There's just the heart.

SR: I have to ask you about "Hallelujah."

LC: That song also comes out of the same place as "crack in everything" and "Ain't No Cure for Love." It says, "And even though it all went wrong, I'll stand before the lord of song with nothing on my tongue but hallelujah." I guess that kind of sums it up for me.

SR: You've heard k. d. lang sing it.

LC: Oh I just love that version.

SR: It is magnificent.

LC: It's just glorious.

SR: She's glorious.

LC: She does that to most of the things she sings but that is a wonderful moment when she sings that song on her last album. It's just beautiful.

SR: So with all of these things going on, Leonard . . . you were concealed for a while. I guess you're back to being revealed for a little while. Are you hot again?

LC: I've never even used that word about myself most of my life but things are tough now and if you want to survive in the marketplace, first of all you have to acknowledge that there is a marketplace and that there are people who operate it and manipulate it. I can't get into it that way.

SR: And I can't ask you about it either, really.

LC: I don't know how it's done and I've had this curious relationship with a number of people, which is the way I look at it. And it seems to be a substantial number of people. So I can address them in exactly the terms that . . . I won't even say appropriately because I don't even know that it's appropriate but just in the terms that appear, that come to me. And I hope I can continue to do that.

SR: When you were up on Mount Baldy with your spiritual leader Roshi—

LC: My old friend Roshi, he's ninety-eight.

SR: He's still alive.

LC: Oh, he's still alive. He said to me, "Excuse me, I forgot to die." He's at the top of his form. That's an inspiration. I never thought of him as my spiritual leader but as someone who exhibits the unusual capacity to thoroughly understand your own predicament. We all try to do that to the people in our lives but it's an art or a skill like anything else and some people have that.

I was never interested in Buddhism. I had a perfectly good religion but I was interested in Roshi's remarkable and unusual interest in other people because I didn't feel I was at home anywhere. So I wanted to avail myself of that hospitality. If he'd been a professor of physics at Heidelberg, I would have learned German and studied in Heidelberg but he happened to be a Zen master so I put on the robes and I entered the monastery and I did what was necessary and appropriate to be able to enjoy his company.

SR: When you came down from the mountain, how did it change how you went through your day?

LC: There's a tremendous respect in that tradition which appealed to me very much. I cooked for Roshi for many years.

SR: What did you make him?

LC: Well, he had to have a lot of protein at his age. So I cooked a lot of fish. He liked tuna and salmon. I used to make a lot of teriyaki salmon.

SR: Did you make him a Red Needle [the drink Cohen created]?

LC: Roshi taught me a lot about drinking. Roshi is a great drinker and he taught me to discern, at least in the early stages of the evening, between let's say the tastes of Hennessy and Martell cognac. He'd test me. But I could never get him interested in red wine. He drank the poisonous raw sake, which he cherished. I could never really embrace sake drinking. If your heart has been nourished by the highs of Bordeaux, it's hard to really get into sake.

SR: A Red Needle, I understand, is your drink.

LC: I invented the Red Needle in Needles, California. I can't make it anymore. I can construct a facsimile of the Red Needle now. Basically it's tequila and cranberry juice and a little bit of soda water to give it a bit of a fizz and some fruit. But when I invented it and proselytized it, I was the evangelist of the Red Needle for a number of years. And it took off. But I've forgotten now. Like most things. Like an opinion—I can come up with an opinion if pressed and generally my opinions are cowardly now. If I'm in a certain kind of environment, I will certainly embrace the ideas that are current at that moment and completely reverse myself. But the Red Needle has fallen into disuse.

SR: I'm so sorry.

LC: There are other practitioners of the Red Needle who can accomplish it.

SR: You've said that even with Alzheimer's, Irving Layton's voice couldn't be silenced.

LC: No. There is something about Irving that is so amazing. When I went to see him in his last days, he hadn't recognized me for a while but before that, I visited him at the hospital. We found a place to smoke. I was helping him light his pipe. His hands were trembling and he says to me, "Have you noticed some decline in your sexual appetite?" This must be about eight years ago and I said, "I have, Irving, somewhat." He said, "I'm relieved to hear that, Leonard." I said, "So I take it, Irving, that you yourself have noticed some decline in your sexual appetite." He says, "Yes,

I have." I said, "When did you first begin to notice it?" He said, "Oh, about the age of sixteen or seventeen." [*Rogers laughs.*]

But it's a curious and mysterious disease, Alzheimer's. I don't have any particular insight into it but the last time I visited Irving, I brought him some cheese Danish. I was with [his friend] Musia Schwartz who was so devoted to him. I cut it up and put it down in front of him. He said, "Thank you very much." And some orange juice. He said, "Thank you very much." And I had the feeling that he was very peaceful. He really enjoyed that cheese Danish. He didn't look up. . . . I just felt that he'd gone beyond the social conventions. It wasn't as though it were some kind of enlightened or spiritual silence. It wasn't that at all. It was just the sense that nothing need be said or can be said. It's not that it was taken for granted. It's more that it just was the way it was and it was completely all right with him. And the only invitation that was in the air was for it to be all right with you too. And I just sat there completely relaxed while Irving felt no need or obligation to acknowledge my presence. That's the last time I saw him.

SR: So you've been able to deal with the unfairness of the way he went out.

LC: These things we simply cannot penetrate. I thought his exit was very graceful. It was silent and maybe unfair but the mind was at rest in some way. This incredible mind that had imagined Canada for all of us . . . it seemed to be at rest.

SR: Can I ask you one question about Canada?

LC: Sure.

SR: Years and years ago, you said Quebec was a country and Canada still had to work on it. That's not a direct quote but what do you think?

LC: Quebec—one language, one religion, one location, one history, one culture—had a legitimate *claim* to calling itself a country while Canada was a *new* kind of formation. These new great ideas that we have in North America, in the United States and Canada, of a different kind of society that is not specifically governed by these tribal obligations, is also wonderful. And if we can accommodate a country in our other formation, it would be a tremendous human achievement, if we could accommodate all kinds of expressions but especially the Quebecois expression. I know everybody's pissed off.

SR: "Not this again."

LC: "Not this again" or "let them go" or "let us go" or "it isn't working and it's time for the divorce." And there's much to recommend everybody going their separate ways. And we're in a period in history where everybody's invited to go their separate ways. I think we should try to do it together. It's much more interesting for us to accommodate one another and the challenges will invite many more interesting kinds of expression than if we do go our separate ways. That's just my two cents.

SR: It's almost an opinion.

LC: I don't care.

SR: I want to thank you very much for this time. And, again congratulations. Your award [is] gleaming in the background behind your head. Thank you, Mr. Cohen.

LC: Thank you.

COHEN CLIP
On His Early Influences

"I read a lot of Lorca at the time and a lot of Isaiah and apocalyptic religious literature appealed to me. The prayer book, the synagogue, the labor movement, collectors like Alan Lomax, singers like Pete Seeger, the *People's Songbook*, the Almanac Singers. On the European side, singers like Amelia Rodriguez and the flamenco singers, the fado singers, the French chanteurs. Those were the influences."

—interview with Michael Silverblatt, *Bookworm*, KCRW-FM (Santa Monica, California), June 24, 2006

LIFE OF A LADIES' MAN

SARAH HAMPSON | May 26, 2007, the *Globe and Mail* (Toronto)

"When I set off to interview Cohen in his home in Montreal, I couldn't have known how long I would have with him or where the conversation would go," Sarah Hampson told me. "He was emerging from his reclusive period. He was known for disliking media. So all of this interview came as a surprise. I was there for close to five hours, and toward the end, the discussion veered off into romantic advice—for me. He had asked me a little about my life. I had recently divorced after an eighteen-year marriage.

"'You just need to find someone to go to dinner with, to sleep with from time to time,' he began.

"'Maybe I should go younger,' I suggested playfully.

"'It's a good idea,' he said. 'At a certain point in someone's life, it's very refreshing. There are a lot of young men who like older women, and really want that experience and that kindness that only childbearing and the real abrasive education of life can give somebody.'

"He told me about meeting [French writer and film director] Marguerite Duras, who had a boyfriend forty years her junior at the time," Hampson recalled. "'That's one of the things that takes a little bit of courage, but it's worth cultivating,' Cohen said. 'You should just think, "This is really nice for me." So, think, "Yes, you want to sleep with me? Lovely. You're eighteen? OK, that's maybe too young. OK, maybe twenty-four? Lovely, how lovely."'

"It was a sweet, funny exchange," Hampson said, "and we laughed. Later, he took me on a small tour of his house. I loved the tiny bathroom with a tub in a crawl space under the stairs leading to the third floor, and I mentioned how inviting the tub looked. I am a big bath person, I told him. 'Come back anytime,' he said in his casual manner.

"When I returned to Toronto, I emailed him to thank him for giving me so much of his time. 'Don't forget the promise of the bath,' I wrote cheekily, thinking I would never get a reply.

"Ten minutes later, it arrived: 'I'll get the towels ready.'

"'And the candles, Leonard?' I typed.

"'Will have to check with the fire department,' he wrote back.
"I printed out the exchange and filed it away for safekeeping." —Ed.

The park is like a poem: self-contained and spare. Smokers sit on benches in the morning drizzle. Pigeons swoop over a small gazebo, under the limbs of stately trees. There is a solemn-looking house, three stories high with a grey stone facade. It's the only one that faces this park in the east end of Montreal, and it's his. There are two big front doors, side by side. No numbers. No bell. No indication which one is right. You just pick, and knock.

There is more than one way into the world of Leonard Cohen, and on this day in late April, they are all open.

Cohen, now seventy-two, novelist, poet, and singer/songwriter, is a cornerstone of Canadian culture, but he dances in our heads mostly unseen, like a beautiful idea. It is rare that he makes himself available for scrutiny.

Here he is, though, a gentleman of hip in black jeans and an unironed dress shirt beneath a pinstriped grey-flannel jacket. Atop his thick white hair, combed back off his deeply lined face, a grey cap sits at a jaunty angle, and in the breast pocket of his jacket, instead of a handkerchief, he keeps a pair of tinted granny glasses. Standing in the cramped foyer to which both front doors open, sporting a wry, knowing smile, he politely ushers you into the house (once partitioned into two dwellings) that he has owned for over thirty years.

Now is a new Cohen moment, and while he acknowledges that his increased creative activity is partly to compensate for the millions he lost in royalties at the hands of his former manager, he seems to be enjoying the attention. Next week, as part of Toronto's Luminato festival, his drawings get their first exhibition, at the Drabinsky Gallery. There's a new concert work by Philip Glass, inspired by Cohen's art and poetry from his 2006 *Book of Longing*, which was published after a thirteen-year silence. In 2004, he released his seventeenth album [counting compilations and concert recordings], *Dear Heather*.

Earlier this year, expanded editions of his first three albums hit the market, as did the critically acclaimed CD, *Blue Alert*, that he worked on with his lover, Hawaii-born songstress Anjani Thomas.

There is nothing off limits in a discussion with Cohen. Sit with him, and the candid revelations come in conversation, in an exchange that is both as playful and solemn, as rich and layered as his work. Over a bottle of Château Maucaillou, Greek bread, a selection of Quebec cheeses, and a fresh cherry pie, bought for the occasion from the local St-Laurent Boulevard merchants, you learn that he prefers to sleep alone; that he is no longer looking for another woman; the real reason he secluded himself in a Buddhist monastery for almost five years; and that a small, faded portrait of Saint Catherine Tekakwitha, the seventeenth-century native woman and heroine of his novel *Beautiful Losers*, hangs on the wall in his kitchen, above a table holding a fifties radio and a telephone with an oversize dial pad.

He will entrance you in the stillness of a moment that stretches to five hours, and in the end, because you happened to ask, playfully, he will say sure, come back any time for a soak in the claw-footed tub, one of several in his house, that sits in a closet of a bathroom under the slope of the stairs.

"I think of it all as notes," Cohen says in his rich, deep voice. Seated at a long pine table in the dining room, which overlooks the park, he is talking about his drawings in a casual, almost shy way.

A collection of self-portraits, landscapes, objects, and portraits of women, sketched throughout his life—in Greece, when he lived on the island of Hydra; on Mount Baldy, at the monastery outside of Los Angeles where he was under the tutelage of Zen master Kyozan Joshu Roshi; in Montreal; in L.A., where he has a second house; and during travels in India—they will be sold in signed, limited-edition prints.

"There were years when I would do a self-portrait every morning. I have hundreds of them. It was just a way to start the day with a kind of device to wake up."

"Like a cigarette?"

"Instead of a cigarette."

He quit four years ago, on a doctor's advice.

"I do miss it," Cohen says. "Much longing," he adds, almost in a moan. (He once wrote a poem about the "the promise, the beauty, and the salvation of cigarettes.") "I said I'd start smoking again at eighty-five." He allows a pause. "If I make it."

He continues to flip through a copy of *Book of Longing*, which contains many of the drawings, several that have been manipulated and colored with Photoshop on his laptop. "Here's a good one," he points out, reading the words beside a self-portrait of glum bewilderment, dated Nov. 18, 2003. "Back in Montreal. As for the past, children, Roshi, songs, Greece, Los Angeles. What was that all about?"

His self-portraits never depict him as happy.

"Well, who is? Is this unique to me?" he asks with a soft chuckle. His friend and fellow poet, the late Irving Layton, once described Cohen as "a narcissist who hates himself."

"I was able to speak to myself in a very frank sort of way," Cohen continues. "I would do it while I brewed my coffee. I would set up this little wood Wacom tablet, and a mirror, a little mirror, and I'd just do a very quick sketch and then, what that sketch suggested, I would write something."

The drawings are "transcendent decoration," he says, touching one on the pages with the tip of a forefinger. "If it has any value at all, it's because it's harmless and doesn't invite any deep intellection." He points to various sketches, one of a Hires root-beer can, another of a candlestick, his granny glasses, a Rolex watch he saw in a magazine. "I have always loved things, just things in the world. I always just love trying to find the shape of things."

And the nude women? "I would just see a beautiful woman photographed in a pornographic magazine. I would see a figure in *Playboy* or something like that, and I'd just take the form." He draws a breath like an inhalation of cigarette smoke, holding it for a moment, exhaling in a sigh. "I rescue her. I put her back in the twelfth century, where she belongs," he says, half-joking. "You know, I couldn't get anyone to undress."

Cohen closes the book, places it on the table, and lifts his eyes in an expression of calm anticipation. Every question, he greets like an invitation to make himself understood. Leonard Cohen, the icon, is a concept he likes to toy with, as if it is both him and not.

"I got this rap as a kind of ladies' man," he says lazily and without irony, at one point. "And as I say in one of the poems, it has caused me to laugh, when I think of all the lonely nights" at the monastery. "As if I'm the only guy who ever felt this way about women," he continues, with a smirk. "As if I'm the only person who ever had some sort of deep connection with the opposite sex."

"Have you learned a lot from women?"

"Oh, yeah. You learn everything from women."

"Everything?"

He leans in. "It is where you move into uncharted territory." He shrugs slightly, his small, neat hands held in front of him. "The rest is just reinforcing wisdom or folly that you have inherited. But nobody can prepare anybody for an encounter with the opposite sex. Much has been written about it. You can read self-help books, but the actual confrontation as a young person with desire, this appetite for completion, well, that is the education."

"And what a ruse that desire for completion is," you suggest, "because ultimately, you're still left with yourself."

"What's left of it," he puts in, laughing.

Cohen sits back in his chair, his ideas as well-worn and familiar as old sweaters. "Of course, women are the content of men, and men are the content of women, and most people are dealing with this—whatever version of that longing there is. You know, of completion. It can be spiritual, romantic, erotic. Everybody is involved in that activity."

Cohen exudes an air of permission. Nothing unsettles him. He will explain all: the eclectic collection of objects in his house—the black-and-white picture of the dog on the pine sideboard (it's of Tinky, the Scotch terrier he grew up with) that sits beside a modernist sculpture in silver by his childhood friend, Mort Rosengarten, that stands next to an antique pot, inscribed with Arabic symbols, which his father liked and that came from his mother's house when she died.

Ask him about the graphic signatures, or chops, as he refers to them, that he designed and stamps onto several of the drawings. Perhaps they are too private to explain. They look like a secret code. "Not at all. Not at all," he murmurs. "This one is the old Chinese writing of my monk's name, Jikan," he says, pointing to one. "It got into the press as the silent one, but it just means ordinary silence." The poet as an absence of communication. Roshi, who assigns the names, likes irony, presumably.

"Yes, could be," Cohen says. A beat of silence. "Since Roshi doesn't speak English, it's almost impossible to discern what he means."

"These two interlocking hearts, I designed for the cover of *Book of Mercy*," his 1984 poetry collection, he says, moving along as he describes another chop. "I established this Order of the Unified Heart, that is a kind of dream of an order. There is no organization. There's no hierarchy. There's just a pin [for] people of a very broadly designated similar intent."

"And yours is?"

He thinks for a minute. "To just make things better on a very personal level," he says. "You're just not scattered all over the place. There is a tiny moment when you might gather around some decent intention."

"And what has been your most decent intention?"

He places his hands on the edge of the table. "I can't think of any right now. There must be one or two."

"Beauty, maybe."

"Beauty, certainly," he responds.

It is often said that Cohen is hard to define. There's Cohen, the son of a prominent Montreal clothier and the grandson of a Jewish scholar. Cohen, the law-school dropout. Cohen, the novelist, the poet, the songwriter. Cohen, the sexual bad boy who becomes a monk.

But he disagrees. "I always felt it was of one piece. I never felt I was going off on a tangent." He admits, though, that he "drifted into things. I suppose there has been an undercurrent of deliberation, but I don't really navigate it." According to legend, it wasn't until he encountered folk singer Judy Collins, in 1966, that he decided to publicly perform songs he had played for friends. The following year, she introduced some Cohen songs on her album, including his big hit "Suzanne." It was in 1968 that he released his first album [*Actually, 1967. —Ed.*]

Cohen didn't seek out a musical career as much as it seems to have found him. Which is what is happening now with his drawings. He appears to have fallen into a whole new career.

He takes in this observation, looks out the window for a moment and then brings his attention back into the room.

"That's why I say free will is overrated," he drawls in his smoky voice.

"It was terrific. The best kind," he says. "We had these appetites that we understood, and it was wonderful that they were taken care of. It was a moment where everybody was giving to the other person what they wanted. The women knew that's what the men wanted."

Don't ask how the subject of casual sex in the sixties came up. It was part of the unfolding of the Saturday afternoon, the laziness of it, like an endless meal of many courses, which you keep expecting to end but never does. You cover one subject, and thank him for his time, thinking he may be tired of talking now, but he doesn't take the opportunity to say good-bye. "Here, relax, eat," he will say. "Have more wine. Would you like a piece of cherry pie?" And then the conversation continues.

"If you could have it so much," I ask, "didn't that devalue it?"

Cohen offers a frank expression. He could be talking about apples. "Well, nobody gets enough of anything," he explains matter-of-factly. "You either get too much or not enough. Nobody gets the right amount, in terms of what they think their appetite deserves."

"But it lasted just a few moments," he says about that time. "And then it was back to the old horror story, whatever it is that still exists. You know, I'll give you this if you give me that. You know, sealing the deal: what do I get, what do you get. It's a contract."

Cohen's sexiness, powerful still, is in his accessibility. His open-door atmosphere of hospitality—an invitation to authenticity, to say and ask what you want—makes him an age-appropriate ladies' man. He is interested in people, in what they think, and he will ask about their lives. But his manner is not invasive or louche. He borders on paternal, or would, that is, if your dad liked to write about cunnilingus and fellatio as if they are fancy Italian appetizers.

"Believe me, what you want is someone to have dinner with," he advises on having a relationship later in life. "Sleep with from time to time, telephone every day or write. It's what you set up that is defeating. Make it very modest. And give yourself permission to make a few mistakes. You know, blow it a bit. Have a few drinks and fall into bed with somebody. It doesn't have to be the final thing."

Thomas appears several times. "See you later, sweetheart," Cohen calls softly to her when she leaves with a friend to go shopping. Rosengarten, whom he has known since their childhood growing up together on Belmont Street in affluent Westmount, and who now lives nearby, drops in for a chat and some food.

A little later, a light knock. "Ah, a tap tap tapping at my chamber door," Cohen says as he gets up. A graduate student, a young man in his twenties, who has written a dissertation on Cohen in his native Italian, has sought him out. Speaking to Cohen in French, he explains his work; gives him a copy; asks if he can speak to him some time at length for future papers he wants to write. Cohen assures him he can. Asked to sign an autograph, he bends down nimbly on one knee in the foyer to do so.

It is not the Cohen of his lyrics or of his sullen self-portraits who moves about this house of austere aesthetic. He is a gentleman to his partner, the friend in the neighborhood, a gracious host. It is in his humanity, his feet of clay, that he is most comfortable.

He talks easily about his earlier years, unburdened by nostalgia. "My constitution is what saved me," he says of the time he used a lot of drugs, especially during the writing of *Beautiful Losers* in 1966. "I'm not a really good drinker or a really good junkie. My stomach just doesn't permit it. I was very lucky in that respect, because a lot of people I know, especially in those turbulent times, just didn't survive it. "

Similarly, he displays no longing or fondness for his time on Mount Baldy. He left the monastery in the late nineties. Not because he couldn't find what he was looking for. Rather, he says, "I had completed that phase of my training."

He had gone there to cure himself of his excesses. He worked in the kitchen and as a secretary to Roshi. But it was not all about serenity. "They're not saints, and you aren't, either," he says of his fellow monks. "A monastery is rehab for people who have been traumatized, hurt, destroyed, maimed by daily life that they simply couldn't master. I had been studying with Roshi for thirty or forty years, but when I actually decided to live with him and really commit myself to the daily life—I did always do that for several months of every year—but when I decided to do it full-time, I had just come off a tour in 1993, and yes, I felt dislocated. I had been drinking tremendous amounts on the road and my health was shot."

Cohen, who has two grown children from his long-term relationship with Suzanne Elrod—not the Suzanne of his famous song—is a grandfather now. Cassius Lyon Cohen was born a few months ago. Still, there's something more at play beneath his palpable equanimity. And it might be as simple as this: the man is happy.

"I always had a background of distress, ever since I was young," he admits. "What part that played in becoming a writer or a singer or whatever it was that one became, I don't know. I didn't have a sense of an operational ease," he continues. About life? "Just about one's work or one's capacity to earn a living; a capacity to find a mate or find a moment of relief in someone's arms," he says, trailing off.

He looks up. "I don't know what happened," he says sweetly. "Something very agreeable happened to me. I don't know what the reason is. That background of distress dissolved." He leaves a small silence, then offers a mischievous smile. "I'm worried now that my songs are too cheerful because I'm feeling well. I think I may be irrelevant pretty soon."

Has Thomas, who is forty-eight, played a part in that happiness? "That might very well be," he allows. He met her in 1984, when she was singing backup for him. They didn't become lovers until 1999. "When the background of distress dissolves, you're able to see people more clearly."

"People who love you, you mean?"

"Yeah, or don't," he says. "You're able to appreciate the authentic situation. You can just see things more clearly. It's a veil that drops. You're not looking at everything from the point of view of your own suffering."

Relationships are often difficult, he says. "I find that people want to name it. The woman is saying, 'What is our relationship? Are we engaged? Are we boyfriend and girlfriend? Are we lovers?' And my disposition is, 'Do we really have to have this discussion, because it's not as good as our relationship? We were having a good time until you brought this up.'

"But as you get older, you want to accommodate, and say, 'Yeah, we're living together. This is for real. I'm not looking for anyone else. You're the woman in my life.' Whatever terms that takes: a ring, an arrangement, a commitment, or from one's behavior, by the way you act. You make it clear by minute adjustments. A woman goes by. You can look, but you can adjust so that it's not an insult, an affront, or a danger. So you're continually making those adjustments, so that you don't make anyone suffer. You're with somebody, and you want to make it work. I'm not interested in taking off my clothes with a woman right now."

He and Thomas live together, but they have separate bedrooms on different floors of the house. "I like to wake up alone," Cohen explains. "And she likes to be alone. We are both impossibly solitudinous people."

If advancing age and his love of Thomas have promoted happiness, so too has Buddhism. What Cohen has developed is a practice of detachment. "You have to take responsibility because the world holds you accountable for what you do," he explains at one point. "But if you understand that there are other forces determining what you do, then there's no pride when the world affirms you, no shame when the world scorns you. Also, when someone does something to you that you really don't like or that hurts you, well, a feeling of injury may arise, but what doesn't is hatred or enmity, because those people aren't doing it, either. They're just doing what had to be done."

Just like this interview. It has been arranged, and so he will do it, graciously, without hesitation, annoyance, or impatience. Finally, when you insist you must leave, he worries if you are dressed warmly enough for the cold weather. He gives you one of his scarves, and goes upstairs to retrieve an old Gap sweater he wants you to wear. He calls you darling. He finds a pin for the Order of the Unified Heart and gives you one, and a ring, too, with the same design.

Earlier, he had explained that even if despair has lessened, challenges remain. "This isn't very different from the monastery," he says, referring to his current situation. "It's the same kind of life, which is sometimes difficult, like everybody else's. It's a struggle for significance and self-respect, and you know, for righteous employment, to be doing the right thing."

Part of that, clearly, is inviting people, strangers even, into his house of unadorned walls, simple white curtains, and old wood floors, nourishing them with food and ideas and hours of delightful conversation, and then sending them back out into the world, the one with the smokers and the drizzle and the pain.

HE'S YOUR MAN

GILLIAN G. GAAR | June 2007, *Harp* (US)

"It's easy for me to remember every press junket I've ever been on, because there have been only three of them," Gillian Gaar told me. "And they all came out of the blue. For this one, there I was, in early 2007, trying to figure out how to drum up a little more writing work, when I was contacted by Fred Mills, then an editor at the now-defunct *Harp* magazine, asking if I'd be interested in flying to L.A. to interview a bona-fide legend: Leonard Cohen. Well, yes.

"I was met by a car when I arrived, with a driver who regaled me with stories of celebrities he'd driven around. It was a rare taste of glamour—all I was missing was a bottle of chilled champagne in the back seat.

"The interview was to spotlight not only the reissue of Cohen's first three albums, but also the release of *Blue Alert*, the third album by his then girlfriend, Anjani Thomas, a collection of atmospheric moody jazz that I had loved. I'd been told it was important to include Anjani in the article, so I began the interview by speaking with her, naturally seguing into talking with Leonard as he not only cowrote the songs on *Blue Alert*, he produced the album. And if he didn't seem predisposed to talking about his own past at length, he acknowledged that it was a necessary element in promoting the upcoming reissues. He was thoughtful, soft-spoken, and incredibly gracious—one of the most charming people I've ever met. My only regret was that we didn't have more time to spend together—perhaps sharing those martinis he talks about.

"Before we said good-bye," Gaar added, "he signed the book of his poetry that I'd brought along, *Let Us Compare Mythologies*, writing: 'Gillian, thanks for the talk.'"

Here's the result of that talk, which sheds light on the nature of Cohen's collaboration with Anjani and explains why his own debut could have turned out quite differently. —Ed.

When people speak about Leonard Cohen, their comments often take on a decided tone of reverence. "This is our Shelley, this is our Keats,"

Bono is seen saying in Lian Lunson's *I'm Your Man*, the acclaimed Cohen documentary/tribute concert film. It's a sentiment you'll find repeated throughout, as when Bono's U2 bandmate the Edge notes, "He's got this almost biblical significance." Over the course of a career that's produced notable recordings like "Suzanne," "Bird on a Wire," "The Future," and "Hallelujah," admiration for Cohen's work only seems to increase, generation after generation.

But the man who inspires such devotion is himself soft-spoken and low-key in person, not to mention unfailingly courteous and polite; prior to an interview at his daughter's antique shop, Boo Radley, on Melrose Avenue in L.A., he pauses to pick up my fallen coat, murmuring, "Oh, don't put this on the floor. It's a beautiful red." And while Cohen is not given to extemporizing at great length, or overindulging in self-analysis, once he's settled in a chair near an old manual typewriter bearing a notice reading "Not for sale," he is relaxed, gracious, and quite willing to talk.

As it happens, there's a lot to talk about. In addition to *I'm Your Man*, now out on DVD, this year also sees the publication of the fiftieth-anniversary edition of Cohen's first book of poetry, *Let Us Compare Mythologies*, and Columbia/Legacy's reissue of his first three albums, *Songs of Leonard Cohen*, *Songs from a Room*, and *Songs of Love and Hate*. In June comes the world premiere of *Book of Longing*, a concert piece with music by Philip Glass, based upon Cohen's poetry book of the same name, published last year.

But right now, Cohen's most interested in talking about another project, the closest thing to a new album from him since 2004's *Dear Heather*.

Blue Alert is the major-label debut by his girlfriend, Anjani Thomas (who's solely credited by her first name on her records) and indeed, at leonardcohen.com it's her music you hear playing on the site, not his. The lyrics are by Cohen, with Thomas composing the music and accompanying herself on piano. It's the kind of highly atmospheric, jazz-influenced album you can imagine being played in a cocktail lounge, the kind of record you don't want to play until after sundown.

"Yeah, it's good for solitude, it's good for quiet moments," Cohen says of the record, as his eyes catch sight of some antique cocktail glasses on a nearby table. "It's good with a drink. I wouldn't mind filling one of these with a martini, for instance. You didn't bring a martini, did you?" (Alas, I didn't.)

Thomas, who hails from Hawaii, first worked with Cohen in 1984, as a backing vocalist on *Various Positions*, and the subsequent tour. Initially, she was not very familiar with Cohen's work. "I'd heard other artists covering his material," she says. "I really liked Roberta Flack's cover of 'Suzanne.' But he was one of the few artists that never came to Hawaii. I had no idea of his prominence until we got to Europe [on tour] and I saw the reception he received, which was overwhelmingly gracious and warm and reverential. That made me sit up and go, 'Who is this guy?'"

But after two more albums (1988's *I'm Your Man* and 1992's *The Future*), Cohen took a break, retiring to the Mount Baldy Zen Center, where he eventually was ordained as a Buddhist monk. Thomas took her own sabbatical from the music business at the same time. After years based in New York City, working both as a solo artist and with others (including Carl Anderson and Osamu Kitajima), she found that jobs had become scarce and she relocated to Austin. "I always liked Texas," she explains. "And I said, 'If I could have some kind of normal nine-to-five life I might as well go to someplace that I like, and I really liked it there.'"

After five years, inspiration returned, and Thomas began working on her first solo album (perhaps not coincidentally, her relationship with Cohen began around the same time). "I'd never had a record deal, and I thought, 'Boy, if I don't do this now, I think I'm going to regret it my whole life," she says. "So I sold my little house and used the money to make the record." *Anjani* came out in 2000, followed by *The Sacred Names* in 2001, released on her own record label, Little Fountain Music. She describes the albums as "folk-jazz oriented but nothing approaching the gravitas of *Blue Alert*. And both of them sold about ten copies!"

One can see the roots of *Blue Alert* on Cohen's *Dear Heather*, on which Thomas plays a prominent role; his drawing of her adorns the cover, and she performs on most of the tracks, as well as cowriting two songs. "Nightingale," which appears on both albums, offers a ready means of comparing their performing styles; Cohen's version, after its a cappella beginning, suddenly becomes a countryish romp, while Thomas's take exhibits a cool restraint, coupled with a smooth, beguiling vocal (interestingly, Thomas arranged both versions).

It was around this time that Thomas found a completed song lyric on Cohen's desk, and was particularly taken by the opening couplet: "There's perfume burning in the air / Bits of beauty everywhere." "It was the most mysterious and visually enticing lyric," she says, and she immediately asked Cohen if she could write music for it. "I had seen a lot of Leonard's lyrics and I never had the temerity to ask for a shot at one before," she says. "I really to this day don't know what overcame me, but something said, 'This is so beautiful, I'd love to have a crack at it.'"

Cohen admits he "wasn't thrilled with the idea" of someone taking lyrics he'd planned to use for himself. "Even Anjani," he says. "I wasn't overjoyed, because it's hard to come up with anything, as you know. And people are always asking me for lyrics, it goes on a lot." And even after finishing a demo, Thomas remained uncertain about Cohen's reaction. "I was nervous," she says. "Now you opened your big trapper! Because he'd never done a jazz tune *per se*, and I thought, 'Oh man, I'm really not sure about this.' But I played it and he instantly brightened up and said, 'It's a masterpiece, it's perfect.' And I thought, 'Great, I've really got a song that you can sing.' I thought I would just do some demos and then he would put his vocal on it. And he said, 'Oh, it's great, but I could never sing that,' and I thought, 'Well, I guess that was a futile exercise.' But then he said, 'No, we'll put it aside. And we'll see.'"

"I was really impressed by the demo," explains Cohen. "It was a very different sound. I knew Anjani was a good singer, but I didn't know she was that good. And when I heard she was that good, I surrendered to the project. Because something really happened to Anjani's voice. It's strange. It doesn't often happen that somebody moves from competence into a unique excellence."

With Cohen's encouragement, Thomas trawled through his writings, mostly drawing on unfinished pieces the two would then work on together. "We just sort of edited each other," she says. "More often than not, he'd have to change the lyric. And once he changed the lyric, I'd know where the music had to go. In 'The Golden Gate,' for example, originally there was a line about Zelda and Scott Fitzgerald. And I said, 'Can we get some other names? 'Cause the Fitzgeralds are just throwing me for a loop.' He didn't want to rewrite, but eventually he did. And once he did, I went, 'OK, here it is.'"

The album was coproduced by Ed Sanders (who'd worked on Thomas's previous records) [*Not the Ed Sanders who cofounded the Fugs. —Ed.*], Thomas and Cohen, marking the first time Cohen's produced an artist other than himself. "It's more that I had the power of veto," Cohen stresses. "Anjani was not convinced that a record this unadorned could please, so occasionally we tried using other instruments. And that's when my real producer's activity came in; I would say 'Let's try it.' But when we'd hear it, it would just get in the way of what Anjani was doing. She's a very fine keyboard player and arranger, so anything we put on top of it obscured the whole moment. It's quiet! And now it's hard to find things that are quiet and beautiful. It's fun to get overwhelmed by a groove and get into something, but this has some very special qualities.

"I don't know if kids will like it, but it's not designed for the market. It's just what it is."

Philip Glass saw an early draft of Cohen's *Book of Longing* book in the nineties, and as Cohen notes, the composer "was very, very interested in it." At the time, however, the two men were headed along different paths. "I went into the monastery, and he had other projects. And then he wrote me and said, 'I remember those poems. Are you doing anything with them?' And I told him that the book was coming out and I sent him a manuscript. And he said, "I'd like to make a song cycle out of it," and I said, "Of course." It was very casual. I just said yes."

The show, which premieres at Toronto's Luminato Festival June 1–3 before going on a brief tour, will feature an ensemble of singers and musicians, Cohen's own prerecorded voice, and a set based on drawings in the book. "Philip played me the demos a couple of months ago," Cohen says. "Very, very beautiful. But it's not my position to critique Philip Glass. He's one of our greatest composers. I think it will be entertaining. But it really is Philip's project. I'm just delighted that the poems touched him in such a way that he felt like producing them in a different medium."

And while he prefers to look ahead to his next venture ("I'm not a very nostalgic person," he says in the *I'm Your Man* film), both documentary and reissues did have Cohen reexamining his life and career, though he says with a chuckle, "I really didn't look very hard." Though his first three albums are now considered landmark works, Cohen regards the reissues with a measure of detachment. "It's a convention of the record companies," he says with a shrug. "They put out the early albums again, if they seem to have lasted. And they've done a good job with these. But I haven't really been that involved with it."

Adding bonus tracks to reissues is another record company "convention," and one Cohen readily admits he "wasn't delighted" with: "I thought the albums could stand as they are." But in the case of the first two albums, the bonus tracks offer some new insights as to how they might have turned out in that they were recorded by different producers than those who ended up working on the final albums. *Songs of Leonard Cohen* was originally going to be produced by John Hammond, who had a heart attack soon after recording began. And Cohen recorded early versions of "Bird on a Wire" and "You Know Who I Am" (rerecorded for *Songs from a Room*) with David Crosby. "I just bumped into him," Cohen explains. "I was introduced to him, I think, by Joni Mitchell. And I said, 'I've got a song, do you want to help me put it down?' and he said sure.

"And then I don't what happened, but I ended up in Nashville," Cohen continues. "I'd bumped into [Columbia producer] Bob Johnston; I wanted to get out of town, and he said Boudleaux Bryant, who wrote 'Bye Bye Love,' had a little cabin that he was renting for forty dollars a month, it's pretty, did I want to go? I said yeah, so I moved down there for a couple years. If I'd stayed in Los Angeles perhaps I would've worked with David Crosby. But I really wanted to get out of town. Those are the paths you take. I didn't know that part of the world, Tennessee. I bumped into people I would never have met under any other circumstances, the cowboys and people living out in the country."

Those who have worshipped the albums for forty years might be surprised to learn that Cohen remains critical of his own performance. "On the first record I thought the voice was all right," he says, "but something was happening on the second album with my voice; I didn't like the sound of it. On the third one the voice was a little bit better. Now, I feel more charitable to the little guy who was trying to put it together. And the songs are good. People liked them; you can't quarrel with that. I'm very happy that the records have lasted long enough so that it's felt that they're worthwhile looking at, worthwhile listening to."

And Cohen also notes that the bonus tracks gave him a new perspective on his work. "The [bonus] song on the first record called 'Store Room,' I didn't really understand it," he says. "Well, I did understand it, but I guess there was something I felt was obscure about it, that I don't feel now. I feel that the guy was right on, and I understand why that song deserves a hearing. The recurring line is 'Just a man taking what he needs from the storeroom.' In a way, that's what's happening. People are acting with a kind of sense of end days, of final days, of desperation. And they're taking what they need from the storeroom. The people that have the storeroom are trying to lock it up, and the people who don't have it are trying to break into it."

The Canadian-born Cohen won't be drawn into a direct discussion of America's current political climate. ("I'm a guest here, so it's not appropriate for me to speak about it, a country that has been so gracious to me.") But in his understated fashion, a clue to his views emerges when he's asked how he regarded America while growing up. "Well, Canadians see themselves as more sane, more gentle, more courteous," he says. "I usually spend a lot of time in Montreal [where Cohen was born], but matters kept me here for the past year or two. I usually spend long periods of time there, and often in the winter, 'cause it's very, very quiet then—and if you don't have to wait at a bus stop and go to work in the morning it's really great! There's much to recommend the country. Montreal is probably the best city around. And we're not at war. It's a very different feeling. Though actually there are young men and women now on the battlefield in Afghanistan, but . . . it hasn't ripped society apart yet."

Perhaps appropriately for a man who's been lauded for his "biblical significance," Mel Gibson's Icon Productions coproduced *I'm Your Man*, meaning the film was potentially funded by profits from *The Passion of the Christ* (and Cohen's "By the Rivers Dark" did appear on *Songs Inspired by the Passion of the Christ*). "That would be OK with me," he says. "But

I think Lian really put it together on a shoestring. I believe Mel Gibson is a friend of hers, and his name on it I guess gave it a certain credibility." And he's amused to hear the film received a PG-13 rating for "some sex-related material." "Oh yeah, really? Where?" he asks. "Strange, when you consider. 'Sex-related' compared to what?"

We decide the "sex" material in question must be Cohen's drawings, some of which have naked women, or possibly the reference to oral sex in "Chelsea Hotel No. 2."

Those eager for Cohen to record his own work again should be pleased to learn that the film's concert sequences have inspired him to consider touring in support of his next album, tentatively set for release later this year. "Yes, yes," he confirms. "I haven't been out since '93. The years went by and I thought 'I'll never go out again.' But every so often you do have that itch. You've heard that saying in rock and roll: they don't pay you to sing, they pay you to travel. But you forget about that stuff. The actual concerts are always compelling. If you've got good musicians, and you're playing, and people know the songs, and they want to hear them live, it is a wonderful thing. And so I'm drawn to that."

But pushed to talk about the album now in progress, Cohen again demurs. "Generally speaking, I don't have anything to say about those things," he says. "I wish I had something interesting to say. But I'm just plugging along, trying to put something together." Ed Sanders is equally circumspect: asked how the new work compares with *Dear Heather*, he merely notes it's "a lot different.

"But the recording's fun!" he adds. "Leonard and I have a good time. We sit down and we discuss a lot of topical and nontopical things and then occasionally we're interrupted by a little recording. So that's the way we work."

And Cohen also makes it clear he's not going to be rushed, evincing a thoughtfulness that explains both the lengthy gaps between projects and the care that makes his resultant work so enduring. "I'm not so interested in my own ideas," he says. "I can trot out opinions like the next guy in a conversation sometimes, although I'm reluctant. When I hear myself talking, I'm not so interested in my opinions. So there's some other level of perception that is deeper than an opinion. That's what I find songwriting is about, is to get rid of the slogans, even the clever ones, even the sophisticated positions, and get to feelings and understandings that are just a little bit beneath the radar of opinions or intellection.

"So that's why it takes a long time," he continues. "Before I can discard a verse, I have to write it. I don't have the conceptual skill to see something and discard it. I have to plug away and write it, and then discard it. Even if it's good, I don't like it if it has a slogan. Anything that resembles an easy position, that's not interesting. So I'm not interested in my opinions, but I am somewhat interested in what I can uncover that is under the opinions.

"That's where I like to go."

COHEN CLIP

On Returning to the London Stage

"It's been a long time since I stood on a stage in London. It was about fourteen or fifteen years ago. I was sixty years old—just a kid with a crazy dream. Since then I've taken a lot of Prozac, Paxel, Welbutrin, Effexor, Ritalin, Focalin. I've also studied deeply in the philosophies and the religions. But cheerfulness kept breaking through."

—from onstage monologue on *Live in London* DVD, 2008

COHEN WORE EARPLUGS TO A DYLAN SHOW?

BRIAN D. JOHNSON | June 4, 2008, interview | June 12, 2008, macleans.ca (Canada)

On March 10, 2008, Lou Reed inducted Cohen into the Rock and Roll Hall of Fame, commenting, "We're so lucky to be alive at the same time as Leonard Cohen." Cohen came to the podium and said, "This is a very unlikely occasion for me. It is not a distinction that I coveted or even dared dream about. So I'm reminded of the prophetic statement of Jon Landau in the early seventies. He said, 'I have seen the future of rock and roll and it is not Leonard Cohen.'" Cohen was of course paraphrasing Landau's famous quote about how he had seen the future of rock and roll and its name was Bruce Springsteen. After the audience (which included Landau) stopped laughing, Cohen went on to cite apropos lyrics from his "Tower of Song": "Well my friends are gone, and my hair is gray / I ache in the places where I used to play . . ."

All that may have been true—his hair was certainly all gray—but Cohen, now seventy-three, was actually right in his prime musically. Moreover, he had embarked on the sort of rigorous concert tour you'd expect from a thirty-year-old rocker.

Backstage after a concert at Hamilton Place in Toronto, *Maclean's* magazine's Brian D. Johnson asked Cohen what had prompted him to go out on the road again. But first Johnson had a question about the singer's apparel. —Ed.

Brian D. Johnson: Tell me about the hat.

Leonard Cohen: I've been wearing a fedora for a long, long time. This particular hat is from a little hat store just opposite my daughter's antique store in Los Angeles. They have a very good hat store there.

BJ: You never used to perform with a hat.

LC: I've never performed with a hat. But I always wore a hat. I started wearing the hat more and more, independent of these preparations. I stopped wearing a fedora after 9/11. I didn't think it was appropriate to wear this kind of hat, and I switched to a cap.

BJ: Why?

LC: I don't really know. It seemed to be too dressed up for a situation that was closer to mourning than any other situation. So I didn't feel like getting dressed up. I always wore a suit, but I stopped wearing a fedora after 9/11.

BJ: It's useful onstage. It allows you to pay homage. Doffing it to the audience and the band.

LC: I started wearing it a lot around the house. I don't go out much. But I usually get dressed every day.

BJ: Now you're going out a lot, to say the least.

LC: Now I'm being sent like a postcard from place to place. It's really wonderful. [*Laughs.*]

BJ: After fourteen years off the road, what brought you back?

LC: Well, one of the things was that pesky little financial situation, which totally wiped me out. So I'm very grateful that I had a way to make a living, because that was indicated in very powerful terms. It wasn't the prime motivator. Thanks to the help of Robert Kory, who is unique among lawyers in that he deferred his fees until the situation was resolved, which is not just unusual but unheard of, I would say, for a lawyer in Los Angeles. So he was able to somehow right the shipwreck. As it turned out, I could have gotten by.

But all the time, even when I was in the monastery at Mount Baldy, there were times when I would ask myself, "Are you really never going to get up on a stage again?" It was always unresolved. It would arise. Not daily, not even monthly. But from time to time, I'd see my guitar. I was still writing songs. But the idea of performing was starting to recede further and further back. One of the reasons was that I was so wiped out physically by the end of my last tour because I was drinking heavily. I was drinking about three bottles of wine by the end of the tour.

BJ: Three bottles a day?

LC: Before every concert. I only drank professionally. I never drank after the concert. I would never drink after intermission. It was a long tour. It must have been sixty to seventy concerts.

BJ: Why did you need to drink?

LC: I was very nervous. And I liked drinking. And I found this wine. It was Château Latour. Now very expensive. It was even expensive then. It's curious with wine. The wine experts talk about the flavor and the bouquet and whether it has legs and the tannins and the fruit and the symphonies of tastes. But nobody talks about the high. Bordeaux is a wine that vintners have worked on for about a thousand years. Each wine has a very specific high, which is never mentioned. Château Latour, I don't know how I stumbled on it, but it went with the music, and it went with the concert. I tried to drink it after the tour was over, and I could hardly get a glass down. It had no resonance whatsoever. It needed the adrenaline of the concert and the music and the atmosphere, the kind of desperate atmosphere of touring— desperate because I was drinking so much! I had a good time with it for a while, but it did wreck my health, and I put on about twenty-five pounds.

BJ: So now what do you do with the anxiety that you were quelling with drinking before? Were you anxious coming into this tour?

LC: I was anxious. But I never really believed that it's entirely in one's hands anyway. I do trust in whatever those components are that buoy you up for the occasion. I am anxious. I don't mean to suggest I'm not at all anxious. But the anxiety is not devastating, as it was before.

BJ: How did you prepare for this tour?

LC: I hadn't really picked up a guitar in any serious way for many, many years. I had to restring all my guitars. And then I got my chop back. I only have one chop. Which [bass player and musical director] Roscoe Beck has now been able to duplicate. He's worked on it for many years.

BJ: He copped your chop?

LC: He copped my chop. . . . So I started practicing guitar. My only regret is that I have a lot of new songs but I didn't get a chance to rehearse them with this band. We're going to rehearse in August and September and I'll be able to include these new tunes. I've written most of a new album. I've recorded three tracks. But this band is so good that I'll probably rerecord the tracks that I did. It's such a privilege to play with these guys.

BJ: You've been working in a room for years; now you're on a stage. What are the pros and cons?

LC: This way, without drinking and smoking, it's a very, very different situation. Anyone who's been a heavy drinker and heavy smoker and has the good fortune to survive that and give it up knows what a very different kind of daily existence one has. I was smoking a couple of packs of cigarettes a day. And I was drinking heavily on these tours.

BJ: The smoke has added a lot of character to your voice.

LC: I lost a note or two in the bass register when I gave up smoking. But I've found some higher registers. I can't go as low, but I can go higher. I've never thought of myself as a singer anyway. . . . I've been free from those considerations because so many people over the years told me I don't have a voice. I kind of bought that. I never thought that much about it to begin with. I knew I didn't have one of the great voices. As my Damon Runyan-esque lawyer used to say, "None of you guys can sing. If I want to hear singing, I'll go to the Metropolitan Opera."

BJ: What's the song that presents the toughest challenge?

LC: The tough one for me is "Suzanne." My chop has not come back completely. I'm playing an acoustic electric guitar. It's pitched right. It's right for my voice. People have asked me what's it like to sing "Suzanne." It's a question I don't fully process, because I don't have the sense that I'm just doing it again. It's hard to sing it. It's hard to enter it. Because it's a serious song. I'm alone singing it. And it brought me . . . in my own curious magical universe it is a kind of doorway. So I have to be very careful with it. I can't speak too much about it because I can't put my finger on the reason, except to say it is a doorway, and I have to open it carefully. Otherwise, what is beyond that is not accessible to me.

BJ: It's not special because it's about one particular woman?

LC: It was never about a particular woman. For me it was more about the beginning of a different life for me. My life in Montreal, and my life wandering alone in those parts of Montreal that are now very beautifully done up and in those days, it was the waterfront. I used to wander around down there and I used to go to that church a lot.

BJ: So it's holy ground?

LC: It's holy ground. You don't want to linger on those matters because they have a significance that could be spoiled by explication.

BJ: Going back on the road after fourteen years—what else made you do it, aside from financial considerations?

LC: I thought it would be now or never. If I didn't do this year, I don't think I'm going to do it when I'm seventy-five, or seventy-seven, or eighty. It was hard for me to say never. It was like, "Wait a second, this is what you've spent your whole life doing. And what you're trained to do." I'm at that age where "never" had a really strong resonance.

BJ: You started this tour in smaller centers in eastern Canada. Was it a warm-up leg?

LC: There's no such thing when you're appearing in front of an audience. It would be insulting. Our band was warmed up. We had three months of rehearsal. [Keyboard player] Neil Larsen said most bands rehearse for a couple of weeks, and then it usually takes ten or twenty concerts for the band to jell. We jelled in the rehearsal hall. God forbid that I would walk out onto a stage and think that this is a warm-up. So from the first concert, which was in Fredericton [capital of New Brunswick, Canada], maybe the show's tightened, and the rhythm of the show has been more accurately defined, but it was no warm-up.

BJ: You and Bob Dylan were in Saint John's [in Newfoundland, Canada] at the same time, playing consecutive shows.

LC: I went to his concert. It was terrific. I've been to many Dylan concerts. This one, there was a walkway from the hotel to the auditorium, so you could enter into this private area, the people who had boxes. We were in one of those boxes. First of all, I've never been in a private box in an auditorium. That was fun. And a lot of members of the band came. But it was very loud. Fortunately, Raphael [Gayol], our drummer, had earplugs, and he distributed them. Because our music is quite soft and that's what we've been listening to for three or four months.

As Sharon Robinson said, Bob Dylan has a secret code with his audience. If someone came from the moon and watched it, they might wonder what was going on. In this particular case, he had his back to one half of the audience and was playing the organ, beautifully I might say, and just running through the songs. Some were hard to recognize. But nobody cared. That's not what they were there for and not what I was there for. Something else was going on, which was a celebration of some kind of genius that is so apparent and so clear and has touched people so deeply that all they need is some kind of symbolic unfolding of the event. It doesn't have to be the songs. All it has to be is: remember that song and what it did to you. It's a very strange event.

BJ: Back in the sixties, there was talk of you being a Canadian Bob Dylan. Didn't you make that analogy yourself at the time?

LC: No. That got into the press. I'd never say that any more than I'd say I want to be the next William Yeats or the next [Canadian poet] Bliss Carman. You know how that arose? There was a party at [Canadian poet] Frank Scott's house. I had a record of Bob Dylan, and I brought it to this party. There were all these poets, [Irving] Layton, and [Louis] Dudek, and maybe Phyllis Webb. It was probably *Bringing It All Back Home*. It was one of his early records. I said, "Fellas, listen to this. This guy's a real poet." I put the record on, and it was greeted with yawns. They said, "That's not a poet." I said, "No, I insist, let me play it again." They said, "Do you want to be that?" That's how it arose. But it's not my syntax. Anyway, they didn't like it. But I put it on a few more times, and by the end of the evening they were dancing.

BJ: You said that an audience brings a lot to someone like Bob Dylan. They bring a lot to you as well.

LC: Yes they do. As I said in the concert, this is every musician's dream, to stand in front of an audience and not have to prove your credentials, to come into that warmth. Of course, it creates other anxieties, because you really want to deliver. There's a lot to live up to. But it is quite a rare thing.

BJ: Are you still undepressed?

LC: Yes, it's held.

BJ: Do you need antidepressants?

LC: No. I find I can't even drink a glass of wine. It interferes with my mood. On Friday night I'll have a glass of wine with my family when we celebrate the Sabbath. A sip or two. I don't know what has happened. Occasionally I'll take hard liquor. I can take a whiskey or a vodka. But I can't drink wine the way I used to. I regret it in some ways. [Guitarist] Bob Metzger and I used to drink a lot together on tour. I don't know why that is. It just doesn't go down well anymore.

BJ: How did you stop drinking? Did you go into a program?

LC: I lost my taste for it. Just like cigarettes. I lost my taste.

BJ: Did you do anything physically to prepare for this tour?

LC: I have a half-assed routine that I try to go to. I miss it every other day. But I try to keep in shape.

BJ: What's your daily ritual on the road?

LC: The thing I'm most worried about is losing my voice. So I tend not to talk between concerts. I never did like going out much. So I really love that moment when I close the door of the hotel room.

BJ: So it's not the old sex, drugs, and rock-and-roll lifestyle, with young girls throwing themselves at you?

LC: But there are lovely communications . . . what you see behind you [notes and flowers from fans]. Many gifts come. It's very touching.

BJ: It's an ascetic life?

LC: Yes it is.

BJ: No temptations?

LC: The Devil laughs if you say there are no temptations. I do cherish those moments when I can just relax in the hotel room. Because there are a lot of details that have to be taken care of aside from just getting up onstage. You're dealing with a number of human beings whose well-being and safety you're concerned about. There are people I like to meet and talk to in the crew and the band.

BJ: You're moving a lot more onstage.

LC: One of the surprises was getting to know these songs again. I hadn't really looked at them for a long, long time. The songs are good. They hold up and you can get into them. I've never really thought of touring as a musical event. It was life on the road. It was temptation. It was drinking, camaraderie. It was the feeling of being in a motorcycle gang. There was that aspect to it which simply doesn't figure now. The music became really important on this tour. I was able to see that these songs really do move, and you can enter them, and there really is a place to live in them, and a place to move in them. And with musicians like I have, and the kind of rhythm section I have, it invites you to move. There is one dancer in our group, Sharon Robinson. She used to dance for Ann-Margret.

BJ: You once told me you've got to beat the band back. That seems no longer the case.

LC: I was drunk a lot of the time. The thing I was worried about was the drum and the bass would turn up. It was very hard to keep the band quiet. Occasionally like racehorses on the homeward track, I never used to blame them, but it was the nature of the beast that the guys want to open up. And because I hadn't rehearsed with this kind of precision and for this duration, I was always worried about them overtaking me. Also it's a different atmosphere. The precision is cherished by these musicians. No one is galloping.

BJ: What's your relationship status these days?

LC: With Anjani?

BJ: Yes.

LC: It's a good relationship. I've known her for a long, long time. She's just finished six songs of her own for a new album. She went to a little cabin in Wyoming for the last month and has written this album. So I'm very anxious to hear it.

BJ: How did your art exhibit do?

LC: It did very well. And continues to do well. It was one of the reasons that I didn't have to go on tour. I was able to pay a lot of lawyers. Not Robert Kory [whose fees are deferred]. I had detectives, forensic accountants, tax specialists.

BJ: If all of that hadn't happened . . . would you be doing this?

LC: Probably not.

BJ: It put a fire in your belly?

LC: Yes. It got me out into the world. I was retreating. It wasn't a retreat from creative activity. It was certainly a retreat from public life.

BJ: Was that a good thing?

LC: Sure. We're not running the show. I don't recommend losing everything as a spiritual discipline. But if it happens to you there are some features that are quite surprising and quite nourishing.

BJ: Do you still see Roshi?

LC: I celebrated his birthday, his hundred and first birthday, April 1. He's in New Mexico but he'll be back in Mount Baldy shortly. He gave me some advice years and years ago, which I didn't heed. I believe it was the '79 tour. He was in the dressing room with me drinking cognac. He taught me to drink cognac. But I was drinking a tumbler of cognac like it was water. He hit my thigh very hard and said, "Body important." [*Laughs.*]

COHEN CLIP

On Ownership of His Songs

"My sense of ownership with these things is very weak. It's not the result of spiritual discipline; it's always been that way. My sense of proprietorship has been so weak that actually I didn't pay attention and I lost the copyrights on a lot of the songs."

—from "On the Road, for Reasons Practical and Spiritual," by Larry Rohter, the *New York Times*, February 25, 2009

TV AND RADIO INTERVIEW

JIAN GHOMESHI | April 16, 2009, *Q with Jian Ghomeshi*, QTV (Quebec), CBC Radio One (Canada)

Cohen followed a good year with an arguably even better one: In 2009, he was touring world-wide and giving some of the best performances of his career. There's ample evidence of that on *Live in London*, which Columbia issued in CD and DVD formats on March 31. (And if you want to see just how far Cohen had come as a performer, check out the fascinating but embryonic *Live at the Isle of Wight 1970*, which was released on CD, DVD, and Blu-ray a little more than six months later, on October 19, 2009.)

Around the time of *Live in London*'s release, he spoke at his Montreal home with Canadian radio and TV personality Jian Ghomeshi about his current tour, his career, and what he had lately been referring to as his life's third act. —Ed.

Jian Ghomeshi: Leonard Cohen . . . it's a great pleasure to be here with you.

Leonard Cohen: Oh, well, thanks for coming over. I appreciate it.

JG: You're very generous to let us come and invade your home and sit inside your house. Thank you for this.

LC: You're most welcome.

JG: I'm thinking about you and your last year. You've just returned from India and you've played New York and I know you were in L.A. and you've been on tour for almost a year now. Does this house that you have owned or been in on and off for thirty-five years represent something of a haven, a retreat for you?

LC: Well, I think everybody's home does, but yes. I'm very happy to come back here.

JG: What do you do when you first get back to this house?

LC: Change the light bulbs. [*Laughs.*]

JG: But this is the cozy retreat?

LC: Yeah. My kids were brought up here a good part of the time. My grandchild comes here. I have a washing machine that everybody in the neighborhood uses.

JG: Still?

LC: Mmm hmm.

JG: You ever consider giving the house up?

LC: Well, you do from time to time. A Montreal house takes a lot of care. You've got to worry about pipes freezing and roofs leaking, so sometimes I think I'm not here long enough to justify the care it takes but that feeling evaporates as soon as I come into the place.

JG: Tell me about this tour, this journey that you've been on. It started around May of last year. It continues. You're doing a bunch more dates coming up. You seem to be having a good time onstage. You just played the Beacon Theatre in New York for three hours plus. You did the same thing when you were here in Montreal last summer. What have you learned being back onstage for the first time in fifteen years?

LC: It's hard to teach an old dog new tricks, as you know. I don't know if I've learned anything but I've been grateful that it's going well. I've got good musicians, great singers, and hospitable audiences and it seems to be going well. You can't ever guarantee that it's going to continue going well because there's a component that you really don't command in these affairs.

JG: What component is that?

LC: Some sort of grace, some sort of luck, some sort of spirit that informs the enterprise. It's hard to put your finger on it and you don't really want to put your finger on it. But there is that mysterious component that makes for a memorable evening. And somehow we've been lucky or graced to have that kind of evening that means something to you more than the fact that you've just done another concert. We'll be doing our hundredth concert in Austin and then we've got another hundred to go. And that'll take us to the end of October probably.

JG: Have you been surprised by just how well this tour has done? It's not the greatest of moments economically for artists who are touring. And you of course are a musical legend. You're known around the world but it's not just in New York and in Montreal and in Los Angeles that the shows are doing well. You're selling out shows in Saskatoon, in Victoria, and in London, Ontario. You're an urban Jewish kid from Montreal who in 2009 is selling out all over the place. What do you make of that?

LC: Well, beyond a general sense of gratitude I don't really analyze the mechanism. I'm just happy that it's going well. Because, as you know as a musician yourself, you never know what's going to happen when you step on the stage. You never know whether you'll be able to be the person that you want to be or that the audience is going to be hospitable to the person that they perceive. So there are so many unknowns and so many mysteries connected. That's even when you've brought the show to a certain degree of excellence. Everybody's well rehearsed, everybody knows the tunes, but still you never know what's going to happen.

JG: I want to ask you about where you're at in life. In 2001 in the *Observer* newspaper, you referred to this stage of your life as the third act and you quoted Tennessee Williams as saying life is a fairly well-written play except for the third act. You were sixty-seven when you said that. You're seventy-four now. Does that ring more or less true for you still?

LC: Well, the beginning of the third act seems to be very, very well written. But the end of the third act, of course, when the hero dies [*laughs*]—

each person considering himself the central figure of his own drama—that, generally speaking from what one can observe, can be rather tricky. My friend Irving Layton said it's not death that he's worried about—it's the preliminaries.

JG: Are you worried about the preliminaries?

LC: Sure. Every person ought to be.

JG: Let me come back to that. If you're accepting the third-act role, let's go back to the first act for a second. Maybe not actually to the beginning of the first act. I want to pick up at the beginning of your musical career because something that's very interesting about you as a singer and a musician is that by the time you started professionally singing, you weren't a teenager—you were a man in your early thirties and you made this decision . . . of course, you're well known as a writer and a poet [by then] but this was a brand-new career for you that you were starting in your thirties. How fearful were you of starting a second career at that point?

LC: Well, I've been generally fearful about everything so this just fits in with the general sense of anxiety that I always experienced in my early life. When you say I had a career as a writer or a poet, that hardly begins to describe the modesty of the enterprise in Canada at that time. We often mimeographed our books. An edition of two hundred was considered a bestseller in poems. So one had a vocation, one had some kind of calling, but you couldn't properly call it a career. At a certain point, I realized that I'm gonna have to buckle down and make a living. I didn't really know how to do this. I'd written a couple of novels and they'd been well received but they'd sold maybe three thousand copies.

JG: Award winning . . .

LC: Well, some of them won an award or two and the reviews were good but the sales were very, very limited. So I really had to do something and the only other thing I knew how to do was play guitar. So I was on my way down to Nashville. I loved country music. I thought maybe I'd get a job playing guitar. And I'd been in Greece for a long time. I was kind of out of touch with what was going on. When I hit New York I bumped into what later was called the folksong renaissance. There were people like Judy Collins and Dave Van Ronk and Dylan and Joan Baez. There were wonderful singers around and I hadn't heard their work. That touched me very much because I'd always been writing little songs myself too but I never thought there was any marketplace for them.

JG: Some people would think it's ironic to go into music to make money given that it's not necessarily the most lucrative of professions for most artists either.

LC: No, in hindsight it seems to be the height of folly to resolve your economic crisis by becoming a folksinger. I had not much of a voice either. I didn't play that great guitar either. I don't know how these things happen in life. Luck has so much to do with success and failure.

JG: People talk about the fact that you've written songs that you've almost grown into as you get older—that you were writing beyond your years, and performing so, when you started your music career. Did that have something to do with the fact that it wasn't happening when you were seventeen—it was happening when you were in your midthirties? In other words, how did starting a musical career in your thirties inform what you were writing and presenting?

LC: I always had the notion that I had a tiny garden to cultivate. I never thought I was really one of the big guys so the work that was in front of me was just to cultivate this tiny corner of the field that I thought I knew something about, which was something to do with self-investigation without self-indulgence. I never liked the latter too much as a mode. Just pure confession I never felt was really interesting but confession filtered through a tradition of skill and hard work is interesting to me. So that was my tiny corner and I just started writing about the things that I thought I knew about or that I wanted to find out about. So that was how it began. I wanted the songs to sound like everybody else's songs. I was very much influenced by women's background voices.

JG: You were influenced by women's background voices?

LC: Yes, I liked those songs that had that feel. Those are the songs of the fifties. So those were the sounds I wanted to try to reproduce. Also, my own voice sounded so disagreeable to me when I listened to it that I really needed the sweetening of women's voices behind me.

JG: Are you over that—your voice sounding disagreeable?

LC: No, not at all. Not yet. Maybe a bit later.

JG: You say . . . you've always been fearful of everything. When did you give yourself permission to think of yourself as and call yourself a legitimate singer and musician?

LC: Well, you cycle through these feelings of anxiety and confidence. If something goes well in one's life, one feels the benefits of the success. When something doesn't go well one feels remorse. So those activities persist in one's life right to this moment.

JG: Meaning there's days you still don't feel legitimate?

LC: Legitimacy is another question. I have a strong sense that I exist. So that's as legitimate as I need to be but when you're out there in front of the public you're going to get a whole lot of responses and at this stage of the game I have a pretty thick skin. I prefer praise to criticism but I'm really ready for both.

JG: Sticking with that first act but moving into the second part of it, into the seventies, you become quite prolific, you put out a few records. . . . A lot of the songs that you write seem inspired by, written for, or written about women. I'm thinking of Suzanne, I'm thinking of Marianne. You've spoken with such awe at the beauty and power of the women who've inspired you. Have the women in your life been a source of your strength or weakness?

LC: Good question for every man. It's not a level playing ground for either of us, for either the man or the woman. Love is the most challenging activity that humans get into. We have the sense that we can't live without love, that life has very little meaning without love. So we're invited into this very dangerous arena where the possibilities for humiliation and failure are ample. So there's no fixed lesson that one can learn about the thing because the heart is always opening and closing. It's always softening and hardening. We're always experiencing joy or sadness so there's no jackpot in the whole enterprise. You're either going to have the courage [or not], because after a certain amount of time, the accumulation of defeats in this realm are going to be significant. So I think people that—in spite of the defeat, in spite of the impossibility of establishing reasonable contacts with the other—are fortunate enough to be able to continue to do that are indeed fortunate. But there are lots of people that close down. And there are times in one's life when one has to close down just to regroup.

JG: Are there times when you've lamented the power that women have had over you?

LC: I never looked at it that way. There's times when I've lamented, there's times when I've rejoiced, there's times when I've been deeply indifferent. You run through the whole gamut of experience but for each other, men for women, women for men, and we are the content of each other. And most men have a woman in their heart and most women have a man in their heart. There are people that don't. There are monks that don't. But most of us cherish some sort of dream of surrender. But these are dreams and sometimes they're defeated and sometimes they're manifested.

JG: It seems like an obvious question but do you think love is empowering?

LC: It's a ferocious activity where you would experience defeat and you experience acceptance and you experience exultation. And a fixed idea about it will definitely cause you a great deal of suffering. If you have the feeling that it's going to be an easy ride, you're going to be disappointed. If you have a feeling that it's going to be hell all the way, you may be surprised.

JG: You were coming to the fore of the public imagination at a time of free love, a great time of sexual liberation, and you famously had a lot of powerful relationships with different women. Do you regret at times not having a lifelong partner? [*Cohen begins singing Edith Piaf's "Non, Je Ne Regrette Rien."*] Not at all?

LC: No. I don't have a sense of my life as a story that was written and that I'm reading. I'm not a sentimental guy. I'm blessed with a certain amount of amnesia and I really don't remember what went down. I know that it's engraved in some kind of cellular level and it's operating and it's there but I don't review my life that way.

JG: I want to move into the second act and ask you about some of the difficult times you had. You've talked about clinical depression that you had and I'm thinking about the 1990s, even in the face of a very successful record that you made in 1992, *The Future*. Do you think dealing with depression was an important part of your creative process?

LC: Well, it was a part of every process. It was the central activity of my days and nights. It was dealing with a prevailing sense of anxiety, distress, a background of anguish that prevailed.

JG: How important was writing to your survival?

LC: It had a number of benefits. One was economic. It wasn't a luxury for me to write, it was a necessity. But in writing, if you can discard the slogans that naturally come to you, especially in a highly politicized time like we are [in] now, where gender politics and regular politics and environmental politics . . . where there's a good thing to say about everything if you're on the right side. These times are very difficult to write in because the slogans really are jamming the airwaves. So writing is a very good way—

JG: What do you mean by the slogans?

LC: Well, what is right, what is the good position. It's something that goes beyond what has been called "political correctness." It's a kind of tyranny of a posture. A kind of tyranny that exists today of what the right thing should be. So those ideas are swarming through the air today like locusts. And it's difficult for the writer to determine what he really thinks about things, what he really feels about things. So in my own case, I have to write the verse and then see if it's a slogan or not and then toss it. But I can't toss it until I've worked on it and seen what it really is. So I [employ the] process of writing the verse and discarding it until I get down to something that doesn't sound like a slogan, that doesn't sound like something that's easy, that surprises me.

JG: If you think about those difficult times—and you can do that now through the lens of what seems to be a pretty positive place you're in today—what do you consider your darkest hour?

LC: I wouldn't tell you about it if I knew. Nothing comes to mind. I dare not . . . even to talk about oneself in a time like this is a kind of unwholesome luxury. There's so much suffering right now. To talk about my darkest hour in the face of what's going on in most of the places in the world now seems to be an area that leaves me quite indifferent. I don't think I've had a darkest hour compared to the dark hours that so many people are involved in right now. Large numbers of people are dodging bombs, having their nails pulled out in dungeons, facing starvation, disease. *Large* numbers of people. So I think we've really got to be circumspect about how seriously we take our own anxieties today.

JG: Well, let me ask you what you would tell others. You're famously mentioned in Kurt Cobain's song, "Pennyroyal Tea": "Give me Leonard Cohen afterworld so I can sigh eternally." After he committed suicide in the nineties, you said you wished you had spoken to him, that you might have been able to "lay something on him." What would you have said to Kurt Cobain?

LC: I don't know what I would say to him but the sense of solitude and hopelessness that comes out of that sense of isolation could probably have been penetrated by a certain kind of company, just a certain kind of sympathetic company. But you can read the life you're living but you cannot change a word.

JG: You've been musing on your own mortality in your lyrics for some time now. I'm thinking back to 1988 and "Tower of Song" where you famously wrote, "My friends are gone, my hair is gray / I ache in the places where I used to play." That was twenty years ago. How much do you reflect upon your own mortality now?

LC: You get a sense of it. The body sends a number of messages to you as you get older. I don't know if it's a matter of reflection. That implies a kind of peaceful recognition of the situation. Occasionally there's a stab of pain or an ache and you remember that this is not going to go on forever. But

I'm not really given to reflection on those. My friend Irving Layton was very concerned with immortality and posterity. And as I read his work now, I think that he will achieve what he wanted, which was not an eternal life based on his work but certainly an extended life. But I never had those concerns.

JG: A couple of decades ago, in a CBC interview, you were asked, "What are you more sure of now than when you were a teenager?" And you said, "Death." [*Laughs.*] You have been thinking about it for a while. So are you *more* sure now?

LC: Am I sure that I'm going to die? Yes.

JG: Well said. Is there a way to prepare for that?

LC: Well, like with anything else, there's a certain degree of free will. You put in your best efforts to prepare for anything but you can't command the consequences. So yes, there are whole religious and spiritual methodologies that invite you to prepare for death and you can embark upon them and embrace them . . . but I don't think there's any guarantee that it's going to work. Because nobody knows what's going to happen in the next moment.

JG: Back to that fear: Are you fearful of death?

LC: I think any reasonable person is going to [be]. It's not so much death, as Layton said—it's the preliminaries. Of course, everyone has to have a certain amount of anxiety about the conditions of one's death—the actual circumstances, the pain involved, the effect on your heirs. But there's so little that you can do about it. It's best to relegate those concerns to the appropriate compartments of the mind and not let them inform all your activities. We've got to live our lives as if they're real, as if they're not going to end immediately, so we have to live under those . . . some people might call them illusions.

JG: Bringing us back to the present day and that Tennessee Williams quote. And you've said, "How it ends is nobody's business. It is generally accompanied by some disagreeable circumstances."

LC: Yes, that seems to be the way it is.

JG: I guess the latest disagreeable circumstances, if 2005 can be considered the latest, were these financial difficulties that you had. You were defrauded by someone you personally worked with closely for many years. . . . Was it important to you to rebuild the nest egg when that money was gone?

LC: Well, it was presented in much more urgent terms than that. It was a matter of financial survival so I didn't sit around thinking it's important to build the nest egg; it's important to produce some income. So I got busy and I was able to put some things into motion. But as I said, you can put forward your best effort but there's no guarantee that the circumstances are going to yield the results that you intend. Nobody can do that. So I put in my best efforts and luckily they've been rewarded with a certain amount of financial remuneration.

JG: And this current tour is very lucrative. You seem like such a modest man. Your house is certainly modest. It's Spartan. You don't seem to require a lot. How important is material wealth to you at this point?

LC: You can't ignore it. I like to live simply but that's not a virtue; it's just a preference. There are people who like to have vast marble halls and ballrooms and that sort of thing. That kind of living has never attracted me. So I don't consider it anything special to live simply. I love this house. It's been very kind to me and my children over the years. I'm sorry that you blacked out the windows [for the TV broadcast] because this is a lovely view of the Parc du Portugal. It's a really nice place to live. It is simple but that's just a preference.

JG: Let me ask you about "Hallelujah" for a moment because it's been an interesting year for "Hallelujah." If it hadn't been a song that Canadians and people around the world have been singing—versions by Jeff Buckley, Rufus Wainwright, k. d. lang—it took on a whole new energy, a song that you wrote in 1984, this past Christmas. Cover versions appeared as number one and number two on the UK bestseller charts and your version was also in the Top 40 from 1984. What did you make of that?

LC: I was happy that the song was being used, of course. There were certain ironic and amusing sidebars because the record that it came from, which was called *Various Positions,* that record Sony wouldn't put out—they didn't think it was good enough. It had songs like "Dance Me to the End of Love," "Hallelujah," "If It Be Your Will," but it wasn't considered good enough for the American market and it wasn't put out. So there was a certain mild sense of revenge that arose in my heart. I was happy about it. But I was just reading a review of a movie called *Watchmen* that uses it. And the reviewer said, "Can we please have a moratorium on 'Hallelujah' in movies and television shows?" And I kind of feel the same way.

JG: [*Laughs.*] I was going to say, ". . . to which you placed a stern phone call saying, 'No! Let's keep it going.'" It's interesting . . . the song kind of transcends musical genres. It's not a typical pop song but not only does it not seem to go away, it seems to grow in its popularity with each year. I know it's one of your favorite songs.

LC: I like the song, I think it's a good song, but I think too many people sing it. I think people ought to stop singing it for a little while.

JG: What is the magic of "Hallelujah"?

LC: I don't know. One is always trying to write a good song and like everything else you put in your best effort but you can't command the consequences. It took a long time. I think the song came out in '83 or '84. And then the only person who seemed to recognize the song was Dylan, and he was doing it in concert. Nobody else recognized the song until quite a long time later, I think. When was Jeff Buckley's?

JG: In '92.

LC: So it's almost ten years later. I knew his father [the late folksinger Tim Buckley] very well, incidentally. They were both fine young men and I think John Cale, whom I knew personally . . . he asked me for a bunch of lyrics and I sent him a whole bunch. Where did he put it out? Is his in *Shrek* or is that Rufus Wainwright's?

JG: That's a good question. I think it's Rufus's, yeah.

LC: In *Shrek* it's Rufus's?

JG: There is a John Cale one that's in a movie too, though, I think.

LC: I don't know about this. Anyway, they're both beautiful versions. I think John Cale's might be in the movie and Rufus's on the soundtrack. There was some curious distribution of the song between those two singers. But they're both great singers. I was in the room when k. d. lang sang it at the Canadian Songwriters Hall of Fame. That *really* touched me.

JG: Do the songs ever feel like possessions? Is there ever somebody working with your writing that you don't appreciate?

LC: I'm not sure that has ever happened. I had a very modest career for most of my life and I was always happy when someone did one of my songs, so that overrode most of the critical concerns I might have had. In fact, my critical faculties went into suspended animation when someone would do one of my songs and I generally was just delighted. And I still feel that way.

JG: Leonard, in 2001, you told the story of your affection for watching eighty-two-year-old Alberta Hunter sing love songs in New York.

LC: That was great.

JG: And you said at the time, "I love to hear an old singer lay it out and I'd like to be one of them."

LC: That's right. I would like to be. She was around eighty-two, I think. Yes, I would love to hear me at eighty-two. [*Laughs.*] That would be good.

As I get older, I like to hear stories from the elderly. I'm reading Irving Layton's poems now over again, especially the poems he wrote toward the end of his life, and they're deep and deeply instructive, not in a pedagogic way but in some kind of information for which the heart is hungry.

JG: You say you hope to hear yourself at eighty-two. What do you hope to sound like at eighty-two?

LC: Alberta Hunter.

JG: [*Laughs.*] You've got your model. We've been talking about three acts. Is there ever a fourth act? You seem like you've got a lot going on still.

LC: There might be a fourth act but we'll leave that to the theologians.

JG: Leonard Cohen, it's a great pleasure to sit here with you. Thank you again for inviting us into your home.

LC: You're most welcome. Have you got enough?

JG: I think so. Thank you very much.

LC: Oh, most welcome. A pleasure. Did we get anything that's interesting? Because if we didn't let's go on. We might get something interesting.

JG: Well, you wouldn't talk to me too much about death. I was trying to learn from that. I've always been terrified.

LC: Really?

JG: Yeah, once or twice a year I wake up in the middle of the night and freak out like I'm on this treadmill toward death and it's something I can't control and I don't know how to deal with it.

LC: If someone could guarantee me that the preliminaries will not be too disagreeable, I'd look forward to . . .

JG: Really?

LC: Yeah.

"ALL I'VE GOT TO PUT IN A SONG IS MY OWN EXPERIENCE"

DORIAN LYNSKEY | January 19, 2012, the *Guardian* (London)

Another first-rate concert video, *Songs from the Road*, appeared on DVD and Blu-ray in 2010. Then, on January 31, 2012, Columbia released *Old Ideas*—only the twelfth studio album of Cohen's nearly half-century recording career—which reached number three on the US *Billboard* charts, his highest ranking there ever. The album also climbed to number one in Canada—his first chart-topper in his native country—as well as in Belgium, the Czech Republic, Holland, Finland, Hungary, New Zealand, Norway, Poland, and Spain. It hit number two in Australia, Denmark, Ireland, Sweden, and the UK. Not bad for a seventy-seven-year-old singer.

Shortly before the album's release, London-based journalist Dorian Lynskey received the news he'd been anticipating for a long time: he'd be meeting with Leonard Cohen.

"For many years, he had topped my wish list of interviewees," Lynskey told me, "but it looked increasingly unlikely that I'd ever have the pleasure. Though he talked to the press at length to promote *I'm Your Man* and *The Future*, he returned years later, happier but considerably more press-shy. Perhaps he felt that by this age his reputation spoke for itself so there was no need to subject himself to another grilling.

"In late 2011," continued Lynskey, "I was told I could fly to Los Angeles to attend a playback of *Old Ideas*, where I might get a few minutes with Cohen, but that plan fell through. Then there was the prospect of Paris. Again, it was debatable whether I would get any time with him but Paris wasn't so far away so it seemed worth a try and I could at least write a profile of him using existing sources and press conference quotes.

"After the predictably witty and enjoyable Q&A session [with multiple journalists]," Lynskey recalled, "Cohen's manager beckoned me to one side and said that because he was a *Guardian* reader, he had convinced Leonard to answer a few questions in private. I consulted my dream list of questions and pared them down to five as I was ushered into an opulent hotel suite and seated opposite Cohen. If he was reluctant to talk he hid it well. His courtesy was as old-fashioned and elegant as his suit, and his humor was as lively as I expected but clearly came from a calmer place than it had back when he was haunted by depression.

"The timer on my voice recorder told me at the end that we'd talked for just six and a half minutes but he gave me more good quotes than most musicians can muster in an hour. As you would imagine from his lyrics, he's not a man to waste words. I left the room not disappointed by the brevity of the encounter but elated that it had happened at all. A photograph of the two of us in conversation hangs on my office wall—a reminder of how thrilling and moving the job of sitting down with a favorite musician and asking a few questions can be." —Ed.

On Leonard Cohen's grueling 1972 world tour, captured in Tony Palmer's documentary *Bird on a Wire*, an interviewer asked the singer to define success. Cohen, who at thirty-seven knew a bit about failure and the kind of acclaim that doesn't pay the bills, frowned at the question and replied: "Success is survival."

By that reckoning, Cohen has been far more of a success than he could have predicted. There have been reversals of fortune along the way but forty years later he enters an ornate room in Paris's fabled Crillon Hotel to a warm breeze of applause. Looking like a grandfatherly mobster, he doffs his hat and smiles graciously, just as he did every night of the 2008–'10 world tour that represented a miraculous creative revival. The prickly, saturnine, dangerously funny character witnessed in *Bird on a Wire* has found a measure of calm and, as he often puts it, gratitude.

These days, Cohen rations his one-on-one interviews with the utmost austerity, hence this press conference to promote his twelfth album, *Old Ideas*, a characteristically intimate reflection on love, death, suffering, and forgiveness. After the playback, he answers questions. He was always funnier than he was given credit for; now he has honed his deadpan to such perfection that every questioner becomes the straight man in a double act. Claudia from Portugal wants him to explain the humor behind his image as a lady's man. "Well, for me to be a lady's man at this point requires a great deal of humor," he replies. Steve from Denmark wonders what Cohen will be in his next life. "I don't really understand that process called reincarnation but if there is such a thing I'd like to come back as my daughter's dog." Erik, also from Denmark, asks whether he has come to terms with death. "I've come to the conclusion, reluctantly, that I am going to die," he responds. "So naturally those questions arise and are addressed. But I like to do it with a beat."

Cohen falls into the odd category of underrated legend. To his fans, including many songwriters, he is about as good as it gets, but he has never enjoyed a hit single or (outside his native Canada and, for some reason, Norway) a platinum album. He has said that a certain image of him has been "put into the computer": the womanizing poet who sings songs of "melancholy and despair" enjoyed by those who wish they could be (or be with) womanizing poets too. These days the database will also note that he wrote "Hallelujah," a neglected song on a flop album that, via an unlikely alliance of Jeff Buckley, *Shrek*, and *The X Factor*, eventually became a kind of modern hymn.

Its creator was born in Montreal on September 21, 1934, three months before Elvis Presley. When he first shopped his songs around New York, the ones that became 1967's *Songs of Leonard Cohen*, agents responded: "Aren't you a little old for this game?" By then he had already lost his father while very young, met Jack Kerouac, lived in a bohemian idyll on the Greek island of Hydra, visited Cuba during the Bay of Pigs invasion, and published two acclaimed novels and four volumes of poetry. In short, he had lived, and this gave his elaborate, enigmatic songs a grave authority to younger listeners who sensed that he was privy to mysteries that they could only guess at. He was neither the best singer nor the best musician nor the best-looking man around, but he had the charisma and the words, and the eroticized intelligence. Perhaps because his style owed more to French chansonniers and Jewish cantors than American folk, he was always more loved in Europe than North America. An early write-up in folk gazette *Sing Out!* remarked: "No comparison can be drawn between Leonard Cohen and any other phenomenon."

Under interrogation he would explain certain details in his songs, such as whether his friend's wife Suzanne Vaillancourt [*née Verdal* —*Ed.*] really served him "tea and oranges" (kind of: she drank a brand of tea flavored with orange peel) or whether Janis Joplin really gave him "head on the unmade bed" in the Chelsea Hotel (yes, but he later regretted his ungallant candor), but never their meanings.

He still resists explaining them and his relentlessly dry self-deprecation works as a very effective, very entertaining shield. Two nights after the Paris playback, Cohen appears at one in London, hosted by Jarvis Cocker. A fan since adolescence, Cocker keeps running up against Cohen's reluctance to delve too deeply into the "sacred mechanics" of songwriting, lest they stop working. Songs come painfully slowly to him, and when he has a good idea he perseveres with it: "Hallelujah" took around two years and eighty potential verses. During the playback, a screen shows pages from his notebooks, full of scribbled amendments and discarded verses. "There are people who work out of a sense of great abundance," he says. "I'd love to be one of them but I'm not. You just work with what you've got."

Cohen's modest star began to wane with 1977's raucous *Death of a Ladies' Man*. In the studio a crazed Phil Spector held a gun to Cohen's head and the producer handled the songs just as roughly. Columbia Records mogul Walter Yetnikoff declined even to release 1984's *Various Positions* (the one with "Hallelujah"), reportedly explaining: "Look, Leonard, we know you're great, but we don't know if you're any good." But his next album, *I'm Your Man*, was both. Armed with synthesizers, acrid wit, and a voice that now sounded like a seismic disturbance, he was reinvigorated just in time to enjoy an avalanche of praise from younger admirers including Nick Cave and the Pixies. But on songs such as "First We Take Manhattan," "Everybody Knows," and "The Future," his depression took on geopolitical proportions. He told the journalist Mikal Gilmore: "There is no point in trying to forestall the apocalypse. The bomb has already gone off." In Paris someone asks him what he thinks about the current economic crisis and he replies simply: "Everybody knows."

In 1993, resurgent and well-loved but in a dark frame of mind, Cohen disappeared from the public gaze. He spent the next six years [*Actually, closer to five. —Ed.*] in a monastery on Mount Baldy, California, studying with his old friend and Zen master Kyozan Joshu Sasaki, whom he calls Roshi and who is now a resilient one hundred and four years old. "This old teacher never speaks about religion," Cohen tells the Paris audience.

"There's no dogma, there's no prayerful worship, there's no address to a deity. It's just a commitment to living in a community."

When he came down from the mountain, his lifelong depression had finally lifted. "When I speak of depression," he says carefully, "I speak of a clinical depression that is the background of your entire life, a background of anguish and anxiety, a sense that nothing goes well, that pleasure is unavailable and all your strategies collapse. I'm happy to report that, by imperceptible degrees and by the grace of good teachers and good luck, that depression slowly dissolved and has never returned with the same ferocity that prevailed for most of my life." He thinks it might just be down to old age. "I read somewhere that as you grow older certain brain cells die that are associated with anxiety so it doesn't really matter how much you apply yourself to the disciplines. You're going to start feeling a lot better or a lot worse depending on the condition of your neurons."

Can it really be that simple? Can the mood of his classic songs really be explained by unfortunate brain chemistry? He recently told his biographer Sylvie Simmons that in everything he did, "I was just trying to beat the devil. Just trying to get on top of it." As well as Judaism and Zen Buddhism, he briefly flirted with Scientology. He has never married but has had several significant relationships, including Joni Mitchell, actor Rebecca De Mornay, and the woman with whom he had two children in the early seventies, Suzanne Elrod (no, not that Suzanne). He was a serious drinker and smoker who experimented with different drugs. On his 1972 tour, as documented in *Bird on a Wire*, he christened his band the Army and they in turn dubbed him Captain Mandrax after his downer of choice.

In that film he appears fractious and exhausted: a "broken-down nightingale," addressing audiences with irritable humor. Yet on his comeback tour he looked profoundly grateful for every cheer or clap. "I was touched by the reception, yes," he says. "I remember we were playing in Ireland and the reception was so warm that tears came to my eyes and I thought, 'I can't be seen weeping at this point.' Then I turned around and saw the guitar player weeping."

The tour was partly triggered by financial necessity after his business manager siphoned off almost all of his savings. Was he reluctant to go on the road again? "I don't know if reluctance is the word but trepidation or nervousness. We rehearsed for a long, long time—longer than is reasonable. But one is never really certain." He hopes to play more concerts and to release another album in a year or so. He is already older than Johnny Cash was when he released his final album; soon he'll creatively outlive Frank Sinatra. On the back of one of his notebooks he has written: "Coming to the end of the book but not quite yet."

In Paris, after the press conference, I'm discreetly ushered into a back room for a rare interview alone with Cohen. Up close, he's a calming presence, old-world courtesy mingled with Zen, and his smoke-blackened husk of a voice is as reassuring as a lullaby. I ask him whether he wishes the long and painful process of writing his songs would come more easily.

"Well, we're talking in a world where guys go down into the mines, chewing coca and spending all day in backbreaking labor. We're in a world where there's famine and hunger and people are dodging bullets and having their nails pulled out in dungeons so it's very hard for me to place any high value on the work that I do to write a song. Yeah, I work hard but compared to what?"

Does he learn anything from writing them? Does he work out ideas that way?

"I think you work out something. I wouldn't call them ideas. I think ideas are what you want to get rid of. I don't really like songs with ideas. They tend to become slogans. They tend to be on the right side of things: ecology or vegetarianism or antiwar. All these are wonderful ideas but I like to work on a song until those slogans, as wonderful as they are and as wholesome as the ideas they promote are, dissolve into deeper convictions of the heart. I never set out to write a didactic song. It's just my experience. All I've got to put in a song is my own experience."

In "Going Home," the first song on *Old Ideas*, he mentions writing "a manual for living with defeat." Can a listener learn about life from his songs?

"Song operates on so many levels. It operates on the level you just spoke of where it addresses the heart in its ordeals and its defeats but it also is useful in getting the dishes done or cleaning the house. It's also useful as a background to courting."

Is a cover of "Hallelujah" a compliment he has grown tired of receiving?

"There's been a couple of times when other people have said, 'Can we have a moratorium please on "Hallelujah"?' Must we have it at the end of every single drama and every single *Idol*? And once or twice I've felt maybe I should lend my voice to silencing it but on second thought no, I'm very happy that it's being sung."

Does he still define success as survival? "Yeah." He smiles. "It's good enough for me."

THE WORKS OF LEONARD COHEN

STUDIO ALBUMS

1967	*Songs of Leonard Cohen*
1969	*Songs from a Room*
1971	*Songs of Love and Hate*
1974	*New Skin for the Old Ceremony*
1977	*Death of a Ladies' Man*
1979	*Recent Songs*
1984	*Various Positions*
1988	*I'm Your Man*
1992	*The Future*
2001	*Ten New Songs*
2004	*Dear Heather*
2012	*Old Ideas*

COMPILATION ALBUMS

1975	*Best of Leonard Cohen*
1997	*More Best of Leonard Cohen*
2002	*The Essential Leonard Cohen*

LIVE ALBUMS

1973 *Live Songs*
1994 *Cohen Live: Leonard Cohen in Concert*
2001 *Field Commander Cohen: Tour of 1979*
2009 *Live in London*
2010 *Songs from the Road*

BOOKS

1956 *Let Us Compare Mythologies*
1961 *The Spice-Box of Earth*
1963 *The Favorite Game*
1964 *Flowers for Hitler*
1966 *Beautiful Losers*
1966 *Parasites of Heaven*
1971 *Selected Poems: 1956–1968*
1972 *The Energy of Slaves*
1978 *Death of a Lady's Man*
1984 *Book of Mercy*
1993 *Stranger Music: Selected Poems and Songs*
2006 *Book of Longing*
2009 *The Lyrics of Leonard Cohen*
2011 *Poems and Songs*
2012 *Fifteen Poems*

CONCERT VIDEOS

2009 *Live in London*
2009 *Live at the Isle of Wight 1970*
2010 *Songs from the Road*

Note: Cohen is also featured in films he did not produce, including *Ladies and Gentlemen, Mr. Leonard Cohen* (1965), *Bird on a Wire* (1974), *The Song of Leonard Cohen* (1980), *I Am a Hotel* (1983), and *I'm Your Man* (2005).

ABOUT THE CONTRIBUTORS

Elizabeth Boleman-Herring is publishing editor of WeeklyHubris.com, a columnist for *Huffington Post*, and author of *The Visitors' Book (or Silva Rerum): An Erotic Fable*. An academic for thirty years, she has also worked steadily as a founding editor of journals, magazines, and newspapers, and is the author of fifteen books in diverse genres. Boleman-Herring is a Traditional Usui Reiki Master and an Iyengar-Style Yoga teacher (who, through GreeceTraveler.com, leads trips to Greece); and, as "Bebe Herring," she has been a jazz lyricist for the likes of Thelonious Monk, Kenny Dorham, and Bill Evans.

Born in London in 1950, **Mick Brown** has contributed to such publications as the *Sunday Times*, the *Guardian, Esquire,* and *Rolling Stone.* He now writes on a wide variety of cultural subjects for the *London Daily Telegraph* magazine. He is the author of six books, including *American Heartbeat: Travels from Woodstock to San Jose by Song Title, The Spiritual Tourist, The Dance of 17 Lives,* and, most recently, *Tearing Down the Wall of Sound: The Rise and Fall of Phil Spector.*

Adrienne Clarkson is a Canadian journalist and stateswoman. She has been a producer and broadcaster for the Canadian Broadcasting Corporation and is a former governor general of Canada.

Bill Conrad is a semiretired music journalist and publicist who lives and continues to write in Jacksonville, Florida. He has worked with record executives and producers Jimmy Bowen and Ken Mansfield. His years with country star Waylon Jennings are the focus of a memoir in progress. A list of his film and print credits is at IMDb.com under William F. Conrad.

Stina Lundberg Dabrowski is a professor of television at the Stockholm Academy of Dramatic Arts. She is also an award-winning journalist, writer, producer, and TV host. Dabrowski, who has been a popular figure on Swedish television since 1982, has interviewed Muammar al-Gaddafi, Hillary Clinton, Nelson Mandela, Yasser Arafat, Mikhael Gorbachev, Al Gore, David Bowie, Norman Mailer, and many other luminaries.

Writer, critic, and biographer **Sandra Djwa**, who holds a PhD from the University of British Columbia, taught Canadian literature at Simon Fraser University from 1968 to 2005. In 1973, she cofounded the Association for Canadian and Québec Literatures. Djwa is best known for her articles on Canadian poets like Margaret Atwood and for her biographies of distinguished Canadians, including F.R. Scott and Roy Daniells. Her latest book, *Journey with No Maps: A Life of P. K. Page*, was published in 2012.

Chris Douridas garnered attention in the 1990s as host of the daily *Morning Becomes Eclectic* program on Santa Monica, California's KCRW-FM, where he has also served as program director. Douridas has been an A&R executive at DreamWorks Records and has produced soundtracks for many popular films, including *American Beauty*, *Shrek 2*, and *As Good as It Gets*. He has had television acting roles and he hosted the inaugural season of PBS's *Sessions at West 54th*.

Gillian G. Gaar is a Seattle-based writer and photographer. Her books include *She's a Rebel: The History of Women in Rock & Roll*, *Green Day: Rebels with a Cause*, *The Rough Guide to Nirvana*, *Return of the King: Elvis Presley's Great Comeback*, and *Entertain Us: The Rise of Nirvana*. She has contributed to many publications, including *Mojo*, *Rolling Stone*, and *Goldmine*, and she served as project consultant/historian for Nirvana's 2004 box set *With the Lights Out*.

Vicki Gabereau has been a popular Canadian radio and television talk-show host for more than three decades. Her book *This Won't Hurt a Bit* collects her conversations with the "famous, not-so-famous, and should-be-famous."

Jian Ghomeshi, who lives in Toronto, hosts the national daily cultural-affairs talk program *Q* on CBC Radio One and Bold TV. The show, which he cocreated, has become the highest-rated morning program in CBC history. Ghomeshi has written opinion pieces for the *Washington Post*, the *Globe and Mail*, the *Toronto Star*, the *International Herald Tribune*, and other publications. During the 1990s, he was a member of the popular Canadian folk-rock group Moxy Früvous.

Mikal Gilmore, one of America's leading music journalists, has written for *Rolling Stone* since the 1970s. He is the author of *Night Beat: A Shadow History of Rock and Roll* and *Stories Done: Writings on the 1960s and Its Discontents*. His 1995 memoir, *Shot in the Heart*, recounts his destructive childhood and relationship with his older brother Gary, who in 1977 became the first man to be executed in the United States after restoration of the death penalty. It won the *Los Angeles Times* book prize and the National Book Critics Circle Award.

Toronto-based **Barbara Gowdy** is a novelist and short-story writer whose bestselling books include *Falling Angels*, *The White Bone*, *The Romantic*, and *Helpless*.

Brett Grainger is a freelance writer and a recipient of a National Magazine Award in Canada. He is the author of *In the World but Not of It: One Family's Militant Faith and the History of Fundamentalism in America*. Grainger, who lives in Narberth, Pennsylvania, has a doctorate in the history of religion from Harvard University.

Richard Guilliatt is a journalist and author whose work has appeared in many leading newspapers and magazines including the *Times*, the *Sunday Times Magazine*, the *Independent*, the *New York Times*, the *Los Angeles Times*, and the *Wall Street Journal*. He is the author of *Talk of the Devil—Repressed Memory and the Ritual Abuse Witch-Hunt* and coauthor with Peter Hohnen of *The Wolf—How One German Raider Terrorized the Allies in the Most Epic Voyage of WW1*. He lives in Sydney, where he is a staff writer at the *Weekend Australian Magazine*.

Jack Hafferkamp lives and works in China. On certain Tuesdays he sings and plays some of Leonard Cohen's songs ("the easy ones") in the Red

Lion bar and restaurant in Wuxi "where most of the people have never heard them or even understand them," since they're being sung in English. "That's OK," Hafferkamp says. "I often think I don't understand them, either."

Montreal-born **Sarah Hampson** is a columnist with the *Globe and Mail*, Canada's leading national newspaper, which she joined in 2007. Before that, she freelanced for the *Globe and Mail*, the *Observer* in London, and many other publications. She has interviewed more than five hundred celebrities and won several National Magazine Awards in Canada. Her memoir, *Happily Ever After Marriage: A Reinvention in Midlife*, was published in Canada in 2010. Her website is hampsonwrites.com.

Though **Patrick Harbron** did some writing early in his career, he is known for his photography. His iconic images of Bruce Springsteen, Eric Clapton, Ray Charles, David Bowie, the Rolling Stones, and hundreds of other rock artists have been featured on album and DVD covers and in such periodicals as *Rolling Stone, Time, LIFE, People*, and *Business Week*. He has produced three books of photography and has photographed for television and film clients such as HBO, ABC, Sony, NBC, Netflix, Disney Films, and Warner Brothers. Harbron, whose work is on view at the Morrison Hotel Gallery in New York and the Analogue Gallery in Toronto, is a faculty member at the International Center of Photography. The New York Public Library for the Performing Arts offered an extensive exhibit of his rock music photography in 2012. His websites are patrickharbron.com and rockandrollicons.com.

Alan Jackson is a UK-based freelance journalist who has been interviewing musicians, actors, and other public figures for nearly thirty years, and for a variety of publications, most regularly among them the *London Times*, the *Observer*, and the *Mail on Sunday*. His interview subjects have ranged from Madonna to Peggy Lee, Bob Dylan (three times) to Justin Timberlake, and Chris Brown to Dusty Springfield. Examples of his work can be found at alanjacksoninterviews.com.

Brian D. Johnson has been a writer for *Maclean's*, the Canadian weekly news magazine, since 1985. He has also been a filmmaker, a columnist for the *Globe and Mail* in Toronto, and a broadcaster and producer with

CBC Radio. He left journalism for some years to perform as a percussionist with rock and reggae bands and has published three nonfiction books as well as a collection of poetry and a novel. He has written for such magazines as *Toronto Life, Saturday Night,* and *Rolling Stone* and has won three Canadian National Magazine Awards. He is currently president of the Toronto Film Critics Association.

Thom Jurek, who served as senior editor for Detroit's *Metro Times* from 1990 to 1996, has been affiliated since 1999 with All-Music Guide (allmusic .com), where he is a staff writer. He grew up in and around Detroit, and has been writing about music since he was fifteen. He has contributed to such periodicals as *Rolling Stone, Creem, Musician, Spin, American Songwriter,* and *Interview.* He is the author of two collections of poetry: *DUB* and *Memory Bags,* the latter with the late French artist Jacques Karamanoukian. His fiction has been anthologized in *Storming the Reality Studio: A Casebook on Cyberpunk & Postmodern Science Fiction.*

Longtime music journalist and record producer **Harvey Kubernik** is the author of *This Is Rebel Music, Hollywood Shack Job: Rock Music in Film and on Your Screen,* and *Canyon of Dreams: The Magic and the Music of Laurel Canyon.* His newest book, *Turn Up the Radio!: Rock, Pop, and Roll in Los Angeles 1956–1972,* was published in 2014. He coauthored *A Perfect Haze: The Illustrated History of the Monterey International Pop Festival.* He has published more than a thousand music- and pop culture–related articles and served as a consultant for television and film documentaries.

Arthur Kurzweil is a writer, teacher, and publisher. He was editor in chief of the Jewish Book Club from 1984 to 2001. His writing can be found online at arthurkurzweil.com.

John Leland, who has worked for the *New York Times* since 2000, previously served as editor in chief of *Details,* a senior editor at *Newsweek,* an editor and columnist at *Spin,* and a reviewer for *Trouser Press.* He is the author of *Hip: The History* and *Why Kerouac Matters: The Lessons of On the Road (They're Not What You Think).*

Dorian Lynskey has been writing about music and culture since 1996 for titles such as the *Guardian, Q,* and *Spin.* He is the author of *33 Revolutions*

Per Minute: A History of Protest Songs and *The Guardian Book of Playlists*. He lives in London.

Alberto Manzano created the Spanish translations of Leonard Cohen's *The Spice-Box of Earth*, *Book of Mercy*, *Stranger Music*, and *Book of Longing*. He is the author of *Leonard Cohen The Biography* and *Conversations with a Survivor*, a compilation of articles and interviews with the singer. In 1966 he worked with the flamenco singer Enrique Morente on adaptations of Cohen's songs for the record *Omega,* and in 2007 he produced the homage album *According to Leonard Cohen*, which featured such artists as Jackson Browne, John Cale, Anjani Thomas, Perla Batalla, Santiago Auseron, Adam Cohen, Constantino Romero, and Elliott Murphy. Manzano met Cohen in 1980, traveled with him on several European tours, and visited him in Hydra and in Los Angeles. Manzano's latest book on Cohen, *Lorca and Flamenco*, was published in 2012. He has translated more than a hundred books of rock lyrics and is the author of three books of poems.

Ray Martin has been one of Australia's most popular TV journalists for decades. He hosted *The Midday Show with Ray Martin* from 1985 to 1993.

Kristine McKenna is a Los Angeles–based writer and curator. Her fourteenth book, *Tripping: Clothing & Costume in the American '60s*, is slated for publication in 2014. She is currently editing a collection of writings by artist David Salle and working on a monograph on artist Joe Goode.

Robert O'Brian has been a journalist for more than thirty years. In addition to Leonard Cohen, his interview subjects have included Bill Moyers, Paul Simon, Buckminster Fuller, B. F. Skinner, Joan Baez, Al Green, Alan Lomax, Ken Burns, Willie Nelson, and Frank Zappa. He is the author of the novel *Jack Kerouac's Confession*. He lives in New York City with his wife, journalist Ilaina Jonas.

Robin Pike was born in Cheltenham, England, and educated at Cheltenham Grammar School, where he was a contemporary of the Rolling Stones' Brian Jones. He is currently collaborating with Paul Trynka in writing a biography of Brian. Pike has been a teacher of chemistry and with his friend David Stopps started Friars, a now world-famous rock music club in Aylesbury. Later Pike ran Division One Club, a launch pad for bands such as Primal Scream. He lives in Hertfordshire, England.

London-based **Alastair Pirrie** is a writer, producer, and director of more than six hundred hours of British and international network television. He has produced television programs with Paul McCartney, Stevie Wonder, Mick Jagger, Elton John, and many other prominent rock artists; presented radio shows on BBC Radio One, Capital Radio, and other stations; authored novels; and lectured on media at Cambridge University.

j. poet is the pen name of a music journalist, poet, short-story writer, and singer/songwriter. His work has appeared in hundreds of publications, including *Berkeley Barb*, the *San Francisco Chronicle, Creem, Crawdaddy!, DRUM, Folk Roots, Magnet, Native Peoples, Pulse!*, and *SOMA*. He lives in San Francisco and says he loves hot music, spicy food, tropical climates, and his wife, Leslie.

After winning the Jerome Lowell Dejur prize for fiction at the City College of New York and the Deems Taylor award for journalism from ASCAP, **Bruce Pollock** went on to found and edit the popular magazine *GUITAR: For the Practicing Musician*. He has published three novels and eleven books on music, including *Working Musicians, By the Time We Got to Woodstock, If You Like the Beatles*, and *The Rock Song Index: The 7500 Most Important Songs of the Rock Era*. His latest book is *A Friend in the Music Business: The ASCAP Story*.

Valerie Pringle, one of Canada's best-known broadcasters, hosted *Midday* on CBC-TV from 1984 to 1992 and *Canada AM* on CTV from 1994 to 2001. She then helped produce, write, and host documentaries and series on CTV and CBC-TV. Now involved full time in not-for-profit work for several foundations, she was appointed a member of the Order of Canada in 2006 for her communications and volunteer work. In 2012, she received an honorary doctor of laws degree from Ryerson University, from which she graduated in 1974.

Jennie Punter lives in Toronto, where she edits *Musicworks*—a magazine about Canadian and international experimental new music and sound art—and covers Canadian film and TV industry news for *Variety*. Since

2001 she has also worked in documentary film research and production. Punter studied classical piano for fourteen years, during which time she also fell in love with punk and started collecting vinyl. From 1991 to 2004 she wrote extensively on popular music as an editor for the North American monthly *Music Express* and as a freelancer for the *Toronto Star* and the women's magazine *Flare*.

Wayne Robins has been a journalist specializing in music for more than forty years. Since his first paid assignment—reviewing the Rolling Stones' 1969 Oakland show for the *Berkeley Barb*—he has written for *Creem, Rolling Stone*, the *Village Voice, Crawdaddy!, Zoo World*, the *Colorado Daily, Komsomolskaya Pravda*, Japanese magazines *Plus One* and *Music Life*, the *Boston Phoenix*, and MSNBC.com. The author of three books, he spent twenty years as the pop critic for *Newsday/New York Newsday* and has taught writing at NYU and copyedited at *Billboard*. His biggest thrill was playing air guitar with Keith Richards.

Shelagh Rogers, who joined CBC Radio in 1980, has hosted and appeared on many of its broadcasts. She currently hosts its weekly program on books and literature, *The Next Chapter*.

Paul Saltzman is a two-time Emmy Award–winning film and television director-producer with more than three hundred productions to his credit. His first feature was the award-winning documentary *Prom Night in Mississippi*. His second feature was 2012's *The Last White Knight*. In 1965, he did civil rights work with the Student Nonviolent Coordinating Committee in Mississippi. In 2010, he cofounded the nonprofit Moving Beyond Prejudice. His most recent book, *The Beatles in India*, features a photographic document of the quartet's 1968 visit to that country.

Vin Scelsa, one of the most important figures in the rise of freeform FM radio, is the longtime host of the New York–area program *Idiot's Delight*, which airs on WFUV and on Sirius/XM satellite radio. He has worked at such stations as WLIR, WXRK, WNEW, and WABC (which became WPLJ). In 2007, the year he celebrated the fortieth anniversary of his first broadcast, he received the prestigious ASCAP Deems Taylor Radio Broadcast Award.

Tom Schnabel helped introduce world music to American audiences as the first music director and host of *Morning Becomes Eclectic* (1979–'91) at the influential KCRW-FM in Santa Monica, California. He is the author of *Stolen Moments: Conversations with Contemporary Musicians* and *Rhythm Planet: The Great World Music Makers,* and has written for such publications as the *Los Angeles Times, Downbeat,* and *Esquire.* He has produced world music CDs, provided music supervision for advertising and movies, served as program advisor for the Hollywood Bowl and Walt Disney Concert Hall, and taught in Los Angeles and Paris. Schnabel, who holds an MA in comparative literature from UCLA, now hosts weekly online music shows for KCRW and writes a blog for its website called "Rhythm Planet."

Karen Schoemer is the author of *Great Pretenders: My Strange Love Affair with '50s Pop Music.* Her journalism and criticism have appeared in the *New York Times, Newsweek, New York* magazine, *Rolling Stone,* and many other publications, as well as the anthologies *Innocent When You Dream: The Tom Waits Reader, Rock She Wrote: Women Write About Rock, Pop, and Rap,* and *Da Capo Best Music Writing 2000.* A resident of Columbia County, New York, she contributes essays about upstate life to the quarterly magazine *Our Town* and hosts a weekly music show on WGXC-FM and wwgxc.org.

Jordi Sierra i Fabra has sold more than ten million books in his native Spain. His hundreds of titles include biographies, histories, works for children, and poetry collections. He has followed the rock scene since the 1960s and has founded such music periodicals as the *Great Musical, Disco Express, Top Magazine,* and *Popular 1.*

Deborah Sprague found her musical passion early on, as a preteen peeking through the windows of the nascent avant-rock scene of Cleveland, where she discovered Pere Ubu, the Pagans, 15-60-75, and many more. Thus fueled, she headed to New York City at age seventeen, began writing for multiple fanzines, and wound up as editor in chief of the late, lamented *Creem* magazine. In succeeding years, her work has appeared in publications as varied as *Rolling Stone, Variety,* the *New York Daily News, Spin,* and *Newsday.* She has also contributed essays to books, including

The Trouser Press Guide to '90s Rock and *Kill Your Idols: A New Generation of Rock Writers Reconsiders the Classics.*

Robert Sward, the winner of a Guggenheim Fellowship, is the author of twelve books, including the novel *A Much-Married Man* and *Four Incarnations: New & Selected Poems*. His fiction has been heard on National Public Radio's *The Sound of Writing*. Sward teaches for Cabrillo College and the University of California Extension in Santa Cruz.

London-based **Steve Turner**, who has written for *Rolling Stone*, *New Musical Express*, and many other periodicals, is the author of such books as *The Man Called Cash*, *Angelheaded Hipster* (a biography of Jack Kerouac), and *A Hard Day's Write: The Stories Behind Every Beatles Song*.

Suzanne Vega's critically acclaimed, self-titled debut album, which appeared in 1985, went platinum in the United Kingdom. The follow-up, *Solitude Standing*, featured the worldwide hit "Luka" (number three in the United States). She has since released nine more studio albums, the most recent of which is *Close-Up, Vol. 4: Songs of Family*. A Leonard Cohen fan since age fourteen, Vega contributed a reading of his "Story of Isaac" to the 1995 tribute CD *Tower of Song*. A long and noteworthy 1992 conversation between the two artists is posted at suzannevega.com.

Steve Venright's books of poetry and short prose include *Spiral Agitator* and *Floors of Enduring Beauty*. As well as being an author and visual artist, he has released several recordings through his Torpor Vigil record label, including Samuel Andreyev's *The Tubular West* and *Dreaming Like Mad with Dion McGregor: More Outrageous Recordings of the World's Most Renowned Sleeptalker*. Venright was born in Sarnia, Ontario, in 1961, and says he hasn't been the same since.

Patrick Watson has been a Canadian television and radio personality, writer, producer, and director for nearly half a century. He was chairman of the Canadian Broadcasting Corporation from 1989 to 1994.

Jon Wilde was all set for a career as a professional footballer "until a painful toe injury put paid to all that." Instead, he has enjoyed a long and varied career in journalism, specializing in interviews with the world's leading hell-raisers, including Dennis Hopper, Richard Harris, Oliver Reed, George Best, Keith Richards, and Harvey Keitel. Wilde is interviewer-in-residence at *Mail on Sunday*'s *Live Magazine*. He lives in Hove, England, with his spaniel, Banjo, and a lively assortment of cats and rats.

In 1966, **Paul Williams** founded the hugely influential *Crawdaddy!*, the first national American magazine of rock criticism. He later published more than two dozen books, including *Outlaw Blues, Das Energi*, and the three-part *Bob Dylan: Performing Artist*. Williams died in 2013.

Chicago native **Paul Zollo** is a recording artist for Trough Records and has cowritten songs with such composers as Steve Allen, Darryl Purpose, and Severin Browne. His song "Being in This World"—which appears on his first solo album, *Orange Avenue*—is a duet with Art Garfunkel. Zollo is the author of several books, including *Songwriters on Songwriting, Conversations with Tom Petty*, and *Hollywood Remembered*. His first volume of photography, *Angeleno*, will be published in 2014. Zollo, who serves as the chief editor of Bluerailroad.com and senior editor of *American Songwriter* magazine, lives with his wife and son in Los Angeles.

ABOUT THE EDITOR

Jeff Burger edited *Springsteen on Springsteen: Interviews, Speeches, and Encounters*, which Chicago Review Press published in 2013. He has been a writer and editor for more than four decades and has covered popular music throughout his journalism career. His reviews, essays, and reportage on that and many other subjects have appeared in more than seventy-five magazines, newspapers, and books, including *Barron's*, the *Los Angeles Times*, *Family Circle*, *Melody Maker*, *High Fidelity*, *Creem*, *Circus*, *Reader's Digest*, *Gentlemen's Quarterly*, *All Music Guide*, and *No Depression*. He has published interviews with many leading musicians, including Bruce Springsteen, Tom Waits, Billy Joel, the Righteous Brothers, Roger McGuinn, Tommy James, Foreigner's Mick Jones, and the members of Steely Dan; and with such public figures as Suze Orman, James Carville, Sir Richard Branson, F. Lee Bailey, Sydney Pollack, Wolfman Jack, and Cliff Robertson.

Burger has been editor of several periodicals, including *Phoenix* magazine in Arizona, and he spent fourteen years in senior positions at *Medical Economics*, the country's largest business magazine for doctors. A former consulting editor at Time Inc., he currently serves as editor of *Business Jet Traveler*, which the American Society of Business Publication Editors named one of the country's best business magazines in 2011 and 2013.

Burger, whose website is byjeffburger.com, lives in Ridgewood, New Jersey. His wife, Madeleine Beresford, is a teacher and puppeteer. The couple have a son, Andre, and a daughter, Myriam.

CREDITS

I gratefully acknowledge the help of everyone who gave permission for material to appear in this book. I have made every reasonable effort to contact copyright holders. If an error or omission has been made, please bring it to the attention of the publisher.

"TV Interview," by Adrienne Clarkson. Originally broadcast on *Take 30*, CBC, May 23, 1966. Copyright © 1966. Printed by permission of Canadian Broadcasting Corporation.

"After the Wipe-Out, a Renewal," by Sandra Djwa. Originally published in the *Ubyssey*, February 3, 1967. Copyright © 1967. Reprinted by permission of Sandra Djwa.

"Ladies & Gents, Leonard Cohen," by Jack Hafferkamp. Originally published in *Rolling Stone*, February 4, 1971. Copyright © 1971. Reprinted by permission of Jack Hafferkamp.

"Famous Last Words from Leonard Cohen (The Poet's Final Interview, He Hopes)," by Paul Saltzman. Originally published in *Maclean's*, June 1972. Copyright © 1972. Reprinted by permission of Paul Saltzman.

"Cohen Regrets," by Alastair Pirrie. Originally published in *New Musical Express*, March 10, 1973. Copyright © 1973. Reprinted by permission of Alastair Pirrie.

"Leonard Cohen," by Pat Harbron. Originally published in *Beetle* magazine, December 1973. Copyright © 1973. Reprinted by permission of Pat Harbron.

INDEX